EXPLORING LANGUAGE ARTS IN THE ELEMENTARY CLASSROOM

EXPLORING LANGUAGE ARTS IN THE ELEMENTARY CLASSROOM

John Warren Stewig
University of Wisconsin, Milwaukee

Holt, Rinehart and Winston
New York   Chicago   San Francisco   Philadelphia
Montreal   Toronto   London   Sydney
Tokyo   Mexico   Rio de Janeiro   Madrid

Library of Congress Cataloging in Publication Data

Stewig, John W.
   Exploring language arts in the elementary classroom.

   Includes bibliographies and index.
   1. Language arts (Elementary) I. Title.
   LB1576.S797 1982   372.6   82-15609

ISBN 0-03-057462-5

Copyright © 1983 by CBS College Publishing
Address correspondence to:
383 Madison Avenue
New York, N.Y. 10017
3 4 5 6   038   9 8 7 6 5 4 3 2 1

CBS COLLEGE PUBLISHING
Holt, Rinehart and Winston
The Dryden Press
Saunders College Publishing

For permission to use copyedited materials, the following authors, artists, publishers, and photographers are acknowledged with thanks.

p. 82: Illustration from Lenore Blegvad (compiler), *This Little Pig-A-Wig, and Other Rhymes About Pigs.* Text copyright © 1978 by Lenore Blegvad; illustrations copyright © 1978 by Eric Blegvad. A Margaret K. McElderry book (New York: Atheneum, 1978). Reprinted with the permission of Atheneum Publishers.
p. 83: Illustration from "This Little Pig Had Roast Beef," from *Ring O' Roses* by L. Leslie Brooke. © Frederick Warne & Co., Ltd., London. Reprinted by permission of the publisher.
p. 102: Illustration from Mary L. O'Neill, *What Is That Sound!* Text copyright © 1966 by Mary L. O'Neill; illustrations copyright © 1966 by Lois Ehlert (New York: Atheneum, 1966). Reprinted with the permission of Atheneum Publishers.
pp. 117-118: The poem "Cat" by Mary Britton Miller, copyright by the Estate of Mary Britton Miller.
p. 118: The poem "The Mysterious Cat" by Vachel Lindsay, reprinted with permission of Macmillan Publishing Co., Inc. from Vachel Lindsay, *Collected Poems.* Copyright 1914 by Macmillan Publishing Co., Inc.; renewed 1942 by Elizabeth C. Lindsay.
p. 149: Illustration from the book *Beauty and the Beast* by Madame de Beaumont, illustrated by Diane Goode. Reprinted with permission of Bradbury Press, Inc., Scarsdale, N.Y. 10583.
p. 150: Illustration by Errol Le Cain from *Beauty and the Beast* by Rosemary Harris. Copyright © 1979 by Errol Le Cain. Reprinted by permission of Doubleday & Company, Inc.
p. 185: Photo reproduced by permission of Hart Day Leavitt.
p. 190: Illustration from the book *Three Aesop Fables* by Paul Galdone, published by Clarion Books, Tichnor & Fields: A Houghton Mifflin Company, New York. Copyright © 1971 by the author.
p. 195: The poem "Snakes and Snails" from *Bird in the Bush* by Grace Tabor Hallock. Copyright 1930 by E. P. Dutton & Co., Inc. Renewal, 1958, by Grace Tabor Hallock. Reprinted by permission of E. P. Dutton, Inc.

PREFACE

The purpose of *Exploring Language Arts in the Elementary Classroom* is to describe a wide variety of instructional strategies for involving children in exploring their language. It is based on the assumption that language is a vital and vibrant phenomenon, the study of which can be an exciting adventure. To young children the world is a fascinating encounter, and they study it with an intensity at which adults marvel. The study of language, an integral and important part of the child's world, could be a similarly fascinating subject. The schools' pervading concern with acquiring proficiency in the outward forms of one type of language too frequently deadens a child's interest in language. To pique that interest, and the interest of teachers, is my purpose.

Chapter 1 describes how infants learn their language, and the proficiency children have developed by the time they reach school. The implications of this proficiency for school language programs are described. Chapter 2 challenges readers to think deeply about the purposes of an elementary language program, and the processes of planning such a program. Learning objectives growing out of these processes can further the purpose of this book. Chapter 3 describes a language curriculum for early-childhood education which builds on and develops children's interest in language. The remaining chapters of the book deal with various specific facets of the language arts. Separate chapters are included for such diverse aspects of language as listening, handwriting, drama, and composition. These are set apart from each other to emphasize their importance. The teaching suggested, however, emphasizes an integrated approach to language arts. The final chapter is concerned with a specific school population, the linguistically different child.

The Chapter Supplements are a unique feature of the book. These short reports were written by undergraduate students preparing to be teachers. In these firsthand accounts, the writers describe ways they involved different groups of children in exploring language.

Two other features of the book are specifically designed to increase the teacher's interest in exploring language. At the end of each chapter, "Suggestions for Further Exploration" are included, which direct your language study to other areas related to the chapter. Sometimes these will direct you to materials that challenge the assertions made in this book. In addition, all the references in the "Related Reading" sections of the book are annotated, in the hope that this will whet your appetite to explore further.

Language: multiple, contradictory, always changing, a tool for thought, and reflective of the individual. These and many other things, but most of all—exciting. Children are immersed in language from the time their mothers hold and comfort them with soothing sounds until they reach school. For too many boys and girls, language then turns into something dull and frustrating. In the hope of keeping an interest in language alive, I have prepared this book, which encourages you to go exploring language with your children. Where will the exploration lead? No one but you and your children can know. Some directions have been suggested, but the possibilities are limited only by the limits of language itself.

It is a pleasure to acknowledge three valued colleagues, whose work influenced the development of this book. Drs. Ruth and Harlan Hansen wrote Chapters 3 and 10 in an earlier version of the book and those chapters in this edition are based on that earlier work. Similarly, Dorothy Huenecke wrote Chapters 2 and 13 in the earlier version, and those chapters in this edition are based on that work.

Beyond the colleagues identified by name are a score of unnamed classroom teachers, kindergarten through eighth grade, teaching in a number of different school systems, who graciously found time in busy schedules to try ideas for me. Whatever sense of reality this text has is directly due to their willingness to test ideas and give me honest feedback about children's reactions. My work is improved immeasurably because of their generous help.

Finally, to David Boynton and Herman Makler of the editorial staff, and to many others in the technical areas of Holt, Rinehart and Winston's College Department, I extend my gratitude for helping make this book a reality.

J.W.S.

CONTENTS

1
CHILDREN
AND LANGUAGE LEARNING

2
CURRICULUM
IN THE LANGUAGE ARTS

3
LANGUAGE IN
EARLY CHILDHOOD EDUCATION

4

LISTENING

5

ORAL LANGUAGE

6

SPONTANEOUS DRAMA

7

WRITING WITH CHILDREN

Contents

8
THE NECESSITY
FOR PRACTICAL WRITING

9
HANDWRITING

10
SPELLING

11
LEARNING ABOUT
LANGUAGE THROUGH LITERATURE

12
VOCABULARY

Contents

13

GRAMMAR AND USAGE

14

LANGUAGE AND THE
LINGUISTICALLY DIFFERENT CHILD

EXPLORING LANGUAGE ARTS IN THE ELEMENTARY CLASSROOM

CHILDREN
AND LANGUAGE
LEARNING

It was a hot summer day, and three-year-old
Melissa was "helping" her daddy mow the lawn.
He paused to wipe the sweat from his forehead,
and noticed the curious preschooler staring at his
shirtless chest. "Yes, my stomach is hairy," he
said. With a note of disappointment, she replied:
"My tummy doesn't have a name."

Such is the interest with which children approach the task of
learning language. By age three, inquisitive Melissa had already become an
active language learner, observing adults' use of language and using it
herself. In this chapter we will focus on some of the ways children develop
language.

The doting parents lean delightedly over the crib, making encouraging
sounds and words to their progeny. A common sight. Yet few mothers or
fathers realize the child is energetically learning. From the moment of birth,
announced by a bellow of protest, the infant is beginning one of the most impressive learning tasks attempted by humans—the acquisition of language.
From this noisy beginning until the kindergartner enters school, a prodigious
feat is accomplished—the child learns language.

In the beginning the child lies in the crib and uses tongue and lips to make
a variety of sounds, many of which are unintelligible to adults. The child is
learning the entire time: listening to sounds, making sounds, combining
them in new and ingenious ways—always experimenting. After this early experimentation, sounds are strung together into words; gradually speech
becomes more intelligible. As mobile and curious preschoolers, children continue their learning; words on a string of thought are made into sentences.

Although estimates vary among linguists and language scholars as to the
age at which a child "knows" the language, agreement is general that the

Talking about objects of interest leads to increased oral fluency in early childhood. (Used with permission of the photographer, Richard D. Bradley.)

kindergarten child is in command of most of the language forms adult speakers use. One linguist comments: "After the age of six there is relatively little in the grammar or syntax of the language that the average child needs to learn, except to achieve a school-imposed standard of speech or writing to which he may not be accustomed in his home environment."[1] Another author goes even further, saying that: ". . . rules learned in school are only the conventions of an educated society. They are arbitrary finishing touches of embroidery on a thick fabric of language that each child weaves for herself before arriving in the English teacher's classroom" (Moskowitz, 1978). These contentions sound a bit extreme at first, for we know that the school devotes much instructional time to teaching children about their language. Why teach children about their language if they already know it?

To answer this question, we must distinguish among three terms: *competence*, *performance*, and *knowledge*. Children do, indeed, have unconscious *competence* in language (the ability to produce appropriate

---

[1] John B. Carroll, "Language Development," in *Child Language: A Book of Readings*, eds. Aaron Bar-Adon and Weiner F. Leopold (Englewood Cliffs, N.J.: Prentice-Hall, 1971), pp. 200–211. An extremely wide-ranging collection, dating from 1927 to 1969, the book includes articles at many different difficulty levels, some exceedingly technical and some easy to read.

linguistic forms in a given situation). Berko (1958) among others, demonstrated that children have basic linguistic competency by the age of six. *Performance*, in contrast, is the child's actual *use* of language in any given situation. Because of factors involved in a real situation, perhaps fear, confusion, boredom, or antipathy, the child may not fully utilize his or her linguistic competence (Wells, 1979). The term *knowledge* means the child's conscious awareness of the structure, inner workings, and classification schemes describing language. Though children come to school linguistically competent, and in various situations may demonstrate their competency by their actual performance, conscious understanding (knowledge) of how language functions is beyond them at this age.

CHILDREN'S LANGUAGE AND THE TEACHER

If the majority of language learning takes place before a child enters school, why is the process of concern to teachers? If teachers at all age or grade levels knew more about early language growth, language arts-reading programs in schools might be considerably different than they are know.

If teachers knew how much language children actually have, and the degree of their linguistic sophistication, changes in teaching strategies could result. Today large groups of children sit, listening to the teacher talk. Instead, small groups of children could be talking together as they enlarge their language patterns by verbalizing questions, opinions, thoughts, and doubts. Today large numbers of children are frustrated because they cannot decipher those unintelligible marks in beginning reading books. Instead, so many children could experience the joy of seeing their own fluent language spring into new life in different forms on paper.

The study of language acquisition can reveal techniques for the teaching of reading and language arts. To develop this idea, the remainder of this chapter will review what is known about language acquisition and draw implications about ways teachers can build on the language children speak. To accomplish this purpose, the chapter is organized into sections:

1. what children learn in acquiring the *structure* of English,
2. what children learn in learning some *functions* of English,
3. *how* children learn the structure and functions of English, and
4. implications for teachers.

STUDYING CHILD LANGUAGE

Though interest in language is not new, the study of child language, and particularly the processes through which language is learned, began recently. As long ago as 1787, Tiedeman, a philosophy professor at the University of Marburg, published the first significant studies of child language, a set of observations of children's speech patterns. Despite this early beginning, only within the last twenty years has the question of how children learn language attracted widespread attention.

In these two decades many research studies began to provide answers to the question of how children learn language. As a result of intensive investigations by a growing band of scholars, we know many interesting facts about children's learning of three major components of language: phonology (the sound system), morphology (the system of word forms), and syntax (the system of sentence structure).[2] Developmental stages have been identified, and acquisition procedures described. Because knowing about this may help you build on the language competencies children have, some significant ideas about children's language acquisition are examined here.

WHAT CHILDREN LEARN IN ACQUIRING THE STRUCTURE OF ENGLISH

As young children talk, they gain command of their language. The sound system of English (phonology) is the backbone of the child's language. It is commonly assumed that the child's cry at birth is the first sound made. But evidence shows that as early as the fifth month after conception, the fetus emits noises (Wilkinson, 1971). By the fourth month after birth, it is easy to distinguish comfort and discomfort sounds in the child's cooing. By then, the child is well on the way to babbling.

Infants babble sounds—some remotely resembling English, others bizarre combinations to be eliminated from the "sound vocabulary" later as they sense adults do not use them. At this age such experimentation with sounds is almost a full-time occupation. This babbling serves three purposes:

1. It is enjoyable, and provides the equivalent of play for the young child.
2. It provides practice in the skill of making sounds.
3. It provides a stream of sounds, some of which parents reinforce, while others atrophy or decrease because they are ignored.

Stages in the development of phonemes have been identified, though in this, as in other aspects of language growth, the *order* of acquisition is usually invariant, but the *time* of acquisition varies considerably. For instance,

---

[2]In addition to this chapter, a very brief, though complete description of these three major components of language is included in William M. Austin, "The Suprasegmental Phonemes of English," in *Culture, Class and Language Variety*, ed. A.L. David (Urbana, Ill.: National Council of Teachers of English, 1972), pp. 83–88.

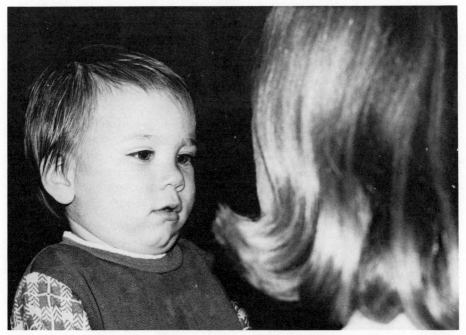

Many chances to interact verbally with an adult are a necessary stimulus to language fluency in infants. (Used with permission of the photographer, Richard D. Bradley.)

the phoneme /m/[3] always proceeds the acquisition of the phoneme /th/; /m/ can be acquired between one-and-a-half and three years, while /th/ can be acquired between five and eight years of age. One researcher[4] points out that all statements of stages need to be examined to determine if they are stating when the sound first appears, when it is usually mastered, or when all children can produce the sound.

Not only does the child produce separate sounds, but in addition, listening skills and responding to speech are developing. One researcher showed that children aged four to five months can distinguish between male and female voices (Kaplan, 1969).

As young children listen, they hear parents use pitch (level of sound), stress (emphasis), and juncture (pauses) to communicate meaning. Even before they understand all the basic meanings of words, children begin to

---

[3]Linguists find it useful to distinguish between sounds, and the letters used to represent them. Slash marks around a letter indicate that a sound is being represented. /m/ represents the sound we hear at the beginning of the word *man*. In some cases the differences are more noticeable. The sound /th/, as in the word *thing*, is quite different than the sound /th/ as in the word *then*, though both sounds are represented by the letters *th*.

[4]Eric K. Sander, "When Are Speech Sounds Learned?" *Journal of Speech and Hearing Disorders*, February 1972, *37*, 55–63. Another important factor is whether a child can use a speech sound in spontaneous language, or only in responding to a predetermined word list.

understand these suprasegmental signals. Evidence exists which indicates that infants pick up the "feeling-tone" transmitted by parents' speech before individual word meanings are learned. This can occur as early as six to eight months of age (deVilliers, 1979).

DEVELOPMENTAL STAGES

Psychologists have studied the stages through which children move from early exploration of sounds to forming recognizable words. As with any list of stages, the reader must here keep in mind that the stages are relatively constant, though the rate may vary greatly. For example, the author of the following developmental sequence maintains that though phrases begin to appear between twenty-one and twenty-eight months, some normal children may not begin to speak in phrases until four years.

Table 1-1 DEVELOPMENTAL STAGES OF LANGUAGE

Age in Months	Nature of Language
4	coos and chuckles
6 to 9	babbles, produces such sounds as /ma/ and /da/; reduplicates common sounds
12 to 18	small number of "words;" follows simple commands and responds to "no"
18 to 21	from about 20 words (at 18 mo.) to 200 words (at 21 mo.); understands simple commands; forms two-word phrases
24 to 27	vocabulary of 300 to 400 words; two to three words in phrase; prepositions and pronouns
30 to 33	fastest increase in vocabulary; three- to four-word sentences; word order and grammatical agreement approximate language of surroundings
36 to 39	vocabulary of 1,000 words or more; well-formed sentences using grammatical rules, though not all have been mastered; grammatical mistakes less common

Source: Adapted from Eric H. Lenneberg, "The Natural History of Language," in *The Genesis of Language*, edited by Frank L. Smith and George A. Miller (Cambridge, Mass.: MIT Press, 1966), p. 222.

It is critical that teachers understand that such developmental sequences as the one above indicate usual progressions, but that the rate of progression through the sequence varies greatly. Weeks (1974) gives an incisive longitudinal study of a gifted child with a measured intelligence quotient of 139, followed over a four-year period. She details the significantly delayed development in phonology, morphology, syntax, and semantics, though

these were not pathological, since the child was in other ways superior in ability. In her conclusion, Weeks cautions that teachers must be especially careful not to judge late-developing children as intellectually limited.

Such developmental stages as those described above tell us *when* a child may be at a particular level of competency, and *what* he or she can do at a particular age. Knowing when a child may be at a particular stage does not, however, give any insight into *how* this happens. Several researchers have attempted to answer this question, and their findings will be considered later. Before considering *how* acquisition takes place, we need to consider what else, besides phonology, children acquire in the structure of English.

CHILDREN AND WORD FORMS IN ENGLISH

Morphology, the study of word forms, is a fascinating aspect of English. Before we become adults, we must master such regular verb forms as *play* and *played*, in addition to such irregular ones as *sing* and *sung*. Verbs are not the only kinds of words in which morphological changes occur. Nouns also inflect, or change form. Sometimes we add sounds plus a corresponding letter to make a plural (boot, boots), sometimes we make internal changes (foot, feet), and at other times we do nothing (deer, deer). In addition, adjectives, adverbs, and pronouns demand form changes. The learning task confronting young children is formidable to say the least!

When do children learn these rather elaborate procedures? Teachers often assume they "teach" children about this aspect of English. In reality this is another feature of English which is largely learned by children before they enter school. In this, as in other aspects of language acquisition, the order is predictable, though the rate varies.[5]

In a pioneer study which examined this aspect of English, Berko (1958) devised a test to determine the extent to which children could control English morphology.[6] She wanted to find out if children had internalized the morphological system and could generalize to new cases or if, rather, they could demonstrate only rote memory of particular words. To do this, she used made-up or nonsense words which illustrate the four most common aspects of morphology:

1. plural and possessiveness of the noun
2. third person singular of the verb
3. progressive and past tense
4. comparative and superlative forms of the adjective

Question-answering tasks were devised, with small line drawings to illustrate each question. Some sample items (corresponding to numbers above) included:

1. "This is a gutch. Now there is another one. There are two of them. There are two _____."
2. "This is a man who know how to naz. He is nazzing. He does it every day. Every day he _____."
3. "This is a man who knows how to zib. What is he doing? He is _____."
4. "This dog has quirks on him. This dog has more quirks on him. And this dog has even more quirks on him. This dog is quirky. This dog is _____. And this dog is _____."

---

[5]This point is clearly made in "Acquisition of Morphology: Sequence," a film from the series, *Language of Children*. National Resource and Dissemination Center, University of South Florida, Tampa 33620. The series includes viewing guides, observation worksheets, and tips for classroom application.

[6]Though her research has been replicated several times, Berko's original study remains of the most interest. See: Jean Berko, "The Child's Learning of English Morphology," *Word*, 1958, *14*, 150–177. A further aspect of the study is her investigation of children's understanding of compound words. These results indicated children often have private and unshared meanings for such words, which interfere with communication because of their extremely personal nature.

Berko tested four- to seven-year-old children orally and found they had little difficulty performing the task. She discovered, in contrast to findings in other tests of language ability, that in her test no significant differences existed between boys and girls. The children demonstrated they had internalized the system of English morphology. Berko concludes, ". . . there can be no doubt that children of this age operate with clearly delimited morphological rules."

Despite the fact that children do operate with such morphological rules, early childhood teachers must remember that developing such internalized, unarticulated rules is a long-term process. Children hear adult speakers, experiment themselves with forms (Malmstrom, 1977), and evolve a system of rules through trial and error. Such experimentation is apparent in the use of past tense forms, a common source of errors which reveals the child is attempting to build a system. At first children hear and learn the correct form. Yet all of us have heard a child use such forms as *goed*, *wented*, *eated*, and *felled*. These represent overextensions of regular forms. Children frequently make such "mistakes" as they attempt to develop an understanding of how the complex system of English verb forms operates (Kuczaj, 1977). Eventually, for most children, this overregularization corrects itself as boys and girls internalize the rules for irregular verb forms.

Children's speech often indicates to us that they are experimenting with the language, trying to master the forms. Five-year-old Jonathan was devouring the last crumbs of the dessert. "Mom, this is the goodest pie you ever made." She responded, "Jonathan, there is no such word as goodest." He thought about it for a minute, and then asked, "How come I can say it then?" Such an interchange, and others like it which occur in school settings, point out the intrepid use of language through which children fashion their own linguistic competency. As parents or as teachers, we need to be responsive to such efforts. Ways of working with children will be suggested later in this chapter.

CHILDREN AND THE GRAMMAR OF ENGLISH

Grammar is a term used differently by linguists than it is commonly used by the general public. It is often used in informal conversation to mean how people talk. More technically, linguists define grammar, which is based upon how people talk (usage), as a description of the ways in which the components of language function. Here we shall use it in a more limited way, however, to refer only to a child's understanding of word function and syntactical relationships.

Adults speak, using all the word classes, arranging them in elaborate patterns difficult to analyze. It was contended earlier that children, perhaps by six years of age, also use all these form classes and a wide variety of syntactical patterns. When do children begin to use these elaborate structures?

Children begin by producing sounds which are gradually combined to make wordlike forms. These one-word utterances, called *holophrases*, stand for a thought which is more complete than the single word form might indicate. The more complex meaning, apparent only when a listener is actually in the situation, is affected by intonation. For example, when a child sitting in the highchair says the word "milk," it could mean:

1. "Mommy, may I have more milk?"
2. "Mommy, look at me, I've finished my milk!"
3. "Oh, dear, I spilled my milk."

In each case, the intonation of the single word, milk, will be different. The mother, actually in the situation, has no trouble interpreting the message, though when the word is written down and read later, the meaning is not apparent.

Holophrases represent the beginning of syntax. These holophrases merge into short phrases, often two words in length, in what is sometimes called *telegraphic* speech (Simmons & Lawrence, 1981). This in turn leads into more fully developed sentences.

There is evidence that in traveling toward a fully developed adult syntactic structure of English, children move through a simpler system of their own. Studies indicate that before such classes as noun, verb, adjective, and adverb are mastered, an intermediate step is necessary. This was, during the last decade, widely referred to as the *pivot and open class* grammar stage.

By eighteen months, the two-word phrases which children say can be divided into two groups. The larger of these is called "open" words; these can be said with other open words, or can appear with pivot words. Such words as boy, sock, mommy, other, yellow, and lettuce are include in this group. The second, smaller group is made up of "pivot" words, which must always appear with an open word. Such words as allgone, byebye, off, fall, pretty, a, dirty, this, and here, are included in this group. Though certain words appear frequently in either pivot or open class, such classification is not universal. When a word is a pivot word for a particular child, it is always a pivot word for that child, though the same word might be an open word for a different child.

A fascinating aspect of pivot-open grammar is that it occurs not only among English-speaking children, but also among such other children as those speaking German, Russian, Finnish, and Samoan. Although the terminology and descriptions vary, several researchers in children's language comment on the existence of this preliminary grammatical form. (Compare Bloom, 1970, and Brown, 1970.)

Recently, some researchers have begun to question the adequacy of this concept, in describing comprehensively the process of acquisition at this stage. First, it appears that the description is too simple to accommodate all children—the language patterns of some children do not fit this description (Bowerman, 1973). Second, the description comments on the structure, but not on the relations between the words (Bloom, 1973). The simplicity of the pivot-open description does not distinguish between mommy sock (in which mommy is an adjective modifying sock) and mommy sock (in which mommy is the agent who will put the sock on the child). Pivot-open grammars are thus an example of how linguistic concepts are changing as new data are gathered (Dale, 1976).

The development of syntax, the arrangement of words into sentence order, presupposes understanding words as independent building blocks. At what point do children perceive words as separate entities, apart from the stream of speech in which they are embedded? While children may understand the import of a sentence because of accompanying suprasegmental "messages," at what point do they begin to understand separate words? Several studies have attempted to find an answer to this question.

One study used sixty-six children of four-and-a-half to five years of age as subjects. The children were asked to separate a phrase into word units, and then to reverse the units. If the children could perform the task, they were demonstrating knowledge of words as independent units. Though the evidence was not completely conclusive, the researcher found enough children experiencing difficulty with the task to suggest that apparently children perceive in larger units than words, and have difficulty in determining a word as a discrete unit (Huttenlocher, 1971).

This lack of ability in understanding words as separate units is seen by some writers as causing difficulty in learning once children reach school. Bereiter and Engelman (1966), authors of a highly structured language program for culturally disadvantaged children, postulate that such children speak, not in distinct words, but rather in whole phrases or sentences which function like giant words. The authors maintain that these giant words cannot be taken apart by the child and recombined and transformed in different ways. Yet children must be able to use language in this way to compete in school. To develop this ability, the authors have created a highly controversial program, for which they claim notable results. Becker (1977) has more recently described the outcomes of such programs.

Other alternatives to educating children for whom standard English is not a first dialect are suggested by Cullinan et al. (1974). The program described, tested with culturally different black children, was based on a philosophy of unconditional acceptance of the language children bring to school. Activities were designed to expand children's language to include standard English while maintaining proficiency in Black English. The statistically significant results achieved establish the effectiveness of this approach.

Some syntactic understandings are simple, i.e., adjectives always precede—never follow—nouns in English. Others are more complex. Adults, for example, order adjectives preceding a noun in a string, but that ordering is usually intuitive, rather than conscious. When several adjectives come before a noun, we arrange them, but some placements are mandatory while others vary freely. Which comes first in a string: size, age, color, composition, or nationality? There are rules for this, but they are largely inherent, and unreflected upon. Interestingly, three-year-olds show a mastery of this order. In tests of ordering, up to 82 percent of their usages were the same as adult usages.[7] This is yet another example of the kinds of innate language abilities children bring to school.

Learning the syntactic rules of the first language is a task all children must perform. Some children, those being raised in bilingual homes, have another task—learning a second set of syntactic rules. Recently researchers have been studying the nature of this process. Lindholm (1980) reports that two- to six-year-old bilinguals were not hampered by this ostensibly more difficult task. The researcher reports that when rules in English and Spanish were of equal difficulty, they were learned simultaneously. When rules pertinent to a structure were more complex in one language than in the other, the more complex ones were learned later. The encouraging finding for teachers is that the bilingual children in this study acquired the structural rules of English no later than monolingual English speakers.

WHAT CHILDREN LEARN IN LEARNING SOME *FUNCTIONS* OF LANGUAGE

As children grow older their speech becomes more intelligible, and adults have a tendency to focus on their meaning, rather than on forms. Teachers of young children often focus on *what* a child says, rather than on how he or she says it. In so doing, some developmental phenomena as significant as those in earlier language acquisition may be missed.

A study done by the eminent Swiss psychologist Jean Piaget (1965) resulted in his formulation of a theory of child language. Rather than dealing with acquisition of basic grammatical forms, this theory is concerned with describing the child's ability to shape sentences for an audience. In this construct, formulated after observing children in school classes, all language is seen as belonging to one of two categories. Piaget believes all children pass through two stages, the *egocentric* stage and the *socialized* stage.

In the *egocentric* stage the child is unconcerned about whether he or she has a listener, making no attempt to determine the view or interest of the hearer. There are three types or categories of egocentric speech:

1. *repetition*, in which the child repeats sounds for the sensual pleasure of talking, including words which make no sense
2. *monologue*, in which he or she talks as though thinking aloud and no attempt is made to address anyone

---

[7]Meredith M. Richards, "Adjective Ordering in the Language of Young Children," *Journal of Child Language*, 1979, 6, 253–277. Ninety children (aged 3 to 7 years) performed three tasks: imitation, comprehension, and production. Closest to adult usage was the ordering by 3- and 6-year olds. Less consistency was apparent in the language of 4- and 5-year-olds, apparently a time of testing. Development of this skill is not simply linear, as might be expected.

3. *dual or collective monologue*, in which an outsider is always present, though in serving as a stimulus to talk, the outsider is expected to neither attend nor respond. In such a situation the child is talking aloud in the presence of others, but ignores their indifference or responses

The last category is very familiar to nursery school and kindergarten teachers. For example, when a group of children are painting at a table, the physical presence of a group stimulates children to talk. The children may describe what they are doing: "Now I'm painting the house's roof. See the green—it's dark. Now the brown chimney, way up at the top." Such talking may go on for extended periods of time, but no response is expected from others in the group.

In the second stage, *socialized* speech, the child is responding or interacting with others. There are five types of socialized speech:

1. *adapted information*, in which the child actually exchanges thoughts with others
2. *criticism*, including all remarks made about the work or behavior of others
3. *commands, requests, and threats*, in which a definite interaction is apparent between one child and another
4. *questions*, including most asked among peers, which require an answer
5. *answers*, to real questions with interrogation marks

Piaget acknowledged that, as with all classification systems, his was open to the criticism of arbitrariness. Nonetheless, its value to teachers is obvious; it provides us with a way of thinking about children's language, and organizing our observations (Smith, 1974).

At what point does a child pass from one stage to another? As in other developmental stages, children take varying lengths of time to pass through the stages. A linguistically advanced child may enter the socialized stage long before one who has less language ability. In addition, the transition from one stage to another is not always permanent. That is, a child whose speech has been primarily socialized for some time may revert to the egocentric stage as a security measure. When a family breaks up in divorce or perhaps upon the arrival of a threatening new baby, the child who has been using socialized speech may return to egocentric speech until the problem has been dealt with.

One conclusion related to these stages may seem surprising to teachers of young children. Piaget has stated that *monologue*, one of the types of egocentric language, plays an important part in the language of children between the ages of six and seven. Further, he feels that egocentric language may account for nearly half of the total spontaneous speech of the child at the age of six-and-a-half. Is such the case with American children's language patterns today? This remains an interesting question which could be researched.

Research into children's language, based on Piagetian concepts, is reported by Donaldson (1978), who notes that in questioning situations, children often give seemingly contradictory responses. She points out that we often interpret utterances on the basis of both our knowledge of states of affairs, as well as knowledge about language. ("No one got in without a ticket," is not interpreted literally, because of what we know about the situation.) Children's knowledge of language is less sure than that of adults, so they rely more on their knowledge of states of affairs.

Child language is also the professional concern of another researcher, M. M. Lewis. He commented on the phenomenon called *dual monologue* by Piaget, the speech carried on as the child does something. The activity may be painting a picture, building a block city, or pushing a truck around the floor; speech is a concomitant part of the action. Lewis says, ". . . this self-addressed speech is more than an accompaniment to action . . . it is part of the action, which is thus both nonlinguistic and linguistic. The words are a means by which a child is helped to direct his attention, to regulate what he is doing, to 'think aloud'" (Lewis, 1969).

This phenomenon is also described by Luria (1959), a respected Russian psychologist, who called it *directive*, or *planning speech*. Though the terminology is different, it refers to a single phenomenon. Luria says this speech is used by children to anticipate their actions and to block out distractions as they carry out plans.

These writers agree that, though this type of speech becomes less frequent as children grow older, it does not completely disappear. Many times adults find themselves verbalizing, even though they are alone. Such "talking-to-one's-self" is common, but usually ignored. Yet it is the counterpart of early speech described by these authors. Related to this subvocalized "talking-to-one's-self" is the entirely internalized *inner speech* described at length by Vygotsky (1962). In this type of thinking in pure meaning, words are used in an elliptical, economic fashion. One communicates only with oneself; such speech is described by this respected Russian language scholar.

MORE RECENT RESEARCH ON LANGUAGE FUNCTIONS

Researchers have focused much attention on what and how children learn language. Some of the results were reported here, concerning how and when children learn to use particular language components of vocabulary and grammar. These components are in a way surface features of language. They are external, easily observed, and quantified.

Recently, however, researchers have been devoting considerable attention to a more complex and more interesting aspect of language—how a child learns the semantic system in language, or learns how to convey meaning.

Much of this interest has been stimulated by the research and writing of M. A. K. Halliday, and some of his findings should be of use to teachers.

Much of child language can be studied in relative isolation. Size of vocabulary (reported more fully in Chapter 12) can be tallied from tape recordings of elicited speech gathered by a researcher in a testing situation. Growth in composing skills can be assessed using the written product, with no children present.

Halliday, among others, has recently been saying that a significant part of language, what a child can *mean* (as contrasted with what he or she can *say*), cannot be studied unless we observe how a child uses language in a particular situation, to accomplish particular functions. These researchers have been analyzing adult uses of language, and then looking for parallel uses among child speakers. To gather this sort of data, they have, in the words of another researcher, " . . . [tried] to get as near as possible to the place and time of the language process." (Stibbs, 1980, p. 21). The research shows that mastery of semantics, or the way we encode meaning in language, is a more complex process than we have previously noted.

Halliday (1973) identified seven functions of language, including:

1. *instrumental*, in which language is used as a means for getting something done. Sentences beginning "I want . . ." are examples of this category, in which the speaker uses language to satisfy material needs.
2. *regulatory*, in which the speaker uses language to regulate the behavior of others. Stages in this category include unstructured demands, ordered sequences of instructions, and converting sets of instructions into rules.
3. *interactional*, in which even very familiar speakers (like mothers and their children) use language to mediate between self and others. An interesting exception is twins, who apparently do not need overt language to interact.
4. *personal*, in which the speaker is aware of language as a form of his or her own individuality. In this function, the speaker is offering himself or herself publicly through language.
5. *heuristic*, in which language is used as a means of investigating reality. This is not simply giving facts, but also explaining facts, and using language to learn. Halliday comments that by age five children already know the concept of question and answer, or language as a way of finding out.
6. *imaginative*, in which the speaker uses language to create the environment. In this category, the reality is in the child's mind, and he or she uses language to make things as they feel. Telling stories and engaging in dramatic games are examples of this category.
7. *representational*, in which language is used to convey a message or to express a proposition. This is the only use of which most

adults are consciously aware, yet Halliday asserts this is often the least important use to children.

Systematic observation in elementary classrooms would undoubtedly reveal children using language for most of these purposes. The problem with this classification system, as with most, is that language is so complex that any one utterance often combines more than one of the functions. Studies of children's language use show that by the age of eighteen months, children have learned to use categories 1 through 4 and are beginning to use categories 5 and 6. Only category 7 is not evident in their speech by that age.

A second useful aspect of the work of Halliday and his colleagues is the attention they call to the relative importance of these functions in different cultures. In an introduction to the work of British linguist Basil Bernstein, Halliday comments that there

> . . . may be differences in the relative orientation of different social groups towards the various functions of language in given contexts, and towards the different areas of meaning that may be explored within a given situation. (Halliday, 1978, p. 106)

That is, for any particular subculture, certain functions of the language may receive relatively greater emphasis. This has implication for classroom teachers working with students from minority cultures. Halliday comments that the major problem with minority speakers is not a deficit in the surface features of language (vocabulary and grammar) but rather a different choice of which meanings to encode. The minority culture from which the child comes may in fact emphasize different language functions as critical, in contrast to the school, which may emphasize others as most crucial. Clearly, middle-class, predominantly Caucasian classrooms seem to place primary emphasis on *representational* uses of language. That may indeed not be the function most important to the child's culture. At the very least the teacher ought to be aware that such differences in emphases may exist.

HOW CHILDREN LEARN THE STRUCTURE AND FUNCTIONS OF ENGLISH

What processes does the young child employ in acquiring language? Of what importance is the environment in this acquisition? Among authorities there is much debate about the answers to these two questions.

In trying to answer the question of how children learn language, Lovel (1968) tested 180 children from ages two through eight, on ten grammatical concepts. He found significant differences in the children's ability to perform the tasks. Children were asked to:

1. *imitate* what the researcher did
2. *comprehend* what the researcher asked
3. *produce* the contrast for which the researcher asked

In all case, the following relationship was found:

$$I > C > P$$

That is, ability to imitate (I) was greater than the ability to comprehend (C), which was greater than the ability to produce (P). Apparently, the ability to imitate is perfected first, with the ability to produce being perfected last.

Children are intrepid in trying to produce language; they are not content with simple imitation. We have all heard a child try a sentence that was intelligible, but not grammatically correct. Children frequently use such sentences as:

"Where I can put them?"
"Where I should put it?"
"What he can ride in?"

These are proof that imitation, while important, is not the only process involved. These sentences are not formed through simple patterning, since no adult would say them. Rather, they indicate that the child is attempting to produce sentences of his own. Child grammar is not an adult grammar and, accordingly, the sentences are not identical to those adults would produce. The important thing about such sentences is that they reflect the grammar children do have. They tell us something about the development of the child (Bellugi, 1968).

What is it that impels children to produce language? One point of view, which stresses the importance of biology, is described by Lenneberg (1964), perhaps the best-known advocate of this theory. There is a significant group of researchers which believes much of language acquisition is determined biologically and is not appreciably affected by the environment. Lenneberg summarized the reasons for this belief. The importance of biological considerations is evidenced by:

1. the developmental schedule apparent in children. Both the onset, and the order of developmental milestones are invariable.
2. the difficulty in suppressing language. The ability to learn language is so deeply rooted that children learn it even in spite of handicaps. Studies of children with several types of handicaps indicate that despite these, language is acquired.
3. the fact that language cannot be taught. Despite many efforts to teach language to animals, it seems that nonhuman forms of life cannot acquire true language (de Villiers, 1979, pp. 117–125).
4. the existence of language universals. Despite superficial differences, all languages are based on the same organizing principles of semantics, syntax, phonology, and morphology.

Lenneberg's studies indicate language is relatively independent of intelligence, and that the basis for language capacity might well be transmitted genetically. Lenneberg concedes that children do, indeed, differ:

1. in their inclination to talk
2. in their vocabulary
3. in what they have to say

These factors may well be affected by the environment. Basic mastery of the linguistic system does not, however, differ greatly from child to child, because of this innate biological impulse to language.

In contrast, such other researchers as Cazden (1981) have investigated the role environment plays in language development. They studied differences between language development in middle-class children, and those who are socially and economically disadvantaged. Such differences appear to be great, and they become apparent at an early age.[8] Interest in causes of such differences has led researchers to examine children's environments to find which factors enhance language development.

Brown and Bellugi (in Emig, 1966), examined types of interaction which exist between mothers and preschool children; their work increases our understanding of the role imitation plays in language use. In this early study, and in other more recent ones, interaction between mothers and children has been the norm. Evidently fathers interact so minimally with children that their influence on child language is not significant (Cahir & Shuy, 1981). The verbal interaction between pairs of mothers and children from eighteen to thirty-six months of age was taped. Then, verbal interaction was analyzed to determine if mothers act in any predictable ways with their young children. As a result, the researchers were able to describe quite completely some typical modes of behavior.

Much that happens between mother and child is a process of *imitation and reduction*. The mother says a sentence, and the child imitates it, in the process reducing some of the less important elements.

MOTHER'S SENTENCE	CHILD'S IMITATION
1. "Fraser will be unhappy."	1. "Fraser unhappy."
2. "That's an old time train."	2. "Old time train."
3. "It's not the same dog as Pepper."	3. "Dog Pepper."

The child preserves the word order, or syntax, of the mother's original sentence. He imitates, "Fraser unhappy," rather than "unhappy Fraser." Usually, the child retains the nouns, verbs, and the adjectives in the mother's model. Word classes most frequently omitted are inflections, auxiliary verbs, articles, conjunctions, and prepositions. There is similarity between these young children's sentences, and the abbreviated sentences adults use in

---

[8]See "Improving Home and Preschool Influences on Early Language Development," by Sandra Anselmo in *The Reading Teacher*, November 1978, pp. 139–143. The author comments that as early as the age of two years, significant differences in language abilities are apparent, and these seem to correspond to the amount of mother-child interaction.

sending telegrams. In both cases, high information words are retained. Words which contain the biggest information loads and, incidentally, which receive the heavier stress in the sentences, are imitated. Words with low information value, and which receive less stress, are omitted.

Another process which occurs frequently is *expansion*. Brown and Bellugi discovered that mothers often take a phrase or idea-fragment said by their child, and make it into a complete sentence, supplying what they assume are the missing words.

CHILD'S FRAGMENT	MOTHER'S EXPANSION
1. "Mommy eggnog."	1. "Mommy had her eggnog."
2. "Sat wall."	2. "He sat on the wall."
3. "Pick glove."	3. "Pick up the glove."

An interesting parallel exists between this process and the previous one. In both, the syntactic arrangement is maintained, though in this case the mother adds auxiliaries, prepositions, verb forms, and articles.

Much of the verbal interaction between mothers and children seems to be cyclical. The mother says a sentence and the child repeats, while reducing the number of elements included. The child says an idea fragment, and the mother expands it, adding necessary elements. The frequency with which the process occurs, and the resulting growth in child language, suggests that this type of interaction is an important influence as the child acquires language. Implications of this process for teachers of reading and language arts will be discussed later.

Another study of verbal interactions between mothers and children showed that social class affects the acquisition of specific vocabulary (Flegg, 1980). A study of thirty-two mother-and-child pairs revealed that professional-class mothers used more global labels, more description, and more functional definitions than did working-class mothers in talking about pictures with their children. The researcher concluded that these differences in socialization strongly influence a child's cognitive strategies and vocabulary.

Another pair of researchers explored mother-child relationships, examining in particular differences between middle-class and lower-class mothers. While the preceding studies were of verbal behavior, this study examined nonverbal behavior. Such behavior forms a significant part of early communication, since much that transpires between mother and child is nonverbal. Schmidt and Hore (1970) examined three areas of communication:

1. body contact
2. body closeness
3. glancing behaviors

Such communication elements as these are more difficult to study than verbal behavior, due to their transitory nature. Because of this, mothers and children were videotaped. Lower-class mothers used more body contact, while middle-class mothers, whose language was more complex, used more glancing behaviors. The authors point out that such differences in mothers' behavior may well influence the language behavior of the children.

Another researcher, while not denying the importance of a model in children's language acquisition, points out that simple modeling may not adequately describe the process. Klima sees the process, even among the very young, as a sophisticated one in which children use data to form generalizations. According to Klima (in Zale, 1968), children study the innumerable examples of language around them and make deductions about the language system. He says: "In a sense, the child is like a linguist, making and rejecting hypotheses about the language . . . after 10 years, the child knows all the principles of the English language. The child obviously poses the right questions and in the right order."

Another writer whose description of the process extends our understanding is Britton (1970). He talks of language *improvisation*, as children take forms they hear and make variations on them, searching for regularities in English. Britton says, "It would seem to be nearer the truth to say that they imitate people's method of going about saying things than to say that they imitate the things said."[9]

One researcher feels that neither the nativist position of Lenneberg, nor the behaviorist position which emphasizes the importance of modeling, is complete of itself. Wells (1980) instead contends that both points of view ignore the socially situated context in which the child learns to control language by exchanging meanings through shared, purposeful activities. He points out that children's experiences with objects are always embedded in a social context. Indeed, children are inducted into the culture through interaction with adults in an environment in which language is a form of action. Unsatisfied with the effects of expansion on child language, Wells has been experimenting with what he calls *recasting* language. The child says a sentence, i.e., "The bunny chased fireflies." The adult responds, "The bunny did chase fireflies, didn't he?" Such verbal interaction seems to result in more complex verbs in the child's language.

Such a brief sketch of language acquisition can do little beyond illustrate some major ways children grow as they make what has been called a miraculous journey from the crib to the kindergarten. Many of the language processes involved are still being explored; many questions remain unanswered. For the teacher, knowledge of this language acquisition is crucial.

Children, at any age, are active, talking producers of language. Though

---

[9]J. N. Britton, *Language and Learning* (Coral Gables, Fla.: University of Miami Press, 1970), p. 42. The quote is from the chapter "Learning to Speak," pp. 33–96. The summaries of Piaget's and Vygotsky's studies of children's language in this eminently readable book are a fine introduction to more complex works.

there may be some rough edges, some forms not yet controlled, they have a capacity for language we must respect. The language-reading curriculum we offer must be more concerned with building on what boys and girls already possess, than in having them analyze someone else's language. That curriculum must help students gain an increasing sense of power in saying what they want to say in original, innovative ways. How does what we know about language acquisition give direction to language arts programs?

IMPLICATIONS FOR TEACHERS

As teachers, we need to be aware of children's language as an object of study. The research indicates we know much about the language forms children acquire before they come to school, and the processes used in such acquisition. Children's language *can* be studied. For teachers, this suggests we need to be aware of ways we can informally study that language, both oral and written, to determine its adequacy in terms of the school situation and in terms of developmental levels.

In thinking about any group of children, we can ask ourselves questions about their ability to use language in the classroom. About *phonology* we might ask, "How effectively do these children use pitch, stress, and juncture (pause) to enhance communication?" This is a necessary question since simple exhortations to "read expressively" seldom result in changed behavior! We need to devise activities that will make children more aware of, and more effective users of pitch, stress, and juncture. For example, we can use sentences open to a variety of interpretations, and explore subtle shifts of meaning as children experiment with different ways to use their voices. The sentence, "That's a pretty green dress you have on today," can convey six different meanings, depending on which word receives the heaviest stress.

For *morphology*, we might ask, "Do these children understand the full range of form possibilities in words?" Such a question leads to exciting possibilities in vocabulary development. We might take a word suggested by a child, and explore all the form changes possible. Children expand their language capacities as we help them activate their understanding of morphology. The word *time*, for example, can be changed in initial, medial, and final positions. Knowing how to use morphological principles, we can make the words *timed*, *times*, *timing*, *timer*, and *retimed* from our base word. Or, take a basic word pattern and have upper primary children think of all the different words which result from shifting the initial sound. Given the word *cat* (CVC pattern), we can make eleven other words using this basic pattern. An exhaustive treatment of morphological possibilities is included in Dale (1971).

For *syntax*, we might ask, "Do these children use the full possibilities of sentence expansion and transformation?" Many authors have described ways children can take simple sentences they have written and enlarge them, or change their form to make more varied writing. For example, we might take a sentence from a story written by a child, "The dog chewed on his bone."

21

The sentence can be expanded in the noun phrase ("The big ugly dog chewed. . . ."), in its verb phrase (". . . chewed hungrily on his big bone."), or in both phrases ("The small red-haired dog chewed noisily on his enormous bone.") In addition to expansion, the sentence can be transformed. A question can be made into a statement, and a positive statement made into a negative one, among other possibilities. These techniques build logically on expansion skills which can be developed in the early years.

Teachers are also interested in determining how children's language relates to developmental levels which have been identified. This is not formal achievement testing of what the school has taught, but rather informal analysis of stages of innate language maturity. One such description of developmental levels for preschool children is included on page 6. Other studies of children's language levels are available (see, for example, Chomsky, 1969). Teachers familiar with Chomsky's findings could assess how their children compare with other children. Awareness of such developmental levels can help us avoid spending time teaching children language forms they will acquire naturally later. Chomsky's research indicates that the ask/tell distinction is not firmly established in many ten year olds, though it is established in some five-year-olds. Knowing this, we see there is no point in spending instructional time teaching second-graders about this feature of English since they will acquire it naturally later. Awareness of developmental levels will also show when a child is experiencing a significant developmental lag which needs individual remedial attention. Chomsky discovered that pronominalization is firmly established by the age of five-and-a-half; a child above this age who has trouble with pronouns probably needs special help. On the other hand, to spend instructional time on pronouns with fourth-graders, as suggested by one published language arts series, is clearly a waste of time for most children.

Chomsky deals with the mechanics of sentence building; larger cognitive concerns are also important. Lovel (1968) described the relationship $I > C > P$. The ability to imitate (I) is greater than the ability to comprehend (C) which is greater than the ability to produce (P). Concerning comprehension, we must avoid assuming that a child understands what we, or other children have said. In some instances the instructional language used by the teacher may be misunderstood; we sometimes think children have comprehended when perhaps they have not. Acquisition research suggests children hold highly idiosyncratic meanings for compound words (Berko, 1958), and that they have difficulty with phonological and syntactic ambiguity (Schulz, 1973). Understanding figures of speech is also a problem (Stewig, 1980). If children don't respond to directions or questions, it may well be because the teacher has assumed they understand when in fact they don't. As a pair of authors says so well, ". . . the child can have peculiar islands of accuracy amid a sea of confusion" (de Villiers, 1979). To avoid this problem, we adapt our instructional practices to enhance the possibility that children do understand us. In giving directions, for example, effective teachers often try to re-say the instructions, consciously using different language. Or they may ask a child to retell the directions, a comprehensive check that will reveal if the child understood the message.

Lovel's description, $I > C > P$, reminds us that our final goal in language-reading programs is not comprehension, but production. That is, we want to enhance children's ability to *use* language, both oral and written. Analysis tools are available to determine the effectiveness of oral language (Melear, 1974) and written language (Carlson, 1973).

As teachers analyze children's language, they can determine the kinds of production activities students need. For too long many language programs have emphasized knowing about language, instead of active production of language. Analyzing parts of speech, completing work sheets requiring correct word forms, and identifying "best" topic sentences, are examples of knowing about language.

We have ample research evidence that children develop language competencies by practicing them. This means many opportunities to practice reading with less time spent on answering low-level questions about what was read. It means more time speaking in small groups with less time listening to the teacher, who is already a proficient speaker! It also means more time expanding sentences they have written with less time learning names for parts of speech, or parts of a sentence.

Another way to develop language competencies is to build on the information Halliday provides about language function. We could look beyond such surface manifestations of language as vocabulary and grammar, and investigate the uses children make of language in the classroom. We can ask several questions about current language arts instruction:

1. How many of the language arts activities we plan for students engage them in using language for *representational* purposes? Critics of schools suggest this is the pervading language use in schools.
2. How often do we set up situations in which children use language *heuristically*? Reports from British Infant Schools seem to indicate this use of language is more common in British than in American schools.
3. How often do children have the opportunity to use language *imaginatively*?
4. What sorts of activities can we plan that would involve children in *personal* uses of language? (Be careful to reread the distinction between this and imaginative uses. These are *not* the same in Halliday's classification, though we often in overly casual fashion equate them when talking about language.
5. What is the balance, especially at the upper grades, between *interactional* language and more solitary language uses? Informal observations suggest that interactive uses of language become increasingly rare as children leave primary grades.

MODELING

Teachers need to be aware of their role as language models, their language being a tool to stretch or expand the child's language. Related to reading, this means demonstrating an interest in, and a fondness for reading. In some classrooms, learning to read is a grim affair, as too much emphasis on mastery of skills drives out pleasure. To counteract this, classroom teachers read widely to children, sharing the delights to the ear of the cadences in spoken words. Listening to the variety of ways skilled writers use English is a pleasure for children, especially those whose reading skills are not fully developed. Children delight, for example, in the expressive language in *The Amazing Bone*,[10] long before they understand the meaning of every word the author uses. From context they can determine that "the old gaffers" describes the elderly farmers depicted in the picture. Besides pleasure, such listening forms important input, as children assimilate, albeit unconsciously, the many ways language can be used. In addition to the time the teacher reads, children are also encouraged to read to each other, for the shared pleasure which results. Sixth-graders with limited reading skills enjoy going to the kindergarten to read: the young children gain language input, the older ones gain needed practice in reading. Another kind of reading occurs when the teacher schedules time when all—the teacher included—stop to read something of interest.

Regarding oral language, teachers see their language in two ways: (1) as a model of standard English, and (2) as a model for speech expansion. In modeling informal standard English, the teacher should be especially aware of ways the dialect spoken locally is different from standard English spoken elsewhere. While they avoid criticizing children for localisms in their speech, teachers will want to model a variety of standard English which is not locally bound. For example, once when supervising student teachers, I noticed one was having much trouble getting children to write *pin* and *pen* in their spelling list. Listening carefully to the student teacher revealed that she pronounced the words identically, as did her students. The reason the children had difficulty with encoding the words into written English was that there was no difference in their oral speech! In addition to such regional variations, the teachers should also be aware of such ethnic variations as Black English, especially when the dialect is different from the teacher's. Many helpful analyses of such variations are becoming available (Cullinan, 1974). Ways of working with children who speak a primary dialect different from the teacher's are being suggested.

Another example is given by Hohmann (1979), who feels a model of language precision is critical for teachers. She cautions that we must not let

---

[10]William Steig, *The Amazing Bone*. New York: Farrar, Straus and Giroux, 1976. The work of Steig is an effective example of works which because of their picture book format are appropriate for children before most of them can decode the words themselves.

An important kind of language input is the book language children hear as teachers read aloud. (Used with permission of the Racine (Wis.) Unified School District.)

context substitute for language. For example, when teacher and children are next to each other in the classroom, minimal verbal instructions for moving a piece of furniture are sufficient. The teacher could say, "Take that one over there," and the child, seeing the teacher gesture at both the chair and its intended destination, could comply. To develop language, however, it is much more effective if the teacher says, "Take the biggest chair and put it next to the table with the globe on it." This accomplishes the task, but also provides a model of precise adult language for the child to hear.

In using language as a model for speech expansion, the teacher uses vocabulary and syntax that is not limited to what the children already know —vocabulary and syntax that illustrate new possibilities. To choose a simpler word children already know in preference to a more expressive word they may not know does children no favor. Similarly, to purposely simplify speaking patterns when talking to children prevents them from being exposed to more mature syntactical patterns (Granowsky, 1970). In fact, one author suggests that teachers consciously make their speech more complex as the school year progresses. "Such an increase in complexity could provide a programmed text for introducing children gradually to progressively more abstract and difficult syntactic relations" (Moore, 1973).

Such modeling in the teacher's speech is crucial, but there is another equally important aspect to expanding children's language. This is the character of the teacher's direct response to something a child has said. Brown and Bellugi (in Emig, 1966) describe the importance of adults expanding children's syntactically minimal utterances into more complete utterances. When early childhood education teachers were trained to expand by elaborating on children's sentences, significant growth in child language occurred. If the technique works with preschool children, we should explore using it with older children. Thus, when a child says a simple sentence, the teacher could consciously expand the child's sentence in response (Frost & Kessinger, 1976). To the child who says, "I brought you these flowers," the conventional thank-you yields little in expansion possibilities. To say, "I'm so glad you brought me these yellow and red flowers with the tiny black centers," provides the kind of expansion that leads to language growth. Preschool teachers do this expanding often; with teachers of older children it occurs less frequently, though it is a technique worth exploring further.

Another, and perhaps more difficult, way for the teacher to model language is to think of the uses of language Halliday described. If the teacher models only a limited range of language functions, children's uses of language will not be expanded. It is probably safe to say that teachers' language most often falls into the instrumental, regulatory, and representational categories of language use. Yet these are only three of the seven identified by Halliday. In what ways could we, as teachers, provide examples of our own use of language for interactional, personal, heuristic, and imaginative purposes?

A BASE FOR LANGUAGE AND READING

The program in reading and language arts must grow from the child's own language. Because it is easy to confuse *competency in* language with *knowledge about* language, some teachers assume children must be taught how to use language. Nothing could be further from the truth. From several points of view, children are competent language users. Long before they come to school children are in command of English phonology. From the wide variety of sounds made as a baby, the native-speaking child of six has eliminated the non-English sounds, and practiced conventional English phonemes; he or she can pronounce all the sounds necessary as an adult. Vocabulary estimates vary widely, but all indicate children's important mastery of morphology. The kindergartener may come to school with as many as 12,000 words in his or her lexicon, encompassing all the form classes used by adults. Studies of syntax indicate competence; children use all the basic sentence patterns before the age of six. They form questions by the age of two, and construct complex sentences shortly after the age of three (Moore, 1973). What do such competencies suggest about the nature of the language arts program?

A crucial task in reading is to help children learn about the relation between the oral language they use and the written language others have used

Individual students need many opportunities to enhance their oral fluency through story dictation experiences. (Used with permission of the photographer, Richard D. Bradley.)

in books. An easy way to make this relation apparent is by making use of children's dictated language in initial reading instruction. Stories dictated by the total group, or by individuals, can serve as a basis for instruction. The child composes orally, sees talk being written down, and then practices reading what was written. The interdependence of the two forms is thus established. There is research evidence that this procedure results in significant gains in reading (Smith and Adams, 1974), and in oral language (Stauffer & Pikulski, 1974). Dictation techniques also work with older children who have not yet developed their full reading potential. These children can make up stories, dictating or writing them, and practice reading them to younger children in school. Such cross-grade involvement provides reading and composition experiences for the older children and encourages good listening habits when the stories are shared with younger ones.

The task in language arts instruction is to continue developing the abilities children bring to the classroom. To do so teachers might provide extensive experiences in creative drama and choral reading, which challenge children to explore their voices by using them expressively.

In drama we lead children through a series of experiences beginning with basic movement problems, continuing through pantomime, and on to more complex story dramatization and improvisation. Children develop their abilities to use voice to evoke a character, create and sustain a mood, and establish setting and plot sequence (Siks, 1977). In addition to using their voices, children learn in drama to use their bodies for communication, nonverbal "language" being an important component. Schmidt and Hore (1970) studied nonverbal communication because they recognized it was important; school language experiences must help children further develop their competencies in this area. One goal of a language arts program is to help children expand their definition of language beyond an oversimplified concept of written language, which we realize is not the only way to communicate (Stewig, 1979).

In choral reading, movement is minimal, but gesture and facial expression augment the spoken word. As the teacher selects poems or prose appropriate for interpretation by the group, the children should be involved in deciding how the literature will be presented.[11] Klima (in Zale, 1968) and Britton (1970) speak of children making guesses about language, trying ideas and accepting them, depending on their usefulness. Both authorities stress the need for children to understand that language is both convergent and divergent; i.e., it may be used to close in on a solution to some problem, or to propose a variety of novel possibilities.

In schools we should be careful to set up some language situations in which there is no one right answer. We want children to make a hypothesis and try it. Given a poem to be read chorally, we can interpret it in several different ways, varying the uses we make of pitch, stress, and juncture. The teacher presents the poem as a problem to be solved and children suggest their ideas. In working with the entire class, each child's idea is tried, until eventually the most effective way of reading the poem is determined. Another approach is to divide the class into several small groups, encouraging each to work out their own ideas. Sharing these and comparing similarities and differences would be helpful in stimulating discussion abilities. Other comments about choral reading are included in Ross (1980).

PROGRAM BALANCE

Effective teachers understand the balance necessary between group and individual activities in language arts programs. In the current trend toward individualization in schools, those of us responsible for teaching these subjects should keep in mind that some experiences in language must be group experiences. Individualized reading has many proponents, yet time spent working alone on skill development must be balanced by time spent sharing the literature which is read. Some language skills like spelling and handwriting can indeed be effectively learned individually. But time spent this way must be balanced by such group endeavors as creative dramatics, choral reading, and oral reporting, which challenge children to work together—planning, solving problems, and presenting the results, all the while using

---

[11]John Warren Stewig, "Choral Reading: Who Has the Time? Why Take the Time?" ERIC Document Reproduction Service No. 165 110, 1978.

language. Why is group experience necessary in the reading-language arts program?

Language is by nature a group activity, not an individual one. We talk *to* somebody, even if we talk to ourselves. Children grow to language competency by interacting with others. Yet many new materials and instructional programs are essentially individualized materials and programs. The trend is not new.

As a supervisor some years ago in a school nationally known for its individualized program, I saw children at all grade levels working methodically through mimeographed learning packages. For the most part, these children, progressing at their own pace, were interacting with their learning package and their book. They read the learning package directions, studied prescribed texts and related trade books, engaged in writing activities, and took mastery tests at the completion of units.

This trend toward the production and use of individualized language materials has accelerated recently; it is not uncommon to find children engaging in much individual work in language. While there is a rationale for using such materials in skill areas like spelling and handwriting, teachers must take care that these do not dominate language programs. The most important parts of language cannot be learned alone, but must be learned in interaction with others. The teacher wanting to base a language arts program on early acquisition research is careful to balance the individual development of some minor skills with large blocks of time devoted to interactive group activities. For most adults, language is a group experience, and in our current rush to individualize, we must keep in mind the communal nature of language, as we plan programs for children.

SUMMARY

What you have read is summary, outline, and forecast. It is a summary, albeit brief, of a complex, rapidly developing field: language acquisition research. It is a brief outline of some ways this research could affect classroom procedures, if teachers were aware of the researchers' findings. And it is a forecast of what you, a classroom teacher, might do to help your children build on the language skills they bring to your classroom. Basing language programs on these skills can make for an exciting new approach, pleasant for you and your children, and resulting in continued growth in language strengths for your children.

Suggestions for Further Exploration

1. Read Piaget's *The Language and Thought of the Child*, some details of which are summarized in this chapter. What aspects of the research lead you to accept or reject parts of his theory about child language? What features of the research are similar to the Brown and Bellugi study?

2. Observe in a preschool or kindergarten situation for a short time. Record all the speech of at least two children. Attempt to analyze it in relation to Piaget's two categories—egocentric and socialized language. Do the children you observed use more egocentric language than the subjects in his study, or less? Are there some sociological aspects of life in the United States today which might affect how much of each type of language children use?

3. A reference to the work of Bereiter and Engelmann was included in this chapter. In contrast, see the article by Sara Moskovitz, "Some Assumptions Underlying the Bereiter Approach," *Young Children*, October 1968, pp. 24–31. She cites the danger of accepting a rigorous appearing approach without examining its theoretical or empirical underpinnings. A more recent description/ evaluation is in *Contemporary Influences in Early Childhood Education* by Ellis D. Evans (New York: Holt, Rinehart and Winston, 1975, pp. 142–152). Which of these seem to make the most convincing case?

4. The contention was made in the chapter that by the time they enter school, children use all the major sentence types (questions, statements, commands, exclamations; simple, compound, complex). Read about these types. See *Teaching Elementary Language Arts*, 2nd ed., by Dorothy Rubin (New York: Holt, Rinehart and Winston, 1980, pp. 231–232). Then observe the speech of some young children. Do those in your sample really make use of all the types?

5. Some writers believe the inability to deal with words as discrete units impedes the school progress of disadvantaged children. Bereiter and Englemann are among them. Make a comparison between their statement about this issue and the work of Basil Bernstein, a British sociologist, who has written about the same problem in British speech. You might find it helpful to read his *Class, Codes and Control* (New York: Schocken Books, 1975). How are the two positions similar or different?

6. The Berko study (see Bibliography) offers insights into children's language competency. Take some of the items from her test and use them with a group of nursery school or kindergarten children. What similarities or differences do you find between the children you test and the results she reported?

7. Analyze several lessons in a published language arts series. What percentage of lessons seem designed to build on children's language competency? What percentage attempt to increase knowledge about language. Compare your results with those of other students.

8. Find a first-grade child with whom to work. Have him or her dictate a story to you about some topic of interest. Compare the sentence structure in the dictated story with the sentence structure in the reading book the child is using. What similarities do you notice? What differences exist?

9. Select one of the pieces of research or writing which are briefly described in this chapter for further study on your own. Are there factors in the research design, or assumptions made in the writing, which raise doubts in your mind about the conclusions reached?

Suggestions for Further Reading

Anisfeld, Moshe and Tucker, G. Richard. "English Pluralization Rules of Six-Year-Old Children." *Child Development* 38 (1967): 1202–1217.

One of several studies based on work by Berko, this study tested production and recognition of words. It shows that children are in control, but not in complete control of their language by the age of six. Children were asked to deduce plural forms from the singular model and singular forms from a plural model; children did better on the first than on the second task.

Beck, M. Susan. "Baby Talk: How It Grows." *Parents* (April 1980): 52–55 + .

A summarization of the stages of language development from the neonate through the four-year-old. The first stage begins with the baby learning the sounds of the native language. When cooing and babbling, babies are learning language. In fact, babbling children can produce all the sounds used in every language in the world. The article discusses the specific pattern of learning sounds. Young children are able to make nonrandom sound substitutions. Two- and three-year-olds know when to make a particular sound a particular way, i.e., the voiceless /th/ in *three*, or the voiced /th/ in *them*.

At two, children's sentences show knowledge of word position, recurrence, possession, and verb phrases, the beginning of the grammar of language. A detailed presentation of the grammar stages of two- through four-year-olds is provided. Four-year-olds are mastering the meaning of language. These children are capable of metaphors, of making up "jokes," and learning about bizarre semantic combinations. In conclusion, the author points out that one of the most remarkable principles in language development is that while children are learn- ing language they are also active discoverers, who express themselves with originality.

Bissex, Glenda L. *Gyns at Wrk: A Child Learns to Write and Read.* Cambridge, Mass.: Harvard University Press, 1980.

A detailed case study of the processes involved when the author's son learned the two basic skills: reading and writing. Her descriptions show clearly the rigor re- quired as children master literacy. The book's three parts reflect: (a) the child's development in writing, especially invented spellings; (b) growth in reading; and (c) the relation between these two processes. The author questions the neat, orderly compartmentalization of learning broken down into small steps and rewarded too often characteristic of school language programs. The child's growth did not follow a neat progression; rather it was characterized by plateaus, leaps forward, and regressions. Unlike programs which minimize error possibilities, this child was constantly testing himself in situations which allowed for errors. As a result, the author argues strongly for viewing errors as sources of information about instruction.

Bloom, Lois. *One Word at a Time.* Mouton, 1973.

The author has taken a small segment in the language sequence and studied it intensively through the observation/anecdote technique. Studying the language of her own and three other children, she compiled an impressive amount of detail regarding the process by which children move from speaking single words to more complex syntax. In the process, she questions the validity of holophrasic speech, and pivot and open grammar, as concepts which are inadequate descrip- tions of the process of acquisition.

Bolles, Edmund Blair. "The Innate Grammar of Baby Talk." *Saturday Review* 55 (March 18, 1972): 53–55.

The writer, a former Peace Corps worker in Tanzania, offers informal observations about language acquisition. Though his comments are derivative of works by Chomsky, the interpretation in light of linguistic patterns in Tanzania is engaging.

Chomsky, Noam. "Language and the Mind." *Psychology Today* 1(9) (February 1968): 48–51.

An eminent linguist describes language acquisition as the process of theory construction. Chomsky feels the child discovers theories of language using only small amounts of data at a time when he or she is incapable of complex intellectual achievements in other domains. This complex theory building is relatively independent of intelligence or the course of experience.

Dale, Philip S. *Language Development.* Dryden Press, 1976.

The author's easy-to-follow style and clear explanations of complex theories make a fine introduction to the topic. Dale's enthusiasm for his topic should develop similar enthusiasm in readers. Most chapters conclude with at least one related reading, presenting another point of view.

Davis, Alan (ed.). *Language and Learning in Early Childhood.* Atlantic Highlands, N.J.: Humanities press, 1977.

This book presents findings of the Educational Research Board of Scotland, including conributions from 65 educators and researchers. The volume deals with fundamental issues, empirical studies, and practical suggestions for encouraging young children's language and learning. Editor Davis supplies a thoughtful general introduction, as well as separate introductions to each section, resulting in a concise, accessible summary of the extensive work being done in this field. A few topics include: language and the disadvantaged, implications for the future of language education, and recent research on the development of spoken language. The extensive bibliography is useful in directing further reading.

deVilliers, Peter A. and deVilliers, Jill G. *Early Language.* Cambridge, Mass.: Harvard University Press, 1979.

The authors have written in an informal style, designed to allay undergraduates' fears that child language is an arcane subject. From their opening anecdote, to a brief bibliography only 157 pages later, this paperback is reassuringly simple. The deVilliers are dealing with complex questions, i.e., "How does the child learn language so well in so short a time?" Nonetheless, they assume no prior background, and the simple, few-footnote style is easy to read. This is clearly the most accessible of the published introductions to the topic. A longer review of this text, and some background information about the authors is included in *The Chronicle Review*, April 16, 1979.

Ervin-Tripp, Susan. "Language Development." In *Review of Child Development Research*, edited by L.W. and M.L. Hoffman. Russell Sage Foundation, 1966.

The chapter offers a complete consideration of very early language development. The section on phonological development is easier to understand than usual. The explanation of the way learning is a sequence of progressively finer discriminations of sound differences is helpful. Sections on syntactical and morphological development point out that the age at which control of the language is accomplished varies with different languages. The chapter closes with a section on language functions, including comments on speech as an accompaniment to action. Material on style variations in different situations has implications for classroom teachers.

Hopper, Robert T. and Naremore, Rita C. *Children's Speech.* Harper & Row, 1973.

A clear explication, with helpful commonplace analogies, of more complex theories of language acquisition. The section on deep and surface structure, and transforms is especially helpful to novice readers. Another section of potential usefulness to teachers is on children's understanding of language functioning within specific contexts.

Kessel, Frank S. *The Role of Syntax in Children's Comprehension from Ages 6–12.* University of Chicago Press: Monographs of the Society for Research in Child Development, Series 139, Vol. 35, #6, September 1970.

The author examined children's acquisition of three structures in English: the ask-tell difference, the eager-easy difference, and ambiguous sentences, using a population of 50 middle-class children. Results showed that children acquired understanding of the structures earlier than the children used by Carol Chomsky in her earlier study.

Lavatelli, Celia Stender. *Language Training in Early Childhood Education.* ERIC Clearinghouse on Early Childhood Education, 1971.

A valuable summary of language development research is included in Chapter 1. Chapter 2 is also helpful, containing a clear explanation of the difference between deep and surface structure. The child's understanding of the transformation process is explained and some suggestions on how to teach this idea are included.

McDonell, Gloria. "Relating Language to Early Reading Experiences." *The Reading Teacher* (February 1975): 438–444.

Reporting on an interdisciplinary seminar sponsored by IRA, the author begins by describing the relation between reading and language, attributing earlier failures in reading instruction to artificial separations of the two processes. She reviews research in language acquisition, pointing out ways learning to read is like, and unlike, learning to talk. The importance of teachers reading a variety of materials to children is pointed out. Principles of teaching reading using the child's language are included.

McNeill, David. "The Development of Language." In *Carmichael's Manual of Child Psychology*, edited by Paul H. Mussen. New York: John Wiley, 1970, Vol. 1.

Probably the most complete summary source available, this does refer readers to a summary by McCarthy (second edition, 1954) for coverage of earlier research. This chapter describes telegraphic and holophrastic speech, pivot and open class, and other early grammatical classes, with extensive recapitulation of significant related research. A description of the language-acquisition device formulated by Chomsky is helpful. The way language is processed through this, as hypotheses are generated regarding the regularities underlying speech, is also described. The role of parental speech is examined, with attention to ways this speech is filtered through the child's developing system of rules. Other topics include negation and question transformations, and the minimal information available on semantics. The chapter requires a fairly sophisticated understanding of linguistics, or a willingness to "dig out" the sometimes abstruse points being explained, despite the author's admirably lucid writing style.

MacGinitie, Walter M. "Language and Development." *Encyclopedia of Educational Research*, edited by Robert L. Ebel. New York: Macmillan, 1968.

The author summarizes the most significant research in this area; the result is a valuable introduction to a complex field. His reservation about accepting without question research which has been done is important. Much research has been done with unusually bright children (often the investigators' own children) in somewhat atypical situations (alone with adults in a problem-solving context). Thus, results must be interpreted cautiously. All children may indeed go through the stages described, but the ages at which this happens with more typical children may be different.

O'Donnell, Roy C. "Language Learning and Language Teaching." *Elementary English* (January 1974): 115–18.

The author summarizes briefly what is known about language acquisition from birth through age six, commenting on the completeness of the process while acknowledging gaps which exist. He draws clearly the distinction between learning language (production) and learning about language (knowledge about), as described in this chapter. The latter is less important than the former, in his opinion. The distinction between writing and speech—commonly overlooked—is clearly made. In closing recommendations for language arts curricula, the author recommends planned freedom in oral language discussion.

Osser, Harry et al. "The Young Child's Ability to Imitate and Comprehend Speech." *Child Development* 40(4) (December 1969): 1063–1076.

The researchers used middle-class white, and lower-class Negro subjects, four and five years old, who responded to production and recognition tasks. Data were analyzed taking into account the major nonstandard English dialect differences. Despite this compensation, the LCN group made more errors on both measures than did the MCW; decoding an unfamiliar dialect penalized the LCN group. There were substantial differences in both groups between imitation (production) abilities and recognition abilities.

Pflaum-Connor, Susanna. *The Development of Language and Reading in Young Children* (2nd edition). Columbus, Ohio: Charles E. Merrill, 1978.

After a brief introduction to the major theories forming the foundation of language acquisition, the author reviews significant empirical studies. Piaget's concept of *assimilation*, the process by which new input is molded into a present cognitive structure, and *accommodation*, the process by which thought patterns are changed to accommodate new input, are thoroughly discussed. Piaget's task of object permanence is imperative to prespeech behavior: children cannot use a

word to represent something if they are not capable of representing symbolical-
ly. Other experts whose work is presented include deZwart, Vygotsky, Bruner,
and Lenneberg. The book is an invaluable introduction to the field.

Rodd, Linda J., and Braine, Martin D. S. "Children's Imitations of Syntactic
Constructions as a Measure of Linguistic Competence." *Journal of Verbal
Learning and Verbal Behavior* 10 (August 1971): 430–433.

This research is typical of much language study: intensive experimentation with
small groups of subjects concerning complex grammatical questions. The researchers used male and female subjects, ages 21 to 28 months, in an attempt to
clarify relationships existing between production and imitation abilities.
Children do not simply echo adult models heard; imitation is an active process
of assimilating and reorganizing model utterances.

Rupley, William H. "Language Development and Beginning Reading Instruction."
Elementary English (March 1975): 403–408.

The central position of reading in elementary classrooms is acknowledged,
followed by an explanation of reasons why success in reading is directly linked
to the child's oral language fluency. A contrasting view, claiming that acquisition of language is quite unlike acquisition of reading, is presented. The distinction between print and speech is described; programs based on children's speech
are recommended. An extensive list of references is appended.

Bibliography

Bar-Adon, Aaron and Leopold, Weiner F. *Child Language, A Book of
Readings.* Englewood Cliffs, N.J.: Prentice-Hall, 1971.
Becker, Wesley C. "Teaching Reading and Language to the Disadvantaged—
What We Have Learned from Field Research." *Harvard Educational Review*
47 (November 1977): 518–543.
Bellugi, Ursula. "Linguistic Mechanisms Underlying Child Speech." In
Language and Language Behavior, edited by Eric M. Zale. Englewood
Cliffs, N.J.: Prentice-Hall, 1966.
Bereiter, C. and Engelmann, S. *Teaching Disadvantaged Children in the
Preschool.* Englewood Cliffs, N.J.: Prentice-Hall, 1966.
Berko, Jean. "The Child's Learning of English Morphology." *Word* 14 (1958):
150–177.
Bloom, L. *Language Development: Form and Function in Emerging
Grammars.* Cambridge,Mass.: MIT Press, 1970.
Bowerman, M. *Early Syntactic Development.* Cambridge, England: Cambridge
University Press, 1973.
Britton, James N. *Language and Learning.* Coral Gables, Fla.: University of
Miami Press, 1970.
Brown, Roger. *Psycholinguistics.* New York: Free Press, 1970.
Cahir, Stephen R. and Shuy, Roger W. "Classroom Language Learning: What
Do the Researchers Know?" *Language Arts* 58(3) (March 1981): 370.
Carlson, Ruth K. *Sparkling Words.* Geneva, Il.: Paladin House, 1973.
Cazden, Courtney B. *Language in Early Childhood Education.* Washington, D.C.:
National Association for the Education of Young Children, 1981.

Chomsky, Carol. *The Acquisition of Syntax in Children from Five to Ten.* Cambridge, Mass.: MIT Press, 1969.

Cullinan, Bernice, ed. *Black Dialects and Reading.* Urbana, Ill.: ERIC Clearinghouse on Reading and Communication Skills, 1974.

Cullinan, Bernice et al. "Language Expansion for Black Children in Primary Grades: A Research Report." *Young Children* (January 1974): 98–112.

Dale, Edgar. *Techniques of Teaching Vocabulary.* Chicago: Field Educational Publications, Inc., 1971.

Dale, Philip S. *Language Development.* New York: Holt, Rinehart and Winston, 1976.

de Villiers, Peter A. and deVilliers, Jill G. *Early Language.* Cambridge, Mass.: Harvard University Press, 1979.

Dil, Anwar S. *Language Acquisition and Communicative Choice.* Stanford, Conn.: Stanford University Press, 1973.

Donaldson, Margaret. *Children's Minds.* New York: W.W. Norton, 1978.

Emig, Janet A. et al. *Language and Learning.* New York: Harcourt, Brace and World, 1966.

Flegg, Janet. "Mother-Child Interaction Studied." *Communication Quarterly* (Fall 1980).

Frost, Joe L. and Kessinger, Joan B. *The Young Child and the Educative Process.* New York: Holt, Rinehart and Winston, 1976.

Geest, Ten van der. *The Child's Communicative Competence.* The Hague: Mouton, 1973.

Granowsky, Seena. "Kindergarten Teachers as Models for Children's Speech." *The Journal of Experimental Education* (Summer 1970): 23–28.

Halliday, M.A.K. *Explorations in the Functions of Language.* London: Edward Arnold, 1973.

Halliday, M.A.K. *Language as Social Semiotic.* London: Edward Arnold, 1978.

Hohmann, Mary et al. *Young Children in Action. A Manual for Preschool Educators.* Ypsilanti, Mich.: High/Scope Press, 1979.

Huttenlocher, Janellen. "Children's Language: Word-Phrase Relationship." In *Child Language, a Book of Readings,* edited by Aaron Bar-Adon and Weiner F. Leopold. Englewood Cliffs, N.J.: Prentice-Hall, 1971.

Kaplan, E.L. "The Role of Intonation in the Acquisition of Language." Ph.D. dissertation, Cornell University, 1969.

Klima, Edward S. "Knowing Language and Getting to Know It." In *Language and Language Behavior,* edited by Eric M. Zale. New York: Appleton-Century-Crofts, 1968.

Kuczaj, Stan A. "The Acquisition of Regular and Irregular Past Tense Forms." *Journal of Verbal Learning and Verbal Behavior* 16 (1977): 589–600.

Lenneberg, Eric H. *New Directions in the Study of Language.* Cambridge, Mass.: MIT Press, 1964.

Lewis, M.M. *Language and the Child.* London: National Foundation for Educational Research, 1969.

Lindholm, Kathryn J. "Bilingual Children: Some Interpretations of Cognitive and Linguistic Development." In *Child Language* (Vol. 2), edited by K.E. Nelson. New York: Gardner Press, 1980.

Lovel, K. "Some Recent Studies in Cognitive and Language Development." *Merrill-Palmer Quarterly* 14 (April 1968): 123–138.

Luria, A.R. and Yudovich, F.I. *Speech and the Development of Mental Processes in the Child*. London: Staples press, 1959.

Malmstrom, Jean. *Understanding Language*. New York: St. Martin's Press, 1977.

Melear, John D. "An Informal Language Inventory." *Elementary English* (April 1974): 508–511.

Moore, Timothy E. *Cognitive Development and the Acquisition of Syntax*. New York: Academic Press, 1973.

Moskowitz, Breyne Arelen. "The Acquisition of Language." *Scientific American* 239(5) (November 1978): 92–108.

Piaget, Jean. *The Language and Thought of the Child*. Cleveland, Ohio: The World Publishing Co. (Meridian Books), 1965.

Ross, Ramon R. *Storyteller*. Columbus, Ohio: Chas. E. Merrill, 1980.

Schmidt, Wilfred H. and Hore, Terence. "Some Nonverbal Aspects of Communication between Mother and Preschool Child." *Child Development* (September 1970): 889–896.

Schultz, T.R. "Development of the Ability to Detect Linguistic Ambiguity." *Child Development* (December 1973): 728–733.

Siks, Geraldine Brain. *Drama with Children*. New York: Harper & Row, 1977.

Simmons, Barbara and Lawrence, Paula S. "Beginning Reading: Welcome Parents." *Childhood Education* (January/February 1981): 156–160.

Smith, Frank L. and Miller, George A. *The Genesis of Language*. Cambridge, Mass.: MIT Press, 1966.

Smith, Grace. "Listening to the Language of Children." *Young Children* (March 1974): 133–140.

Smith, Lewis and Adams, R.W. "Experience Approach to Reading." *Instructor* (November 1974): 72–73.

Stauffer, Russel and Pikulski, John. "A Comparison and Measure of Oral Language Growth." *Elementary English* (November/December 1974): 1151–1155.

Stewig, John Warren. "Nonverbal Communication: 'I *See* What You Say.'" *Language Arts* (February 1979): 150–155.

Stewig, John Warren. *Read to Write: Using Children's Literature as a Springboard to Writing*. New York: Holt, Rinehart and Winston, 1980.

Stibbs, Andrew. *Assessing Children's Language: Guidelines for Teachers*. London: Ward Lock Educational and National Association for the Teaching of English, 1980.

Vygotsky, L.S. *Thought and Language*. Cambridge, Mass.: MIT Press, 1962, pp. 17–19.

Weeks, Thelma E. *The Slow Speech Development of a Bright Child*. Lexington, Mass.: Lexington Books, D.C. Heath, 1974.

Wells, Gordon. "Apprenticeship in Meaning." In *Child Language* (Vol. 2), edited by K.E. Nelson. New York: Gardner Press, 1980.

Wells, Gordon. "Variation in Child Language." In *Language Development*, edited by V. Lee. London: Croom Helm, 1979.

Wilkinson, Andrew. *The Foundations of Language*. New York: Oxford University Press, 1971.

Zale, Eric M. *Language and Language Behavior*. Englewood Cliffs, N.J.: Appleton-Century-Crofts, 1968.

CURRICULUM IN
THE LANGUAGE
ARTS

No single source of information is adequate to
provide a basis for wise and comprehensive decisions about the objectives of the school. (Tyler,
1950, p. 4)

The language arts occupy an important place in elementary
school programs. The term *language arts* includes the primary communication skills of reading, spelling, and speaking as well as such unifying skills as
creative writing, drama, and interpretive listening. How these skills can be
integrated into a harmonious entity, forming the basis for the majority of
human learning, is a major curriculum concern (Rank, 1979). For classroom
teachers wrestling with the problem of a desirable interrelationship among
the language arts *and* the relation of language skills to other skills, several
questions are perturbing. These are typical:

What language skills are really important for learners at any particular
   stage of development?
How can the broad outlines of what is important be specified in detail?
Which instructional materials can best help me attain my purposes?
How can I teach spelling to learners who aren't really interested?
How much should I stress reading? Is one approach more effective than
   another?
Do I have to teach drama?
How should I use the graded language arts series adopted by the school
   system? (Moss, 1975)

Another list of such questions is provided by Petty (1976). General
answers to such questions can be sought through the study of a rational ap-

proach to curriculum development. As these questions show, curriculum development is a process involving decisions about: What? When? For whom? How? Prior to concern with these questions, however, comes the most fundamental question: Why? The field of curriculum points to ways of dealing with this question also.

RATIONAL CURRICULUM DEVELOPMENT

In a rational approach to curriculum, consistency is the hallmark. Consistency is required in the curriculum decisions made at various levels of responsibility. The basic level is society or the community which a school serves. Following directly from the societal level is the institutional level, including such school personnel as superintendents and principals. One of the major responsibilities at this level is the management of the schools in ways consistent with the community's value orientation. In an era when financing public schools is becoming more precarious, administrators know schools must reflect the community's values. The next level of decision making, the instructional level, consists primarily of teachers. Among the major responsibilities of the teacher is the identification of purpose, the design of methods to attain purpose, and the evaluation of progress toward the desired purpose, all of which need to be in harmony with the community's expectations. Figure 2-1 presents a model based on Goodlad and Richter (1966) to illustrate this relationship.

A closer examination of these levels can emphasize the need for consistency. The *societal level* is represented by such agencies as school boards and the local, state, and federal government. These agencies might determine general aims to be pursued, but they are not usually concerned with specific proposals for attaining these aims. A typical product from this level of decision making is a statement of goals for a school system, prepared by the local board of education. As an example, the Cincinnati Public Schools *Language Arts* guide (1975) includes such general goals as: "To foster good listening habits," "To increase use of Standard English," and "To recognize that language can be a powerfully influential tool."

The *institutional level* involves decisions made by central office and

FIGURE 2-1 *A Conception of the Curriculum Decision-Making Process*

Levels of Decision Making	Areas of Decision Making
Societal Level	Values
Institutional Level	Goals
Instructional Level	Objectives
Instructional Level	Teaching Strategies
Instructional Level	Evaluation

supervisory personnel, administrators, or curriculum committees. These decisions are made for types of learners rather than for specific children. Decisions might be made regarding the types of composition experiences eight-year-olds should encounter. Such decisions might specify the organization of the language arts content, i.e., by eighth grade all students should have been introduced to predicate adjectives. Such decisions might also specify general approaches, i.e., one school might choose a bidialectical approach in which students learn to speak Standard Dialect as opposed to another approach in which children use their own dialect (Vacca, 1975). A typical product from such a group is a curriculum guide. Such guides are periodically evaluated by a committee of the National Council of Teachers of English (Winkeljohann, 1980).

At the institutional level, knowledge about learning theory, philosophical concepts, contemporary society, and subject matter can be used in decision making, but information about individual learners in specific situations is unavailable. Decisions are made for hypothetical learners who are prototypes of individuals.

The *instructional level* involves decisions made by a teacher or team of teachers who have direct responsibility for specific children. Curriculum decisions at this level include those relating to specific objectives and the feasibility of a particular activity for a specific group of learners. For example, the teacher may be using a guide which lists the objective: "The students will use the correct mechanics of speaking before a group." (Clark County, 1977) It is up to the individual teacher to select from among the activities suggested those which seem most appropriate to help the class attain the objective. In this case, information about individuals is an important source of data.

Instructional Level Decisions

It is at the instructional level that teaching occurs and that the learners can be found. This is undoubtedly the level of decision making of most interest to readers of this book. To examine it in greater detail, four classic questions having great relevance for the teacher should be studied:

1. What educational purposes should the school seek to attain?
2. What educational experiences can be provided that are likely to attain these purposes?
3. How can these educational experiences be effectively organized?
4. How can we determine whether these purposes are being attained? (Tyler, 1950)

To put it another way, the identification of direction or purpose is the essential first decision required of the teacher. His or her purposes should be consistent with those of the institution. Following this, the development and organization of educational experiences or learning activities is needed.

FIGURE 2-2 *Conception of the Relation among Preinstructional, Instructional, and Postinstructional Curriculum Decisions*

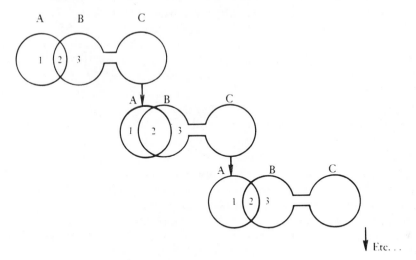

A = what is planned (preinstructional)
B = what occurs (instructional)
C = evaluation (postinstructional)
1 = what is planned that does not occur
2 = what occurs that has been planned
3 = what occurs that has not been planned [1]

Last, evaluation is necessary to determine whether the specified purposes have been attained. This process is illustrated in a model from Duncan and Frymier (1967) shown in Figure 2-2.

If A and B are congruent, everything that has been planned occurs in the teaching situation and everything that occurs in the teaching situation has been planned. In actuality, this rarely happens. More frequently, much of what has been planned occurs, but much unanticipated instruction also occurs (Huenecke, 1969). One of the major reasons for considering the above four questions is to reduce (not necessarily eliminate) the inefficiency and ineffectiveness which result when there is little consistency between preinstructional and instructional decisions.

The instructional level of curriculum decision making forms the focus of this book. More precisely, much of the rest of this book is devoted to learning activities or teaching strategies in the language arts.

---

[1] One pair of authors has vividly described this aspect of curriculum, in writing about students who learn "in spite of school," despite fragmented skill programs unrelated to children's experience. See "Real Communication—Key to Early Reading and Writing," by Nancy L. Roser and Julie M. Jensen, *Childhood Education*, November/December 1978, pp. 90–93.

But how does the teacher decide which strategies are appropriate in a given situation, with particular students? Clearly, there are vast numbers of teaching strategies and resources, but teachers operate with limited time facilities and resources. For example, one curriculum guide (St. Louis, 1975) suggests twelve different materials that could be used at the fifth-grade level to teach synonyms/antonyms. Not all of these will be appropriate for all learners. In addition, the teacher will not find all of these fit his or her ideas about teaching. To resolve what may be a source of conflict, teachers should reach decisions about strategies with conscious knowledge of their own values and goals.

Although classroom teachers are influenced by societal values and institutional goals, they need to examine their own values and goals to deal rationally with the curriculum decisions that bombard them. Teachers' personal values and goals need to be congruent and/or complementary to the society and institution being served if the teacher is to remain happy and mentally healthy. It is no small wonder that rationality is to be desired under such conditions as these! Figure 2-3 illustrates the dilemma.

In the sections that follow, values, goals, objectives, teaching strategies, and evaluation techniques will be examined.

FIGURE 2-3 *The Curriculum Decision Dilemma at the Instructional Level*

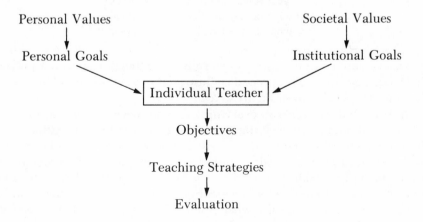

VALUES

In today's ever-changing, fluid society, it is unwise to generalize about group values, expectations, or mores since many of these may be ethereal. Shifts in societal values have been hypothesized by many writers.[2] The value shifts

---

[2]See bibliography entries for Mead, Packard, Reich, Toffler, and Whyte.

A group of teachers listens to a presentation about a new set of curriculum materials (Used with permission of the Racine (Wis.) Unified School District.)

they have suggested, particularly in relation to such topics as work, sex, money, and family structure, have had a vital impact on what society expects from education.

It is very difficult to determine contemporary values or hypothesize future direction. A major problem in assessing societal values is that they can best be viewed historically. It is virtually impossible to determine current mores or values, particularly if they differ from those that have become conventional.

For the classroom teacher, local community values and expectations may have more relevance than those of the larger society (Hunkins, 1980). In a country as vast as the United States, including virtually every type of geography, topography and climate, populated by people from every walk of life, having within its borders members from many religious and ethnic groups, the views of the local subculture may be far more influential than those of the larger society. For example, Wallace (1979) states: "The teacher's role is that of discussion leader, guide and observer, reminder, and encourager, rather than final authority." This statement is reflective of some views, but is not reflective of local attitudes in other areas. Teachers may find themselves teaching in some areas where parents do, in fact, want them to serve as final authorities. Assessment of these views and how they contribute to an educational environment is a necessary prerequisite for rational curriculum development.

Personal Values

As indicated in Figure 2-3, evaluation of one's own personal values is needed also. Attitudes, beliefs, and values are terms often used interchangeably in discussing the "feeling" dimension of humans. In actuality, the difference among these terms is probably one of degree rather than kind. *Attitudes* are fairly transient responses to certain situations; *beliefs* are somewhat more stable and deep-seated. *Values* refer to the deepest and most meaningful human feelings; they affect not only one's thoughts, but actions as well.

Seven criteria a feeling must meet in order to be classified as a value are suggested in the book *Values and Teaching* (Raths et al., 1966). The criteria include:

CHOOSING

1. freely
2. from alternatives
3. after thoughtful consideration of the consequences of each alternative

PRIZING

4. cherishing, being happy with the choice
5. willing to affirm the choice publicly

ACTING

6. doing something with the choice
7. repeatedly, in some pattern of life.

Three major criteria are stressed. First, values must be chosen, not imposed. Second, the person holding a particular value must be proud of it. Third, feelings classified as values must be manifested in behavior; if a feeling is not supported in action, it is not a value.

A rationale for much human behavior can be found in the individual's values though identifying these is not easy. Introspection may yield the identification of several feelings that meet the valuing criteria. In addition, *Values and Teaching* describes numerous strategies that can be used in the value-clarification process. The book is an excellent resource for teachers who want to examine values with their students, but it is also useful in suggesting procedures for examining one's own values.

In the investigation of personal values, it is important to keep in mind that *no area of human concern is irrelevant in dealing with values in relation to education.* Although values concerning individual worth, work, and intelligence have an obvious relation to the classroom behavior of the teacher, any affective area has relevance in the interaction among human beings, especially in schools. In *Values and Teaching*, ten areas are identified that are particularly fertile for yielding data about values:

1. money	6. politics and social organization
2. friendship	7. work
3. love and sex	8. family
4. religion and morals	9. maturity
5. leisure	10. character traits

If a person can become increasingly aware of his or her feelings in relation to such topics as these, self-knowledge will increase. For teachers, this awareness may aid in identifying what is important for education. Clarification of such ideas results in the establishment of educational goals. In addition, teachers can choose to help students clarify their own values in relation to such topics as the above, by using drama in the language arts program (Duke, 1978).

EDUCATIONAL GOALS

Educational goals are broad statements that generally identify desirable ends of education. Goals are long range; it may be intended, for example, that goals be attained by the end of twelve years of schooling (Hansen & Kimpston, 1981).

Innumerable sets of goals have been developed. Virtually every school district has a list which they have either developed or adapted from another source (Northern Valley, 1976). Although most of these sets of goals are very similar, it is, nonetheless, crucial for teachers to examine carefully what has been outlined as important by their school district. As a result, curriculum decisions at the instructional level can be congruent and/or complementary with those made at the institutional and societal levels.

National Sources of Goals

Educational goals may be developed by the federal government through such activities as the White House Conference on Education. National education organizations also formulate goals to reflect the thinking of their members. Statements of goals or purpose may be obtained from such organizations as the International Reading Association, the National Council of Teachers of English (Glatthorn, 1980) and the Association for Supervision and Curriculum Development (Wiles & Bondi, 1979).

Goals from these sources may be widely publicized and discussed, but there tends to be less follow-through on them than on district-wide or state goals. In general, the farther removed the source of goals at the institutional level from the situation where they are to be implemented, the less likely they are to be translated into objectives at the instructional level.

State Department Goals

Another source for goal statements is state departments of education. In the state of Georgia, for example, the Georgia Board of Education developed a set of goals appropriate for "children and youth—to live successfully in Georgia and United States of 1985 and beyond" (Division of Planning, 1970). To accomplish this, four tasks were undertaken:

1. The examination of the social, economic and political life of Georgia.

2. The projection of the probable social, economic, and political life in Georgia through 1988.
3. The identification of goals for education; the knowledge, skills, and values that will enable the citizen of Georgia to live successfully in the future.
4. The projection of the type of education system necessary to achieve the desired goals.

As a result, a list of seventy-seven goals was developed. Some which might appropriately be the concern of the language arts are included below:

1. *The Individual and Himself*
   The individual possesses the ability to read, speak, write and listen.

2. *The Individual and Others*
   The individual possesses the ability to understand and cope with dissent.

3. *The Individual and His Physical Environment*
   The individual possesses an appreciation of the beauty of nature.

4. *The Individual at Work*
   The individual possesses pride in workmanship and accomplishment.

5. *The Individual at Leisure*
   The individual uses as a listener, participant, and/or observer one or more of the arts or crafts in recreational and leisure time activity.

Teacher Goals

Regardless of the source of goals, each teacher needs to define for him or herself what he or she believes are the important outcomes of a long-term educational experience. Generally, the major task is not identifying worthwhile goals but ordering priorities among them. Examining basic feelings and values may expedite this perplexing task. Whether goals are formulated by individuals or institutions, however, several common elements are generally considered:

1. The nature and concept of the society in which these goals will operate.
2. An image of the type of person education is striving to create
3. The structure and amount of knowledge available at any particular time. (Keith et al., 1968)

As they are cited in this section, goals are statements identifying such broad behaviors that they offer only *macroscopic* (or large, general) direction for the teacher. To be practical in terms of everyday use, goals need to be refined into objectives that provide *microscopic* (or small, particular) direction (Lazarus & Knudson, 1967). Translation of goals into detailed objectives takes place on the instructional level of decision making as described in the following sections.

INSTRUCTIONAL OBJECTIVES— ONE APPROACH

Instructional objectives are statements of intent for specific learner behavior. They vary from goals in that they are more specific—so much so they can realistically be attained in thirty minutes to an hour of instruction.

Decisions pertaining to instructional objectives require much teacher time and consideration. In specifying objectives, teachers have access to many aids: textbooks, curriculum guides, programmed materials, and objectives exchanges.[3] Regardless of the expertise of those who prepared these materials, however, one essential component is lacking—only the professional teacher in the situation has access to the specific learners. Knowledge of students' needs, interests, and abilities is crucial at the instructional level.

Mager Objectives

A widely used format for stating objectives is based on *Preparing Instructional Objectives* by Robert Mager (1962). Essentially, three components are required:

1. the conditions under which an identified behavior is to occur
2. a readily observable behavior
3. the criteria of acceptable performance

The first phrase in these objectives is a description of the conditions under which the behavior should occur. The conditional phrase identifies the situation in which the learner is to demonstrate attainment of the behavior. Examples of conditional statements include: "Given a human skeleton. . . ," "After viewing the film 'The Five Chinese Brothers'. . . ," and "After the class has agreed on a title for the picture. . . ."

The second phrase identifies the desired learner behavior. Using Mager's format, it is imperative that the behavior be observable. The following behavioral terms are useful in stating this type of objective:

---

[3]One such source was described in "The Instructional Objectives Exchange: Progress and Prospects," a symposium presentation given at the American Educational Research Association Annual Meeting in Minneapolis, March 1970, by W. James Popham. The paper describes the work of a nonprofit corporation in California which collects and distributes such objectives.

write	perform	dissect
recite	verbalize	assemble
list	arrange	reproduce
construct	circle	complete
rephrase	pantomime	underline

The last phrase describes minimal acceptable performance. If the established criterion is not achieved, the objective has not been attained. Criterion performances most often are described in quantifiable terms; the concept of percentages is useful in this regard, though at least one English Education expert has contended that all behavioral objectives should be stated in binary terms: pass or fail, happen or not happen, present or absent (Hoetker, 1970).

It should be clear that these are highly structured statements requiring a high degree of specificity. This fact contributes significantly to the *usefulness* of these objectives as well as to their *uselessness*. That is, these statements should be used only when a precise, predictable outcome is desired, for instance, in such areas as punctuation, spelling, grammar, and pantomime. The following objectives serve as examples:

1. Given a paragraph with no punctuation at the end of sentences, the student should be able to place a period, an exclamation point, or a question mark correctly in thirteen of the fifteen sentences.
2. When presented with the words orally, the student should be able to write spelling words with 100 percent accuracy.
3. Given a page with ten sentences (both active and passive), the student should be able to label the sentences with 90 percent accuracy.
4. When given a slip of paper with a description of a common activity written on it, the student should be able to pantomime the activity so that the other students can correctly identify what he or she is pantomiming within one minute.

This type of objective has questionable value when individuality of response is desired. Mager objectives should be used in situations where an accurate outcome is possible. They are appropriate *only* in convergent situations where correct information is obtainable. In situations where there are a large number of answers or where accurate information is unobtainable, this type of objective is unsuitable.

INSTRUCTIONAL OBJECTIVES — ANOTHER WAY

A second widely used format for stating objectives is based on the taxonomies of educational objectives which classify human behavior into three realms:

cognitive, affective, and psychomotor.[4] In contrast to the Mager-type objective, when the cognitive and affective taxonomies are utilized, behaviors are identified that are *not* readily observable. Nonobservable intellectual and emotional behaviors from the taxonomies are specified for which behavioral indicators must be identified when evaluation is made.

Further, the conditions under which the behavior is to occur and the criterion performance are not identified. Thus, use of the taxonomies results in an objective statement that specifies only the behavior and the content to which it is to be applied. Examples of this type of objective and a discussion of the taxonomies follow.

Cognitive Taxonomy

The cognitive taxonomy lists six major categories of cognitive or intellectual behavior, which are sequential and cumulative. They represent a hierarchy of behavior; each behavior prepares for the next while including all those that precede it in the classification. Objectives based on the cognitive taxonomy can be employed in virtually any area of the language arts. Even for such skills as penmanship—which basically requires muscular coordination—knowledge is required. The major cognitive levels, examples of behavior at each level, and sample objectives are presented below (Bloom, 1956):

1.0 KNOWLEDGE

Knowledge involves recalling such things as specifics, methods, processes, or structure. It is concerned with bringing to mind appropriate material. Little, if any, alteration of the material is required.

Objectives stated at this level could employ such behavioral terms as:

a. define

b. recall

c. recognize

Sample objectives:

The student should recognize capital letters in cursive writing.

The student should recall the definitions of the following terms: transformational grammar, syntax, word class.

2.0 COMPREHENSION

This level involves understanding the literal message of an idea, including the ability to translate, interpret, and extrapolate.

Objectives stated at this level could employ such behavioral terms as:

a. translate (verbalize mathematical symbols, etc.)

b. draw inference

---

[4]See bibliography entries for Bloom, Krathwohl, and Simpson.

c. generalize
d. summarize
e. draw conclusions
f. predict

Sample objectives:

The student should generalize about the writing style of E. B. White.

The student should translate a reading story into a play.

3.0 APPLICATION

Application involves the ability to use abstractions in concrete situations. The abstractions could be general ideas, rules, methods, principles, or theories which need to be remembered and applied.

Objectives stated at this level could use the term:

a. apply

Sample objectives:

The student should apply knowledge of short vowel sounds as found in the consonant-vowel-consonant pattern in figuring out new words that follow that pattern.

The student should apply knowledge of suffixes to make the following words plural: . . .

4.0 ANALYSIS

This level involves breakdown of material into constituent parts so the relation among parts is clear. Such analyses will illuminate the basis and organization of the material.

Objectives stated at this level could employ such behavioral terms as:

a. classify
b. identify elements
c. detect (fallacies, causal relations, etc.)

Sample objectives:

The student should classify the following words into their word class: . . .

The student should identify the common elements in "The Three Little Pigs," "Snow White and the Seven Dwarfs," and "Little Red Riding Hood."

5.0 SYNTHESIS

Synthesis involves the putting together of elements and parts of a whole. This process combines elements to form a structure that is new to the learner.

Objectives stated at this level could employ such behavioral terms as:

a. design
b. integrate
c. propose

d. formulate

e. create

Sample objectives:

The student should create an original story using the format of a fairy tale.

The student should integrate at least two propaganda techniques into an original TV commercial.

6.0 EVALUATION

This level involves making judgments in terms of *internal* evidence (organization, consistency, etc.) or in terms of *external* evidence with reference to standards of criteria.

Objectives stated at this level could employ such behavioral terms as:

a. distinguish

b. assess

Sample objectives:

The student should evaluate the effectiveness of the metaphors in a poem containing at least three metaphors.

The student should evaluate a TV commercial using criteria he or she establishes.

Affective Taxonomy

The same general assumptions forming the basis of the cognitive taxonomy also apply to the *affective taxonomy*. That is, levels presented below are sequential and cumulative (Krathwohl, 1964).

1.0 RECEIVING

At this level the learner is sensitized to the existence of certain phenomena and stimuli. The learner is willing to receive this stimuli while remaining neutral or in a state of suspended judgment.

Objectives stated at this level could employ such behavioral terms as:

a. aware of

b. conscious of

c. sensitive to

Sample objectives:

The student should be aware that poetry can be written in many forms.

The student should be sensitive to the fact that there are many interpretations of Robert Frost's poetry.

2.0 RESPONDING

Responding involves doing something with or about the phenomena.

Objectives stated at this level could employ such behavioral terms as:

a. obeys
b. accepts
c. enjoys
d. participates
e. is interested in
f. appreciates
g. rejects
Sample objectives:
    The student should participate willingly in a spelling game.
    The student should enjoy reading.

3.0 VALUING

At this level the learner displays a particular behavior consistently in appropriate situations.

Objectives stated at this level could employ such behavioral terms as:
a. desires
b. is committed to
c. is devoted to
d. values
Sample objectives:
    The student should value the right of everyone to express individual opinions.
    The student should be committed to taking care of the books in the room.

4.0 ORGANIZATION OF VALUES

As more and more values are internalized, situations arise where more than one value is relevant. At this level, the learner is continuously involved in organizing his or her values into a hierarchy or harmonious relationship.

5.0 CHARACTERIZATION BY A VALUE OR VALUE COMPLEX

At this level of internalization, the values that have been previously organized control the learner's behavior to the extent that he or she can be described or characterized according to these values. The learner acts according to these values without conscious thought. A total philosophy or world view is developed. This level takes a long time to achieve and is changed only by a traumatic experience.

Instructional objectives based on the first three levels of the affective taxonomy can be used for any area of the language arts. Levels four and five are not appropriate when considering instructional objectives because they involve long-range behaviors. Because objectives are statements of purpose that can realistically be attained after one or a few sessions, the more advanced affective behaviors cannot realistically be attained under these conditions. Instead, these levels are better described in statements of goals that identify long-range outcomes.

Psychomotor Domain

The third area of human behavior is the *psychomotor domain*, which includes the motor skills or those requiring muscular coordination.

Objectives using psychomotor behaviors apply most obviously to these language areas: penmanship, articulation, enunciation, and the decoding dimension of reading. The major levels, behavioral terms within each level, and sample objectives are listed below (Simpson, 1966-67):

1.0 PERCEPTION
This level is parallel to the first level of the affective taxonomy. It refers to the process of becoming aware. Which sense or combination of senses form the avenue of awareness is important in this domain. Behavioral terms that can be used include:
a. hears
b. sees
c. feels (touches)
d. smells
e. tastes
Sample objectives:
The student is visually aware of the difference between "B" and "D."
The student hears the difference in format between free verse and conventional poetry.

2.0 SET
A set involves preparatory readiness or adjustment for a particular kind of action or experience. A set can be *mental*, requiring prerequisite knowledge; *physical*, requiring appropriate anatomical adjustment; or *emotional*, requiring a willingness to respond. In addition to terms from the first level of the cognitive taxonomy and the second level of the affective taxonomy, the following may be used:
a. assumes the position
Sample objectives:
The student should position the paper correctly before beginning the penmanship lesson.
The student should locate the reading story after the page number is given.

3.0 GUIDED RESPONSE
This level involves the overt behavioral performance of the learner under the guidance of the instructor. This behavior may be the result of imitation or trial and error. The following behavioral terms can be used at this level:
a. imitates
b. follows along as demonstrated
c. discovers

Sample objectives:

The student should imitate the figures "D" and "B" on paper as the teacher demonstrates them on the blackboard.

The student should imitate the sounds the teacher makes.

4.0 MECHANISM

At this level, a particular learned response has become habitual so it is part of the learner; the learner has developed confidence and skill in this behavior. Any behavioral terms indicating a single action can be used at this level.

Sample objectives:

The student says a spelling word before spelling it aloud.

The student projects his or her voice clearly when participating in creative dramatics.

5.0 COMPLEX OVERT RESPONSE

At this level, a complex motor act can be performed with a high degree of skill. Appropriate behavioral terms are those that signify complex actions performed skillfully.

Sample objectives:

The student should be able to set up the puppet stage alone.

The student should be able to choose appropriate tapes and use the tape recorder correctly at the listening station.

Three Taxonomies

In many instances, a simple lesson will incorporate objectives from all three domains, as illustrated in the following lesson for a primary group:

The learner should recognize new words in a reading story.
(Cognitive taxonomy)
The learner should be interested in reading a new story. (Affective taxonomy)
The learner should be able to pronounce the new words.
(Psychomotor taxonomy)

CONTRASTS AND CAUTIONS

There are several distinct differences between the objectives based on Mager and those based on the taxonomies. Mager's objectives require three components: a statement of behavior and content, the condition under which the behavior is to occur, and the minimal acceptable performance. The taxonomic objectives consist of only the first of those components. This is not to say that when taxonomic objectives are utilized, consideration is not given to learning conditions and their evaluation. These factors merely are not included in the statement of purpose itself. Thus, when taxonomic objectives are used, in addition to the objective itself, explicit attention must be given to the teaching environment designed to provide for the attainment of the objective. Mager's conditional phrase identifies contexts allowing for the attainment of the specified behavior. A separate statement is needed for this purpose with taxonomic objectives.

A similar situation exists with regard to evaluation. Mager's third phrase describes the minimal acceptable performance of the objective. When taxonomic objectives are utilized, identification of an evaluation technique for assessing performance needs to be detailed apart from the objective.

Another contrast between the two types of objectives concerns the behavior. In Mager's approach to objectives, the behavior must be readily observable. This is not true for the cognitive and affective taxonomies. With both types of objectives, however, inferences are made about unobservable behavior. With the Magerian format, the inference is made that "listing" or "reciting orally" is an indication of certain cognitive processes. If this were not the case, there would be little value in the listing or reciting. With objectives based on the cognitive taxonomy, the intellectual process is identified and the overt behavior that gives evidence of this behavior is inferred. "Reciting out loud" may be inferred as evidence of "recalls"; so indeed may "lists." One of the strengths of taxonomic objectives is that they allow for a variety of ways in which an intellectual or affective behavior can be expressed. Many examples of this variety of expression are included in the next chapter.

A third difference between the two types of objectives relates to the number of learners for whom the objectives can appropriately be designed. In general, taxonomic objectives can be formulated for a larger number of students than can Mager-type objectives which eliminate the appropriateness of one objective for many students because of their high degree of specificity. Any given taxonomic objective can apply to many students for several reasons. *First*, because there are a variety of ways in which a particular cognitive or affective objective can be expressed, many students can be accommodated within one objective. Thus, if "summarize" is the desired behavior, some students can summarize orally, others can summarize in paragraph form, and others by outlining. All three situations can provide evidence of the learner's ability to summarize. A *second* reason taxonomic objectives can be applied to many students is that no criterion needs to be established. This means different degrees of accuracy and different amounts of work can be accepted from learners who possess different needs and abilities. One guide (Indiana, 1978) includes this objective: "In a group discussion, the students participate as leaders by summarizing the progress of the group." Because no criterion is established, students working toward this objective can attain different degrees of accuracy and do different amounts of work. Because Mager-type objectives are so specific, any one objective can be applied only to a small group (Mason et al., 1980).

Cautions

Several cautions regarding objectives need to be voiced. Objectives have been discussed as statements of purpose for learner behavior that the teacher formulates apart from the learner. This need not be the case. In many instances, it is highly desirable that students for whom the objectives are intended be included in the formulation process.

Objectives detail purpose and give direction to instruction. When an objective is developed, it is assumed that the learners for whom it is intended have not achieved the behavior specified. *At no time* should an objective be formulated under the following conditions: (1) it is reasonably impossible for the student to attain the objective (Pratt, 1980, p. 185); (2) the student can already perform what is specified in the objective. In both cases, a teacher abrogates his or her responsibility if he or she violates these conditions.

An increasing problem with objectives is that they have more and more been used for a purpose other than the one suggested here. Objectives should be used to specify desired learner behaviors, or what the student will do in the learning situation. A problem arises when such objectives are used to generate mastery test items for each objective (Shawnee Mission, 1975). It is readily apparent that if teachers know test items will be written to assess particular competencies, they will teach those competencies. As one author points out, this model assumes that the whole, generalized ability is the sum of the parts (Algozzine, 1981). Any teacher of language arts knows that language competency is far more than the sum of the parts of specific language skills.

Finally, the whole area of instructional objectives needs to be kept in proper perspective. *Objectives are a means to an end, not an end in themselves.* If the practice of writing objectives becomes ritualized to the extent that concern for the quantity of objectives or their format takes precedence over the content and quality of the objectives, the purpose of the objectives is lost.

TEACHING STRATEGIES

Teaching strategies, educational experiences, and learning activities are generally synonymous terms referring to activities designed for students for the purpose of attaining specified behaviors. Here, again, consistency is of the utmost importance. Teaching strategies should be planned that seem likely to encourage desired learner behavior as specified in objectives.

Although it is impossible to predict that a given type of learning will result from a given teaching strategy, thoughtful analysis reveals that some strategies more than others are apt to promote certain behaviors. Clear definition of objectives is essential for such an analysis.

When objectives specify intellectual behavior, analyses based on the cognitive taxonomy can yield useful data. Overgeneralization is hazardous but, in most cases when learning at the knowledge level is sought, lectures, discussions, or reading assignments can be appropriately incorporated into teaching strategies for the attainment of knowledge. These strategies are invariably content oriented and often teacher centered. When higher level cognitive behaviors are sought, less teacher-centeredness is desirable.

A parallel can be drawn for behaviors classified at the higher affective and psychomotor level. Thus, as you proceed through the levels, more and more individual interpretation is required. Strategies that encourage independence and freedom are most likely to encourage the attainment of these behaviors.

No specific strategies are discussed here because in the chapters that follow a wide variety of teaching strategies are presented. As readers incorporate many strategies into their repertoires of teaching behaviors, it is hoped they will be aided in the selection of which strategies to employ under which conditions by the curriculum principles presented in this chapter.

EVALUATION

Evaluation of students' abilities and progress presents some of the most perplexing problems encountered in teaching. Questions of reliability, validity, and objectivity plague the teacher. Far too often the term evaluation conjures up images of standardized and teacher-made tests. This is truly unfortunate as evaluation involves judgment that can be made based on evidence from many sources, not just test results.

When the model for rational curriculum decision making, illustrated on page 39, is employed, one major aspect of the evaluation of instruction stands out above all others: *evaluation must always be done in relation to objectives.* Judgment of achievement should be made only in relation to what has previously and thoughtfully been defined as desirable achievement.

Evaluation of Mager-Type Objectives

If the Mager-type objective format is used, questions of evaluation are encountered from the beginning. Decisions about identification of criterion performance and methods for evaluating behavior are made as the desirable behavior is identified.

As cited earlier, this type of objective is most useful for specifying skills. Evaluation thus becomes a relatively simple matter because deciding whether a student can read a particular story orally, for example, is accomplished by obvious means.

A major consideration with Magerian objectives is the criterion performance. Generally, 100 percent accuracy is too much to realistically expect for all students for whom the objective is intended. On the other hand, if the expectation of the criterion performance is lower than 85 percent, it is questionable whether the objective is appropriate. Another objective for which greater accuracy can be realistically expected might be better. The establishment of uniform minimal performances tends to limit Mager objectives to small groups of students.

Evaluation of Cognitive Objectives

Movement through the levels of the cognitive taxonomy takes one from generally convergent to generally divergent situations. For this reason, evaluation of the lower levels is often easier to obtain than of the higher levels. This is because solutions requiring convergent thinking involve data that can usually be verified or authenticated.

For example, in either oral or written form, students can be readily evaluated for the following behaviors:

ability to recognize the initial consonant sound of /d/ (knowledge)
ability to recognize iambic pentameter (knowledge)
ability to recall the main characters of the story (knowledge)

Less congruent but still relatively easy behaviors to evaluate include:

ability to translate what is happening in a picture into words (comprehension)
ability to summarize the peculiar features of fairy tales (comprehension)

Evaluation becomes more difficult in a divergent situation as the possibilities for being correct increase. Thus, when students are to assess a poem using a given set of criteria, personal interpretation and application of the criteria can result in as many different yet "correct" assessments as there are students.

Evaluation of Affective Objectives

It is with the *affective taxonomy*, however, that the greatest problems of evaluation occur. It is impossible to assume at the stage of identifying affective behaviors how the manifestation of that behavior may appear in the student. The way an individual might express attitudes or appreciations is indeed uncertain. For example, one guide includes: "Develops appreciation for the writing of others." (Alabama, 1976) The ways this objective is manifested could differ. For example, while listening to a writer read a story, an intent gaze might be an indication of enthusiasm by a generally passive child, but it could indicate boredom on the part of another. Evaluation in the affective realm is further complicated by the fact that attitudes which have no opportunity to be expressed in school may be possessed by a student. It would be foolish to assume under these conditions that the attitudes are lacking.

It is in the affective realm that many of the joys of teaching occur. When an apathetic child becomes enthusiastic over a picture, a song, a field trip, the teacher can know a very special satisfaction. When a child shyly hands the teacher a poem he or she wrote the night before, hours of hard work are suddenly rewarded. Surely such behaviors are to be cherished whenever they occur, even if their achievement cannot be readily systematized or assessed.

Few would deny the importance of student interest or involvement. Thus, the necessity for identifying affective behaviors in objectives seems apparent even in the face of many difficulties to be found in attempting to evaluate them.

SUMMARY

Decisions about *what* to teach and *how* to teach are among the most pressing in education. Such decisions become more difficult as community members become increasingly vocal about demanding that schools perform one task or another. At various levels of decision making, such pressures must be taken into account. At the *societal* level of responsibility, the value orientation or mores of the community influence decisions about what should be taught in a general way. At the *institutional* level, the tasks of school administrators include more specific designation of content as well as some consideration of instruction, the manner in which content is presented.

It is at the *instructional* level of decision making where teachers operate. One of their major responsibilities is to specify content and desirable student behaviors (Kneller, 1974). They also need to organize content and, based on knowledge about their specific students, determine which instructional strategies are most likely to attain the specified behaviors.

As readers progress through this book, they may become increasingly aware of the many possibilities available to teachers. As you face decisions about purpose, content, learner behavior, and teaching strategies, you should attempt to act consistently with societal and institutional expectations. Further, each decision you make needs also to be consistent with your other decisions.

Suggestions for Further Exploration

1. Determine whether the following curriculum decisions should most appropriately be made at the societal, institutional, or instructional level:
   a. Should students be allowed to read controversial books?
   b. What should the sixth-grade students do in spelling on Wednesday?
   c. What language arts textbook series should be ordered for the school?
   d. How should creative writing be evaluated?
2. Choose such an area of language arts as creative writing. Formulate at least six questions that a teacher must deal with in this area at the instructional level.
3. Following is an example of an educational goal: "The student should be able to express himself or herself with ease." Formulate five instructional objectives for it.
4. For one month, collect newspaper and magazine articles that deal with purposes or goals for education. Categorize and analyze them.
5. Locate the teacher's manual for an elementary language arts textbook. Categorize the objectives according to the three taxonomies and the level within each category. Can you draw any conclusions from your classification?

6. Read *Classroom Questions: What Kinds* by Norris Sanders (see annotation, p. 178) for a presentation of the types of questions to ask to elicit thinking at the various cognitive levels. Develop questions in a language arts area at each level.

7. Read *On Writing Behavioral Objectives for English*, edited by Maxwell and Tovatt (Champaign, Ill.: National Council of Teachers of English, 1970). The chapter entitled "On Hunting and Fishing and Behaviorism," by Robert F. Hogan is particularly well written. As a result of reading this and comparing it with what is presented in this chapter, determine for yourself which approach detailed in the above book presents the more convincing case about objectives.

Suggestions for Further Reading

Christensen, Jane. "Color and Spirit." In *Needs of Elementary and Secondary Education in the 1980's*. Washington, D.C.: U.S. Government Printing Office, 1980, pp. 453-462.

The author, a department chair in a junior high school, opens with the point that curriculum, apart from its natural dynamic setting between teacher and students, often seems to lack life. As implemented in real settings, curriculum is a dynamic intersection between the disciplined, structured sequence of the craftsman, and the freedom and invention of the artist. The true challenge for the teacher is to provide for both. Every field of study contains the basics of craftlike structure, and the basics of artistic freedom. Both are interdependent and equally important. The real danger today is that one is losing out to the other.

The subject matter, which ideally has colored the mind and heart of the teacher, is the vehicle for bringing curriculum to life. The teacher's contagion allows the whole process to flourish. To continue to do this, teachers need retraining and revisioning. A critical problem is how the teacher can stay alive and vital in a situation fraught with problems. Christensen suggests eight ways to revitalize the teacher. Each is valid, though in this brief compass, she was not able to explore fully sources of funding which would make these good ideas workable, since each would cost additional money. Her concluding argument is that we cannot measure only small, easy-to-measure pieces of teaching and learning in simplistic testing and call it "whole." That is the real danger in current trends of "back to basics," which her article counteracts so effectively.

Conroy, Pat. *The Water is Wide*. New York: Dell Publishing, 1972.

The paperback that followed the movie "Conrack" enables additional audiences to follow the adventures of a teacher on his initial foray into the struggle to overcome both the hazards of a status-quo Superintendent of Schools and a school full of children, all black, who speak only Gullah, our only acknowledged Afro-American dialect. The problem of what to teach such students (curriculum) and how to teach it (instructional strategies) is compellingly treated.

Genishi, Celia. "Letting Children Communicate: The Synthesis of Language Skills and Language." *Language Arts*, September 1979, *56*, 628–633.

In planning curriculum, teachers must distinguish between teaching specific language skills and enabling children to develop and use the language they already have. Analyzing recent research and being cognizant of increased demand for basic skills and measurable objectives, Genishi calls for language curricula in which teaching skills and cultivating children's language are carefully synthesized. The article is extremely helpful for those teachers who may be somewhat warily facing the back-to-basics issue as they plan language arts programs. Increased public demand for accountability in education too often translates into satisfactory performances on standardized achievement tests. The result is a return to more formal, traditional curriculum and methods. Although the author does not elaborate on specific planning strategies for creating a balanced program, she does focus on some techniques used by three effective language arts teachers which provide some guidance and motivation.

Hoffman, M. J. "The Harmful Effects of Traditional Language Arts Teaching Methods When Used with Disadvantaged Afro-American Children." *Elementary English*, May 1970, *47*, 678–683.

A degree of linguistic sophistication on the part of the classroom teacher is not only desirable but indispensable if some harmful effects of traditional language arts curricula are to be avoided in respect to the disadvantaged Afro-American pupil. This article suggests that teachers lack sophistication in working with such students because their training does not adequately prepare them. More adequate preparation will help teachers to:

1. discover the existence of language learning problems of which he or she was unaware earlier.
2. learn the reasons for one's own lack of awareness
3. understand why faulty common-sense assumptions are made
4. comprehend the nature of language learning problems in general

The author concludes with a discussion of the language sophistication desirable in a teacher.

Johnson, K. R. "When Should Standard English Be Taught to Speakers of Nonstandard Negro Dialect?" *Language Learning*, June 1970, *20*, 19–30.

The hypothesis of this paper is that disadvantaged black children should not be taught standard English until adolescence or the secondary grades. Johnson specifically discusses some of the reasons standard English instruction should be delayed, including the difficulties children have in learning another dialect of a language because of the subtle differences between standard English and nonstandard English. Johnson lists many things that the language arts program should concentrate on for these children, including encouraging black children to use their own nonstandard Negro dialect. At the intermediate level, the teacher should plan activities that point out differences in language systems as children learn that there are varieties of English. No value judgment need accompany these differences. It is at this level that instruction in hearing the differences between standard English and nonstandard Negro dialect should begin. The author feels that standard English should be taught as an alternate dialect to be used in appropriate situations, rather than a replacement dialect.

Madden, Peter. "Magazines and Newspapers for Children." *Childhood Education*, April/May 1977, 328–336.

> In planning curricula, teachers sometimes rely too heavily on available textbooks. In contrast, magazines and newspapers can provide up-to-date factual information in more depth than is possible in books. In this article, the author presents full bibliographic information, including source and cost, for 125 periodicals. A brief annotation is included for each. The list includes magazines, like *Dance* and *Ebony*, that are essentially for adult readers.

Zais, Robert S. "Content." In *Curriculum: Principles and Foundations*. New York: Thomas Y. Crowell, 1976, pp. 322–349.

> Opening this chapter, the author points out that until 1960 no aspect of school received as little attention among professional educators as subject matter. He notes, for example, that teachers were fully prepared to deal with new *methods* of teaching math, but totally unprepared to deal with new *content*. Current tendencies to separate and elevate "knowing how" from "knowing what" appear unjustified. Some definitions of content exclude skills (processes) and affects (values) while other definitions include these. As curriculum planners we tend to select *content* (record of human knowledge) in terms of its importance to us as adults. *Knowledge* is increased/deepened meaning which results from our transaction with content. The problem is that the learner may generate entirely different knowledge as a result of contact with the content we select. This results, for example, in English grammar (being): "taught and retaught throughout all of school life, for students to pass their grammar examinations, and then to graduate from high school knowing no grammar." Another significant question he raises: Should curriculum include content from both the disciplines and from informal sources (less organized and less vigorously validated information)? Related specifically to English education, one might raise two related questions: (1) Is there such a body of informal sources about language which traditional English programs overlook? (2) Are such informal sources in the process of working their way into the formal content of the English program?

Bibliography

Alabama State Department of Education. *Alabama Course of Study. Language Arts K–12*. Montgomery, 1976, p. 58.

Algozzine, Jane. "Viewpoints." *Language Arts*, January 1981, pp. 4–5.

Bloom, Benjamin S. (ed.) *Taxonomy of Educational Objectives, Handbook I: Cognitive Domain*. New York: David McKay, 1956.

Cincinnati Public Schools, Department of Curriculum and Instruction. *Language Arts*. Curriculum Bulletin No. 105, 1975, p. 13.

Clark County School District, Department of Instructional Services. *Language Arts*. Las Vegas, Nevada, 1977, pp. 6–10.

Division of Planning, Research, and Evaluation. *Goals for Education in Georgia*. Atlanta: Georgia Department of Education, 1970.

Duke, Charles R. "Educational Drama, Role-Taking, and Values Clarification," in *Educational Drama for Today's Schools*, ed. by R. B. Shuman. Metuchen, N.J.: The Scarecrow Press, 1978, pp. 63–86.

Duncan, James K. and Frymier, Jack R. "Explorations in the Systematic Study of Curriculum." *Curriculum Theory Development: Work in Progress, Theory into Practice*, Vol. 6. Columbus: College of Education, The Ohio State University, 1967.

Glatthorn, Allan A. *A Guide for Developing an English Curriculum for the Eighties*. Urbana, Ill.: National Council of Teachers of English, 1980.

Goodlad, John I. and Richter, Maurice N., Jr. *Development of a Conceptual System for Dealing with Problems of Curriculum and Instruction*. Cooperative Research Project No. 454, United States Office of Education. Los Angeles: University of California and Institute for Development of Educational Activities, 1966.

Hansen, Harlan S. and Kimpston, Richard D. "An Educational Contradiction: Is What Schools Say They Teach What They Really Teach . . ." Minneapolis: College of Education, University of Minnesota, 1981, p. 7.

Hoetker, James. "Limitations and Advantages of Behavioral Objectives in the Arts and Humanities." In *On Writing Behavioral Objectives for English* (J. Maxwell and A. Tovatt, editors). Urbana, Ill.: National Council of Teachers of English, 1970, pp. 49–59.

Huenecke, Dorothy M. "The Relation of Teacher Expectations to Curriculum Guide Implementation." Ph.D. dissertation, University of Wisconsin, 1969.

Hunkins, Francis P. *Curriculum Development: Program Improvement*. Columbus, Ohio: Charles E. Merrill, 1980, pp. 65–86.

Indiana Department of Public Instruction. *Basic Objectives in Language Arts K–12*. Indianapolis: Division of Curriculum, 1978, p. 15.

Keith, Lowell; Black, Paul; and Tiedt, Sidney. *Contemporary Curriculum in the Elementary School*. New York: Harper & Row, 1968.

Kneller, George F. "Behavioral Objectives? No!" In *Curriculum Planning: A New Approach* (edited by Hass et al.). Boston: Allyn and Bacon, 1974, pp. 225–228.

Krathwohl, David et al. *Taxonomy of Educational Objectives, Handbook II: Affective Domain*. New York: David McKay, 1964.

Lazarus, Arnold and Knudson, Rozanne. *Selected Objectives for the English Language Arts, Grades 7–12*. Boston: Houghton Mifflin, 1967.

Mager, Robert F. *Preparing Instructional Objectives*. Palo Alto, Cal.: Fearon Publishers, 1962.

Mason, Betty O. et al. "Competency-Based Approach to Language Arts: Pre-Kindergarten through Grade Five." In *Three Language Arts Curriculum Models* (B. J. Mandel, editor). Urbana, Ill.: National Council of Teachers of English, 1980, pp. 23–34.

Mead, Margaret. *Culture and Commitment: A Study of the Generation Gap*. Garden City, N.Y.: Natural History Press, 1970.

Moss, Joy. "A General Language Arts Program in an Informal Classroom." *The Elementary School Journal*, January 1975, pp. 239–250.

Northern Valley Regional High School District, Closter, N.J.: *Language Arts Curriculum Guide, Performance Expectations, K–12*. ERIC Document Reproduction Service No. 140 329, 1976.

Packard, Vance O. *The Pyramid Climbers*. New York: McGraw-Hill, 1962.

Petty, Walter T. (ed.) *Curriculum for the Modern Elementary School*. Chicago: Rand McNally, 1976.

Pratt, David. *Curriculum: Design and Development*. New York: Harcourt Brace Jovanovich, 1980.

Rank, Janice. *One That Works! An Integrated Program of Basic Skills.* ERIC Document Reproduction Service No. 173 762, 1979.

Raths, Louis E.; Harmin, Merrill; and Simon, Sidney B. *Values and Teaching.* Columbus, Ohio: Charles E. Merrill, 1966.

Reich, Charles A. *The Greening of America.* New York: Random House, 1970.

Roser, Nancy L. and Jensen, Julie M. "Real Communication—Key to Early Reading and Writing." *Childhood Education*, November/December 1978, pp. 90–93.

St. Louis Public Schools. *Teacher's Guide for Language Arts, Grades 4–8*, 1975, p. 32.

Sanders, Norris M. *Classroom Questions: What Kinds?* New York: Harper & Row, 1966.

Shawnee Mission, Kansas Public Schools. *Elementary Language Arts, 4–5: Sequencing and Keying of Language Arts; Test Specifications for Criterion-Referenced Testing.* ERIC Document Reproduction Service No. 114 843, 1975.

Simpson, Elizabeth. "The Classification of Educational Objectives, Psychomotor Domain." *Illinois Teacher of Home Economics*, Winter 1966–67, *10*, 110–144.

Toffler, Alvin. *Future Shock.* New York: Random House, 1970.

Tyler, Ralph W. *Basic Principles of Curriculum and Instruction.* Chicago: University of Chicago Press, 1950.

Wallace, Eunice (ed.). *Language Arts Guide K–12.* Boise: Idaho State Department of Education, Division of Instruction, 1979, p. 82.

Whyte, William H. *The Organization Man.* New York: Simon and Schuster, 1956.

Wiles, Jon and Bondi, Joseph. *Curriculum Development: A Guide to Practice.* Columbus, Ohio: Charles E. Merrill, 1979, p. 227.

Winkeljohann, Sr. Rosemary. *English Language Arts Curriculum Guides K–12.* Urbana, Ill.: National Council of Teachers of English, 1980.

3

LANGUAGE IN EARLY CHILDHOOD EDUCATION

> In order to educate children who are able to use language in various forms for different purposes, we need to teach the skills essential to reading and writing—and we need to let children communicate. Communication does not occur while they quietly complete worksheets. It occurs when children and adults talk to each other, attend to what others say or write, and express themselves freely. (Genishi, 1980, p. 61)

By its sounds, symbols, and signs, language makes it possible for humans to be distinctive creatures. Language is characteristically human and plays a leading role in most human activity. Because language is vital to becoming a civilized person, adults must provide young children opportunities to acquire language early and then direct them in its use.

Language builds more easily and efficiently when there is a need to communicate and to learn new words to communicate more effectively. The earlier children confront this need to communicate, the sooner they are able to internalize perceptions and store them in their memory. From this language reservoir, children can bring forth new combinations of words as they experience new things, ideas, and situations in the environment.

The purpose of this chapter is threefold: (1) to examine the functions of language, (2) to suggest basic principles upon which classroom teachers can develop language experiences, and (3) to suggest sample practical techniques involving children in the effective use of language. These functions, principles, and techniques must represent a realistic bridge between what is happening inside and outside the classroom. If this is accomplished, the language learned will enable young children to better understand, interpret, and integrate into their environments.

THE FUNCTION OF LANGUAGE

Early childhood education encompasses programs from birth through the primary grades or, in terms of language, from the child's first newborn cry to a more sophisticated and highly solidified language pattern. To understand our professional roles in guiding the early acquisition of language, we need to review the basic functions of language.

Language identifies wants and needs. This function of language is basic to human communication. All humans, from birth, have needs requiring satisfaction. Initially, a gesture, a grunt, or a cry may make known one's desires. But as desires and needs become more complex, or more refined, the child has no alternative but to learn and use language which will insure prompt and full gratification.

Language facilitates the acquisition and exchange of information and ideas. Without language one would have a limited understanding and awareness of life. Language determines one's picture of reality and gives meaning to experience. The fact that no one person can understand or experience all that the world has to offer demands an exchange of information and ideas. This exchange broadens understanding of personal experiences and makes us aware of events not yet experienced.

Language is a means of expressing feelings and emotions. Language is rarely neutral, even in the exchange of information and ideas. Language which conveys a host of affective sensations provides therapeutic release as well as a vehicle to hurt, to humor, to hate, to hail, to convince, to excuse, to taunt, or to love. The greater the language facility, the greater the chance for emotional release and the more directly one's feelings, via language, hit their mark. Teachers need to encourage children to release their feelings, thus enabling them to build appropriate language for this function. Feelings are basic to human nature. To suppress them in the name of classroom control retards the development of the language that serves the function of expressing emotions.

Language is a means of self-identification. The need we have for self-understanding is continual throughout life. All people strive to find out, or attempt to run from finding out, who they are and what their limits and potentials are. Language is tied directly to self-identification in two ways. Initially, it is the language of others which helps build or break a child's self-esteem. Words such as *good, bad; right, wrong; do, don't; can, can't; should, shouldn't* continually remind boys and girls early in life of the kind of person they are perceived as being. It also continually reminds them of the kind of person someone else would have them become. However, as we gain inner dependence, it is our ability to understand, explain, defend, and justify ourselves to ourselves which produces the climate for self-acceptance and worthwhile change. Language facilitates this continual introspection and seeking of inner security as well as enables us to seek external help.

Language is a means of social interaction. Humans are social beings—forced by circumstances and specialization into contact with others. We work with others for a livelihood and seek others for companionship. How well we can communicate our ideas and interests will determine how successful we will be in both endeavors. Language not only aids in communicating with others, it enables us to better understand and accept others in order to work and relax in closer harmony. In addition, language denotes each of us. It is one of the initial measures people use in accepting and rejecting others—not only in the quality of the thought, but in the skills of expression.

Language is a basis for reflective thinking. Language need not be vocal. Many more thoughts and ideas churn internally than ever see the vocal light of day. People constantly reflect on the multitude of situations and problems encountered in all phases of their daily lives. One's ability to put these thoughts into proper perspective allows for a more organized vocalization of them. Such ability also assists in mentally settling minds and putting reflections in some order. The reflective thinking process is enhanced or hindered by the language brought to the task.

Language is a basis for extended thinking. Creativity must operate from a foundation of some sort. We do not create from a void (Torrance, 1970). How well we are able to put together new language combinations is dependent on the number and quality of words available to us. We often expect creative language from children without giving consideration to the need for providing a rich foundation of varied language experiences. These experiences provide the basis for the expansion to new and imaginative language.

Language is adaptable to alternate forms of communication. Although oral language was mainly dealt with in the previous discussion of language functions, oral expression is but one of a variety of methods of communicating. Gesture, graphic, and mechanical code systems intermix to form the multiple communication systems used by humans (Garrey, 1974). Our ability to understand, interpret, and respond to the varied forms rests on our awareness of these alternatives. Children begin to demonstrate ability to perceive and utilize such nonverbal clues as gestures and proxemics between the ages of three and five years (Melson & Hulls, 1975).

The purpose of this brief consideration of the functions of language is to illustrate the broad spectrum that "language" embraces and to give direction in the evaluation and selection of early-childhood language programs.

LANGUAGE APROACHES

Children come to initial education programs with language acquired through a random array of experiences in the home and community. There is a need to systematize experiences so all children develop a broad language base. But at the same time, the unique dialects and idiolects found within the children, their families, and community need to be given their rightful role (Broman, 1978). The teacher of young children needs to identify an approach to language development which will assist in providing optional language experiences. A short discussion of the available alternatives should assist in making decisions regarding the advantages of each approach, and aid the reader in determining which is best for a given situation. As pointed out in Chapter 2, making decisions of what to teach, to whom, and how, is difficult. It is hoped that this consideration of alternatives will make such decisions easier for teachers of young children.

The Language Kit Approach

The language kit, of which the *Peabody Language Development Kit* (Level P–3 to 5 years mental age) is perhaps the best known, provides a total language program (Dunn & Smith, n.d.). The Peabody Kit provides language-development activities to fill a forty-minute period each day throughout the school year. The program functions independently of other content areas and features a systematic segmental approach to language development.

Another example is the *Scholastic Early Childhood Program*, *Language Reading Module*. This box of materials includes an excellent 454-page teacher's guide as well as such materials as puzzles, posters, lotto boards, and duplicating masters. An important feature of the program is informational letters to send home to parents, providing for parent involvement. Also useful for forging a link between home and school are sheets suggesting activities children and parents can enjoy together. The reading component in this program is admirable. It provides significant opportunity to learn for those children who are ready, but does not exert heavy pressure for mastery on those children who are not yet ready.

In the absence of a better plan, kits offer an organized approach to developing language. However, because children come to initial education programs with various language needs, the sequential aspect of the program may be inappropriate for some who are beyond or behind that particular lesson on that particular day (Roser & Jensen, 1978). In addition, it may be that, while the skill is appropriate, the content included in the lesson has little relation to what is happening in the children's environment and, therefore, has little relevance for them.

Perhaps the best use for such programs as these is as supplemental work for individual children with special language disabilities.

The Language Arts Text-Series Approach

Textbook language series have traditionally been introduced at the beginning of third grade. Now, however, it is more typical for publishers to also produce texts for grades one and two. In addition, some publishers are producing kit materials for the early childhood years, correlated with texts for succeeding grades. Continued emphasis on early childhood education will no doubt prompt publishers to explore the development of more programs for the very young. The extension of this subject matter approach into the early years continues to segment learning and often fails to integrate language into the total learning environment.

The Reading Program Approach

In the absence of a broad range language arts textbook, a reading program often doubles as the language program.[1] New vocabulary is presented by the words in the stories and usage parallels the sentence structure of the stories. This can represent a very narrow approach. Language acquisition and use justify their own existence; language development need not be subservient to other content areas. Rather, increased language development should heighten a child's contributions to other parts of the curriculum.

An alternative concept worth considering is *Success in Kindergarten Reading and Writing: The Readiness Concept of the Future*, by Adams (1978). This program, which combines aspects of both language arts and reading, is unlike others described above, not based on a series of books for children to use. Each of the seven grade levels available has a handbook for the teacher. In the guide, the four program modules are described: (1) the alphabet and spelling patterns of written English; (2) written composition; (3) purposeful reading of everyday print (like newspapers); and (4) recreational reading. At the kindergarten level, mastery of reading is not the major concern. Rather, exposure to meaningful print is the important goal. In this program, which features total class participation and then individual work (rather than several small groups), each child writes every day. Low on publisher-prepared sequentially organized materials to be purchased, this does demand a high level of teacher involvement and initiative.

The Total Program Approach

This approach, having great potential for effective language development, is described in detail below. It is based on the premise that the teacher, knowing the children and their language capabilities, is the most logical person to plan the curriculum. In this approach, teachers plan individual language activities, concerning themselves with when and how such activities should occur.

---

[1]Many articles have appeared about both sides of this issue. Arthur M. Enzmann, "A Look at Early Reading," *The Reading Teacher*, April 1971, *24*, 616–620, is among those who have pointed out that the more important question is *how* such early instruction is given. Other sources include Christine LaConte, "Reading in Kindergarten," *The Reading Teacher*, November 1969, *23*, 116–120, and the comprehensive summary available in Delores Durkin, "When Should Children Begin to Read?" in *Innovation and Change in Reading Instruction* (Chicago: The 67th Yearbook of the National Society for the Study of Education, Part II, 1968), pp. 30–71.

THE PROGRAM AS A BASIS
FOR LANGUAGE DEVELOPMENT

The total-education program, which includes the classroom as well as community environment, provides the most legitimate and meaningful basis for language development.[2]

The following discussion deals with the need for establishing a classroom climate that will stimulate children to learn. It *describes* language techniques rather than *prescribes* them because the most effective language development results when a child responds to his or her environment rather than to a kit of language activities and lessons. The key to language development is a stimulating and enriching environment which generates new language patterns.

Any approach to educating young children must rest upon some basic assumptions—or keystones. These provide the rationale for selecting appropriate content, materials, and activities. Without the identification of these keystones, programs may eventually accomplish worthwhile outcomes but in the manner of someone driving to an unknown point without the benefit of a map or concise directions. This is a luxury one may indulge in while on a vacation, but in the elementary curriculum, time is of the essence!

To expose young children to the world around them in the limited time available, professionals need to systematize their approaches, even though such approaches can be individualized and open ended.

The following keystones provide a model for teachers of young children to examine, digest, and compare with their existing or emerging set of basic assumptions. Basic assumptions are similar to the values you were urged to examine in Chapter 2. These assumptions or values need not be absolute; yet, they should be given consideration in establishing early childhood programs that will maximize the language potential of each child. As you read, think about the values you yourself hold. How do your values concerning early childhood language education compare or contrast with those presented in this chapter?

KEYSTONES
Keystone 1

The early years provide the initial direction intelligence, achievement, and attitude patterns will take later on. Therefore, early programs need to address themselves to long-range goals rather than to shortsighted yearly goals.

Benjamin Bloom's review of studies relating the impact of the early environment on later growth patterns concluded that by age nine at least 50

---

[2]For a more complete description see D. C. and M. A. Davis; H. S. and R. M. Hansen, *PLAYWAY: An Interest Center Approach to Initial Education* (New York: Winston Press, 1973), including expanded treatment of learning environments, interest centers, play centers, unit topics, and scheduling.

percent of the general intelligence achievement and attitude patterns measured by age eighteen have been developed (Bloom, 1964). Because many researchers suggest that scores on standardized intelligence tests and achievement measures directly correlate with verbal acuity, the early development of language is crucial. And because the early identification of attitudinal patterns is now receiving greater focus, we must concentrate more on helping children to acquire the language facility needed to internalize, interpret, and articulate their feelings. Further evidence suggests that it is questionable whether any amount of remediation at a later date can compensate for a void of enriching experiences in the early environment.

Keystone 2

A concept of differential treatment makes it possible for the total environment, in and out of school, to be introduced into the early childhood learning classroom. Treatment, in the simplest sense, refers to the degree of depth and scope afforded a certain concept by the activities and materials employed in its consideration (Davis, 1965). Three types of treatment are appropriate in discussing educational situations.

Skill treatment is an overlearned, habitual reaction or conditioning on the child's part. When children are skilled in certain areas, they have mastered the feat. At the early childhood level, there are few areas where children have the ability to become skilled—mainly, in the operational acts of listening, following directions, and persisting; and in the manipulative acts of cutting, pasting, folding, tearing, and marking. Children need to develop the appropriate language to accompany skill development in these areas.

Stories read aloud serve as a stimulus to talk. (Used with permission of the Racine (Wis.) Unified School District.)

71

Foundational treatment sets the stage for a later development. It requires a minimal group understanding to assure that children are ready for further exploration and involvement. Ideas and experiences treated foundationally result in specific vocabulary which a child utilizes orally and mentally for further verbalizing.

Basic readiness areas of reading, writing, and communicating fall under foundational treatment. Because these are important to the child's later progress in school and in life, and because they demand a mental and verbal understanding to some normative level, the development and use of accurate and appropriate language is vital.

Finally, *impressional treatment* intends only to systematically make children aware of materials, topics, and experiences. There is no attempt to define or fix this affective learning because at this age children are unable to draw upon a storehouse of experiences and vocabulary in articulating their innermost thoughts. Early childhood education programs broaden children's horizons during these critical years by exposing them to a wide variety of enriching experiences. When children encounter these materials and topics later in school or life, they may be better prepared to understand them.

The performing arts provide the most logical avenue for impressional treatment. To insist on a foundational or skilled treatment in this area would fail to allow each child to accept, reject, change his or her mind—and would fail to provide the early opportunity to initiate a basic self-value system.

In these days of accountability many educators, politicians, and parents question the notion of impressional treatment. Not measuring objectively every area of the curriculum upsets the cost accounting procedure deemed so necessary by some. Yet the school's job is broader than just "opening up" heads and stuffing in "things." Feelings and appreciations need to be nurtured gently and slowly so each child has the opportunity to identify his own likes and dislikes, independently of what mentors deem "good" or "bad," "worthy" or "unworthy."

The use and development of language during impressional treatment becomes highly individual—and may remain internal and seemingly dormant until the vagueness begins to clear and form a more well-defined pattern. Teachers of young children must not become frustrated because of previous teacher-training practices which placed a heavy emphasis on verbalizing the content of the curriculum. Rather, they should keep sight of the eventual outcomes of effective impressional treatment—a child whose language will reflect the enthusiasm and excitement derived from being immersed in an interest she or he selected.

Keystone 3

A stated curriculum is necessary to identify the content of the program, and a stated or implied vocabulary is necessary for meaningful involvement.

There are many ways of stating—or not stating—a curriculum. Some people feel a curriculum should emerge from children's interests, fixing experiences and related languages as they randomly emerge (Sowards & Scobey, 1968). To others, it is crucial to identify those process skills that are important for understanding and that apply to many situations. Learning and vocabulary are built, in addition, around such concepts as *over, under; large, small; high, low; in, out; behind, in front of;* and so forth.[3] Others would plan and have available a variety of curricular areas in which children could become involved if they so choose. Another approach identifies and applies crucial unit topics but leaves actual learning and application for more appropriate spontaneous small group and individual situations. And finally, there is a strong move to bring the content of grades into the early years with sequential subject matter blocks of time and with children generally progressing in groups at the same rate and by the same method. In each case, the curriculum planner is attempting to answer the questions raised in Chapter 2, though the resulting curricula are very different from one another.

The approach utilizing the systematic unfolding of a unit topic has the optimal potential for laying group foundations while allowing for individual application. A unit introduces the vocabulary for a topic, establishes a way of thinking about the topic, and stimulates ways of observing and identifying in the broader environment. All children are involved in this unfolding while being at various levels of understanding and application. The open-ended quality of the unit allows each child to apply this knowledge in meaningful and spontaneous, not contrived, experiences throughout the unit and school year. This procedure allows children to progress at their own rate through their own sets of learning styles from the previously laid foundations. Each following unit adds more potential for individual application. This is the type of flexible expectation described in Chapter 2 which identifies the advantages of taxonomic objectives in planning a curriculum. Some appropriate unit topics encouraging this individual response will be discussed in the section on learning environments.

The important point to remember is that if language comes from the curriculum, what a child "gets out" of the curriculum in terms of language and vocabulary development will be in proportion to the thought and planning a teacher has "put in."

"Doing your own thing" may be important. Yet in the early years a child's "thing" may be a random, fleeting thing to which adults put too much meaning. To be gently nudged "up and beyond" their present interest, ability, and language level in areas of cognitive, motor, and affective development will allow children to develop more interests and to become more personally involved as growing young adults.

---

[3]Many children's books by Tana Hoban are useful in concept development. Such books as her *Push Pull Empty Full* (New York: Macmillan, 1972) contain few words to accompany dramatic, clear black/white photographs illustrating concepts.

Keystone 4

A one-to-one correspondence must exist between the in- and out-of-school environment so classroom learnings and related language have immediate value to the rest of the child's world. To that end, *resource persons, field exploration*, and *artifacts* must be extensively utilized. No one teacher and no one classroom can hold all the knowledge, expertise, and experience necessary to satisfy the changing needs and goals of our educational programs. Why not, then, tap the community for available sites, skills, and related tangibles to provide a bridge between the classroom and the community? In so doing, we will be fulfilling the often discussed, but seldom realized, goal of "education for life and life for education."

Resource persons can make important contributions to education (Conk, 1977). They leave valuable impressions, add otherwise unavailable expertise and skill, and provide children with a realization of the various roles of adults in society giving students a future glimpse of vocational aspiration and leisure-time interests. They also expose boys and girls to other language models, bringing into the classroom the dialect and idiolect patterns of the community.

The primary function of *field exploration* is to make children actively aware of and involved in curriculum content at its source. They are thus able to experience what is being taught in the classroom and develop and use the vocabulary in its natural situation.

Artifacts provide in-class tangibles representing various aspects of the environment when on-site visits are not possible or are unnecessary. The purpose of these tangibles is to make children aware of and help them understand the role of the artifacts in the environment. By viewing and becoming acquainted with the use of these tangibles, children fix the related vocabulary in their language pattern. They are, consequently, able to examine and verbalize many more aspects of a situation than would be possible with intangible substitutes. Tangibles provide insights into size, shape, texture, weight, density, color shades, and natural phenomena, as well as the specific purpose under study.

Frequently, parents or other guests visit the classroom to explain and demonstrate the use of artifacts or tangibles.[4] For example, during a unit on cutting and pasting, parents may be asked to send cutting and adhesive materials from home. Items ranging from nail clippers to lawn clippers and from homemade paste to carpet tape are included in the collection. As the children explore and become involved with this display, they use the vocabulary associated with the items and begin to understand the role the materials play in their home and community environment.

---

[4]A parent questionnaire, sent out early in the year, often reveals that many parents can serve as resource people. A sample questionnaire is included at the end of this chapter (p. 93).

Classroom visitors, in this case the father of one of the children, can establish a link between the classroom and the outside world. (Used with permission of the Racine (Wis.) School District.)

As the child explores scales, rules, measuring cups and other tangibles provided during a number unit, he or she begins to realize how numbers are used in everyday life and is motivated to learn them.

Hansen and Hansen (1972) investigated the use of the speaker-phone in an elementary school as an alternative to field trips and resource people. This device is called by different names, including Conference Telephone, but all variations work in essentially the same fashion. The speaker-phone has an external receiver and speaker allowing classes to speak with or hear a distant resource person. Using this medium necessitated advance planning with the speaker and advance identification of appropriate questions to initiate the discussions. It was a very effective substitute for going on field trips or bringing in resource people. The upper grades talked to a newspaper publisher regarding editorial policy, a bank president regarding interest rates, and political figures regarding conservation and pollution. The kindergarten group was even more active. They made arrangements for their own field trip by calling the bus and the museum, asked a lumberman to help explain ways to keep their block structure from falling, called the city manager on Earth Day to see what jobs they could perform, and discovered a multiplicity of words when they called a television director to inquire about the special words he uses in his job. These experiences called for planning ahead and for utilizing vocabulary in real-life situations. As a result they had a far greater impact on the students than the contrived "language period" customary in many classrooms.

Teachers need to be aware of the available community resources. Sending questionnaires to parents and community members, talking with parents at conference times, writing parents letters discussing topics under study and suggesting parental contributions are only a few methods a teacher should employ. The task of finding people, places, and things to enrich a topic or activity demands persistence and hard work, but the rewards in learning and related language development make it worthwhile. As teachers continue to seek ways to build bridges between the school and the community, they are able to create learning which is more meaningful for young children (Bartolome, 1981).

Keystone 5

The identification of eight learning environments goes beyond present subject matter concerns and involves both the long- and short-range goals of early childhood education. These learning environments highlight major areas to be emphasized in the total program. Whether they be designated by a systematic Unit Topic, a loosely organized series of activities, or an isolated experience, evidence of each needs to be present if we are to fulfill our goal of providing a total education experience for each child. The eight learning environments are (1) play, (2) physical fitness, (3) contemporary living, (4) basic tools, (5) performing arts, (6) social thinking, (7) service, and (8) scientific thinking.

LEARNING ENVIRONMENTS

Although keystones provide a theoretical basis for curriculum planning and give direction for more specific ways of creating enriching experiences, the eight learning environments take teachers directly into the classroom and involve them more specifically in their work with children. An examination of each learning environment will provide the basis for some practical applications.

Play

Play needs to come back into favor in education programs (Herron & Sutton-Smith, 1971). Whether one calls it individual directed activities, free time, or liberty play, it still means the same thing. It allows children time during each day to freely explore and interact with their environment. It is unrelated to any subject-matter field and should have few rules.

The important thing in play programs is to make available ample stimuli so the children can make worthy selections. This choice allows children to

I like rain and thunder
i go out to play in my sandbox.

Children's composition grows as they dictate sentences about their artwork.

identify their own interests and regulate their own environment. The teacher moves throughout the room as a guide, stimulator, helper, and challenger.

Play obviously encourages language (Genishi, 1979). Too often in group situations, some children are not ready to talk at a particular time, are too shy to talk at a particular time, or are not called upon even at the particular time they *are* ready. The interest generated in free selection and this approach to learning results in a natural spontaneous language development.

Equipment needs to be selected which involves children in the following forms of play and their related language use:

1. *Intellectual play*—books, number and science devices, maps, historical collections
2. *Therapeutic play*[5]—clay, sand, water, punching bags, workbench
3. *Sensory play*—easels, paint, paper, old magazines, collage materials
4. *Aesthetic play*—musical instruments and books, records, art books and prints

---

[5]An engrossing account of the use of therapeutic play in treating an emotionally disturbed child is in Virginia M. Axline's *Dibs—In Search of Self* (New York: Ballantine Press, 1969).

5. *Physical play*—balance beam, jump ropes, tricycles, climbing ropes
6. *Miniature play*—dolls, dress-up clothes, street signs, flowers and vases, items to reproduce lifelike situations

The first five play purposes are self-explanatory. Miniature play, however, requires a brief discussion. The major goal of miniature play is the development and use of language. It is termed "miniature" because it sets up in the classroom miniature reproductions of lifelike situations and allows children to play the roles they see around them.

The traditional miniature play center is the housekeeping corner. Too often, however, this corner outlives its usefulness because it remains a permanent part of the classroom and ceases to stimulate language. The insightful teacher will change the center to incorporate other miniature situations: shoe shop, hat shop, flower shop, beauty shop, travel bureau, first-grade corner, fix-it shop, handicapped corner, and others that restimulate children to discussion and problem solving.

An example of the language use stimulated by miniature play is the following conversation overheard one day in the flower shop. One child, who was being the florist, "I'm really worried, Room 102 ordered a dozen and one-half roses and I don't know how many that is. What should I do?" From another child, who was being the florist's assistant came the answer, "All I know is you'll need a lot of styrofoam for that big of an arrangement."

Physical Fitness

The physical play material mentioned under the previous learning environment was for individual self-selected purposes. In addition, there should be a short, daily, carefully planned physical education period devoted to the development of all children's physical efficiency (Foerster, 1972).

Children need to be instructed orally and by demonstration that physical education includes elements of balance, coordination, strength, relaxation, endurance, body flexibility and projection. As activities are introduced, the children should be made aware of the reasons for the activities, for example, "This heel click will help your flexibility," or "Chinese Get Up is excellent for developing your strength." This procedure provides cognitive understanding and vocabulary development. Marc, a new child in the kindergarten program, was struggling with the "rocking chair," an exercise most of his classmates had mastered. Mike was overheard saying to him, "I know it's hard to do but keep trying 'cuz it's good for endurance and strength."

Contemporary Living

This learning environment focuses on the here and now, not just because children are a part of it but because they need to examine it and put it in some perspective. Children's verbal input includes far more than many adults imagine. As children sit at the dinner table, they hear conversations about such things as unemployment, taxes, jobs, money, autos, government, neighbors, and community situations. We need to help children find their places as they become intellectually and verbally involved with the contemporary scene.

The *calendar* can effectively stimulate language, providing it is a calendar which highlights children's birthdays, field trips, resource persons' visits, and community, state, and national events. A trip through the year, highlighting little-known special days is provided by Sarnoff and Ruffins (1979). Animated discussions result as the children use a linear calendar to keep track of upcoming events as well as solve number problems that arise.

"Four kids are absent today. Let's figure out how many are here today." Or, "It's been ten days since the minister showed us the gestures he uses with deaf people and I can still remember how they sing 'Glory, Glory, Hallelujah' with their hands." To make youngsters aware of other languages when doing calendar activities, put the name for the month in another language under the English word. Or, in doing calendar activities during December, teach children other ways to say "Merry Christmas."

A *news bulletin board* highlights pictures and stories from daily life. Encouraging young children to bring in these items will result in a few contributions, but encouraging parents to assist their children in browsing through the paper for interesting items will be of greater benefit. Newspaper and magazine publishers spend millions of dollars each year to find unique human interest pictures which give a different slant on a subject, set up a problem situation, or distort reality through optical illusion. These provide tremendous discussion stimuli. News stories which highlight special events or children in the news also furnish a meaningful discussion base and supply the added bonus of exposing children to the world around them.

Yet it is amazing how schools will spend untold dollars for commercial pictures and other language-stimulating devices, overlooking the newspapers and national picture magazines which can provide classrooms with more than sufficient material while keeping students abreast of contempary life. A teacher was asked to review some commercial educational materials developed to stimulate language. She used these several days with her kindergarten children with disappointing results. The next day she brought to her class a newspaper picture of the huge outdoor sculpture by Picasso which graces an open square in Chicago. What a lively discussion ensued as the children tried to describe what they thought it was!

Conversation, reporting, and discussion is a three-part technique which substitutes for the traditional "show and tell," "bring and brag," or "pump and prime," and signifies a new approach to this part of the daily program with greater results in language development. Teachers' "show and tell" practices often are not facilitative of language. Do we restrict this practice to: boys on Tuesdays, girls on Thursdays; bring only one item; must say at least three things about it; must speak in full sentences; must speak out loud;

must bring unit item on Monday, news item on Tuesday, personal item on Wednesday. . .?" Such restrictions develop language only on certain days and around certain topics! What about the rest of the day? There is no need to accomplish everything during this period, and it is especially impossible under such arbitrary conditions.

Furthermore, the fifth rock that is brought in, the new shoes, the lost teeth build little new vocabulary and need not be made a part of group sharing. These items may be of great importance, but there are other ways to recognize them, thus eliminating the risk of children grabbing the last thing they see as they leave the house just to have something to "show and tell." A three-part alternative is preferable to this overused technique.

Conversation suggests the need for the teacher to talk with each child as he or she enters the room. During this informal conversation, the teacher can suggest that Jon put the fifth rock he has brought to school on the observation table for his classmates to see; can help Tammy find a comfortable place for the doll she has brought for the third consecutive day; and can exclaim over Brad's lost tooth. In essence, these children do have "show and tell" but not at the expense of the total class's time. This conversation time is also beneficial in uncovering personal information important in dealing with the child, such as a fight in the family, extreme marital problems, or a pending death. Too often this information needlessly ends up being shared with the other children.

Reporting gives those children with items to share the opportunity to explain them to their classmates. Children might report on a news item,

Children enjoy talking informally about objects they have brought to the classroom.

something for the observation table, or an artifact relating to a Unit Topic. These items will result in increased language and information development. As an example, during the number unit, Stephie brought her father's abacus. She reported what it was, demonstrated how it was used, explained that her father got it while visiting the Orient, and showed the children the Orient on the globe.

Discussion, which may be teacher or child initiated, emerges from a need for a common situation. It could, for example, relate to a news article on the President's trip, a "dangerous stranger" in the neighborhood, fire prevention week, famous people's birthdays, or a behavior problem within the group. It provides another opportunity for children to use language and new vocabulary in responding to the topic under consideration.

Basic Tools

The basic tools learning environment includes what has been traditionally called the "three R's" with additional emphasis on the language arts. The major areas in this environment are:

Oral language—what, how, and when it is used
Nonverbal language—everyday and special gestures
Five basic written code systems—graphic (picture) writing (Blass et al., 1981), word writing, idea writing, ABC writing, and electronetic writing (a term used to include recording ideas on film, filmstrips, records, audiotapes, videotapes, and computers).
Scribbles—the developmental phases of writing
Numbers—an idea code system of thinking or recording
Measurement—a standard way of looking at something
Tools for writing—sticks, pencils, pens, magic markers, crayons
Manipulative acts—cutting, pasting, folding, tearing, marking
Operational acts—listening, following directions, persisting

Oral language is such a pervasive element in early childhood classrooms that it may go unnoticed. Yet the teacher has two responsibilities: (a) to provide planned experiences designed to motivate oral language, and (b) to consciously point out links between oral and written language.

To accomplish the first point above, teachers plan experiences to stimulate oral language. One kindergarten teacher took her children on a field exploration to the local museum. The purpose was cognitive, that is, to provide input about dinosaurs. An additional experience was language-related. During the trip, children were encouraged to ask questions. Following the trip, those who wanted to could dictate individual stories about the experience. Allan used oral language to tell the following, and watched with much interest as his teacher enscribed his imaginative story:

Once upon a time I walked outside and I heard a strange noise. I saw a dinosaur. The dinosaur was Tyrannosaurus Rex, the King. He chased me

From The Little Pig-A-Wig *by Lenore Blegvad.*

away. I was *so* scared. He stepped on our hose and fell and skinned his knee. I asked him, "Are you lost from the jungle?" He nodded his head, "Yes." I showed him the way back. And he walked in his cave. His mother spanked him for running away. And then he ate his mother and me!

Several days after the trip, the teacher wrote as the entire group dictated their composite story about dinosaurs:

This is our dinosaur jungle story. Some of the dinosaurs eat meat and some eat plants and flowers. They are going into the jungle to look for food. All of a sudden two Tyrannosaurus Rexes began to fight over meat. One took the meat away from the other one and one got hurt. The unhurt Tyrannosaurus Rex took his food to the cave where he hid it. Then the Tyrannosaurus Rex shared his food with his family.

In both experiences, the teacher was accomplishing the second task identified above. She was making a conscious link between oral and written language. By writing down what the children said, she was helping them see that thought can be expressed in oral words, and then made permanent in written words. By writing as the children could watch her, the teacher was indeed demonstrating several factors about writing. Some children will observe these; others are not developmentally ready to notice that: (a) writing moves from left to right and top to bottom; (b) there are spaces between words and sentences; (c) some words begin with capital letters;

(d) some words are enclosed in quotation marks. Despite the fact that not all children will be ready to notice these conventional aspects of writing, it is critical for teachers to write where children can observe, as well as to talk about some of these mechanical aspects of print, so the link can begin to be made (Schickedanz et al., 1977).

This basic tools learning environment is too broad to be given adequate coverage in this chapter. It might be of value, however, to highlight one sequence of several Unit Topics related to this environment, which can unfold language to children in a logical and historical manner.

A Unit Topic on "Gestures" can involve children in nonverbal communication, including spontaneous everyday gestures, occupational gestures, or interpretive dance and movement gestures. Such nonverbal systems as sign language and finger spelling can also be studied (Kelliher, 1980). Showing a film without sound and having children interpret the story, as well as inviting guests who use gestures in their occupations, adds relevance to this topic.

A Unit Topic on "Talk" exposes children to the many dialects and idiolects in our culture. Children realize that, while people say the same things, they say them differently. Presenting to children a tape recording of many Mother Goose rhymes spoken in various dialects reinforces this notion.

A Unit Topic on "Folktales-Storytelling" introduces children to the oral

This illustration and the preceding one accompany the Mother Goose rhyme, "This Little Pig," from Ring O' Roses: A Nursery Rhyme Picture Book *by L. Leslie Brooke.*

base of language by explaining many versions of folktales. Children create their own versions as they perpetuate this folkway of communication. One kindergarten class heard several versions of "The Runaway." In Russian the story is about a bun; in Norwegian, a pancake; in Scottish, a bannock; and in the United States, a gingerbread boy.[6] After listening to these variations, the children created their own version. In their story, a huge McDonald hamburger rolled out of the drive-in, bragged that it couldn't be caught, was chased by the cook, policemen, children, dogs, and cats. Finally it rolled into the kindergarten, where it was caught and devoured by the children.

Yet another Unit Topic, on "Mother Goose," represents a basic core of literature for the very young, originating from Charles Perrault's collection of folktales published originally in 1697. This unit examines the legends of Mother Goose origins, acquaints children with Father Goose, exposes them to an in-depth collection of Mother Goose literature, and points out the mother-father love function that literature offers.

"Book" is another Unit Topic which exposes children to the full range of this concept. Children examine why books came into being, their history, how they are made, their physical properties, where they can be obtained, as well as authorship and illustrations. Having the children collect a wide variety of books, make their own, visit with author or illustrator guests, and examine artifacts of early book forms, will give them firsthand experience with the topic. In addition, there are fine videotapes to further expand children's awareness of and interest in books (Agency for Instructional Television, 1976, 1977). This early involvement with books should put meaning into the decoding skills of the reading program as children look beyond to the excitement books hold in store.

Finally, a Unit Topic on "Five Basic Written Code Systems" involves children in the examination of graphic writing, word writing, idea writing, alphabet writing, and special writing such as shorthand and mechanical systems. Children communicate in all five writing codes, realizing the circumstances under which each does a more effective job (Stewig, 1978).

These six Unit Topics provide scores of activities for language development. The teacher must be cautioned, however, that young children are not involved in these topics at a skilled level. The *foundational* and often *impressional* treatment of these topics give children an initial awareness of language. This awareness may stimulate a greater involvement in the skills when children see them as a means to a greater end.

The important job for teachers of young children is to know the content of

---

[6]Almost any tale is available in several versions. In doing this one with children, you might use Ruth Sawyer, *Journey Cake, Ho!* (New York: Viking Press, 1953), "The Wee Bannock" in *More English Fairy Tales*, ed. Joseph Jacobs (New York: Schocken Books, 1922), "The Pancake," in *The Arbuthnot Anthology of Children's Literature*, ed. Zena Sutherland (Chicago: Scott, Foresman, 1976): 238–239, or "Mr. Bun" in Tasha Tudor, *The Tasha Tudor Book of Fairy Tales* (New York: Platt and Monk, 1969): 57–59.

these topics, to involve children in the vocabulary of each area, and to provide tangible resource persons, field exploration, and problem-solving situations so the vocabulary becomes fixed through proper and appropriate use. There are many sources available describing the content in each of these basic tool areas.

Performing Arts

This impressionally treated area lends itself to many classroom guests, as children are exposed to the word of expression through dance and movement, music, art, literature, folkcraft, and industrial arts.

Guests who play musical instruments, paint, sculpt, sew, carve wood, create imaginative settings, or form industrial products provide language in the descriptions of their skills as well as in the vocabulary attached to the related equipment.

An "Artist of the Month" or "Composer of the Month" can elicit personal reactions to many artists and their works while building language as the children relate these reactions to their own value system (Stewig, 1980).

Materials available during play will allow children to select avenues of expression in a performing arts interest area. Records and tapes of all varieties of music and literary forms should be available. Comparing the various illustrations of a common story lets children respond to literature in a different way. In addition, the teacher may present the same story in different ways: orally, in book form, on film, and in record format. Following such a variety of presentations, a discussion of which form brought the book alive for each child requires that language beyond just the words or pictures of the story be used in making judgments.

Links can be established between the performing arts. Visuals, especially reproductions of artists' paintings, can serve as motivation for another art, that of writing. Gather and mount such reproductions, making them available at the composing center, so the children can choose a favorite painting and write about it. Among the reproductions on a third-grade composition table was one of the French painter Henri Matisse's *Goldfish* (p. 86). During free time, Theresa chose this painting, and wrote:

> Once upon a time there was a glass of water. And inside that glass of water lived four goldfish. Under the glass was a plate with plants on it. Under the plate was a table. Around the table were pink, red, and green flowers. There were plants all around too.
>
> The goldfish said, "I wonder when Sarah's going to feed us? I hope she feeds us soon because I feel sick." She felt sick not because she was hungry. It was because she was going to have a baby. She had a baby. She felt much better then. Now there were five little goldfish all in a jar.

Treated impressionally, the performing arts allow children to use language gained from contact with artifacts and artists to build a personal

Henri Matisse, Goldfish.

value structure. In so doing, it also exposes children to the language of line, form, texture, subject, mood, color, character, beat, shape, materials, and media which are the foundation of the performing arts areas.

Social Thinking

Social thinking involves children in activities which challenge them to look at themselves and their relationship with others. The *process* of social thinking is far more important than the *facts* of social situations, places, and events. The term *self-concept* is often used to describe the emphasis at the initial education level. However, while the concentration is on "self" it must include the broader aspect of self, namely, relationships with other beings.

Activities which involve children in social thinking include the following:

a. Self-description activities—Young children are egocentric, yet seldom have a full conception of their external appearance. Mirrors—full-length, three-way, magnifying, and others—need to be employed to highlight all physical features. A child, listening to his or her own voice on a tape recorder, becomes aware of how he or she sounds to others. Using cameras to record classroom activities encourages children to use language in describing situations which have been photographed. A camera taken on field trips retrieves on-site impressions for in-depth follow-up discussions.

b. Self-esteem activities—Children need opportunities to talk about their capabilities, limitations, interests, wishes, and long-range goals. This introspection encourages recognition of their own uniqueness as well as a feeling of self-worth (South Carolina, 1981). A parent reported the following incident several months after her kindergarten child had been involved in a "Who Am I" unit:

> Tracy had fallen and cut a deep gash in her forehead. While it was in the healing stage, her father in a joking manner called her "scarface." Holding back tears his daughter retorted, "It doesn't matter what I look like on the outside. The important thing is what I'm like inside."

c. Activities related to family—Family pictures help children see common features within the family while highlighting individual differences. And discussing or assuming family roles demonstrates the need for family interdependence.

d. Activities related to people—Children need to be exposed, in person or through graphics, to diverse people. Exposing children to people with varied characteristics sensitizes them to these differences while making them aware of many similarities. If it is true that attitudes are formed at a very early age, teachers must expose children to situations that allow them to see each person's worth beyond the too-easily formed surface biases.

Opportunities to talk informally with others is important as young children develop increased oral fluency. (Used with permission of the photographer, Richard D. Bradley.)

Implied in all of these activities is the need for refining one's relationships with others so each child can effectively function in a world of people and yet retain his or her unique individuality. Because language forms the major element in contact with others, its continual development and refinement is crucial to the social process.

Service

The other aspect of social thinking is thinking about someone else. This should receive systematic handling. Too frequently, service is given little attention in educational programs, yet we expect children to automatically grow up being concerned for others. There are many opportunities for service projects which enable children to use language to convey their feelings and emotions. These projects include sending cards and messages to shut-ins or to senior citizens in care centers, writing group or individual expressions of sympathy after a local or national tragedy, and telephoning a sick classmate or teacher.

Scientific Thinking

Scientific thinking involves children in observing, questioning, predicting, recording, classifying, checking, and generalizing. As in social thinking, the emphasis is on the process, not on the product.

Children need to intellectually, tactilely, and verbally explore a host of natural and sensory phenomena. Supplying appropriate equipment such as microscopes, magnifying glasses, and dissecting tools adds to the experience.

To build scientific vocabulary along with the thinking processes which employ this vocabulary will provide children many spontaneous opportunities throughout the year to apply this knowledge. Even though adults tire of the young child's asking the question "why" over and over again, they should not turn the child off by ignoring such questions. Instead, turn these questions into opportunities for children to seek their own answers. In so doing, the "whys" will slowly be replaced by self-sustained active inquiry. And new language will grow with each new discovery.

The preceding discussion of keystones and learning environments is intended merely to whet the appetite for further exploration. An entire year's educational program cannot be spelled out in a few pages. However it is hoped this discussion will form the basic framework from which teachers can derive language objectives and activities that are appropriate and relevant to their particular classroom of children.

Oliver Wendell Holmes said that "Language is a temple in which the soul of those who speak it is enshrined" (Kin, 1955). Teachers of the very young need to assist children in reflecting more than just words. Rather, they must nurture language which allows effective expression of the inner depths of each child's heart and mind. Only then can language truly be considered an art!

A tacit assumption in this chapter has been that most children will come to the classroom with "normally" developed language skills. The program described is essentially a *developmental* one, designed to provide a rich array of experiences to further extend a child's competency in and enthusiasm for language. Realistically, however, the teacher must be aware that, even at this early stage, some children will manifest language problems needing *remedial* attention.

DIAGNOSING EARLY LANGUAGE DEFICIENCIES

The major task of teachers of young children in the area of language deficiencies is to be aware of potential problems and seek professional assistance immediately. Some language deficiencies left unattended for several years solidify into deep-rooted patterns that become increasingly difficult, if not impossible, to redirect as time goes by.

Teacher education institutions give too little education in the remediation of language deficiencies, except to specialists. Most classroom teachers are, therefore, unqualified to handle the language problems of their students. A rule of thumb to follow is to call for professional assistance on all suspected language problems.

Many school systems make the service of psychometrists, psychologists, or speech clinicians or therapists available. Let the professional decide if testing is necessary and suggest classroom techniques that will aid in overcoming the identified problem.

Of what language problems should a teacher be aware? Following is a sample list:

Problems for referral to a speech clinician—irregular syntax; lack of plurals, possessives, and connectives; not including all sounds, especially s's and th's which are not acoustically intense; garbled speech and the lack of articulation; and pronounced speech defects.

Problems for referral to a psychologist—a child who never talks; immature language patterns (baby talk, two- or three-word sentences); a child's continued third-person referral to himself; tangential associations (responding with speech unrelated to topic); not understanding words; and not following directions.

In some cases, several professionals may need to work together to diagnose and suggest remedies for the problem. And some problems, especially in the area of suspected mental retardation, are difficult to diagnose at this early age because professionals need to hear speech patterns which often the child has not yet acquired, to help identify a more deep-rooted problem.

If testing is required, there are several language tests available (Buros, 1978). The *Illinois Test of Psycholinguistic Ability* is representative of a comprehensive language test measuring two levels of speech organization: meaningful and automatic-sequential. At the meaningful level, three abilities are tested—decoding (Do fish swim?), encoding (Show me what you do with this. [hammer]), and association (Soup is hot, ice cream is _____). "Here is an apple, here are two _____" is an example of automatic-sequential. The age span of the ITPA is two-and-a-half to nine years of age.

The *Peabody Picture Vocabulary Test* is representative of tests of understood vocabulary. Word comprehension or understood vocabulary is measured by having a child point to pictures, one of which represents the word given. The age span of the Peabody Test is two-and-a-half to eighteen years of age.

The *Templin-Darley Screening and Diagnostic Tests of Articulation* are representative of tests to measure articulation levels of children three to eight years of age. This and a wide variety of other tests are described and evaluated for quality by Mavrogenes et al. (1976).

A representative example of a language deficiency test is the *Slingerland Language Disability Test* for children of five to fourteen years of age. Finally, the *Engleman Concept Inventory* is a sample of tests of concept development for children ages four to seven years.

Early diagnosis and professional help are essential! Certain language problems of young children, if not treated early, may result in fixed lifetime language deficiencies. The teacher plays a crucial role in diagnosing language problems in time for professional assistance to redirect them into positive language patterns.

SUMMARY

This chapter has dealt mainly with creating an enriched classroom environment to stimulate vocabulary and language use. While some practical ideas are included, the objective is to identify the content areas in which children need conceptual learning and to identify related language facilities for these content areas. It is hoped that the sample ideas will spark teachers to create many more.

A brief discussion of the basic functions of language was included to review the varied ways language is used. Another brief discussion of language program approaches emphasized the need for evaluating and selecting approaches which will produce the most comprehensive results. Thinking about the merits of various early childhood programs always needs to be placed in the context of thinking about the children for whom the program is planned (Verzaro-Lawrence, 1980). In the final chapter we shall return to this issue, considering at length the differing student populations.

The approach identified in the present chapter as having the most potential for language development is the "total-program approach." The total-program approach identifies basic keystones upon which the content rests and provides the major learning environments from which concepts and language are derived. The learning environments of play, contemporary living, physical fitness, basic tools, performing arts, scientific thinking, social thinking, and service provide this learning and language foundation.

The need for remediation of language problems at a time when they can be more easily overcome was stressed and it was suggested that teachers become familiar with diagnostic tools and refer children to specialists, when necessary.

The role of the teacher in early language development is crucial. Teachers must identify content crucial to the needs of children. They must gather resources which allow children to approach the content from many avenues. And, through the classroom environment, they must constantly challenge children to acquire and use language as they meet new situations and solve new problems.

In providing the climate that offers a broad range of language experiences and in guiding each child's exploration of this environment, the teacher will help ensure that all children have the opportunity to reach their full language potential.

Suggestions for Further Exploration

1. Review the available language arts series which include materials for preschool and kindergarten levels. Analyze the content to determine how effectively the approach relates the children's language development to their environmental language needs.

2. Keystones of an early childhood education program were suggested in the chapter. Identify basic assumptions of keystones *you* deem essential for an effective early childhood education program. How do your keystones compare with those suggested in the chapter?

3. Learning environments serve to identify the major focuses of a program and the language needed to articulate each focus. Are the suggested eight learning environments all inclusive? Develop your own set of learning environments and compare with those suggested.

4. Talk with several preschool and kindergarten teachers. Have them describe their approaches to language development. Compare their approaches with the language-program approaches reviewed earlier in the chapter.

5. The chapter includes some sample classroom activities within each learning environment. What other ideas for classroom activities or play tangibles did the described activities generate in you? List several of these new ideas for each learning environment.

6. Select one content area within the learning environments. Search the community for available artifacts, resource persons, and field exploration sites related to that topic. Describe the kinds of language learnings you could plan as a result of contact with these artifacts, persons, and sites.

7. Secure a camera (instamatic-type cameras use film cartridges and do not require settings). Take slide pictures of people in the community who use nonverbal communication or gestures in their occupations. Consider referees, music conductors, police and firefighters, airport ground crews, and others. What kinds of messages can such people communicate without using spoken words?

8. Familiarize yourself with representative language development tests. Talk with a school psychologist and a speech clinician about the common and uncommon speech and language problems they diagnose and treat.

COMMUNITY RESOURCE QUESTIONNAIRE*

Name _____

Address _____

Phone _____ (home) _____ (office, if appropriate)

Listed below are several classifications in which parents and other interested community members can assist in expanding classroom study. Resource persons, field exploration, and artifacts provide firsthand experience with topics. This enables children to bridge the classroom environment with the home and broader community environments. Please respond in those areas of your interest and expertise.

1. Hobbies _____

2. Collections _____

3. Play musical instrument _____

4. Travel—where _____

    slides _____

    pictures _____

    artifacts _____

5. Do you speak (read) a foreign language? If so, which _____?

6. Occupation _____

    Would a visit to your place of work be worthwhile and possible? _____
    Would you be willing to visit the classroom to discuss or demonstrate?

    _____ yes _____ no

    What days are best for you? _____
    Would you need transportation? _____
    Would you be available for a classroom telephone call, if appropriate?

    _____ yes _____ no

*Thanks to Dr. Ruth Mork Hansen for permission to reprint this form.

SAMPLE PARENT LETTER

June 1, 1982

Dear Parents:

In the next few weeks children in our class will be exploring "Who Am I?" and "Names." The objectives of these units will be to establish foundational recognition of individual's names, differences between people, specific word recognition of names, self-image roles, and family contributions to each child.

Enjoy listening and conversing with your child about names, your child's self-image, and his or her individual behavior. Please provide needed information about interesting and unusual family names. If you have kept a family record or family photo album, permit these to be shown by your child in our self-expression center. Whenever you can, supply interesting family experiences concerning family names. Tell these to your child.

A special project, *Who's Who in the Kindergarten*, will be undertaken. Information for this project will need to be supplied by you, the parents. Could you find time to write a brief outline about your child, including entire name, nickname, reason for selection of name, birth weight, and little tidbits about your child's unique personality?

Once I had a child in class who discovered her middle name was *Eden*. This is the exact way she reported this information to her classmates: "My middle name is Eden, and Eden means beautiful, and . . . and . . . and when my daddy first saw me he thought I was the most beautiful thing he had ever seen."

These letters to you from school will be sent quite regularly. Each letter will be mailed through your child as a special postman or postmaid. Consider them as special delivery messages with tender loving thoughts on how we all can make school experiences very important.

Sincerely yours,

Ruth Hansen
Peter Hobart School
St. Louis Park, MN

Paragraph 1 of home-school letters sets the specific information about Unit Topics and related school events.

Paragraphs 2 and 3 give parents ideas and suggestions to do at home concerning the unit focus. Specific artifacts and resources which they may supply for adequate treatment of the curriculum are described. Requests for artifacts should be completely on a voluntary basis because many parents have a multitude of home tasks to do. Encourage only relevant materials to be provided, using the objectives of each unit as guides.

Paragraph 4 relates a true-to-life school experience illustrating how this unit has been experienced by other children in past instruction.

Paragraph 5, a couple of sentences, adding a personal communication between teacher and parent-family, is effective. The teacher adds such footnotes as Artist of the Month, needs for empty cans for easel painting, and other learning materials that most parents willingly supply upon request for each unit and special event in the curriculum.

The closing lines remain professional. Such letters to parents will vary in style because of each writer's personal pattern. It will be well to consider this form of communication as a blend between personal friendly letter writing and professional business communications. As you vary your style and personal form, keep in mind that it is best these letters not become overly personal or overly professional in either *style* or *form*.

Suggestions for Further Reading

Alleen, K. Eileen. *Mainstreaming in Early Childhood Education*. Albany, N.Y.: Delmar Publishers, 1980.

Enactment of public laws mandating education for all handicapped children beginning at age three now make it more important than ever that early childhood teachers know how to meet the needs of such youngsters. This book provides a comprehensible introduction to the issues involved in providing programs for handicapped students. The tasks of identifying, assessing, and individualizing programs for such children are completely discussed, suggesting not only what should be done, but also what shouldn't be done. The discussion of specific disabilities the early childhood teacher may encounter is helpful. The book includes many specific skills to teach to children.

Docter, Virginia D. "Tracing Our Heritage." *Insights into Open Education* 12(4) (December 1979): 2–4.

As part of a social studies project, this teacher of third/fourth grade had children interview older members of the community, to familiarize students with artifacts, processes, and ways of life no longer current. The questions—developed by children—could be incorporated into a parent letter.

Ginsburg, Herbert. *The Myth of the Deprived Child*. Englewood Cliffs, N.J.: Prentice-Hall, 1972.

The author discusses use and abuse of IQ scores and other measures with deprived children. He concludes that poor children's language is not generally deficient in important respects and that many enjoy a rich verbal heritage.

Herron, R. E. and Sutton-Smith, B. *Child's Play*. New York: John Wiley, 1971.

Current research on play is described. Reports on the value of play in cognitive learning and the review of Piaget's concept of play are noteworthy.

Knott, Gladys P. "Nonverbal Communication During Early Childhood." *Theory into Practice* 18(4) (October 1979).

Few studies are available describing children's acquisition and development of nonverbal abilities. The author defines paralanguage, proxemics and kinesics, and then groups summaries of what research is available under these headings. Nonverbal elements can serve three functions in children's communication: substituting, complementing, or supporting verbal elements. The teacher of early childhood needs to be aware that students make more overt use of these nonverbal elements than adults do. There are sex-linked differences: girls use more gestures than do boys by the time they come to school. An important implication for teachers of learning disabled students is that deficits in understanding and using nonverbal communication may retard acquisition of verbal language. Though teachers often assume children acquire nonverbal language by themselves, studies reveal that some children may require teacher help in using this mode of communication.

Landreth, Catherine. *Early Childhood, Behavior and Learning*. New York: Alfred A. Knopf, 1969.

For a comprehensive overview of the early years development in all areas, this book provides research to support child development as well as overviews of various approaches in studying children.

Larrick, Nancy. "Wordless Picture Books and the Teaching of Reading." *Reading Teacher* (May 1976): 743–746.

To see if children really like these books and if they give positive support to reading, the author interviewed four teachers and their pupils. She concluded that to four-year-olds such books are a boon; they learn to handle books and to move from front to back and left to right. Sixth-graders preferred books with words.

Leeper, Sarah et al. *Good Schools for Young Children*. New York: Macmillan, 1969.

This guide for working with three-, four-, and five-year-old children discusses language arts activities and other content areas.

Michaelis, S. U. et al. *New Designs for the Elementary School Curriculum*. New York: McGraw-Hill, 1967.

This text gives a comprehensive overview for becoming familiar with skills in all subject matter areas. These skills then need to be translated into appropriate content and activities.

Munro, Margaret. *The Psychology and Education of the Young American*. New York: Elsevier-Dutton, 1969.

An excellent foundation book with a chapter on the nature of language dealing with language acquisition and use. It also discusses language deprivation and disorder.

Opie, Iona and Opie, Peter. *The Oxford Nursery Rhyme Book*. Oxford: The University Press, 1955.

Eight hundred rhymes and songs, including several variants of the same verses, are grouped into nine sections. The Opies comment on the importance of illustrations for children, who frequently ignore a verse without a picture. The art of Thomas Bewick, who brought wood engraving to its zenith in the 17th century, is featured; engravings are by contemporary artist Joan Hassel.

Todd, Vivian and Heffernan, Helen. *The Years Before School: Guiding Preschool Children*. New York: Macmillan, 1970.

A preschool methods text that contains a good section on language development as well as suggestions for the entire curriculum program.

Bibliography

Adams, Anne H. *Success in Beginning Reading and Writing.* Santa Monica, Calif.: Goodyear Publishing Co., 1978.

Agency for Instructional Television. *Spinning Stories* (1976) and *Book, Look and Listen* (1977). Bloomington, Ind.: A.I.T.

Bartolome, Paz I. "The Changing Family and Early Childhood Education." *Childhood Education* (May/June 1981): 262–266.

Blass, Rosanne J. et al. "Showing Children the Communicative Nature of Reading." *The Reading Teacher* (May 1981): 926–930.

Bloom, Benjamin. *Stability and Change in Human Characteristics.* New York: John Wiley, 1964.

Broman, Betty L. *The Early Years in Childhood Education.* Chicago: Rand McNally College Publishing Co., 1978.

Buros, Oscar Kristen. *The Eighth Mental Measurements Yearbook.* Highland Park, N.J.: Gryphon Press, 1978.

Conk, Judith A. S. "Using Community Language Resources in the School." *Theory into Practice* 16(5) (December 1977): 401–406.

Davis, D. C. *Patterns of Primary Education.* New York: Harper & Row, 1965.

Dunn, Lloyd M. and Smith, James O. *Peabody Language Development Kit— Manual.* Circle Pines, Minn.: American Guidance Service, Inc.

Foerster, Leona M. "As They Move They Learn." *Instructor* (March 1972): 59.

Garvey, C. "Some Properties of Social Play." *Merrill-Palmer Quarterly* 20 (1974): 163–180.

Genishi, Celia. "Letting Children Communicate: The Synthesis of Language Skills and Language," in *Basic Skills in Kindergarten: Foundations for Formal Learning.* (ed. by W. B. Barbe, et al.) Columbus, O.: Zaner-Bloser, Inc., 1980, pp. 57–62.

Genishi, Celia. "Young Children Communicating in the Classroom: Selected Research." *Theory into Practice* 18(4) (October 1979): 244–250.

Hansen, Harlan S. and Hansen, Ruth M. "The Speakerphone in the Elementary School." *Elementary English* (December 1972): 1262–1265.

Herron, R. E. and Sutton-Smith, B. *Child's Play.* New York: John Wiley, 1971.

Kelliher, Nancy. "Another Way to Talk." *Early Years* (April 1980): 18–19.

Kin, David (ed.). *Dictionary of American Maxims.* New York: Crown, 1955.

Mavrogenes, Nancy et al. "A Guide to Tests of Factors That Inhibit Learning to Read." *The Reading Teacher* 29(4) (January 1976): 343–358.

Melson, Gail F. and Hulls, Johanna. "Speaking Through Space: Non-Verbal Communication in the Preschool Child." Dallas, Tex.: Paper presented at the National Association for the Education of Young Children Annual Convention, November 1975.

Roser, Nancy L. and Jensen, Julie M. "Read Communication—Key to Early Reading and Writing." *Childhood Education* (November/December 1978): 90–95.

Sarnoff, J. and Ruffins, R. *Light the Candles! Beat the Drums!* New York: Scribner's, 1979.

Schickedanz, Judith A. et al. *Strategies for Teaching Young Children.* Englewood Cliffs, N.J.: Prentice-Hall, 1977.

South Carolina Department of Education. *State Objectives Reading Writing and Mathematics, Grades K–12.* Columbia, S.C.: South Carolina Department of Education, 1981.

Sowards, G. and Scobey, M. *The Changing Curriculum and the Elementary Teacher.* Belmont, Calif.: Wadsworth Publishing, 1968.

Stewig, John Warren. "Illustrator of the Month," in *Children and Literature.* Boston: Houghton Mifflin, 1980, pp. 61–64.

Stewig, John Warren. *Sending Messages.* Boston: Houghton Mifflin, 1978.

Torrance, Paul F. *Encouraging Creativity in the Classroom.* Dubuque, Iowa: William C. Brown, 1970.

Verzaro-Lawrence, Marce. "Early Childhood Education: Issues for a New Decade." *Childhood Education* (November/December 1980): 104–109.

LISTENING

To me it is especially curious that in the
classroom we spend more time teaching writing
than reading, more time teaching reading than
speaking, and the least time, if any at all,
teaching listening.

Meanwhile, not only outside of school but
right in the classroom, we do more listening than
speaking, more speaking than reading, and more
reading than writing. A perfect negative correla-
tion between education and life. (Johnson, 1972)

Almost from the moment a newborn infant is laid in its crib,
it is intently at work taking in information through our most-used receptive
channel—the ears. Though this first listening is crude compared to the
sophisticated, inferential listening adults do, it is a beginning. As children
grow, their listening processes develop as they sense, sort and begin to act
upon the aural signals they receive.

By the time children go to school, they have listened for uncounted hours,
largely on their own initiative. As with speech, most children receive little
direct instruction in the home about how to listen. Despite the fact that most
listening habits are assimilated unconsciously rather than taught, the child
has learned the necessity of listening to learn. In this as in other areas,
however, there are marked differences in how much the child has learned.

In some homes, children are encouraged to listen. Parents are around who
listen and respond to what the child says. Dinner time is an occasion for talking and listening. The groundwork is laid, albeit unconsciously, for the idea
that listening is a courtesy paid to the speaker. Duker (1969) has pointed out,
"Generally it is agreed that parents who listen to their children tend to be the
best teachers of good listening habits."

In other homes, little or no premium is put on listening. Sometimes children from minority homes have poorly developed listening skills.[1] Their families may be fragmented because of instability and seldom gather for leisurely exchange of talk. If the home environment is crowded with young children, it is usually permeated with noise. Apparently children from such surroundings often "tune-out" the noise and, consequently, their listening skills develop slowly.

A DISTINCTION IN TERMS

Before proceeding, a distinction must be made between two terms, *hearing* and *listening*. Though these are often used interchangeably, they refer, in fact, to two distinctly different abilities. *Hearing* refers to the physical reception of the sound waves through the ear. *Listening* refers to both the process of hearing and of responding as the listener reacts to the physical stimuli or uses the information he or she has heard. There are many classifications of listening, called either types or levels.

Some years ago Strickland (1969) identified four different types of listening, characteristic of both adults and children. *Marginal* listening is the kind children in an open classroom setting do when they go about their own work, yet are still aware that others in the classroom are doing other tasks. A major component of the early childhood language arts curriculum is *appreciative* listening in which classes listen to the teacher, or perhaps to a tape or record, as a story or poem is presented. *Attentive* listening is essential when as teachers we are giving instructions or directions, and when children themselves are participating in discussions or planning sessions. Finally, *analytic* listening is essential when children need to detect an author's purpose, identify propaganda devices, or analyze bias or point of view. Specific activities designed to encourage attentive and analytic listening are described later in this chapter.

The number of these classifications and accompanying terminology vary with each writer. Which classification system is used makes little difference. The important thing to remember is that while most children with whom you work can hear, few will be good listeners. This is the point at which your responsibility as a teacher of listening is apparent.

THE CHILD AS LISTENER IN SCHOOL

As any kindergarten teacher can tell you, there is a wide difference in listening ability among children. This difference remains apparent at all grade

---

[1]Such children do less well on listening tests, even after instruction. See Arlene K. Feltman, "The Effect of Reinforcement on Listening Skills of the Culturally Deprived" (Master's thesis, The Ohio State University, 1967). Though the groups designated as "deprived" responded favorably to tangible rewards, their group scores were lower than those of "average" groups.

Illustration accompanying the poem "What Is the Sound of a Giggle?" in What Is That Sound! *by Mary L. O'Neill.*

levels, though the spread seems to widen as children grow older. Whom can the teacher expect to be a good listener?

Before children can be effective listeners, they must be able to hear adequately. A continuing job of every teacher is to be alert for signs of children with hearing problems. One estimate is that between 5 and 10 percent of all children may be hearing impaired (Green & Petty, 1975, p. 118).

Especially at the beginning of a school year, as the teacher starts working with a new group, one task is to determine if any of the children in the room have hearing problems. This is important at any grade level, for hearing problems develop at varying times. A child's hearing loss may not have been detected by previous teachers, especially if it only recently became apparent. Detecting hearing problems is not a simple task, as different children may:

1. have trouble hearing different types of sounds,
2. hear with different efficiency at different times, due to such physical conditions as being overly tired, and
3. manifest their hearing problems in different ways.

The teacher looks for signs which indicate that rather than being an inattentive listener, the child may have a hearing impairment which needs referral to a specialist. For example, the child may:

1. have trouble hearing /th/ words, which contain the softest sound in the language.
2. have a problem hearing consonant sounds, as they are softer than vowel sounds in words.
3. have trouble understanding long sentences. Children with hearing problems can usually cope only with short sentences (Van Riper, 1978).
4. have problems in voice production, including:
   a. abnormal pitch, intensity or quality of the voice,
   b. unusual speech rhythm, or
   c. persistent articulation errors (Travis, 1971).
5. have trouble making a distinction between different phonemes.
6. have memory-span problems and cannot remember sequences. For example, the sequence activity, suggested on page 114 would prove difficult to children with hearing problems.
7. gesture frequently to make ideas or wants known.

If such signs are evident, the teacher refers the child to the speech-and-hearing therapist employed by the school system or suggests to the parents the need to take the child to a doctor for hearing tests. The teacher makes such recommendations, even though some children suspected of having hearing problems may simply be poor listeners. One writer has reported: "According to some ear specialists, it may be that more than half of proclaimed deafness is nothing more than inattention" (Lundsteein, 1979). If hearing tests reveal no pathological problem with the child's hearing, the teacher must help the child to listen attentively. Those children whose listening skills are underdeveloped are a major focus of this chapter.[2]

Even among children whose hearing is adjudged "normal," there is a wide range of difference in listening ability. What types of children may the teacher expect to listen well?

The child who is intelligent is apt to be a good listener (Duker, 1969). Though the exact nature of this relationship is uncertain, several researchers have found a significant relationship between listening skills and general intelligence. The child who is a good reader is also apt to be a more skilled listener than other children (Brown, 1965). As both are receptive language skills, it is logical to posit such a relationship, which is in fact borne out by research studies. Sex differences are evidently not as apparent in this

---

[2]For children whose hearing is impaired, special attention beyond the training of the teacher is required. For a teacher with such a child in the room, the following may be of help and may serve as a reference for parents: Jacqueline Keaster and Gloria Hoverstein, *Suggestions to the Parents of Pre-School Children with Hearing Impairment* (Rochester, Minn.: The American Academy of Opthalmology, 1971). An inexpensive pamphlet that covers many areas of concern, this suggests games and exercises parents can share with their hearing-impaired children.

language skill as in some others. After six weeks of instruction in a sequential listening program, Hollow (1955) found no significant differences in listening ability between boys and girls in her 200-child sample.[3]

LISTENING DEMANDS

People frequently react to comments about the necessity of improving listening skills by wondering why this is a concern: Since everyone listens, why worry about it? One valid reason for helping children improve their listening skills is that we listen a large part of our lives, both in school and as adults.

A study done in schools indicates the important role listening plays in the lives of children. The researcher Wilt (1950), who studied 568 children in sixteen classrooms, investigated the amount of time spent in each of the language arts. In addition, she studied the relation between what *actually* happened in the classroom and what teachers *thought* happened in their classrooms. She discovered that children spend an average of more than two and a half hours listening during a five-hour school day. Especially interesting is the fact that this time was more than twice that estimated by teachers. Though the Wilt study is now an older one, it has not been replicated on a large scale. What are conditions like in schools in the 1980s? It is safe to assume that children still spend a good part of their school lives listening. The amount of time spent listening to a teacher in a group setting may have diminished. However, recent emphases on individually guided instruction may actually have increased the amount of time children spend listening to media essential for such programs.

Wilt's study was done in self-contained classrooms, surrounded by permanent walls, shut off from exterior noises by doors which could be closed. Her study, as she acknowledges (1974) needs to be replicated in today's open classrooms, where the problem of noise control is probably much greater. Smith (1979) in a review of all aspects of nonverbal communication, reports that in a study of junior high school students, 75 percent of the respondents reported noise as the major problem in their schools.

A smaller study investigated the amount of time devoted to the various language arts in the classrooms of 266 teachers (Van Wingerden, 1965). The order of priority was:

first—reading
second—writing
third—speaking
fourth—listening

---

[3]Contrary evidence is presented in Larry L. Barker, *Listening Behavior* (Englewood Cliffs, N.J.: Prentice-Hall, 1971), p. 45. Barker's discussion of fifteen factors which affect listening is a valuable reference.

Of the respondents, 52.9 percent reported that there was "little" direct planned listening instruction in their program. This study, done in a limited geographic area, may have few implications for the entire country. It does, however, raise questions about what conditions are: a nationwide study should be undertaken soon. Apparently, though much time has elapsed since these studies, little change has occurred in the teaching patterns in the elementary schools.[4] Listening instruction remains on the bottom of the list; children still spend much time doing something for which they receive little instruction ("Secrets of Being a Better Listener," 1980).

A survey by Brown (1967) revealed that less than one percent of the total content of elementary language arts textbooks is devoted to listening instruction. Because this is the case, teachers too seldom know how to teach listening. In studying secondary schools, Steil (1977) found instruction in listening to be "nonexistent to minimal at best." This chapter will point out some ways teachers can work to improve listening skills.

Children listen much of the time they are in school. Is the same true of adults? An early study pointed out clearly the importance of listening in the lives of adults. Rankin discovered that 68 percent of his subjects' waking hours were spent in some form of communication.[5] The types and percentages were:

1. listening, 45 percent of the total
2. speaking, 30 percent of the total
3. reading, 16 percent of the total
4. writing, 9 percent of the total

If such a study were replicated today, what would be the results? Because of the increase of such passive entertainment as television, the percentage of time spent in listening has probably increased. We do not know for sure, but apparently to function well both in school and the adult world, the child needs well-developed listening skills: such skills are increasingly called into use in other important areas. A study by the University of Michigan Research Center indicates that over 40 percent of the public's political information is

---

[4]One hundred and sixty Minnesota teachers estimated that their students listened 58 percent of the school day. See "Elementary Classroom Teachers' Attitudes Toward the Instruction of Listening Skills," by Verne Shea. Unpublished Specialist Degree paper, St. Cloud State University (MN), 1980.

[5]Paul T. Rankin, "The Importance of Listening Ability," *English Journal* 17 (October 1928): 623–630. Though it was done with a small sample, several more recent studies done with larger samples have replicated his results, indicating the validity of his pioneer work. See Donald E. Bird, "Are You Listening?" *Office Executive* 40 (April 1955): 18–19, or Lila R. Breiter, "Research in Listening and Its Importance to Literature" (Master's thesis, Brooklyn College, 1957).

gathered from radio and television (Duker, 1971). With the brevity and (some say) bias of electronic media, it is apparent that critical listening is of utmost importance to our society.

Yet another reason for stressing the importance of listening is that much content is lost after listening occurs. It has been estimated that only one week after listening to an oral presentation, the average listener has forgotten 25 percent of what he has heard. After a month's interval, fully 50 percent of what was retained has been lost. Not only do we need to listen often, but we also lose much of what we have heard.

LISTENING: A PROBLEM

In addition to demands for listening on both children and adults and evidence that wide differences in listening ability exist, some features of the act of listening create problems. One of these is the nature of the listening process. Earlier, the fact was mentioned that children who are good readers will often be good listeners. This is logical because both are receptive skills. There is a fundamental difference between the two, however. The listener usually cannot control either the rate of presentation or the number of repetitions. In reading, the child can control both. If something makes no sense, he or she can reread, and then reread again, pausing to consult a dictionary to determine the meaning of a crucial word. Such luxury is not the listener's prerogative. The ephemeral words are spoken at a rate selected by the speaker, and it is often impossible to hear the same thing over again. It is true that tape recordings or records allow the child to control the number of repetitions. However, in more usual situations when listening to a person speak, the listener must "catch it on the wing."[6]

The converse problem, of the speaker going too slowly so the listener loses interest, has also been noted by several authorities. Common estimates are that we can listen comfortably at rates from six to ten times faster than a speaker can speak. This discrepancy has been investigated by researchers who have demonstrated that in test conditions subjects can listen at rates up to 450 words per minute (Orr, 1956). Such studies make use of mechanically compressed speech, eliminating the problem of high pitch which usually results when records or tapes are played at too fast a speed. Though the ability to listen and comprehend compressed speech has been well established, no use of this information has been made in the elementary school to this time.

---

[6]Paul S. Anderson and Diane Lapp, *Language Skills in Elementary Education*. New York: Macmillan, 1979, p. 99. This point and many helpful suggestions for listening activities make this book a valuable one for teachers. The section on the teacher's voice quality (pp. 111–113) is well worth reading.

IS IMPROVEMENT POSSIBLE?

Given that children listen with varying effectiveness but that many demands to listen are placed on *all* children, one question occurs. Does direct instruction in how to listen result in improved ability? According to the evidence presented by Brown (1967), apparently authors of elementary materials for children don't believe so because they devote little attention to improvement of this skill.

In spite of this neglect of listening, several research studies indicate listening is a teachable skill. These are summarized by Duker (1968) in a book useful to teachers. Duker surveyed 1,332 articles about listening and concluded that considerable agreement exists among researchers: the skill of listening can be taught, and the results of such teaching can be measured.

A study by Childers (1970) is representative of those demonstrating the value of teaching listening skills. Using a large group of children (N = 111) including a wide variety of intelligence levels, Childers tested listening ability before and after a series of lessons designed to increase listening skills. Children in all the groups improved their listening skills significantly. An analysis of other studies on the effects of listening is provided by Marten (1978).

Apparently listening is a necessary skill that can be improved through direct instruction. Many teachers want to help their children do this. The question remains: How does one go about this task? There are basically two approaches to listening: (1) use of a commercial program, or (2) creation of a program by the classroom teacher.

COMMERCIAL PROGRAMS

A distinguishing feature of most commercial programs is their highly sequential, organized nature. Such programs: (a) identify a specific set of listening subskills to be improved; (b) often specify procedures for teacher and pupil; and (c) typically make provision for evaluation of how well the skill is learned.

TEACHER-MADE PROGRAMS

Commercial programs provide a solution to the problem of a teacher with too many subjects to prepare in too short a time. In a real sense, however, no such program meets the specific needs of the children in a particular classroom as effectively as can one created especially by the teacher in that situation.

A major advantage of a teacher-made program is its *flexibility*. As teachers sense children's listening problems, they can alter and adapt the sequences of experiences in response to the needs of the particular group. Sample listening experiences are included in this chapter. These should not be followed prescriptively but may suggest some ideas to try, once you determine the listening needs of your children. It is hoped that the sequence will encourage you to think about other experiences you can plan for your group.

SETTING THE STAGE

Whether in preparation for a listening lesson or in the context of listening for directions in a subject-matter-related lesson, it is crucial to set the stage for careful listening. Much inattentive listening occurs because the speaker proceeds without preparing the listeners adequately.

Before beginning, make sure to compensate for any physical distractions. This suggestion seems self-evident; in actuality children are often required to listen in less than ideal conditions. Lundsteen (1979) comments that:

> [I]t is not uncommon for children to be expected to listen far beyond the time of their likely attention span with lawn mowers going or children playing outside the window, with noise-amplifying flooring, sweltering weather (unairconditioned), or over-heating—every imaginable kind of inhibition to attention.

As a teacher you need to be aware that children have grown accustomed to shutting out sounds. Ecologists express growing concern about noise pollution; children among others shut out the high-level noises pervading our atmosphere. This is not surprising when we consider that overall loudness of environmental noise is doubling every ten years. Quiet eludes us: in addition to loud noises, we are constantly bombarded by the ubiquitous mechanized music which fills the spaces in restaurants, elevators, and waiting rooms. That is among the less offensive; many noises in our environments approach deafening levels.

Even in school, children *must* tune out. The task of finishing an assignment while other children, perhaps no more than fifteen feet away, are reading orally, is not an easy one. Since children have learned to ignore sound, when you are planning a lesson in which they must listen, you need to set the stage carefully so that they can listen.

To begin a unit on listening, some teachers find it helpful to explore what children know about the task. A second-grade teacher asked her class two simple questions which elicited much motivating discussion. She asked "Why should we listen?" Her children contributed these responses:

To know what people are doing
To know what people talk about
To get different ideas
To know what made you scared
To get warned of trouble coming
To understand more

The teacher then asked her class, "When should we listen best?" Among her students' responses were these:

When teacher talks
When something's real, real important
When someone helps
When there's a fire drill so I know where to go
When someone reads a good story
During a discussion
When my coach gives us directions
Watching TV

In addition to setting the stage, it is important that teachers set the *expectation* of listening attentively. Frequently, children ask over and over again to have simple directions repeated. When the teacher acquiesces, the result is less efficient listening habits. It is crucial to establish in children's minds that directions and instructions will be given once, and once *only*. Naturally this cannot be done precipitately: some warning must be given and practice in listening attentively must be provided (Burnham, 1981).

The teacher can easily talk with the children, perhaps pointing out that he or she had to repeat instructions several times and does not intend to continue doing so. The teacher should systematically reduce the number of times directions are repeated until most of them are given only once. This encourages careful listening to all instructions.

Children also need to be prepared by being informed about the *purpose for listening*. Some brief introduction, stating the nature of the instructions and why they should listen, will help the children establish the purpose for listening. Do not entreat boys and girls to listen "Because listening is important," but rather "Because when I have finished giving the directions there are three activities you are to do." This procedure puts listening into a very practical framework: children begin to realize that unless they listen, they will be unable to accomplish the task.

What to do with the child who does not listen, even though directions are repeated only once? The remedy is to maintain the policy, telling the child to find out from some other child what the instructions were. The bother of being interrupted by a child who has not listened soon annoys others who have, and they are not slow to let the nonlistener know they don't want to listen for him or her.

Probably one of the most significant things a teacher does to encourage good listening habits is to be a good listener herself. It is unreasonable in children's eyes, as in those of an adult, to ask others to do something we ourselves don't do. Yet too often teachers, preoccupied in many tasks, ignore the child speaking or reading. A student teacher once personified such preoccupation in a negative way: While a child was reading aloud during a reading session, the young teacher got up from her chair, walked halfway across the room, wrote an additional direction she had forgotten on the

chalkboard, walked back and sat down in the reading circle. You can imagine the child's feeling! Not only did this reinforce in the child's mind that
what he was doing was not important, but it further reinforced the idea that
listening was not important to the teacher.

Every teacher should model effective listening, but this is probably
especially necessary for teachers of children from culturally different backgrounds. The teacher *must* listen attentively in order to establish good listening habits. Many children grow up in crowded living conditions where the
air is filled with the sounds of many people and the intrusive noise of a television set. The quieter atmosphere of the classroom where the teacher, an
adult model, listens to the child may in fact be the only place he or she enjoys
an adult listening ear.

Teachers of culturally different children must keep in mind that evidence
of listening varies from culture to culture. Hall (1969) comments that
members of a culture manipulate such things as posture and eye contact differently, though often teachers of different cultural groups may be unaware
of this. Information about such differences in European cultures has existed
for some time. Other groups' evidences of listening have not been widely
studied. Hall warns that teachers of Mexican-American, Puerto Rican, and
black children must be aware that ways of showing one is listening vary in
these cultures:

> Basically the informal rule for black culture goes somewhat as follows: if you
> are in the same room with another person, or in a context where he has
> ready access to you, there are times when there is no need to go through the
> motions of showing him you are listening because that is automatically
> implied.

Sensitive teachers of such children will do their best to learn what these
culturally induced manifestations are in order to facilitate learning.

A SEQUENCE OF SKILLS

Earlier it was pointed out that there are two basic approaches to teaching or
refining listening skills. One approach is for the teacher to develop a listening program for the children. What follows is a sequence of listening skills
which may be used as a base for a listening program, though it is not intended that any class would necessarily follow the sequence completely, or
in this exact order. The teacher, working closely with a group over an extended period of time, can easily determine if the children are profiting from
a particular segment of the sequence and thereafter either condense, expand,
or eliminate it.

Listening to Natural Sounds

Begin a sequence of listening experiences by having your children stop whatever they are doing and simply listen to all the sounds they can hear around them.[7] The group can then discuss the sounds they heard, perhaps listing them on the chalkboard. Encouraging the children to listen to the variety of sounds they hear on the way to school is helpful. Or, you might find it interesting to take the children, blindfolded, on a walk around the school. Afterward, the boys and girls can dictate their stories about the experience. Some first-graders dictated these accounts:

I went to the bathroom. I heard the toilet flushing, and I heard the
   tissue, and the water.
I went to the gym. People were talking, and there were lots of
   people. I heard Mr. _____'s voice. I heard people talking.
I heard talking and a piano from the kindergarten room.
I heard when I bumped my head.
I heard our room door close.

Eugene

We walked in the bathroom. I heard people walking, and washing
   their hands, and putting paper in the garbage can.
We went to the music room. People were singing.
We went to the gym. People were running. I heard Mr. _____
   say, "We don't start to run yet."
When we came in the room people said, "Where were you going?"

Chris

To make such experiences more complex, urge your children to think about what conditions might affect sounds (time of year, of day, atmospheric conditions). Children can become very sophisticated listeners as a result of such activities. One day when we were doing this activity, I was surprised to find a child in my fifth-grade class correctly identify, not only that a sports car had been started outside our window, but also what *kind* of a car it was—very well-developed listening skills, indeed. Such experiences as these make children *aware* of the variety of sounds which surround us and sensitize them to information we can gather through our sense of hearing.

---

[7]This can indeed be done by parents with children long before they come to school. Having children listen to sounds around the home is one of several activities suggested in *Getting Ready to Read* by Susan M. Glazer (Englewood Cliffs, N.J.: Prentice-Hall, 1980). Teachers may want to recommend this book to parents for the many useful language activities it suggests.

Using a listening station, several children can listen to a record as they follow along in their books. (Used with permission of the photographer, Richard D. Bradley.)

Listening to Created Sounds

Children enjoy contributing objects to a "Listening Box." Several objects hidden from sight in a cardboard box can be used to make sounds children are asked to identify. Begin simply, perhaps with a scissors, and move to more complex sounds. Eventually children can tell the difference between the sound made when a metal lid is opened (for instance, the kind on a bandage box) and the sound made when a plastic lid is opened (for instance, on a refrigerator storage box).[8] To begin, the teacher should provide the objects, but quickly the children take over, and bring to class a variety of objects to put in the "Sound Box." Such an activity can sensitize children to rather minimal differences in sounds which are similar. They enjoy being "sound detectives."

In one second-grade classroom, children listened to the sound of a scissors. The teacher asked them for words to describe the sound, and the children contributed:

clicking	snipping
snapping	clipping

---

[8]It is often wise to have children listen to sounds from similar but slightly different sources. Listening to different kinds of clocks, for example, sensitizes children to minute differences in sounds. Use the film "Once Upon a Time" (Texture Films, Inc., 1600 Broadway, New York 10019), 11 min., color. This exploration of varied facets of time includes unusual clocks and timepieces of all ages. You might have your children make a collection of clocks in the classroom to use as the basis for a sound-discrimination lesson.

Then she asked them to tell what kind of a sound it was, to focus on the qualities of sound. The children said the sound was:

quick	short
sharp	harsh
high	unpleasant

As a next step, the teacher asked her children if this sound was like any other sound they knew. Boys and girls compared it to:

jaws chewing	birds chirping
cupboard snapping	bacon sizzling
clicking closing	

Another day the same teacher shook a bottle of vitamins. The children described the sound as:

loud	it has more than one part
dull	a rattling kind of noise
low	

When asked what the sound was like, the children gave these comparisons:

popcorn popping	shaking a Pringle's Potato Chip can
a rattle	rocks falling
a train	going through beads with your fingers
a maraca	

A sound-matching experience can grow from objects and lead into writing. Make a sound discrimination set by filling pairs of plastic eggs with objects such as beans, thumbtacks, erasers, cotton, or raisins. Let the children match those pairs that have the same sound. If plastic eggs are hard to obtain, use small film cans, pill containers with the plastic covered by strips of construction paper, or small match boxes. After the children have matched the sounds, have them describe the sounds verbally or write down words that represent the sound they have heard.

Listening to Voices

A simple game can be played by having children listen to voices to determine who is speaking (Burk, 1971). The teacher instructs the children to close their eyes. Then the teacher walks quietly around the room, stopping to tap one child on the shoulder. After returning to the front of the room, the teacher has the child say three or four sentences, and the other children guess who said them. It is a simple game, but it does encourage careful listening, particularly as the only clue the children have is an aural one. Such listening to voices can provide an entrée into dramatization, as children listen to voices and then improvise, or role-play, a characterization of a person based on the voice (Peavy, 1974).

With older students, teachers can initiate tape exchanges with classes in other parts of the country. Such tapes provide opportunities for children to listen to other boys and girls whose dialects are different than their own (Rogers, 1972).

Developing Words to Describe

In the preceding and other listening activities, the teacher works toward developing a vocabulary which describes sounds children have heard. This is slow to develop; some of the less specific words come first. "It was a loud sound," or "It was a soft sound." On the other hand, students can be led to see that we can describe several aspects of sound:

> *Pitch.* The highness or lowness of the sound. Comparisons can be
> made, and when listening to three sounds, words like high,
> higher, and highest or low, lower, and lowest can be encouraged.
> *Timbre.* Children should be encouraged to describe the quality of
> the sound—is it a soft sound, a harsh sound, a raspy, or buzzy, or
> singy sound? These terms may sound rather imprecise, but the
> point is to encourage boys and girls to put into words the sense
> impressions they have taken in through their ears. For a teacher
> to insist on the one word that seems most appropriate to him or
> her would be to defeat the purpose of the exercise.
> *Duration.* All sounds can be characterized as constant or intermit-
> tent, and children can be asked to describe the nature of this
> aspect of the sound. If it is intermittent, can the pattern of sound
> and silence be described in words? Many listening activities of this
> nature can be planned with a music teacher, who will be happy
> to suggest experiences in which children listen to various musical
> instruments. If you have no music teacher, consult any of the
> elementary music series noting especially the listening sections
> provided.

Listening for Sequence

It is simple to encourage attentive listening in quasi-game situations by having children listen to sequences and then tell or write what they have heard. Kindergarteners can listen to simple sequences made by rhythm instruments and then tell what they heard. The teacher might play a sequence: bell, then drum; bell, drum, drum; or drum, drum, bell. Do this first in the open and later behind a small screen to focus the attention on listening (Zigmond &

Circi, 1968). The sequences can become more involved as the children's ability increases.

With older children, you may read a string of numbers: 2, 7, 11, 4, 9. Begin with a short string and gradually increase it, being sure to vary odd and even numbers. Read the sequence evenly at first, and then try patterning with the voice, 2, 1, / 4, 3, 4, / 7, 9; or 3, 2, 1, / 2, 5, / 7. Encourage your children to discuss such questions as: "Which way is easier to remember—when the numbers are read evenly, or in a patterned sequence?" Children find that the challenge of listening and remembering the sequence is enjoyable and attentive listening is encouraged.

Try sequencing with a simple series of directions, which you read while the children listen and respond. When you begin, three directions may be enough; see how far you can extend this. A sample series might include:

1. middle name
2. our classroom number
3. the name of the street you live on.

With older children who have had more practice, such a sequence might include:

Write your:
1. age
2. the number of years you've lived there
3. your mother's first name
4. the product of 7 x 9
5. your favorite food
6. your middle name
7. your shoe size.[9]

Sometimes a sequence of sounds (or noises) can be used as a stimulus for composition. *Sound Stories and the Sound Library* (Educational Noises and Sounds, Inc., P.O. Box 591, San Clemente, CA 92672) is an example. This tape includes five "stories" and a sixth segment of miscellaneous sounds. There is a rough order of events in the five stories, though these are open enough to stimulate several possible interpetations. Use one of the stories as motivation for your total group and then put the tape at the listening station so the children can compose individually later.

A different kind of sequence—this one numerical—is presented in *The Nickle Nackle Tree* (Dodd, 1976). In a book of nonsense creatures who in-

---

[9] In "'Huh? Wadja say?' Index to Better Listening," *Instructor* (October 1974): 59–68, additional sequence activities recommended include listening for detail, for main ideas, and to make inferences. The many suggested activities are arranged roughly into difficulty levels, and many of the simpler ones can be used by primary teachers.

A motocycle goes reen, reen. EMH
I like that sound.

After having children listen to sounds, have them draw a favorite subject that they relate to those sounds.

creasingly clutter up the page, the author provides an alliterative counting rhyme somewhat reminiscent of Lewis Carroll. The book needs to be read aloud for the delicious sounds it creates. One teacher of first grade used this to develop her children's ability to hear rhyming words. Then the book served as a basis for a group-dictated oral composition:

One fickle-fack bird eating ice cream
Two bob-a-loo birds having a dream
Three wird birds swimming in a pool
Four noodle birds singing in school
Five nickle tickle birds tickling in the tree
Six stick birds as white as white can be
Seven digitor-dird birds doing problems on their knees
Eight dickapick birds playing with their keys
Nine ningle-nangle birds curling their hair
Ten tickle-tackle-tee birds kissing a bear
Eleven geezle-gum birds sucking their thumbs
Twelve turtle-gurtle birds eating some plums.

Listening to Anticipate

The ability to anticipate is closely linked to the ability to extract meaning while listening. A child may learn to anticipate when presented with a piece of poetry in which some of the words are left out. The purpose is to encourage children to use whatever clues they can garner in trying to guess what the missing word might be.

For example, the teacher might read the following poem, and leave out the italicized words. Children are then encouraged to offer their suggestions about what word might logically fit into the blank, based on what they have heard.

CAT
by Mary Britton Miller

The black cat yawns,
Opens her jaws,
Stretches her legs,
And shows her claws.

Then she gets up
And stands on four
Long still legs
And yawns some more.

She shows her sharp teeth,
She stretches her lip,
Her slice of a tongue
Turns up at the tip

Lifting herself
On her delicate toes
She arches her back
As high as it goes.

She lets herself down
With particular care,
And pads away
With her *tail* in the air.

(in Hopkins, 1981)

It is unnecessary to insist that children give the one word the poet chose. There is often more than one answer possible; encourage your children to discuss reasons they think their answer is most likely. In addition to listening for missing words, children can also listen for missing phrases. In the following poem, for example, children need to listen attentively to gather information about the pattern of the poem, so they can anticipate what will come next. They are to fill in the italicized lines.

THE MYSTERIOUS CAT
by Vachel Lindsay

I saw a proud, mysterious cat,
I saw a proud, mysterious cat,
Too proud to catch a mouse or rat—
Mew, mew, mew.

But catnip she would eat and purr,
But catnip she would eat and purr,
And goldfish she did much prefer—
Mew, mew, mew.

I saw a cat—'twas but a dream,
I saw a cat—'twas but a dream,
Who scorned the slave that brought her cream—
Mew, mew, mew.

Unless the slave were dressed in style,
Unless the slave were dressed in style,
And knelt before her all the while—
Mew, mew, mew.

Did you ever hear of a thing like that?
Did you ever hear of a thing like that?
Did you ever hear of a thing like that?
Oh, what a proud, mysterious cat.
Oh, what a proud, mysterious cat.
Oh, what a proud, mysterious cat.
Mew . . . Mew . . . Mew.

(in Johnson et al., 1977)

Listening to Determine Meaning

There are times when you, the teacher, prepare children for listening by discussing the meaning of unfamiliar words in advance. At other times, encourage children to listen carefully to determine meaning from context. You might read the following:

> Mary and Tom were walking home in the rain. They came to a big puddle on the sidewalk, and he splashed in the middle. Mary was very *indignant*. She made a face at Tom and ran home ahead of him.

Then ask the students to tell which of the following they think is correct:

1. Mary was wet.
2. Mary was confused.
3. Mary was tired.
4. Mary was angry.

Often the meaning may not be entirely clear. In the above example, Mary could be either (1) or (4). The purpose when beginning such exercises is not to pin down one specific meaning, but rather to encourage children to think about what they have heard, discuss the evidence on which they have based their answer, and determine which is the most likely possibility. The materials to motivate such listening and discussion can be made up by the teacher, or they can be drawn from literature.

The teacher might read one of Leo Lionni's stories about a timid mouse, named Theodore, who gained confidence in a devious way. The teacher could then engage children in a discussion about some of the words used. For example, read the following section:

> "Quirp!" said the mushroom.
> "What does it mean?" asked Theodore's friends, dumbfounded.
> "It means," said Theodore, "that the mouse should be venerated above all other animals."
> The news of Theodore's discovery spread quickly.
> His friends made him a crown.
> Animals came from far away with garlands of flowers.
> Wherever he went he was carried on the turtle's back on a cushion of flowers.
> And wherever he went he was venerated above all other animals.

Rather than trying to pose some specific alternatives, as in the example above, simply ask children to tell what they think the word *venerated* means, based on what they have heard. To aid in vocabulary development, you might, after this initial informal listening exercise, have a few children look up the word in a dictionary to find other aspects of the definition.

Critical Listening

A more sophisticated kind of listening requires that children listen critically, to answer questions posed about the material. Many times a shared listening experience may naturally culminate in some oral discussion questions (Fitzgerald, 1979; Cromwell, 1979). In this case, as in the case of a written question the child is to answer, the teacher's goal is to move beyond mere factual questions to ones requiring more involved thinking processes.

After children have listened to the following passage, they might be asked the simple recall questions below, so the teacher can determine how accurately they have listened.

> The cockroach belongs to an insect order that includes the grasshopper, the praying mantis, the cricket, the katydid, and the walking stick. The name of the order is Orthoptera, which means "Straight Wings." Most of these insects have two pairs of wings; the back pair folds like a fan under the long, straight front wings. (Cole, 1971)

Questions:

1. What are some other members of the group to which the cockroach belongs?
2. What does their scientific name mean?
3. How many wings do most of these insects have?

Beyond such basic, factual questions, however, the teacher's goal is to ask more involved questions, requiring critical listening. The Bloom Taxonomy was explained at length in Chapter 2. Sample questions, arranged from Level One to Level Six are included here to illustrate how such questions can be used in stimulating critical listening. The following material might be read to children:

> Sand Paintings, believed to have magical healing powers, are made by the Navajo, the largest of all Indian nations. The sand painters are Navajo medicine men, also called singers. They chant ceremonial songs as they create traditional designs from memory. The paintings are made by carefully dropping dry pigments, powdered stone and charcoal on a bed of clean sand. (Glubok, 1971)

After children have listened to the paragraph, they might be asked the following questions:

LEVEL ONE: What is the largest of the American Indian nations?

LEVEL TWO: Would it be usual to find people other than the medicine men making the paintings?

LEVEL THREE: What might the medicine man's reaction be to a suggestion that new designs be used?

LEVEL FOUR: Given what you know about the art, what can you assume about the relation between materials used and tradition?

LEVEL FIVE: Could you assume the role of a Navajo, and tell a friend of your job as a sand painter?

LEVEL SIX: How could you tell if sand paintings were effective in accomplishing their purposes?

Such activities lead to more sophisticated thought about what was presented, as children develop the ability to ask themselves such questions as:

1. What is the reliability of the source? Is the material drawn from books or people who are qualified in the area of their presentation?
2. What is the relevance of the argument? Good listeners try to determine what helps make the point and what is simply extraneous.[10]
3. Is the speaker using language emotively to cloud my thinking, so I won't remember the actual facts which are presented?[11]

The above materials are factual, but at times the teacher uses literature when attempting to encourage critical listening. The ability to draw inferences, to extend or extrapolate ideas beyond the basic material in a story, is a mature skill which develops slowly. As the teacher discusses a story the class has shared orally, she or he is motivating children to use what they have heard to answer higher-level questions—the answers for which were not given in the story.

The teacher might use the disarmingly original story *The Bat Poet* (Jarrell, 1964) who, unlike his brothers, has aspirations to write poetry. He encounters an audience for his writing in a neighborhood mockingbird. After reading the entire story for the children, the teacher might ask such questions as the following:

---

[10]This distinction can be made with television commercials. Worthwhile listening lessons can be planned involving children in listening at home in the evening, and then discussing in class the next day what they observed. Recently I noted such an example in a commercial for a washing machine, the advantage of which was its smooth enamel washing drum, perfect for permanent press clothes. In reality, all washers feature such drums.

[11]This material is adapted and expanded from Anderson and Lapp, *Language Skills in Elementary Education*, p. 104.

How do you think the bat might react if he encountered somebody in trouble on his nightly flights? What evidence do you have in the story about the nature of his personality?

Do you think the mockingbird was genuinely interested in the bat's poems? What clues do you have? At what points in the story is there a difference between what he says and what he does? Would he have reacted differently if the poems hadn't been as well written?

An interesting and quite systematic adaptation of the idea of using the Bloom Taxonomy as a means of teaching thinking skills to bilingual children is described by Streiff.[12] Lessons were planned for Navajo and Mexican-American children to help them learn to ask the full range of questions in the taxonomy. These children, who had been in kindergarten ESL programs, participated in this listening program designed to help them move from pattern drill into more sophisticated thinking patterns.

In the first stage of this listening comprehension program, students listened to a brief introduction to the story material and then generated questions about it. In later stages in the program, they generated questions—at various levels of the taxonomy—while listening to the story material. A final stage in the program was to apply focused anticipation questions in such other content areas as math, science, and social studies.

The teachers' reactions indicated enthusiastic approval of this listening/question strategy program for use with Navajo and Mexican-American students.

TEACHERS EVALUATE THEMSELVES

In this, as in other curricular areas, the teacher is—like it or not—a model for children to emulate. This is fine when the teacher is also an attentive and appreciative listener. If such is not the case, he or she may unconsciously be fostering poor listening habits among the children. Because listening habits, like much habituated behavior, often remain unexamined, a checklist for teachers is included here. The teacher is encouraged to confront questions in two areas:

How Effective Am I as a Planner?

1. Do I realize children may have difficulty listening attentively for long periods of time? Can I plan my sequence of learning activities with variety so that listening is a pleasant and not overly lengthy task?

---

[12]Streiff, Virginia H. "Question-Generation by First Graders," in *Bilingualism in Early Childhood* (Mackey & Andersson, eds.), Rowley, Mass: Newbury House Publishers, 1977, pp. 272–286. Other chapters of interest to teachers of bilingual children include descriptions of programs offered in several different places in the United States.

2. Do I plan my presentation carefully so children listen to one thing at a time? Are my instructions planned with clarity so children can easily understand them?

3. Are my explanations carefully given throughout, clear and concise? Have I planned more than one way to say something, so if children do not understand the first time, I am prepared with an alternative?

4. Do I set aside some times during the day when a child may come to me and share something orally? Do I work to establish a rapport which encourages such oral sharing and listening?

How Effective Am I as a Presenter?

1. Do I encourage good listening by limiting the amount of talking I do?[13]

2. Do I use changes in pitch, tempo, and volume of my speaking? Can I manipulate these paralinguistic elements to hold the children's attention? Do I also consciously use kinesics to add richness to my speech?

3. Do I give children time to think when I ask a question? Can I endure some "empty spaces" while children cope with the verbal problem I have presented? Or does silence threaten me, so that I have to fill it up with talk?

4. Do I wait to get the attention of all the children before I begin to speak? Have I eye contact with the majority of the listeners before I begin?

5. Do I remember to give some positive response to each speaker without needlessly summarizing or paraphrasing what was said?

6. Do I make sure that when only one child has difficulty understanding, I clarify for him or her later, rather than interrupting the train of thought of all the children while I explain?

7. Is my speech free of repeated expressions or phrases which are unnecessary or offensive? Among many teachers two common expressions are "You know . . ." and "Listen . . . ."

8. Do I listen attentively to children when they talk, and express my interest and appreciation in what they say?[14]

---

[13]Studies of the amount of talking teachers do reveal that two-thirds of the time it is the teacher who is talking. Teachers asks eight questions for every question asked by a child. See Stephen M. Corey, "The Teachers Out-Talk the Pupils," in *Listening: Readings*, compiler Sam Duker (New York: The Scarecrow Press, 1966). Teachers have found it possible to change their behavior in this. See Karen Drury Norris, "Shut Up, Teacher," *Today's Education* 60 (November 1971): 46.

[14]A highly apparent part of this is eye contact. A survey of 350 elementary children showed that the largest number chose, "She looks at me when I am talking," as the way they knew they had the teacher's attention. See, "Hey, Did You *Really* Hear That Kid?" by Charles Galloway and Truman Whitfield in *Instructor* (October 1976): 84–86.

The above is not to suggest that the teacher's job is primarily that of presenter or dispenser of information. Such was the case fifty years ago; ideas about the teacher's role are changing quickly. Nonetheless, there are times a teacher should present information, and such presentation ought to be as effective as possible. Thinking about the above questions may help teachers increase their effectiveness.

CHILDREN EVALUATE THEMSELVES

It often helps to involve children in evaluating listening habits. Discussions about what group members think constitutes a good listener can begin at the kindergarten level, and children can draw up lists that can be posted in the classroom and reviewed periodically.

In first grade, for example, such a list is often quite simple. One drawn up cooperatively by a first-grade class and their teacher resulted in these rules:

Am I a good listener? If so, I:

1. Look at the person who is talking to me.
2. Don't talk until it is question time.
3. Think about what the person is saying.
4. Keep my hands and feet quiet.

It is readily apparent to adults that such criteria do not necessarily ensure attentive listening. It is very possible to be listening attentively while not looking at a speaker. However, at this level, when we are trying to build listening habits, it is more *likely* that good listening will occur if the child listener maintains eye contact with the speaker.

As children become older, the list of points included on the chart can become more sophisticated. A fifth-grade class drew up the following list:

Do you think you are a good listener? If you are, you do these things:

1. Prepare to listen physically and mentally.
2. Anticipate the plan or organization of the talk. Listen for cues the speaker gives.
3. Listen for a summary. If the speaker doesn't give one, try to make one yourself.
4. Take brief notes on information talks.
5. Think of questions to ask the speaker. What else do you want to know?[15]

---

[15]Teaching children to ask questions of the speaker can help them improve their understanding of ambiguous messages. See "How Children Learn to Listen . . ." by Marsha Ironsmith and Grover Whitehurst, *Developmental Psychology* 14(5) (1978): 546–554.

6. Think about how the things the speaker said are like or unlike what you already know.

STANDARDIZED LISTENING TESTS

Teachers should evaluate their own listening skills and encourage children to evaluate theirs—but at times they may wish for some more methodical ways of evaluating children's growth in listening. Some commercial listening programs provide for evaluation. If the teacher has evolved a teacher-made program, he or she will also need to plan a means of evaluating its effectiveness. Is this enough? Some teachers may not feel so, and, as a result, search for a standardized test in listening. Such tests are widely available in other skill areas; there is an abundant selection of reading tests, for example. Little is available, however, to a teacher interested in assessing listening.

One possibility is to use the listening section from the *Sequential Tests of Educational Progress* (Princeton, N.J.: Cooperative Test Division, Educational Testing Service). The test attempts to measure three factors:

1. *Comprehension:* identifying main ideas, remembering significant details, and sequence of ideas
2. *Interpretation:* understanding the implications of main ideas, details, and the interrelationships between ideas
3. *Evaluation:* judging the validity of ideas, the organization of materials, and recognizing the intent of the speaker

The classroom teacher administers the test; children respond to multiple-choice questions. One problem inherent in the testing is that there may be considerable variation from classroom to classroom, depending on how effective the teacher is in administering the test. The rate and mode of presentation may affect the reliability of the test. One writer suggested this limitation could be overcome by having the materials presented on tapes by a trained reader (Wilkinson, 1969). Another limitation of the test is that the longest time it requires children to listen is five minutes; children are often involved in listening for longer periods than that, even in an elementary classroom. As a result of these factors, there is some doubt as to whether the test really tests listening. Reservations about this test have been expressed by Kelly (1965). The teacher must use it with caution and interpret the results with care, but since it is virtually the only such test available at this time, it is important to be aware of it.

The teacher combines both informal in-class observation of pupil listening behavior and more formal test responses, because some children do better in one situation than in another. Lundsteen (1971) reminds us that:

[I]t is likely that in testing situations some of the "best" listeners may have high mental ability and are normally relatively inattentive under nontest circumstances; and some others simply do poorly in a test environment.

SUMMARY

Listening could be called the most elusive of the language skills. A distinction, too seldom made, exists between hearing and more complex listening. Listening problems which need specialized attention do exist in the elementary school, though most children fall within a normal range. These normal abilities are used to meet the early and continuing demands to listen well. Listening is the skill most used by both children and adults. This presents a dichotomy, since few children experience a regular, planned sequence of lessons to enhance listening, despite research which shows this skill can be improved. One means of improvement is the commercial listening kit materials. Another approach is for teachers to design listening programs: the major portion of this chapter presented a program of listening skills. After setting expectation that children will listen, linked with clearly stated purposes for listening, teachers can lead children through a sequence of listening experiences of increasing difficulty. Children should listen to environmental sounds, to created sounds, and to voices, as they develop a vocabulary to describe what they have heard. More complex activities involve students in listening to sequence, to anticipate, to determine meaning, and, finally, to listen critically. The chapter concluded with sections on teachers evaluating themselves, and children evaluating themselves.

Many demands are made, and yet too few children leave the elementary school as efficient listeners. Reasons for this were suggested and ideas about improving the skill were given. To write and read about an aural skill can be frustrating, but I have done so in the hope that you will translate these ideas into a vital listening program in your classroom.

Suggestions for Further Exploration

1. Select a story or a piece of informational writing of interest to you; practice reading it until you are satisfied with the results. Obtain a recorder and make a tape of your reading. Wait a week or so, then listen critically to the recording. Is it the kind of reading to which children would listen with interest? If not, what aspects of your presentation need work?

2. If you have access to a class, plan a short lesson and give it, recording it either on audiotape or videotape. The advantage of videotape is that it allows you to monitor your use of kinesics. Review the recording. Does the presentation encourage attentive listening, or are there elements you think need further work?

3. Electronic music, piped into most public places, is so all-pervasive we seldom notice it. Yet in some ways it can be looked upon as noise pollution. Check to see if there is a supplier of such sound in your community. Call and arrange an interview with one of the staff. What rationale is given for such music? (An affirmative statement is "Music for Working" by William Wokoun in *Science Journal*, November 1969, pp. 55–59.) Can the people who provide this service

also provide documentation about its value? On what basis do they justify this service to those who consider using it?

4. Much concern has been expressed recently about noise pollution. You might be interested in reading about this problem. See William Burns, *Noise and Man* (Philadelphia: J.B. Lippincott, 1973); David Lipscomb, *Noise: The Unwanted Sounds* (Chicago: Nelson-Hall, 1974); or M. Barbara Scheibel, *The Unseen Enemy* (West Haven, Conn.: Pendulum Press, 1972).

5. Is the average classroom a quiet place in which to listen and work? In preparation for a visit to a school to answer this question, read "How to Keep School Noise at the Right Level," by Ronald L. McKay in *The Nation's Schools* (March 1972): 64–69. Then, observe in the school and note the sources of noise pollution. Think up some ways these could be minimized, if not eliminated.

6. The Montessori approach is based on education of the senses—including listening. You may find it interesting to read about the work of this pioneer educator. Of special note is her approach to developing listening skills, described in *The Montessori Method* (Cambridge, Mass.: Robert Bently, 1964): pp. 203–206, 209–214.

7. Research quoted in this chapter asserts that there is no significant difference between boys and girls in listening ability (Hollow, 1965). Contrary evidence is presented in Larry L. Barker, *Listening Behavior* (Englewood Cliffs, N.J.: Prentice-Hall, 1971, p. 45). Read both, and then observe in a classroom. Can you notice any overt difference between boys and girls in: who they listen to, how much, and how they show they are listening?

Suggestions for Further Reading

Bednarz, Barbara. "Project Sound Makes It." *Elementary English* 48 (January 1971): 86–89.

Pointing out that listening to sound is related to creative writing, the author lists thirty-one musical selections which can be used as starters to elicit writing from children.

Berg-Cross, Linda and Berg-Cross, Gary. "Listening to Stories May Change Children's Social Attitudes." *The Reading Teacher* (March 1978): 659–663.

A study exploring the effect that listening to picture books about social values (sex, role stereotyping, friendship, death, and risk-taking) has on children's attitudes. 120 children took pre- and post-tests to measure their attitudes. Four picture books were read individually to the children. No discussion took place while the story was being read or afterwards, but spontaneous questions from the child were answered. The attitude change from pre- to post-test was significant. Across all stories, experimental subjects changed well over half their answers on the two tests. Expressed attitudes and values of four- to six-year-olds can be significantly changed by listening to and looking at a picture storybook which espouses different attitudes. These changes occurred even *without* discussion, a finding contrary to previous research. The socializing aspect of these books suggests that parents and teachers take more seriously books they introduce to children.

Campbell, E. "Teaching Listening: A Case Example." *Audiovisual Instruction* 13 (November 1968): 1003.

The article describes a program for inner-city children which centered on poor listening habits including: tuning out, doing other things instead of listening, not thinking critically, and listening to words instead of ideas. This program was designed to increase the listening skills, encourage maintaining attention, and develop an appreciation of the children's culture.

Devine, Thomas G. "Listening: What Do We Know After 50 Years of Research and Theorizing?" *The Reading Teacher* (January 1978): 296–304.

Reporting on nearly three dozen pieces of writing about listening, ranging in date of publication from 1926 to 1977, the author concludes that though much is known about listening, little is done about it. He describes listening tests; teaching techniques; the relation to intelligence, to reading, and to thinking; and the status of listening instruction in the U.S. His comment on skills sequences is revealing: though many of these make logical sense, very few have been validated through research.

Farrell, Muriel and Flint, Shirley H. "Are They Listening?" *Childhood Education* 43 (May 1967): 528–529.

An article stressing the importance of listening with a purpose. Several musical games are described to teach discrimination between pitches, timbres, tone qualities, tempo changes, and differences in rhythm.

Funk, Hal D. and Triplett, DeWayne. *Language Arts in the Elementary School: Readings.* Philadelphia: J.B. Lippincott, 1972.

This paperback brings together four important nomothetic articles suggesting to the teacher what should be done about listening.

Hamachek, Don E. "How to Get Your Child to Listen to You" and "How to Listen to Your Child." *Today's Education* 60 (April 1971): 33–48.

An excellent resource for teachers—as it will cause them to reexamine their listening behaviors—and for them to recommend to parents. Written in easily readable, concise fashion, both articles have a practical emphasis.

Hennings, Dorothy Grant. *Communication in Action.* Chicago: Rand McNally, 1978.

In her usual highly readable style, the author opens a helpful chapter by considering types of listening, with clarifying examples of each. Particular literature selections for developing different listening skills are recommended. The strength of this writing, as in Henning's earlier books, is the practicality of her classroom activities. There are simple, introductory activities included, as well as more complex critical listening skills for older children.

Herman, Wayne L. "The Use of Language Arts in Social Studies Lessons." *American Educational Research Journal* 4 (March 1967): 117–124.

During a six-week unit topic, the author had three judges record what went on in fourteen randomly selected fifth-grade classrooms. Results showed that in these social studies classes, children were listening and speaking 78.8 percent of the time, and were reading only 13 percent of the time. Slow learners were called on a significantly smaller number of times than were bright children.

Kelly, Charles M. "Listening: Complex of Activities—and a Unitary Skill?" *Speech Monographs* 34 (November 1967): 455–466.

The author contends, in contrast with the statement in this chapter, that listening tests really tell us very little of value. He offers a wide-ranging critique of the literature and concludes that such a complex skill cannot be adequately assessed by the relatively crude measures available.

Konopa, Valerie and Zimering, Stanley. "Noise—The Challenge of the Future," *Journal of School Health* (March 1972): 172–176.

The detrimental physical and psychological effects of noise on people, especially the effect on teenagers listening to loud rock music, are described in scientific detail understandable to the layperson. Citing this as the most noise-exposed generation ever reared in the western world, the authors describe government efforts to control this problem.

Lamberts, Frances et al. "Listening and Language Activities for Preschool Children." *Language, Speech and Hearing Services in Schools* (April 1980): 111–117.

Opening with a summary of the kinds of language growth related to listening skill, the authors point out that children have greater difficulty attending to auditory than to visual information. They comment on the dearth of available auditory training materials for young children. Then they describe a set of materials, including pictures, slides and cassette tapes, which they developed. These materials included people, indoor, animal, music and outdoor sounds for picture matching experiences. In addition to picture matching, students also view a sequence of pictures, listen to a sequence of sounds, and cross out the missing sound. Using these materials with preschool children, the authors report that the combination of sound and pictures made it possible to maintain children's attention, even when materials were used repeatedly over long periods of time. Lamberts and her colleagues feel these materials help balance the predominantly "eye biased" elementary curriculum.

Lundsteen, Sara W. "Critical Listening and Thinking: A Recommended Goal for Future Research." *Journal of Research and Development in Education* 3 (Fall 1969): 119–133.

Research and writing in this area are confused and confusing, and the lack of agreed-upon definitions is partly the cause. The author reviews the significant research, including that of Kellogg, Saadeh and Reddin, and gives an overview of her own extensive research. She identifies the need for teachers to develop their own critical listening skills so they can help children improve this skill.

Lundsteen, Sara W. "Language Arts in the Elementary School." In *Teaching for Creative Endeavor*, edited by W.B. Michael. Bloomington, Ind.: Indiana University Press, 1968.

Long known for her concern about and insights into listening, the author advocates a creative problem-solving approach to teaching listening. Many activities are described, as well as some brief notes about what research says to the teacher.

Mial, Dorothy J. and Jacobson, Stanley. "Accent on Listening." *Today's Education* 57 (October 1968): 67–69.

The authors stress the importance of listening for *content* (facts and figures), *feeling* (how what the speaker is talking about affects him), and for *process* (what the speaker is trying to accomplish). Several games and techniques are included to improve students' skills in doing this.

Russell, D.H. and Russell, Elizabeth F. *Listening Aids Through the Grades*. New York: Teachers College Press, Columbia University, 1979.

Newly updated by Dorothy G. Hennings, herself an author of several imaginative texts, this handy paperback still contains the most comprehensive collection of listening activities in existence. Expanded to include 232 activities, this is divided generally into kindergarten, primary and intermediate grade sections, and into levels of listening skill. The introduction is interesting because of its analysis of the similarities and differences between reading and listening.

Smith, Charlene W. *The Listening Activity Book*. Fearon Publishers, 1975.

A practical small paperback full of teaching suggestions. "Ten Basic Listening Experiences" presents types of activities, with the suggestion that the teacher can easily adapt these to other story material. A section specifically designed for primary grades precedes two which are more appropriate for intermediate grades on evaluating advertisements and checking the facts. The succinct mini-lessons could be cut apart and attached to file cards for easier accessibility, if desired.

Wolfgang, Aaron. "The Silent Language in the Multicultural Classroom." *Theory into Practice* 16(3) (June 1977): 145–152.

The author's basic premise is that teachers must be aware that factors beyond the spoken word affect whether a message is received or not. When teachers move into another culture, they become aware that many things taken for granted can no longer be counted upon. Teachers of culturally divergent groups need to be aware that use of proxemics (distance) differs from culture to culture, as do the kinesics a speaker uses. Eye contact, for example, may indicate a listener is paying attention, but it may also mean, as in the Puerto Rican culture, something quite different. The author urges native speakers of English to be aware that students whose first language isn't English may need time to translate questions or directions from one language to the other.

Books for Children

Baylor, Byrd. *The Other Way to Listen*. New York: Scribner's, 1978.

This poetic text consists of short, conversational responses to nature. Peter Parnall's distinctive settings and insightful portraits depict an old man and a young boy as they speak together of the need to take time to listen. The boy learns to listen with the old man's help. Alone, he hears a sound he cannot write down, for it would not make a word. The book is, once again, Parnall's insightful tribute to the idea that spareness is effective. The minimal lines in the sketches are brightened with yellow orange. The short text is equally spare, without an unnecessary word.

Borten, Helen. *Do You Hear What I Hear?* New York: Abelard-Schuman, 1960.

Borten's evocative prose, richly laden with unusual similes, is here turned to description of a wide variety of sounds. From the sound of a daisy's petal falling to the roar of trucks, she leads readers to an appreciation of the wealth of information and sensuous delight our ears afford us.

Branley, Franklyn M. *High Sounds, Low Sounds*. New York: Thomas Y. Crowell, 1967.

When doing a listening unit, it is often possible to interest children in the science of sound. Branley's book does an admirable job of making complex matters simple. The experiments he suggests will intrigue children. The illustrations, done in Paul Galdone's usual relaxed style, are a valued and integral part of the book.

Breitner, Sue. *The Bookseller's Advice*. New York: Viking Press, 1981.

A humorous tale of the problems caused when the kindly old bookseller doesn't hear what is said to him. Not inattentive listening, but rather a hearing loss, results in misunderstandings. Everyone consults the bookseller, the wisest man in the village. They follow his advice, honoring his wisdom. But the advice goes wrong when he doesn't hear what people are asking. The minor mishaps turn out satisfactorily, allowing the bookseller to continue enjoying his esteem.

Brown, Margaret Wise. *The Summer Noisy Book*. New York: Harper & Row, 1951.

The story of little Muffin, an appealing pooch of indeterminate origin, and the sounds he hears on his way to the country and while he is there. To involve the children, the story gives the sound and then asks them to guess what makes that sound. Cheerful pictures in full color by Leonard Weisgard are a happy addition. This is from a series of books: see *The City Noisy Book*, *The Country Noisy Book*, *The Indoor Noisy Book*, and *The Quiet Noisy Book*.

Elkin, Benjamin. *The Loudest Noise in the World*. New York: Viking Press, 1954.

Prince Hulla-Baloo who lives in Hub Bub, the noisiest city in the world, has a doting father. The prince wants the loudest noise in the world for his sixth birthday present. This requires elaborate arrangements involving millions of people. Unfortunately, the plan goes awry, but the resulting present is the most beautiful one in the Prince's whole life.

Guilfoile, Elizabeth. *Nobody Listens to Andrew*. Chicago: Follett Publishing, 1957.

The charming misadventures of Andrew, who tries valiantly to tell everyone his important message. All are too busy to listen, until he finally bellows out the news about the bear under his bed. The response such news causes completes the slim book.

Johnson, LaVerne. *Night Noises*. New York: Parents Magazine Press, 1968.

Especially appealing to very young children, this slender tale recounts the adventures of a little boy upstairs in bed, who plays a game of listening to noises and trying to identify what they are. Particularly good for fostering basic auditory perception.

McGovern, Ann. *Too Much Noise*. Boston: Houghton Mifflin, 1967.

Two-color illustrations with black-ink line tell the story of an old man in an old house that creaked, squeaked, and made many other noises. After suggestions from the Wise Man didn't work, the old man solves his own problem.

Miller, Lisa. *Sound*. New York: Coward-McCann, 1965.

Part of the publisher's "Science Is What and Why" series, *Sound* uses a simple, attractive approach to help young children learn about sound. Easy experiments (i.e., tying a piece of sewing thread to a doorknob to experience sound and vibrations) make this readily understandable. *Frequency, wavelength,* and *echoes* are words explained and illustrated in vivid orange and pink by Tomie de Paolo. Teachers will want to do the activities in a group setting, though individual children will find the book attractive enough to read again independently.

Myller, Rolf. *A Very Noisy Day*. New York: Atheneum, 1981.

A very special new book effectively translates sounds into visual representations. Using a variety of type faces, sizes and colors of type, the author recounts the adventures of Fred, an inquisitive dog whose day was both good and bad. From the first yawn of the morning until the contented snoring when the day is done, each of the sounds Fred hears and makes is presented visually. Clever page placement enhances the varieties of type which encode the sounds visually. Especially helpful in establishing a relation between sound and print.

O'Neill, Mary L. *What Is That Sound!* New York: Atheneum, 1966.

From the crash of the first poem to the thump of the last, the author's writing resounds with vibrant noise. She explores the unusual: wail, bleat, riffle, and twang. More common sounds are reshaped by the poet's unique vision into a fresh experience.

Perera, Thomas and Perera, Gretchen. *Louder and Louder. The Dangers of Noise Pollution*. New York: Franklin Watts, 1973.

Black-ink drawings by Leonard Shortall whimsically illustrate points made in this easy-to-read book which assumes no prior knowledge. Six brief chapters deal with such topics as "What Is Sound?" and "Can We Quiet Noise Pollution?" For intermediate grade readers, this could encourage students to search for sources of noise pollution in their school or home. An index makes it easy to refer back to sections read earlier.

Rand, Ann and Rand, Paul. *Listen! Listen!* New York: Harcourt, Brace and World, 1970.

Bold, abstract graphics in limited forms sensitize children to sounds around them. Done in poetry, this book characterizes the sounds with an imaginative array of descriptive words, like "scrithity-scratch." It can be used to motivate students to make up their own sound words.

Russell, Solveig P. *Sound.* Indianapolis: The Bobbs-Merrill Co., 1963.

Simple illustrations in blue and dark green accompany the text which discusses what sound is, how vibrations make movements called sound waves, and the things which serve as conductors of sound. There is ample treatment of echoes, of qualities of sound (pitch and volume), of ultrasonics and supersonics. The writing is clear and words are adequately defined in context. Most appropriate for third grade and up.

Showers, Paul. *The Listening Walk.* New York: Thomas Y. Crowell, 1961.

A little boy, his pipe-puffing father, and their old dog walk around the city. Sometimes the noises are soft: the sound of the dog's toenails on the sidewalk; sometimes they are loud: the boom of a jet. Always they are fascinating to the boy, who uses his ears to sense the city in an unusual way. The pictures by Aliki, though limited in color, are fresh.

Shulevitz, Uri. *Oh What a Noise.* New York: Macmillan, 1971.

Through a surrealistic setting the nameless little hero wanders from bedroom to bathroom to brush his teeth. On the way he encounters a noisy menagerie including cats, whales, parrots, monkeys, donkeys, lions, and giants. The noise accumulates until its cacophony is deafening. All subsides gradually, as he returns sleepily to his bed.

Slepian, Jan and Seidler, Ann. *The Junior Listen-Hear Program.* Chicago: Follett, 1967.

Five picture books, boxed together, develop listening and auditory-discrimination skills. *The Silly Listening Book* develops gross listening. *An Ear Is to Hear* is for discriminative listening. *Bendemolena* is for listening to vocal play. *The Hungry Thing* is for listening to rhymes, and *Ding-Dong, Bing-Bong* develops discriminative listening to word pairs. The humorous tone of all the books is delightfully abetted by the charming illustrations of Richard Martin. *The Teacher's Source Book* is included in the package. Another series, the *Listen-Hear Books,* for older children, deals with particular sounds which may present difficulties to the younger child.

Spier, Peter. *Gobble, Growl, Grunt.* New York: Doubleday, 1971.

In an eye-catching succession of brilliantly colored pages, the illustrator has portrayed over 600 animals and the sounds each makes. Valuable both for its visual
stimulation, and for the familiarity it encourages with a wide diversity of
sounds.

Tresselt, Alvin. *Wake Up, City!* New York: Lothrop, Lee and Shepard, 1957.

A sensitive evocation of the city just before dawn; as the sky brightens a variety
of noises begin and increase in number and intensity. Children will enjoy making the sounds that go along with the narrative. The sketchy pictures in limited
color by Roger Duvoisin provide a variety of views. See also: *Wake Up, Farm,*
by the same author-illustrator team.

Zolotow, Charlotte. *If You Listen.* New York: Harper & Row, 1980.

A pleasant, impressionistic treatment of the variety of sounds a young girl hears
as she follows her mother's advice to listen to: church bells; a fog horn from a
river miles away; one petal falling off a rose; and a train rushing by in the
night, among other sounds. The chalk illustrations by Marc Simont are as appealing as the text which deals obliquely with the small girl listening because
she is lonely for her absent father.

Bibliography

Brown, Charles T. "Three Studies on the Listening of Children." *Speech Monographs* 32 (June 1965): 129–138.

Brown, Kenneth L. "Speech and Listening in Language Arts Textbooks."
Elementary English 44 (April and May 1967): 336–341, 461–465.

Burk, K.W. "The Speech Clinician and Voice Therapy." Paper presented at
Eastern Washington Conference on Voice Disorders in School Age Children.
Spokane, Wash., March 1977.

Burnham, Larry D. "To Hear or Not." *Teacher* 98(5) (January 1981): 68–69.

Childers, Perry R. "Listening Ability Is a Modifiable Skill." *Journal of Experimental Education* 38 (Summer 1970): 1–3.

Cole, Joanna. *Cockroaches.* New York: William Morrow, 1971.

Cromwell, Doris G. and Au, Kathryn. "Using a Scale of Questions to Improve
Listening Comprehension." *Language Arts* (January 1979): 34–43.

Duker, Sam. *Listening Bibliography*, 2nd ed. Metuchen, N.J.: The Scarecrow
Press, 1968. This unique resource compiles annotations for 1,332 articles and
studies about listening.

Duker, Sam. "Listening." In *Encyclopedia of Educational Research*, edited by
Robert L. Ebel. New York: Macmillan, 1969, pp. 747–751.

Duker, Sam. "The Art of Listening." In *Listening: Readings*, compiled by Sam
Duker. Metuchen, N.J.: The Scarecrow Press, 1971, vol. 2, p. 151.

Fitzgerald, Thomas P. "Critical Listening Activities: A First Step in Language
Arts." ERIC Document Reproduction Service No. 185 587, 1979.

Glubok, Shirley. *The Art of the Southwest Indians.* New York: Macmillan, 1971.

Green, Harry A. and Petty, Walter T. *Developing Language Skills in the
Elementary Schools.* Boston: Allyn & Bacon, 1975.

Hall, Edward T. "Listening Behavior: Some Cultural Differences." *Phi Delta
Kappan* 50 (March 1969): 379–380.

Hollow, Sister Mary Kevin. "An Experimental Study of Listening Comprehension at the Intermediate Grade Level." Ph.D. dissertation, Fordham University, 1955.

Hopkins, Lee Bennett (sel.). *I Am the Cat.* New York: Harcourt Brace Jovanovich, 1981.

Jarrell, Randall. *The Bat Poet.* New York: Macmillan, 1964.

Johnson, E. et al. *Anthology of Children's Literature.* Boston: Houghton Mifflin, 1977.

Johnson, Wendell. *Living with Change: The Semantics of Coping.* New York: Harper & Row, Inc., 1972.

Kelly, Charles M. "An Investigation of the Construct Validity of Two Commercially Published Listening Tests." *Speech Monographs* 42 (June 1965): 139–143.

Lionni, Leo. *Theodore and the Talking Mushroom.* New York: Pantheon Books, 1971.

Lundsteen, Sara W. *Listening—Its Impact on Reading and the Other Language Arts.* Urbana, Ill.: National Council of Teachers of English, 1979.

Marten, Milton. *Classroom-Relevant Research in the Language Arts.* Washington, D.C.: Association for Supervision and Curriculum Development, 1978.

Orr, David B. et al. "Trainability of Listening Comprehension of Speeded Discourse." *Journal of Educational Psychology* 56 (1956): 148–156.

Peavy, R. Vance. "Listening and the Classroom Teacher." In *Learning to Read. Reading to Learn*, edited by Ollila et al. Victoria, B.C.: Vancouver Island International Reading Association, 1974, pp. 148–159.

Rogers, Richard. "New Friends via the Tape Recorder." *Instructor* (June/July 1972): 40.

"Secrets of Being a Better Listener." *U.S. News and World Report* (May 26, 1980): 65–66.

Smith, Howard A. "Nonverbal Communication in Teaching." *Review of Educational Research* 49(4) (Fall 1979): 631–672.

Steil, Lyman K. "A Longitudinal Analysis of Listening Pedagogy in Minnesota Secondary Public Schools." Ph.D. dissertation, Wayne State University, 1977.

Strickland, Ruth G. *The Language Arts in the Elementary School.* Lexington, Mass.: D.C. Heath, 1969.

Travis, Lee Edward, ed. *Handbook of Speech Pathology.* New York: Appleton-Century-Crofts, 1971.

Van Riper, Charles. *Speech Correction.* Englewood Cliffs, N.J.: Prentice-Hall, 1978.

Van Wingerden, A. "A Study of Direct, Planned Listening Instruction in Four Counties in the State of Washington." Ph.D. dissertation, Washington State University, 1965.

Wilkinson, Andrew. "Listening and the Discriminative Response." In *Claremont Reading Conference 33rd Yearbook*, edited by Malcolm P. Douglass. Claremont, Calif., 1969.

Wilt, Miriam E. "A Study of Teacher Awareness of Listening as a Factor in Elementary Education." *Journal of Educational Research* 43 (April 1950): 626–636.

Wilt, Miriam E. "Listening: What's New?" In *Language and the Language Arts*, edited by deStefano and Fox. Boston: Little, Brown, 1974, pp. 79–86.

Zigmond, Naomi K. and Circi, Regina. *Auditory Learning.* San Rafael, Calif.: Dimensions Publishing Company, 1968.

ORAL LANGUAGE

The young father was impatiently calling the
family's two puppies into the house. "Come on,
come on, come on," while his three-year-old
daughter watched. Several months later, wanting
to hurry her dawdling exit from their automobile,
he said, "Come on, Lisa, come on, come on." She
looked up at him and responded, "But Daddy, I'm
not a dog."

The true story, related by an embarrassed father, himself a
high school English teacher, demonstrates how early in life children are at-
tuned, albeit unconsciously, to the subtleties of oral language. As they listen
to adults speak, they are assimilating intuitively such elements as pitch,
stress, and juncture.

DEVELOPING THE ART OF ORAL LANGUAGE

This chapter focuses on enriching the basic skills in oral language which
most children bring to school. It is generally agreed that most children are in
command of the basic structure of their language before they start school.[1]
Children have used their listening skills to hear and master the sounds of

---

[1]A comprehensive statement about young children's language acquisition is by Vera P. John
and Sarah Moskovitz, entitled "Language Acquisition and Development in Early Childhood," in
Linguistics in School Programs, The Sixty-Ninth Yearbook of the National Society for the Study
of Education, Part II (Chicago: The University of Chicago Press, 1970), pp. 167–215. Though difficult reading, this provides a wealth of information for the persistent reader. A section on the
contribution linguistics makes to school programs will help teachers interested in learning how
to use linguistic understandings.

English, with the exception of the voiced and voiceless /th/. They have acquired an impressive array of syntactic constructions: movable noun phrases, past tense, plural markers, progressive form, and verb complements, among others (Yawkey, 1981). Young children have experimented with a variety of ways of enscribing ideas (see Clay reference, Chapter 7). They have used language to serve all the functions for which adults use it (see Wilkinson reference, Chapter 1). While there still are, at that time, some significant gaps in the skills which children possess, basic linguistic competency is essentially established. Our task, therefore, if we are dealing with a group which has this competency, is to provide an array of experiences that will allow students to move beyond such basic competency to more masterful fluency. The teacher provides experiences which challenge students to extend, enrich, and elaborate the language patterns they already command.

THE PRIMACY OF ORAL LANGUAGE

An examination of some common facts about oral language which are too often overlooked will reveal the reason linguists have for some time identified oral language as *the* language. This form, and not the written form which is a symbolization removed from the actual language, merits our attention for several reasons:

1. Oral language is the most commonly used mode of expression. Studies indicate that as adults we use oral communication more frequently than written language.[2]
2. Oral language is the first form children learn and, for many, remains the mode in which they feel most secure.
3. Oral language is the form all peoples develop. Of 2,796 languages in the world, all have an oral form, though only about 153 have developed a written form.[3]

ORAL LANGUAGE BEFORE SCHOOL

Young children often, in informal settings, play with language, using it for the aural qualities it provides, rather than for the message it conveys (Schwartz, 1977). This gamelike use of language is apparent when, for ex-

---

[2]This was established some time ago and remains true. In 1929, Paul T. Rankin reported that subjects spoke almost three times as much as they wrote. ("Listening Ability," Proceedings of the Ohio State Education Conference, pp. 172–183.) More recently a study by Ralph G. Nichols, "Do We Know How to Listen?" *The Speech Teacher* 10 (March 1961): 118–124, established that every seven out of ten minutes we are conscious, we are communicating verbally.

[3]In Mario Pei's *The Story of Language* (New York: Mentor Books, 1965), the author discusses in readable fashion many aspects of the 2,796 languages we speak. You will find the chapters on dialect and on place names helpful in stimulating children's interest. Information about the number of written languages is from the *New York Times Encyclopedia Almanac*, 1970.

ample, a child playing with a boat starts to chant, "boat, moat, gloat, rote, tote, smote." The child doesn't intend to convey a meaning to others near enough to hear, but rather simply is experimenting with forming new words, chanting the rhyming sounds for the pleasure in mastering the formation. Using the tongue, teeth, and lips in different ways to make different sounds is common. This kind of experimentation with phonemes is more common than is play with syntax, in which the child repeats and varies sequences.[4]

Unfortunately this kind of experimentation with oral language decreases as the child grows older and enters grades in school where written language is emphasized. We encourage a related kind of directed experimentation with oral sounds, for instance, when we ask children to manipulate pitch, stress, and juncture in preparing a choral reading (Johnson, 1979). This helpful kind of planned curricular experience is an example of building on what children do naturally before they come to school.

ORAL LANGUAGE IN THE CURRICULUM

Though it is apparent that children need to go beyond basic language skills to develop oral fluency, it is only recently that elementary school language arts curricula have begun to shed their emphasis on written language and reflect the importance of the oral form. It is still, unfortunately, true that neither elementary textbooks nor curriculum guides give the teacher enough encouragement to work on such oral aspects of language.

Brown (1967) examined the content and emphases in elementary language arts series textbooks and concluded that although editors and writers, "state explicitly and imply that oral communication should be stressed . . . Nevertheless, actual emphasis in the books does not support this." Brown studied fourteen different language arts series and as a result concluded, "it is apparent that writing and grammar are emphasized more than speaking and listening." This emphasis is in spite of numerous studies, to be discussed in the chapter on grammar, which point to the inefficiency of conscious teaching of grammar as a means of improving language fluency. Such an emphasis on the written language is not universal. In Germany, for example, emphasis on the spoken word over reading and writing has been constant during the past century (Fishman, 1972, p. 348).

The study by Brown is an older one, but it has not been replicated. In newer language arts materials, revised content and emphases are placing greater priority on oral language activities but written language activities still predominate. Another pervading influence is the curriculum guide, and an examination of these found that "there is rarely any evidence of a

---

[4]Another statement about such language play, which hastens the development of meta-linguistic awareness, is in "Play with Language and Metalinguistic Awareness," by C. Cazden, in *Dimensions of Language Experience*, edited by C. Winsor (New York: Agathon Press, 1975), pp. 3–19.

deliberate sequence designed to develop oral skills." More recent than Brown's study, Davidson's (1968) analysis reaffirms that the teacher interested in developing oral fluency in a sequential and structured way apparently receives little and rather intermittent support from both curriculum guides and language texts.

Probably one reason for the minimal emphasis on oral language is that, to date, little has been done with identifying the separate components of oral fluency. And little is available in organized fashion related to the following questions:

1. What specific oral competencies should children develop as a result of contact with the oral fluency strand in a language-arts curriculum?
2. What are the most efficient ways of developing the desired competencies? What experiences, contacts, problems, and challenges should children encounter to further oral fluency?
3. What kinds of measurement and evaluation of oral fluency are appropriate? How could we measure the specific competencies to determine if our program is effective?

Walter Loban, in a fresh and direct article written especially for classroom teachers, commented on the problem of evaluation in oral language.

> Developing adequate means of evaluating growth in oral skills will be especially essential, for until anything is evaluated it is unlikely to receive much emphasis in the total teaching scheme. "Give me the power to evaluate and I will control the curriculum," is a memorable saying. The boundaries of the curriculum inevitably shrink to whatever is evaluated, and at the present time oral proficiency is scarcely evaluated at all.[5]

Though Loban's article was written some time ago, a search of the literature about oral language reveals that even now attention to this vital area is minimal.

There are least two reasons for this evaluation problem. The first is the *complexity* of the oral message, and the second is its *transitory* nature. Any oral message is made up of a wide range of subcomponents: the basic oral sounds, the paralinguistic elements, and such little recognized components as gesture and kinesics. Thus, analyzing oral communication for evaluative purposes is a much more complex task than analyzing written communication. *Second*, the transitory nature of oral communication militates against effective evaluation. Once a message is frozen in writing it can be considered

---

[5]Walter Loban, "Oral Language Proficiency Affects Reading and Writing," *The Instructor* (March 1966): 97ff. This brief article, filled with practical suggestions, emphasizes building classroom activities on the research in the area. The suggestions about sentence manipulation and about children hearing a variety of adult readers as models will be helpful.

at leisure, reexamined, and pondered. Unless one has audiotape equipment and, indeed, preferably videotape equipment for preserving those nonverbal aspects of language, evaluation is almost impossible. Once something is said, it is lost. Until teachers can find the time and have use of facilities to tape students' oral communication so this data can be analyzed later, effective evaluation in the oral area will be limited.

Despite the problem of few oral language curricula, and few means of evaluating growth in oral language, this critical area needs teacher attention. Children's verbal fluency directly affects their teachers' evaluations: "It appears that a lack of language fluency may affect school success negatively because teachers tend to judge children on such qualities as speed, pitch and intonation." (Weeks, 1974). In addition, success in oral language is related to other curriculum areas, especially reading (Ribovich, 1976). It is difficult to understand how reading programs can overlook this important link between children's oral ability and their ability to read. Because of these two important factors, the next part of this chapter will outline briefly a curriculum in oral language.

WHERE TO BEGIN: INFORMAL CONVERSATION

The nursery and kindergarten teacher's role in oral language is one of encouraging children's spontaneous oral language while helping increase their fluency in using words to say what they want to say (Williams, 1977). Most young children will be anxious to talk with the teacher, with other children, and in small-group situations. Thus, the most important thing teachers do to increase oral fluency is to demonstrate interest in what children want to share.

The teacher does this in several ways. Children must have a listening ear as frequently as they need it (Hohmann, 1979, p. 154). If the teacher is elbow deep in mixing fingerpaints, it is absolutely crucial to suggest another (and more appropriate!) time for children to share their ideas. Thus, the teacher says something like, "I can't talk with you right now, Bobby, or the paint will dry out, but come and sit by me when we have milk and I can listen then." It's admittedly true, in fact almost inevitable, that by milk time, which may be only ten minutes away, Bobby will have forgotten what he wanted to say. Nonetheless, the teacher has established in the child's mind that what he has to say is significant, even if something prevents the teacher from listening at the exact moment the idea occurs.

Another way teachers demonstrate to children the importance of oral language is by the informal oral conversation groups they form and encourage. Draw two to six children together, perhaps to observe something, to reflect upon someone's idea, to share part of a book, or to help solve a problem. The purpose in these groups is to provide a milieu in which children learn the delight of, and incidentally, some of the informal rules that govern small-group conversation or discussion.

The majority of early childhood teachers seem imbued with the desire to

Small-group discussion about topics of interest to students enhances oral fluency. (Used with permission of the Racine (Wis.) Unified School District.)

facilitate this type of informal conversation and discussion. The same is not, unfortunately, true of teachers of other grades. What are the values of informal conversation groups, and why should all teachers encourage them?

The values accruing from such informal conversations are many. Frequently, a strengthening of *self-concept* occurs as children learn to interact with a group of peers. The child learns to cope with situations verbally, instead of withdrawing or having a tantrum, which may have sufficed at home. Another value is the *language learnings* which may occur as children find out, for example, that though their ideas may be clear to them, they may not be equally clear to their listeners. *Conceptual learnings* are another value of informal conversation groups, for instance, when one child talks about a topic another child has never encountered, or discusses an unfamiliar aspect of a familiar topic, or when another way of viewing a topic is suggested.

Any and all these learnings can and do occur without the teacher being in the group. While it is true that, if there, she or he can help expand and relate any learnings which are occurring, the teacher is not the crucial element in the group. As Lindberg (1965) says so well, there are many talkers in any elementary classroom, and teachers who regard themselves as *one*, but not even the most important one, will allow children to learn on their own.

There is no reason to assume that, once children enter the primary school, these same values are not available from small-group conversations, but it is rare indeed to see much time specifically provided for such activities above the kindergarten level. This dichotomy between what we see as valid learn-

ing in kindergartens and do not accept in other grades is becoming inten-
sified because of increasing concern over "basics."

Play corners are a commonly used means of motivating informal conversation among young children. Unfortunately, such corners too frequently remain unchanged. The objects (kitchen equipment, clothes for dressing up,
and other regalia to encourage language) are the same from the beginning of
the year to the end. Davis et al. (1973) suggest varying the equipment in the
play corner, which should be more facilitative of language. In addition to
the ubiquitous housekeeping equipment, the authors suggest changing the
corner into "learning" centers: a role-playing center, a handicapped center,
a hospital, shoe shop, beauty salon, flower show, white elephant, or a school
play center.

Such informal conversation groups will, perhaps later in the school years,
and certainly by the primary grades, be augmented by more formal conversations motivated by the presence of classroom visitors. Teachers should plan
to invite guests to the room whose language, vocations, hobbies, ethnic
backgrounds, or travels can augment a unit being studied. During interaction with such visitors, children's language must be focused to communicate
with someone unfamiliar, who may not necessarily share the same frames of
reference as the child. One expert has said: "Outsiders to the classroom community—transients like visitors—can play an important role in sustaining
the need to communicate more explicitly than classmates might require"
(Cazden, 1975).

MORE FORMAL CONVERSATIONS: SHARE-AND-TELL

Share-and-Tell is one of the most abused practices in elementary schools. It
is probably no exaggeration to claim that in most classrooms it is a complete
waste of time. Yet this is unfortunate, for the activity has much potential
and the language learning it offers to young children is wide ranging and
long lasting (Edelsky, 1978). Surely when teachers work on this skill, they
are helping students develop an ability of much use in adult life, for we all as
adults engage in variations of this technique in sharing with our peers
something that delights us. Why, then, is the elementary share-and-tell
period too frequently such a listless preoccupation, frequently enforcing
wandering attention upon something of interest to neither the possessor nor
the listener? Answers to this question lie primarily in the techniques
employed by the teacher.

To be of maximum effectiveness, teachers should:

1. Give undivided attention to what is going on. While the temptation
may be great to balance the attendance register or to enter information on
health records, the teacher must always give each sharer his or her full attention. This is because, at first, the activity is *informal*, but it is also *directed*.
It is not free and spontaneous, though these are qualities the teacher is trying
to develop. Such qualities are learned, and the teacher has to guide the
discussion by making appropriate comments (Higginbotham, 1977), by ask-

ing leading questions, perhaps holding part of the article for the child. The teacher is an *active*, not a passive participant. As children develop the skill of taking part, the teacher's role lessens. By the time the practice has served its purpose, eliciting a free flow of discussion, the teacher will be involved only minimally.

2. Develop the ability to ask intelligent, probing questions. Not such questions as: "Who gave you the book, Tom?" or "When did you get the firetruck, Anne?" These elicit one- or few-word replies, and do not help expand oral fluency. Rather, ask such questions as: "What else can you tell us about the truck, Anne?" or "Have you heard any other stories like the one in Bobby's book? How are they like each other?" or "What do you suppose you might have done if the same thing had happened while you were at the parade?" Such questions are not easy to ask, but this skill can be developed. Teachers interested in such questioning skills can refer to several helpful sources. The best known is the *Taxonomy of Educational Objectives* (Bloom, 1956). While not devoted specifically to questioning techniques, this is helpful to teachers who want to improve their questioning ability.

Share-and-tell should focus on children's language, although the teacher should feel free to participate (Lee & Rubin, 1979), sharing information about a hobby or perhaps a trip. Another helpful idea is to invite classroom visitors to provide language stimulus. One kindergarten teacher had an "Old-Fashioned Day," inviting grandparents to share-and-tell. Some came prepared only to tell of days gone by, others brought pictures or showed how to perform a now unfamiliar skill. One played a guitar and sang a song learned during an Appalachian childhood. Similarly, a third-grade teacher invited a retired teacher who had worked with Hopi children in the southwest. He brought souvenirs, including drawings students had made. It was a valuable language interaction experience, enjoyed by both the retired teacher and the children, who were on the edge of their seats as he told of daily life in an Indian school.

THE IMPORTANCE OF QUESTIONS

It seems obvious that anyone intending to teach should be able to ask stimulating, open-ended questions. Research has demonstrated that such is not the case. The ability is neither native nor easy to develop. Research done on classroom questions in general (Gall, 1970), questions asked in reading classes (Guzak, 1967), and even questions asked in art classes (Clements, 1965), indicate that many teachers need to improve the open-endedness of questions they ask.

Response to questions also varies in differing cultures. Weeks (1976), reporting on her interviews with Yakima Indian children and non-Indian children, commented on alternative ways to respond. Anglos tended to talk immediately after a question had been asked; Yakimas tended to pause, to formulate a response. Indians who didn't know the answer to a question responded, "I don't know," while Anglos changed the subject.

From Ukrainian Folk Tales *by Marie Halun Bloch. This illustration is from a book that contains many stories suitable for telling. Several of the stories have refrains that children can set to simple melodies.*

RESPONDING TO STORIES

Teachers of young children sometimes make the mistake of asking the wrong question after reading a story. To ask, "Did you like the story?" is unhelpful and doesn't accomplish anything. Most children, anxious to please the teacher, will answer "yes." For the one or two obstreperous children anxious to attract attention, their emphatic "*no*" serves their purpose, but not the teacher's.

Instead, a helpful question to initiate response after students have listened to a story is, "What were you thinking?" This allows students to respond with feeling reactions about the story, with cognitive responses (perhaps noting a similarity to another story), or an evaluative response (perhaps in telling something they noticed about how the story was read). Any such reaction is encouraged, as we lead into other, more specifically focused questions.

Teachers use questions to stimulate discussion about many topics. Research justifies discussing literature with children; such discussion expands vocabulary. Fisher (1972) used six primary classrooms in which children listened to the teacher read, and then discussed what was read. Following a twelve-week period, boys in her experimental groups made significant increases in vocabulary growth.

Strickland's (1971) research involved black, linguistically different kindergarten children in listening to the teacher read literature and discussing it afterwards. These experiences helped students expand their language repertoire to include standard English, without negating their own home dialect.

QUESTIONS AND CULTURE

In the preceding two sections, and elsewhere in this book, teaching strategies are suggested which have been tested in a variety of classroom settings, with children from differing socioeconomic statuses. Most of the children in these settings, however, were speakers of standard English. Another factor has significant effect on the questioning and other verbal strategies teachers use: The ethnicity of both students and teachers critically affects how teachers interact with students and how students respond. Some teachers work in classrooms in which the majority of children are from a culture other than their own, and such teachers need to be especially aware of how this difference should influence their use of language. Ethnologists, social scientists who enter a culture and study it from within, are finding important information about language and societies which should be useful to teachers.

For example, how students perceive and respond to questions may be quite unlike how the teacher perceives and responds to questions, if teacher and children are from two different cultures. As a result of her five years of study as a participant observer in a community, Heath (1982) found that a considerable difference existed between the questions teachers asked and those parents asked in the home. The main difference was not topical, but rather functional. The working-class black parents in Heath's study did not use questions to elicit a response when they already knew the answer. This was, however, a common questioning strategy among teachers. Clearly when boys and girls in the community Heath studied came to school, they perceived and had to adjust to a significantly different function of questions than they had experienced at home. Probably one of the reasons why some children have difficulty in school is not because they lack an intrinsic language ability, but rather because they are unwilling or unable to perceive and adjust to such different uses of language. Helping teachers become aware of and responsive to their language use as it differs from that of their students is an important concern. Much of the material in the last chapter of this book will consider this important concern.

DEVELOPING DESCRIBING COMPETENCIES

Many different activities can lead to oral fluency. Describing is one competency that can be expanded and enlarged as the teacher helps children toward fluency.

Describing People

Children enjoy the opportunity to observe people and then use words to create oral descriptions. (Such activities may culminate in written activities for older students.) For the primary child this is essentially a two-step procedure. First, the teacher works on simple describing. Tell your children to secretly pick a friend and observe that friend in spare moments. Later, each child can give an oral description while others guess the identity of the child being described.

When beginning the activity, have the children observe randomly. Accept and encourage all reporting. After they have developed some facility in this process, help the children categorize or organize the descriptors they have been using as an aid to further improvement. Ask, "What kind of things about the person have we been including in our descriptions?" and list the answers. When posted in the room, the list will help develop this skill.

A slightly more involved task is *comparing*. A child can choose two "subjects," observe likenesses and differences, and attempt to create an oral impression of both children.

Describing Objects

Students can be challenged to describe objects, which presents a different sort of challenge. Bring in a large box with assorted objects and allow each child to describe one of them for the rest of the children, who can then guess what the object is. It's important to remember that, even though this can be a delightful game, the main purpose is *not* the guessing but rather the developing of describing competencies. Therefore, at some time after the children have enjoyed playing the "game," the teacher draws from them a list of elements which should be included in a good description. Such a list would include many aspects of the subject. Later, children should be encouraged to bring more objects for the "Describing Box."

In addition, at some time during this activity, the teacher helps children understand that descriptions can be made in two different ways, *finite* and *comparative*. The sample statements below indicate how various elements might be described.

TABLE 5.1 TYPES OF DESCRIPTIONS

Finite	*Comparative*
A. Size "The object is about six inches long."	"The object is about as long as a water glass is tall."
B. Color "It's blue with a lot of black mixed in it."	"It's the color of the sky just before a thunderstorm."
C. Texture "It's made of lots of small peaks arranged close together in a regular pattern."	"It's like a rough kind of sandpaper."

Describing Pictures

Pictures are one type of object which can be described. Because they are more visually complex than most objects, they deserve special attention as motivation in developing skill in describing. At first, teachers and children can talk about the visual qualities of the pictures. Later, teachers can consciously use the pictures as a discussion stimulus. Reproductions of paintings are a rich motivation to talk.

Children are shown pictures and encouraged to move through a three-step procedure: first simple *describing*, then *comparing* two illustrations, and finally *valuing*. This last term means a statement of preference. The teacher is developing the fluency which enables the child to say: "I like this picture because. . . ." As adults, we often make statements beginning, "I like. . ." but only rarely do we move to the more sophisticated statement including a fluent reason for this preference.

Almost any picture can stimulate describing skills. An easy way to begin this activity has been described in an article that establishes the rationale for this oral language experience and includes a list of materials (Stewig, 1973). The rationale for moving children through a sequence of increasing difficulty in developing skills of describing, comparing, and valuing, may be helpful to teachers interested in initiating such a program. Using illustrations from children's books is an easy way to assemble materials to develop these skills. Specific materials for a poem ("The Owl and the Pussy Cat"), a fable ("The Hare and the Tortoise"), and a folk tale ("The Three Billy Goats"), are described.

It is a simple task to select a pair of books in which different illustrators depict the same tale. We might use Quackenbush's version of the *The Steadfast Tin Soldier* (1964) in which this popular artist provided strong woodcuts in red, dark blue, and black, arranged in large, double-page spreads with a strong sense of pattern. In contrast, we could encourage boys and girls to compare the pictures in ink line with applied color by Marcia Brown (1953), softer and looser than those by Quackenbush. After they have studied the illustrations, ask your students to describe the similarities and differences they notice. Some elementary series do involve children in such describing activities. Easton and Klein (1981) ask children to use words to describe a picture, while Conlin and LeRoy (1978) solicit words from the children themselves.

Another challenging oral language experience is to ask the children to compare and contrast two film versions of the same story. A third-grade teacher used a black-and-white silhouette version of *Thumbelina*, and a four-color animated version of the same tale. Following this, the class constructed this chart:

From Beauty and the Beast *by Madame de Beaumont.*

HOW WERE THEY DIFFERENT?

Black/White Version	*Four-Color Version*
pictures were old-fashioned; silhouettes; more detail	colors were brighter; could see faces
story teller did the talking	many voices could be heard
Thumbelina had pretty clothes	she wore a short blue nightgown like in "The Flintstones"
there were five or six fish; the fish said, "Ha, ha, ha."	there was only one fish; the fish didn't talk.
Thumbelina was on a lily pad; the butterfly pulled her	Thumbelina was on a nutshell
Toad wanted his son to marry Thumbelina.	Frog wanted to marry Thumbelina himself
she played with the birds and bugs in the summer; animals were nice to her	beetles captured her; thought she was ugly; pushed her off the leaf

Black/White Version	Four-Color Version
not included	Thumbelina was swinging on a web; spider cut it and she fell; went away on a dandelion seed
when reaching the mouse's house, the mouse invited her in	mouse did not invite her in; she had to beg to get in
mole was rich	mole was not rich
went to live with the flower spirits	there was no ending; they just flew away

From Beauty and the Beast *by Marianna Mayer.*

HOW WERE THEY THE SAME?

In both: Thumbelina was born on a flower.
She was put in the lily pad.
The fish chewed on the stem.
She went to live in a mouse's house in the winter.
A bird rescued her.
The mole wanted to marry her.
She went to live in the south.

Describing Voices

A kindergarten teacher used a record, *Mother Goose* (Ritchard) with her class. She asked her children to focus on what kinds of voices the readers had. Following this, the children described the voices. A recording of "The Crooked Man" was read by Boris Karloff. Children commented: "It sounded scary." "It is an ugly voice." "It was down a little." After listening to "The Three Little Kittens," read by Celeste Holm, children said: "It sounded wavy." "Her voice went up and down." "She sounded like a baby."

Observing and Describing Language

One important aspect of a language program ought to be the study of language itself, an entity worthy of consideration. As a scientist might study animal or plant forms in the laboratory, so linguists utilize scientific techniques of observation and hypothesis to study language. To do this it is essential to secure a "chunk" of material to study.

An easy way to study language is to arrange for a tape exchange with a group of children in another part of the country. A student teacher with whom I worked evolved a successful unit with fifth-grade children. She contacted a teacher in another state and the classes prepared tapes about their cities as a social studies project. For more than a week these children were involved in gathering material, sifting sources, collaborating in writing, and practicing reading their own writings before recording their program. The project entailed a wide variety of oral and written language skills.

Beyond the social study learning, however, the student teacher was able to develop some interesting study of language. After the social studies content had served its purpose, the student teacher had her children focus on language by having them listen *just* to the sound on the tape, ignoring the content. This task proved a bit difficult, perhaps because the children were not used to studying oral language, and so they listened to the tape several times. As they did this, the student teacher had the children identify specific speech items they could discern that were different from their own. After they had listed these items on the chalkboard they categorized the items. The speech on the tape revealed differences in the three major classifications or building blocks of language:

1. *morphology*—there were specific word forms that were different.
2. *syntax*—there were some sentence constructions which were different.
3. *phonology*—there were many pronunciations or sound differences that were apparent.

The children enjoyed discussing these differences and learned from the experience. Some of the learnings were general, i.e., speech can be studied. Some of the learnings were quite specific. After the teacher questioned them, the children realized that it was in the vowel phonemes where the greatest differences occurred between the other children's speech and their own. As a result of this project, these children experienced working the way linguists work: collecting data in the form of recorded speech and analyzing that data to see what patterns occur. Certainly all of this took place on a very simple level compared with the work of professional linguists. Yet such a project must be regarded as both a significant and somewhat unusual language experience. It transcended the usual mundane experiences with workbook pages and gave children insights into the vital force of language.

FIELD EXCURSIONS

When teachers plan field trips they are setting up a situation in which questions are critical, and in which children can use their describing competencies. Oral language is central as children draw up a list of questions to which they would like answers as a result of the trip. During the excursion, they should be encouraged to ask questions, of the host/guide or resource person, of the teacher, or of other adults who are helping supervise. When they return to the room, the children need time to dictate group chart stories, or to record individual impressions of the experience on cassette tapes. In so doing, they can describe what they saw, felt, smelled, touched, and tasted during the experience. All the while they are doing this, they will be using their listening skills as they interact verbally with others in the group. An informal oral report to younger children might be appropriate culminating activity for upper primary students.

Upper grade students can be involved in a more structured program of oral interviewing. Eighth graders in one Vermont school embarked on a year-long program of gathering oral history (Wolkomir, 1974). Because the language arts teacher sensed the area was rich with older adults who had detailed memories of times past, she involved her classes in gathering information about life as it used to be. During the process, the children interviewed, took photographs, wrote letters, made entries in their personal journals, discussed progress in class, and made public presentation of their taped interviews. A multifaceted use of language enriched their oral and written skills.

CHILDREN CREATE BEAUTY WITH THEIR VOICES

More time is now spent in passive consumption of electronic media than on arts created by the individual. Thus, a suggestion to provide time for children to explore and extend the range, power, and expressiveness of their voices is apt to go unheeded. Yet it is indeed true that children can create beauty with their voices. This section makes some specific suggestions to help children achieve great satisfaction from the expressive qualities of their voices.

Oral Reading

A teacher can read to the class each day for a variety of purposes, including sharing a wide spectrum of literature children might not otherwise encounter. Equally important is to provide a model of an adult as reader so students may find this activity pleasant.

In addition to being a pleasant language activity, such oral reading serves another valuable purpose. Children from homes in which parents are engaged in literacy activities like reading, had "significantly clearer comprehension of the purposes of written language than children from homes where literacy behavior was less likely. . ." (Ollila, 1980, p. 23). Several studies have shown that children whose parents read to them have a head start in reading readiness. We know that all children do not come from homes in which parents read to them, so as teachers we must read, to compensate.

Even five minutes a day results in a vast quantity of literature being shared during the year. For example, if you were to read just one poem a day for an entire school year, children would encounter about 180 poems, more than most children encounter in their entire elementary school career. If you read prose for just five minutes a day, sharing about five or six pages, imagine how many books your children could encounter in a year! Neither plan would be good as described, for a program of reading must include a variety of forms. The figures are included simply to make the point that vast quantities of literature, of whatever form, can be shared with children if teachers will do this on a regular basis.

The Teacher as a Model for Oral Reading

As with storytelling, the purpose of oral reading is not only for children's passive pleasure. It extends to involving upper primary children in reading to the group. This is not reading around the circle in reading class, but rather more expressive creation—choosing something the young reader wants to share with others. To make this sharing more effective, the teacher brings to conscious level what children have assimiliated unconsciously about effective oral reading. Through discussion, draw from your children some things an effective oral reader does. These can be formalized in a chart

Experiences reading favorite stories aloud to classmates provides groundwork for later storytelling experiences. (Used with permission of the Racine (Wis.) Unified School District.)

posted in the room. Children might identify some of the following. The reader:

1. establishes eye contact with listeners before beginning.
2. tells something interesting about the selection (perhaps the reason for choosing it) before beginning.
3. has practiced enough in order to read fluently without excessive dependence on the book—the book is a reminder or a cue card, not a crutch.
4. uses the voice effectively to catch and hold interest. With younger children this point may be identified very simply: "His voice told us when he ended a sentence." With older children, it will be discussed in more sophisticated fashion—"She stressed the important words," or "He used the pauses effectively."

It is not necessary to discuss oral reading techniques with the entire group; not all children will be ready to begin at the same time. Work with a small group, but post the chart where everyone can see it. This will stimulate other children's interest.

The teacher should help children select something to read, keeping in mind the child's individual reading ability and what has been read in class recently. This should be as pleasant an experience as possible for all children. Thus, if a child has chosen something too difficult, suggest something closer to his or her reading level.

Provide time for children to practice. Like many oral arts, oral reading requires practice. Students need time alone to practice, to manipulate pitch, stress, and juncture in a variety of ways to bring life to the printed word.

Provide time for children to evaluate their own work before reading aloud. Make available an easily operated cassette tape recorder. Boys and girls find listening to themselves as revealing as do adults; the child is sure to find different ways to read the material as a result of using the tape recorder.

STORYTELLING

The ultimate purpose in sharing stories orally with children is the same purpose as that of oral reading. In both activities the teacher tries to establish in children's minds that these oral activities are worth the time and concern of an adult. The final goal is to motivate the children so they will want to assume responsibility for the activity. To achieve this goal the teacher provides a model, and in the case of storytelling this involves learning and telling stories to the class.

Selecting a Story to Tell

The first step is to choose a story *you* like—one that captures your imagination. Read through several stories, and then set the project aside. After a while, one or two of them will come back to you—you should probably learn one of these.

Preparing the Story

There are three basic steps in preparing the story. The first is to divide the story into *units of action.* As you read any story you will notice that most seem to divide into an easily definable series of actions, or episodes. These can be summarized in brief note form, and then the sequence of units of actions or episodes can be learned. This procedure, for most people, will prove to be a more efficient way of learning the story than simply trying to begin at the beginning and memorize to the end.[6]

The story used here as an example is a delightful old favorite, *The Fisherman and His Wife* (Jarrell, 1980), summarized in units of action below. This should illustrate the procedure which can be applied to almost all stories.

ACTION ONE
Fisherman encounters flounder, who begs for his life; fisherman frees him and fish swims off.

---

[6]Children's ability to comprehend and recall stories is one of the topics in "Remembrance of Things Passed: Story Structure and Recall," by Jean S. Mandler and Nancy S. Johnson, *Cognitive Psychology*, Vol. 9, 1977, pp. 111–151. As children listen to stories, they develop schemata which act as general frameworks within which comprehension takes place. These schemata are reorganized over time, as the story is retrieved for retelling.

ACTION TWO
·Wife berates her husband for not asking for something in return for freeing fish. Husband returns to sea; calls fish who returns and agrees to provide a better home, the request of the wife.

ACTION THREE
After being happy for some time, wife becomes disgruntled and tells husband he must return to fish, asking for a "great stone castle." Husband protests, but at last agrees.

ACTION FOUR
Husband calls the fish, who returns to shore, and complies with fisherman's request. He returns home, and wife is ensconced in great stone palace.

ACTION FIVE
The next morning, wife decides she will be king. Sends her husband to the fish with her request.

ACTION SIX
Husband returns to the sea; calls fish who comes to shore and grants the request. Fisherman returns home to an even bigger castle, with more elaborate trappings.

ACTION SEVEN
Wife is happy only until husband returns; as soon as he is there, she demands that she be made emperor, and the hapless husband has no choice except to return to the fish with another request.

ACTION EIGHT
Husband calls fish, who comes to shore and grants the request. Fisherman returns home to find wife emperor presiding over a fine polished marble castle.

ACTION NINE
Wife is happy until the next morning, when she decides she must be "like the good Lord." Husband, with trepidation, follows her command to return to the fish.

ACTION TEN
Husband returns to side of sea; calls fish, and conveys request. Fish, having been tried beyond endurance, tells fisherman the consequences of his wife's greed.

Exact Wording

The second task is to identify those sections which do need to be memorized verbatim. This may include some words, some repeated phrases, or perhaps some larger sections. In this particular version of the tale, the fisherman calls the flounder:

> Flounder, flounder in the sea,
> Come to me, O come to me!
> For my wife, good Ilsebill,
> Wills not what I'd have her will.

We retain such elements as they are in the story because to eliminate them is to destroy some of the essence of the story. Many folk and fairy tales will include elements like this, but they will not be difficult to learn.

Learning the Story

The task of memorizing a story in its entirety is indeed formidable, especially today when demands for more "practical" activities press upon us all. The delightful thing about storytelling is that few stories need to be memorized, though many may have short sections, as identified above, which will be learned exactly. Despite these sections, most stories are more interesting to listener and teller alike if the teller learns the essence of the story and allows it to unfold in a slightly different way each time he or she tells it.

Once units of action are identified, these can be learned in an easy, conversational tone, using any words that come easily to you. It is simple enough to learn the units of action. Write them on index cards and carry them around with you. Then each time you have a few minutes, you can review the action and the sequence. Reread the cards, while you are waiting for a red light, for the checkout at the line at the grocery, for an appointment with the doctor, for the elevator to arrive. Using a procedure like this, I find it usually takes me about a week to learn such a story as the one summarized above.

Gestures

An additional way to enhance the story is to use simple gestures when they seem appropriate (Groff, 1977), and facial expressions (Post, 1977). Some authors recommend subordination of gestures because of their feeling that storytelling must not become drama. Despite this opinion, judicious use of some gestures can enhance a story. While such gestures must not obscure the story, or become intrusive, certainly each individual can use good judgment in this matter. Arbuthnot (1972) feels that gestures enhance a presentation, but they must be geared to the age group. She summarizes: "But they [gestures] probably should diminish to the vanishing point with older children."

This section on storytelling assumes that the audience can hear. To make children aware that this is not always the case, you could lead them into a study of sign language, a way of "telling" a story to the deaf. Teachers report that preschoolers (Hagino, 1980) through junior high students (Rubinstein, 1979) take to learning sign language with gusto.

Children's oral language fluency is enhanced when they sing songs integral to stories the teacher is telling. (Used with permission of the photographer, Richard D. Bradley.)

Music

An additional way to enhance the telling of stories is to create simple tunes for songs the characters sing. Songs occur with frequency in children's literature.[7]

For this particular story, it is logical to set to music the repeated refrain with which the fisherman calls the flounder from the depths of the sea. Instead of using the refrain cited earlier, I chose a simpler set of words (Grimm, 1963) and set these to an easy-to-sing melody.

---

[7]A brief survey of folk and fairy tale literature reveals that many of these tales include songs. You might enjoy making up simple tunes for any of the following songs. (1) There are several songs in "The Widow's Lazy Daughter," in *Favorite Fairy Tales Told in Ireland*, ed. Virginia Haviland (Boston: Little, Brown, 1961). (2) The song in the Brothers Grimm *Rumpelstiltskin* (New York: Harcourt Brace Jovanovich, 1967). Pictures by Jacqueline Ayer, in a subdued but not somber pallette, are particularly evocative of a different time and place. (3) The doleful song in "The Cauld Lad of Hilton" is in marked contrast to the more usual cheerful songs in *Fairy Tales from the British Isles*, ed. Anabel Williams-Ellis (New York: Frederick Warne, 1960). (4) The awful creature in "Ruddy-my-Beard" sings a menacing song in *Tales from the Welsh Hills*, ed. Ellan Pugh (New York: Dodd, Mead, 1968). (5) The mocking monkey sings in "Born a Monkey, Live a Monkey" in *West Indian Folk Tales*, ed. Philip Sherlock (New York: Henry Z. Walck, 1966). (6) Finally, for a more ambitious project that may need the aid of your music teacher, try setting to music the carol in Kenneth Grahame's *The Wind in the Willows* (New York: Scribner's, 1960).

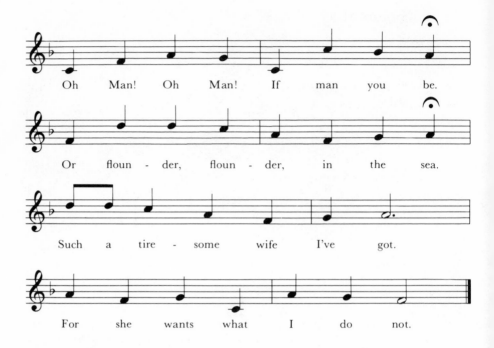

Oh Man! Oh Man! If man you be.

Or floun - der, floun - der, in the sea.

Such a tire - some wife I've got.

For she wants what I do not.

Simple tunes like this are easy to create and serve two purposes. *First*, they capture children's attention and provide for active involvement in the story. Even very young children enjoy singing along with the storyteller. In this story, the song is sung five times, and in a group of four-year-olds with whom I recently worked, the children who could not really learn the melody during the first telling of the story, nonetheless enjoyed singing some of the words.

Second, such songs reinforce in children's minds that creating or composing music, as composing in other art forms, is a logical school activity. As the teacher, you can teach these songs to the children before you tell the story, either by simply singing the song without accompaniment, or by playing the melody on the autoharp or some other instrument. The final goal is not the teacher as performer, but rather the child as composer of simple tunes.

Recent emphases in music education have included composing music, as well as the more conventional singing activities (Painter & Aston, 1970). Children enjoy making up melodies, and when a melody composed by a group of children can be utilized in a storytelling session, it provides an additional impetus to create.[8]

---

[8]Having the children set poetry to music, after singing many of the song-stories available, is described in "Action Activities" by Mildred Laughlin, in *Learning Today*, Spring 1976, pp. 76–78. Introduce the process using such favorites as *Frog Went A-Courtin'* and then have children make music for *Millions of Cats*, *Horton Hatches an Egg*, and others suggested by this author.

The Teacher as Storytelling Model

While storytelling is a pleasant activity serving the useful purpose of expos-ing children to a wealth of literature they might not otherwise encounter, regular storytelling serves another purpose. Children see the teacher as a storyteller. This demonstrates for them that storytelling is an acceptable and pleasurable activity for adults. Especially in the early primary grades when children try to emulate the teacher, this practice helps establish storytelling as a legitimate activity in the minds of children.

CHILDREN AS STORYTELLERS

The teacher's goal is to encourage children to begin telling their own stories. As kindergarten teachers encourage children to talk during share and tell periods, they are encouraging spontaneous oral composition. Let children tell short stories, which often will be only two to six sentences in length at the beginning, to lay the groundwork for more formal storytelling later.

In addition to encouraging children to make up their stories, the teacher may use particular materials to motivate stories. An interesting way to do this is by way of several tradebooks which have pictures but no printed story line. An example is *Pancakes for Breakfast* (dePaola, 1978). Others by Mercer Mayer (1967, 1969) are also particularly helpful in eliciting stories from children. As one author points out:

> These books provide a story structure—plot, characters, theme . . . and so provide the necessary framework on which [children] build their stories. . . . From the experience gained, [children] learn how the elements of the story interconnect and build on each other.[9]

Cullinan goes on to point out that such stories told orally into a tape recorder, then transcribed into type, provide reading material for the child who told the story, and for other children who may be interested in learning to read the story.

One kindergarten teacher regularly includes time for children to dictate stories to her, after they have viewed a wordless book. Early in the year she shared *Bobo's Dream* (Alexander, 1970) with her children. This is a gentle, realistic story of a small black boy who, accompanied by his dog, goes on a pleasant journey to the park where they enjoy a book and a bone, and then cope with problems. Soft-edged illustrations in gray, brown, and orange are realistic.

---

[9]Bernice E. Cullinan et al. *Literature and the Child.* New York: Harcourt Brace Jovanovich, 1981, p. 480. See also the helpful list of suggestions of material appropriate for choral speaking. The authors suggest ways children can dramatize stories they have read, and also ways written expression can grow from children's books.

After sharing the book with her group, the teacher left it on the table so children could look at it again when they chose to. In the following days, some children came to dictate a story to her. Bradley told the following:

John said that Bobo should come because they were going somewhere. They went to the store and got some bread. They paid the man and went away with the bread. The boy gave the bone to Bobo and Bobo sucked the bone and John read his book. John was reading the book while Bobo sucked the bone and then a big dog came along nicely. But then he took the bone with a growling face. Bobo was very mad while John was reading the book. He put his paw on John's arm. Then John looked too. The other dog had the bone and John said, "Give me the bone," to the other dog. Bobo was barking with a growling face. Then they got the bone and walked away while Bobo was sucking on his bone. He licked John and thanked him for getting the bone for him while the bone was on the ground and he was holding the page down. He looked at the book while Bobo was sucking on the bone. Then he was looking at his back too while Bobo was sucking on his bone. Bobo went to sleep while he was sucking on his bone and dreamed that the football players were playing football. One of them had the football in his hand and was running. Then one of them almost caught the ball and then they almost won the game. Then one of them threw it at some boys and hit one of them. Then he dreamed that they were very mad and took the football away. Bobo dreamed that the bigger kids wouldn't give the football back. He tried to take it while he was trying to catch one of the other football players. Bobo dreamed that he opened one of his eyes and John was shouting with a football in his hand saying, "Come here!" Then he looked and was mad. He woke up and thought he was big while he was dreaming and he got mad because he woke him up. He was so big and the other kids looked at him and were very scared because he was so big. He threw the football back at them and they ran away as fast as they could. Then they hopped on his back and hugged him and then he held up the football and they went away. Then the other dog came along and Bobo put his paw on his bone while John was almost finished with his book. Then the other dog looked at him and he barked because he thought he was bigger than him. Then they went away while the other dog was licking his fur.

There are some gaps in this narrative retelling which are unclear unless one reads the account while looking at the pictures. Nonetheless, this is impressive oral language for a five-year-old. It indicates the completeness with which children will retell stories if given an opportunity to dictate a response.

The sample provides interesting insights into a five-year-old's language capabilities. Note the relational terms:

> "reading the book *while*. . ."
> "and *then* a big. . ."

There is also effective use of descriptive terms:

> ". . . then a big dog came along nicely."
> ". . . took the bone with a growling face."

The child indicates an ability to deal with a variety of ideas in one syntactic unit. Notice the sentence.

> "He licked John and thanked him for getting the bone for him while the bone was on the ground and he was holding the page down."

This is complex language, showing the influence of adult language models. It also indicates a rationale for providing time to dictate stories to the teacher. It will be several years before the child will be able to write this complex a sentence.

Older children also enjoy retelling wordless book stories. In *Lost* (1975), artist Sonia Lisker has encoded in soft shades of brown, yellow, and orange the slight story of a child accidentally separated from his family at a zoo. One teacher of third grade shared this with her class. She had previously arranged with the school's kindergarten teacher for each of her students to be paired with a younger child. The older students then retold the tale in their own words, recording the story on cassette tape so the teacher could listen later.

In addition to using wordless picture books as stimulus to compose, they can also be a diagnostic reading readiness tool. When children's oral language in dictating stories begins to approximate more formal language (book talk), the child is ready to read (McDonell, 1978). With older children, dictated stories give teachers insight into the children's ability to infer (Jett-Simpson, 1976).

Retelling the Tale

With young children, a useful stimulus to oral language is retelling a story in their own words (Wagner, 1970). One kindergarten teacher read *Goldilocks and the Three Bears* (Cauley, 1981) to her class. Afterward, some of the children dictated their own retelling of the tale. Scott told the following:

The mother bear made some porridge but the porridge was too hot. So, the bears went for a walk in the woods. A little girl came from a little house, to the house of the three bears. First she went to the papa bear's porridge, but it was too hot. Then she went to the middle-sized bowl of porridge. Then she went to try the wee little baby's porridge and it was just right. Then she went upstairs. They had three chairs — papa's size, mother's size, and a baby size. First Goldilocks went to the papa bear's chair. It was too hard. Then she went to the mama bear's chair. Then she went to the baby bear's chair. She broke the chair all up! Then Goldilocks went to the next room. She went in the papa bear's bed, and it was too hard. Then she went in the mama bear's bed, but it was too soft. Then she went to baby bear's bed. This bed was just right. Goldlilocks fell asleep. Then the three bears came. Papa bear said, "Somebody's been drinking my porridge." Then they came to mother bear's porridge. Mother said, "Somebody's been drinking my porridge." Then baby bear said, "Somebody's been drinking my porridge and they drank it all up!" Then baby bear said, "Somebody's been sitting in my chair and they broke it all into pieces!" Then they went to the next room. Papa bear said, "Somebody's been sleeping in my bed." Mama bear said, "Somebody's been sleeping in my bed." Baby bear said, "Someone's been sleeping in my bed and here she is now!" Goldlilocks blinked her eyes and saw three bears. She ran out the window. She ran and ran and she would never go to the forest again.

Such story retellings can be taped, so the story can be listened to again, by its creator, or by other children. If encoded in writing, it can be illustrated and placed in a "story corner" so it can be reenjoyed later. In addition to such pleasant outcomes, story retelling can also be helpful to the teacher interested in assessing language growth. Pickert and Chase (1978) point out that comparing story retellings by a child over a period of time will tell the teacher something about the child's (1) comprehension, (2) organization, and (3) expressive abilities. This is another justification for oral retelling as part of the curriculum.

Dictating the Ending

A particularly effective way to elicit dictation is to read a story up to an exciting place and then stop and ask children how they would finish it. The activity can be done in a group, or individual students can complete the tale. Then the actual ending can be compared and contrasted.

A teacher of kindergarten children read *A Color of His Own* (Lionni, 1975), to the point where the two chameleons are wondering what they should do to solve their problem. Lionni's usually sensitive design here depicts the story in stencilled watercolor, recounting the discontent of a pair of chameleons who long for their own color. Five-year-olds dictated the following endings:

The green chameleon was the brown chameleon's dad. Then they
both went home. They asked mom chameleon if they could go to
a carnival. She said they could go. So they went to the carnival
and won some prizes. The dad won a can of paint and painted
the brown one and everybody was happy. The End!!

Tracy

So the chameleons headed towards a paint can. The color was
yellow. The paint can tipped and all the paint was all over. The
sun was hot and the paint dried. They started heading for Florida.
They fell in love and lived yellow all their life.

Ricky

In *Carrie Hepple's Garden* (Craft & Haas, 1979), the author created a suspenseful story around a common childhood experience, having to retrieve a toy from the yard of a feared older neighbor. A teacher of second-graders read the story to the point where Carrie is confronting the children, and asked her students to finish the story. Notice the following endings are told almost entirely in dialogue:

"Should we ask?" "Yes," said the little girl. "Well, do you want the
ball?" "Yes, Yes," said the boy. "O.K. then, but next time ask and
don't step on my flowers."

Monique

"We came in to get our ball," they said. "What are you crawling
for?" "We thought you were a mean creepy and spooky witch."
Then Carrie started to laugh. "Me, a mean witch? You can have
your ball. Oh, and come back to play with the cat and look at
my garden."

Richard

"What are you doing here?" "We were going to get our ball in your
garden." "Well, you're not, because I don't like people trappeling
(*sic*) all over my plants. You'll never get the ball." "But, how will
we get it?" "Just ask," and they did. For the rest of the time the
children just asked her and she did it.

Cindy

Parallel Plot Construction

In this technique, equally useful in motivating either oral or written composition, a literature model is provided. With their teacher, children extract the plot. In the process, specific details are stripped away, and the level of abstraction is raised so units of action can serve as a basis for a story by the children. The original story is fleshed out with details: setting, characterization, and resolution, which are the children's own.

Some stories have very simple structures. In *The Gingerbread Boy* (Galdone, 1975), for example, the plot line is: (1) an old person makes a food; (2) the food runs away; (3) the food encounters someone (either person or animal, depending on version) who wants to eat it; (4) the food escapes; (5) (repeat of 3 and 4—this is repeated differing numbers of times); (6) the food is captured and eaten. Primary boys and girls would enjoy an opportunity to dictate their own stories based on this plot pattern.

Other, more complex stories are appropriate for intermediate-grade students. You might read *The Bears on Hemlock Mountain* (Dalgliesh, 1952). Fourth-grade children listened to that story, and afterward analyzed the plot. The main character, sent to fetch something that is needed from some distance, accomplishes the task but on the way home encounters a danger, from which the character is saved by an adult. Those of you familiar with the particulars of the story will note the abstract way the action is summarized. This is done to provide a facilitating framework, a structure around which children can arrange whatever details they want to include. After analyzing the story, some children dictated their oral stories into cassette recorders. Kim's story, which she divided into chapters, incorporates going up and down a hill, as in the original story by Dalgliesh.

WHEN PETER GOES TO HIS GRANDMA'S

One day Peter got sent up to his room for breaking a window by throwing a snowball through it. Later his mother said, "Come down stairs and go to Grandma's for me. Put on your snowsuit, mittens and scarf." "Mom, what am I supposed to get?" "A pound of butter, Son," said his mother. "Do you know where Grandma's house is?" Peter knew, so he set off.

Chapter Two

"Harold, I sent Peter over Indian Hill," Peter's mother told his father. "I heard that there is a loose tiger there," said his father. Clip, clop, Clip, clop, Clip, clop, went Peter's boots. "Well, now that I am up the hill," said Peter, "all I have to do is go down." Just then Peter saw a shadow in the snow. Then came another shadow, and another. Peter thought, "What is that?" Out popped the shadows. It was only a family of rabbits. Peter was so relieved that he petted the rabbits. Then he kept on walking to Grandma's house.

Chapter Three

Peter walked down the hill. When he got to his grandma's, he knocked on the door. "Hello, Peter," said Grandma. "How did you get here?" she asked. "I walked," said Peter. "You walked! Well, you must be hungry. Come and have a cookie," said Grandma. He hoped she would bring brownies, too. After Peter ate his cookies, he asked for the pound of butter. Grandma gave him the butter. "Now, you had better get going, or your mother will be worrying," said Grandma. "Why don't I take two pounds, in case mother runs out," asked Peter. "O.K.," said Grandma, "but now you hurry home."

Time for the news on the radio. "Now for today's news report: A tiger has escaped from the zoo." Clip, clop, Clip, clop, Clip, clop, went Peter up the hill. Then Peter saw another shadow. It was the tiger.

Chapter Four

Peter ran, and the tiger ran. Peter climbed a tree, and the tiger climbed the tree. Then Peter thought of an idea. "Why don't I throw some of the butter down? Then the tiger would take the butter and go away." So Peter threw one pound of butter down on the ground. The tiger licked up the butter and went away.

"Harold, I think you should go and look for Peter," his mother told his father. "Yes, I'm putting on my boots," said Peter's father. Peter thought, "How am I going to get down?" When he heard his father call, "Peter, Peter," he called back, "Dad, I'm here." "It's a long story," said Peter. "I'll tell you when we get home." So they got home safely and Peter told his story. And his mother never sent him on another errand.

WHAT-IF QUESTIONS

Another effective way to elicit stories from children is to pose "What-If" questions (Torrance & Meyers, 1970). The teacher can present one of these either early in a day or the week, and provide time later for children to tell their story in answer to the question. The goal in making up "What-If" questions is to provide an open-ended structure. This might seem to be a contradiction of creativity. Such is not the case. The fact that a question *is* posed adds structure to the story-telling, but the open-ended nature of the questions encourages the child's creativity.

Recently college juniors created the following "What-If" questions, which proved effective in eliciting stories:

1. What if you could be anything in your kitchen?
2. What if when you touched anything it spoke to you?

3. What if every time you tried to talk, music would come out instead?
4. What if you were one inch tall?

Here are some stories told by children with whom this set of "What-If" questions was used:

1. I would be a refrigerator, and this is what I would do. It was supper time, and mother got the plates, and the forks, spoons, and knives out. She made hamburgers and french fries. Then she sat cokes on the table. She was going to the refrigerator. She opened the door and went to get the catsup, but I didn't want her to have it. I held onto it. She pulled and pulled and pulled. She said, "Let me have it." So I let her have it. I told the catsup to take off his lid. So he did, and red catsup went all over her head.

Debby, Grade Five

2. Once there was a little doll and I wanted to talk to her. One day she said she wet her diapers. I was so surprised that I fainted. Then she said, "I think I have to dump a pail of water on her face." Then I woke up and I saw her with a pail of water in her hand. I was about to say, "Don't dump the water on me," but she did. I was so mad I said, "I'll get you sometime." But she said, "Shame, shame, on you." And she said, "Are you going to change my diapers." And I said, "Yes." And we lived happily ever after.

Marcie, Grade Three

3. One night I was choking a lot. I was trying to call my mom but I just couldn't. Then I started to scream really loud, but the only thing that I could do was talk music. Songs were coming out of my mouth and not words. I was singing the music of the McDonald's song and lots of other kinds of music. I tried and tried to call my mom but I couldn't. Instead I rolled off the bed and hit my head. I stopped screaming. I woke up and I could talk normal now. It was just a bad dream!

Alberta, Grade Two

4. If I were one inch tall I would ride worms to school. A sandwich would be a feast and last at least a week. A flea would be a frightening beast, if I were one inch tall.

Michael, Grade One

The teacher can also encourage students to create their own "what-if" questions, once they understand the procedure. Children delight in making up this type of question. The following were among those made up by a fifth-grade class:

1. What if you woke up one morning and you were very bold?
2. What if you were a clock without a face?
3. What if you had to spend the rest of your life in an area no larger than a refrigerator—what would you choose to keep you company?
4. What if you noticed an interesting opening in a row of bushes—where would it lead?

Focusing attention on children's ability to compose orally lays the ground-work for later written composition. Oral composing needs to continue through the grades, as children's ability to "talk a story" will almost always outstrip their ability to write one. This is especially noticable at the early grades, where handwriting is still a problem. A teacher of second grade used *Stone Soup* (Lindquist, 1970) with her students. She asked children to both dictate, and to write, a further adventure for Pell, the wily boy who outsmarts those who don't want to share. Notice the differences between what the children could write, and what they could tell:

Handwritten: "He kept walking and walking until he got to another village to teach them how to make soup." (Joe)

Dictated: "Then he was walking, and he came to another village. They didn't have no food. A lot of people were dying, so he made some food with his soup stone. Then he said if they had any carrots and they had none but he had some. Then he served it out. Everybody like it, so he gave the soup stone to them." (Joe)

Handwritten: "Pell went to the country to see how the country is and he wanted something to eat and they wanted something too and he gave a stone rock to them and they gave him a stone rock. (Eugene)

Dictated: "Pell went to another country to see how it was. Pell said to some people, do they have any food? They said, "No." They said that is what they need. They need some food, and then Pell said, "We need a pot and some fire, and we need some wood, and we need some water." Then Pell dropped a stone in. Pell started up the fire, and then it boiled. He needed some salt, and Pell said that he needed some vegetables. Then he needed some more vegetables, and more, and then they wanted to eat but they couldn't. It wasn't done, and then Pell wanted to taste it. He

167

tasted it, and it was done. They started eating it, and then they wanted some more. Then they wanted some more, and some more, and then they wanted something to eat, but it was gone. Pell was gone. Then he came back and gave them the stone. (Eugene)

This discrepancy is common, and continues throughout the primary grades. To encourage full expression of children's ability to compose, we must provide dictation experiences even though we also teach students to encode their thoughts in writing.

Most of the foregoing has considered storytelling with elementary age students, though Jennings (1981) reports on the effectiveness of storytelling with delinquent preteenagers.

CHORAL SPEAKING

Choral speaking or choral reading are two terms used interchangeably which refer to saying a piece of poetry as a group. A rich diet of poetry as part of the oral reading program is one of the best ways to develop interest and enthusiasm for the art of choral speaking (Bamman, 1964). With poetry, as with some other forms of literature, reading aloud is the most effective way to experience it. Poetry is not effective read silently. Teachers need to transform poems from a thing in space, into sounds in time, because, "It is the performance of the poem which *is* the poem" (Salpen, 1964).

The kindergarten teacher, reading many poems to the children, will discover them repeating some of the words, or perhaps even a phrase or two. The teacher should encourage this, but participation at this level remains simple. Groups enjoy saying simple rhymes together, perhaps from Mother Goose.[10] It is appropriate for the teacher to help them learn to say a poem orally even before they know how to read (Heinrich, 1976). Formal work in choral reading is more logically a concern of the primary and intermediate grades.

Children may be divided into many types of groupings for choral reading: unison, refrain and chorus, dialogue or antiphonal, line-a-child, or solo voices with choirs (Stewig, 1981). Any teacher with a good poetry anthology will find some useful poems, but some are suggested here in case you have never tried locating poetry for this purpose. For *unison* reading you might like to try: "There Was a Crooked Man"(Brooke, 1976); for *refrain* and *chorus*, the repeated line "A-chewing, A-mooing to pass the hours away," in "Cows" (Stephenson, 1968). For *dialogue* or *antiphonal* reading, try the

---

[10]There are innumerable versions of Mother Goose verses. One of special appeal is by Brian Wildsmith (New York: Franklin Watts, 1964). Sensuous color and bold design delight the eye. In marked contrast is Tasha Tudor's introspective and intimate version (New York: Henry Z. Walck, 1944).

Saying a poem together chorally as a child leads the group is a useful oral language experience. (Used with permission of the photographer, Richard D. Bradley.)

whimsical "I Eat Kids Yum Yum!" (Lee, 1977) with its unexpected reversal. For *line-a-child*, "When Dinosaurs Ruled the Earth" (Hopkins, 1978) is particularly appropriate. The poem "Let's Go to the Wood" (Blegvad, 1978) is especially good for *solo voice with choir*.

Scoring a Poem

As a composer decides which instrument will play a specific part in a musical score, so the teacher will decide—at least at the beginning—which children will say what lines.[11] It is important to specify that the teacher will do this at the beginning, for children will soon have ideas about how the poem should be divided. The teacher encourages these ideas and takes the time necessary to try out the variety of ways boys and girls suggest. A group of children recently evolved the following way of dividing this poem as the way they liked best after experimenting with several ways of saying it:

---

[11]A useful resource is "Let's Say Poetry Together," catalogue #10-AR-1, available from Educational Activities, Inc., Freeport, NY 11520. This introduction to choral speaking shows ways a group can be divided. A book of poetry accompanies the tape.

CAT OF CATS
by William Brighty Rands

Group A	I am the Cat of Cats. I am	
	The Everlasting Cat!	*Group B*
Group C	Cunning, and old, and sleek as jam,	
	The Everlasting Cat!	*Group B*
Group D	I hunt the vermin in the night—	
	The Everlasting Cat!	*Group B*
Group E	For I see best without the light—	
	The Everlasting Cat!	*Group B*

(Hopkins, 1981)

Marking the Poem

Teacher and children alike may find it helpful to go through the poem and mark it, so they will remember how they want to read it, once a favorite way is agreed upon. A rudimentary working system makes it easy to remember how a poem is to be done:

   / = a slight pause

   // = a complete stop

   ∪ = a continuation of the voice so that the thought is continued to the next line

   ∧ = a heavy stress on the word

   ∨ = a lighter stress on the word

   < = voices get louder

   > = voices get softer

I am the Cât of Câts. I am ∪
The Everlasting cat!/
Cunning, and öld, and sléek as jäm,
The Everlasting cat!/
I hunt the vérmin in the night—//
The Everlasting cat!/
For I see best without the light—//
The Everlasting cat!//

   To begin, children will need to stick closely to the poem to gain expressive ability in this art. As the teacher senses students are developing the skill to read or speak chorally, they can be encouraged to add sounds to enrich the poem.

Creating Verbal Obbligatos

Many poems lend themselves to the creation of verbal obbligatos. The term obbligato, borrowed from music, means a persistent background motif. Usually this refers to a repeated theme played by an instrument against the major melody in a piece of music. In choral reading, it means having some children repeat at patterned intervals words or sounds to heighten the mood or evoke the image. For example, in "Trains" (Sutherland, 1976, p. 51), children may repeat the words "clickety-clack" in a rhythm they have created, as the rest of the students say the poem. One group of children with high voices repeats the clickety-clack in one rhythm while another group with lower-pitched voices repeats the same words at a different rhythm. This provides a background while the third group says the poem.

Other poems that lend themselves readily to the enhancement of obbligatos are the three cat poems included in Sutherland (1976, pp. 36–37). Experimenting with mew, meow, and other cat sounds in different pitches and different rhythms can result in a very rich obbligato background for the poems. A more involved background is necessary for "Three Little Puffins" (Sutherland, 1976, p. 74), which mentions panting, puffing, chewing, and chuffing—all in one poem! Children enter with enthusiasm into planning this intriguing collection of sounds as they vary rhythm and pitch to create an obbligato which may surpass the poem in interest.

Finally, no teacher interested in choral speaking will want to miss the delightful challenge in "Jabberwocky" (Zalben, 1977). There are all manner of beasts: toves, mome raths, borogroves, jubjub birds, in addition to the fearsome Jabberwocky. Children have created fantastic obbligatos of much complexity as they imagine sounds in rhythm for each of the animals included.

In this activity children are creating a sound experience in which the emphasis is on using a piece of poetry as a departure point for a complete creative expression. Certainly the same careful attention must be given to the basic reading of the poem as in simple choral speaking, but beyond that children are free to create as imaginative a group of sounds as they can.

Mention should be made of the valuable uses a tape recorder can serve. As children create their obbligatos, they get wrapped up in the excitement of creation and performance, so a recorder is necessary. The teacher captures the sounds on tape so, after the children have done the poem in one way, they may listen to it, reflect upon it, and discuss it. As they do this, new ideas for different ways to do the piece will occur to them. Perhaps someone will suggest adding something, another person will suggest deleting something; yet another may feel altering some part of the total poetry experience would help. As the children reshape, rework, listen and reshape again, the piece moves from its first tentative beginnings to a finished choral sound experience, alive as only children's imagination can bring something to life.

COMBINING FORMS: A POETRY EXPERIENCE

One of the most challenging of oral language experiences for children is that of putting together sounds or music and the spoken word in a poetry tape. Children can also set stories to background music (Foster, 1980) but we shall use poetry here, because poems are shorter.

The project, clearly described in a short article written by a classroom teacher, involves children in selecting a poem and preparing it as a finished product. The steps are as follows. The child:

1. selects a poem.
2. plans the sound or music background for it. If using music, the goal is to get some piece which intensifies the mood of the poem. The type of ubiquitous sounds which surround us in restaurants and elevators everywhere today should be avoided.
3. records the sounds or music. Children can do this by taking a cassette to the sound, if it is one not present in the classroom. A child might want a ticking clock, perhaps for use in "The Duel," about the Gingham Dog and the Calico Cat (Sutherland, 1976). If you use records for background, you can dub the sound on the cassette tape.
4. practices the poem, varying the three paralinguistic elements of pitch, stress, and juncture, until achieving a satisfying interpretation.
5. makes the final tape, using either another cassette recorder or a reel recorder. While playing the background on one tape, the child reads the poem aloud and the two are recorded on the other tape (Thuet, 1971).

The procedure is simple, and easily within the capabilities of intermediate grade children. You will need to demonstrate the procedure first and then supervise the actual recording with the children. Practice in reading the poems and in recording the background sounds can be done on an independent basis as the children have time. In addition to recordings of music, the teacher may want to explore the possibility of obtaining some sound effects records. There are many of these available.[12] The cost is no more than that of regular records, and a few would be a good addition to the school library collection.

As the poems most frequently will be short, several can be put on one tape. Children can, if the recorder available is equipped with earphones,

---

[12]Consulting the current issue of Schwan Record Catalogue (issued monthly) will give you a current list of such records. Some that have proved especially useful are *Sound Patterns* (Folkways 6130), *The Sounds of London* (Folkways, FD 5901), *The Storm* (Audiophile Records), and *The World of Man* (Folkways FC 7431).

listen to the poems when they have free time. Intermediate grade children are also delighted to have an opportunity to present their finished poetry tapes to younger children; a session spent sharing the poems with younger children is rewarding to both groups.

This preceding section has stressed the art of choral speaking. In addition to this, however, there is some evidence that such group approaches may result in significant measurable gains in reading ability, especially among minority children (Hoover, 1978).

READER'S THEATER

More involved than choral speaking, *reader's theater* is appropriate for upper intermediate grades, when children can handle the demands of reading a script interpretively (Burns & Roe, 1979). Unlike the simultaneous reading in choral speech, in reader's theater individual children take a part. Using only their voices and minimal gestures, they interpret the author's message (Larson, 1976). Reader's theater does not involve staging, costumes or lighting; rather, readers usually sit in a semicircle facing the audience, and use pitch, stress, and juncture to evoke a character. A complete description of this oral art is included in McCaslin (see Chapter 6 for reference).

NATIVE SPEAKERS OF OTHER THAN ENGLISH

The suggestions for activities in this chapter have been planned, field tested, and results described for classrooms in which most of the children bring fluency in English. While the level of fluency varies considerably, nonetheless in many classrooms teachers work with children for whom English is their native, or home, language.

Because of increasing concern over the educational fate of all children, educators are focusing efforts on children who come to school speaking languages other than English as their first language. Until this time, schools in general have been notably unsuccessful in assimilating such children, and in developing their ability to use oral English. Campbell (1970) has commented:

> The results of such instruction and testing are well known. By the end of six years of elementary school, a great number of these students were tragically behind their English-speaking counterparts in their academic achievement and were prime candidates to drop out of school. . . . The most common assumption has been that it is unreasonable to expect a child to acquire the fundamentals of education in a language he does not understand.

As a result of growing awareness of the number of children who come to school without a command of English, educators have developed different kinds of programs. One of these, English as a Second Language (ESL), uses foreign-language teaching techniques to add English to the children's speaking repertoire. Campbell concedes that the results of such programs have been mixed, at best. Another approach, which actually includes a variety of different ways of working with children, is bilingual education, in which the emphasis is on providing instruction in the child's native language. Both of these will be discussed at length in Chapter 13.

SUMMARY

Most children bring to school a vigorous oral language, shaped by the language of the home, and adequate for most of the child's purposes. The task of the school is to expand on these oral competencies, and in some cases to add standard English to the child's home language. Informal conversations, and more formal "Show-and-Tell" call on the teacher's ability to use questioning techniques to draw out boys' and girls' oral language. Structured experiences in developing describing competencies are one sort of activity that enhances native oral abilities. Oral reading by the teacher provides needed literary language input. Such reading leads naturally into storytelling, first by the teacher and then by the students. Choral reading experiences enhance appreciation of poetry while also developing the expressiveness of students' voices. The rewards are many: increased understanding and freedom of response to literature, development of drama skills, growth in language competencies, and increased ability to portray ideas through pantomime and gesture.

Suggestions for Further Exploration

1. The statement that oral language is *the* language is an oversimplification. Record some speech and transcribe it. What elements of speech cannot be transcribed? What can we communicate in writing but not in speech?
2. Describing was one oral-language component considered in this chapter. Others include fluency—stringing thoughts together coherently. Identify more components and make up activities to develop them in children.
3. Read E. Edwards' "Kindergarten Is Too Late," *The Saturday Review of Literature* 51 (June 15, 1968), pp. 68–70 + . Develop a rationale of the need for a four-year-old language program. Role-play with another student as the superintendent opposed to the idea.
4. Select a book you enjoy and plan several questions related to the book which would require children to operate on levels other than recall.
5. Children's taste in poetry may differ from that of teachers. See R.C. Nelson, "Children's Poetry Preferences," *Elementary English* (March 1966), pp. 247–252. Select six poems you think are appropriate for choral speaking and identify reasons you think so.

6. Storytellers communicate through gestures as well as their voices. Follow the steps outlined for learning a story. Tell it to a group of children, recording your telling. Then tell it to another group, having someone videotape it. What things about your effectiveness can you learn from comparing the two?
7. Make up ten "What-If" questions. Use them with children to motivate storytelling. Record and analyze results to determine which questions were effective and which were not. Why?
8. Find a group of children to observe. While watching them interact verbally, note the use they make of (1) a variety of sentence patterns; (2) nonsense syllables, repetition, syllable substitution and other word "play"; (3) paralinguistic features; and (4) kinesics. You should be able to notice the nature and extent of the vocabulary used, and the role of the teacher in furthering or inhibiting language growth.
9. The study by Brown is by now an older one. Are his statements about the lack of emphasis on oral language still valid? Select the most recent elementary language arts series available to you, and after reading the article describing his procedures, try to analyze one grade level of the series.

Suggestions for Further Reading

Baker, Augusta and Greene, Ellin. *Storytelling, Art and Technique.* New York: R.R. Bowker, 1977.

This is a brief but very complete treatment of the topic. Easy-to-read, and drawn from their own extensive experience, the authors offer eminently practical advice. An introductory section provides historic background, and a series of questions and answers potential storytellers might ask is included. Selection, preparation, and presentation are the most valuable sections for teachers. There is emphasis on mainstreaming children with special needs. Read this to compare/contrast with the equally fine *Storytelling* by Ruth Tooze (Englewood Cliffs, N.J.: Prentice Hall, 1959).

Bauer, Caroline Feller. *Handbook for Storytellers.* Chicago: American Library Association, 1977.

This complete compendium of techniques is written with enthusiasm and liberally illustrated. The author describes basic methods but also includes audio and visual aids. There are sections on how to plan programs for young listeners to integrate creative drama into the storytelling session. While some readers may have reservations about Bauer's use of gimmicks to attract and hold attention, there is no question the book includes something for everyone.

Blake, James Neal. *Speech Education Activities for Children.* Springfield, Ill.: Charles C. Thomas, 1970.

Though Chapter Seven, specifically related to speech disorders, may not be of interest to the classroom teacher, the rest of this small book will be. Contents range from oral reading to debate, and attention is given to dramatic activities and storytelling.

Britton, James. *Language and Learning*. Coral Gables, Fla.: University of Miami Press, 1971.

Britton (like Halliday, below) defines three stages of oral language development—*Expressive Speech*, largely egocentric; *Transactional Stage*, with dialogue used to inform, persuade, teach and learn; and *Poetic*, in which individuals react to the total, including past experiences. These phases move from language as participant to language as spectator. Adults can be both. As spectator, says Britton, "There is an increasing ability to handle the possibilities of experiences."

Colwell, Eileen. *A Storyteller's Choice*. New York: Henry Z. Walck, 1965.

The teacher will find any of the twenty stories in this collection of unusual interest to children. But the book's strength is the concluding material: a section on the author's ideas about the art and on specific notes for each story. In the latter, Colwell indicates approximate telling time, difficulty level for the teller, appropriate audience age; in addition background on the stories and suggestions to improve the telling of each is provided.

Haley-James, Shirley M. and Hobson, Charles David. "Interviewing: A Means of Encouraging the Drive to Communicate." *Language Arts* (May 1980): 497–502.

Reports on a planned sequence of interviews through which first graders improved listening, speaking, reading, and writing skills. Guidelines are provided for teachers interested in such a program.

Hall, Edward T. "Learning the Arabs' Silent Language." *Psychology Today* (August 1979): 45–54.

The author, long acknowledged as an expert in nonverbal communication, here describes the difference between a low context culture (like ours) and a high context culture (like the Arabs'), and conflicts which result when this difference is not understood. Kinesics, proxemics, and haptics are far more crucial in a high context culture; to ignore them impedes understanding.

Halliday, M.A.K. *Learning How to Mean, Explorations in the Development of Language*. London: Edward Arnold, 1975.

The author analyzed ways children use oral language to develop skill in different functions of language. Halliday says: "The early development of the grammatical system has been thoroughly explored. What has been much less explored . . . is how the child learns dialogue." Language acquisition and development pass through three stages—*Origin of Language*, *Transition Stage*, and a stage he calls *Into Language*. Adult language occurs without being tied to the immediate environment. The functions of language are developed by the same author in *System and Function in Language* (London: Oxford, 1976), including instrumental (satisfying needs), regulatory (controlling others), interactional (cooperating), personal (expressing the self), heuristic (organizational), imaginative (creating), and representational (informative).

Henry, Mable Wright, ed. *Creative Experiences in Oral Language*. Champaign, Ill.: National Council of Tealchers of English, 1967.

Chapters on a variety of topics are contributed by several specialists, including a preface by the editor. The section on creative dramatics is the strongest and

176

most extensive, but the chapters on choric interpretation and storytelling will be of help. The scoring of poems is a useful guide to teachers who have not done choral speaking.

Hunter, Madeline. "The Elements of Effective Communication." *Childhood Education* 46 (December 1969): 158–61.

The author identifies four elements in communication: the message, encoding, transmission, and decoding. She stresses the help which awareness of these can be to teachers, both in developing their own communication skills and those of their children. The importance of language in sharpening perception is noted, and a useful section on nonverbal clues for the decoder is included.

King, Helen Lamar. "Story Tellers, Story Writers." Grand Forks, N.D.: University of North Dakota, 1979. Eric Document Reproduction Service No. ED 169 561.

Written and oral stories of forty-six third-graders were studied to answer the question: How can children be helped to develop and improve effective writing skills? King does not feel that teaching grammar or usage improves the acquisition or development of language, but instead emphasizes artificial language performance, removing language from its natural context. The author advocates the "natural language context" stresses by James Moffett, because oral forms provide such a context for language development.

Petty, Walter T. *Research in Oral Language.* Champaign, Ill.: National Council of Teachers of English, 1967.

A useful compilation of articles that appeared originally in *Elementary English*. This volume serves as a summary of research in several aspects of oral language. Each article summarizes other pieces of research less accessible to the teacher than is this volume.

Possien, Wilma. *They All Need to Talk.* New York: Appleton-Century-Crofts, 1969.

The author deals with the entire range of oral activities, from more structured reporting, to more free drama activities. The paperback is rich in specific examples of actual classroom experiences, and the varied uses of children's literature is another strength.

Rich, Dorothy. "Spurring Language Creativity in Young Children." *Young Children* 23 (January 1968): 175–177.

Emphasizing preschool through primary-grade language learning, the article offers many ideas for stimulating oral language. Much emphasis is placed on active involvement. The relationship between language and observation, memory and sensory experiences is explored, with suggestions for activities. The use of pictures for stimulating storytelling is described.

Ross, Laura. *Scrap Puppets.* New York: Holt, Rinehart and Winston, 1978.

Clearly illustrated, this book describes four basic kinds of puppets, with variations within each section. A list of materials precedes the directions for making each puppet. Included are a List of Terms, Table of Contents, Index, and a related reading list.

Sanders, Norris M. *Classroom Questions—What Kinds?* New York: Harper & Row, 1966.

Practical and comprehensive. Chapters focus on questions for memory, translation, interpretation, application, analysis, synthesis, and evaluation. Aimed at social studies, it is also useful for the language arts.

Sawyer, Ruth. *The Way of the Storyteller.* New York: Viking, 1962.

Includes an analysis of storytelling as well as stories adapted for telling. Although lacking in specific directions, the book is a charming reminiscence about the long, successful career of a master storyteller.

Scott, Louise Binder. *Learning Language Skills.* Manchester, Mo.: Webster Publishing, McGraw-Hill, 1971.

A sequentially organized program designed to develop oral language fluency in young children, this offers a set of four different levels, for children ranging in age from four to eight. This focuses attention on listening, making sound discriminations, using sentence patterns, noticing likenesses and differences, classifying, telling stories, and reasoning. As with some other programs, components of each set may be purchased separately.

Seymour, Dorothy Z. "A Fresh Look at 'Show and Tell.'" *Young Children* 23 (May 1968): 270–271.

Seymour advocates teaching children the difference between information which belongs in offhand conversations and that which can contribute to the learning of other children. She offers specific suggestions for dealing both with the shy and the aggressive child, and emphasizes the need for organization of the sharing period; this was long thought to be unnecessary.

Shedlock, Marie L. *The Art of the Story-Teller.* New York: Dover, 1951.

This version of a now classic work merits attention, as much for its legible and attractive format as for its content. Though the book was written many years ago, both the section explaining Shedlock's ideas and the selection of stories adapted for telling are unique. The chapter on artifices (techniques) for capturing and holding interest is valuable, as is the chapter on questions asked by teachers.

Skull, J. and Wilkinson, A. "The Construction of an Oral Composition Quality Scale." *British Journal of Educational Psychology* 39 (November 1969): 272–277.

Most available evaluation scales in this area are old; all were troubled with the problem of recording the speech. This attempt, which deals only with standard English, is for fifteen-to-sixteen-year olds. Sample talks of short duration were given without notes, which children had a week to prepare on tape. The amount of agreement between the assessors suggests that teachers could use this scale by comparing their own students' recorded tapes with the sample tapes.

Smith, Janet. "Classroom Help for the Non-Verbal and Speech Delayed Child." *Early Years* (October 1979): 74–76.

The article focuses on environmental and functional causes of delayed speech (or mutism). Easy, informal teaching procedures help the classroom teacher assess the nonverbal strengths and weaknesses of students, and identify children who should be referred for more intensive evaluation. Informal tests include auditory discrimination and memory; phonetic knowledge; verbal skills; and self-concept assessment. Activities are included to elicit speech from the child who is organically and functionally able to speak, but does not.

Szasz, Suzanne. *The Body Language of Children.* New York: W.W. Norton, 1978.

Teachers rarely notice children's physical clues to how they feel, tending to focus on verbal responses and gross motor behavior. The superb photography in this book creates empathy with the subjects, with text providing a lexicon of nonverbal communications. Szasz clearly states she knew what caused the response she captured on film. By adding words to the photographs, she hoped to provide a guide to the interpretation of children's behavior. Her success in doing so is impressive.

Storytelling Materials

Writing about an aural and visual art, storytelling, is less effective than experiencing it directly. For this reason, the following annotations about materials related to storytelling are included. As you develop your storytelling skills, you may wish to see and listen to these:

"The Art of Storytelling." Available from Farmhouse Films, P.O. Box 30893, Honolulu, Hawaii 96820. 20m, color.
The narrator in this film is a mother relating her own experiences of learning to tell stories to her daughter, to counteract the competition of television cartoons. She cautions that this is not easy, even though it may appear so, and she suggests several practical steps. The film also includes two male storytellers, important since children may perceive this to be a female art form. The film shows audiences ranging in age from preschoolers through adults, also an important subliminal message about the persuasiveness of this art.

"Rumpel-Stilts-Kin," from *Grimm's Fairy Tales.* Available from Spoken Arts, New Rochelle, NY 10802. S.A. Miniatures, #300.
Narrator Eve Watkinson, who has a very resonant voice, effectively changes her voice to enact different characters in this retelling. There is simple harp music as an introduction, though the rest of the record is backgroundless, a pleasant statement about the effectiveness of the human voice alone. A refrain is provided, and you might like to have your class set this to music. A print version of the tale is provided so child readers can follow along.

"Storytime." Available from Great Plains National Instructional Television Library, Box 80669, University of Nebraska, Lincoln, NB 86501. A series of 32, 15-minute, color videotape programs.
Storyteller Joan Beasley is a very "pure" storyteller, i.e., no gestures or props, just the voice alone. She relies on the effect of the storytelling, eschewing any attempt to teach requisite vocabulary before beginning. The accompanying teacher's manual provides activities that are at most a page in length. Could be used as a motivation for children to tell stories themselves.

Other annotations of visual materials are included in "Introducing Children to Books via Television," by Pauline B. Gough. *The Reading Teacher* (January 1979): 458–462.

Bibliography

Alexander, Martha. *Bobo's Dream*. New York: Dial Press, 1970.

Arbuthnot, May Hill. *Children and Books*, 4th ed. Chicago: Scott, Foresman, 1972.

Bamman, Henry A. et al. *Oral Interpretation of Children's Literature*. Dubuque, Iowa: William C. Brown, 1964.

Blegvad, Lenore. *This Little Pig-A-Wig*. New York: Atheneum, 1978.

Bloom, B.S., ed. *Taxonomy of Educational Objectives: Handbook I—Cognitive Domain*. New York: David McKay, 1956.

Brooke, L. Leslie (ill.). *Ring O' Roses*. London: Frederick Warne, 1976.

Brown, Marcia (ill.). *The Steadfast Tin Soldier*. New York: Scribner's, 1953.

Brown, Kenneth L. "Speech and Listening in Language Arts Textbooks." *Elementary English* 44 (April 1967): 336–341.

Burns, Paul C. and Roe, Betty D. *Reading Activities for Today's Elementary Schools*. Chicago: Rand McNally, 1979.

Campbell, Russell N. "English Curricula for Non-English Speakers." In *Report of the 21st Annual Round Table*. Washington, D.C.: Georgetown University Press, 1970.

Cauley, Lorinda Bryan. *Goldilocks and the Three Bears*. New York: Putnam, 1981.

Cazden, Courtney B. "Concentrated vs. Contrived Encounters: Suggestions for Language Assessment." *The Urban Review* 8 (Spring 1975): 28–34.

Chomsky, Carol. *The Acquisition of Syntax in Children from Two to Ten*. Cambridge, Mass.: The M.I.T. Press, 1969.

Clements, Robert D. "Art Teachers' Classroom Questioning," *Art Education* (April 1965): 16–19.

Conlin, David A. and LeRoy, A. Renee. *Our Language Today*. New York: American Book Co., 1972.

Craft, Ruth and Haas, Irene. *Carrie Hepple's Garden*. New York: Atheneum, 1979.

Dalgliesh, Alice. *The Bears on Hemlock Mountain*. New York: Scribner's, 1952.

Davidson, Dorothy. "Trends in Curriculum Guides." *Elementary English* 45 November 1968): 891–897.

Davis, David; Davis, Madeline; Hansen, Harlan and Hansen, Ruth. *Playway: Education for Reality*. Minneapolis: Winston Press, 1973.

dePaola, Tomie. *Pancakes for Breakfast*. New York: Harcourt Brace Jovanovich, 1978.

Easton, Lois Brown and Klein, Marvin. *Expressways*. Oklahoma City: The Economy Co., 1981.

Edelsky, Carole. "Teaching Oral Language." *Language Arts* 55(3) (March 1978): 291–296.

Fisher, Carold J. "The Influence of Children's Literature and Oral Discussion in Developing Oral Language of Kindergarten, First-, and Second-Grade Children." Ph.D. dissertation, Ohio State University, 1972.

Fishman, Joshua. "What Has the Sociology of Language to Say to the Teacher?" In *Language in Sociocultural Change* (selected by Anwar S. Dil). Stanford: The University Press, 1972.

Foster, Harold. "The New Literacy." *Early Years* (February 1980): 25–27.

Galdone, Paul. *The Gingerbread Boy*. New York: Seabury Press, 1975.

Grimm, The Brothers. *Household Stories.* New York: Dover Publications, 1963.

Groff, Patrick. "Let's Update Storytelling." In *Language Arts* (March 1977): 272–277.

Guzak, Frank J. "Teacher Questioning and Reading." *The Reading Teacher* 21(3) (December 1967): 227–234.

Hagino, Janice L. "Educating Children about Handicaps." *Childhood Education* (November/December 1980): 97–100.

Heath, Shirley Brice. "Questioning at Home and at School: A Comparative Study." *Doing the Ethnography of Schooling: Educational Anthropology in Action* (ed. George Spindler), pp. 102–131. New York: Holt, Rinehart and Winston, 1982.

Heinrich, June Sark. "Elementary Oral Reading: Methods and Materials." *The Reading Teacher* (October 1976): 10–15.

Higginbotham, Dorothy and Reitzel, Armeda. "The Emergence of Decentration in Children's Social Speech." ERIC Document Reproduction Service No. 144 408, 1977.

Hohmann, Mary et al. *Young Children in Action. A Manual for Preschool Educators.* Ypsilanti, Mich.: High/Scope Press, 1979.

Hoover, Mary Rhodes. "Characteristics of Black Schools at Grade Level: A Description." *The Reading Teacher* (April 1978): 757–762.

Hopkins, Lee Bennett. *I Am the Cat.* New York: Harcourt Brace Jovanovich, 1981.

Hopkins, Lee Bennett. *To Look at Any Thing.* New York: Harcourt Brace Jovanovich, 1978.

Jarrell, Randall. *The Fisherman and His Wife.* New York: Farrar, Straus and Giroux, 1980.

Jennings, Tim. "Storytelling, A Nonliterate Approach to Teaching Reading." *Learning* 9(9) (April/May 1981): 49–52.

Jett-Simpson, Mary. "Children's Inferential Responses to a Wordless Picture Book: Development and Use of a Classification System for Verbalized Inference." Ph.D. dissertation, University of Washington, 1976.

Johnson, Ken et al. *Language.* Lexington, Mass.: Ginn and Co., 1979.

Kelliher, Nancy. "Language at Their Fingertips." *Early Years* (April 1980): 18–19.

Larson, Martha L. "Reader's Theater: New Vitality for Oral Reading." *The Reading Teacher* (January 1976): 359–360.

Lee, Dennis. *Garbage Delight.* Boston: Houghton Mifflin, 1977.

Lee, Dorris M. and Rubin, Joseph B. *Children and Language.* Belmont, Calif.: Wadsworth, 1979.

Lindberg, Lucille. "Oral Language or Else." *Elementary English* 42 (November 1965): 760–761.

Lindquist, Willis. *Stone Soup.* New York: Western Publishing, 1970.

Lionni, Leo. *A Color of His Own.* New York: Pantheon Books, 1975.

Lisker, Sonia O. *Lost.* New York: Harcourt Brace Jovanovich, 1975.

Mayer, Mercer. *A Boy, a Dog, and a Frog.* New York: Dial Press, 1967.

Mayer, Mercer. *Frog, Where Are You?* New York: Dial Press, 1969.

McDonell, Gloria M. and Osborn, E.B. "New Thoughts about Reading Readiness." *Language Arts* (January 1978): 26–29.

Ollila, Lloyd O., ed. *Handbook for Administrators and Teachers. Reading in the Kindergarten.* Newark, Del.: International Reading Association, 1980.

Paynter, John and Aston, Peter. *Sound and Silence.* Cambridge, Mass.: The University Press, 1970.

Pickert, Sarah M. and Chase, Martha L. "Story Retelling: An Informal Technique for Evaluating Children's Language." *The Reading Teacher* (February 1978): 528–531.

Post, Robert M. "The Reading Teacher as Oral Interpreter of Literature." *The Reading Teacher* (December 1977): 303–307.

Quackenbush, Robert M. (illus.). *The Steadfast Tin Soldier*. New York: Holt, Rinehart and Winston, 1964.

Ribovich, Jerilyn K. "Comprehension of Syntactic Structures in Oral Language and Its Relationship to Reading Comprehension in First Grade Children." ERIC Document Reproduction Service No. 144 103, 1976.

Ritchard, Cyril et al., readers. *Mother Goose*. Caedmon Records, TC 1091.

Rubinstein, Robert E. "Talk with Your Hands." *American Education* (August-September 1979): 34–36.

Salpen, Donald. "A Study of an Oral Approach to the Appreciation of Poetry." Ph.D. dissertation, University of Minnesota, 1964.

Schwartz, Judy I. "Metalinguistic Awareness: A Study of Verbal Play in Young Children," 1977. ERIC Document Reproduction Service No. 149 852.

Stephenson, Marjorie. *Fives Sixes and Sevens*. Chicago: Rand McNally, 1980.

Stewig, John Warren. "Choral Speaking: Who Has Time? Why Take Time?" Paper presented at the Third Great Lakes Regional I.R.A. Conference, October 1978. ERIC Document Reproduction Service No. 165 110.

Stewig, John Warren. "Teaching the Language Arts." In *The Elementary School*, edited by Frost. Boston: Houghton Mifflin, 1969, pp. 364–382.

Stewig, John Warren. "Choral Speaking: Who Has the Time? Why Take the Time?" *Childhood Education* (September/October 1981): 25–29.

Strickland, Dorothy S. "The Effects of a Special Literature Program on the Oral Language Expansion of Linguistically Different, Negro, Kindergarten Children." Ph.D. dissertation, New York University, 1971.

Sutherland, Zena (rev.). *The Arbuthnot Anthology of Children's Literature*. Glenview, Ill.: Scott, Foresman, 1976.

Thuet, Barbara S. "The Music of Poetry." *The Instructor* (April 1971): 83.

Torrance, F.P. and Meyers, R.F. *Creative Learning and Teaching*. New York: Dodd, Mead, 1970.

Wagner, Joseph A. *Children's Literature through Storytelling*. Dubuque, Iowa: William C. Brown, 1970.

Weeks, Thelma E. *The Slow Speech Development of a Bright Child*. Lexington, Mass.: Lexington Books, D.C. Heath, 1974.

Weeks, Thelma E. *Discourse, Culture and Instruction*, April 1976. ERIC Document Reproduction Service No. 128 144, 1976.

Williams, Frederick et al. *The Sounds of Children*. Englewood Cliffs, N.J.: Prentice-Hall, Inc., 1977.

Wolkomir, Joyce. "Students Record 'Way It Used to Be.'" *Christian Science Monitor* (May 20, 1974): F-2.

Yawkey, Thomas D. et al. *Language Arts and the Young Child*. Itasca, Ill.: F.E. Peacock, 1981.

Zalben, Jane Breskin (illus.). *Jabberwocky*. New York: Frederick Warne, 1977.

SPONTANEOUS
DRAMA

The class of nursery school children was enthusiastically responding to their teacher's suggestion that they become cars in a used car lot. She
came around, turned on the "key" of each one,
and drove them around the block before returning them to the "lot." Three-year-old Larissa
bucked and bumped when it was her turn. Then
she explained that she was a "cold car," so stopped, patted herself on her jacket, until she was
"all warmed up." Then she and the teacher drove
smoothly around the block.

WHY IS DRAMA A LANGUAGE ART?

This chapter states that spontaneous dramatics is one of the language arts;
more accurately, dramatics *should be* part of the language arts program. To
understand this difference, one must examine the nature of language arts
programs in the elementary school.

A curious aspect of these programs is that their emphasis is somewhat out
of touch with adults' use of language. Linguists have long pointed out the
primacy of oral language, that is, the importance of speech. They call attention to the fact that most adults use language orally. This is true whether
they are a college professor leading a discussion or an automobile mechanic
discussing with his service manager the reason for a particular repair. For
most of us, we use, *most* of the time, whatever oral proficiency we have
developed. A look at elementary language arts programs reveals this is not
generally true of these programs.

Many language arts programs share similar features. Teachers most often
use one of the nationally distributed hardback basic language texts by a major publisher. Frequently, they will also use a spelling book, while somewhat

less frequently, they will give either cursory or compulsive attention to one of the many handwriting series. In many language arts programs, written work is pervasive. In too many basic texts there is little emphasis on oral arts—listening and speaking.

Several writers have commented on the need to develop sequential programs in listening (Sowards & Scobey, 1968), in oral language (Possien, 1969) and in dramatics,[1] but little has been accomplished in these areas. These areas, and the related speech skills so crucial to most adult speakers, are most frequently ignored in elementary curricula. Further, while it is true that some children do get rather limited experiences in oral language (during the show-and-tell period for example); recurring drama experiences are seldom a regular part of language arts programs.

Because language is primarily spoken, language programs that do not give children chances to talk are inadequate. The addition of drama to the language arts curriculum can provide numerous opportunities for development of language. This does not mean that dramatics develops *only* language abilities, for there are many benefits derived when it is included in the school curriculum.

Definition

We have been talking about drama in the elementary school, but the exact nature of the process being recommended may be unclear. We are thinking about spontaneous, or improvised drama as opposed to formal playmaking. Improvisation is the informal, though not unplanned, response on the part of a child to some material, motivation, or stimulus. The response can be oral (Side, 1969) or physical—through bodily movement. The main characteristic of the responses is that they are improvised. This type of experience is basically made up of the following components:

COMPONENT 1: THE MATERIAL
Material is motivation of some nature and usually appeals to children's senses. The teacher may use the following materials:

A. A poem (Mandelbaum, 1975) or part of a story to motivate children. In using prose selections, the leader is always aware of the need to condense and simplify, for most selections are too long to be used in their complete form. The leader pares the story down to the "bare bones" of the plot, to bring it to manageable length for playing.

---

[1]Ann M. Shaw, "A Taxonomical Study of the Nature and Behavioral Objectives of Creative Drama," *Educational Theatre Journal* (December 1970): 361–372. The first quite convincing attempt to apply behavioral objectives to creative dramatics. People in the arts, generally, view such specific statements of objectives with skepticism. In an era where parents are increasingly questioning what schools are doing, such statements do, however, help justify drama.

This photograph could be used as a visual stimulus for dramatization.

B. A visual stimulus of some nature. Teacher-leaders have used reproductions of paintings, a photograph (any from Leavitt & Sohn's book, 1964, as the one above, would be useful), or perhaps an object (a mask borrowed from a historical society, or a piece of African sculpture).

C. The sense of touch, for example, by having children interpret in movement the surface textures of a piece of wood, corduroy, glass, corrugated cardboard, or tweed.

D. The sense of smell, when the teacher has children pantomime their reactions to odors. Actual odors are preferable to imagined ones, and children easily create impromptu scenes built around a character's reaction to olfactory stimulation.

E. Even the sense of taste, a seldom utilized avenue of learning in schools. Taking such a simple taste as that of a lemon, for example, the teacher can give children an opportunity to react.

These, then, are sources of material to which the leader turns in preparing material for spontaneous drama. What does he or she do with these basic sources, however?

COMPONENT 2: THE DISCUSSION-QUESTIONING SEGMENT

After exposing the child to the motivation, and indeed sometimes *as* this is going on, the discussion occurs—spontaneous, unplanned, but directed by the leader through questioning. A teacher might use such questions as the following (keyed to the examples given in the preceding material):

A. Do you have any clues in the story as to what the characters are like? How could this story have ended differently?

B. What are some words we could use to describe the main character? What might have happened before the picture was taken? What might happen now? What could happen next?

C. What does the surface of the material feel like? Is it regular? If not, do the irregularities form a predictable pattern? By using your body in recurring up-and-down movements, could you represent the contrast between the two levels of the corduroy?

D. Give the children paper cups filled with unfamiliar spices such as cumin, savory, and chervil, and let the children smell these and express their thoughts about them. What do they smell like? Where might you encounter an odor like this? What types of people could be there? What would they be doing?

E. In working with the taste stimulus suggested, in this case, of a lemon, the teacher might explore with the children such questions as: Who is tasting this? Where are they? Are they alone? Why? What happened prior to this to lead the person to want to taste the lemon? Was it simple curiosity—or was something more involved? What happens after they taste the lemon? What kind of action could it lead into? Are there things which could happen as a result of this action?

Remember that these are simply sample questions, not designed to be followed prescriptively by a teacher interested in emulating what is described here, but only as *examples*.

Similarly, there is no *one* right answer to a question. Though this chapter is full of questions, there are no answers provided. This is because the teacher's primary concern is to elicit many responses, to get at the diversity of ideas available when working with children.

COMPONENT 3: THE ACTUAL PLAYING OF AN IDEA

This component varies greatly, depending upon the age of the children, the amount of experience they have had with drama and their leader has had in directing it, where the lesson happens in the sequence of drama experiences, and the creativity of the children.

Sometimes children will respond with movement, either representative or abstract.[2] Ehrlich (1974) suggests a variety of introductory exercises that use movement to ease children into more sustained playing of dramatic scenes.

---

[2]Teachers find *Movement in Time and Space* (16m, b&w film available from Time-Life Films, New York) provides an enlightening introduction to ways movement activities can lead to drama.

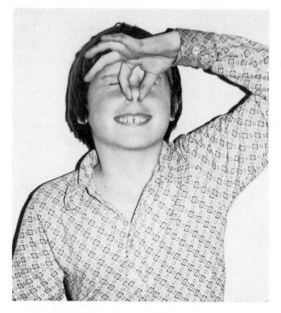

In informal classroom drama, we ask students to consider, "How would the character show an idea without words?"

At other times they will pantomime[3] and convey a thought or idea with gestures and facial expression. At still other times, children will be moved to add dialogue to their playing, to supplement the more basic bodily communication.

The above variations are not to be thought of as stages, for, if they are progressive at all, it is only in a very rough way. Though it does appear that dialogue is among the last of the dramatic elements to appear, groups and individuals will make use of one or several of these possibilities at different times, depending both upon the type of motivation and their response to it at a particular moment.

COMPONENT 4: EVALUATION

There are basically two types of evaluation in creative drama: *concurrent* and *terminal*.

Concurrent evaluation is of two types, teacher evaluation and group evaluation. By observing children working, the teacher can note which children are successful in capturing an idea and conveying it, and further encourage the group by positive comments. Make such general comments as: "My, I see so many cats and they *are* being very different," or "I can really feel the lightness in your bodies as you move—it comes across well." Or such specific comments as: "What an effective frog Billy is being," or "Mary's bird is flying so well."

---

[3]"The Mime of Marcel Marceau," a 23-min. color film featuring the work of this best-known pantomimist, is a fine way to introduce children to this aspect of drama. Available from Learning Corporation of America, New York.

Group evaluation occurs when teachers sense a need to consolidate something particularly effective, when they want to help the group shift direction, or simply feel that the children need a change of pace. Teachers can draw students together, usually in close physical proximity to encourage their participation in this transitory quiet period, and briefly share their reactions to what has been going on. Sometimes the the discussion starts with a very specific question: "What could we do with our legs to make them seem more like a horse?" At other times teachers can ask more general questions: "Did you like what you were doing?" This phase of the session is short, rarely more than a few minutes in length, but it both helps the children return to thinking more analytically about what they have been doing and helps change directions or make a transition to related but different activities.

Terminal evaluation occurs at the end of each session. On paper this looks like a logical and fairly easy thing to accomplish—in actual practice, it is not.

The leader may find it takes quite a while to arrive at the ability to lead an evaluation session that should be a summing up of what already has been accomplished and of what remains to be accomplished. Children and teacher together discuss what they did which was particularly effective, what was honestly attempted but did not turn out to be effective, and what skills, ideas, thoughts, and feelings remain to be worked on at the next session.

It must be emphasized that this is not the teacher evaluating the children, but the teacher and children evaluating *together* how the session went (Fariday, 1968).

Terms

In previous sections, terms have been used which may have been unfamiliar to you; some attention to these is necessary. The most common title for what this chapter is about is *creative dramatics*, but this term—though widely used—is avoided here. There are two reasons for this:

First, "creative" has been misapplied to such a variety of different phenomena that it is almost impossible to establish a clear, denotative meaning for it (Way, 1981). People bring a variety of reactions to the term, including some negative ones; therefore, we will not use it here.

Second, drama should *always* be creative, so as an adjective the word creative is redundant. If we accept different types of creativity, then all drama, from the informal dramatic play of preschool children to a finely disciplined Shakespearean performance, and including such mundane activities as lighting and scenery construction is, in fact, creative.

In this book, drama activities are described as spontaneous (Lud & Ulrich, 1980). That is intentional, to point out the need for an intuitive, flexible, adapting, and dramatic experience which is truly spontaneous. A dictionary definition reveals that *natural* is listed as one synonym for spontaneous, and it is a good word to use in describing such experiences. Drama leaders are concerned with evoking in children a natural, spontaneous response to the chosen motivation. This is akin to the free, unstructured response of young children's imaginative play, so respected in nursery school and so quickly discouraged in first grade. The teacher-leader does not formulate ahead of time what the children's response to the material ought to be, but rather plans a motivation and builds a dramatic experience as the children's natural responses to that motivation come forth. This use of the term does not, however, mean that the drama *program* is spontaneous, or unplanned (Fineberg, 1969). The teacher realizes boys and girls need a stimulus to be creative. Many writers have pointed out that children cannot create in a vacuum, but must be exposed to some sort of stimulus.[4] So the role of the drama leader is to locate and select from among the available motivations the one which will be most effective. This requires preplanning, but not of the entire lesson.

The foregoing is a general definition of informal drama for children. There are, in addition, some quite specific related terms which will help to further clarify the nature of this art form.

Another term used throughout this chapter is *leader*. This term is used because for too many people, the role of "teacher" is largely a didactic one, mainly occupied with dispensing of information. The too common picture is of the teacher standing in front of a group of children and talking *at* them. This is not an effective way to lead a drama session which requires some different abilities than you customarily use when you are teaching more conventional subject matter. These will be pointed out in following sections.

INTERPRETING VERSUS IMPROVISING

To some, the term improvising may seem a cumbersome way to say "act out," and frequently teachers respond to ideas in dramatics by saying "But I do that all the time in my reading classes." There is a rather subtle distinction to be made, however, between interpreting a story and improvising one.

It is, of course, true that many elementary teachers encourage literature interpretation in their reading classes. This takes many forms. It may vary from simply assigning certain children to read each of the character parts in the story to allowing a group excited about their "play" to enact the story, without using the book as a cue card (Cornwall, 1970). In these activities a crucial element is successful and accurate interpretation, enactment, or recreation of the author's statement and intent.

---

[4]Maurie Applegate, *When the Teacher Says Write a Poem* and *When the Teacher Says Write a Story* (New York: Harper & Row, 1965). The opinion about the necessity of triggering creativity is widely held; it is as well expressed by Applegate as by anyone. Several of her books are listed in the bibliography for the next chapter and are of interest, though they are not directly related to dramatics activities.

From Three Aesop Fox Fables *by Paul Galdone.*

In working with "The Fox and the Grapes" (Galdone, 1971), the teacher who talks with children about how they can convey the anger of the thwarted fox, what sounds and bodily movements they can utilize to show this, is still working with interpreting, not improvising.

When, however, asking the children, perhaps after simple enactment as described above: "Can you imagine what might have happened if the grapes *had* fallen into the fox's paws?" the teacher is moving into improvisation. The teacher is asking the children to extend, to extrapolate, to enrich the basic materials with ideas of their own making. This is the point at which the group is moving from interpreting to improvising.

Perhaps another example will clarify the distinction. Allowing children to choose parts and read a story interpretively is doubtlessly valuable. In such a story as the *Midas Touch*, children revel in impersonating the greedy king and his pathetic daughter. Some limited attention can be given to voice quality, inflection, and other aspects of oral interpretation. Usually the teacher limits the number and extent of these periods devoted to exploring the story's dramatic qualities. Since the results of such an experience are less tangible than those obtained when skill teaching takes place, even a teacher who may sense that the children are learning from the experience, moves ahead to more practical considerations. Consequently, those children who might have been anxious to "get inside" the skin of the avaricious king and explore greed and its consequences are left behind.

Spontaneous *improvisation* is the major emphasis in drama (Shuman, 1972–73), entirely different from interpretation as it involves going beyond the basic material. Taking the theme of the *Midas Touch* story, there are a variety of possible questions.[5] Children could easily respond to such as these:

1. Why do you imagine the king was so greedy? What might have made him this way?
2. How did the king react to other people? (You will recall that in the story we do not see him interacting with other people.) What was he like to his servants; the townspeople?
3. In what other ways could he have solved his problem?

Children would enjoy improvising these ideas. The teacher might use some of the questions to stimulate discussion; others would encourage children to "act out" their responses, creating additional episodes which could occur before, during, and after the basic story.

No matter what specific questions are used to begin a session, the teacher can move from interpretation to improvisation. In essence we ask students to extrapolate, to extend or expand, to take some basic material and go beyond it. Children draw from within themselves ideas, thoughts, feelings, and conclusions based on, but not found in, the basic material.

One aspect of improvisational drama must be emphasized here. Though dramatics *may* lead into creative theater, it is a completely separate entity. There should be no intent, for example, that simple improvisation on a new ending for a favorite fairy tale will lead into a fully costumed and lighted adaptation of a scripted play for parents. Children may eventually mature from simple spontaneous creation of a new character in the story "Stone Soup,"[6] to authorship of a new version of "Little Red Riding Hood," presented to the rest of the school, but if such does occur, it must happen because of the children's desire to do so.

Teacher-leaders, in fact, must be constantly wary that they succumb neither to their own need nor those of the principal or PTA president to mount a production for an audience. Some groups may evolve a semifinished

---

[5]A useful section on such material is in "Myth and Dramatization," *Competency and Creativity in Language Arts: A Multiethnic Focus* (Nancy Hansen-Krening. Reading, Mass.: Addison-Wesley, 1979, pp. 190–198). The emphasis is on drawing from children's own cultures — here as a basis for drama; elsewhere as a basis for speaking and writing. Each section begins with a rationale and is followed by annotated references and lesson plans which are up-to-date and imaginative.

[3]Marcia Brown's illustrations for this old tale (New York: Scribner's, 1947) lend a clearly defined aura of the "strange country" in which the story is set. For a suggestion about how to use this tale with learning disabled children, see Behr et al., 1979.

play. When this happens naturally, as an expression of children's interest, there is little harm in allowing the sessions to progress in this direction. It is, however, imperative that leaders continually examine their motives to make sure it is the children who are making a more formal "play" seem important.

Throughout this chapter spontaneous drama *sessions* will be mentioned, another purposeful terminology change. The term is used to avoid calling them lessons, for far too many people bring negative connotations to the word "lesson." Instead, drama sessions are referred to for two reasons:

1. There is not a specific "chunk" of material to be covered in a given time span, whether its span be a single session, a month's experience, or a year's work. The teacher does have a plan, but, as will be pointed out later, it must remain flexible so adjustments can be made as the session progresses. This is in contrast to academic lessons, the learning dimensions of which are all too frequently established by curriculum planners, subject-matter experts, textbook writers, and the teacher in the grade higher than the one you teach.

2. The mental "set" of both teacher-leader and students is different than that in a conventional academic lesson. In such a lesson children too frequently "take-in" whatever is presented, even if it is learned as the result of an *inquiry-oriented* process. In a drama session the leader is presenting something, but only for the purpose of motivating children. There is no intent that they should remember content details in the material. Confronted with a visual image, an aural message, or a tactile sensation, children engage in a process of drawing from within themselves responses and reactions, selecting the most appropriate of these and playing them out while interacting with other children. If, after using the material in a session, the children do remember details of names, occurrences, and sequences, this is a dividend but is not a purpose of the sessions.

The Inclusive Quality of Spontaneous Dramatics

In addition to unique terminology, there are several qualities of informal drama that are unusual enough to require some description.

Perhaps one of the most distinguishing qualities of classroom dramatics, setting it apart from other theater activities, is its inclusiveness. Opportunity is provided for all children to participate, and the premium is not on the potential actor but rather on the ability to take an idea and react spontaneously to it. This latter ability is one which most, if not all, children can develop. Authors have described encouraging results with learning-disabled students (Snyder, 1977) and with second-language speakers (Turkewych & Divito, 1978), for example.

The key word in the preceding paragraph is opportunity, for it is crucial that, even with very young children, it be an opportunity, and not a requirement. The leader first makes a genuine attempt to involve all children in the

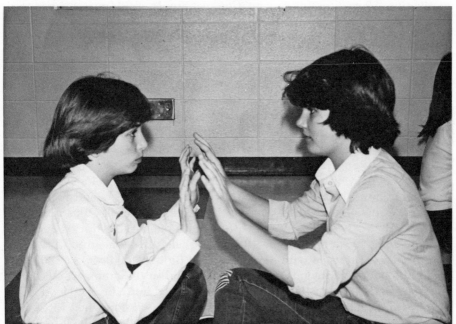

Students rehearse an improvisation before sharing it with others in the class.

group. This includes allowing those timid or as yet unresponsive children to play inanimate objects, if this gives them security. The teacher works diligently to involve all children, though sometimes this does not succeed. Since we are attempting to release children's creative potential, and *not* simply add another compulsory subject to the curriculum, it is perfectly acceptable if a child wants to retire to a corner with a book, rather than participate. Usually the eavesdropping begins quickly enough, and seeing others enjoying themselves, the child chooses to rejoin the group.

The goal is to engage all children in this activity. Sometimes teachers need to bide their time and wait, but keep trying to involve all children, since all boys and girls can both contribute to the activity and learn from it.

At times this inclusive quality involves the teacher, who participates as one of the characters, and in the guise of that character leads the playing. Wagner (1978) says that through *teaching-in-role*, the leader can encourage children to reflect on their actions, help them problem solve in resolving drama conflicts, and expand oral language by having participants explain their decisions.

The Ongoing Quality of Spontaneous Dramatics

The dramatics leader has a plan for the session. Among less experienced leaders this should be rather carefully written out, to detail stimulus, motivation, procedures, and evaluation techniques. With more experienced leaders, this plan may be more simply an idea of the direction for the lesson. In both cases, however, the leader remembers there is another session coming later.

This means that, though the session is by no means devoid of purpose, it is also by no means considered a failure if that exact purpose is not reached in *that particular session*. There will be other sessions and, providing something of benefit occurred, the leader can be content and work with the original idea again later. Perhaps an example will clarify this characteristic.

Suppose a teacher is working with the idea of mood, using the story of "Little Red Riding Hood."[7] The main purpose might be to help children sense the mystery of the forest and how the trees, growing closely together, allow only dim filtered light to sift through to the narrow and rocky path beneath. Suppose also, however, that in attempting to play this idea with children, they become fascinated with the idea of characterization and considering what Little Red Riding Hood was really like. One group I worked with became concerned with how Little Red Riding Hood could be so gullible, so oblivious to obvious danger signals, and so the group worked on a characterization of a slightly more alert Little Red Riding Hood. The devious wolf had a much more difficult job in our version when Little Red Riding Hood took on some of the sophistication natural to the children who

---

[7]The teacher might be interested in using the version included in Edna Johnson et al., *Anthology of Children's Literature* (Boston: Houghton Mifflin, 1977), pp. 313–314. This is another large anthology of children's literature which any teacher in elementary school would find indispensable.

were improvising. The leader should not be dismayed when changes like this occur. It is true that she or he intended to work on mood, but it is also true that because there is no specified content to be "covered," the leader can have another session on mood later. Perhaps in a second session, the class could work with the variant by Hogrogian (1967).

The teacher can, next session perhaps, choose another story. For example, use "The Three Bears" (Brooke, n.d.). Also set in a forest, this story is good for work on mood. Because most teachers tailor the spontaneous drama program as they go, the leader is not bound by considerations of "finishing" something by a given time. And leaders need not rush on to something else, fearing what the teacher next year will expect the children to have learned.

The Recurring Quality of Spontaneous Dramatics

There are certain basic recurring ideas, strands, or organizing elements that pervade drama programs at any level. These are mood, plot, characterization, rhythm, and unity. Because they recur, a kindergarten child as well as juniors in college are concerned with these elements. Once while working with a group of kindergarten children, I used Grace Hallock's poem about snakes (Sheldon, 1966).

SNAKES AND SNAILS
by Grace Taber Hallock

Through the grasses tall and slim
All about the water's rim,
Lie the slimy secret trails
Of the water-snakes and snails.

We delighted in moving through the mind-created swamp grasses as threatening snakes. However, this particular group of kindergarten children was ready for more. So we talked about snakes. Some of the questions we considered were:

1. Are all snakes alike?
2. If not, how are they different?
3. How would a heavy, fat old rattler, soaked in the sun, move?
4. How would this be different from a lithe young grass snake?
5. How would you move differently if you were hungry, than if you were full of a foolish mouse dinner?

These and other questions stimulated the children to think of differences, and we were on our way to a simple understanding of characterization. Similarly, though they had worked on characterization previously, a sixth-grade class especially enjoyed further chances to develop skills of characterization. This time we used the nonsense rhyme about the old lady so silly she swallowed a whole menagerie (Westcott, 1980).

POOR OLD LADY
Unknown

Poor old lady, she swallowed a fly.
I don't know why she swallowed a fly.
Poor old lady, I think she'll die.

Poor old lady, she swallowed a spider.
It squirmed and wriggled and turned inside her.
She swallowed the spider to catch the fly.
I don't know why she swallowed a fly.
Poor old lady, I think she'll die.

Poor old lady, she swallowed a bird.
How absurd! She swallowed a bird.
She swallowed the bird to catch the spider,
She swallowed the spider to catch the fly,
I don't know why she swallowed a fly.
Poor old lady, I think she'll die.

Poor old lady, she swallowed a cat.
Think of that! She swallowed a cat.
She swallowed the cat to catch the bird,
She swallowed the bird to catch the spider,
She swallowed the spider to catch the fly,
I don't know why she swallowed the fly.
Poor old lady, I think she'll die.

Ordinarily we would consider sixth-graders too sophisticated for such a poem, but in this case it proved a good vehicle for character extension. As I read the poem we laughed over it, and then we sang an impromptu version of it that the children had learned in music class. And then we explored some questions:

1. What is the old lady really like?
2. Was she always as silly as she is now?
3. If not, what made her the way she is?
4. What problems has she? How does she react to these problems?

After a spirited discussion of the old lady's foibles, we divided up into small groups. One of the groups invented a problem for the hungry old lady, and the other group created her response to the problem, thereby establishing their conception of her character. The drama session also provided many opportunities for creating other characters in some way involved with the old lady.

The Process Quality of Spontaneous Drama

In spite of the danger of unnecessarily raising the dichotomy of process versus content, it seems important to point out that informal drama is a process for elementary school children rather than a content area with specific grade or level expectation.

While for college students and teachers there is content *about* informal drama to be learned (McCaslin, 1980), the same is not true in the case of drama used with elementary students. Drama is primarily a process, used with *many* contents, to attain artistic response from children. Boys and girls do learn about such things as characterization, mood, plot, conflict, and rhythm. They learn things about these drama techniques, however, using any content. For example, it does not matter whether the leader uses *Snow White* (Heins, 1974) or *Cinderella* (Montresor, 1965) to develop ideas about characterization. The leader might use *Sleeping Beauty* (Hyman, 1977) for mood development. If none of these interests the group, the teacher may choose an entirely different story.

VALUES OF DRAMATICS

Many writers have described effectively and at some length the social and emotional values which accrue when children participate in drama on a regular basis (Hoetker, 1969). Almost any of the books mentioned in this chapter include a rationale for establishing dramatics as part of a child's education. An early, pace-setting book contains a convincing statement of the values of drama experiences. Though older, Geraldine Siks's book (1958) remains a basic statement that should be read. The same philosophic commitment to the individual's growth through drama is basic to her *Drama with Children* (1977).

Siks's books are among several introductory books dealing with drama in general. See, for example, the fine new book by Heinig (1981). Because these statements of the values of drama are widely available and because the emphasis in this chapter is on drama as a language art, only brief mention of the other reasons will be included here. Certainly for a comprehensive view of dramatics, the reader should do some background reading in the other recommended books.

The child's *creativity* can be developed by exposure to drama as explained earlier in the section dealing with the reason for calling this spontaneous drama. Several people have pointed out the need for encouraging creativity (Crary, 1969), have discussed how to do this (Kneller, 1965), and have identified conditions for encouraging creativity (Strickland, 1969); the reader is referred to these statements.

Another social value developed by dramatics is *teamwork*, the very heart of drama. As children work with others, they learn to modify their ideas, plans, and thoughts as they are exposed to the ideas, plans, and thoughts of others. This needs little encouragement by the teacher, as the child soon discovers that the group with candor and impartiality exerts the discipline necessary for effective playing.

Another value often identified is that drama provides children with healthy channels for the *expression of emotions*. When working *on* ideas in drama, the child can also work *out* frustrations, fears, and inhibitions, which ordinarily must be kept in during more conventional school classes. Seeing that characters in motivational materials share some common problems can be encouraging to a child.

Drama also provides for the development of *reasoning powers* for, as children analyze the appropriateness of what has been done in the session, they begin to evaluate, to formulate alternatives, and to develop the ability to choose the most appropriate of the alternatives.

All these abilities are crucial, but because they have been so well explicated elsewhere, they will not be developed more fully here.

Instead, we turn now to the *language learning* this art form can foster.

DRAMA AND LANGUAGE GROWTH

Young children engage in dramatic play even before they enter nursery school. Informally they assume roles—of mother, of father, and of other adults they observe, and they interact with peers in "trying on" adult roles. Dramatizing needs to be encouraged because of the language growth it stimulates. As Schickendanz (1978) points out, children generate more verbal language during dramatic play than in any other situation. Wise teachers can build upon the potential for language learning as they begin to structure experiences that bring children and drama and books together.

An experimental study done by William E. Blank (1954) points out clearly some of these learnings. Blank studied three aspects of children's development: voice qualities, personality factors, and vocabulary. Under voice qualities he included articulation and flexibility of tone. Two groups of school children took part; one met weekly during the school year for drama (the experimental group) while the other did not (the control group). Blank administered pre- and post-tests and found that the experimental group showed a mean improvement over the control group significant at the .01 level. Dramatics had been effective in stimulating growth in voice quality, personality factors, and size of vocabulary. The two language factors are of most interest to us, and will be discussed further.

It seems, then, that one approach to justifying drama as an integral, rather than a peripheral part of an elementary language-arts program is the possibility it offers for growth in language. What particular aspects of language growth does drama encourage?

Vocabulary Growth

According to Blank, one aspect of language growth that drama encourages is vocabulary development. Certainly teachers must be concerned with this because of the crucial relationship between vocabulary development and success in school. By vocabulary development we do not mean, however, learning specific lists of words. We have ample evidence this is not effective (Petty, 1968). What we need, instead, is the passionate involvement with words and the wonder at what they can do which makes coming across an unknown word a challenge rather than a bore.

What is your curiosity quotient about words? Take these as examples:

Have you ever noticed someone's *obliquity*?
Have you ever wanted to be a *mugwump*?
Have you ever *excoriated* anything?

How many of them do you know? Do they intrigue you so that you would like to know more about them?

How are we to achieve this involvement with words so we develop adults whose curiosity is piqued by unfamiliar ones? Certainly not, as mentioned earlier, by drilling children on lists. Spontaneous dramatics can provide one way. Much of the literature used as stimulus for drama will result in an exposure to new and unfamiliar words. Ward (1957) says that in using literature to stimulate dramatics, "the children will take hold of as much of the original language as they are able for the sound of it is fascinating to them."

In using drama to further vocabulary growth, we are not after specific words to be memorized but a captivating exposure which sensitizes children to the "lure and lore" of words.

Several excellent examples are contained in the book entitled *Push Back the Desks*. In this first example, the author describes how he worked with kindergarten children:

> From my meager linen closet I sacrificed a good white sheet to make a dramatic entrance into the kindergarten. . . . As a roaming language-arts teacher I was able to indulge in such activity. . . There I was in the middle of the kindergarten covered with my last good sheet, in which two holes had been cut out for my eyes. I saw twenty-two pairs of eyes looking at me. "I am a friendly apparition," I slowly stated. "What's that?" asked five-year-old Tony. They all started to talk at once, of course, so I asked them to sit in a circle, and I sat in the center. I proceeded to whirl about in a flashing dervish manner and explained to them that for Halloween I was going to be a very friendly apparition. "What do I look like?" Finally Annette guessed that I was dressed as a ghost. They then took turns wearing the large sheet and . . . flew through the kindergarten air as friendly apparitions. It was simple for them to accept apparition as a good kindergarten word. (Cullum, 1967)

Certainly this is simple dramatization—the very beginning steps, but even at this stage children take delight in responding to words.

It is one thing to let boys and girls respond with fervor to words, and it does build a sensitivity to them, but do these words remain with a child? Cullum feels they do and describes results he achieved with kindergarten children:

> It was exciting to see them go home during the school year as twenty-two eerie apparitions . . . well-trained pachyderms . . . (or) proud, snorting stallions . . . they carried their big words home to astounded parents, grandparents, and older brothers and sisters. They were proud of their new words. Together we had added six-ty new words to their speaking vocabulary. At the end of the year I devised a test to see how well they had retained their big words. Without any review, over ninety percent of the class scored one hundred. The words were still alive.

In summary, what the drama leader accomplishes, then, is to share words with children, and as Lewis (1968) says so well "the pupils are off their guard . . . and it is then that something is not learned, but absorbed through the intuitive channel."

Paralanguage

Another area of children's growth in language through dramatics is paralanguage—pitch, stress, and juncture. Leaders work to help children understand *pitch*, the high or low sound; *stress*, the accent in a word; and *juncture*, the stops or pauses between words. Students grow to a conscious knowledge of how they can use this expressive overlay on language. Prob-ably all children, except those with severe emotional and/or learning prob-lems, unconsciously assimilate the basic features of paralanguage along with other early language learning. Most children come to school as fully in con-trol of paralanguage as they are of the more basic verbal symbols of language. Beyond this basic mastery, however, school provides children with scant opportunity for conscious practice in manipulating these three elements to convey ideas more expressively.

Why should children learn something of these features of our language? Linguists agree they are critical factors in communication. For instance, psychologist Albert Mehrabian estimated that of the total impact of the message, 7 percent is accomplished by basic verbal symbols, while 38 per-cent is conveyed by vocal overlays of pitch, stress and juncture—that is paralanguage. In addition, he estimates that 55 percent of the message is determined by the accompanying facial expression called *kinesics*, which we will consider later. Apparently only a small portion of the message is transmitted by the basic verbal symbols.

If these extraverbal factors are crucial in communication, then it is ap-parent children should practice using them, so they can grow to be more ef-fective in using their language.

Examination of basic language textbooks reveals that little is done to make children aware of how they can achieve desired effects of manipulating pitch, stress, and juncture. Much work is included in these books about correct usage, but little is done with helping children experiment with these three elements of paralanguage to become more effective speakers of English. There are, happily, a few interesting exceptions among more recent texts.

Children do know about these factors subconsciously, but we are concerned here with their *conscious control* in order to create desired effects. By stimulating children to improvise dialogue for a variety of people, dramatics helps raise to conscious level the idea of the diversity of people's language.

Sometimes these learnings come up incidentally, in sessions involving experimenting with voices necessary to a particular story. Using the *Three Billy Goats Gruff* (Asbjornsen & Moe, 1957) with young children, for example, such questions as the following can be explored:

1. What does a troll sound like?
2. Do all trolls sound the same? Does a river troll (as the one in the story is described) sound the same as a forest troll? How would a cave troll sound different?
3. How does a father troll sound when he is content after a filling dinner of succulent goat?
4. How does a mother troll sound when she is nagging her obstreperous offspring to do what she tells them?

Children find such questions as these delightful. They provide opportunities to create story line spontaneously, but more important, they allow the children to explore paralanguage, to play with and speculate upon speech of this created troll family and to see how imaginative they can be in creating trolls with their voices.

Sometimes these learnings can be stimulated purposely, as when we show pictures of people, and ask the children to create voices, manipulating pitch, stress, and juncture to make the character live. Confronted with a picture and having only visual clues, the child is challenged to create a person, using the three elements of paralanguage to augment the basic verbal symbols.

In such experiences students can learn consciously ideas about paralanguage, which were previously known, but at an unconscious level. These are ideas of which far too many adults remain unconscious. We use paralanguage as adults every day and if we can teach children how to manipulate the three elements consciously, we shall be teaching them how to use one of the most expressive devices of a marvelously flexible language.

Kinesics

Another aspect of language about which children can learn in spontaneous dramatics is kinesics. Lefevre (1970) defines the term to include:

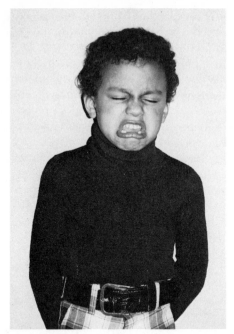

Introductory mime experiences motivate children to communicate nonverbally.

all bodily gestures, nudges, nods, finger, hand and arm signals, shrugs, and facial gestures such as winks, smiles, sneers and leers—the whole gamut of expressive actions, so important in . . . interpretation and in the small events of daily life.

Some psychologists estimate this aspect of language may account for up to 55 percent of the meaning of the message. Despite this, and the universal use we make of this part of language, an examination of elementary language materials reveals that, like paralanguage, kinesics is seldom a matter of much concern in language series. Using dramatics can make up for this lack, as children examine characters in depth and work to convey their understandings through extralinguistic features.

To alert children to the importance of kinesics, you might use *Face Talk, Hand Talk, Body Talk* (Castle, 1977). Many large, clear black-and-white photographs accompany the simple text, showing children communicating nonverbally. Augment these photos with others you collect of adults using kinesics, and discuss with children the nonverbal messages being conveyed.

In working to develop sensitivity to nonverbal messages, don't be surprised if girls, more than boys, respond to these ideas with more interest and ability. Researchers have discovered that in test situations girls as early as third grade showed better ability than boys in "reading," or interpreting the nonverbal clues shown on film (Rosenthal, 1974).

To sensitize them to this important aspect of communication, we plan

202

drama experiences in which children must use kinesics to create characters. A group of fourth- and fifth-grade children recently worked with the old folktale entitled "The Stone in the Road" (Ward, 1952, pp. 152–154) and concentrated especially on the reaction of the villagers to finding the stone in the otherwise meticulously maintained kingdom. Their leader talked with them about nonverbal means they could use to develop characterizations of the villagers as, in this session, each child chose to be one of the villagers. The differences in the shrugs, hand and arm movements, frowns and gestures, and other kinesics made obvious to the observer the character of the soldier, scholar, carpenter, and other inhabitants. In the evaluation session following the improvisation, the children learned much from comparing the way one child's characterization differed from that of another child's.

Spontaneous Oral Composition

A more encompassing goal than the specific ones mentioned earlier is that of encouraging growth in the child's ability in spontaneous oral composition, that is, impromptu or extemporaneous invention. We work for this goal when we work with plot development. Ward (1957) says that giving children experiences in thinking on their feet and expressing ideas fearlessly is an important concern of drama. She further notes:

> when older children are asked what . . . [drama] is worth to them besides being so enjoyable, they often think first of this objective because they feel so strongly the need both for the poise which comes from being articulate and the power it gives them among their fellows.

One way Ward suggests developing this ability is to allow a child to give a lead sentence, for example: "The boy was uncertain about what to do now." Without allowing the child who contributed the sentence to explain it, the leader selects volunteers to build an impromptu scene around the sentence.

Another successful way to develop the ability to compose orally is to take a piece of literature and present an additional problem related to it. For example:

1. What would have happened if the goat couldn't get across the bridge?
2. How else could Midas have solved his problem?
3. What would have happened if the slipper had fit Cinderella's sister's foot?
4. Who could have come to the aid of the gingerbread boy as he rode across the river on the fox's back?
5. Who else besides the knave might have stolen the Queen's tarts— why?

Children respond easily to this type of problem and, in the process, develop oral proficiency.

Recently, I used this approach with third-grade children. The motivation was the old Mother Hubbard rhyme (Lobel, 1968). The rhyme, as you remember, reads:

> Old Mother Hubbard went to her cupboard,
> to get her poor dog a bone.
> When she got there, the cupboard was bare,
> and so the poor dog had none.

The question to the children was: Instead of simply letting the poor dog go hungry, what *else* might Old Mother Hubbard have done? Among the more inventive responses suggested, which lent themselves to playing in dramatics were these:

1. She went to the butcher and asked for a job. He was in need of help, and so he hired her to cut meat from the bones. At the end of the day she got to keep the bones.
2. She planted a garden in which she grew many vegetables. The extra ones she sold at a stand and used the money to buy bones for her dog.
3. She went out begging from door to door, asking for a penny at each house. The townspeople were embarassed to give her just a penny, so they gave more. When she was through collecting she had so much money she built a mansion and bought bones.
4. Since she didn't have bones she made some porridge, and it was so good, the dog ate that instead.

Or try using a piece of literature and having children make up dialogue for characters in the story. In *Owl at Home* (Lobel, 1975), simple though well-meaning owl has a strange "visitor." Read the story to your children, and then have them make up the dialogue between Owl and his friend, to whom he tells the strange story the next day. In a first-grade classroom, two children made up the following dialogue:

First pair: Owl—Eugene   Bird—David

Owl is asleep in the chair when he is awakened by a knock at the door.
OWL: Who is it?

BIRD: The bird.

OWL: *(opening door)* Have a seat.

Bird and Owl sit down.

OWL: Know what? There was two bumps in my bed.

BIRD: Probably a ghost.

OWL: And know what? When I moved my foot, my right foot would move and move. And then I would move it again, and it would do it again.

BIRD: It's probably a water bed.

OWL: Then, know what? I raised up my covers. I looked, and it was gone; and I raised it down and it was right there; and it was gone and I just had my foot.

BIRD: You probably put your feet up.

OWL: Then I was getting cold, and I put the cover back on, and it was there again.

BIRD: Take the bed down.

OWL: And then, know what? I jumped on it, and jumped on it; and I said, "Bump, go away!" Then, know what? The bed broke, and I didn't have no bed. Then I ran downstairs, and I slept downstairs.

BIRD: Ask someone to fix your bed.

OWL: Then I slept and I had a dream; and I had a dream about bumps, bumps, just bumps. Then I made my first dream, and the dream is about bumps in my bed.

BIRD: And they are probably visible.

OWL: I need someone to fix my bed. I'm tired.

BIRD: I'll fix your bed.

OWL: Would you?

BIRD: My dad will.

OWL: Will you bring your dad over, and he will fix it?

BIRD: Yes.

OWL: I am sleepy.

Bird leaves.

Children can become proficient in this kind of spontaneous oral composition, though certainly this skill is slow to develop and difficult to measure. Perhaps the few ideas discussed here will motivate you yourself to even more creative approaches to stimulating spontaneous oral composition. Other suggestions for having children create dialogue for characters are given by Forseth (1976).

After children have dramatized, they can be led to write down what the drama showed. In one third grade the teacher used the "Old Mother Hubbard" idea described above. When the dramatizing was over, the children encoded the ending they had seen in their own words:

From The Comic Adventures of Old Mother Hubbard and Her Dog *by Arnold Lobel.*

She went shopping and bought the dog a hamburger. When she got back the dog was pretending to be a puppet with strings hanging from him because he attached them with tape. Then she went to the puppet place and took the dog with her and pretended to be a puppeteer to show all the people when they came to see the puppet show. When they saw the puppy with strings on him, they laughed their heads off. And they all had to go to the doctor.

Tracie

Mother Hubbard looked in a different cupboard but she didn't see any bones. So she went to her next door neighbor and asked if they had any bones but they said "No." So she went to her grandma's and asked her but she said, "No." And she went upstairs and asked her grandson, but he said, "No." And he said, "Why don't you ask Grandpa!" So she went downstairs in the TV room where he was watching TV and she asked him and he said, "Yes!"

Mara

SOME OTHER USES FOR DRAMATICS

Now that we have considered at some length the specific language uses of classroom drama, we will refer briefly to other uses of drama because "drama is also at the service of other areas of the curriculum" (Heathcote, 1971). The perceptive teacher is able to see many subject areas in which to use dramatics. One inventive leader interested in social studies helped intermediate children to a better understanding of themselves when they worked with the idea of fear, in interpreting feelings as they set foot on the white-grained edge of an unfamiliar continent. Another helped children evolve some sensitive rhythmic patterns based on the concept of number bases in mathematics. The group, divided into different bases, interwove, moved, split, regrouped, and enjoyed working with the concept on paper after they had interpreted it rhythmically.

Still a third teacher helped kindergarten children in a simple fashion respond to the ebullience of a Sousa march and later led sixth-graders in a sensitive response to the brooding and evocative counterrhythm in Ravel's *Bolero*.

In science, another leader helped second-grade children improvise on the life cycle of flowering plants and enriched the topic considerably by helping children understand the rather subtle differences between larkspur and hollyhock, fuchsia and dandelion, and how to interpret their responses to outside influences. The hollyhock and the larkspur responded to the effect of the wind, for example. The children understood and played the differing effects of the sun on the shade-loving fuchsia and the sun-loving dandelion.

Other drama leaders have found opportunities to incorporate drama into other areas of program. While there are many applications of this art in the curriculum, the ones of most concern here are those integral to the language-arts program. Readers interested in other uses for dramatics will find the articles in the "Suggestions for Further Reading" section helpful in explaining the wide scope of drama in the elementary school.

SUMMARY

Two things have been attempted in this chapter.

First, to provide a brief description of spontaneous drama, detailing the diverse activities included under the general title, so you may have a clear idea of the activities you are encouraged to do.

Second, to identify the many types of language growth that may result from using drama as an aspect of your language-arts program.

There is no limit to the amount of language growth possible through spontaneous drama—if the leader is eager to undertake such an adventure with the same willingness as the children will be to participate.

Suggestions for Further Exploration

1. The definition of drama given in this chapter is informal and process oriented. Assume that you are a teacher interested in spontaneous drama and are asked to explain it at a parent-teacher meeting. Evolve your own definition which should be more specific than the one given in this chapter.
2. The chapter makes the point that in longer prose selections, the leader's job is always to condense and tighten the action and plot, to reduce it in length to a manageable size for playing. Choose a folk or fairy tale and do this while retaining all the essential action and characters.
3. Where else, besides in the context of drama, have you heard the word *creative* used? With a few other people in class, try to establish a denotative meaning for the word, noting your agreements and disagreements. Can you agree on a connotative meaning? Reading Paul Torrance's *Guiding Creative Talent* (Prentice-Hall, 1962) might clarify your ideas.
4. Earlier in the chapter the word mugwump was introduced just to pique your curiosity about an interesting word. Since by now you know what it means, try planning a drama session around the imaginary adventures of a mugwump. How would you introduce the idea to the children? What questions could you ask to motivate them?
5. One of the most successful ways to get children to think about paralanguage is to show them pictures of distinctive-looking people and let them create voices for the unknown persons. Look through magazines for pictures that will stimulate children to create voices and experiment with paralanguage.
6. The Old Mother Hubbard rhyme was chosen because its plot led to a crisis point at which children could problem solve. Find several other stories that could be used in the same way. Locate the crisis point in each one and create some motivating questions to encourage children to solve the problem.
7. In discussing Little Red Riding Hood, reference was made to *mood* as a dramatic element. Choose six other stories you feel would help children understand the concept of mood, and create motivation questions for each that would help the children understand what mood is and different ways mood can be evoked.
8. Readers' Theater is a dramatic activity in which oral interpreters present a literary script using their voices and minimal body movement, usually while seated. Read *Readers' Theater Handbook* by Leslie Coger (Scott, Foresman, 1973) and then apply these ideas in a class to see how they work for you.

Suggestions for Further Reading

Allen, Elizabeth G. and Wright, Jone P. "Just for Fun: A Creative Dramatics Learning Center." *Childhood Education* (February 1978): 169–175.

Creative dramatics activities improve oral reading, arouse interest in stories, permit children to "live" literature, give them opportunities to elaborate on and explore further their relationships with reading, and enhance reading programs with added interest and vitality. Examples of drama and reading used together demonstrate how children discover things they had unknowingly misunderstood, and then realize their interpretation was not the only one justified by the text. By dramatizing answers to inferential questions, children observed several interpretations of the same situations, read to decide whether to agree/disagree with the interpretation, corrected misinterpretations, and sharpened comprehension.

To organize a creative dramatics learning center, a number of materials/supplies are necessary, obtained either through the home or school. Some needed materials are: wigs, clothing, hats, puppet materials, writing supplies, tape and audiovisual equipment. The physical aspects of such a center are described in the article.

Allen, Joan Gore. "Creative Dramatics and Language Arts Skills." *Elementary English* 46 (April 1969): 436–437.

The writer reports on her work with a fourth-grade class that wrote a play based on a story, of the learnings generated in this activity, and of her belief that teachers need not lay down formal rules for this procedure. Students, when involved, do not realize the amount of work they are accomplishing as part of the enjoyable activities.

Barlin, Anne and Barlin, Paul. *The Art of Learning Through Movement.* Van Nuys, Calif.: Learning Through Movement, 1979.

Two dancers with extensive drama backgrounds offer a wealth of specific suggestions to the teacher interested in movement. Each activity is described clearly, and careful attention is given to preparation, explanation of the movement, further development, and musical accompaniment. The last is provided, for many of the activities, on two records which come with the book. A bright, encouraging book, distinguished by clear and open format.

Brady, Bee. "The Play's Not the Thing." *Grade Teacher* 85 (March 1968): 82–83.

Brady identifies several purposes for creative drama. She advocates using stories to motivate because she feels that pictures are too static; her suggestions on how to choose a story are valuable; Kipling and Stevenson stories are recommended.

Bush, Catharine S. "Creative Drama and Language Experiences: Effective Clinical Techniques." *Language, Speech and Hearing Services in Schools* (October 1978): 254–258.

A speech and language pathologist reports on her five years' experience using informal classroom drama with children who have communicative disorders. Describing ways of getting children with unlike speech problems to work together to informally dramatize stories they have read, Bush talks also of such specific problems as articulatory modification. Yet she works on these in natural-language situations in contrast to more typical one-to-one clinical arrangements. Children can work on fluency problems, practicing pitch, inflection, cadence, and intonation, as they enact stories. In the process, their language becomes more complex and lengthy. Children's own dictated or written stories can be starting points for improvisations in which children can practice skills. She suggests each drama experience end with an evaluation session, discussing with children the concepts and skills worked on in the session.

Byrne, Barbara. "Opening the Special Classroom Door." *Design for Arts in Education* (March-April 1981): 9–15.

Opening with an anecdotal account of a drama specialist meeting her newly assigned special-education class for the first time, the author leads into a consideration of the needs of such children. Observing differences between mainstreamed and other students, she distinguishes between *disabilities* and *handicaps*. Students' needs differ depending on whether they belong in one of two groups: (a) those who have never made it into the mainstream, and (b) those who failed out of it. For the first group, drama can develop educational skills. In addition to requiring the educational uses of drama, children in the second group need its therapeutic benefits. Aesthetic/artistic values of drama are important since such children, often isolated physically in schools and lacking mobility, are deprived of adequate opportunities to explore their artistic potentials. The article closes with some specific suggestions about drama activities adaptable to work with mainstreamed boys and girls.

Chambers, Dewey W. *The Oral Tradition: Storytelling and Creative Drama.* In the series *Literature for Children*, edited by Pose Lamb. Dubuque, Iowa: William C. Brown, 1977.

Chambers deals competently with both arts included in the title and, in the section devoted specifically to drama, identifies readiness activities leading into drama, describes procedures in planning the crucial first session, and relates at length the description of an actual fourth-grade work with a folktale. Drama leaders will find both the section on classroom climate and on the steps involved in creative drama helpful.

Daniels, Stephen. *How 2 Gerbils, 20 Goldfish, 200 Games, 2,000 Books and I Taught Them How to Read.* Philadelphia: Westminster Press, 1971.

A fascinating firsthand account by a teacher of black ghetto children, which should be of interest to anyone who wants to teach culturally different children. Though the major focus is on reading, the section on role-playing or psychodrama will be of interest to the drama teacher.

Davis, Sandra A. "Pied Piper Way to Reading." *High Points* (Winter 1968): 8–10.

Working with two comparable groups of intermediate-grade children, this teacher provided drama and music activities that led to reading for one group; and for the other a highly motivating experience which did *not* include drama. Scores on a standardized reading test, administered at the close of a four-month treatment period, indicated that the group whose reading activities grew out of drama and music scored higher than did the control group. The author achieved a statistically significant improvement in reading scores.

Dixon, John. "Creative Expression in Great Britain." *English Journal* 57 (September 1968): 795–802.

Dixon believes that writing should use feelings as well as thoughts which arise from personal experiences. Improvisation, he contends, helps students penetrate roles and, therefore, offers the possibility of changing their attitudes about subjects.

Feitstritzer, Patricia. "Entering the World of Children." *Momentum* (May 1979): 11–23.

Drama as it could be—integral, not peripheral, to education—is described in this article telling of the work of the Austrian philosopher Rudolph Steiner. In the Waldorf schools based on his ideas, now numbering 165 around the world, the arts of storytelling and creative dramatics are basic. In addition to their use in language arts and history, they are part of the content and methods of science and math. A class may spend as much as eight weeks (daily classes) on a single story, as the teacher uses the material to challenge curiosity and aid concentration. Children use drama techniques to illustrate, among other things, grammatical concepts. Another part of this experience is Eurthmy, a language of gesture originated by Steiner.

Harris, Peter, ed. "Drama in Education." *English in Education* 1(3) (Autumn 1967).

A valuable article on drama in primary schools opens this comprehensive yet small publication that gives American readers an insight into drama programs in Great Britain. One article, "Sit Down, Sidney," is particularly helpful as it deals with children doing seated pantomimes—one solution to the problem of inadequate space. The magazine is published by the National Association for the Teaching of English, the British equivalent of our National Council of Teachers of English.

Hunt, Douglas and Hunt, Kari. *Pantomime.* New York: Atheneum, 1964.

In simple, nontechnical writing, the authors explore the art of pantomime from its earliest beginnings among prehistoric cave dwellers to its most recent manifestations on television. Though the chapters are brief (5-7 pages), and specific sources are not footnoted, each of the distinctive mime forms is treated in a believable and interesting way.

Prentice, Walter C. and Tabbert, Jon C. "Creative Dramatics and Reading: A Question of Basics." *Insights into Open Education* (November 1978): 1–11.

To support dramatics in the elementary curriculum, the authors cite research which concludes that play increases the child's repertoire of responses to the environment, and has value for subsequent adaptive responses. Creative drama incorporates the same elements of play that contribute to the cognitive and affective development of children, providing a link between a child's learning experiences outside and inside the school.

A teacher's primary role is to provide a structure within which drama can take place, starting slowly. Warm-up exercises with which to begin appear in the Appendix.

The authors relate reading to drama; they advocate using creative dramatics *before* reading a story. By discussing and acting out ideas and events to be encountered in a story, children bring more understanding to the story. Thus they can interact more thoroughly with the author's words, and come away with a better sense of story, and of how it relates to their own lives.

Smith, Elaine Campbell (ed.). "Drama and the Schools: A Symposium." *Elementary English* 49 (February 1972): 299–306.

This article is composed of papers by three different authors, representing an overall, broad view of drama and education. Drama encourages involvement by direct participation (improvisation, role playing, pantomime, characterization) and by indirect participation (empathic responses to drama presentations).

One author provides broad goals for a theater in education program, including aesthetic, pedagogical, and psychological values. Another author identifies five developmental behavior patterns that should result in dramatic activities for children. Impression behavior results from lessons based upon the five senses. Expression behavior includes the control of voice and body. Communicative behavior shares thoughts or feelings. Social behavior includes role playing in order to identify with other people. Creative behavior is shown by fluency, flexibility, originality and elaboration.

Weisheit, Marilyn. "Knowing Is Experiencing," *Childhood Education* 44 (April 1969): 489–500.

Weisheit relates the experience of a kindergarten teacher using egg hatching as motivation for a creative dramatics experience. Children pantomimed and developed a story on the basis of their observations.

CHAPTER SUPPLEMENT

AN EXPERIENCE WITH DRAMA

by Darrell Merkel
Mayflower Mill Elementary School
Lafayette, Indiana

Student teachers often are hesitant to try drama with children because it seems to an observer to be disorganized and chaotic. Good drama experiences are not so, as this chapter points out. Nevertheless, the seeming confusion that occurs when children are involved in drama sometimes discourages the inexperienced student teacher from planning drama experiences. In addition, too few cooperating teachers do drama, so the student teacher often does not have a model to emulate.

The selection that follows describes the experiences of a junior-year student teacher doing drama with children. Although he received little encouragement from his cooperating teacher, Merkel was able to lead the children in a successful sequence of drama experiences. Perhaps his enthusiasm will encourage you to try planning some experiences for your children.

Children are potentially creative. They have sensitivity, imagination, and a desire to express their feelings and responses openly and imaginatively. Too often this creative urge is stifled by the teacher, the school, or some other environmental influence; consequently children don't develop their creative abilities. The job of the teacher, therefore, is to develop, not inhibit, the child's creativity, sensibility, and imagination. Children need to express themelves creatively. One way they can do this is to experiment with their bodies and voices. A natural outlet for this experimentation is creative dramatics. Through creative dramatics, a child can improve social attitudes and relationships, gain greater self-confidence and emotional stability, improve vocal and physical expressions and develop independent thinking and personal creativity.

Creative drama is an area of the school curriculum for which a potential teacher or inservice teacher does not need extensive training and background. My own interest in dramatics began while participating in high school formal play productions. I developed experience in characterization and learned set construction techniques, costuming, and makeup. In my second year of college I was introduced to creative dramatics as a part of the elementary school curriculum—in a course I was taking to learn methods and materials for teaching all areas of language arts. I studied the topic of creative drama and found it an interesting and valuable part of the language arts program. I participated also in some informal creative drama sessions. My interest grew as a result of this involvement, and because of this, I structured a semester project around the subject. This involved research, organizing lesson plans for the primary grades, and testing them with students in a classroom setting. The lessons were utilized in three traditional classrooms in an average middle-class situation. The positive results encouraged me to take a more active interest in creative drama.

During an eight-week student teaching assignment, I was able to actually integrate creative drama into a language arts curriculum. The school was an open-concept building in a rural community utilizing team teaching in grades kindergarten through three. Grades four, five, and six combined to form one team with differentiated staffing. In addition, the help of interns, student teachers, teacher aides, and paraprofessionals was integrated throughout all seven grade levels. I was assigned to grade four and instructed to teach all areas of the curriculum excluding art and music. All fourth-graders had language arts instruction for five thirty-minute periods every week. The Monday and Friday periods were devoted wholly to spelling. The other three days were generally used for grammar. Creative drama had never been introduced in any form and many of the teachers were not aware of its existence as part of the curriculum.

Fourteen children were selected from the fourth-grade sections by the two certified language arts teachers. Chosen randomly from different ability groupings, many of the children had been exposed to drama only through such productions as Christmas plays. I completed my plans to present a final outline of my project to the school administration for their approval and consent to proceed. The school requested this evidence, being somewhat skeptical as to the values of such a program and of the physical requirements placed on rescheduling room assignments.

I set up a series of eight lessons that would involve children in sixteen thirty-minute sessions. For each I organized *group goals*, that is, what a session was to help children learn to do. I also had specific *drama goals* establishing the dramatic abilities each session was designed to encourage. I then selected materials needed to fulfill my objectives: audiovisual machinery, sources of literary material, pictures, books, and props that might be utilized. Next, I prepared a brief description of the method that might be used. I use the word "might" since these were not rigid guidelines but suggested sequences, including questions and comments for each lesson. Through student reaction, the sessions could proceed in many different directions.

The introductory lessons in creative dramatics ranged from relatively simple activities to more complex dramatizations. They were flexible enough, however, to be included at any convenient time as an adjunct to the language arts curriculum, responding to the interests and demands of the children.

I then submitted an outline, an example of which follows, to the administration. The outline lists session numbers, the main emphasis of that session, and the stimulation or motivational device that would be used in the presentation.

Session Number	Main Emphasis	Stimulation
1–2	Introduction to creative drama; learning to use the body to do interpretive movement.	Present words that describe animal movement. Children become animals indicative of these words (e.g., slump, slither, glide).
3–4	To increase abilities in interpretive movement; introduction of the idea of mood.	Play a tape recording containing many different types of music. Ask the children to assume the mood of each recording through facial expression and bodily movement (e.g., classical could be light and happy whereas blues is sad).
5–6	To increase abilities in interpretive movement; further development of mood.	Discuss the poem "The Sandhill Crane,"[1] after which the children will dramatize the animal movements in the poem as it is read.

---

[1]Mary Austin, "The Sandhill Crane," in *The Arbuthnot Anthology*, edited by Zena Sutherland (Chicago: Scott, Foresman, 1976, p. 38).

Session Number	Main Emphasis	Stimulation
7–8	Major emphasis is on mood.	Present pictures that suggest some unspecified danger dealing with the lives of people. Children's discussion of the pictures will provide basis for dramatic interpretation.
9–10	Characterization is the main emphasis. Plot introduced.	Show children different types of hats, some indicative of a specific occupation or role (e.g., cowboy). Others, not indicative, can be whatever the child makes them. Children portray different roles to interact and create a story line.
11–12	Characterization, plot, incidental dialogue.	Show slides of different people from which the children will speculate about that person's character. The discussion provides the groundwork on which a later improvisation about the person's life will occur.
13–14	Combining characterization, plot, dialogue and mood.	Create a story line in response to a picture. Children are in total control of the manipulation of characterization, plot, dialogue and mood. They must create their own material.

Because of omitted and shortened class periods—the project took place during the Thanksgiving and Christmas seasons—I did not complete the outlined program. Many sessions were shortened because of practice for the Christmas play. Others were omitted completely with no available time for "makeup" sessions. As a result, sessions thirteen and fourteen were combined into one session, which became the culminating lesson. What follows is an outline of the lesson for that session.

A. *Group Goals*

1. To correlate creative dramatics with other areas of the curriculum—particularly language arts and social studies.
2. To increase skills of intragroup cooperation necessary for group improvisation.

215

B. *Drama Goals*

1. To present pictures that stimulate children to create a dramatization of life in this unnamed culture.
2. To continue developing in children increasing competency to use the dramatic elements to create and play a story of their own devising.

C. *Materials*

Slides taken from pictures in Kari Hunt and Bernice Carlson, *Masks and Mask Makers*. Nashville, Tenn.: Abingdon Press, 1961. Background information from Matthew Baranski, *Mask Making*. Worcester, Mass.: Davis Press, 1962.

D. *Method*

Begin with a discussion of the artifacts and the lives of their creators to stimulate ideas that will later lead to playing out some aspects of these lives.

Questions and comments for prompting thought:

"By looking at the masks on the screen, can you tell me anything about the people who made them?"

"What are the masks made of? How are they painted? For what purposes could they be used?"

"Although we don't know much about these people, can you imagine where they live? How? Do they live in family units like ours? Are there many children in the family?"

"What could their homes be like? What are they made of? How are they built?"

"What kind of food might they eat? How is this food prepared? How do these people get their food?"

"How could the people travel? Are there roads? How do they get from village to village?"

"What do the people look like? How do they dress? Why? What are their clothes made of? How do they wear their hair? Can we tell their occupation or duty in their community by what they are wearing?"

At any point in the discussion, the children should be free to dramatize their answers. Gradually string these ideas together until the children have created an improvisation about the life, or some aspect of the life, of these unidentified people. The materials, although from actual Indian cultures, need not be identified for the children during the session so as not to stifle creative thought. At another time the correct information may be supplied. I found this most important because the children were able to let their imaginations work and to create their own culture when supplied only with three slides and several flat pictures of masks. I supplied the actual information about the people who were associated with the masks in a social studies class that followed the creative dramatics sessions. The children were very surprised how near their interpretations were to the real information. A unit on American Indians and in particular, Indians in Indiana, followed in social studies. Dramatics were then used in that class to personalize the information. In language arts class we followed up with lessons about Indiana in creative writing sessions and developed spelling lists using words frequently encountered when studying Indiana. In reading classes, the children did independent reading in fictional Indian material, and then reported to the class the subject and sometimes the story line of the book through dramatics.

I found the response to my program to be tremendously positive. All the children showed excitement, enthusiasm, and interest and demonstrated a willingness to participate and cooperate. Even the shy ones began to develop an eagerness to dramatize their ideas and express themselves verbally by the end of the short program. They were beginning to work well as a group and their attitudes toward each other improved. Since there were only fourteen children in the program, the other children did not receive this kind of instruction. They talked to my group, however, and told me they would like to do something with dramatics. This is why I followed my creative dramatic sessions with some related dramatic activities in the classroom so that all the children could become involved.

The teachers' reactions, disappointingly, were not as enthusiastic or encouraging. Throughout my student teaching at the school, despite my invitations, my sessions were never observed by the teachers I was working with. I was rarely questioned as to the purpose or procedures involved in the project, although some teachers did say the program sounded "interesting," but insinuated in other discussions its lack of practicality in their own programs.

I found, however, the experience to be successful and worthwhile. It helped me gain a better understanding of the advantages and limitations of creative dramatics and of the potentiality children have for creative expression. I understand this ability in many children as a result of having worked with them in other, more structured subject areas, in which they displayed less creativity. I was pleased to see the reasoning abilities each displayed. Their ideas often were very sophisticated, which prompted my alertness and total involvement throughout each activity. I feel that I could never have gained the depth of insight into creative dramatics I now have if I had only read about it and not become involved. One's ideas grow when watching and listening to children as they work.

The following are suggestions I would make to anyone beginning a program of creative dramatics.

1. Every person has the ability to be creative if he or she is not afraid to let it show. There can be no right or wrong way in being creative. Therefore, don't fear teaching creative drama. A sincere effort will have successful results.

2. Express to the children that sincerity is the key to their performance. It is hard to judge sincerity so, if in doubt, don't assume the action was insincere.
3. Remember to evaluate the action and not the child. Nothing stifles creative thought, I've found, more than to criticize the child. If you feel the action was not good, ask questions that would elicit creative responses to correct or improve the action.
4. When starting a program, I found it easier to begin with animate objects, since children are naturally full of motion. Don't expect too much of the children on your first try. Often what looks feasible on paper won't work with a particular group. You must be willing to adjust to the capabilities of your group.
6. Don't talk about doing it, get involved!

Bibliography

Asbjornsen, P.C. and Moe, J.E. *Three Billy Goats Gruff* (illus. by Marcia Brown). New York: Harcourt Brace Jovanovich, 1957.

Behr, Marcia Ward et al. *Drama Integrates Basic Skills.* Springfield, Ill.: Charles C. Thomas, 1979.

Blank, William Earl. "The Effectiveness of Creative Dramatics in Developing Voice, Vocabulary and Personality." *Speech Monographs* 11 (August 1954): 190.

Brooke, L. Leslie. *The Story of the Three Bears.* London: Frederick Warne, n.d.

Castle, Sue. *Face Talk, Hand Talk, Body Talk.* Garden City, N.Y.: Doubleday, 1977.

Cornwall, Virginia. "Magic Road to Class Dramatics." *Instructor* (March 1970): 65–66.

Crary, Ryland W. *Humanizing the School: Curriculum, Development and Theory.* New York: Alfred A. Knopf, 1969.

Cullum, Albert. *Push Back the Desks.* New York: Scholastic Magazines, 1967.

Ehrlich, Harriet (ed.). *Creative Dramatics Handbook.* Philadelphia: Office of Early Childhood Programs. The School District of Philadelphia, 1974.

Fariday, M.J. "Creative Dramatics: An Exciting Newcomer in the Elementary Curriculum." *Minnesota Journal of Education* 48 (January 1968): 20–21.

Fineberg, Rose M. "Creative Drama Needs a Building Process." *Language Arts* (February 1976): 184–186.

Forseth, Sonia. "Cinderella, Shave off Your Mustache." *Language Arts* 53(2) (February 1976): 172–174.

Galdone, Paul. *Three Fox Fables.* New York: Seabury Press, 1971.

Heathcote, Dorothy. "Drama," in *Challenge and Change in the Teaching of English*, edited by A. Daigon and R. LaConte. Boston: Allyn & Bacon, 1971.

Heinig, Ruth Beall. *Creative Drama for the Classroom Teacher.* Englewood Cliffs, N.J.: Prentice-Hall, 1981.

Heins, Paul. *Snow White.* Boston: Little, Brown, 1974.

Hoetker, James. *Dramatics and the Teaching of Literature.* Champaign, Ill.: National Council of Teachers of English, 1969.

Hogrogian, Nonny. *The Renowned History of Little Red Riding Hood.* New York: Thomas Y. Crowell, 1967.

Hyman, Trina Schart. *The Sleeping Beauty*. Boston: Little, Brown, 1977.

Kneller, George R. *The Art and Science of Creativity*. New York: Holt, Rinehart and Winston, 1965.

Leavitt, Hart Day and Sohn, David A. *Stop, Look and Write!* New York: Bantam Books, 1964.

Lefevre, Carl A. *Linguistics, English and the Language Arts*. Boston: Allyn & Bacon, 1970.

Lewis, C. Day. "The Poem and the Lesson." *English Journal* (March 1968): 321–327.

Lobel, Arnold. *The Comic Adventures of Old Mother Hubbard and Her Dog*. Englewood Cliffs, N.J.: Bradbury Press, 1968.

Lobel, Arnold. *Owl at Home*. New York: Harper & Row, 1975.

Lud, Mara and Ulrich, Judy. "Drama in Your Classroom." *Early Years* (March 1980): 64–66.

Mandelbaum, Jean. "Creative Dramatics in Early Childhood." *Young Children* (January 1975): 84–92.

McCaslin, Nellie. *Creative Drama in the Classroom*. New York: Longman, 1980.

Montresor, Beni. *Cinderella*. New York: Knopf, 1965

Petty, Walter T. et al. *The State of Knowledge about the Teaching of Vocabulary*. Champaign, Ill.: National Council of Teachers of English, 1968.

Possien, Wilma M. *They All Need to Talk*. New York: Appleton-Century-Crofts, 1969.

Rosenthal, Robert et al. "The Language Without Words." *Psychology Today* (September 1974): 64–68.

Schickendanz, Judith. " 'You Be the Doctor and I'll Be Sick': Preschoolers Learn the Language Arts Through Play." *Language Arts* (September 1978): 713–718.

Sheldon, William D. et al. *The Reading of Poetry*. Boston: Allyn & Bacon, 1966.

Shuman, R. Baird. "Drama in the Schools: A Well-Spring of Creativity." *Journal of English Teaching Techniques* (Winter 1972–73): 16–22.

Side, Ronald. "Creative Drama." *Elementary English* 46 (April 1969): 431–435.

Siks, Geraldine Brain. *Creative Dramatics: An Art for Children*. New York: Harper & Row, 1958.

Siks, Geraldine Brain. *Drama with Children*. New York: Harper & Row, 1977.

Snyder, Alice B. "Let's Do Drama." *The Pointer* 21(3) (Spring 1977): 36–40.

Sowards, G. Wesley and Scobey, Mary Margaret. *The Changing Curriculum and the Elementary Teacher*. Belmont, Calif.: Wadsworth, 1968.

Strickland, Ruth G. *Language Arts in the Elementary School*. Lexington, Mass.: D.C. Heath, 1969.

Turkewych, Christine and Divito, Nicolina. "Creative Dramatics and Second Language Learning." *TESL Talk* 9(3) (Summer 1978): 63–68.

Wagner, Betty Jane. "The Use of Role." *Language Arts* 55(3) (March 1978): 322–327.

Ward, Winifred. *Playmaking with Children*. New York: Appleton-Century-Crofts, 1957.

Ward, Winifred. *Stories to Dramatize*. Anchorage, Ky.: Children's Theatre Press, 1952.

Way, Brian. "Drama as a Sense of Wonder." *Language Arts* (March 1981): 356–362.

Westcott, Nadine Bernard. *I Know an Old Lady Who Swallowed a Fly*. Boston: Atlantic Monthly Press Book, 1980.

WRITING WITH
CHILDREN

The written word
Should be clean as bone,
Clear as light,
Firm as stone.
Two words are not
As good as one.

(L'Engle, 1972)

Few adults use written language with as much precision and effectiveness as Madeleine L'Engle; the task for child writers seems even less attainable. Yet samples of writing included in collections indicate that some children express themselves in written words honed to effective expression. How does this composing ability develop? In this chapter we shall examine the nature of the writing program in the schools and its effect on child writers.

Children's writing can be divided into two types for purposes of clarification and consideration. Whether these types are labeled creative and practical, imaginative and utilitarian, or innovative and functional is not important; in any case, the writer is simply trying to establish a dichotomy in the reader's mind. In one type the emphasis is on children's power to invent or fashion something new, different, unique, or unusual. In the other type, because of a different intended purpose, mechanics and form must be proportionately more important. Each of these types of writing demands slightly different behavior from the teacher. To adequately consider each type and point out how you can encourage children to write better, each will be considered in a separate chapter.

EARLY WRITING

Classroom practice in composition has changed dramatically over the years; at one time pencils were a rarity in kindergartens. Little or no encouragement was given to encoding thoughts in written form by first- and second-graders. This is despite the fact that over fifteen years ago a reading expert pointed out ways writing aids reading.[1] Hildreth said: "In the initial stages of learning to read any experience with writing benefits reading, no matter what methods are used in reading instruction." She went on to emphasize that writing, which serves as a bridge between the parts of language (taught in reading), and the wholes of language, enhances reading skills. Writing aids memory of letter and word forms, increases discrimination of similar appearing words, and minimizes reversals and other confusions.

Despite the wisdom of Hildreth's comments, writing languished in early primary classrooms. Until too recently, teachers assumed reading skills were their major priority. Writing seemed beyond most young children. The ollowing is probably typical of pervading attitudes:

> If anyone had told me two or three years ago that first grade children could write and read their own stories during the first quarter of any school year, without benefit of many months of formal reading instruction, I would have considered the idea ridiculous.

writes a first-grade teacher in New Hampshire (Caroselli in Haley-James, 1981, p. 60).

Today, in contrast, there is much interest in planning opportunities for children to write, and in studying the stages through which students progress in learning to write. This change has come about as increasingly effective observation revealed that many young children experiment with "writing" long before it is included in school curricula.

Early childhood classrooms provide many opportunities for boys and girls to:

1. see the teacher encoding thought in writing, as she or he takes both individual and group dictation, recording thoughts and feelings that provide a base for reading practice;
2. experiment with different kinds of paper and writing tools (pens, pencils, crayons, flo-pens, adhesive and transfer letters, sticks dipped in paint) in centers to which they go when they have free choice time; and

---

[1]"Early Writing as an Aid to Reading," by Gertrude Hildreth, *Elementary English*, 1964, *40*, 15–20. This suggests specific writing activities related to learning the alphabet, mastering phonics skills, solidifying a sense of left-to-right progression; it is characterized by the practicality of Hildreth's suggestions.

3. participate in planned writing experiences designed to motivate them to do different kinds of writing.

Further, teachers use informal classroom environments to observe children in different types of writing experiences, noting both the strategies students use in attempting to spell words (Beers & Beers, 1980), and to write entire sentences (Clay, 1975). In establishing a primary-grade writing program, teachers plan experiences in *imaginative* and *practical* writing.

WHAT IS IMAGINATIVE WRITING?

The question may seem superfluous, and yet to give some attention to a definition seems a wise idea. In creative writing, children make up, invent, devise, originate, or in some other way respond to a stimulus. The response may be a poem, a short story, a descriptive paragraph, or a play. The important element is that the child encounters the motivation and, using his or her own ideas, builds upon it.

Since this is the case, we need to identify more particularly some possible stimuli, or means of motivation. As in other areas of the language arts, if we think of the five senses, we have a point of departure (Rukavina, 1977).

1. The sense of *sight*. Teachers frequently use pictures or other visual stimuli to evoke imaginative writing. Many magazines have pictures that can be used, and a concerned teacher has a picture file to go to (or to which children may go) in search of a picture that will evoke creative writing. As a general rule, pictures in which something happens, has happened, or is about to happen, are more effective than simply "beautiful" views or landscapes. The latter offer little in the way of potential plot development.

A natural beginning to writing about pictures occurs when teachers provide wordless picture books (Mallett, 1976–1977). Engaging children in the process of translating from the artist's visuals to their own words is a valuable language challenge. As an example, we could use *Bubble Bubble* (1973), another of Mercer Mayer's appealing books for very young children. After examining the pictures, first-grader Eugene wrote the following:

> The boy was walking, and he saw some bubbles. He got up on a stool, and then he saw the bubbles up in the air. He saw the Magic Bubble Maker. He was surprised. Then he bought one, and then he ran along. He made some bubbles. Then he made a kangaroo, and then he made all kinds of stuff: car, boat, choo choo train, clown, shoe. Then he made a airplane and then shoe house. Then he made a snake. The snake tried to get him. He was trying to bite him ferociously. Then he made a cat, and then the cat scared him away. The cat was trying to get the boy. Then he made a elephant, and the elephant scared the cat away. Then the elephant was trying to get the boy, and then the boy made a mouse, and he scared away the elephant. Then the mouse was

trying to get the boy, and the boy popped it. Then he poured it all out and put it in the garbage. Then the dragon came up. Then he walked away, a long way, and went home. The dragon stayed there.

Though we usually think of wordless books for very young children, some are more complex, and can easily serve as stimuli for composition with upper primary children. *The Joneses* (Ramage, 1975) uses black line with restrained touches of solid pink, orange, and green to tell about an unusual family. After studying the pictures, Marnie, a third-grader, wrote the following:

Once upon a time, in the City of Oceiano lived a family named the Joneses. The Joneses had 30 children, all of which are very rowdy! Everyday early in the morning, father gets up and says goodbye to mother who is going to work. Mother drives a submarine! "Have a good day, dear husband," said mother. "Have a good day, dear wife," said father. As father shuts the door he lets out a sigh of relief. "Boy, am I glad the children are asleep now."
At 7.00 A.M. the children awaken and half of them get ready for school. While the children wash up, father cooks breakfast. Once Ray smelt the scrambled eggs he charged downstairs to the kitchen followed by Bobby, Cookie, Caryl, and Kim. Meanwhile, mother waved goodbye as she stepped quickly into the bus. When the 18 children were ready for school they went and fooled around for awhile until father said, "The School Bus is here!" Kevin was the first child down followed by Sally, Terry, Judy, Steven, Cheryl, Kathy, Mike, Jack, Jackie, Mary, Cary, Keith, Patty, Corinne, Ray, and Kim. Meanwhile, on the other side of town, the bus drives up on the dock and the bus-driver yells, "Last stop boat dock, everyone off!" Mother gets off the bus and steps onto the pier. Back at the house the children are calmly playing. Nobody knows where Cookie, Dolly, and Billy are. Randy, Sandy and Kris are up in their room sleeping. Bobby, Tiny and Ron are playing some game they can't pronounce. Nan is playing her older brother's clarinet. Tim is standing on the couch. Lee is making marks on the carpet with a Tonka trunk. That's when Cookie and Billy ran into the room. Cookie ran and got her teddy bear, then she went back to her room. Billy was doing flips and standing on his head while father was downstairs ironing clothes in the soundproof laundry room. Meanwhile mother paddles to her submarine on a life boat. She chats with her partner as she steps onto the submarine.
Dolly loved animals; she adored them so much that she always let the bird out of its cage. Today she opened the door. "Hello Birdie," said Dolly. The first thing the bird did was to bite Dolly's

finger, then flew away. While Dolly was chasing the bird, father
was downstairs feeding Sandy.

While back at the dock, mother started the submarine. The ocean
was silent. The submarine emerged into the deep, dark, silent
water. Meanwhile at home Dolly is still chasing the bird. In the
master bedroom Cookie and Billy were jumping on the big brass
bed. While on the submarine mother is humming the song,
Yankee Doodle Dandy, while at the bottom of the ocean laid a
big huge sea monster. Back at the house poor Dolly is still
chasing the bird but the bird flew out of a hole in the panel.
Back downstairs in the master bedroom Cookie and Billy are still
bouncing away. Then all of a sudden the bed gave out and Billy
fell right through. He also broke the panel.

Back at the submarine the sea dragon got hungry. Boy did he get
hungry! He started on his way up to attack. Poor old Dolly ran
right out the panel after the bird but with her luck, she caught
the panel. Now besides Billy falling, Cookie fell too. The sea
dragon made it to the submarine and he chomped it right in half.
Mother frantically screamed for help. The submarine started
heading towards the bottom of the ocean. Dolly is still hanging
but crying for help. I guess the Joneses need a new master bed
because this one has two holes in it. On mother's submarine,
mother is sad as she sits on the bottom of the ocean. The dragon
is still chomping on the wood. Dolly is ready to give up but out
of the blue, well, I should say out of the white comes little birdie
to the rescue. Mother saves little Cookie and Billy. But they're
still not out of trouble. The sea dragon got mad. "I can't stand
these old boards, I want the Joneses," said dragon. Birdie saved
Dolly from her misery and flew her back to the house. "Coming
in for a landing, watch out, I have an overload," said Birdie.
Mother sees the dragon and she shoots a missile at it. Dolly and
Birdie get in the house and greeting them are father, Lee and
Candy.

Mother, Cookie and Billy ride back into the panel watching the
dragon blow-up. Everybody was happy that Dolly was okay and
Birdie was back. All that missile did to the dragon was blow
away the bad part of him and it took out the good part. The
good part of the dragon swam down and went into mother's submarine. The children started setting the table while father played
with the younger kids. Meanwhile, mother drives away with the
dragon, Cookie and Billy. The table's all set and everybody is
waiting for the three. The four Joneses walk onto the dock and
start for home. The family greets them as they walk to the front
door. Everybody sits down to eat. After they ate they talked
about adopting the dragon and calling him Dandy because that

day mother was humming Yankee Doodle Dandy. They all agreed. Dandy read a book. They all got tired so they walked upstairs and went to bed. "Goodnight, Brother Dandy," said Corrine.

Note that in her word retelling of the picture story, Marnie has successfully recreated an elaborate plot, and added interesting details.

A more difficult task is capturing in words the moving images of film. A teacher of third grade showed a version of *Thumbelina* to her students with the sound turned off. Then children were to recreate the adventure in their own words.

Once there was a bird singing on a branch. That day a bee was near a flower. The bee backed up from the flower. A little girl came out and saw the bee bump into a flower. The girl climbed down and fell. She ran to a lake and dunked her feet in. A frog popped out. He looked around and saw the little girl. He ran after the girl. The girl climbed in a shell. The frog looked at it. Then he picked it up and took it to the water. He swam to his lily pad and set it down. He swam away under water. The girl peeked out of the shell. She climbed out, looked around. A fish came and she asked him if he would push her down the stream. He said, "O.K." and he did it. A bee came and took her off. He took her to his home. He asked her something and they laughed at her. The bee pushed her off. She landed on a web. She swung back and forth. She fell off and caught a cloud. She dropped on a flower. That day it was cold and breezy. She fell off and saw a home. She ringed the doorbell. A mouse answers the door. The mouse lets her in. The mouse takes her to her bedroom. She falls asleep on a rock. She gets up and the mouse tells her to sweep the floor. She was spinning with the broom. The mouse falls asleep. The girl runs and sees a bird. The mouse's husband saw the girl. The girl runs and hugs the bird. The man mouse walks up to the bird. The bird flies away with the girl. The bird is back on his branch.

Lisa

Children's written composition are useful as a means of studying variability in production. Using the same film, a teacher of second grade had children write their retelling. Notice the differences in the following stories, in both variety of vocabulary, in the amount written, and in syntactic variation. Though both of these writers were chronologically the same age and in the same classroom, their writing ability differs markedly.

One day a girl from a flower. She got down from her flower and
walked away from her flower. She walked to the pond. A frog
came up and chased her and she climbed into the nut and frog
took the nut and swimmed to a lily-pad and put the nut . . . it.
She called for help. A fish—the fish pushed her. A bee got her.
He pushed her. A storm came. She went in a mouse's house. A
bird was in it. . .(?). . went to the bird. The bird opened his eyes
and flew away with the girl.

Charity

It was a wonderful morning and all the birds chirped. Thumbelina
was in a flower when a bee knocked on her flower. She opened
the flower. The bee got so scared he flew away. Thumbelina
climbed down. She walked to the pond and put her feet in. Then
she saw a frog. The frog tried to get her. Thumbelina ran into a
shell. The frog tried to open the shell, but he couldn't. So he took
the shell. He put the shell on a lily pad and swam away. Some insects saw her. Then they grabbed her. Two insects were laughing
and laughing. Thumbelina got so scared she fell off. She landed
on a spider's web. The spider took a scissors and cut the web.
She landed on a flower and the petals flew away. She took hold
of one petal and sailed away with it. She landed in a flower. She
climbed down. She saw a little house. She knocked. Mrs. Mouse
opened the door. "Come child and have a good night's sleep."
"O.K." She went to bed. When she woke up she did lots of work.
Mrs. Mouse was tired, so Thumbelina went upstairs. She saw
something black. She rubbed it because she thought it was soft.
Then it began to move. It was a bird. Mr. and Mrs. Mouse were
mad. Mr. Mouse tried to get Thumbelina. Thumbelina jumped on
the bird and flew away.

Heather

2. The sense of *hearing*. Records can stimulate the flow of thought that
may lead to expressive writing. Sometimes try using just sounds and then talk
with children about such questions as: In what places might we hear such a
sound? What kinds of people could be in such a location? For what purposes? What kinds of things might they be doing there? Why? With whom?[2]

Or, you might prepare a cassette tape with disparate sounds (i.e., a dog
barking, a phone ringing, a can opener grating, and a dish breaking).
Children can weave these into a story of their own.

At other times, you might use a storytelling record and stop it before the

---

[2]Examples are *Sounds of Animals* (Folkway Records FX6124), *Sound Patterns* (Folkway
FX6130), and *Voices of the Satellites!* (Folkway FX6200).

A *blindfolded sense walk can provide stimulus for a writing experience. (Used with permission of the photographer, Richard D. Bradley.)*

end to let children write their own conclusion.[3] Even very young children can do well in finishing a story with their own creative ending; this technique is widely recommended.

3. The sense of *touch*. In developing descriptive skills, it is often wise to give children the challenge of describing the feel of something. To isolate the sense of touch, some teachers use blindfolds, so children focus only on whatever information their hands give them. The exercise works with individuals or groups. If working in groups, the children can compose a description and read it to the other children to see if they can guess the material being described.

This is easy to do with children because they delight in bringing items to school for the "feel" box. If you keep a box accessible where they can contribute items whenever they see something of interest, you will always have a supply from which to draw.

4. The sense of *taste*. A profitable experiment in expressive writing is to allow children to describe tastes, with the purpose of encouraging them to observe carefully and develop a telling description. Samples of herbs, spices,

---

[3]There are many such records and tapes available. Three I have found to be special favorites of children are *Joy to the World* (Christmas Legends) told by Ruth Sawyer (Weston Woods #707c), *Best Loved Fairy Tales*, by Charles Perrault (Spoken Arts #847), and *Ruth Sawyer, Storyteller* (Weston Woods, #701-702c).

vinegar, and other substances can be handed out in small paper cups. After children have developed the ability to describe what they have tasted, they can be encouraged to weave this into a story. They can be asked such questions as:

Who could be tasting this? Why?
What brought the person to taste this?
What could happen as a result?
Where might this be happening?

5. The sense of *smell*. Children can observe smells at several locations (Cassedy, 1979). Have them observe at home, in the school, or outdoors. One teacher led her children blindfolded around the school, to see if they could determine where they were by the smells in different locations. They discussed the places they had been, the smells they couldn't recognize, and later wrote a group description of the smells of the school.

6. A *combination* of the senses. Teachers often find that using more than one sense results in increased ideas for writing. They have used such films as "Rainshower,"[4] "The Hunter and the Forest"[5] and "Let's Write a Story"[6] to good advantage in motivating writing. The charming "Alexander and the Car with the Missing Headlight,"[7] which features strikingly original art work by children, can be used effectively to motivate other adventures for Alexander. "The Loon's Necklace"[8] is especially effective with older children in having them write their own folktales.

These are simply some possible motivations to encourage imaginative writing. No one author can give you all the ideas you will need for creative writing. Several other sources are included in the chapter bibliography that will help start children on the journey toward becoming effective writers.

THE NECESSITY FOR WIDE READING

The process of creative writing can be thought of as a two-part process: a *taking-in* part and a *giving-out* part. The teacher is active in stimulating the second, or *giving-out* part, as the previous section pointed out. But in a more far-reaching and less-direct way teachers also are influential in the *taking-in* part. This part of the program entails reading to the class on a regular basis.

It is crucial that the teacher read to the group: every day is really minimal. *What* is read is not nearly so crucial as the fact the teacher reads: poetry, fiction, biography, newspaper articles, perhaps a diary excerpt or

---

[4]Churchill Films, 15 minutes, color, sound.
[5]Aktiebvlaget Svensk Film, 8 minutes, black and white, sound.
[6]Churchill Films, 11 minutes, color, sound.
[7]Weston Woods film, 14 minutes, color, sound.
[8]Crawley Films, Ltd., 11 minutes, color, sound.

even something interesting from an encyclopedia—anything and everything. We do this because some of this reading will touch children in ways that more direct motivation closely linked to the actual process of creative writing may not (Cramer, 1975).

The rationale for this reading, plus some comments about reasons teachers don't read to children are put forth in delightful if slightly acerbic fashion by Root (1967). As he so aptly writes, there are at least three reasons reading is crucial:

1. Many types of writing must be heard in order for their full beauty to be accessible; poetry and plays fall into this category. Without such reading aloud of these and other forms, children may never be exposed to the particular delights available in these forms. Read *The Crest and the Hide* (Courlander, 1982) aloud so children can hear the beauty of the language included in these African folktales.

2. The contents of many books is appropriate before the reader is able to cope with the complexities of the printed page which they offer. Root mentions *Charlotte's Web* (White, 1952), and to this should be added the delightful works of Milne (1926) and *The Wind in the Willows* (Grahame, 1908). Share these with your children or, by the time they become competent enough to cope with the print, they may be put off by the topic. No one should have to wait until they're adult to discover these joys!

3. There are exciting bits of literature too far from the beaten track for most children to discover alone. If you doubt this, look over the list of Newbery and Caldecott winners for a start. How many of these have your children exclaimed over? Each has something unique to offer—perhaps you can widen your children's exposure by reading to them. In addition to these, make sure your children encounter *The American Institute of Graphic Arts Awards* books, and the *New York Times Book List*. The *Lewis Carroll Shelf Awards* name other excellent books that may not have been explored.

Probably the most difficult thing for teachers to do is to have the restraint to keep quiet after sharing something with the group. The natural tendency is to talk about the work, to point out the imagery, the figurative language, and to belabor all those "interesting" vocabulary words. To do so often destroys the magic of the moment and turns the reading time into yet another teaching time.[9]

The relationship between what you've read and expressive writing will be, for the child, tangential if not nonexistent on a conscious level. That's fine—leave it that way. The purpose here is not to provide conscious patterns for children to emulate, or direct instruction in forms, but rather to

---

[9]This point is made by John Coe, "In Their Own Way," *Childhood Education*, March 1978, 54, 225–228, who reports on ways writing is integrated into the British primary school curriculum. A major point is that flexible amounts of time need to be available as children are writing.

provide an enriching experience that may affect some children. The key word is "may," for we have no real way of knowing what effect all this reading has on individual children. And this is the way our work frequently is when we are concerned with learning in the affective realm. We are not concerned here with things easily measured, with missing addends to be found or with elusive pitches to be matched, but rather with enlarging children's consciousness by exposing them to experiences they might not otherwise encounter. In this, as in much of our teaching, we are offering children a chance to grow beyond what they were when they came to us, and, in the final analysis, the decision to accept or reject must be the child's. We do know that, as teachers of writing, we are sure that an enlarged and expanded self leads to more creative writing, and that is our goal.

WRITING GROWS FROM READING

At other times we choose a piece of literature specifically because it provides a motivation for students to write. With very young children we begin with simple retelling in their own words. The task of listening to a story, and then retelling it may seem simplistic, but in actuality it gives children valuable experience in sequencing, remembering detail, and translating from the aural to a written mode.

Plot Completion

A second type of literature-based composition is ending a story. We read to an exciting place, then stop and ask the children to finish the plot. A teacher of sixth-grade students used *Theodore and the Talking Mushroom* (Lionni, 1971). She read the story to the point where Theodore's friends revile him and then asked the children to finish the adventure. Brian wrote the following:

From Theodore the Talking Mushroom *by Leo Lionni.*

Theodore finally stopped in a place called Chicago. There wasn't any trees, just buildings. So Theodore went to explore one of the buildings. He went in a door that said, "Secretary" and found piles of papers and a bird in a cage. He felt sorry for the bird and decided to be its friend. When the lady that was playing with a big machine got done, she left, and Theodore unlocked the bird. Theodore gave him some bird feed but the bird said, "I'm sick of bird feed!" So Theodore got the bird some soda from the soda machine.

Theodore wanted to explore the rest of the city so he said "bye" to the bird and went to explore. Theodore found a smaller building that said Pet Shop. He went in and found a glass box. He went in it and started to run around on a little wheel. Then the lady that was playing the big black machine came in, looked at Theodore and gave another lady some green paper. She took Theodore and the cage and put it by his friend, the bird, and that's where he stayed.

Mike wrote:

Theodore kept running until he ran into a cornfield. One day, while in the cornfield, he heard a whirring noise. All of a sudden, some thrashers missed him by inches! He ran as fast as he could but the thing was too fast. He was swept up and landed in a big pile of corn. He was in the reaper on a tractor. After a while, he was put in a silo to store the corn. He got to the side and found a tunnel leading under the corn. He went in and kept walking. He tried to stop but couldn't. He seemed to be sliding forever. Pretty soon he landed on the bottom with a thump. He had his eyes closed and didn't want to open them. He fell asleep. When he woke, he found a face looking at him. It was another mouse. The mouse ran off and Theodore followed. He didn't walk far when he walked into a mouse living room.

There was a father and mother mouse with five children mice. He instantly liked one of the children that was his age. After a couple of months he got to know her. Her name was Theresa. He asked her father if he could marry her and he said "Yes." They had a beautiful wedding and lived happily ever after.

BECOMING THE CHARACTER

Much literature is written in third person, the voice of the impersonal, all-seeing and all-knowing narrator. You can read such a story to children, and have them rewrite part or all of the tale, recasting it in the more personal first person. The task of writing as if they were one of the characters is an interesting challenge for boys and girls.

Fairy tales work particularly well for this purpose. A sixth-grade teacher read *Cinderella* (Hogrogian, 1981) to her children. Eric retold it in the following way:

Once upon a time there was a young prince. This prince had a little
   boy named Bernard. Bernard wanted to know how his father met
   his mother, Cinderella. So the prince said he would tell him.
"We met at a ball at the castle. Your mother and I danced all
   evening until midnight, when your mother ran off and disap-
   peared."
"Why did Mother run away?" asked Bernard. "Where did she go?"
"Maybe I'd better tell you the story your mother told me about that
   day before the ball. Cinderella lived with her stepmother and two
   stepsisters. They are your grandmother, Phoebe, and your Aunts
   Prunella and Drunella. Years ago, they were unkind to your
   mother and expected her to do all the chores."
"What chores did Mother have to do?" asked Bernard.
"She swept the floors, dusted the rooms, cleaned the fireplace,
   cooked and did the dishes. On that day, years ago, your mother
   had to help Grandmother and your aunts get ready for the big
   ball."
"Was Mother invited to the ball too?" Bernard wanted to know.
"Your mother was invited too, but Grandmother kept her too busy
   to get herself ready to go," said the Prince.
"Mother must have felt sad," said Bernard.
"Yes," said the Prince, "she cried to herself. All of a sudden, there
   appeared in the room, a lovely lady who said she was
   Cinderella's godmother."
"Child," said the godmother, "dry your tears and let's get you ready
   for the ball!"
"Boy, I wish I had a fairy godmother!" said Bernard. "How did she
   get Mother ready in time?"
"She waved her magic wand and changed your mother's ragged,
   dirty dress into a beautiful gold-colored ball gown with a very
   full skirt. On her feet, your mother found she was wearing a pair
   of glass slippers. Cinderella's godmother then changed a pumpkin
   from the garden into a carriage and six mice into white horses. A
   rat became a fat jolly coachman. Your mother was now ready for
   the ball. But her godmother warned her, "Be home by midnight,
   because at that hour, the carriage will become a pumpkin, the
   horses will become mice and the coachman will become a rat."
"That's why Mother ran away so quickly at midnight!" said Bernard.
"Yes, so quickly that she lost one of her slippers, and I realized that
   I did not know the young lady's name," said the prince.
Bernard said, "How did you find her?"
"I sent out my courtier to try the slipper on every young lady in the
   kingdom, until she was found. When he went to your grand-

mother's house, Aunt Prunella and Aunt Drunella tried on the slipper but it did not fit. Cinderella asked to try it on and while your aunts laughed, the courtier slipped the slipper right onto her foot. It fit!"

"What happened next?" Bernard wanted to know.

"Cinderella and I were married soon afterwards here, at the castle," said the prince.

"Did Grandmother, Aunt Prunella and Aunt Drunella come?" asked Bernard.

"Oh my yes, they asked your mother to forgive them and she did. They were at the wedding and so were my parents, your grandfather David and grandmother, Daphane."

"Someday I will become King, and your mother, Queen. When you grow up, you will become King," said the Prince.

"That's a great story, Father. I'm glad I asked," said Bernard.

A teacher of fifth-grade students read *The Sleeping Beauty* (Hyman, 1977). After hearing it, boys and girls retold the story as if they were one of the characters. Leonore wrote:

My story starts out when Queen Isabelle and King George IV had a baby. I am the "Old Fairy" and I wasn't invited to the party.

I knew they wanted a baby badly because I worked for them for ten years. That's where I got my wickedness. In the kitchen where all the herbs and spices were, was that potion. I drank a little and all of a sudden I started turning old. My fingers were wrinkling right in front of my very eyes. And my back started caving in. And my personality turned wicked.

Now I was the "Old Fairy" and none of my sisters liked me. They were very young and beautiful. And when the queen and king didn't invite me to see their daughter, and invited my fairy sisters, I got so mad! I had to think of a mean spell, so I hobbled over to my broomstick and flew off to the castle, with black smoke trailing behind me. On my way to the castle I thought about putting the king and queen's baby to sleep. When I got to the castle, I decided she would fall asleep by pricking her finger on a spinning needle. I announced this to the king and queen in front of the whole court. Everyone was really shocked, but I didn't care. I enjoy being wicked.

A few years later, in one of the old rooms, I was prepared with the spinning needle and everything else. And the child pricked her finger and fell asleep. A few years later, I found out my spell put the whole castle to sleep. Well, I finally did something to spite that old king and queen! And I was glad! My wish came true, everyone fell asleep in the kingdom. Now, that whole dumb castle would be forgotten!

Except for one thing. If a hundred years didn't quite pass by, a

prince could kiss the princess and the whole castle would wake
up. I hope and pray that no prince will see that castle. But no
prince would, it would probably be so covered with moss that no
prince would see it. Anyway, I hope he doesn't.
But one day a prince found that castle, and kissed the princess. But
that wasn't what made me mad. The thing that made me mad
was that my fairy sisters told him where the castle was. Now, I
have to think of a punishment for my fairy sisters!!

In addition to retelling folk tales, Lewis (1979) suggests children write as
if they were a historic explorer. Her statements about the effectiveness of this
type of writing task with second graders challenges long-held beliefs that
young children cannot transcend the here-and-now. Her book is especially
effective in describing the nurturant environment necessary to encourage
very young writers.

Parallel Plot Construction

In this technique, a story with a strong plot pattern is read to children.
Together the class and teacher list the plot elements, stated more generally
than in the story. The elements provide a structure within which children
can work, adding their own details to make a new variation on the model
story. *Periwinkle* (Duvoisin, 1976) provides such a useful structure. After
listening to the story, the children made a list of plot elements. Then Karen
wrote the following account:

Once there was a big hairy lion that was Orangish Yellow. But there
was a small mouse that was all gray. One day this gray mouse
met this big big lion. "Hello, big lion," said the mouse. "Hello,
small mouse," said the lion. "Come to my house for dinner. I'm
always lonely," said the lion. "O.K.," said the mouse. They went
to the lion's house. The lion said, "Here's meat." "I want some
cheese." "I said meat," said the lion. "Well, you are the best
friend I ever had. I guess I'll have meat." "That's fine with me,"
said the lion. Did the mouse like the meat? We never knew.

In *Simon Boom Gives a Wedding* (Suhl, 1973) the main character wants
to have the very best of everything, and that wish leads to disastrous results.
Children were asked to write a story in which a desire for the best (or most)
leads someone into trouble. Rachel, a sixth grader wrote:

Aunt Em lived on a corner street, with a funny little house with no
chimney. She was very picky and just loved furs. So far she had
117 furs. All of them were just perfect. On March 26, she went to

buy her 118th fur. She wanted a calico cat fur. (She didn't like cats very much!) So she decided to go to the fur shop. Well, when she got there, there weren't any calico cat furs. So then she went to the pet shop and bought a calico cat!

On her way home she wore the cat around her neck.

Soon the cat got tired of being wrenched around this lady's neck. So the cat decided to make a big racket, and that's just what she did.

As Aunt Em went down the streets, everyone was staring at her, because of this noise-making cat around her neck. But Aunt Em really thought that everyone was staring at her because of her beautiful fur coat.

That night Aunt Em wore the cat around her neck when she went to see a play at the theater. During Act 2, Aunt Em began to itch. What had happened is that the cat had fleas, which descended on Aunt Em. Soon Aunt Em was howling in misery, she itched so much. Everyone was staring at her. Aunt Em was embarrassed. And to add to everything else, the cat jumped out of Aunt Em's arms and sped across the room and ran away. Everyone soon was chasing the cat. By the end, everyone was pooped.

Aunt Em was furious! However, she began to laugh because it was really funny indeed. Soon everyone was laughing, too. Everyone kept on chasing and chasing the cat. No one could catch her. Finally, somebody caught her. Of all people it was a little boy, who was sucking a green lollipop. Aunt Em took the cat back, and gave the boy a five dollar bill. Then she thanked the boy. Then he left. Then Aunt Em paid for all the damages the cat had done and took the cat home.

Aunt Em didn't care anymore if she had a calico cat fur or not. She just loved her cat, and both of them lived for a long time thereafter.

WRITING FABLES

Using the fable as a literary model can motivate effective writing. Read some fables aloud, perhaps from a fine new collection with impressive full-color illustrations by Holder (1981). Then have children extract the characteristics of this form: fables are short tales featuring animal characters who personify human vices/virtues. The moral of the story is consciously stated. Then have boys and girls write their own fable. Third-graders wrote these:

Once there was a dog. The dog spied a cat. Now this cat was very big and would make a good meal for any dog. The cat was thinking about a mouse she spied. All the sudden the dog ran after the cat. The cat still wanted the mouse so while the cat was being chased by the dog, the mouse was being chased by the cat. There was a lot of rumbling and grumbling. It turned out that nobody got their meal. The moral of the story is that if you want your meal, you better not have your meal have his meal in mind.

Kay

Once upon a time there were two frogs named Bill and Jane. One day Bill invited Jane for lunch and they had fly soup. Every frog just loves fly soup, especially Bill and Jane. It was especially good that day, because the flies were just caught and fresh. After their lunch at Bill's, Jane invited Bill for lunch the next day. They had fly sandwiches which were very good also because Jane's a great cook. The moral of the story is: Treat people how you would like to be treated.

Michelle

CHANGES IN COMPOSITION

The relative importance of creative writing in the schools today can legitimately be questioned. While much has been written about it, even a cursory look at most elementary language arts programs reveals that writing has yet to carve out for itself a significant position in the elementary curriculum (Graves, 1978). Why is this the case?

A look at the history of composition suggests some answers to this question. Early in the 1920s, many writers began to emphasize the need to add writing experiences of a creative nature to the elementary curriculum. One of the first people pointing out this need was Hughes Mearns (1958) in a book which still makes fascinating reading. Mearns's book was the beginning of a whole series of encouraging books by gifted teachers, blessed with insight into the conditions necessary for encouraging children to create and skilled in drawing from children writing of rare insight and beauty.

Generally these early books shared three concerns. They all gave some attention to the *conditions* necessary for encouraging creativity. They addressed themselves to the role of the teacher, to means of stimulating writing, and to practices to be avoided.

Second, these books emphasized the necessity of *accepting* all efforts and encouraging the children. Burrows (1964) in a quotation fairly typical of these writers said:

It follows that because we permit each child to say what he wants to say in his own way, we, for our part, must accept graciously whatever he writes . . . an eager acceptance of their stories . . . we accept them as we would any other gift—with warm appreciation. Criticism is as inappropriate in this situation as it would be at Christmas time.

Third, these writers all agreed on the minimal importance of *mechanics*. The suggestions was that work on skills, punctuation, spelling, or grammatical considerations, must take place in periods separate from creative writing. The feeling is that marking papers for these points will surely destroy any impetus a child has to create.

Sharing these three common concerns, the books also shared a common shortcoming—they did not generally provide for any kind of a *sequential development* in children's writing. The teacher was left with interesting ideas, which when used often resulted in evoking creative expression. Basically there was one element missing—a progression or sequence of development. That is, though a child's writing may have improved in some ways, perhaps due to maturity, there was little or no discernible improvement because of the program itself. As a result, the teacher garnered occasional pieces of genuine beauty but could see no observable growth toward writing power.

This may be one reason creative writing has remained a stepchild in the curriculum: a pleasant endeavor of interest to both the teacher and child, but not a central concern.

A NEWER APPROACH

Within the last few years composition has been taking a new direction. This new direction results from the uncomfortable awareness of many adults

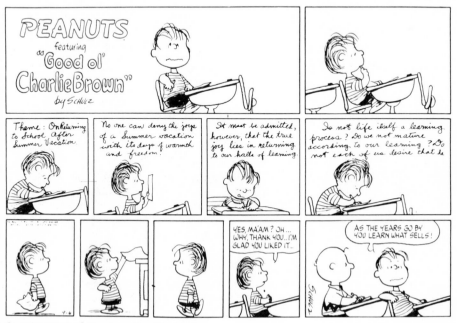

© 1970 United Feature Syndicate, Inc.

that, although many children have had some experience with composition as part of the language arts curriculum, all too few write well as a result. Indeed, as Hochstetler (1971) says so emphatically, far too many children: ". . . reach sixth-grade level without being able to construct good clear sentences either orally or in writing. What is probably more detrimental to the . . . expression is his inability to examine and edit his sentences critically."

Evans's article is a succinct and forceful statement of the need for a planned program to develop writing skills.[10] When talking about skills he is not concerned primarily with the basic mechanics of punctuation, grammar, and syntax, but rather with developing in children the ability to write tellingly about what they have observed carefully. While he does not in the confines of this short article describe the exact nature of the organized writing program he advocates, his plea for consciously teaching children how to observe, write, and rewrite is a compelling one.

Two other authors have expanded their ideas into a sequential program. Moffett and Wagner (1976), in an excitingly different book, have challenged readers to rebuild the language arts curriculum around writing. They believe children should observe keenly, describe analytically, and revise critically. In addition, they write convincingly of children's ability to work in small groups as they help each other edit, to a more extensive degree than is usually the case. These authors make a clear distinction between editing and correcting, which is helpful to teachers trying to experiment with this approach.

The basic problem involved is that so far no generally agreed-upon sequence of writing skills to be mastered at the elementary level has been identified. People in mathematics and music education, for example, have identified quite definitely the specific skills and their order of acquisition. In language arts, skills in spelling and handwriting have also been ordered sequentially. Such ordering is rare in creative writing, though the writings mentioned here begin such a task.

Actually, the foregoing dichotomy between free and more structured approaches to imaginative writing is an artificial one, set up primarily to throw into relief the distinguishing characteristics of each point of view. It is possible to take the best of each approach and weld them into a richer experience than either would provide alone. It seems apparent that neither provides a completely satisfactory approach, but together they provide a means of improving the composition program.

---

[10]Robert Evans, "A Glove Thrown Down," *Elementary English*, May 1967, 523–527. The author points out the fallacy of assuming that children can write significant prose without direct instruction and makes a convincing argument for structuring beginning writing experiences around careful observation of objects.

Teachers as Writers

There is a growing feeling that at times it is important for teachers to write along with the children.[11] This accomplishes two purposes. First, it shows children that the teacher values composition. As the class—and the teacher—write, children can see that the teacher feels the task is important enough for him or her to participate. Second, such participation allows teachers to assess the difficulty level of the assignment. Often teachers may tend to assign tasks they themselves would never have attempted. Actually trying something themselves that they have asked children to do provides valuable information about the validity and difficulty of the task.

EDITING AND CORRECTING

To understand this new approach to writing, the teacher must understand a fundamental but often overlooked distinction between two terms: *editing* and *correcting*.

It is safe to say that most of what happens to writing after the first draft falls into the category of correcting. For far too many children, writing is a two-step process—creating or setting the ideas down and correcting or repairing the way these ideas look on paper. Thoughtful teachers have long been aware that such attention to the mechanics of proper punctuation, spelling, and even more sophisticated matters as phrase relationships, seems to have one effect: it discourages pupils from wanting to write more (Tway, 1980). Studies have shown empirically what some teachers have known intuitively for years: the more emphasis is placed on mechanics or correcting, to use our term, the less writing may ensue. The increasing concern over "basics" on the part of parents, intensifies the problem.

This places the teacher in a dilemma: How to encourage writing that abounds in creative, vigorous ideas, and yet which presents the ideas in a form that communicates well? The skillful teacher knows that giving back papers to be corrected should occur as an option for those children who receive satisfaction from seeing papers displayed in the room or around the school. Naturally if they wish such pleasure—and children can understand this—then they must do their potential reader the favor of putting the writing into standard English, or risk remaining unread (Horn, 1974).

The skilled teacher also knows, however, that there are myriad ways writing can legitimately be improved, through expanding or clarifying the

---

[11]A major part of the Bay Area Writing Project involves teachers in writing themselves. One of the responses to national concern over children's lack of composition ability, the project is training teachers to be better at teaching composition. A report about the project is included in "How to Improve Student Writing," by Shirley Boes Neil in *American Education*, October 1976, 6–12.

thought expressed. We call this process *editing*. Undoubtedly the most complete and definite statement about editing has been given by Moffett and Wagner (1976), who place creative writing at the very core of the language arts program. In their book, creative writing *is* the language program, to oversimplify a bit. While such emphasis on writing is interesting, such a curriculum in language arts may not be possible for most teachers. If, as a teacher, you are not comfortable with such a single-minded position, perhaps the materials in this chapter will give you some ideas about how composition can be a more vital part of the language arts program. Considerable time will be spent on editing because of its importance in the writing process.

Whenever a child has written something, it can probably stand some editing. Note please that the previous sentence does not read "should be edited." There is a vast difference between pieces that *can* be edited (all writing, at all times) and those pieces that *should* be edited (some writing, sometimes). It is the fine discernment in telling when and how which cannot be legislated.

What do we mean by editing? Very precisely, we mean changing, altering, adapting, adding to, or taking away from what was originally there. We mean revising, reshaping, relocating, and redoing in order to say more exactly what we wanted to say originally.

Teacher advocates of this process approach to writing have students compose regularly. The writing is filed in a manila folder, one for each child writer. At intervals, the teacher asks boys and girls to select one piece from their folder which they would like to bring to finished form. Then teacher and child can edit the work. To sustain interest in revision, the piece of writing needs to be important to the student (Kirby & Liner, 1980). During the writing conference, children can be led to ask themselves some questions.

1. Which of my sentences say what I want to say the "best" way they can? Are there some which don't really say anything at all? Are there places I've expected a reader to jump wider gaps in action than anyone can safely jump? Is there a way I can rearrange my sentence to make it more interesting (funny, engaging, descriptive, unexpected, shorter, longer, tanatalizing)?[12]

2. Are there words in my story which need to be made stronger? For example, *nice*, that pale modern-day descendant of the vigorous Middle English adjective meaning wanton, is now so anemic it can seldom hold its own in a sentence. Children can be helped to see that many words need to be weeded out of their writing vocabulary because they are today too feeble to be effective.

3. Is there anything in my story as a whole that (a) needs to be somewhere else or (b) doesn't need to be included at all? In this, of course, one is trying

---

[12]The materials in *Language Explorations for the Elementary Grades* (A Curriculum for English) (Lincoln: The University of Nebraska Press, 1966) are particularly helpful in developing this sense of how sentences can be edited.

to get children to do basic plot revision, to think about what happened to whom, when, and why.

All of this is so different from the usually rather picky insistence on mechanics. It is quite unlike the too frequent harping about, for instance, agreement of verb tense with subject (which incidentally is more profitably approached from the point of view of the thoughts expressed than from the side of "correctness" or rules). It is also so different from asking children to follow through such uninspired activities in a language arts book as asking them to pick out the "best" topic sentence, an uncertain task at best.

What we are asking children to do is to step back from their work, take a hard look at it, and then impartially make some value judgments about its quality. This is, as anyone who has ever attempted it knows, an exceedingly difficult task. It is, however, one which in the long run proves to be worth the time expended on it. The teacher should realize that this ability develops slowly over a long period of time. If you want to develop the ability in a group which has never worked this way before, it may well take an entire year to bring children to the point of achieving the objectivity necessary for successful editing.

The teacher, thus, is aware of the goal—stimulating children to write more—and it is only by writing and then editing that children learn to write more effectively.

This editing procedure is more important than mechanical correctness in creative writing, and profits from the teaching of specific mechanical skills, which is done when children are engaged in practical writing. That is, having received specific, organized, and sequential exposure to the mechanical skills in the other segment of their writing program, children are able to use these skills as they compose. Techniques for teaching such skills will be discussed later.

EVALUATING CREATIVE WRITING

Three types of evaluation need to be considered: (1) the children evaluating their work, (2) the teacher evaluating children's work, and (3) the teacher evaluating his or her own work. Whether the teacher prefers having children work at editing alone or in groups, this procedure leads naturally into evaluation. Children evaluating their own work is listed first because it is the most important type of evaluation. This type is closest to the way adult writers work. Writers seldom rely mainly on extrinsic evaluation but, as is the case with other creative people, rely primarily on their own intrinsic evaluation of their work. This is not to deny the importance of such people as editors in helping writers examine their work, but simply to say that the major evaluative effort rests with the creator.

Our job then is to help children learn to evaluate their own work. Basically, this is what the series of questions below is designed to do.

The term *evaluation* suggests an extensive procedure taking place over a period of time. This is facilitated by having children keep a folder of their work so they can evaluate at intervals the progress they have made. If the teacher encourages children to keep samples of writing, he or she can have individual conferences with children in which they evaluate their writing.[13]

In reviewing a child's creative writing, the teacher can help the young author think about the following questions:

Questions Related to the Plot

1. Are the ideas in my stories becoming more interesting? Am I learning to make things happen sequentially so the reader can follow easily?
2. Am I learning how to make plots go in more than one direction? Can I sometimes start at the end of my story and work backward, or in the middle and go in both directions, instead of always having to start at the beginning and work toward the end?
3. Am I learning how to write different kinds of plots including both realistic and fantasy ones? Am I learning how to write plots which both boys and girls find interesting?

Questions Related to Characterization

1. Do my stories show I am learning how to write about a variety of people?
2. Are my people becoming more believable? Do they do and say things which *might* happen within the confines of my story as I've written it?
3. Am I improving in my ability to make people more real? Do the details I include seem to make the people alive, rather than flat like silhouettes?
4. Do I ever try to personify something? Can I convincingly make something inanimate come to life?

Questions Related to Setting

1. Am I improving in my ability to look at some object and write a clear, concise description that will share my impressions with a reader?
2. Am I becoming able to combine descriptions of several objects into a unified paragraph that helps my story?
3. If I write made-up descriptions, are they getting better at making a reader "see" the objects or situation I am describing?

---

[13]The suggestion is made in "How to Help Your Child Become a Better Writer," Suggestions for Parents, a pamphlet available from the National Council of Teachers of English (1111 Kenyon Road, Urbana, Ill. 61801), n.d. This inexpensive pamphlet can be made available at the beginning of a school year to explain the writing program.

4. Am I developing the ability to reread what I have written and to eliminate detail that I may like but which doesn't help my story?

The teacher makes use of some of the above questions during editing conferences with the children. It is not necessary to use all all of these, or to use them in the order presented (King et al., 1973). In addition, further questions need to be written for *mood* in the story, *climax* and conclusion in the story, and *conversation* in the story.

As teachers help children evaluate their own work, they are also

Children write about experiences they know first-hand. This is a page from Gripping Tales of Living with Seizures, *a book written by epileptic children.*

243

evaluating so they can decide which children need further work in specific writing skills (Searle & Dillon, 1980). These conferences are used to determine which children need to be grouped for more experiences, in a group working on description, for instance. A review of a child's work may indicate that the child doesn't need further work on description but does need further work on plot or dialogue. Thus, the teacher, in addition to using the conferences as a time to help children evaluate their own work, also uses them as a time to determine what the child needs to do next.

The teacher also uses the conferences as a way of evaluating his or her own work, to assess strengths and weaknesses of the composition program as a whole. If few children can write convincing dialogue, planning of the program must have been weak in that area. If many children are able to write convincing climaxes and conclusions, the teacher can shift focus to emphasize some other aspect of writing. Therefore, while the major purpose of conferences is to help children develop the power to analyze their own work, they also are a technique for evaluating teacher effectiveness.

If teachers find it difficult to schedule time for individual conferences with each child, "person-to-person" contact can be increased by cassette tapes. The teacher can read the student writing, and comment orally on the tape, which can be listened to any time the child writer has free time (Murray, 1974).

PUBLISHING WRITING

One way to help children share their writing is by seeking nationally distributed, commercial publication of their writing. While this is clearly not an avenue available to, or desirable for, all students, it is a distinct possibility for those with exceptional talent. *Stone Soup, the magazine by children*,[14] is published in a pleasant, small format which features typeset stories and drawings by boys and girls. Wide margins and large type make the stories look good. The publishers also issue *The Editor's Notebook*, a companion volume providing suggestions about ways to use the magazine as a basis for a comprehensive writing and art program.

CHILDREN AND LITERARY FORMS

Related to the idea of a structured and sequential program is the thought that children can and should be taught to write specific literary forms.

One of the most accessible of these is the *simile*, because making comparisons using the terms *like* or *as* is relatively simple. Many language arts books teach this form to children.[15]

---

[14]Published five times a year by the Children's Art Foundation (126 Otis St., Santa Cruz, CA 95060).

[15]See, for example, Mildred A. Dawson et al., *Language for Daily Use*, Book 5, pp. 258–259; David A. Conlin et al., *Our Language Today*, Book 6, pp. 78–82; Ken Johnson et al., *Language*, Book 6, pp. 127–128; Harold Cafone et al., *Language Skills and Use*, Book 5, 100–103.

One easy way to teach this idea is by using an audiovisual approach. We have had singular success by using the text, *A Picture Has a Special Look*.[16] Though originally intended to sensitize children to a variety of art media and their distinctive characteristics, this text is written using many similes. The available film strip is used as motivation, followed by a discussion of the author's similes. To follow up, a record about similes is used.[17] Some third-grade children recently created the following similes after this introductory motivation:

1. as simple as	writing *a* an egg pulling grass
2. as tight as	a belt that is too small for you shrunk pants
3. as thin as	the letter i a stamp
4. as mean as	a horse that kicks
5. as small as	plankton
6. as stupid as	a potato

This motivation seems effective at all levels. Recently college juniors in a language arts methods class, trying the motivation themselves before using it with children, wrote the following:

As misunderstood as a cat in a fishbowl.
As disappointing as an empty mailbox.
A character as fake as a frozen TV dinner.
As definite as a little boy with his first tricycle.
As simple as a bald head.
As promising as a bag of jelly beans.
As busy as an electric typewriter.

Another form children can learn to write is the *metaphor*, although this is a bit more difficult because the comparison is not directly stated.[18] An article by Stewig (1966) may offer some helpful suggestions when you motivate children to write metaphors.

---

[16]Helen Borton, *A Picture Has a Special Look* (New York: Abelard-Schuman, 1961). This is also available as a filmstrip-record combination (SF-54C) from Weston Woods Studios.

[17]Use #9, "Metaphors and Similes—Imagery!" from the record and filmstrip set, *What Is Poetry*, CFS-501, available from Coronet Instructional Media.

[18]Some elementary language series attempt to help children with this idea. See, for example, Mildred A. Dawson et al., *Language for Daily Use*, Book 5, pp. 260–261, 280; Eric P. Hamp et al., *Language Basics Plus*, Book 6, pp. 268–269; Ken Johnson et al., *Language*, Book 5, pp. 103–105.

Lena's Poem

I don't have any pets –
But
I want to pretend,
when I bring one home
then I'll have a pet –
then I'll have a cat
and a dog!

Yaron's Poem

My mom and dad and I
went somewhere –
there was a cat
by my window.
My dad saw it and yelled.
It wasn't listening –
It just sat right there!

The cat woke me up
last nite –
I didn't scream about it,
I just dreamed about pets.
It was a terrible dream.

POETRY

Poetry writing presents a unique problem for teachers, for as Gooch (1974) says: "There seem to be more students with antipathy to poetry than there are with a dislike of drama, short stories, and novels." This is a strange phenomenon, for when young children come to nursery school or kindergarten, most respond enthusiastically to Mother Goose rhymes. Somewhere before they leave sixth grade too many children develop an antipathy to poetry (Stewig, 1980).

Some teachers have found that helping children write unrhymed poetry maintains interest in the form. Freed of the constraints of rhyme, many children can express their ideas in the succinct form characteristic of poetry. One teacher of five- through seven-year olds read them much unrhymed poetry. Children then dictated the following:

Mirror

I see myself in the mirror.
I pretend that there is another
    person in the back.
She looks at me
    and sees me.
Maybe she wants to get
    out.
if I could.

Krissy

To a Cheetah

I'll get you a job, Cheetah.
Do you see?
You will guard me.
You will keep me young
    and beautiful.
Oh, so beautiful.
Do you see, Cheetah?

Anne

246

By the way in which she arranged their dictated language on the paper, this teacher emphasized that poems have a different form than other writing.

Teachers of older students have used *haiku* as a motivation for children to write their own.[19] With practice, fourth-graders wrote these:

Sailing above the clouds,
Soaring so very lightly,
Is a tiny bird.

Laurie

The lion is full
He had some deer for supper
He will go to sleep.

Jeri

Cinquain is another commonly taught form (Livingston, 1975, 1976). Cinquain is a five-line form with a 2, 4, 6, 8, 2, syllable pattern. Seventh-grade students wrote the following:

Growing
Isn't it great?
Sprouting like many weeds,
Catching up to your parents' size.
It's great!

Tim

People
Frightened of things,
Do not know what to do,
Scatter around like litter
Turmoil.

Lonny

Words, a 1977 film from Churchill Films, shows third- and fourth-grade students composing a group cinquain, and then saying it together chorally.

You might involve older students in writing nursery rhymes, which can then be shared with younger listeners in the school. Some seventh-graders of limited language ability wrote the following based on the pattern of "Little Miss Muffet:"

Scared Tommy Snyder
saw a black spider,
creeping on down the hall;
Tommy turned off the light
The spider screamed with fright,
And then he ran into the wall.

Sheryl

Littel Mel cood'nt spel
his teecher coodnt ether.
They listened to birds and
learned all the words,
and Mel became an opera
singer.

Don

There have been many periodical articles describing approaches to writing haiku, sijo, cinquain, and diamante. These are often written by classroom teachers reporting on successes they have had, and so they generally are very helpful and need no further word of explanation here. Several are included in the chapter bibliography.

---

[19]See the filmstrip-tape, "Writing Haiku and Other Short Poetry—Elementary," #10-AR-7, Educational Activities, Inc., Freeport, NY 11520.

```
IFLAGFLAGFLAGFLAG
IFLAGFLAGFLAGFLAG
IFLAGFLAGFLAGFLAG
IFLAGFLAGFLAGFLAG
II
II
II
II
II
II
II                        SHIPSHIPS
II                        HIPSHIPSH
II                        IPSHIPSHI            SHIPSHI
II                        PSHIPSHIP            PSHIPSH
II                        SHIPSHIPS            IPSHIPS
II                        HIPSHIPSH            HIPSHIP
II                        IPSHIPSHI            SHIPSHI
II                        BOATBOATBOATBOATBOATBOATBOATBOAT
II                        BOATBOATBOATBOATBOATBOATBOATBOAT
II                        BOATBOATBOATBOATBOATBOATBOATBOAT
II                        YACHTYACHTYACHTYACHTYACHTYACHTYACHTYACHT
II                        YACHTYACHTYACHTYACHTYACHTYACHTYACHTYACHT
II                        YACHTYACHTYACHTYACHTYACHTYACHTYACHTYACHT
II              VESSELVESSELVESSELVESSELVESSELVESSELVESSELVESSEL
II              VESSELVESSELVESSELVESSELVESSELVESSELVESSELVESSEL
STEAMERSTEAMERSTEAMERSTEAMERSTEAMERSTEAMERSTEAMERSTEAMERSTEAMERSTEAM
SAILBOATSAILBOATSAILBOATSAILBOATSAILBOATSAILBOATSAILBOATSAILBOATSAI
CANOECANOECANOECANOECANOECANOECANOECANOECANOECANOECANOECANOECANOE
 OCEANLINEROCEANLINEROCEANLINEROCEANLINEROCEANLINEROCEANLINEROCEANLI
 ROWBOATROWBOATROWBOATROWBOATROWBOATROWBOATROWBOATROWBOATROWB
 AIRCRAFTCARRIERAIRCRAFTCARRIERAIRCRAFTCARRIERAIRCRAFTCARRIER
 CORYDORYDORYDORYDORYDORYDORYDORYDORYDORYDORYDORYDORYDORY
////////////////////////////////////////////////////////////////////
WWWWWWWWWWWWWWWWWWWWWWWWWWWWWWWWWWWWWWWWWWWWWWWWWWWWWWWWWWWWWWWWWWWWWW
AAAAAAAAAAAAAAAAAAAAAAAAAAAAAAAAAAAAAAAAAAAAAAAAAAAAAAAAAAAAAAAAAAAA
VVVVVVVVVVVVVVVVVVVVVVVVVVVVVVVVVVVVVVVVVVVVVVVVVVVVVVVVVVVVVVVVVVVVV
EEEEEEEEEEEEEEEEEEEEEEEEEEEEEEEEEEEEEEEEEEEEEEEEEEEEEEEEEEEEEEEEEEEE
SSSSSSSSSSSSSSSSSSSSSSSSSSSSSSSSSSSSSSSSSSSSSSSSSSSSSSSSSSSSSSSSSSSS
```

This sample of concrete poetry is made from all of the different words for ship. *It will help the child coordinate his or her typing, learn new words, and watch spelling.*

SUMMARY

Recently many writers have focused attention on early writing; this chapter opened with a description of ways to set an environment for young children that motivates them to write. Imaginative writing is frequently a response to the senses. Wordless books and writing about films are responses to visual stimuli; other writing problems can be devised based on the other senses. Reading to children provides literary input that influences the understanding of form. In addition, literature can be a base for writing experiences, and the chapter suggests particular books to use. Other composition techniques include translating a story from third- to first-person narration, adding a character, writing another adventure, and parallel plot construction. The section on imaginative writing closes with a distinction between editing, or rearranging content and correcting, or repairing mechanics. Finally, evaluation questions to help the teacher and child writers were suggested.

Suggestions for Further Exploration

1. Obtain some samples of children's stories. In each case, try to determine which aspects of the story need the kind of editing described in this chapter. Remember it is crucial to pick the elements *most* in need of attention: belaboring the details in one piece of writing too extensively can cause children to lose interest.
2. Select a motivation of your own in one of the five sense categories mentioned. Plan carefully the questions you will ask to encourage children to think about the motivation. Make sure the majority of the questions are open-ended ones which will allow for a wide variety of responses. If possible, use the motivation with a group of children to determine the effectiveness of your questions.
3. A good way to understand the difficulties inherent in any art form is to try doing it yourself. Study the materials available about some of the structured poetry forms, and then try to write some poems yourself. After you have done this, analyze the difficulties you encountered. How does being aware of your own difficulties change the way you would approach these forms with children?
4. Gather a collection of unrhymed poetry to use with children. Try to find poems of this type at different levels of complexity, appropriate for use at different ages. This is important because children too frequently feel that to be poetry, writing must rhyme. Most poetry writing is bad because of this idea.
5. To develop the ability to write convincing details and description (created as opposed to observed) take a myth you find interesting and develop it into a fully detailed story. Expand the setting, plot, and characters, trying to retain the essence of the original.
6. Take any story which includes several characters. Mary Norton's *Bed-Knob and Broomstick* (New York: Harcourt, Brace, 1957) is a good example. If you have access to a group of children, share the story with them, and then let them choose which character they would like to be. Let them rewrite an episode in the story from that character's point of view.

Suggestions for Further Reading

INEXPENSIVE PAPERBACKS ABOUT CHILDREN'S WRITING

Many people have written about children's composition. The following paperbacks are recommended:

Applegate, Maurie. *When the Teacher Says Write a Poem.* New York: Harper & Row, 1965.

The potential audience for this book is junior high school students, and Applegate's argument is that "poetry is for you." The sections on rhythm, and the pictorial nature of poetry are especially good. Though designed for an older age group, the book has many ideas of interest to elementary teachers.

Applegate, Maurie. *When the Teacher Says Write a Story.* New York: Harper & Row, 1965.

Written in Applegate's usual evocative style, this book includes both adult and children's writing in copious amounts. Particularly useful is the chapter on character development and the section on checking writing before considering it finished.

Arnstein, Flora J. *Children Write Poetry: A Creative Approach.* Dover, N.Y.: Dover Publications, 1967.

The author reports on many years of experience sharing poetry and helping children write it. She deals deftly with the problem of the ideas children develop about themselves which interfere with creative expression. A good section is included on helping children evaluate their own standards, both for their writing and their adult poetry.

Arnstein, Flora J. *Poetry in the Elementary Classroom.* New York: Appleton-Century-Crofts, 1962.

Suggestions on how to interest children in poetry, to encourage poetry writing, and to compensate for inadequate backgrounds in poetry are designed to bolster teachers' confidence in their ability to handle this topic. Includes many examples of poems written by children.

Burrows, A.T. et al. *They All Want to Write: Written English in the Elementary Classroom.* New York: Holt, Rinehart and Winston, 1965.

This older book, frequently updated because its message is so basic and fresh, reports the work of four teachers who concerned themselves with writing before it became generally accepted in the elementary curriculum. A concern for the mental health of children and the release which creative writing can provide permeates the book.

Carlson, Ruth K. *Sparkling Words.* Paladin House Publishers. Available from the National Council of Teachers of English, Urbana, Il., 1979.

The author deals with fostering divergent thinking creative approaches to poetry writing. Most of the approaches recommended have grown out of classroom teachers' experimentations.

Carlson, Ruth K. *Writing Aids through the Grades.* New York: Teacher's College Press, 1970.

The author provides valuable help in getting and keeping the flow of expression going through motivations keyed to children's own personal experiences—and suggests ways to overcome the difficulties of grammar, structure, and spelling without stopping the creative flow.

Clay, Marie M. *What Did I Write?* Auckland, N.Z.: Heinemann Educational Books, 1975.

Despite the title, the book is not about handwriting. Rather, it describes some of the insights children gain during first contacts with written language. Many examples in the text illuminate points at which children may be confused by the system of English orthography. Clear reproductions of children's actual first attempts at writing illustrate (in Chapter 3) six concepts the author finds prevalent in most early attempts to encode thoughts. The author follows the development of young children from first attempts at making individual letters through phrase and sentence making. One of the most useful sections is Chapter 7, "Application," which draws implications of this informal and observational research for classroom practice. There is a list of references, and the index makes rereading by topic easy.

Cassedy, Sylvia. *In Your Own Words. A Beginner's Guide to Writing.* Garden City, N.Y.: Doubleday and Co., Inc., 1979.

The author, herself a published writer of books for children, here presents a comprehensive look at the writing process. After introductory chapters on observation skills drawing from sensory input, the book is divided into two major sections, prose and poetry. In the prose section, she deals with both genre (myths) and literary elements (characterization); the same genre (haiku) and elements (rhythm) approach is carried through the second section. The writing is spritely and humorous. The book is laced with myriad examples from famous writers, and others made up by Cassedy to illustrate specific points she is making. A must read for students interested in writing!

Glaus, Marlene. *From Thoughts to Words.* Champaign, Ill.: National Council of Teachers of English, 1965.

Another book of ideas compiled by a classroom teacher, these enrichment activities stimulate an interest in language. The first section encourages observation in a variety of situations, the second concentrates on word activities and a third presents ways of introducing children to authors.

Henderson, Harold G. *Haiku in English.* Champaign, Ill.: National Council of Teachers of English, 1967.

The author's modestly sized volume is illustrated throughout with tasteful black and white drawings. Henderson begins with a lucid explanation of Japanese Haiku, and another chapter of English Haiku presents a clear contrast. Teachers will find the chapter on how to teach Haiku particularly helpful, as much because of the sample poems as for the clear and easy to follow instructions.

Jackson, Jacqueline. *Turn Not Pale, Beloved Snail: A Book about Writing among Other Things.* Boston: Little, Brown and Co., 1974.

The author suggests a variety of approaches to learning to write, and uses excerpts from her own writing, and that of her children, to make her point. Her approach is humorous and anecdotal. The book is full of commonsense ways to turn an informal urge to write into writing.

Leavitt, Hart Day and Sohn, D. *Stop, Look and Write.* New York: Pathfinder-Bantam, 1964.

A book of black-and-white photographs divided into twenty sections, each of them prefaced by comments directed to the high school students for whom it was originally intended. Described by the authors as a "beginner's course in how to see," the book provides a wealth of photographs of use to the elementary teacher.

Mearns, Hughes. *Creative Power: The Education of Youth in the Creative Arts.* Dover, N.Y.: Dover Publications, 1958.

This reprint of the original edition (1929) details the author's innovative work many years ago at Columbia University; an amazingly fresh treatment of writing poetry, plays, and other creative expression. Mearns brings a truly gifted insight into children's potential to create, and his book is inspiring encouragement to all who want to do likewise.

Petty, Walter T. *Slithery Snakes and Other Aids to Children's Writing*. New York: Appleton-Century-Crofts, 1970.

The contents are as useful as the title is catchy. Chapters on building blocks and on tools of the trade are full of useful ideas. The authors deal with transforming and combining at the sentence level, and with larger forms, including poetry.

Smith, James A. *Creative Teaching of the Language Arts in the Elementary School*. Boston: Allyn & Bacon, 1973.

Smith's book (from a series of seven devoted to all curricular areas) is primarily a handbook of techniques, which includes many examples written by students. The list of ways to motivate children, the section on judging quality in writing, and the material about using questions are particularly helpful.

Stegall, Carrie. *The Adventures of Brown Sugar: Adventures in Creative Writing*. Champaign, Ill.: National Council of Teachers of English, 1967.

A spritely account of the skills pupils encounter with creative writing on an extended basis—from the moment the idea of their book was conceived, through the many sessions of learning skills, to the final culmination in their own book. A delightfully encouraging account of how an insightful teacher can make language arts live.

Studacher, Carol. *Creating Writing in the Classroom*. Palo Alto, Calif.: Fearon Publishers, 1968.

Practical suggestions and procedures for enriching the creative climate of the classroom. There are chapters on description, writing stories and poetry, creative writing projects, and setting and maintaining the creative climate. Methods applicable to students at all levels of achievement in the elementary grades are included, as well as many examples of student writing.

Wolsch, Robert A. *Poetic Composition in the Elementary School: A Language Sensitivity Program for Teachers*. New York: Teachers College Press, 1970.

A language arts consultant encourages the teaching of poetic composition as a means of developing the whole child, because writing poetry heightens children's awareness of themselves, their surroundings, and their language. The author reports his own experiences with children. This is a much-needed guide for elementary teachers.

PERIODICAL BIBLIOGRAPHY

Ackerlund, Sylvia. "Poetry in the Elementary School." *Elementary English*, 47(5) (May 1969): 583–587.

The author stresses the necessity of including poetry in the language arts program and offers suggestions on how to teach poetry more effectively. Included are such ideas as relating poetry to classroom situations, using poems for pantomime and dramatization, and encouraging children to write their own poems.

Allen, R. Van. "Let Not Young Souls Be Smothered Out. . . ." *Childhood Education* 44 (February 1969): 354–357.

Creative writing experiences help children realize no one else can really say what they themselves want to say. Each child should be allowed to develop his or her own style of expression. Writing can develop imagination, build self-confidence, provide for emotional expression, develop the aesthetic sense, deepen appreciation of other people, and bring balance to educational activities.

Dearmin, Jennie T. "Teaching Your Children to Paint Pictures with Words." *Grade Teacher* (March 1965): 26–27.

The article relates the experiences of a teacher in using the cinquain form with her fourth- and sixth-grade children. This brief report, dealing with what the author calls a "dwarf poetry" form, is nonetheless sufficient to whet the appetite of a teacher interested in motivating his children to write this type of poetry.

Freeman, Jayne. "Elementary Classroom Editing Groups." *Teacher* (October 1979): 77.

The author uses "editing groups" in her fourth-grade classroom. Students can be very effective teachers of other students, and using peer groups provides for a positive feeling toward writing. Peer-group reinforcement and interaction appear to be more effective than teachers' corrections of grammatical errors and vocabulary use. First, the teacher demonstrates the entire editing process by choosing one student's writing for examination by the class. The teacher also discusses positive behavior techniques to be used in the groups, as well as a code for correcting papers. After studying corrections, all students copy the story correctly. Next, the teacher assigns students to groups in which they will meet after they have written. In the groups the student's task is to find errors and give suggestions for improvement. Freeman feels students "accept responsibility for the quality of their work" with this technique.

Gamble, Linda B. "'Speaking' Creative Languages." *Teacher* (November 1978): 88, 90, 92.

Group composition of poetry is the central core of a multifaceted approach described by this first grade teacher/author. After listening to nonsense and rhythmic poetry, the author then has children do a class cinquain. Having composed orally, the children then do an individual written poem. After that, each child recommunicates the message of his or her poem in another "language." Choosing art, movement, music, or dance, the child translates the original message into another form.

Glickman, Janet. "A First Grade Haiku Project." *Elementary English* 47 (February 1970): 265–266.

Simple in form and direct in thought, Haiku, the old Japanese poetry form, requires that children be very exact in what they are saying. The article relates a beginning attempt that integrated art and oral language using this form in the first grade.

Hopkins, Lee Bennett. "Two Creative Verse Forms." *Instructor* 78 (March 1969): 76–77.

The *Sijo* poetic form was produced by the Yi Dynasty of Korea in the fourteenth century. In English translation it is written in six short lines, each line containing seven to eight syllables, for a total of forty-eight syllables. The first part of the word *cinquain* means the number five in French and Spanish. This refers to its five lines. Each has a specific number of syllables and a specific purpose. The author offers suggestions for how to teach these forms to children.

Reisberg, Carol L. "Poetry Cards." *Media and Methods* (November 1978): 45–47.

This technique for analyzing the words and images of a poem "provides an opportunity not only for students to appreciate why a poem was written the way it was, but also to exercise their own poetic skills by exploring other words and images that may have been used." The teacher chooses a poem and deletes a certain number of nouns, verbs, and adjectives. Packets of cards consist of words deleted from the poem and alternate choices. The students, working in groups, choose words to complete the poem, share each group's choices, vote on the best one, and compare their poems with the original. This technique provides an exciting way to see how parts of speech function in a line of poetry, how words color each other, how images are created, and even how a poet thinks.

Shapiro, Phyllis P. "The Language of Poetry." *Elementary School Journal* 70(3) (December 1969): 130–133.

The author speaks of poetry as an experience and suggests ways the reader may gain the most from experiences with poetry. She also stresses the important use of sound and meter in poems as compared to their use in normal language communication.

Sharples, Derek. "The Content of Creative Writing." *Elementary School Journal* 68(8) (May 1968): 419–426.

The article deals with the question of how creative writing should be judged. Sharples states that since judgment must stem from individual development, the degree of progress made in creative writing must be based on the child's previous performance. He also suggests that the teacher must present the stimuli to encourage the child to make this progress.

True, Sally R. "Sijo." *Elementary English* 42(3) (March 1966): 245–246.

This article introduces the Korean poem form, the Sijo. In English translation Sijo is a six-line, nonrhyming poem dealing with deep thought and revealing emotions. This is done mainly by using such contrasts as sun to rain, mountains to water, or earth to sky. The teachers who introduces Sijo to students will not only be sharing the beauty of nonrhyming poems, but also encouraging children to use nature symbolism.

AN INTEGRATED LANGUAGE ARTS UNIT

by Carolyn Holland
Klondike Elementary School
West Lafayette, Indiana

With a great deal of enthusiasm for audiovisual techniques I plunged wholeheartedly into a project that turned out to be a wonderful learning experience for all involved.

My student teaching was in a departmentalized situation in which my cooperating teacher and I taught reading and language arts to three classes of fifth-graders. Each group spent half the period reading and working in an individualized reading program. The other half was devoted to language arts, and this was my focus.

My supervising teacher gave me *The Lion, the Witch, and the Wardrobe* by C.S. Lewis, with the suggestion that I use it as the core of my language arts instruction for the next eight weeks. I was free to design the unit in any way I felt would make it easier to teach.

After reading the book, I decided the story would lend itself well to condensation, and that the children could probably take the main idea from each chapter and make a poem of it, carrying the thread of action from stanza to stanza. Each class would compose its own version, and the resulting narrative poem would then furnish us with a script. This would be taped by the children and illustrated with a slide set.

Since there were three groups of children involved, I decided to use three different mediums for the pictures so that I could have the varied experience, and so that there would be a basis for comparison of the techniques. One group posed in living pictures for their slides, the second made paper bag puppets, and the third used magazine pictures and original art to illustrate their poem.

It was an ambitious project, so I allowed the plan enough flexibility to change and grow with classroom developments.

BUILDING INTEREST IN POETRY

I had selected poetry as the device to use in the project, so my first step was to stimulate interest in poetry—in reading it, writing it, listening to it. I put up a brightly colored bulletin board using poetry books from the library. These were carefully chosen for their splashy pictures, shortness of verse, and clarity of thought. The books were opened out flat and secured to the bulletin board in random fashion. The object was to get the children to stop and look at the illustrations and see that much indeed can be said in just one line. A sign on the board read, "What Is a Poem. . . .?"

To supplement this, other interest centers were set up. On the windowsill we made a collection of poetry books, started with volumes from the library. Before long, the children were bringing their own favorite poetry books to share with classmates, and our window library became quite representative of all types of poetry.

On a work table we set up a listening post. This was a box wired for sound to which several sets of earphones were connected. It allowed more than one child to listen at the same time. As a matter of fact, eight children listened at one time to poetry records from the library. For some of these records, there were accompanying books. Poetry tapes were also available from our school library. The children signed up to listen, and each child had the opportunity to listen to each record or tape before a change was made.

Out of these exposures to poetry grew the desire for expression. The children began to hand in unsolicited original poetry. We felt this needed recognition, so we invited all classes to participate in making an original poetry book. The children were to write the poems. This was completely voluntary and absolutely no pressure was brought to bear. The poems were not altered or changed by the teachers, nor did we question their motive, style, or content. The poems were free form, and most of our corrections and suggestions were punctuation. Our purpose was to motivate. The response was amazing. Three poems from among the many written are included here.

RAIN

Rain!
It is very beautiful.
Rain!
It tingles your nose.
Rain!
It clatters on the roof.
Rain!
Children go splash! splash!
Rain!
When it rains, mothers worry
That you'll catch cold.
Would you catch cold from rain,
No!

Tina

THE ROLLING CLOUDS

The rolling clouds I see above my head,
As they float over the mountains and
    through the valleys,
Make me wish that I were one of them,
So I could float and see the roaring
    streams and lakes below.
The rippling streams and lakes I see below,
As they wind and wiggle through the
    mountains and vales.
Make me wish that I were one of them,
So I could watch the trees color their
    leaves.
The painted trees I see that drink the
    water from every stream,
As I go winding by.
Make me wish that I were one of them,
So I could stand so straight and tall,
    and watch the birds fly by.

Jim

THE WIND

Have you ever felt the wind?
It can be as soft as a kitten's purr.
At time I don't even know it's there.
But when a trickle of wind goes up my spine,
   I know it's there, somewhere.
Have you ever felt the wind?
It can be as fierce as a lion's roar.
I always know it's there.
The wind practically blows me when I try to talk,
Have you ever felt the wind?

Barbara

We had the poems typed, each on an individual sheet, and each child had the privilege of illustrating it, if he or she chose to do so. A ditto was made so there could be a copy of the book for each child. The best cover for the book was selected from among many submitted, and the activity culminated with a beehive of activity in assembling the book.

STARTING TO WORK

With this introduction, it was time to begin our main project. I introduced *The Lion, the Witch, and the Wardrobe* by telling some interesting facts about the author and his other works. Then I described the successive steps we would take in making a slide set.

We started by putting up a large bulletin board depicting the main characters, which aroused much interest and speculation about the story. One of our most stringent requirements for reading aloud to the children was that they give their undivided attention, so desks were cleared, and we began to read the first exciting chapter of our book, discussing points as we proceeded.

Immediately then, working on the chalk board, I asked the children to list the main ideas in the first chapter so that we could use them as a starting point for our poem. This done, we began to make rhymes or couplets out of the ideas. For example, the story begins by telling about four children who were sent away from London to the countryside during World War II so they would be safe from the Blitz. We turned this into:

Once four children were sent to stay
At a house in the country not far away.

This was a good start. The next part told about the house they went to, the old professor they stayed with, and their feelings about being there, and this description evolved:

257

It was big and spooky with rooms galore,
All of it was theirs to explore—
Boy! This is better than any old war!

The children began to get the feeling. Right away they could see the possibilities, and we raced ahead, completing the poem for that day. I was pleased. So were the children. Enthusiasm was high.

Each day thereafter, we read one or two chapters, always drawing out the main ideas to form a framework for our poetry. To write a poem every day was a demanding assignment for middle-graders, so we used various methods to give variation. Some days, the children were allowed to work in small groups of three or four to make a poem at school; sometimes they did it as homework. Frequently we combined parts of the work from various groups or individuals; sometimes the class was divided and half would work on today's poem, half on tomorrow's. Always there was the privilege of individual work for the more talented.

Also, there was the need to assemble the work daily and make the decision about the final form. We needed today's poem to add to the previous day's poem, which was mounted on a bulletin board so the children could read and reread it and make suggestions for change. An editing committee of volunteers was formed for this work, and it was surprising how adept they became at sorting and assimilating the material.

By the time we finished the book, we had the narrative poem also and were ready to turn our attention to making the slide sets. We gave a ditto copy of the completed poem to each child at this point and explained that the poem now had to be divided into scenes so that a picture could be obtained to represent each segment of the action. They did not find it hard to decide upon the scenes and this was accomplished rather quickly. In one group, it happened that there were five pages of poetry and five rows of students, so one page was assigned to each row as their responsibility. This ensured uniform participation. Each page included at least five scenes. From this point, each of the three classes was involved in different kinds of things that would contribute to their own particular project. I will treat each separately to describe the steps taken.

THREE GROUPS AT WORK

The *living pictures group* was now ready to make their background scenery. Our room had several large four-by-four-foot bulletin boards, so we decided to draw the backgrounds, paint them and mount them on the boards, and to create whatever props were needed from things at hand or from home. Each row was responsible for creating the scenes on its page of poetry. We found that some of the scenery was usable throughout the story, and as it turned out, each row created one scene. This allowed more focus for the children, and the backgrounds they created were most imaginative.

A list of all the characters was written on the board and the children drew lots for the parts. All were free to draw for any part until each got one. The list was extended to include things like trees, flowers, and animals; this gave everyone a responsibility, a costume to make, and a picture to be in. Drawing lots seemed to work better and get more different students involved, even the less capable, than tryouts and popular selection. Each one had an equal chance.

The children made their own costumes from things at hand. If anyone needed an item not available at home, we asked the class, and it was amazing how all our needs were met—and with such imagination and ingenuity.

Now we were ready to take the pictures. Each row posed the characters into the pictures they thought would best represent the scenes in their part. Remember, each row worked on only one page. By using the row system, which included only five or six students at any one time, we kept commotion at a minimum.

We used a Kodak Instamatic camera, completely automatic, two reflector lights, and colorchrome slides, all furnished by the school. The teacher took the pictures, as we felt it important to protect the quality of the pictures. Each group was allowed thirty slides.

The more adept students evolved as helpers of various sorts, assistant directors, prop people, costume or makeup. This afforded a wonderful opportunity for us to delegate responsibility and really involve everyone.

While all this was going on, the students who had speaking parts were practicing individually and together, using a tape recorder to check their progress. A tape recorder is indispensable in doing this because students are sensitive to their own recorded voice and performance, faults and all. The recorder was available to the students individually and as a group, and it didn't take long for them to become quite critical and begin to iron out their difficulties.

As the recording went on, we asked for volunteers from each of the three classes to make one musical background, which would be used by all three groups, under the direction of the music teacher. We obtained a chorus from the combined classes, and they selected background music from among songs they knew, practiced and recorded it in a humming, drumming style. This was dubbed in as background music for the narrative poems.

The mechanics of running the recorder, dubbing the music and sound effects were done by the students themselves. The crew practiced right along with the students who were reading the parts, and by the time the final recording was done, they had all practiced enough together to perform like clockwork. They arranged their desks in a close circle so they could spread out their scripts to eliminate paper noises. The microphone was set up in the middle of the group for uniform recording. This, of course, was under the constant supervision and guidance of the teacher. It required self-discipline and cooperation, but they felt like movie stars and directors, and they loved it!

The *puppet group* made their characters out of lunch bags. We used the small sacks to get uniform puppet size. The trick to making these puppets is to fix a large head about five or six inches in diameter to the bottom of the

259

sack. The legs, body or costume can be made quite small to fit onto the side of the sack. It seems that this proportion makes the most effective puppet.

We gave the children sacks, colored paper, scissors, and paste and told them to make whatever character they wanted to. I made several samples, showing how to curl strips of paper to use for hair, how to make animal whiskers, to fringe the paper, and use scraps and buttons for trim.

Finally, the class selected from among all those made which ones should be used to represent each character. This class used the basic scenery the other class had made but made changes in it to suit their script and their puppet size.

We again used the row system whereby each row directed one page of script, and again it worked out fine. We found out that while one row was working, the others should be occupied reading or with some assignment. At this point, much of the work had been done, and if they were not working on something specific, they sometimes bothered the ones who were.

My original intent was for the *third group* to illustrate their poem with magazine pictures, collages, and original drawings. We realized fairly early that this story did not lend itself to magazine pictures, and decided that original art would be better. Each day, after we read the chapter from the book and outlined the main ideas on the board, the children selected something from that chapter that they wanted to draw a picture of. Sometimes the entire class would have the assignment. Often, half the class would do the pictures one day, the other half the next day. In this way, we had some pictures for every chapter to choose from, plus the magazine pictures they brought in. We kept a good supply of eight-by-eight-inch paper available for these pictures so they would be of uniform size.

We used a Kodak Visualmaker for the filming. This is a special outfit which includes a camera and a metal stand. The camera, which attaches to the metal stand, has a special lens enabling it to make perfectly focused slides of any picture centered under the stand. The picture must be no larger than eight-by-eight inches. This equipment is specialized, but it is easy to use, and many schools have it in their media centers. A Visualmaker camera is virtually foolproof and each child was allowed to photograph the drawings he or she had contributed.

By the time this group finished the book and their story poem, they also had most of their pictures. A good idea is to have the children write a title for their picture on the back of it—and the chapter number for proper identification. After a while, there are enough pictures so that this becomes necessary.

We then selected a committee whose job it was to select the most representative picture to illustrate a chapter. When these were selected, the class helped with final selections and culling.

We used a slide sorter for all three groups to arrange the pictures in order according to the script. Then we played the recorded poem, showing the slides at the same time, making any necessary changes, and marking on the script the exact time to flick to the next scene.

SHARING THE RESULTS

The results were impressive. We had three original narrative poems, each illustrated in a different medium. The children were delighted with the results, but they wanted to see each other's work. They also wanted their parents to see the show, so we decided to have a premiere showing. The project had been fun to do, and the party we had was a fitting climax. The children baked dozens of cookies, made gallons of Kool Aid, cleaned and decorated the room, moved and arranged the furniture, set up equipment, and served happily on any committee.

Their enthusiasm was reflected on the day of the party in the presence of an appreciative overflow crowd. I am sure that none of these children will ever forget their involvement in this project, no matter how small the role they played. It was a real learning experience for all of us.

Note: Another set of suggestions about using *The Lion, the Witch, and the Wardrobe* as a basis for a unit is included in *Response Guides for Teaching Children's Books* by Albert B. Somers and Janet Evans Worthington. Urbana: N.C.T.E., 1981, pp. 75–79. The guide includes suggestions for teaching 27 books. Each unit plan includes sections summarizing the book; giving reasons for using it; describing reading problems (including vocabulary to be emphasized); providing introductory activities; suggesting discussion questions; relating art and media activities; and listing other audiovisual materials based on the book.

Bibliography

Beers, James W. and Beers, Carol S. "Vowel Spelling Strategies among First and Second Graders: A Growing Awareness of Written Words." *Language Arts* (February 1980): 166–172.

Burrows, Alvina Treut et al. *They All Want to Write.* New York: Holt Rinehart and Winston, 1964.

Cafone, Harold et al. *Language Skills and Use.* Glenview, Ill.: Scott, Foresman, 1980.

Cassedy, Sylvia. *In Your Own Words. A Beginner's Guide to Writing.* Garden City: Doubleday, 1979.

Clay, Marie M. *What Did I Write?* Auckland, New Zealand: Heinemann Educational Books, 1975.

Conlin, David A. et al. *Our Language Today.* New York: American Book, 1978.

Courlander, Harold. *The Crest and the Hide and Other African Stories.* New York: Coward-McCann, 1982.

Cramer, Ronald L. "The Nature and Nurture of Creative Writing." *Elementary School Journal* (May 1975): 507–512.

Dawson, Mildred A. et al. *Language for Daily Use.* New York: Harcourt Brace Jovanovich, 1978.

Gooch, Bryan N.S. "The Teaching of Poetry: Problems and Principals." In *Learning to Read. Reading to Learn,* edited by L. Olilla et al. Victoria, B.C.: Vancouver Island International Reading Association, 1974.

Grahame, Kenneth. *The Wind in the Willows*. New York: Charles Scribner's Sons, 1908.

Graves, Donald. *Balance the Basics: Let them Write*. New York: Ford Foundation, 1978.

Haley-James, S. (ed.). *Perspectives on Writing*. Urbana, Ill.: National Council of Teachers of English, 1981.

Hamp, Eric P. et al. *Language Basics Plus*. New York: Harper & Row, 1979.

Hochstetler, Ruth. "Facets of Language—Grammar and Usage." In *Guiding Children's Language Learning*, edited by Pose Lamb. Dubuque, Iowa: William C. Brown, 1971.

Hogrogian, Nonny. *Cinderella*. New York: Greenwillow Books, 1981.

Holder, Heidi. *Aesop's Fables*. New York: The Viking Press, 1981.

Horn, Thomas D. and Fowler, Elaine. "Written Language-Skills are Important." *Instructor* (February 1974): 50–52.

Hyman, Trina Schart. *The Sleeping Beauty*. Boston: Little, Brown and Company, 1977.

Johnson, Ken et al. *Language*. Lexington, Mass.: Ginn & Co., 1979.

King, Martha et al. *A Forum for Focus*. Champaign, Ill.: National Council of Teachers of English, 1973.

Kirby, Dan R. and Liner, Tom. "Revision: Yes, They Do It. Yes You Can Teach It." *English Journal* (March 1980): 41–45.

Larrick, Nancy, selector. *Green is Like a Meadow of Grass*. Champaign, Ill.: Garrard Publishing Co., 1968.

L'Engle, Madeleine. *A Circle of Quiet*. New York: Farrar Strauss and Giroux, 1972.

Lewis, Claudia. *A Big Bite of the World: Children's Creative Writing*. Englewood Cliffs, N.J.: Prentice-Hall, Inc., 1979.

Lewis, C.S. *The Lion, the Witch, and the Wardrobe*. New York: The Macmillan Co., 1950.

Lionni, Leo. *Theodore and the Talking Mushroom*. New York: Pantheon, 1971.

Livingston, Myra Cohn. "But Is It Poetry?" *Horn Book Magazine* (December 1975): 571–580 (Part 1); (February 1976): 24–31 (Part 2).

Mallett, Jerry J. "Hey . . . They Don't Have Any Words." *Ohio Reading Teacher* 11(3) (1976–1977): 6–9.

Mayer, Mercer. *Bubble Bubble*. New York: Parents Magazine Press, 1973.

Mearns, Hughes. *Creative Power: The Education of Youth in the Creative Arts* (2nd ed.). New York: Dover Publications, Inc., 1958.

Merriam, Eve. *It Doesn't Always Have to Rhyme*. New York: Atheneum, 1965.

Milne, A.A. *Winnie the Pooh*. New York: E.P. Dutton, 1926.

Moffett, James and Wagner, Betty Jane. *Student-Centered Language Arts and Reading*, K-13. Boston: Houghton Mifflin, 1976.

Murray, Elizabeth. "But What Does It Mean?" *Instructor* (June/July 1974).

Ramage, Corrine. *The Joneses*. Philadelphia: J.B. Lippincott, 1975.

Root, Sheldon. "What's Wrong With Reading Aloud?" *Elementary English* (December 1967): 929–932.

Rukavina, Joanne L. "Beginner, Perpetual Beginner: Encouraging Children to Write." *Language Arts* 54(7) (October 1977):

Searle, Dennis and Dillon, David. "Responding to Student Writing: What Is Said Or How It Is Said." *Language Arts* 54(7) (October 1980): 773–781.

Stewig, John Warren. "Metaphor and Children's Writing." *Elementary English* (February 1966): 121–123.

Stewig, John Warren. *Read to Write. Using Children's Literature as a Springboard to the Teaching of Writing.* New York: Holt, Rinehart and Winston, 1980.

Suhl, Yuri. *Simon Boom Gives a Wedding.* New York: Four Winds Press, 1973.

Tway, Eileen. "Teacher Responses to Children's Writing." *Language Arts* (October 1980): 763–772.

White, E.B. *Charlotte's Web.* New York: Harper & Row, 1952.

THE NECESSITY
FOR PRACTICAL
WRITING

Writing can be used for different purposes.
Sometimes we use it to express whatever thoughts
and feelings happen to be crossing our minds.
Sometimes we use it to tell a story. And
sometimes we use it to get something done....
Writing in this last sense is called transactional
writing. Sometimes transactional writing consists
of imparting or sharing information, or explaining
something. We lump these functions together and
call them expository writing. Sometimes transactional writing consists of an attempt to persuade
someone to do something or believe something.
This is called argumentative writing. (Temple, et
al., 1982)

Dividing writing into two distinct types is, as the authors of
the above quote would agree, an artificial distinction. Types of writing can
be arranged more appropriately on a continuum from expressive to transactional. On a continuum the distinctions between types can be more subtle.
However, in an effort to provide an easier understanding of the two ends of
the continuum, this book includes two separate chapters on writing. The
first dealt with several types of writing in which expressive aspects are emphasized. In this chapter, we shall turn our attention to writing in which the
author attempts to communicate with the reader in the ways identified
above.

Although a variety of terms are used for this type of composition, it is important to remember there should always be imaginative elements in every
child's writing. Even in something as prosaic as writing an invitation,
children can be imaginative if the teacher allows for flexibility. Even in a letter to an editor, children can be creative if the teacher is encouraging. Even

though we teach specific skills to be followed in writing a report, there is room for imagination.

A pervading concern in this chapter is teaching children specific skills of use in writing. The work on standard writing skills is done in periods separate from expressive writing, so as not to inhibit the writing itself. Teachers know that skills learned will be transferred to the expressive writing.[1]

SKILL GROUPS AND THE MECHANICS OF WRITING

We need to make a distinction here between the way children too often learn skills and the method this chapter advocates. Unfortunately, the overly-common approach is to have children progress page by page through the language arts textbook. This is frequently done because of the mistaken belief that such an approach to mechanics will be effective. Such procedures persist despite the fact that thoughtful writers have pointed out for a long time their questionable merit.[2]

The most helpful approach to mechanics is one called *diagnostic*. That is, the teacher watches children's written work, notices which problems recur, keeps a record of the frequency of these errors, and finally prescribes a remedy (Holbrook, 1973). In the last stage of this procedure, children in small groups do intensive work on the specific problem they share. The characteristic of these groups is their ephemeral nature; children work together only as long as necessary to master the needed skill.

TIME PROBLEM

The most frequent cavil against individualizing any instructional program is lack of time. This is indeed a problem if one sees the textbook as equivalent to the instructional program. Perhaps this is one reason so little in-dividualization occurs in elementary schools.[3]

---

[1]Harriet B. Cholden, "Writing Assignments with Equal Writes," *Elementary English*, February 1975, 52(2), 190–191. Cholden reports that when she taught skills in the context of assignments every child did which were structured and limited in length, improvement in free writing was noted. When children chose what to write about, no correction was made on their expressive writing papers.

[2]Miriam E. Wilt, "Organizing for Language Learning," *The National Elementary Principal*, November 1965, 6–12. Wilt describes clearly the need for such a "diagnostic" approach to skills as described here.

[3]A survey indicated that in 81.5 percent of the classrooms responding, the textbook was the language arts curriculum. Such a lack of individualization of the program unfortunately results in a poorer program than desired. See *The Status of Language Arts* (Dansville, N.Y.: F. A. Owen Publishing Co., 1965). Given parents' concern about the "basics" of education, this percentage may be greater now than when the survey was done.

If, however, the teacher comes to see the textbook as a reference aid, a source of ideas and exercises for children to do, time will be no problem. This is because all those large blocks of time currently spent leading children page by page through the text will now be free time for work on individual problems.

An example may illustrate this point. While observing a student teacher, I saw her give a unit test on contractions, and especially the use of "it's" as a contraction for "it is." As anyone who has observed signs, billboards, and adult writing of all kinds can attest, this is one of the things schools are apparently least adept at teaching—yet it is a simple phenomenon which is easily taught. One child, a fifth-grader, failed the test, but the next day the student teacher scheduled another topic. When I asked her what would happen to the child who got so few contractions right she said: "Oh, it doesn't matter, they'll get contractions again next year." And the student will probably graduate from high school without knowing how to use contractions because no one is sufficiently interested to break this cycle of indifference, stopping to help the child learn this simple skill. The student teacher had dutifully "covered" the pages prescribed in the textbook series at her grade level, and was content to let the next teacher worry about this problem. Instead of determining which small group of children needed help on this specific skill, she held the whole class together, boring some and not reaching others, until the five pages were covered. Then, inexorably, she moved on.

An unsatisfactory approach? Yes, but because she felt the entire group had to use the entire book in sequence, this approach appeared to be logical. Had she tried the skill-group approach described above, she might have been more successful in meeting the children's needs.

SOURCES OF ERRORS

As mentioned earlier, children's writing can indicate areas needing individualized work. The work on mechanics always takes place in a period separate from creative writing time, however, and while examples drawn from children's compositions may be used, these are never identified by author.

The teacher may use some sentences or paragraphs taken from the writing turned in because this lends an air of reality to the skill practice. This should be done anonymously to protect the child who wrote the example from ridicule. Copy the material on a ditto master, write it on a transparency to use in an overhead projector, or use the paper itself (with the name masked out) in an opaque projector. Using such real examples has the advantage of being more interesting to children than examples from a text or made up by the teacher.

Yet another way to accomplish this purpose, if you are concerned that children will discover who wrote the example, is to work with another teacher on this project. If some of your children are having trouble with subject and verb agreement, for example, you can borrow some samples another teacher has gathered. If some of that teacher's children are having trouble with misplaced modifiers, he or she can borrow from you. Usually there will be enough overlap of problems in children of any grade level, so it will not be a problem to obtain samples this way.

DURATION OF GROUPS

There is no stigma to being in a skill group if two conditions are met:

1. *Each person* is working in a skill group of some kind. It is a rare classroom where a number of children don't have some kind of problem. If you do have some children whose written work needs no help, they may need skill-group work in other subject matter.

2. The groups have to be viewed as *temporary*, not permanent. The teacher groups children to learn a skill; when they have learned that skill the group disbands and children regroup to learn a different one. Unfortunately, it may seem some children are always in a skill group. This will be a problem unless you have been able to meet condition one, above. If you have not been able to, and some children feel self-conscious about this, perhaps you should reexamine your priorities and see which of the skills you are expecting these children to learn are most crucial.

LETTER WRITING

Though letter writing has been included in this chapter dealing with practical writing, it belongs as logically with expressive writing because the best letters are indeed creative.[4]

Teachers must be aware that one reason why teaching anything beyond some basic structural considerations related to letter writing is difficult is that ours is not, and has not been for some time, a nation of letter writers. Few children have a model to emulate in this skill. It is a rare person, indeed, who has the leisure or, perhaps more accurately, decides to use that leisure in creating compelling communication in written form. In fact, though many elementary texts still deal at length with teaching children to write invitations and thank-you notes, such forms of communication are becoming increasingly rare in today's society. Consider when you as an adult last received a written invitation of the type still too frequently included in

---

[4]Alvina Burrows makes this point, and offers several suggestions about encouraging children's writing in "Involving the Child in the Language Arts," Album 3 from *Listener Inservice Cassette Library*, available from Listener Corporation, Hollywood, Calif. The album of cassettes also offers help in oral language development.

language arts textbooks. Perhaps such consideration might change your mind about the need to teach such forms to children.

Though there is no particular justification for attributing this decline in letter writing to how the skill has been taught in schools, such is at least a reasonable assumption. It is true that there are certain basic forms that need to be used when writing business letters. These forms can usually be learned at the time children have need of them. In informal letters, however, the emphasis on content which will capture a reader's attention, far too infrequently takes priority over a punctilious attention to mechanical details. Children can be helped to understand that a letter can be as exciting to read as a story.

One way of stimulating children to edit their own personal letters is to have them write a letter to a real person, and then let them work on the letter with a classmate. With their partner, they can edit the letters, using some of the questions proposed on page 241, to increase the effectiveness of their writing. After such editing, the letter is recopied, and must be mailed to give the child a feeling that this is a worthwhile task.

Another way of motivating students to write letters is to initiate a class writing project (Balaz & Dumas, 1979). As early as kindergarten, a class can write to another in a different school district, exchanging pictures, self-portraits, and dictated stories about their class, to which they can sign their names. The children described by Balaz and Dumas learned the parts of a letter, where and how to write addresses and affix stamps, and practiced "rereading" a friend's letter (a preliminary step in editing) before it was sent. At the close of the school year, the pen pals exchanged home addresses, so correspondence could continue over the summer.

A group letter of appreciation, perhaps to the author of a book the class has enjoyed, can be meaningful to students. A first-grade teacher read each of the poems in *Moments: Poems About the Seasons* (Hopkins, 1980) during a week when the season was changing dramatically from spring to summer. The children were encouraged to share their reactions orally if they wished. On Friday the teacher asked the children to think during the weekend about whether they would like to compose a group letter to the author on the following Monday. When Monday came, boys and girls were still so enthused about the poems that they wanted to compose the letter. This is what they dictated to their teacher:

May 24, 1981

Dear Mr. Hopkins:

Our teacher read us your book *Moments*. We like your poems, especially about Spring and Summer, and you are nice. Our favorite poem in the book is "Homework." We also like "Oh Have You Heard," "What Shall I Pack in a Box Marked 'Summer,'" "Crabapples," "New Year's Eve," and "Squirrel."

We would like to know how you could make a book like yours?
    How could we make a book like it? Where did you find so many
    interesting poems, and how do you make poems? How did you
    make the book so good? Is it hard to make a book, or is it easy?
    Do you have to erase sometimes? Where do you work? Where do
    you get all the paper? How do you feel about being a writer?
    Well, that is all the questions. We wish you could come to this
    school.

Sincerely,

Adam	Richie	Megan
Jason	Jill	Betsy
Kelley	Stacye	Dugan
Jon	Geoffrey	Amy
Melissa	Kwanza	Laura

Teacher: Mrs. Barbara Larkin
First Grade
University School

The teacher mailed the letter to the writer, in care of the publisher.[1] Some
time later an envelope arrived from Mr. Hopkins, containing the letter reproduced below, as well as various promotional materials (bibliographies,
illustration reproductions, and bookmarks), which publishers regularly produce about their authors' works. These gave children insights into how this
particular writer works and how books are produced.

From the Desk of
LEE BENNETT HOPKINS

May 30, 1982

TO ALL IN MRS. LARKIN'S FIRST GRADE:

Dear Boys and Girls:

Thank you very much for taking the time to write to me about
    my anthology, MOMENTS: POEMS ABOUT THE SEASONS. It was
    a delightful book to do.

---

[1]Children's trade book publishers are happy to forward letters to their authors. The
publisher's addresses are found in *Books in Print* (New York: Bowker, yearly). Or, personal addresses for many authors can be found in *Something About the Author* by Anne Commire
(Detroit, MI: Gale Publishing Co.).

I look for poetry everywhere. To do a book like MOMENTS
which contains 50 poems, I easily looked at 1,000 poems before I
made the final selection.

You asked so many wonderful questions! Many of them will be
answered on the attached brochures.

Here's wishing you a wonderful Summertime. May it be filled
with lots of good reading including lots of poetry!

Happiness to all . . .

Cordially,

Letters to writers are a pleasant way to expand the classes' contact with a
book and its author. Teachers need to be aware, however, that in contrast to
the personal letter this class received, some authors prefer to have the
publishing house itself send a form letter, so they can spend their time
writing other books.

Other letters of appreciation might be written to the following:

1. The president of the Parent-Teachers Association for new library
   books bought with P.T.A. funds;
2. The school cooks for a particularly tasty new menu in the school
   cafeteria;
3. A child's parent, for coming to the classroom to share slides of a
   trip to a foreign country;
4. The Department of Public Works for the beautiful flowers newly
   planted in the city park;
5. The program director of a local radio or television station for continuing to program a favorite entertainment program;
6. The editor at a publishing house for choosing to publish a new
   book by a favorite author;
7. The governor of the state for proclaiming a week during the year
   as National Education Week;
8. The educational director of the symphony for arranging for a free
   concert for children;
9. The alderman of the ward for coming to school to explain the
   delay in having a stop sign installed in front of the school; or
10. The principal from the School for the Deaf, for coming to point
    out what the class will see during the upcoming field trip.

The same first-grade teacher, always alert for opportunities to make letter writing significant in the lives of her students, overheard two of the children talking at recess one day. One was complaining to the other about an older child swearing. Later that day the teacher suggested to her class that they compose a group letter to the school's headmaster, telling him what they liked about the school and how it could be improved. The following composite letter resulted:

May, 198_____

Dear Mr. Johnston:

We like University School because we have fun things to do and very nice teachers. We like the food and hot lunches. We like having gym every day, and art, library, and music. We like outside because we can play soccer and we have field trips. We have good books in the library and chess club is fun. We like all our math activities. Everyone can make good friends and we learn more things at this school. It is nice to have free choice at the end of the day.

There are things to make this school better like having hobby days more often. We would like to have two recesses, two teachers for each class, and more free time. We want to have school longer so we can have more free choice. If I were you I would say no swearing or you can't come to school. We should change one rule — to be able to wear the thing we want to wear like blue jeans. We would like to see the middle school and lower school follow the directions.

Thank you,

Sincerely,

First Graders at University School

In response to the children's letter, the headmaster came to the classroom and talked in person about their requests. He explained the reasons for wearing uniforms. It is important for children to look nice at school and not try to buy better clothes than someone else. He suggested that the children write a letter to the new head of the lower school about having hobby days more often. Then she could meet with them when she comes in the fall. He said that he would like to have school longer each day also. He was sorry to hear that swearing was a problem and would try to do something about it. The children were glad to know the headmaster better.

The teacher's model as a letter writer is fine motivation to interest children in writing. Teachers find it helpful to communicate frequently with parents, sending home a weekly letter, informing parents of their child's

271

achievements, and of classroom happenings (Hoxworth, 1979). Often such letters result in increased parental attendance at conferences, more relaxed rapport between parent and teacher, and increased parental concern for incomplete work. Seeing the teacher communicate regularly through letters can motivate children's interest in writing themselves.

Another imaginative approach to letter writing is suggested by Ziegler (1976) who expands the idea to include four "audience groupings," in which children write letters to (a) objects (i.e., garbage can); (b) nonhuman organic things (i.e., volcano); (c) people who have died (i.e., grandfather); and (d) figures from history/literature (i.e., Columbus). As a rule, letters should be written to someone from whom the child can expect a response. In the case of Ziegler's suggestions, the challenge is in the composition itself, and no response is possible or expected.

A fifth-grade teacher experimented with Ziegler's categories, and asked her students to choose a category and compose a letter. Children might write to a *natural object*.

Dear Thunder,

Why are you so loud, and why do you scare my little brother? I want to know! I'm getting very angry with you.
Who makes the lightning that comes before you? There must be some good answer for these questions and I want them, SOON!

Yours truly,

Steve

Dear Mr. Cloud,

Good afternoon. The reason I am writing this letter to you is that I have been so curious about you for such a long time that I really must ask you some questions.
What in the world is it like to have an airplane fly through you, and get all its dirt on you? How about when companies have smoke coming out of their chimneys right onto you? What is all of this like? I see you floating all the time. What does this feel like?
I hope to see you soon.

Signed,

Michelle

Another category from which boys and girls could choose was *inanimate objects*.

Dear Spiral Notebook,

Do you remember when I first picked you out at the store? You were so nice and red! I bought you for $1.05, and you came with a pencil.

Your paper is excellent! I use it every day. I am very sorry if I hurt you by ripping the paper out. Do you like being used with my TRUSTY #5 pencil? How about with an MPS TESTING PENCIL? Yuck, you say? Well . . . . . sorry! I'll try a COLORBRITE!

Your faithful writer,

Mackey

Dear Record,

How are you feeling? Scratchy? Understandable since you are always being scratched with needles. At least you're kind of cool. You know, groovy (small laugh). Did you hear "Name That Tune" last night? They were literally playing your song. Well, hear you around.

Your friend,

David

Dear Sneakers,

I'm really sorry about making you all dirty and smelly! I really think you're very helpful and without you I'd have really sore feet! Remember the time when I got *grease,* all over you? I think you guys were ready to untie yourselves and hit me over the head! Well, I just wanted to say thanks for putting up with it all.

Sincerely,

Mafmudye

Dear Pencil,

Hi! My name is Sarah. I use you almost every day. What is it like to have someone just reach out and use you? Does it really hurt you when they break you? Well, in real life when you break a leg, you don't just get sharpened, you have to go to the doctor and tell him what happened, and he'll say I will put a splint on it, or a cast. Do you have any doctor pencils?

I have a mother, her name is Bobby J. _____ . Do you have a
   mother that is nice to you and takes you places? Do you have
   real places besides being put in a desk or on a shelf? How does it
   feel when you have to write on paper? What is it like in a pencil
   sharpener? You know, I would really like to see what it would be
   like to be a pencil.

Yours truly,

Sarah

A third category was to *someone real who has now died.*

Dear Grandpa,

I hope you are doing fine in heaven, because I know that's
   where you are. I am 11 years old now. I pray for you every night,
   and Grandma too. Grandma went to Great America She said she
   had a great time, but I bet it would have been the greatest if you
   would have been there. I love you very much.
You should see my brothers now. Andre is 4, and James Jr. is 2.
   We will all pass away someday, and we will see you then, and we
   can celebrate being together.

Your grandbaby,

Zina

Dear Brian,

I wonder how you feel in the ground? Did you make it to
   heaven? Are you having fun?
Well, down on earth it's okay. It's a dangerous world as always.
   I have pretty nice friends and a real good teacher.
Oh, don't let me forget! It was a sad funeral. People were
   crying and shouting. It was just LOUD!
Well, Brian when I die I hope to see you in heaven and get to
   know you better.

Sincerely,

Tracy Williams

Another category was to a *famous person now dead.*

Dear Wilhelm Roentgen,

I did a project about you, and found you were a very interesting
   person. But when you stuck your hand into the unknown ray, that
   wasn't too smart! (no offense) What you discovered are called
   X-rays today. Boy, do they help us out! Even medical schools
   have them.
I wish you hadn't died when you did, because you could've used
   your brain to find more medical wonders. Maybe we will find a
   ray that will see further than yours, but nothing is better than the
   original!

                              Your favorite studier,

                              James C.

Dear Alexander Graham Bell,

I want to thank you for inventing the telephone. It is a very
   useful gadget. You can use it for so many different things.
Since you invented it, people have improved it, but I'm not
   saying the original one was bad. There are now push-button
   phones. You are able to push buttons instead of dialing the
   number. There is now a more convenient way of holding the
   receiver. Some phones are very modern like the ones that are
   round, some pop out of a box, and others are automatic.
I don't think I could ever live without a telephone. I use it for
   school purposes as well as entertainment.
It must have been hard to put all those wires together and figure
   out how to get vibrations from one place to another in a split
   second. You are some genius!

                              Yours truly,

                              Wendy

Dear Ludwig,

I have all of your records. How does it feel to be an idol to
   musicians? I went to a concert conducted by Lucas Foss. They
   played your Ninth Symphony and Wellington's Victory. It was
   very good.

                              Your fellow musician,

                              Andy

Dear Mr. Goddard,

I really enjoy rocketry and am fascinated by the variety of
rockets we have today. You probably wouldn't have believed the
technology we have in these days. We have a rocket that's been
in space three times and will soon be blasting off a fourth time.
In your days, you barely had any rockets. I'm glad you launched
the first rocket, or we wouldn't have even gotten off the ground.

Sincerely yours,

Sasha

A related imaginative composition task might be to encourage students to write a letter of response, as if they were the recipient of the letter. That could, especially in this last category, encourage students to do further research of their own before writing the response.

REPORT WRITING

Report writing is frequently a problem for teachers. Most reports children write are badly done because techniques of report writing, if taught at all, are taught too hurriedly and too late. It is difficult for many children to understand that writing a report is not the same as copying from an encyclopedia.

A brief anecdote will illustrate the problem. While supervising a student teacher, I listened to some reports of the usual kind—painful readings of long transcripts from encyclopedias, much of which was unintelligible to both the reporter and the victims. As one particularly inept fourth-grader struggled with his list of principal products, faltering over: "The principal products are coffee, tea, and . . . and . . . and . . .," he was unable to read the long word he had copied verbatim but uncomprehendingly from the encyclopedia. Into the painful silence came a very up-to-date future airline attendant who obligingly supplied: "and milk?"

One reason children may fail to write good reports is that far too few understand how helpful outlining can be. Outlining is basically a simple skill and can be taught in first grade if approached correctly. There are two easy ways to do this. *First,* when a teacher works with the idea of sequence in doing an experience chart with children, he or she is providing a useful introduction to outlining. Outlining is, after all, nothing more than setting information down in logical order. After a trip, perhaps to a bakery, help children write down in order some ideas they want to include in their experience story; this is beginning outlining. *Second,* it is helpful as an introductory technique to have children rewrite in their own words a story that has been read to them. Any simple story will do. As the teacher helps her children make an orderly list of the characters to be included, he or she is providing a painless introduction to a skill which, if well learned, will prove eminently useful.

One sixth-grade teacher, concerned about his students' inability to actually write reports, determined to teach the skill in a group setting, building on the outlining skills his students had already developed. He felt that after the skills of organizing material were taught, students could apply them to a topic of their own choosing.

The students were assigned to read two articles about moles, a topic from their science unit. After all students had taken their own notes, the teacher helped the group build an outline together. Then the class wrote an initial draft of the theme cooperatively on the board. The teacher purposely let a week elapse before the class talked about revision. This was to give the students some intellectual "distance" from what they had composed, so they could be more objective about their writing.

During revision the class talked about how they could regroup some of the information so that the report didn't end up with too many short paragraphs. Because some of the students had experienced sentence combining the previous year, they were able as a group to expand upon some of the short sentences found in the first draft. (See chapter 12 on grammar for a more complete description of sentence combining.) Although the class was only average in ability, there were four or five students who really saw how combining and rearranging would improve the initial theme. The following is the resulting revised theme.

The mole, an animal disliked by most people, is ideally suited to its environment. Its pig-like snout, wedged-shaped face, sharp front claws, and powerful rear legs aid the mole, which spends most of its life underground, to make zig-zag tunnels across lawns and fields as it searches for food. Despite poor eyesight and small openings for ears, the mole survives because its body is sensitive to touch. In its underground world touch is more important than sight or hearing.

Fortunately, the mole has but one litter a year which consists of two to five babies. When born, the mole is blind and naked, but within ten days it has light grey, velvety fur. After four weeks the babies leave the nest.

The mole is both useful and destructive. Because of its tremendous appetite, it needs to consume its own weight (anywhere from one and one half to five ounces) every day. Seldom harming plants, it seeks out cutworms, insects, and earthworms. But because it creates ridges in lawns and fields, gardeners and farmers set traps to catch them. At one time they were also caught for their fur, but since the fur did not wear well that practice has ended.

The mole, however, is not easily caught. Since it spends most of its life underground, it is safe from its enemies. When confronted by danger above ground, it can easily escape underground in less than a minute because of its digging ability.

Even though the mole does eat destructive insects and was once sought for its fur, it disfigures lawns and is considered a pest. Pest or not, it is an interesting animal to study.

Having been taught specific skill steps in writing a report, this group of students was then able to apply these skills in writing individual themes on topics of their choice.

MULTIPLE SOURCES

Teachers lay groundwork for intelligent report writing in sixth grade, when, in kindergarten, they use several versions of a favorite story.[5] When they read a variety of settings of "The Three Billy Goats Gruff" for example and discuss with children which they enjoyed most, teachers are helping them see, even if indirectly, that one source is not a final authority (Western, 1980). The teacher continues going to more than one source, talking about likenesses and differences between them, to inculcate the idea that multiple sources add richness to our thinking and experiences.

In one first-grade class the teacher used two variants of an old tale. *The Five Chinese Brothers* (Bishop, 1938) with illustrations by Kurt Weise is well-known. Less familiar is the *Six Chinese Brothers* (Hou-tien, 1979), illustrated with scissors cuts. The teacher read the Bishop book one day and encouraged students to react to it. On the following day she read the version by Hou-tien, and again the class discussed the book. Then they drew up a list of comparisons:

The books are the *same*

both were about brothers
both were Chinese
both had talents
both begged to say goodbye
both lived in villages
in both, someone tried to kill the sons
no names in either story
both tried to chop off the heads
both had stretching legs
both tried to drown a brother

---

[5]Any card catalogue should reveal multiple versions of a single story. The major purpose of using several versions is the enrichment of the literature program which results. A collateral benefit is establishing in children's minds the value of using more than one source.

The books are *different*

one story has five; the other six brothers
brothers had different powers in each story
one had a mother, the other had a father
one used the word "promptly" and the other didn't
in one the man was sick; the other a boy was drowned
one had skin so hard steel bounced off and the other had an iron
    neck
their clothes were different
they had different ways of asking to go home to say goodbye
there was no arm stretching in the first story
one didn't have a person who could hold his breath "indefinitely"

The list represents impressive observation skills on the part of these children, who had never before participated in such a comparing/contrasting experience. Activities in observing similarities and differences lays needed groundwork for high-level thinking and responding skills. Later, as students are reading several sources, they can be encouraged to notice similarities and differences.

MAKING CHOICES

Another composition skill is making preference statements. This involves going beyond simply noting likenesses and differences to a more sophisticated expression of a reason for liking one or the other of the two books. Even in report writing, when expressing an opinion about what they have read, students should see the need to give a reason for their opinion. In the upper grades, students engaged in argumentative writing should be held to giving a reason for their idea. Laying the groundwork for this skill begins early. First-grade children, after seeing both of these books, dictated a reason for choosing one or the other. Among those who chose *The Five Chinese Brothers*:

> I liked them both because they both had happy endings and they
> never could get rid of all those brothers. I like Chinese stories,
> and I know about other countries.
>
> *Ira*

> I liked the *Five Chinese Brothers* because there was more action.
> The boy drowned. One brother was thrown in the water. One
> brother couldn't be burned. The pictures were more colorful.
>
> *Slaven*

Others chose the *Six Chinese Brothers*:

> I liked the *Six Chinese Brothers* because I am six years old. The
> story was exciting because the one who could stretch his leg
> found jewels, and the story had a pearl.
>
> *Marko*

I liked the *Six Chinese Brothers* because the pictures were little
people and they stole a pearl from the king and boiled it. The
father got better. This book had my favorite colors, red and
white.

Joyha

Second-graders who also looked at both books were asked to write down
their choices. Among responses to *The Five Chinese Brothers* were:

I liked *The Five Chinese Brothers* because it had funny pictures . . . .
like when the third Chinese brother got thrown off the boat and
the powers were gooder because the legs could stretch farther. I
like the boats better because the boats were not fancy.

Ian

I liked *The Five Chinese Brothers* because the pictures were more
realistic and the Brothers were big. I do not like little people.
And the book was more exciting because the King is more mean.
The King in *The Five Chinese Brothers* put the boy in whipped
cream and the King in the *Six Chinese Brothers* threw him in the
water, and I liked whipped cream better.

Bill

Among responses to the *Six Chinese Brothers* were:

My favorite book was *The Six Chinese Brothers* because I liked the
pictures. It was exciting and thrilling. It was sad and happy. I
liked it because they are smaller and I liked small people. I was
sad because the King wanted to kill the first brother. I like the
pictures because I like red better than yellow. It was exciting
because when the doctors said, "You will have to get the King's
pearl and boil it in water." That was exciting because I've never
heard of that cure.

Lori

I like *The Six Chinese Brothers* more because the people are funny
and little. The pictures were nice in both books, but the *Six
Chinese Brothers* was more interesting. The Brothers were little. I
liked colors better because I like red, black, and white.
The pictures are beautiful because they weren't plain like the other
book. They both were dressed good. The words were spelled
good. I liked both boys that could stretch their legs. And the one
that could stretch his arms because they were funny. And the

gold pieces. The gold pieces were very shiny and pretty. I liked the King because he had gold pieces and I like gold pieces. And both of the stories had a happy ending.

Amy

Children should not get the mistaken impression that reports are only based on book research, however. Another possibility, using oral language, is to have the children interview someone and then write a report about what was learned. You might introduce oral interviewing as a basis for written reports, by reading "Beezus' Creative Writing," a chapter in a book by the immensely popular Beverly Cleary (1977). This continues the series of Ramona's adventures; here her older sister is completing a school assignment, not unlike one you might assign to your class. A more serious treatment of interviewing is by Haley-James (see Bibliography).

Children later use their practical writing skills when they send letters to various newspapers, ordering single copies of the papers in order to see how differently the same events are reported in different parts of the country.[6] Imagine the shades of opinion represented in newspapers, for example, the day the Supreme Court action on segregation was taken! Though such a project as this is more closely related to social studies, it does entail language arts skills. Whether using actual materials to gather data or using reference books, children can begin to sense the need for more than one source, if the teacher values this.

QUESTIONING

One of the most helpful habits teachers can instill in students is that of making a list of questions to be answered before starting a report. Instead of simply requiring them to sign up for a topic, the teacher helps the children frame a series of questions which should be answered. In doing such a report, boys and girls frequently tend to simply copy the section in the encyclopedia about the topic. There are, however, a whole variety of more particular or specialized questions to which children might want answers, if they were encouraged to speculate about the general topic. For example, in considering a report on the products of Italy, they might explore such questions as:

Are there other products, not of major importance economically, but which are important for other reasons, perhaps aesthetically?

---

[6]Consult Robert U. Brown, ed., *The Editor and Publisher International Yearbook* (New York: The Editor and Publisher Company). It lists all newspapers published in English throughout the world and gives the necessary ordering information.

Are there some which can be produced only in certain places
because of geographical features?
Are there some which are becoming less important? If so, for what
reasons?

When children search for answers to questions *they* have asked, the tendency
to copy from an encyclopedia is less, no matter what the topic.

The only problem with this approach is that the teacher must avoid "implanting" questions in children's minds. The teacher, too, should be able to
suggest some questions, as an ex-officio member of each planning committee, but the process must not turn into a thinly disguised guessing game
designed to place these questions at the head of the list. If you can help your
children with these three ideas: note taking, outlining, and the use of multiple sources, you will very likely stimulate them to do reports with interesting
content—and ones which are good examples of the child's ability in language
arts as well.

SUMMARY

A basic premise of this chapter is that children should be engaged in the
process of interpreting, shaping, and coping with some bits of experience,
to paraphrase a point made by Britton (1970). In a section discussing the
ways writing can help children sort experiences and interpret them, Britton says children are motivated to do this when the experience is meaningful to them. Clearly, to make the experience of looking up information
on a topic a meaningful one, children should be searching for questions to
which they themselves want answers. The section on children's perception
of audience—who they are writing for—is another useful part of this
small booklet. Some problems involved in helping children become more
adept at practical writing were touched on.

In this chapter, concern was chiefly on some larger issues, rather than
on specific skills that should be taught. This is because it is impossible to
specify the exact skills your children ought to learn. The practical writing
skills necessary for one group may be very different from those needed by
another. Also, the time of acquisition may be different for those skills the
two groups do share. This is the reason for the emphasis on skill groups.
What may be the focus of a skill group in one situation may be a truly irrelevant skill for another group. Thus, it is up to you as the teacher to
analyze your children within the context of the community, the school,
and the parents; determine what practical writing skills you think
children may need; and proceed from there. Of course, it is impossible in
one of the most fluid societies the world has ever known to predict what
writing skills your children will need as adults. But the procedure of

analysis and skill-group treatment makes more sense than to assume, a priori, that any set of skills can be established as necessary for all children.

Chapters 7 and 8 must be seen simply as an introduction to a few possibilities in this facet of the language program. Writing, unlike some of the more easily definable and teachable skills of language, is both more elusive and, finally, more rewarding for teacher and child. Because of its complexity, the writing process is more difficult to write about, to read about, and to encourage, than the more routine aspects of a total language program.

Suggestions for Further Exploration

1. Select some common object you are used to seeing frequently. Examine it as if it were the first time you were seeing it. Write a description of it including any observations you make with your senses. Visual descriptors will probably occur to you first: the surface texture, the contours of the object, its dimensions. Do not neglect the other senses: can you describe how it feels, how it tastes, what noises it can make? Don't neglect the off-beat or unusual: the taste of a piece of paper, the sound of a leaf (as you rub your hand against it), the smell of a toothbrush, or the feel of uncooked macaroni.
2. Find several versions of the same folktale and share these with your children. Then have them choose which one they like best and analyze in writing what they liked about their choice. You might try several versions of "Rumplestilt-skin" (including the charming version of it by Evaline Ness, *Tom Tit Tot*, New York: Scribner's, 1965). Another good one is "Cinderella," and be sure to share with your children the unique version by Beni Montressor (New York: Knopf, 1965). His version, with the more complete descriptions of the Baron of Monte-fiascone, his daughters Tisbe and Clarinda, and poor Angelina (renamed Cinderella) make fascinating reading.
3. Is there a writing crisis? Some popular journals declare it so. See "Why Johnny Can't Write," by Merrill Sheils, *Newsweek*, December 8, 1975, pp. 58–63. In contrast, see "Rx for Helping Johnny Write Better," by Matthew Meisterheim, *Elementary School Journal*, September 1977, pp. 5–8. Which of the two makes a more convincing case? Role play a situation involving a teacher, a principal, and a parent, exploring the differences in the articles.

Suggestions for Further Reading

Brandt, Sue R. *How to Write a Report*. New York: Franklin Watts, 1968.

It is difficult to determine which is crisper: the author's style or the illustrator's drawings. There is no doubt that both contribute to making this an extremely valuable tool in teaching what is too often a dull subject. The author's approach is straightforward and the material is well organized, while the humorous il-lustrations help to hold wandering attention. If any book could interest children in the topic, this one should.

Corbin, Richard. *The Teaching of Writing in Our Schools.* New York: Mamillan, 1966.

One in a series planned to answer questions parents ask, this book gives insights into particular aspects of the creative-writing program which may need explaining to parents. The chapter on reasons for a creative-writing program could be used to good advantage, as could the many suggestions in the evaluation chapter.

Foster, Joanna. *Pages, Pictures and Print: A Book in the Making.* New York: Harcourt Brace Jovanovich, 1958.

This small book details in interesting fashion the process from idea to printed page. The author deals easily with the complexities of blanket cylinders, Quoin keys and Smyth sewing, while retaining the readers' interest by her deft style and eye for descriptive detail.

Jacobs, Gabriel. *When Children Think.* New York: Teachers College Press, 1970.

The author describes his experiences in eliciting imaginative thinking from nine- to twelve-year-olds by having them keep journals of their ideas. Selections from the children's journals show the range of their thoughts, the honesty of their views of themselves and their world, and the excitement of recognizing and developing an idea new to them.

Tusan, Stan. *Girls and Boys Write-a-Letter Book.* New York: Grossett and Dunlap, 1971.

For late primary or intermediate grade students, this is a wide-ranging treatment of topics that includes parts of a letter and types of letters (thank you's, pen-pal letters, ordering by mail). Useful in a supplementary fashion when teaching a unit on letter writing.

Yates, Elizabeth. *Someday You'll Write.* New York: E. P. Dutton, 1969.

This charming small book, directed especially to elementary children, gives an introduction to the author as well as to the art of writing. She stresses the importance of reading as preparation and the need to establish clearly a time reference when beginning a story. The section on style is particularly helpful as is the one on selecting the right word for the right spot.

Periodical Bibliography

Cook, Cindie. "Writing in the Elementary School—Why?" *The Reading Teacher* (March 1980): 722–725.

Writing can be a personal way of gaining meaning from experience, a help in understanding print (an essential part of reading), and an aid in establishing meaning. Very young children can "write" with the notion of making a message. Thus writings should begin at the primary level, continuing through all the years of the elementary school, as a natural and legitimate activity, not restricted to certain times, forms, or topics. The author suggests four other principles which help children become successful writers. Students need to: have something to write about, have real reasons to write, trust that their writing will be accepted and valued, and talk before writing. Teachers should attend to the quality and details of writing only when children are fluent and confident writers. The article concludes with five recommended sources of other information about writing.

DeVries, Ted D. "Writing Writing and Talking Writing." *Elementary English* (December 1970): 1067–1071.

DeVries recounts an experiment using tape recorders to help children move through three stages: saying something, hearing it back, and seeing it in writing. Essentially a report on variation on the language-experience approach used for writing purposes instead of reading. There are suggestions on how to increase students' desire to write, including the novel idea that teachers write for and with their students.

Gay, Carol. "Reading Aloud and Learning to Write." *Elementary School Journal* (November 1976): 87–93.

In beautifully crafted prose, the author describes the guilt some teachers feel in giving time to oral reading, worrying that they should be engaged in more "serious" tasks. Next, she develops thoroughly, giving examples, reasons for reading aloud. Weaknesses in basal readers, especially in presenting unnatural language patterns children cannot emulate, are described. Having little oral input that is discriminating and precise, and written patterns which are stilted, students are not motivated to write. The author's antidote: a regular program of reading aloud.

Graves, Donald H. "An Examination of the Writing Processes of Seven-Year-Old Children." *Research in the Teaching of English* 9(3) (Winter 1975): 227–241.

While much has been written about ways to motivate children to write, researcher Graves feels that there has been too little case-study research involving the process of writing. He studied a group of seven-year-old children to see what variables influenced their writing. The sample involved two formal and two informal second grade classrooms in a middle class community. One phase of the research involved 94 children, to assess the general writing habits of the group in terms of writing frequency, assigned/unassigned writing, writing length, and thematic interests. Later, the researcher narrowed the group studied to fourteen children. Fifty-three writing episodes from among this group were observed. Each writing episode consisted of three steps: prewriting (including choosing a theme and discussions with class members), composing (including actual writing, teacher and peer help) and postwriting (editing). In addition, children were asked to review and rank their own writing. Graves concluded that children generally write better in informal environments, with girls performing better than boys in formal settings. Regardless of the environment, unassigned writing is longer than assigned writing.

Gray, James and Myers, Miles. "The Bay Area Writing Project." *Phi Delta Kappan* 59(6) (February 1978): 410–413.

The Bay Area Writing Project (BAWP), created by a group of San Francisco educators representing all levels of instruction, is based on the assumption that most teachers do not teach writing because they have not been trained as teachers of writing. Four assumptions, each validated by educational research, guided the development of BAWP in its summer programs, district programs, national replication sites, and plans for field-based research and publication: (1) curriculum change cannot be accomplished by transient consultants who appear briefly, never to be seen again; (2) a substantial body of knowledge exists concerning the teaching of writing; (3) curriculum materials cannot be "teacher-proof" if real change is to occur; (4) field-based research could make a significant contribution to improvement of instruction.

Hagemann, Meyly Chin. "Taking the 'Wrench' Out of Letter Writing." *English Journal* (March 1980): 38–40.

The author provides practical, in-classroom tips marked by their practicality, to accomplish her main concern: making letter writing an authentic experience. Inexpensive.

Smith, Lewis and Willardson, Marilyn. "Communication Skills through Authorship." *Elementary English* 2 (February 1971): 190–193.

The authors recognize that a young child has always had to be dependent on adults to record his thoughts. The article presents one solution using portable cassette recorders. Separate units were set up in one corner of the classroom, and children were encouraged to dictate any time they wished. Teachers or teacher aides typed the recordings. These typed materials later became the source of reading activities.

Bibliography

Balaz, Pat and Dumas, Barbara. "Making Friends by Mail." *Early Years* (September 1979): 101–102 + .

Bishop, Claire Huchet. *Five Chinese Brothers.* New York: Coward, McCann, 1938.

Britton, James Nimmo. "The Student's Writing." In *Explorations in Children's Writing* (ed. by Evertts), Champaign, Ill.: National Council of Teachers of English, 1970, pp. 21–26.

Cleary, Beverly. *Ramona and Her Father.* New York: William Morrow, 1977.

Haley-James, Shirley and Hobson, Charles D. "Interviewing: A Means of Encouraging the Drive to Communicate," *Language Arts* 57 (1980): 497–502.

Holbrook, David. "Children Write." Cassette tape available from Cambridge University Press, 1973.

Hou-tien, Cheng. *Six Chinese Brothers.* New York: Holt, Rinehart and Winston, 1979.

Hoxworth, Alice. "Try a Friday Letter." *Early Years* (December 1979): 33 +

Temple, Charles A., et al. *The Beginnings of Writing.* Boston: Allyn and Bacon, 1982, pp. 167–168.

Western, Linda E. "A Comparative Study of Literature Through Folk Tale Variants." *Language Arts* (April 1980): 395–402.

Ziegler, Alan. "Letters That Can't Be Delivered." *Teachers and Writers Collaborative* 7(3) (Spring 1976): 26–31.

HANDWRITING

Handwriting is an art open to any amateur for the delight he gets from it himself, and for the further pleasure he gives to others. (Mumford, 1959).

The above quote by a delightfully wry commentator on the American way of life seems strangely out of date now, although it was written only two decades ago. It's a rare individual who has the leisure today to savor the art of the proper shaping of letters. If we notice good penmanship, we may unconsciously be grateful for it, but seldom do we pause to reflect upon the skill of the writer. Even less often do we think consciously about our own writing.

Although our world is unlike Mumford's, and delight in an attractive page is minimal, some valid reasons remain for being concerned with handwriting and how to teach it to children.

PRACTICAL REASONS

Is the street address 732 Vineland Place, or 132 Vineland Place? Is the client on whom you are to call Mr. Thomaus or Mr. Tomans? Is the cough medicine for which you're searching called Myoncl or Myond? So often we find ourselves in such situations, staring in bewilderment at the scribbles on the papers in our hands, unable to decipher the marks. Time and money are lost as we try to interpret our own scrawls or those of others. Postal clerks, pharmacists, plant managers, and secretaries all share the same frustration in dealing with the products of a society which sees no intrinsic value in handwriting, yet pays the penalty for illegibility. The problem of unreadable writing is nationwide and apparently not getting any better. As long ago as 1959 the estimate was that U.S. businesses lost about $1 million *per week* because of scrambled orders, missent deliveries, and clerical mistakes resulting from poor handwriting (O'Brien, 1959). The problem is probably of greater magnitude today. In a more recent survey of 500 members of the National Secretaries Association, 57 percent of the respondents rated their bosses' handwriting either "difficult" or "impossible" to read. The median time spent redoing work because of misread writing was three hours per week (Los Angeles *Times* Service, July 26, 1981).

Adult handwriting may range from such clear and legible samples as Figure 9-1 to the completely illegible scratches of Figure 9-2, taken from the

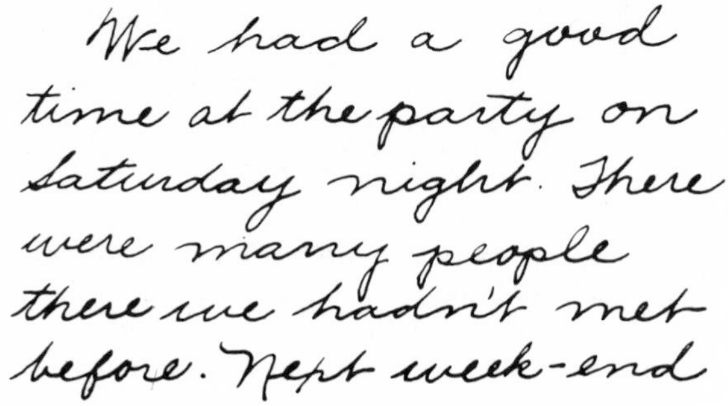

We had a good
time at the party on
Saturday night. There
were many people
there we hadn't met
before. Next week-end

FIGURE 9-1

writing of a professor who communicates daily in writing with many colleagues and students.

Every teacher in elementary school is faced with a wide range of hand-

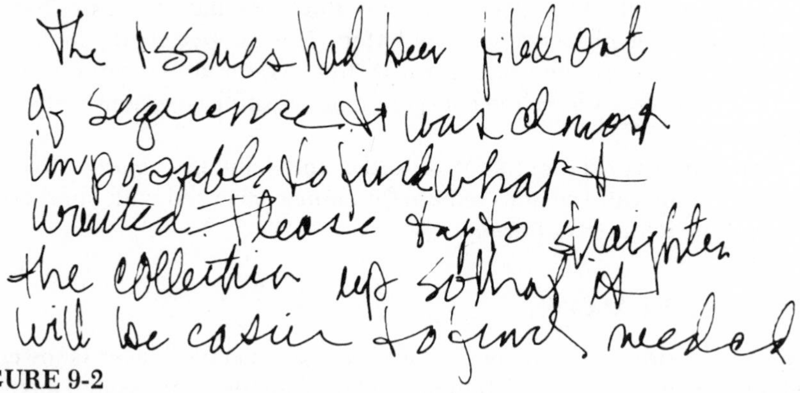

The issues had been filled out
of sequence. It was almost
impossible to find what I
wanted. Please try to straighten
the collection up so that it
will be easier to find, needed

FIGURE 9-2

writing competency, as demonstrated by the samples included in Figure 9-3, all taken from one class of fifth-grade children.

Given the reality that widely differing competencies exist among young children's handwriting and apparently continue to exist among adults, the need for some sort of handwriting instruction is evident. To whom should it be given and for how long? These among others are the questions with which this chapter will be concerned.

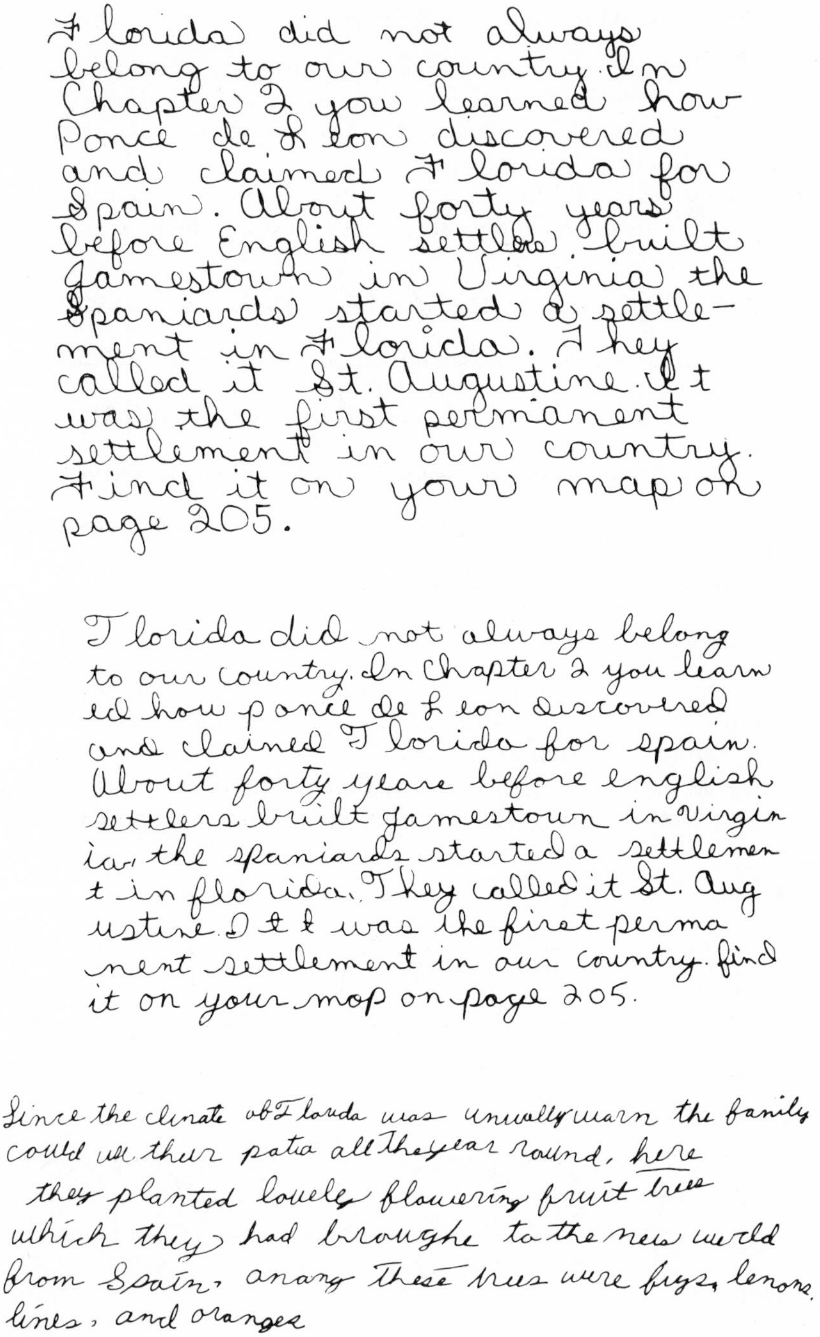

Florida did not always belong to our country. In Chapter 2 you learned how Ponce de Leon discovered and claimed Florida for Spain. About forty years before English settlers built Jamestown in Virginia the Spaniards started a settle-ment in Florida. They called it St. Augustine. It was the first permanent settlement in our country. Find it on your map on page 205.

Florida did not always belong to our country. In Chapter 2 you learned how ponce de Leon discovered and claimed Florida for spain. About forty years before english settlers built Jamestown in Virginia, the spaniards started a settlement in florida. They called it St. Augustine. It It was the first permanent settlement in our country. find it on your map on page 205.

Since the climate of Florida was unusually warm the family could use their patio all the year round. here they planted lovely flowering fruit trees which they had brought to the new world from Spain. Among these trees were figs, lemons, limes, and oranges

FIGURE 9-3

HOW IS HANDWRITING TAUGHT?

Since much of what goes on in schools is evolutionary from ideas and practices of earlier times rather than implementation of new ideas (Ammons, 1969), some investigation of handwriting instruction may help future teachers understand current programs.

For many years, children in this country learned only *cursive* writing (Figure 9-4). This is the connected form we most commonly call "writing."

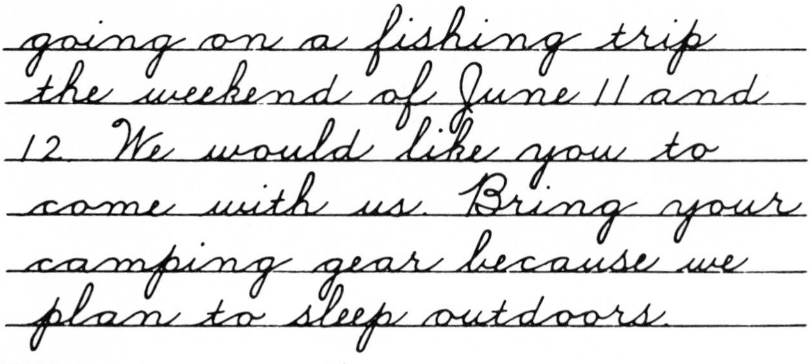

going on a fishing trip
the weekend of June 11 and
12 We would like you to
come with us. Bring your
camping gear because we
plan to sleep outdoors.

FIGURE 9-4

Though young children learned to read from materials set in printer's type, quite unlike the script they wrote, no attempt was made to begin writing instruction with a form similar to type.[1]

It was not until early in this century that children began to be instructed first in one kind of writing (close to print type, Figure 9-5) and then were re-

Eat good fc

Keep clean

FIGURE 9-5

---

[1]An exception to this is the series of books about Babar, the elephant, not set in manuscript-like type, but rather using cursive writing. See, for example, *The Story of Babar* (London: Methuen, 1955).

quired to learn another form (the form widely accepted among adults).[2]

The acceptance of *manuscript* writing, the unconnected form made essentially of straight lines and circles, is remarkable for two reasons:

1. We can pinpoint with accuracy both the date and the person responsible for introducing the idea. One cannot help but marvel at the pervading influence of a dynamic lady from England, Marjorie Wise, who first taught a course in this new method at Teacher's College (Columbia University) in New York in 1922. From this beginning manuscript has spread until its use is almost universal (Enstrom, 1964).

2. The degree of acceptance of this two-form approach to teaching handwriting is almost complete. It is a rare idea or innovation in education that receives almost universal acceptance in schools. A study done some time ago indicates that almost all children learned both forms of writing.[3] While the study is admittedly an older one, there has been no replication of it. Informal observation does not suggest that the situation has changed much.

Thus we see that handwriting instruction is fairly well codified into one approach: that of using an introductory mode (manuscript) and a permanent mode (cursive).

TIME ALLOTMENTS

While there is no general agreement about the amount of time that should be spent on handwriting instruction, it is not unfair to characterize it as minimal. Though school schedules and time durations vary widely, one element which pervades many classrooms is the need to teach many language arts in a limited amount of time. The teacher must provide mandated experiences in reading, mechanics/usage exercises, and spelling. Recent interest in composition has ensured that more children are receiving at least some instruction in writing. Committed teachers try to provide time for listening instruction, for drama, and oral language work. Certainly it is easy to see why the teacher, inundated with so many things to do in so short a time, turns to the sequentially organized handwriting series. Pressed for time and faced with the need to teach the skill effectively, teachers seek materials which will do it easily and quickly. It seems fair to generalize about handwriting instruction as being fairly well codified in approach and taught in minimal amounts of time. Some teachers feel strongly that this is a wise curricular decision (Jervis, 1979).

---

[2]Almost all American children learn both styles, but in a number of European countries children learn only the cursive form.

[3]Virgil Herrick, *New Horizons for Research in Handwriting* (Madison, Wis.: The University of Wisconsin Press, 1963), pp. 19–20. The study revealed that 79 percent of all children learned both forms, with 14 percent learning cursive only and a miniscule 7 percent learning only manuscript.

The foregoing assumes a specific time set aside for handwriting instruction, though casual observation suggests that fewer and fewer teachers are giving systematic, planned instruction, at least beyond the introductory level. Some children may, in fact, be able to practice and perfect their writing ability in the context of other assignments.

With the increased emphasis on mainstreaming exceptional children, however, further thought should be given to providing specially set-aside time periods for handwriting instruction at all levels. One pair of authors has pointed out the problem: "Many mildly handicapped children are inadequate incidental learners and as such will not be able to acquire new skills or alter existing ones without receiving specific instruction. The teacher who is aware of this fact will . . . provide systematic instruction which will teach step-by-step procedures for handwriting acquisition."[4]

As more and more teachers are dealing with larger numbers of children whose handicaps are minimal but real nonetheless, the importance of planning a sequence of handwriting instruction becomes apparent. Not only will teachers plan time for introductory sessions in which letter forms are taught, but maintenance sessions, in which children practice and improve skills previously introduced, will also be planned.

MINIMAL INTEREST

Probably one reason for the state of handwriting instruction today is that neither teachers nor students find it a very rewarding subject. One author identified the reason for teachers' attitudes toward the subject: "Handwriting is an unpopular subject with teachers, probably because adult handwriting tends to be inferior to that of students. . . . (Noble, 1963). Groff (1975) believes that the quality of teachers' handwriting has deteriorated over the years. In addition to the problem of teacher attitude, a recent study indicated that children are not very interested in handwriting. Inskeep and Rowland questioned 550 children in grades four through six and discovered that handwriting was next to the bottom in a list of preferred school subjects.[5]

COMMERCIAL MATERIALS

Teachers should be aware of the commercial series available for handwriting instruction since they typically choose one to use, rather than fashioning their

---

[4]Sandra B. Cohen and Stephen P. Plaskon, *Language Arts for the Mildly Handicapped.* Columbus, Ohio: Charles E. Merrill, 1980, p. 239. This comprehensive handbook of techniques for the classroom teacher gives practical suggestions in oral skills of listening and speaking, as well as written skills, both mechanical and expressive. The spelling chapter, which identifies five different modality preferences mildly handicapped children may favor, is particularly helpful.

[5]James Inskeep and Monroe Rowland. "An Analysis of School Subject Preference of Elementary School Children of the Middle Grades." *Journal of Educational Research* 58 (January 1965): 225–228. An interesting aspect of this study is that through an examination of correlations between IQ and preferences, the authors discovered that this dislike for handwriting pervaded all intelligence levels.

own program. Indeed, some authorities have taken the position that the most crucial determinant of the nature of any handwriting program is the commercial series used (Herrick, 1963).

When the teacher, perhaps while serving as a member of a textbook adoption committee, examines these materials, he or she is struck immediately by the quantity available. There are in excess of sixteen companies manufacturing handwriting materials; among these it should be possible for every committee to find something to their liking.

The commercial materials differ in three aspects:

1. In the individual letter *forms* presented as models to be followed.[6] For instance, we find that both capital and lowercase letters are made differently depending on the series. The letter P, for example, may be made in any of the ways illustrated in Figure 9-6. The letters

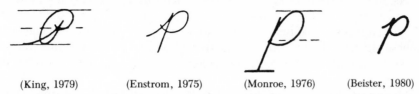

| (King, 1979) | (Enstrom, 1975) | (Monroe, 1976) | (Beister, 1980) |

FIGURE 9-6

B, W, X, and R are others that vary from one series to another.

2. In the *sequence* in which individual letters are presented. Some series introduce all lowercase and then all uppercase forms (Norwick & Bell, 1978). Others introduce a mixture of lowercase and capitals (Enstrom, 1975), and still others introduce each uppercase with its corresponding lowercase form (Bowmar & Noble, 1981) In each case, the rationale for the mode of presentation is "difficulty," though exactly how this is determined is not always clearly explained.

3. In the recommended *method* for making a letter. For example, a child learning to make a manuscript E may learn one of the three ways illustrated in Figure 9-7.

| (Thurber, 1981) | (Norwick & Bell, 1978) | (Barbe, 1979) |

FIGURE 9-7

---

[6]One factor to keep in mind in selecting a series is *simplicity* of form. Most adults tend to modify the style they learned in school in the direction of simpler forms (Askov, 1970).

CHOOSING A SERIES

Making a decision about which series to use is indeed difficult; despite small differences in the three aspects mentioned above, the materials are characterized more by their similarities than by their differences. In fact, one author maintains that because of this: "a teacher using one series rather than another might be somewhat hardput to identify specific advantages of the adopted series . . ." (Lamb, 1971).

The decision-making process is further complicated by the fact that research is limited. We do have some indication of which letters are most difficult, and this information can be used in assessing the materials. The Lewises (1964) did a study in which they determined the difficulty of *manuscript* letters and discovered that q, g, p, y, and j are the most difficult, while H, O, L, o, and l are the least difficult. Burns (1962) examined the difficulty of *cursive* letters, and as a result of his study determined that a, e, r, t, v, n, o, and s are the most difficult. These studies provide a teacher with some data to use in selecting a series. If you are involved in an adoption committee, check to see if these difficult letters are among those taught first or whether they are delayed until later in the sequence when presumably a child has more confidence in the skill.

Beyond these studies, there is little controlled, empirical research to justify materials and methods in handwriting. There is a great quantity of nomothetic writing by experts, but unfortunately little of this is backed up by "hard" data. Until more research is available, decisions about what materials to use and how to use them will probably continue to be made on intuitive bases.

Other materials for handwriting instruction are similarly based on expert opinion rather than research. For some time, children beginning to write were given large wooden pencils on the theory that small muscle coordination was not sufficient for boys and girls to use regular adult pencils. This practice continues, despite studies which demonstrate that handwriting quality is not significantly related to pencil size (Wiles, 1943; Parker, 1973). In fact, children's performance seems to increase when they use felt-tip pens.

The problem of selecting materials is related to the question of methods to use in teaching handwriting. Special methods are needed for left-handed children and for those with special learning needs. In writing about learning disabled students, Tufo (1980) recommended four steps that would be useful to teachers having such children in their rooms. Some experts feel that learning disabled children should begin handwriting instruction using cursive writing (Mullins et al., 1972). As Peck et al. (1980) note: "With mandated mainstreaming of special education children, continued research on the development of handwriting skills among handicapped children is imperative."

One series deserves special mention. *Writing Our Language* by Marion Monroe (1976) is unusual because of its use of actual student handwriting samples. Most available handwriting materials present a model of unblemished perfection, which at times looks as though it might have been created by a machine. The question should be raised about the effect such unrelenting perfection has upon children, and especially upon boys, for whom such perfection is not easily acquired and by whom it is seldom desired.

INDIVIDUALIZING THE HANDWRITING PROGRAM

Typically, handwriting instruction has been given in total-class situations (Addy & Wylie, 1973). The teacher most frequently presents the new letter or combination form using the handwriting series as guide, and all the children work on the same letter at the same time.

Given what we know about the range of individual differences likely to be present in any elementary classroom, such a procedure cannot be maximally effective. What are the alternatives? Some scheme of individualized instruction seems desirable.

There are basically two types of individualization. The first is *rate* individualization, the easier to accomplish. Especially with new materials now available, it is possible for children to move through a specified content at their own speed.

The more difficult type to implement is *content* individualization, due to the reluctance with which we adults relinquish ideas of certain contents being necessary for everyone. It is probably a fair generalization that most individualized learning programs in effect today are ones of rate, not content.

Askov (1970) is firm in pointing out that there are definite advantages when individual instruction is provided. Her review of research revealed that, especially for older children, more gains are made when children's individual problems are diagnosed and specific study strategies are created than when everyone progresses through the same program in the same way.

The Open Concept and Individualization

The idea of open-concept, or multiage grouping, arousing such interest among educators now because of the positive and pervading influence of the British Infant Schools,[7] can lead to individualization of handwriting. One interesting aspect of this approach is that it puts into practice ideas suggested some time ago by forward-looking educators.[8]

---

[7]For a description of how such a grouping facilitates language learning, and especially how one child with more mature skills helps one with less mature skills, see Ann Cook and Herbert Mack, "The British Primary School," *Educational Leadership* 27 (November 1969): 140–143.

[8]Miriam Wilt, "Organizing for Language Learning," in *Issues & Problems in the Elementary Language Arts,* edited by Petty (Boston: Allyn & Bacon, 1968): 39–46. The most striking fact about Wilt's article is that it discusses ideas only now becoming accepted. Her suggestions for multiage grouping with younger children learning from older children in a very free environment were made some time ago, though they are only now being implemented on a wide scale.

Such organizational arrangements capitalize on the help older children, whose skills are firmly established, can be to younger children who may still be learning basic skills.

Teachers in such situations can guide older and more capable students in helping younger ones move at their own rate in acquiring handwriting skills. The teacher may need to present initial lessons in the mechanics of making a particular form, but follow-up practice can be done alone.

One program needs special attention here because it provides not only individualization of rate, but also of content (manuscript, cursive, or typewritten symbols).

An Experimental Program

One of the most noteworthy programs in handwriting, the Hawaii program, was begun several years ago. It is experimental and of interest for two reasons.

The first is that, after they have progressed through a series of group readiness activities, children entering the handwriting program are allowed to choose in which mode they will learn: manuscript writing, cursive writing, or typewriting. Recent correspondence with a member of the Hawaii English Project[9] casts doubt on the strongly held belief that children need to learn manuscript writing and then switch to cursive. Data collected during a five-year period indicates that over 90 percent of the kindergarten children in this state are able to go directly to the cursive script. Follow-up studies on the children who attempt cursive and do not succeed indicates that they also have trouble with the manuscript form, suggesting a need for further readiness activities.

A second feature which distinguishes the program is that it is highly individualized and autoinstructional. Although handwriting experts have for years pointed out the importance of individualization, in actuality one finds that group instruction as mentioned earlier is the more usual method.

In the Hawaii program, after children have chosen the mode (manuscript, cursive, or typewriting) in which they will learn, they make a further choice. They elect to learn using *Flock Cards*, *Writing Books*, or *Film Loops*. All the materials have been prepared or especially adapted for this program. The learner uses the Flock Cards, which include specific directions for making each letter enhanced by the kinesthetic or tactile element; the Writing Books,

---

[9]Information in this section adapted and updated from reports and personal correspondence from Florence Wakuya, Office of Instructional Services, Hawaii English Project, July 22, 1981.

HANDWRITING PROGRAM

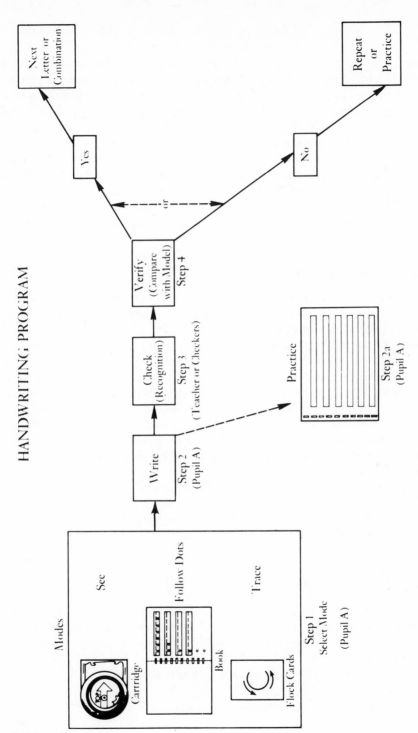

FIGURE 9-8

297

which are similar to conventional handwriting materials; or the Film Loops, each of which presents a single letter in an easily used format that the child may view as frequently as she or he likes. Children work individually and progress at their own rate. There is no group instruction. Instead, the teacher uses the time set aside daily for handwriting practice to assist individual children. After practicing a particular letter or combination form until it is mastered, the child can go to a checker who examines the material. These are salaried staff members who also perform other paraprofessional tasks. The teacher helps with checking but is not alone responsible for all the children. The checker either recommends that the learner go on to another letter, or practice further. The steps in this program are diagrammed in Figure 9-8.

Paraprofessional Help in Individualization

Few teachers work in programs as experimental as the one described above. Yet even in a more conventional program, with some planning and recruiting among parents, more individualization can be effected than if the teacher tries to do the entire program alone. A brief review of school admission forms will reveal which mothers have proficient enough handwriting to serve as assistants in the program. These women can be contacted about helping with the handwriting program. The teacher can spend a few hours on initial instruction with the group of volunteers, who come into the classroom on a regularly assigned basis. The teacher will undoubtedly do the initial presentation on the letter forms. After this, the mothers who have been instructed in how to supervise practice can help individual children work at whatever forms they need to practice.

Another source of help is the school district home economics department. Many forward-looking departments are instituting child study courses as electives. Students enrolled in such courses often need practicum experiences, and can be contacted about helping in elementary classrooms.

THE ISSUE OF TRANSITION

Much of the foregoing, concerned with how handwriting is taught and the materials necessary to accomplish this, is based on a tacit assumption: the use of two forms. It is important to question this practice, despite the evidence cited earlier that the use of two forms is almost universal and despite the fact that few commercial series even admit that perhaps some children should be allowed to learn only one form.

The reasons given for teaching manuscript are logical. These include:

1. There are only two basic shapes to be mastered, the circle and the straight line.

2. There is time for the child to rest between letters, since each letter is disconnected from the others.

3. There is much similarity between this style of writing and the print children read.

4. In natural settings, most children learn to write discontinuous letters first, later connecting the letters. (Hodges, 1981)

Considering the inherent logic of these reasons, we must ask if the advantages gained by learning cursive writing are strong enough to warrant burdening children with learning two systems.

We have empirical evidence that manuscript writing is superior to cursive in some ways. It is more legible than cursive writing, it can be written as fast as cursive, and it can be learned more easily (Anderson, 1966; Jackson, 1971).

In addition, it is difficult to read the research of Templin (1963) without wondering about the wisdom of requiring children to learn both manuscript and cursive writing. Templin examined the handwriting of 378 adults and concluded that: "The transition from the manuscript to the cursive style of handwriting at any age or at any grade level tends to result in less legible adult handwriting."

The main, and indeed only, reason which justifies this dual system of instruction is societal pressure brought to bear on those who use manuscript once they are adults. All sorts of reasons are given for making a transition, e.g., cursive is faster, it is more individualistic, it is a legal requirement on documents. None of these reasons can be defended by empirical data. We are thus confronted with the fact that we ask children to learn two systems simply because many in our society look upon cursive writing as more "adult" than manuscript (Barham, 1974). The question to be considered by teachers is: How long must we use a cumbersome two-style approach, which results in reduced legibility, in order to satisfy an illogical societal demand? The amount of time wasted when one well-developed skill is discarded and another must be learned has to be weighed against the value of this time being spent in more profitable pursuits. Western (1977) deals with this point in arguing convincingly that this time might better be spent helping students improve their ability to compose, that is, to express their ideas.

Changing the Status Quo

Naturally the change from a two-style system of instruction to teaching a single form, or to allowing children to choose which form they will learn, needs to be made at a school-district level. No teacher can effect such a change alone. All teachers and administrators must agree on the wisdom of having children learn one, not two styles. Once such a decision is made,

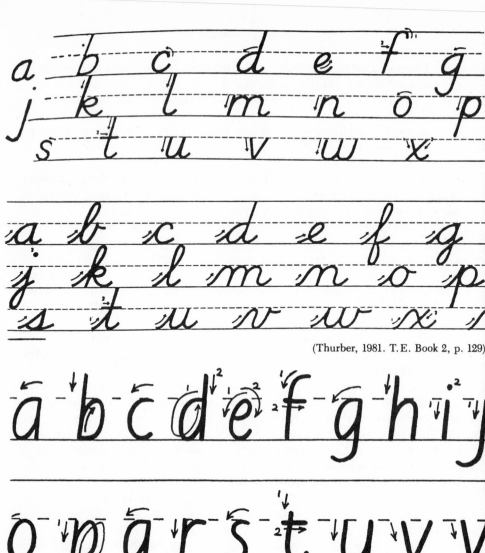

(Thurber, 1981. T.E. Book 2, p. 129)

Paper was invented by the Chinese i
the second century. In Western Europ
it did not become a serious rival to par
ment until the fifteenth century!

(Getty, 1980)

FIGURE 9-9

specific plans must be developed for explaining to parents the rationale for the decision and for enlisting their aid in making the program a success.[10]

It is especially appropriate now to consider this problem in view of the interest in accountability which seems so common.[11] Parent groups throughout the country are requesting and receiving specific statements of what schools are attempting to do and reports about the effectiveness of these attempts. Along with demands that schools increase their effectiveness should go some reconsideration of this issue in handwriting. Time spent instructing students in one system of handwriting, soon to be abandoned in favor of another, cannot be spent on other subjects which are indeed more basic.

Another Alternative

Recently another possibility has become available to those teachers and administrators concerned about the amount of time spent teaching children two systems of handwriting. *Italic* handwriting, a modified, single-form approach neither manuscript nor cursive, seems to be easy to teach and to learn. Italic writing systems are available in several formats. (See Figure 9-9.)

Accepting the Status Quo

Realistically, it is probable that teachers and principals may be unwilling to change to a single style of handwriting, or to allow children a choice of modes as is done in the innovative Hawaiian program. If this is the case, the school staff needs to consider *when* the change from manuscript to cursive is to be made.

Educators must be alert to research that demonstrates conclusively that the *later* the transition is made, the better off the child is. Wilson (1963) speaks for those who believe this in stating that, "The delay of the cursive writing skill increases the mastery of written language each half year it is delayed." Her research indicated that fifth-grade children in her study (N = 147) wrote more words the later they made the transition. She discovered that children who changed as second-graders wrote on the average of 2,623 words. Those who did not change until the end of third grade wrote on the

---

[10]This will not be easy. Patrick Groff, in "Preference for Handwriting Style by Big Business," *Elementary English* 41 (December 1964): 863–864, reports that though business executives expressed a preference for manuscript, parents felt two systems were necessary. See "Parents' Opinions about Handwriting Styles," *Elementary English* 43 (December 1966): 873–876.

[11]Accountability, the idea that schools must assume responsibility for the results of their work, is widely treated in the professional literature. See, for example, R. E. Burgett, "Accountability: Just the Teacher?" *School and Community* 58 (December 1971): 30–31, or R. J. Nash, "Accountability: Next Deadly Nostrum in Education?" *School and Society* 99 (December 1971): 501–504. Both provide a good introduction to a problem that needs careful consideration by teachers.

average of 7,681 words. Clearly, then, the later the transition, the better for the child.

Teachers should be aware that several of these series suggest optional times of transition in the program, and some decision about which to adopt must be made. In addition, all series give very specific suggestions on how to make the transition.

DEVELOPING LEGIBILITY

When working with older children who have learned cursive writing, two approaches to practice are possible. You may decide to use the handwriting series essentially as it is, or you may decide to work on legibility by concentrating on the problems your children have, which is a diagnostic approach.

Research on handwriting has demonstrated that some letters are quite apt to give children problems. The teacher may want to analyze the children's writing to determine which of the children have such problems. Then put the children into skill development groups to work on their specific problems. Children can work with their small skill group until they have mastered the particular troublesome form and then move to another group. When all the children have mastered the form, the group is disbanded.

Horton (1970) studied difficulties in cursive writing among 1,000 sixth-grade children. As a result, it is possible that the following letters will be difficult for your children:

<table>
<tr><td></td><td></td><td>r—This is the most difficult and accounted for 12 percent of all illegibilities.</td></tr>
<tr><td>These letters accounted for 30 percent of all illegibilities</td><td>{</td><td>h
l
k
p
z</td></tr>
</table>

Given such a large percentage of difficulties caused by a small number of letters, Horton concluded that "concentrated effort on a few troublesome letters would produce greater legibility in cursive [writing]. . . ."

Beyond working on specified form problems, however, the teacher is always concerned with a larger problem, that of helping children to *regularize* their handwriting. Legibility is to a large degree dependent upon this regularization or the predictability the reader can expect while reading a particular sample.

There are basically four aspects of handwriting that should be regularized: (1) slant; (2) size; (3) form; (4) spacing.

The question of amount of *slant* forward or backward is not as important as the regularity of the slant. Although some authors are adamant in recommending elimination of a backhand slant, it is difficult to justify this position, provided the backhand slant is regular, i.e., consistent, and not too extreme.

There is no doubt that excessively small or excessively large handwriting presents problems of legibility, but the regularity of *size* is more important.

Similarly, while there may be certain *form* irregularities or peculiarities so unusual that the teacher feels it necessary to help a child eliminate them, it is more crucial that the child be consistent in the form used. That is, if the reader can anticipate the form of a particular letter will always be made the same way, he or she can minimize the problem of reading the writing. If, for example, in a single sample the letter *a* is made three different ways and at random, the legibility problem is greater.

Finally, helping children work on regularity of *spacing* is essential. Again it matters less whether the spacing is compact and tight or loose and relaxed, providing it is regular. When one encounters irregularity of spacing legibility diminishes.

Children can check the regularity of their own slant, simply by drawing lines through the spines of the letters; these lines should be parallel. Figure 9-10 indicates a desired regularity of slant.

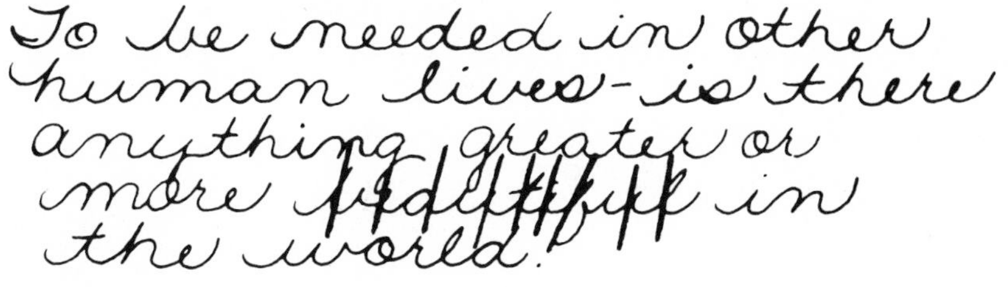

FIGURE 9-10

What one wants to help children overcome is the sort of irregularity in Figure 9-11.

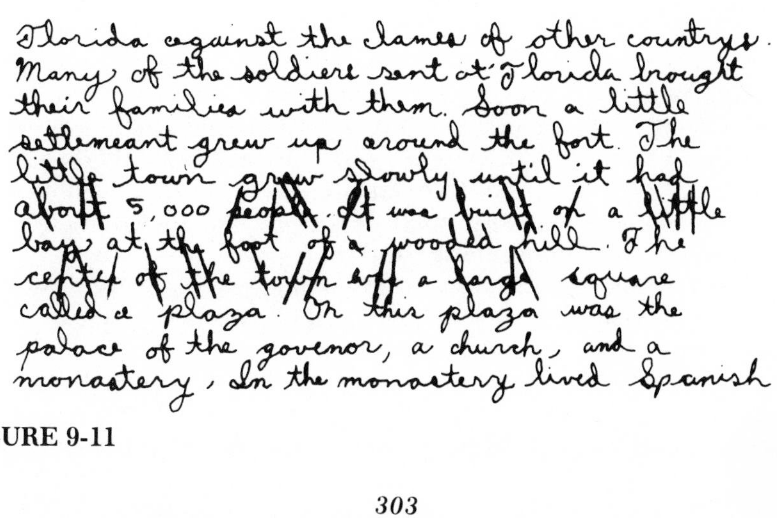

FIGURE 9-11

303

Whether handwriting is large or small is less crucial than that the size is regular. Drawing guide lines (Figure 9-12) can help children check on the regularity of size in their writing.

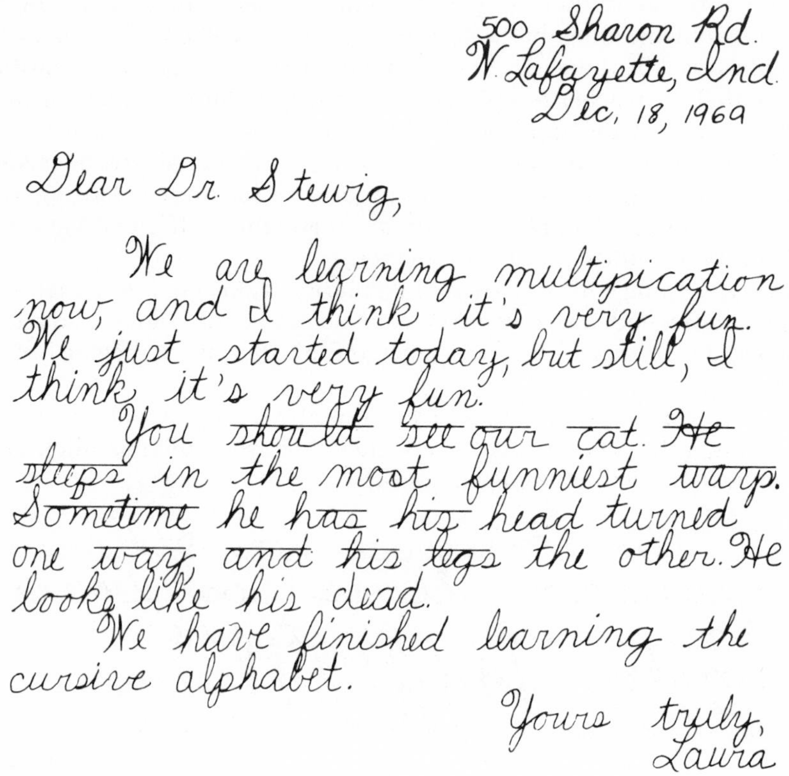

500 Sharon Rd.
N. Lafayette, Ind.
Dec, 18, 1969

Dear Dr. Stewig,

We are learning multiplication now, and I think it's very fun. We just started today, but still, I think it's very fun.
You should see our cat. He steps in the most funniest ways. Sometime he has his head turned one way and his legs the other. He looks like his dead.
We have finished learning the cursive alphabet.

Yours truly,
Laura

FIGURE 9-12

What we want to help children avoid is the sort of size problem illustrated in Figure 9-13.

It is simple to check regularity of form—have your children use a paper punch to put one hole in a small piece of cardboard. This can be moved along a line of writing as it is used to check on the legibility of individual letters. The cardboard serves to block out the surrounding letters. While it is true that within the context of a word we can often make out an individual letter, the goal is complete legibility apart from context. To accomplish this, children need to work on regularity of form.

Regularity of *spacing* is harder to evaluate, because it has to be done visually. The child needs to look not only at single words, but also at lines of writing, to determine if the spacing is regular. Allen and Wright (1974) present an evaluation sheet students may use to assess their progress in handwriting.

Work on these four elements of legibility will result in improved handwrit-

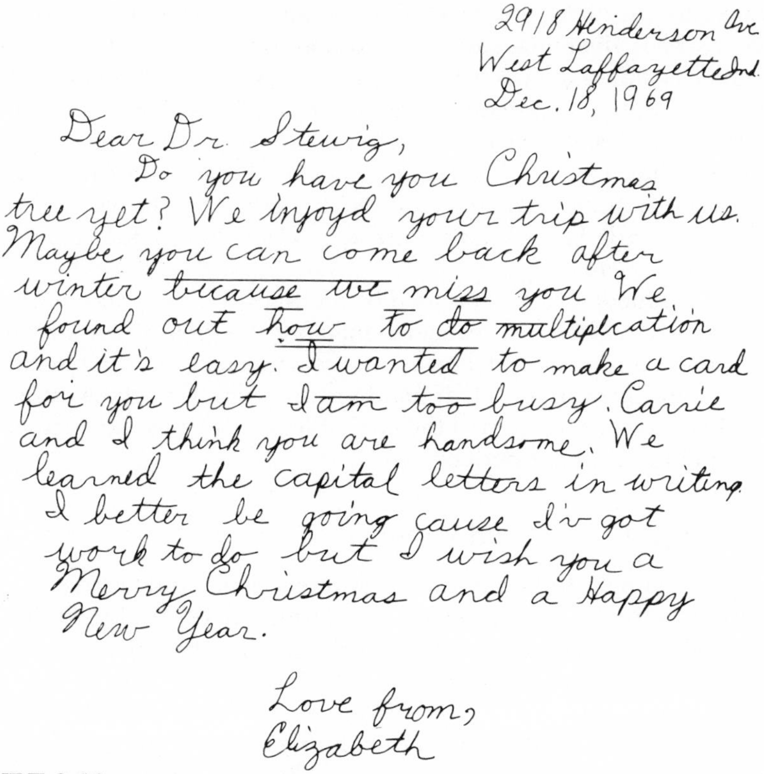

2918 Henderson Av.
West Laffayette Ind.
Dec. 18, 1969

Dear Dr. Stewig,
     Do you have you Christmas
tree yet? We Injoyd your trip with us.
Maybe you can come back after
winter because we miss you We
found out how to do multiplication
and it's easy. I wanted to make a card
for you but I am too busy. Carrie
and I think you are handsome. We
learned the capital letters in writing.
I better be going cause I'v got
work to do but I wish you a
Merry Christmas and a Happy
New Year.

                    Love from,
                    Elizabeth

FIGURE 9-13

ing, though there are other legibility factors teachers may wish to consider. Alignment of letters, quality of the line, letter height, and grip on the writing instrument are considered influential in legibility. Both Askov (1970) and Peck (1980) summarize research on these and other components of legibility.

Variability of Standard

In the emphasis on legibility, it is important to remember the intended audience. In practice work and, indeed, in most of what they write in school, children are writing for other people and thus must write legibly. This is simple courtesy.

Teachers must be understanding, however, and recognize that as adults we all write differently in different situations. When we write a letter to a friend our handwriting is of better quality than when we scribble a grocery list. So, too, as children take notes for a report or do a first draft of a story, they need to be allowed to scratch out their ideas quickly, without being concerned about the quality of their handwriting. Obviously, if one's goal is free and untrammeled expression in creative writing, any attention to legibility of copy can wait until *after* the ideas are safely on paper.

Related to variability of form is variation in speed. Girls apparently achieve a speed advantage early on and maintain it when they are adults. Groff (1963) studied over 3,000 subjects in grades four through eight and discovered that girls consistently write faster than boys. Another study (Gust & Schumacher, 1969) revealed that female college freshmen consistently wrote faster than males. This has apparent implication for the elementary teacher when writing tasks are required of both sexes. Provision for extra time must be made for boys, who are apt to take longer to accomplish an identical writing task.

Finally, the moderation advocated by Smith et al. (1976) summarizes this section: "It is vital that the teacher remember the great variability among learners and keep ends and means in proper perspective. Children vary greatly in coordination, and their handwriting will reflect these differences. The teacher, in working toward the goal of legibility, must be satisfied with progress and not demand perfection."

Who Are Apt to Be Good Writers?

There do not appear to be significant differences in handwriting related to either ethnic or socioeconomic status (Niedermeyer, 1974). Strickling (1974) found that below-average readers made a significantly greater number of handwriting errors than did average readers.

The concern about good handwriting is not simply an intrinsic one, however. A child's handwriting often influences the teacher's judgment about the worth of the paper. Markham (1976) found that when more than eighty teachers and future teachers evaluated student papers, "Papers with better handwriting consistently received higher scores than did those with poor handwriting regardless of the quality of the content."

TYPING IN THE ELEMENTARY SCHOOL

One can view the question of typing by elementary children either as a natural phenomenon of our electronic age or as an impractical idea. Whatever position one holds, there are questions to be raised before a decision can be made on what choice of action should be followed.

Interest in this idea is not new, although the amount of research is limited (Wood & Freeman, 1932). The major question to be answered is: Can children successfully be taught how to type? Wood and Freeman's study gave an affirmative answer to the question, and almost forty years later another study by Tootle (1971) gave the same answer.

What happens to children who are taught to type in the elementary grades? They gain in spelling (Tootle, 1971; Singh, 1975) as well as in creative writing ability. Tootle further found, and Donoghue (1975) also reports, that the *amount* of writing increases. Tootle was reporting on the amount of creative writing, while Donoghue was reporting on the amount of report writing. Donoghue concluded that the reports written by children

Typing a story is a valuable option for children as they are composing. Many students may prefer this to encoding their thoughts in handwriting.

who type average 3.3 times longer than similar reports written in longhand by nontypists. Her further argument in favor of typing is that children can learn to type "at rates which exceed their handwriting rates by as much as two or three times. . . ."

Since it has been established that children can be taught to type at the elementary school level, some methodological questions can be considered (McCall, 1968):

1. *By whom* should typing be taught? Is this a skill one can expect a classroom teacher to teach? Or is it more logical to expect that teachers with special training of some kind would be needed? Or could such teaching be done by tapes, records, or other audiovisual materials?
2. *When* should it be taught? Is this something else to be included in the school day, or should it be offered outside regular school hours? At what grade level should it be taught? Freeman recommended beginning in first grade, as did Haefner (1932). Is this, in fact, the optimum age for beginning such instruction?
3. *To whom* should it be taught? Is this something all children should learn, or should it be offered on an elective basis?
4. *How* are physical considerations to be arranged? The question of financing and where to locate machines are problems that need to be solved.

Proponents of typing in the elementary school make convincing arguments for their case (Martin, 1969; Klyhn, 1968; Switzer, 1979). Despite such arguments, the number of children who learn to type in the elementary school remains small. Is typing instruction at the elementary level an educational idea ahead of its time? Or is it a needless frill suggested by the mechanically inclined? Typing may be either, or something else entirely. Could you develop a rationale for typing instruction that might convince a principal or a group of parents of the need to include it in the elementary curriculum?

STUDYING WRITING SYSTEMS

Maintaining children's interest in handwriting, even if the teacher's enthusiasm is high, is sometimes difficult. The teacher may find it helpful to develop a unit on other systems of writing to revive flagging interest. Children at any grade level can study such a unit, with some adjustments made for difficulty level. This section describes some ideas for such a unit. These must be viewed as suggestions, provided simply to start you thinking. As you work with children, other ideas will occur to you.

It is logical to begin such a unit with a study of other writing systems currently in use. Children can examine samples of other alphabetic systems.[12] They will find it interesting to compare similarities and differences among such alphabets as the Cyrillic, Korean, or Arabic.

In contrast to single letters used to represent sounds, some languages use symbols to represent syllables. Sequoyah, a Cherokee Indian chief, sensed the need for a way to record his language, and so devised an 86-syllable writing system. The unusual aspect of this alphabet is that it is the product of a single person's mind, not the accumulated work of many anonymous peoples over an extended period of time (Jones, 1968).

Students can draw up charts illustrating some of these unfamiliar letters and practice making some of the more unusual ones, including trying to write words or sentences in one of the alphabets.

While doing this, children can study the different pronunciation marks which are used in other languages, including the tilde /ñ/, the macron /ō/, the breve /ŏ/, the diaeresis /oö/, and the cedilla /ç/. Such typographic symbols as the ellipses / . . ./, the dagger /†/, and the section mark /§/, can be noted. For older children, a study of editing marks can be included.[13]

---

[12]A plethora of such materials is available. Some of the trade books on the topic are included in the bibliography.

[13]See Joanna Foster, *Pages, Pictures and Print* (New York: Harcourt Brace Jovanovich, 1958). The entire book, devoted to the processes involved between manuscript and published work, is of interest to children. The chart of proofreaders' marks on page 33 is particularly useful for this unit.

Children also enjoy reading about such *ideographic* systems still in use as Chinese and Japanese. Boys and girls enjoy learning to make their name, or to make symbols for some intriguing words in one of these communication systems. The sample in Figure 9-14 is Chinese:

Woman   Child   Love

FIGURE 9-14

In such a unit, classroom visitors can augment research in books. For example, within your community there will surely be someone who could demonstrate how to write Hebrew (Figure 9-15). If you live in a large community, perhaps there will be writers of other languages. A foreign student from a university or perhaps the grandparent of one of your children will know how to write another language.

FIGURE 9-15

Children are interested in learning how blind people write (Soloway, 1978). It may be possible to borrow a braille typewriter from your local association for the blind. One kindergarten teacher provides a particularly meaningful experience for her children in arranging to have a blind person come to her classroom to demonstrate the typewriter (Figure 9-16). Then the boys and girls in her room usually continue to correspond the rest of the year with their visitor.

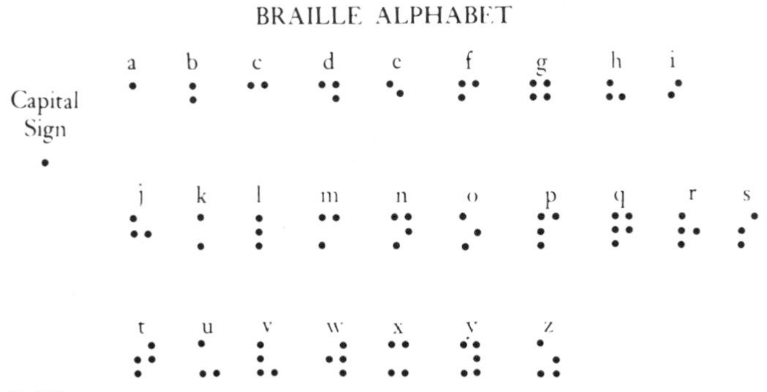

BRAILLE ALPHABET
Capital Sign
a b c d e f g h i
j k l m n o p q r s
t u v w x y z

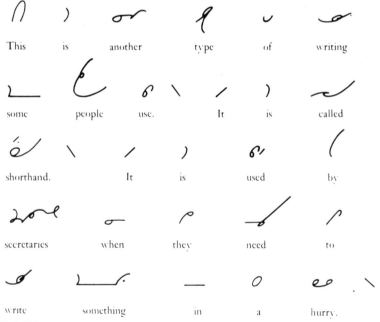

FIGURE 9-16

In addition to these writing systems, children also can learn much about *notation systems,* ways people communicate ideas using written symbols which are nonalphabetic (Stewig, 1978).

It is useful to expose children to some of the following:

1. A secretary, who can illustrate how to take shorthand. Children are always fascinated to see how their names look when written in shorthand. They delight in writing their name this way and older children like to try writing entire words (Figure 9-17).

This is another type of writing
some people use. It is called
shorthand. It is used by
secretaries when they need to
write something in a hurry.

FIGURE 9-17

STUDY IN BODY AND ARM MOVEMENTS

Suggested music: Brahms' "Lullaby."

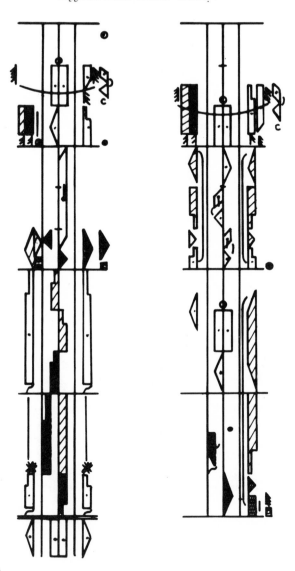

FIGURE 9-18

2. A dancer, who can illustrate how to write *Labanotation*, the system for recording choreographic ideas. Perhaps the dancer could write out a few steps and then show how a dancer translates this into movement (Figure 9-18).

3. A court reporter, who can illustrate how to use a stenotype machine. This ingenious device, which allows the reporter to record as fast as

a witness can speak, always amazes children (Figure 9-19). Older children can be allowed to use the machine after they have been instructed in correct procedures.

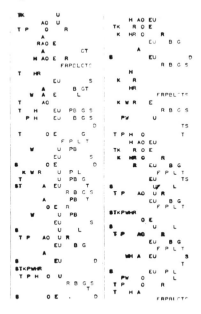

FIGURE 9-19

4. A composer (or perhaps a music teacher or professor) who can show children how the music symbol system can record intricate ideas.
5. An architect, who can show children how to indicate with written symbols many details of importance to both builder and client. With fifth- and sixth-grade children, such study could lead to a coordinated unit directed by the art teacher on house planning, so the symbols can be used.

After studying current writing systems, the teacher may want to involve children in studying ancient writing systems. There are many of these which interest children.

An immediate attention-getter is the boustrophedon arrangement of the ancient Greeks,[14] which involved writing alternate lines backwards (Figure 9-20). The challenge in writing in this fashion will intrigue children.

In studying ancient writing systems chronologically, one can begin with the caves of Altamira in Spain and Font-de-Gaume in France, to which language historians trace humans' first attempts to "write" ideas. The boldly ex-

---

[14]A particularly delightful explanation of this is in *Look and Learn,* the 1966 Childcraft Annual (Chicago: Field Enterprises), pp. 64–65. One of the freshest approaches available to a wide spectrum of language ideas, this bright, colorful, innovative, and imaginative volume belongs on every teacher's desk.

Come over to my house

a gnivig m'I esuaceb

party tomorrow.

FIGURE 9-20

ecuted paintings, flung from one end of the mammoth caverns to another, represent exploits of the hunt. These early attempts are acknowledged in both trade books (Rogers, 1960) and language arts textbooks.

Several correlations are possible between language study and the art program, though the art teacher may not look upon these as "art" per se. After reading about the clay tablets on which the Mesopotamians wrote, children may fashion replicas of the tablets and the V-shaped gouges with which they wrote. Any type of clay (including plasticene) works and tongue depressors make good gouges. Interest is high as children try their hands at communicating in this unusual, albeit cumbersome, fashion. Vegetables can be cut into a variety of letter forms and printed as two-dimensional visual compositions.[15] Any firm vegetable, such as potatoes, carrots, parsnips, etc., can be used. Even first-grade children, who can safely use blunt knives for this purpose, may take part in a project of this type. The printing process may use just letters or may incorporate children's drawings and paintings for more visual interest.

Children can search for typeface samples in magazines, which illustrate visually the quality of words. For instance, they might find examples of lettering which is:

tense	open
elegant	crowded
relaxed	thick
tall	squashed
complex	simple
curving	spiky

To begin, you may suggest certain qualities like those above. Later, the children can suggest qualities and find examples. In addition to stimulating an interest in writing, this activity also can build visual sophistication.

---

[15]Harvey Weiss, *Paper, Ink & Roller* (New York: Young Scott Books, 1958) is of help in this area. A pleasant visual layout and clear instructions distinguish this eminently practical book, which should encourage even the most timid of teachers to adventure into printing experiences of all kinds.

Several other ideas of this nature have been suggested by John Holt, who addresses himself to the question of building and maintaining interest in writing.[16] In the engagingly written section devoted to handwriting, Holt puts much premium on exploration. The question he asks is one we could ask ourselves more often: "How many different ways can you think of to do it?" He suggests we can take a single letter and vary it in three aspects: proportion, slant and weight (thickness). Some ways an A could be varied are included in Figure 9-21.

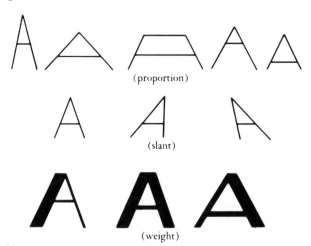

FIGURE 9-21

Holt's ideas about making letters out of a variety of materials are also exciting to read and should result in unusual and stimulating experiences for children.

To conclude this section on developing a unit of study of different types of writing, we could profit by keeping in mind a comment Holt makes: "Nothing, not even a task so seemingly cut-and-dried as making letters, needs to be monotonous, frightening, dull, cut off from the rest of learning, and of life, or from the possibility of imagination, experiment, invention, play." (Holt, 1970, p. 200)

Suggestions for Further Exploration

1. Try an experiment with some materials easily at hand. For the next two weeks, keep all the handwritten envelopes that come to you through the mail. At the end of that time take these (and one *you* have addressed) and arrange them from the most to the least legible. Then try to identify the factors you see as most crucial in legibility.

---

[16]John Holt, *What Do I Do Monday?* (New York: E. P. Dutton, 1970). Holt, who has worked with students from elementary through graduate school, offers a unique way of looking at this topic. The chapters related to the development of self are particularly thought-provoking as are his comments on basing creative writing on oral language.

2. Using a copy of the guidelines provided in Burns et al. (pp. 364–366), analyze two of the handwriting series available to you. Which of them ranks highest, according to their guidelines? After reviewing the series, decide if there are any important factors that are not included.
3. You might be interested in reading something about *graphology*, the study of handwriting for the purpose of character analysis. Be sure to read several sources. Are there areas of both agreement and disagreement among those who write about this topic?
4. Innovative suggestions concerning handwriting are few. One worth examining is by Frank N. Freeman ("On Italic Handwriting," *Elementary School Journal* [February 1960]: 258–264). Read his article and try to identify both the strong and weak points in his argument that favors adoption of this different system.
5. A piece of research referred to in the chapter reported that handwriting was among the most disliked of school subjects. Interview three or four children in each of several different classrooms. Find out what they think about handwriting and their reasons for these attitudes.
6. Find examples in magazines which illustrate to your satisfaction the list of adjectives (p. 313) and make these up into a poster or chart you can use with your children. Could another list of *verbs* be made up and illustrated in the same way?
7. Find a copy of *Words and Calligraphy for Children* by John Cataldo (Reinhold Book Corporation, 1969). This is an excellent source of motivating activities related to words and writing. Try Cataldo's idea of using the letters in the word to depict an animal visually. Then try the project with a class or a small group of children, to get their reactions to the idea.

Suggestions for Further Reading

The Art of Writing. Paris: UNESCO, 1965.

An elegantly designed catalogue for a traveling exhibition, this publication surveys the whole history of written communication. Though the illustrations are in black and white, the paperback book is exciting to look at; the commentary is brief and within the reading level of most intermediate grade children. It is an invaluable source of illustrations.

Cartner, William. *The Young Calligrapher.* New York: Frederick Warne, 1969.

First published in England, this book reflects British interest in elegant handwriting and the lavishly illustrated volume should indeed spark the interest of upper intermediate-grade readers. Large black-and-white photographs range from closeups of writing implements and shots of people in correct writing position to reproductions of early examples of calligraphic writing. Complete sample alphabets, as well as lines of individual letters illustrate different styles and show procedures for making writing from simple labels to complete books. Burnt orange enhances the black and white page, resulting in a beautiful and practical book.

Cataldo, John W. *Words & Calligraphy for Children.* New York: Reinhold, 1969.

A lavishly illustrated record of the ways in which words and art materials can be unified into finished visual expressions. Examples of art work by children from six to seventeen demonstrate how words and letters can become integral parts of paintings, drawings, and other art forms. While some of the techniques, like batik, are not explained in sufficient detail, most of the projects are well within the range of a classroom teacher.

Chang, Raymond and Chang, Margaret. *Speaking of Chinese*. New York: W. W. Norton, 1978.

Fascinating comparison of spoken and written Chinese, by a native speaker and his wife. For over 3,000 years, literate Chinese, who speak many dialects, have shared a common written language, featuring a definite ideogram for each of 25,000 or so words. As China developed contacts with other countries, the disadvantages of this treasured calligraphy became apparent, so systems of Romanization were devised; one of these is included in this book of interest to teachers and mature readers.

Chappell, Warren. *A Short History of the Printed Word*. New York: Alfred A. Knopf, 1970.

Primarily of value as a resource book for the teacher, this extensive and scholarly book will be of interest to intellectually mature intermediate-grade children. Illustrated profusely with diagrams, drawings, samples of typefaces and scripts, and with photographs, it is a rich source of examples in planning a unit on writing. Of particular interest is the complete section on printing: machines, processes, tools, and reproduction techniques are described and illustrated.

Fairbank, Alfred. *The Story of Handwriting*. New York: Watson-Guptil Publications, 1970.

A small, but lucidly written and profusely illustrated book that opens with an account of Sumerian writing from 3100 B.C. From that point, the book deals concisely with all the major writing forms. The writing presupposes no background on the part of readers but details with interest and with few oversimplifications the development of writing.

Fraenkel, Gerd. *Writing Systems*. Boston: Ginn, 1965.

In brief compass, the author explores the history of writing from earliest times, concluding with a treatment of the need for spelling reform in our current alphabetic system. Scattered throughout the book are line drawings, diagrams of ancient syllabaries, and photographs of remnants of writing from several civilizations. The accompanying teacher's handbook includes a bibliography.

Gourdie, Tom. *The Puffin Book of Lettering*. Baltimore, Md.: Penguin Books, 1961.

This delightful little paperback should prove of much interest in motivating intermediate-grade children. It deals with pen, brush, and simple carved letters and explores a variety of forms. The child with determination should enjoy the lettering skill this book encourages. See also Gourdie's *A Guide to Better Hand-Writing* (New York: Viking, 1967).

Kohn, Bernice. *Secret Codes and Ciphers*. Englewood Cliffs, N.J.: Prentice-Hall, 1968.

Middle-grade children will be fascinated by this examination of the types of ciphers (both concealment and transposition ciphers are included), and will be challenged to learn and use the intriguing ways of disguising written communication. Though many of these codes are old, the author concludes with a chapter on codes of our century.

Krieger, David L. *Letters and Words*. New York: A Young Scott Book, 1969.

Bold graphics illustrate a variety of forms for each of the letters of the alphabet, to help children understand the different forms possible. In addition, cut paper silhouette shapes illustrate some of the words included. Words are chosen to illustrate varying letter position: initial, medial, and final.

Mellor, Ann. *Children's Printing*. Newton, Mass.: Educational Development Center, 1969.

Part of the Elementary Science Study project, this slim paperback describes in convincing fashion the encouragement that experiences with the printing process offer to the creative writing of children. Procedures for movable type and silk-screen printing are clearly explained and illustrated with samples by children. Such use of a press is highly motivating to children learning manuscript who need extra practice in recognizing forms.

Montessori, Maria. *Dr. Montessori's Own Handbook*. New York: Shocken Books, 1965.

The educational pioneer whose ideas still have much to say to the classroom teacher, Montessori's presentation of her theory of handwriting instruction is unique and challenges traditional approaches. The section with emphasis on kinesthetic methods is of interest as is one devoted to the acquisition of vocabulary.

Mother Tongue Series. "Problems and Remedies." Segment #4, Time-Life Films, New York City.

This film series, produced for BBC-TV, examines all facets of the popular British Infant School movement. The first ten minutes of the segment are devoted to the type of integrated handwriting program using italic writing common in these schools. Because both the approach and the materials are so different from what is used in American schools, the film is particularly informative.

Ogg, Oscar. *The 26 Letters*. New York: Thomas Y. Crowell, 1971.

The author begins with a recounting of the discoveries of the treasures in the caves of Spain and France, wall and roof paintings, which are humans' earliest attempts at written communication. Between that chapter, and the last on printing and typefaces, is a fascinating account of the struggle to record thoughts in written words. Ogg's style is casual but informative; the abundance of two-color illustrations enhance the topics.

Scott, Louise Binder. *Developing Communication Skills*. St. Louis: Webster Division, McGraw-Hill, 1971.

Teachers will find the book long on practical suggestions and short on theory, but of immediate usefulness in the classroom. The sections on readiness activities for, and kinesthetic teaching of, handwriting are helpful.

Thomas, George L. *Better Handwriting.* Middlesex, England: Penguin Books, 1967.

A brief but intriguing explanation of italic handwriting, in terms simple enough for older intermediate children. The directions and illustrations are clear and easy to follow. Samples written in this hand by both adults and children encourage those trying to master the skill. The paperback format is inexpensive, and this, plus some simple pens could launch interested children on a challenging undertaking.

Wood, Barbara Sundene. *Messages without Words.* Milwaukee, Wis.: Raintree Childrens Books, 1978.

The author begins with prehistoric cave paintings, and includes totem poles as a means of communication. She considers trademarks, and such symbols as the barber pole, and gives brief explanations of their origins. Other ways of sending messages include coats of arms, North American Indian smoke signals, and lighthouse signals, as well as carrier pigeons, kinesics, and gestures. The artwork throughout is in full color, though it is realistic, and not too inspired. There is an Index, a Pronunciation Key, and a Glossary.

Periodical Bibliography

Bell, Mary Elizabeth. "Manuscript Writing after the Primary Grades." *Education* 89 (September 1968): 81–83.

This article gives a brief account of how manuscript writing began and advocates the use of manuscript and cursive writing by children throughout the school year. The author feels that manuscript writing should not be pushed to one side after learning cursive, but should be used in daily lessons. She notes that immature children are not capable of doing cursive, so they should be allowed to use manuscript.

Enstrom, E. A. "Instructional Goals for Handwriting." *Elementary English* 85 (January 1969): 84–85.

Guidelines for designing a worthwhile handwriting program. Legibility, speed, and efficiency in performance are three subgoals, according to the author. In teaching motor skills one must: (1) *teach* the skill; (2) *teach the use of the skill;* and (3) motivate the importance of *using* the skill. Also, he stresses the importance of "overlearning" the skills, in practice sessions. According to Enstrom, the teacher's skill is the first essential in the teaching of handwriting.

Enstrom, E. A. and Enstrom, Doris. "Signs of Readiness." *Elementary English* 48 (February 1971): 215–220.

It is not uncommon to find a child entering kindergarten who has already had some exposure to handwriting. The kindergarten teacher must make sure that any previously learned bad habits are corrected. Do not force the children to write but satisfy the needs of those who desire it.

Furner, Beatrice A. "Recommended Instructional Procedures in a Method Emphasizing the Perceptual-Motor Nature of Learning in Handwriting." *Elementary English* 46 (December 1969): 1020–1030.

According to Furner, instruction in handwriting must stress perceptual development. The students should observe the teacher's movements in making the letter. This instruction involves the use of a problem-solving approach. The visual sensation is reinforced by a verbalization of the process involved in forming a letter. Furner contends that in learning any handwriting procedure, visual, auditory, and kinesthetic stimulation should be employed. Letters having common form characteristics are introduced in groups. The sequence of instruction for grades 1–3 is summarized.

Gaforth, Francis and Hunnicutt, C. W. "A New Slant on the Second R." *Today's Education* 59 (February 1970): 45–46.

The authors feel that good handwriting is dependent on muscle training to only a limited degree and that handwriting seems to be primarily a mental process or an internalization of legible external models.

Learning handwriting in the beginning is more like drawing and the larger the drawing the easier it is to form internal images, so use of the chalkboard is good. Individual work is best after an initial group presentation. Work on the most obvious and easily corrected errors should be done first so the child can achieve success. When legibility is satisfactory, the child can be excused from handwriting instruction.

Krzesni, Joseph S. "Effect of Different Writing Tools and Paper on Performance of the Third Grader." *Elementary English* 48 (November 1971): 821–824.

This study attempted to determine if primary students performed better with a felt pen, a ballpoint pen, or a pencil, and to see if there was a difference in performance between students using lined paper and those using unlined paper. The sample consisted of 120 third-grade pupils. The children wrote a short story about a camera and were given a spelling quiz. There was no significant difference when lined paper instead of unlined paper was used. The performance was better with ballpoint pen and felt pens than with pencils; felt pens were superior to ballpoint pens.

A follow-up study reported essentially the same results. See "Writing with Flair," by Nancy L. Roser and James Britt, in *Elementary English* 52(2) (February 1975): 180–182 ff. The authors' first-grade children wrote more during the six lessons they wrote with felt-tipped pens than the six they wrote in pencil.

Lamme, Linda Leonard. "Handwriting in an Early Childhood Curriculum." *Young Children* (November 1979): 20–27.

Preschool children, often highly motivated to write their names, are eagerly assisted by parents. That interest is understandable and highly commendable; parents need to understand that writing one's name does not necessarily indicate children are ready for formal handwriting instruction. Lamme asserts that without having acquired adequate prehandwriting skills, children may be discouraged, and will probably develop poor handwriting habits, difficult to correct. The author identifies six prerequisite skills: small muscle development, eye-hand coordination, holding a writing tool, basic strokes, letter perception, and orientation to printed language. Teachers are encouraged to familiarize themselves with these, sharing the information with parents, and providing children with opportunities to achieve competence in these pre-handwriting skills. Lamme suggests numerous activities to assist children in skill acquisition, and offers clues to help teachers or parents determine when a child is ready to write.

Otto, Wayne. "Effect of Time of Transition from Manuscript to Cursive Writing upon Subsequent Performance in Handwriting, Spelling, and Reading." *The Journal of Educational Research* 62 (January 1969): 211–216.

The purpose of this research was to determine the best time for the transition from manuscript to cursive writing. The researchers selected children who fell within one of the four common transition periods: first half of the second grade, second half of the second grade, first half of the third grade, and second half of the third grade. Results indicated that late transition was connected with rapid handwriting and early transition with legible writing.

Smith, Martha. "Project that Writing Lesson." *Texas Outlook* 53 (April 1969):24–25.

The author experimented with an overhead projector in first-grade writing classes in an attempt to increase student interest. She found children grasped the writing technique easier with the use of the overhead projector. It helped greatly to have the kinesthetic practice of writing in the air while she demonstrated the proper forms on the projector. With this approach, she also felt she could give more individual help.

Strahan, Mary Anne. "Film Loops to Teach Handwriting." *Instructor* 80 (May 1971): 70–71.

The author reports favorably on the use of film loops that students can work with by themselves, and which teach specific techniques like holding a pen or pencil correctly and the proper formation of letters and words.

The advantage of this approach is that teacher supervision is not needed as the student keeps track of his or her own performance, finds the weaknesses, and then works on a program that will give the needed help.

Tufo, Thomas. "Handwriting and the Special Child." *Early Years* (May 1980): 76–77.

The article provides recommendations for helping the special child develop handwriting skills. They include: (1) Develop relaxation and build confidence. (2) Use a multi-sensory approach. Children need large vertical surfaces, such as chalkboards, to write on. (3) Encourage rhythm and movement. The descriptive count for manuscript and cursive writing (examples given) reinforce how the letters are formed, as well as regulating movement. (4) Aim for fluent legibility. A practical style of writing is not copy-book perfection, rather it is legibility with ease and speed. Finally, the author believes teachers must build confidence and relaxation in their special students, using all their senses in developing the visualizing of letter forms, and free movement in writing.

Umbach, Walter O. "Teaching Penmanship." *School and Community* 56 (November 1969): 48–49.

The author feels the main problem with penmanship instruction today is the poor handwriting of the teachers who aren't being proper models.

The theories and the materials used for handwriting are good, the subject matter is relatively easy, therefore the fault must lie with the teacher. Students whose teachers write well have the advantage, because many students learn to write by copying their teacher. Teachers who scribble tend to produce students who scribble.

Whitt, Barbara M. "Chalk It Up to Copy Copy Copy Writing." *Early Years* (November 1979): 26–27.

The author discusses steps for teaching manuscript printing to first graders, with the teacher illustrating name placement, letter alignment and formation, using alternate lines on the chalkboard. In addition, a copy of the material, such as a poem, is made for each child, because students can more easily copy from a nearby horizontal surface than from such a distant vertical one as the chalkboard. Each page is placed in a transparent plastic holder so copies do not become torn or wrinkled. Later, the chalkboard is used for a combined review of reading, and additional printing practice. Or the child is given lined duplicator master paper with a starter sentence. The child completes the sentence orally while the teacher writes the response. This becomes the child's copy for printing on a piece of writing paper.

Wilson, Louise Ada. "Helping Children with Manuscript Writing." *Peabody Journal of Education* 47 (September 1969): 72–76.

This article looks at both types of handwriting from the kinesthetic point of view. The problem of transition from manuscript to cursive is noted, and a suggestion of how the transition can be made easier for the child is given. An explanation of how the two writings are comparable should help the child. Results are given to back up the suggestions. The article also includes suggestions on how to help the child develop motor skills and how to evaluate writing through descriptive expressions.

WHAT HELP FOR THE SINISTRAL WRITER?

The problem of left-handed children is a recurring one, primarily because of the instructional questions raised when the right-handed teacher must attempt to teach the left-handed child. Though estimates vary according to sources checked, it seems likely that the teacher is apt to encounter more left-handed children today than ever before.[1]

Teachers often wonder about how to determine handedness, about the wisdom of attempting to change handedness, and about appropriate instruc-

---

[1] Estimates range from a low of 2 percent to a high of 11 percent by Gertrude A. Boyd, *Teaching Communication Skills in the Elementary School* (New York: Van Nostrand Reinhold, 1970).

tional techniques. Though some research indicates that the final *product* of the left-handed child may be equal to that of the right-handed child,[2] the problem of how to help the left-handed child remains.

To help the teacher with this problem, we offer the following bibliography. Space prevents comprehensive summaries of the ideas included, but the interested teacher will want to read further in this crucial area.

Anderson, Verna D. et al. *Readings in the Language Arts.* New York: Macmillan, 1968, pp. 172–174.

Burns, Paul C. "Language Arts Research that Should Make a Difference." *Elementary English* 41 (March 1964): 279.

Burns, Paul C. et al. *The Language Arts in Childhood Education.* Chicago: Rand McNally, 1979, pp. 342–345.

Coody, Betty and Nelson, David. *Teaching Elementary Language Arts.* Belmont, Ca.: Wadsworth, 1982, pp. 114–116.

Dallman, Martha. *Teaching the Language Arts in the Elementary School.* Dubuque, Iowa: William C. Brown Co., 1976, pp. 184–185.

Dawson, Mildred. *Guiding Language Learning.* New York: Harcourt Brace Jovanovich, 1963, p. 330.

Donoghue, Mildred R. *The Child and the English Language Arts.* Dubuque, Iowa: William C. Brown, 1975, pp. 356–362.

Drummon, Harold D. "Suggestions for the 'Lefties.'" *Elementary School Principal* 24 (February 1959): 15.

Enstrom, E. A. "The Extent of the Use of the Left Hand in Handwriting." *Journal of Educational Research* 55 (February 1962): 234–235.

Enstrom, E. A. "In Left-Handed Handwriting: The Little Turn that Makes the Big Difference." *Elementary English* 43 (December 1966): 865–868.

Enstrom, E. A. "Misconceptions Regarding Teaching the Left-Handed." *The Catholic Education* 35 (February 1966) 46–48.

Enstrom, E. A. "Research in Teaching the Left-Handed." *The Instructor* 73 (October 1964): 44–46.

Gardner, Warren H. *Left-Handed Writing.* Danville: The Interstate Publishing Company, 1958.

Green, Harry A. and Petty, Walter T. *Developing Language Skills in the Elementary School.* Boston: Allyn & Bacon, 1975, pp. 443–444.

Groff, Patrick. "Spelling and Language Achievement of Left-Handed Children." *Elementary English* 39 (May 1962): 446–469.

Petty, Walter T. and Jensen, Julie M. *Developing Children's Language.* Boston: Allyn & Bacon, 1980, pp. 486–488.

Rose, Karel. *Teaching Language Arts to Children.* New York: Harcourt, 1982, pp. 428–429.

Williams, Neil W. "What Do You Know about Lefties?" *Grade Teacher* 81 (June 1964): 44–45.

---

[2]Patrick J. Groff, "Who Are the Better Writers — The Left-Handed or the Right-Handed?" *Elementary School Journal* 65 (November 1964): 92–96. The author compared writing samples from children in fourth grade through sixth grade and concluded that the right-handed children did *not* write better than the left-handed ones.

Wills, Betty. "Handedness." *Encyclopedia of Educational Research*. New York: Macmillan, 1960, pp. 613–615. See also the section on this topic in the 4th edition (1969) by Otto and Anderson, p. 573.

Bibliography

Addy, Polly and Wylie, Richard E. "The 'Right' Way to Write." *Childhood Education* 49 (February 1973): 253–254.

Allen, Elizabeth G. and Wright, Jone P. "Personalizing Handwriting Instruction. *The Elementary School Journal* (April 1974): 425–429.

Ammons, Margaret. "Communication: A Curriculum Focus." In *A Curriculum for Children*, edited by Alexander Frazar. Washington, D.C.: Association for Supervision and Curriculum Development, 1969, pp. 105–122.

Anderson, Don W. "Handwriting Research: Style and Practice." In *Research on Handwriting and Spelling*, edited by Thomas A. Horn. Champaign, Ill.: National Council of Teachers of English, 1966, pp. 18–28.

Askov, Eunice et al. "A Decade of Research in Handwriting: Progress and Prospect." *Journal of Educational Research* 64 (November 1970): 99–111.

Barbe, Walter B. et al. *Creative Growth with Handwriting*. Columbus, Ohio: Zaner-Bloser, 1979.

Barham, Genevieve. "Writing Cursive—It's the Real Thing!" *Instructor* (October 1974): 71–72.

Beister, Ralf. *Reader's Digest Handwriting*. Pleasantville, N.Y.: The Reader's Digest Association, 1980.

Bell, Mary Elizabeth et al. *I Learn to Write*. Indianapolis: Bobbs-Merrill, 1968.

Bowmar/Noble Handwriting. Los Angeles: Bowmar/Noble Publishers, Inc., 1981.

Burns, Paul C. *Improving Handwriting Instruction in Elementary Schools*. Minneapolis: Burgess Publishing Company, 1962, p. 24.

Burns, Paul C. et al. *The Language Arts in Childhood Education*. Chicago: Rand McNally, 1979.

Donoghue, Mildred R. *The Child and the English Language Arts*. Dubuque, Iowa: William C. Brown, 1975, p. 353.

Enstrom, E. A. *Adventures in Handwriting*. New York: Macmillan, 1975.

Enstrom, E. A. "Print-Handwriting Today." *Elementary English* (December 1964): 846–850.

Getty, Barbara M. and Dubay, Inga S. *Italic Handwriting Series*. Portland, Ore.: Portland State University, Division of Continuing Education, 1980.

Groff, Patrick. "Can Pupils Read What Teachers Write?" *The Elementary School Journal* (October 1975): 33–39.

Groff, Patrick. "Who Writes Faster?" *Education* 83 (February 1963): 367–369.

Gust, Tim and Schumacher, Deborah. "Handwriting Speed of College Students." *Journal of Educational Research* 62 (January 1969): 198–200.

Haefner, Ralph. *The Typewriter in the Primary and Intermediate Grades*. New York: Macmillan, 1932.

Halpin, Glennelle and Halpin, Gerald. "Special Paper for Beginning Handwriting: An Unjustified Practice? *Journal of Educational Research* 69(7) (March 1976): 267–269.

Herrick, Virgil. *New Horizons for Research in Handwriting*. Madison, Wis.: The University of Wisconsin Press, 1963, p. 27.

Hodges, Richard E. *Learning to Spell*. Urbana: ERIC Clearinghouse on Reading and Communication Skills, 1981, p. 13.

Holt, John. *What Do I Do Monday?* New York: E. P. Dutton, 1970.

Horton, Lowell W. "Illegibilities in the Cursive Handwriting of Sixth Graders." *Elementary School Journal* 70 (May 1970): 446–450.

Jackson, Arthur Dale. "A Comparison of Speed and Legibility of Manuscript and Cursive Handwriting of Intermediate Grade Pupils." Dissertation Abstracts 31(9) 4383-A-4384-A, 1971.

Jervis, Kathe. "A Discussion among Four Experienced Teachers." *Insights into Open Education* 12(1) (September 1979): 3.

Jones, Weyman B. *Edge of Two Worlds*. New York: Dial Press, 1968.

King, Fred M. *Palmer Method Handwriting*. Schaumburg, Ill.: A. N. Palmer, 1979.

Klyhn, Joan. "Tiny Typists." *Times Educational Supplement* 2785 (October 1968): 607.

Lamb, Pose M. "Handwriting in Elementary Schools." In *Guiding Children's Language Learning*. Dubuque, Iowa: William C. Brown, 1971, p. 225.

Lewis, Edward R. and Lewis, Hilda P. "Which Manuscript Letters Are Hard for First Graders?" *Elementary English* 41 (December 1964): 855–858.

Markham, Lynda R. "Influences of Handwriting Quality on Teacher Evaluation of Written Work." *American Educational Research Journal* 13(4) (Fall 1976): 277–283.

Martin, Thelma. "Have You Considered Typing?" *The Instructor* 78 (May 1969): 20.

McCall, Margaret. "It Worked for Me." *Grade Teacher* 86 (October 1968): 35.

Monroe, Marion. *Writing Our Language*. Glenview, Ill.: Scott, Foresman, 1976.

Mullins, June et al. "A Handwriting Model for Children with Learning Disabilities." *Journal of Learning Disabilities* 5 (May 1972): 306–311.

Mumford, Lewis. As quoted in Robert O'Brien. "The Moving Finger Writes—But Who Can Read It?" *Saturday Review* (July 18, 1959): 8.

Niedermeyer, Fred C. "Kindergartners Learn to Write." *Elementary School Journal* 74 (January 1974): 130–135.

Noble, Kendrick B. J. "Handwriting Programs in Today's Schools." *Elementary English* 40 (May 1963): 511.

Norwick, Terese D. and Bell, Mary Elizabeth. *I Learn to Write*. New York: McCormick-Mathers, 1978.

O'Brien, Robert. "The Moving Finger Writes—But Who Can Read It?" *Saturday Review* (July 18, 1959): 8.

Parker, Tom S. "The Developmental Nature of Children's Ability to Use Varying Diameter Writing Instruments." *Dissertation Abstracts* 33(7) 3399-A-2400-A, January 1973.

Peck, Michaeleen et al. "Another Decade of Research in Handwriting: Progress and Prospect in the 1970's." *The Journal of Educational Research* 73 (May/June 1980): 283–298.

Peterson Handwriting. Greensburg, Pa., p. 27.

Rogers, Frances. *Painted Rock to Printed Page*. Philadelphia: J. B. Lippincott, 1960.

Singh, M. C. et al. "Using the Typewriter to Improve Reading and Spelling." ERIC Document Reproduction Service No. 186 852, 1975.

Soloway, Rhoda K. "Adopt-a-Letter." *Teacher* (March 1978): 78–84.

Smith, E. Brooks et al. *Language and Thinking in School*. New York: Holt, Rinehart and Winston, 1970, p. 253.

Stewig, John Warren. *Sending Messages*. Boston: Houghton Mifflin, 1978.

Strickling, Gloria A. "The Effect of Handwriting and Related Skills upon the Spelling Score of Above Average and Below Average Readers in the Fifth Grade." *Dissertation Abstracts* 34(7) 3717-A, 1974.

Switzer, Mary Ellen. "Getting Keyed Up about Language Arts." *Early Years* (November 1979): 24–25 + .

Templin, Elaine. "The Legibility of Adult Manuscript, Cursive, or Manuscript-Cursive Styles." In *New Horizons for Research in Handwriting*, edited by Virgil Herrick. Madison, Wis.: The University of Wisconsin Press, 1963, pp. 185–206.

Thurber, Donald N. *D'Nealian Handwriting*. Glenview, Ill.: Scott, Foresman, 1981.

Tootle, John C. "Typewriting in the Written Communication Activities of the Fifth Grade." (Ph.D. dissertation, The Ohio State University, 1971).

Tufo, Thomas. "Handwriting and the Special Child." *Early Years* (May 1980): 76–77.

Western, Richard D. "The Case against Cursive Script." *The Elementary School Journal* (September 1977): 1–3.

Wilson, Louise Ada. *The Journal of Exceptional Education* 31(4) (Summer 1963): 371–380.

Wood, Ben D. and Freeman, Frank N. *An Experimental Study of the Educational Influences of the Typewriter in the Elementary School Classroom*. New York: Macmillan, 1932.

SPELLING

A criticism with which we are all familiar . . . is
that our schools fail to make good spellers. It is
undeniably true that there is a great deal of bad
spelling in our schools . . . results lead one to
doubt seriously the efficiency of the methods of
teaching spelling. (Falk, 1944)

Such a condemnation of the school's apparent inability to
teach children to spell is not unique. Criticism of poor spelling is commonplace among parents, the general public, and those responsible for hiring sec-
retarial and other office help. Recent proponents of the "Back-to-the-Basics"
movement are especially vocal in criticizing lack of spelling skills. Yet, it's
ironic that the complaint above was voiced well over thirty years ago! Concern over spelling continues, as does the search for the most efficient methods
of helping children master this language skill. Definitive answers are not yet
available, but indications of helpful techniques can be considered. This
chapter will examine the nature of the spelling problem and suggest some
ways of helping children acquire the skill.

EARLY ATTEMPTS AT SPELLING

Beginning in the late primary grades, and continuing through the intermediate grades, virtually all teachers teach spelling. Many children are interested in encoding their ideas in print before adults try to teach them to spell.
Recent research shows that, like earlier oral language development, attempts
at writing move through identifiable stages (Beers & Henderson, 1977).

Gentry (1981) suggests that early childhood teachers can observe stages in
the development of spelling:

STAGE ONE: "Deviant Stage," an example of which would be the word monster represented as vtBpA. This clearly shows the child, despite an interest in writing down ideas, has no knowledge of sound-symbol correspondences.

STAGE TWO: "Pre-phonetic stage," in which the child renders one- to three-letter spellings demonstrating some understanding of sound-symbol correspondence. In this stage the word monster might be represented as MSR.

STAGE THREE: "Phonetic Stage," in which the cognitive understanding of the link between sounds and letters is stabilized. The word monster might be represented as MONSTR.

STAGE FOUR: "Transitional Stage," between phonetic and correct spelling, in which though words are often misspelled, they do look like English.

STAGE FIVE: "Correct Stage," in which purposeful writing continues vigorously as formal instruction in spelling is begun.

Gentry contends that by the time children are in second grade they have usually advanced to the fifth stage, and formal instruction can begin. Teachers of younger children can observe undirected attempts at spelling to see how far along the continuum toward correct spelling children have traveled.

Competency in composing and interest in spelling are both furthered when early childhood teachers encourage writing. Some teachers may feel that if children can't spell correctly they shouldn't write. This probably stems from the problems they have when parents criticize papers sent home with misspellings. Despite this, the more writing children do, the more likely they are to be better spellers, for "It is during the act of writing that the rationale and function of spelling becomes most clear to a primary child" (Beers & Beers, 1981).

One way to avoid parental criticism of spelling, which may well stifle children's interest in composition, is to *not* routinely send everything a child writes home; a paper can be brought from first rough draft into completed form, including correct spelling. Other compositions can be saved in a file folder, so the child and the teacher together can review progress made in composition. When a paper is to be shared publicly, either on a school bulletin board, or with parents, correct spelling is necessary. Proofreading is a skill that develops slowly (Yatvin, 1979). Sometimes it helps, after a child has gone over the paper, to begin at the bottom of the page and proofread backward (Tenny, 1980).

FORMAL SPELLING PROGRAMS AND THE SITUATION TODAY

Are children today poorer spellers than those who studied in the one-room school of yesteryear? Sherwin (1969) analyzed nine studies to answer the question: How effective is spelling instruction today? The studies, published between 1926 and 1951, dealt with different school populations in a variety of ways. Unfortunately, the conclusion reached was that the researchers shared a consensus—"the results are beneath what they regard as their legitimate expectations."

Reprinted by permission of Newspaper Enterprise Association.

Why should we be concerned with inaccurate spelling? The contention was made in the chapter in oral language that it is the most common, the most essential form for the child to master. If this is so, why is spelling important at all?

The spoken word, quickly uttered and more quickly lost, has an impermanence that allows for more deviation from a set standard than is possible in writing. Mispronunciations and usage errors are in many situations overlooked, or noticed but tolerated.

The same is not true for the written word. The simple procedure of encoding one's thoughts gives a permanence and thus a specious authority to writing. Errors last longer and because of this are more roundly condemned. People tend to look down upon those who cannot spell accurately. Because of this, and despite the fact we know spelling is a skill not necessarily related to general intelligence and ability, we must help children learn to spell.

Some children have little trouble with spelling; others find it a mystifying task and mortifying trial. There are a variety of reasons for this.

Some Causes

Often spelling difficulty may not be caused by a single reason; several factors may account for continued problems. The teacher should try to determine the causes, and once this is accomplished, the problem can be attacked from more than one direction.

Many children spell poorly because they *listen inaccurately* to the speech of others. In social situations and in weekly spelling lessons, these children listen inattentively. Thus, they do not hear correctly and when confronted with a word in a spelling list, may spell it as they have heard it. For example, if a child listens inattentively, he or she may spell *probly* instead of probably. Similarly, the child who writes *reconize* may *not* be hearing the /g/ sound in the middle of the word. Spelling problems caused by poor listening habits show up when children omit syllables, drop endings, and reverse syllables or letter order. More practice in listening may well result in better spelling.

Students who listen poorly to others may also listen poorly to *their own speech*. For example, someone may say umbrella, but hearing the word inaccurately, the child may add a syllable, resulting in *umberella*. This also leads to spelling problems. Sessions designed to improve listening habits should be accompanied by increased attention to the accuracy of a child's oral pronunciation.

Children with *poor reading ability* are apt to be poor spellers. Though the exact nature of this interrelationship has yet to be defined, it has been documented that children with reading problems are seldom good spellers.[1] Apparently through wide reading, which results in seeing words over and over again in context, good readers unconsciously assimilate the spelling of more words than do children who read less widely. For children with reading problems, more in-class practice or even referral to a reading specialist may result in reading *and* spelling improvement.

As to the *type* of reading instruction which results in the most impressive gains in spelling, one carefully controlled research study indicates that children who learn the language-experience approach to reading become significantly better spellers than do pupils who use basal readers. This superiority is evident in both spelling in written compositions and in spelling lessons (Cramer, 1970).

The child with *poor handwriting* is also apt to have spelling problems. While practicing writing words during spelling classes, such a child encounters difficulties because words can easily be miswritten. This is not

---

[1] The converse is apparent in reports that children's spelling and reading scores have been correlated as high as .63, indicating that those who read well are often superior spellers. Thomas D. Horn, "Spelling," in *Encyclopedia of Educational Research,* 4th ed., ed. Robert L. Ebel (New York: Macmillan, 1969), p. 1289.

because of any cognitive problems of misunderstanding the spelling, but because of the purely mechanical problems involved in putting words on paper. For such a child, an increased amount of time devoted to handwriting practice may also result in increased spelling proficiency. Another way to help children with motor skill problems is to allow them to use manuscript writing during spelling tests, which makes the spelling procedure easier. Even with intermediate grade children who have made the switch to cursive writing, allowing the use of manuscript on spelling tests frequently minimizes problems of handwriting which complicate the spelling task.

The teacher should be aware that in this, as in other areas of learning, *sex differences* will be apparent. As with handwriting, so it is with spelling: boys regularly do less well than girls. This was first noted in 1897 by a researcher named J. M. Rice; it is also commented upon by Personke and Yee (1971). Though it is probably not necessary to institute sex-segregated spelling classes to compensate for this difficulty, the individualized spelling techniques described later in this chapter may help boys achieve more than will traditional methods.

In these examples we have been concerned with problems individual children might have. There is a larger and more universal problem related to spelling English which affects all children.

The Problem of "Fit"

Much of spelling can be summarized as a problem of fit, between the sounds we make as speakers of the language and the symbols we use to write down what we have said. The discrepancy between sounds (phonemes) and symbols (graphemes) is the crucial determinant of how easy or difficult it is to spell a language. Stageberg (1965) defined phoneme:

> The phoneme is easily understood; it is a speech sound that signals a difference in meaning. Consider, for example, the words *dime* and *dine*. They sound exactly alike except for the /m/ and the /n/, yet their meanings are different. Therefore, . . . the /m/ and /n/ . . . are thereby established as English phonemes.

The words *can* and *cap* are two other examples.

In contrast, the term grapheme describes the letters used to record the sounds we make and hear. While the sound in two words may be the same, the way in which they are written may be quite different.

Every language has these two elements, though the similarity of fit between the elements varies in different languages. In some languages, all or almost all of the sounds are recorded in one unvarying way. For example, in such languages as Hawaiian, Turkish, Spanish, and Finnish, there is close correspondence between sounds and letters. Finnish children have minimal trouble spelling because for nineteen phonemes, they have twenty graphemes. Thus the correspondence between sound and written symbol is almost 1:1.[2]

The Problem in English

It becomes apparent that English-speaking children will have more trouble writing their native language than will Finnish children when we consider that though English has 41–45 phonemes,[3] we have only 26 symbols (the alphabet letters) to record what we have said.[4] What causes these sound-symbol irregularities? There are basically three reasons for this phenomenon.

First, because English is an eclectic language, we have borrowed many words from *different countries.* Because the sources are different, the letters for representing the sounds are different. Borrowings in English account for up to 40 percent of the total stock of vocabulary words. This may seem large, until we consider that other languages borrow even a larger percentage of their words. Albanian, for instance, contains only 8 percent native Albanian words; the remaining 92 percent are borrowed.

Words have entered our language at *different times,* and this also resulted in different spellings for similar or identical sounds. One elementary series helps children understand the reason why one group of words, which ends in the same sound, is spelled with two different written endings, -ent and -ant. The reason is because these words entered our language at different times.

Third, spellings and pronunciations for words have *changed* since they were first introduced. (See Hodges, 1981 for further information.) The words *know* and *knight,* for example, were first pronounced with /k/ sounds at the beginning of the words. What was once an essential phoneme has, over the years, become a troublesome silent letter. You could use the poem, "Knot Fair" (Hymes & Hymes, 1964), to introduce this concept to young children.

This problem has been of concern for some time, both to the casual observer and the serious scholar. The following poem illustrates the problem well.

---

[2]In contrast, imagine the trouble youngsters have learning Amharic, widely spoken in Ethiopia, which has a 1,700-year-old alphabet written with 247 characters!

[3]There is some difference of opinion about the number of phonemes in English. Estimates vary from 37 (Norman Stageberg) to 45 (Paul Roberts). The exact number is not so important as the fact that even with the lower estimate, much discrepancy exists in number between phonemes and graphemes.

[4]It has been noted that American English spelling consists of 41 sounds represented by 26 symbols. Yet over 500 different spellings of these 41 sounds exist. For a more detailed description see: "Phonemic Notations and the Roman Alphabet," by Godfrey Dewey in *Education,* April 1968, *88*(4), 296–299.

OUR QUEER LANGUAGE
by Lord Cromer

When the English tongue we speak
  Why is not break rhymed with freak?
Will you tell me why it's true
  We say sew but likewise few;
And the maker of a verse
  Cannot cap his horse with worse?
Beard sounds not the same as heard;
  Cord is different from word.
Cow is cow but low is low,
  Shoe is never rhymed with foe;
Think of comb and tomb and bomb;
  And think of goose and not of choose;
And since pay is rhymed with say,
  Why not paid with said, I pray?
We have blood and food and good;
  Mould is not pronounced like could;
Wherefore done but gone and lone?
  Is there any reason known?
And in short it seems to me
  Sounds and letters disagree.

(in Henry, 1942)

It has been assumed for a long time that such discrepancies as these resulted in English being essentially irregular. We are apt to notice these words (of low regularity) because they occur so frequently.[5] What we are apt to ignore, as casual observers of the language, is the large body of words which are highly regular and occur frequently. Because they are less distinctive, they are less noticeable.

As a result of the assumed irregularity in spelling, materials and emphases in spelling programs formerly made children learn spelling word by word—indeed a formidable task! Little emphasis was placed on learning the predictable patterns in English. As a result, children, especially those with little intuitive grasp of how our language patterns, were overwhelmed by the spelling task and often gave up. It has been estimated that when this practice was common and a child was handed a list containing fifteen words, each of which had to be learned separately, a spelling program from grades two through eight could include an overwhelming total of more than 3,000 such separate acts of memorization (Ames, 1965).

---

[5]Teachers are aware of them because they cause endless problems for children. Anyone who has attempted to teach children how to spell *one, acre, iron, myth,* or *laugh* can attest to the difficulties caused by irregular spellings.

Other Complications

As if the pervasive problem of discrepancy between sound and symbol were not enough, there are other problems a child faces in learning to spell.

One of these is that we sometimes say words in one way, but write them in other ways. An example of this—independent of dialect which will be discussed later—is the word *February*. In America it is almost universal in informal speech to omit the first /r/, while the spelling has remained as if the /r/ were said. We most often say the word: /feb' yoo er ē/, while it is still written as if it were said: /feb' roo er ē/. Such eliminations of sounds are a problem for some children.

A child's *dialect* must be considered because it may make learning to spell more difficult.[6] Several examples may clarify this point. In north central Indiana, many speakers make no difference in the medial sound of two words: /pin/ and /pen/. Since children say only one sound, they will have to learn consciously that this sound is *written* two different ways if they wish to communicate. In eastern New England the words /tot/ and /taught/ are often homophones. In parts of the eastern United States, the terminal /r/ is often completely lost, though it must still be represented in writing. Students may well say /ka/ but they will be expected to write car. The reverse problem, that of an inserted /r/ must be dealt with when children realize that is may be acceptable to say /idear/, but the word must be written *idea*. In parts of the South, the word which is written *tune* is pronounced /tyoon/ with only minimal similarity between sound and spelling. In some parts of the north central area of our country, *horse* and *hoarse* are pronounced as homophones, which complicates spelling for children of that region.

A further problem for all children is that of the "schwa" sound.[7] Four examples are given below. In each case the sound is the same, but the mode of representing it in graphemes is different:

The word:

/but' ən/   where ə is written as o, button
/vur' jə nəl/   where ə is written as a, virginal
/wor' dən/   where ə is written e, warden
/foun' tən/   where ə is written as ai, fountain

---

[6]The teacher's own dialect, particularly when dictating a spelling test, may also complicate the spelling problem. Recently, while working with a group of teachers in Florida, I heard /repoat/ for report, /libry/ for library, and /mere/ for mirror. This was in informal conversations but it does raise the question of how these teachers pronounce such words on the spelling test.

[7]The indeterminate vowel sound or sounds of most unstressed syllables of English, however represented; a neutral vowel written in a variety of ways.

Influence of Linguists

Recently, linguists of many sorts have become interested in the problem of the relationship between the symbols and sounds in our language.[8] One study, notable for the extensive treatment it gives the problem, is sure to have much influence on spelling materials and methods.

Paul Hanna and his associates (1966) have done a study made possible through the use of computers, which indicates that in fact a large percentage of the words we use are regular. The researchers analyzed over 17,000 common American English words and concluded that vowel and consonant sounds and their symbols have regular spellings approximately 80 percent of the time. Such elements as position within a word lower the percentage, however. Only about 49 percent of the words were spelled correctly using the rules. Hanna and his coworkers have created a spelling series (1967) and written a professional book (1971) making practical application of the ideas developed in the study.

Spelling Generalizations?

Is it helpful to teach children phonetic generalizations? As pointed out earlier, the act of learning each new word as a separate task is such a formidable one that it may overwhelm some children. Yet, the question is: Does it do any good to teach children sound-symbol generalizations? The research regarding this, summarized in Personke and Yee's book, is equivocal. After examining many research studies, the authors could not find undisputed evidence that time spent teaching and learning spelling generalizations resulted in superior performance. Reporting one of their own studies, they summarized: "The hypothesis that phonetic instruction provides a positive difference in spelling achievement was *not* confirmed in this study" (Personke & Yee, 1971).

Despite lack of evidence about the efficacy of teaching spelling generalizations, teachers have for some time taught children generalizations about the relationships between sounds and letters. Such attempts have been concentrated in instruction during reading classes, with the idea that understanding such generalizations would help children read better. Certainly there is substantial difference between the decoding process in reading, and the encoding procedure in spelling. Nonetheless, it is interesting to consider the validity of the sound-symbol generalizations children have been learning.

Clymer (1963) studied basal reading series and located 121 different sound-symbol generalizations which were being taught. Of these, he selected forty-five for further study. These were analyzed to determine the percent of

---

[8]The term linguist is an "umbrella" word, a general term including many separate entities categorized together for convenience. There are structural, transformational, comparative, historical, and descriptive linguists, among others.

utility or the frequency with which the generalization did indeed apply. This was done by comparing the number of times they did apply with the number of exceptions that existed. As a result, he concluded that only eighteen of the generalizations had a 75 percent utility and were thus worthy of being taught.

While Clymer cautions that his research cannot be viewed as completely conclusive, it does raise interesting questions about how many and which kinds of sound-symbol generalizations children should learn. We need, apparently, to reexamine some of our cherished old shibboleths. Generations of children learned the old saw: "When two vowels go walking, the first one does the talking." This seems hardly worth teaching when we consider that it has only 45 percent utility (Grief, 1981). Apparently, we must be careful in selecting generalizations to teach. One must always balance the time taken up in teaching and learning these generalizations against the other uses to which such time could be put.[9]

A related, but slightly different approach, is that of teaching spelling *patterns* to children. Several authorities maintain that this approach results in increased spelling competencies.

There are basically four patterns of enough utility to be worth a child's time:

Pattern One: CVC   Examples are the words *cat* and *sad*. This is the most common pattern, a short vowel preceded and followed by a consonant. Once children have played with this pattern, creating many words from the basic pattern, they can experiment with the variations: substitute consonant blends for the initial consonant (such words as *clan*) or for the final consonant (such words as *hand*).

Pattern Two: CVCe   Examples are the words *save* and *plane*. In this common pattern the long vowel sound, surrounded by two consonants, makes a word in which the final e is silent.

Pattern Three: CVVC   Examples are the words *pain* and *leaf*. In this pattern the two medial vowels produce a dipthong or a long vowel sound between the initial and final consonants. Children can substitute consonant blends for the initial consonant (such words as *brain*) and substitute consonant blends for the final consonants (such words as *beast*).

Pattern Four: CV and CVV   Examples are such words as *be* and *go* (CV) and *may* and *see* (CVV). In the second pattern children may substitute consonant blends for the initial consonant (in such words as *flee*).

---

[9]There are many other studies dealing with this problem, including Lillie Smith Davis, "The Applicability of Phonic Generalizations to Selected Spelling Programs," *Elementary English*, May 1972, 49(5), 706–713.

Once students have explored these four patterns, there are innumerable others which they may explore, depending on the amount of time available and the inclination of the teacher.

Exceptions to the Pattern

Having children experience patterns in spelling is not the complete task, however. As they progress through the spelling program, they must be exposed to the idea that in addition to patterns, there are exceptions. The danger in any generalization is that the pattern may be overextended or applied to words for which it is inappropriate. Much inaccurate spelling results from overzealous application of generalizations. The child who spells *bizzy* (for busy), *honer* (for honor), and *ankshus* (for anxious) is only trying to apply what he or she has learned.

Trying to explain the logic behind some of these exceptions is largely futile; many exceptions must simply be learned on a rote basis. For example, children are often taught the pattern: When words begin with an initial /k/ sound, they are spelled with the letter *K* when the letters *i* or *e* follow, and are spelled with the letter *C* in all other cases. The alert child will soon notice, however, that there are exceptions. In such words as *chaos, character,* and *chorus,* the initial *ch* spelling is necessary to represent the initial /k/ sound. This is because such words are borrowings from the original Greek spelling, with the *ch-* retained, instead of modified to fit the more general English system (Corcoran, 1970). Does this make sense? Of course not, if one is searching for logic in a system that developed in piecemeal fashion. The child simply has to learn that there are exceptions to the system. While it would be more convenient for everyone concerned if some of these obscure borrowings were changed in written form to conform to the system, this is unlikely. Therefore, the onus of learning not only the system but also the exceptions falls on the child. An unfair requirement? Probably, but one which is unlikely to be changed! The teacher's job is, therefore, to make the learning of the system as palatable as possible.

Developing Word Families

The position taken later in this chapter is that individualization is the key to a successful spelling program. Such a position does not negate, however, the value of some group experiences designed to help children learn about the basic spelling patterns of high frequency.

To begin with very young children we might use *Andy (That's My Name)* (dePaola, 1973), which in a very unstructured way introduces the child to the idea of word building. This basic phonics concept is here presented in an undidactic picture book, featuring a small boy who takes his name in a wagon. Other children arrange and rearrange the letters into many other words, and illustrate in action the words they have made.

A more structured approach is appropriate for the older boys and girls with whom teachers can develop the concept of word families. This is important, both for the help it brings in understanding underlying spelling patterns, and also for the self-confidence it can foster. Given a basic pattern, students are automatically able to spell many other words. They may be unaware of this family feature in English, and it should be called to their attention, in informal group situations. For example, the teacher might take Pattern One: CVC. Given the fact that children can spell cat, they discover that they can also spell: bat, fat, gat,[10] hat, mat, pat, rat, sat, tat, and vat, or a total of eleven words, rather than one.

Children should be able to come up with nine other words in the family for the word *save* (Pattern Two), six other words in the family for the word *pain* (Pattern Three) and ten other words in the family for the word *may* (Pattern Four). The challenge of finding new words intrigues children, and the resulting contests to see who can come up with the longest list of family words helps children internalize the idea of patterns in spelling and also acts as a helpful motivating device.

All of the foregoing assumes that English spelling is quite rigid and as a generalization this is true. Spelling is undoubtedly one of the least creative aspects of language. Yet there is evidence of more flexibility in spelling than is commonly acknowledged.

The Need for Flexibility

At one time, English spelling was more flexible than it is now. Written records from the sixteenth century reveal that the word we can only spell *guest* today was then spelled in a variety of ways: gest, geste, gueste, ghest, or gheste (Pei, 1954). Such individuality of approach is not condoned in our era.

Today, it is certainly true that there is a body of basic words with invariant spellings which all who wish to be considered educated must learn to spell the "right" way. Spelling is, however, by no means as invariant as most spelling series and too many teachers have led children to believe. The frequency with which people refer to a dictionary as the ultimate authority in determining the "proper" and only way to spell a word is unwarranted spelling dogmatism.

Some time ago one researcher compared the variety of spellings listed in several different dictionaries. As a result, Emery (1958) concluded that many fairly common words may be spelled in more than one way, and even the dictionaries do not agree on the number and spelling of acceptable variant forms. Emery reported that in many cases it was not possible to determine which was considered the common spelling and which the variant.

---

[10]In developing word families with children, they will frequently suggest a word the meaning of which is unfamiliar to them. Since it makes no sense to isolate spelling from other language arts, the teacher uses such occasions to do some informal vocabulary teaching. Widen the experience of children with such words, though don't attempt to fix these in a use vocabulary. Rather, talking about what a gat is and who uses the term, is simply a way of expanding the child's world.

I once examined a currently available dictionary, in an attempt to identify what types of options exist for the speller. One dictionary (Stein, 1967) was used; several would undoubtedly reveal many more options in the spelling of our language.

Spellers have options at all three positions in words; initial, medial, and final. The *initial* position, we find impale or empale is used. In *medial* positions we find the following possibilities: pygmy or pigmy; brier or briar; extrovert or extravert; and knowledgeable or knowledgable. In the *final* position we find theatre or theater; debonair and debonaire; and plow or plough. We find further that as spellers of English we have other options. When we *pluralize*, we may use either colloquiums, or colloquia. When we *change tense* from present to past we may use focused or focussed. There are innumerable such examples in our language.

As teachers, we must be flexible enough to accept such differences for the richness they add to English, and not ignore them because they represent a spelling with which we are unfamiliar. As Sherwin (1969) has said, "It is difficult enough to teach spelling without dissipating one's efforts in correcting supposed errors which are merely alternate forms. The spelling lesson is not an occasion for indulging one's linguistic prejudices."

THE CHANGING ROLE OF DICTIONARIES

Despite the reverent attitudes of Scrabble and crossword buffs, manifest changes in ideas about dictionaries are taking place.

For hundreds of years, dictionaries were looked upon by those who made them (lexicographers) and those who used them as *prescriptive* tools, that is, as the ultimate authority in prescribing how words should be spelled, pronounced, and what they should mean. This attitude about the function of

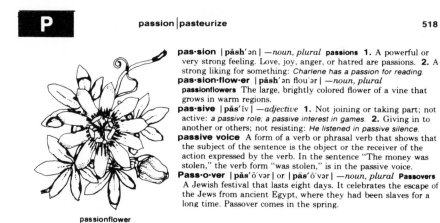

P passion | pasteurize 518

pas·sion | păsh′ən | —*noun, plural* **passions 1.** A powerful or very strong feeling. Love, joy, anger, or hatred are passions. **2.** A strong liking for something: *Charlene has a passion for reading.*
pas·sion·flow·er | păsh′ən flou′ər | —*noun, plural* **passionflowers** The large, brightly colored flower of a vine that grows in warm regions.
pas·sive | păs′ĭv | —*adjective* **1.** Not joining or taking part; not active: *a passive role; a passive interest in games.* **2.** Giving in to another or others; not resisting: *He listened in passive silence.*
passive voice A form of a verb or phrasal verb that shows that the subject of the sentence is the object or the receiver of the action expressed by the verb. In the sentence "The money was stolen," the verb form "was stolen," is in the passive voice.
Pass·o·ver | păs′ō′vər | or | păs′ō′vər | —*noun, plural* **Passovers** A Jewish festival that lasts eight days. It celebrates the escape of the Jews from ancient Egypt, where they had been slaves for a long time. Passover comes in the spring.

passionflower

From Children's Dictionary *(Boston: Houghton Mifflin, 1979).*

dictionaries is summarized by Noah Webster (1828) who wrote in the preface of his dictionary:

> It has been my aim in this work . . . to ascertain the true principles of the language . . . to purify it from some palpable errors, and reduce the number of its anomalies, thus giving it more regularity and consistency in its forms . . . to furnish a standard of [language] . . . redeemed from corruptions . . . and degradations . . .

In contrast, current dictionary makers view their function differently, as *describing* what people actually do with the language, rather than attempting to tell users what they *ought* to do. This newer approach is summarized by the editor of the 1961 edition of *Webster's Dictionary* which stimulated such controversy when it was published. In emphasizing the *recording*, rather than the *prescribing* aspects of the dictionary, the editor comments: "It does not attempt to dictate what usage should be . . . [it is] the record of this language as it is spoken and written."

In addition, he points out that "a definition, to be adequate, must be written only after an analysis of usage. . . ." Finally, in commenting on the elimination of the descriptive labels identifying level of usage,[11] the editor points out that "it is impossible to know whether a word out of context is colloquial or not. . ." (Gove, 1961).

The whole issue of the purpose of a dictionary is dealt with in a book of use to teachers.[12] You may want to read this to expand your understanding of dictionaries. The authors describe in admirably objective fashion the point of view of the lexicographers, and also of their opponents, who contend that in refusing to prescribe usage the dictionary makers are abrogating their rightful authority.

The idea that a dictionary should be looked upon as a recording device, not a law-giving one, is certainly a concept teachers will want to share with children when doing a unit on dictionaries.[13] With older students such a unit must include several different dictionaries, so children can become aware

---

[11]This issue was one of the most heated when the dictionary was first published. Previous dictionaries labeled words as colloquial, slang, nonstandard, idiomatic, etc. *Webster's Third* was the first major dictionary to eliminate many of these labels, feeling that such evaluation was not part of its major task, which was reporting.

[12]Richard R. Lodwig and Eugene F. Barrett, *The Dictionary and the Language* (New York: Hayden Book Co., 1967), pp. 48–65. This interestingly written book provides a pleasant introduction to the wealth of variety available in dictionaries.

[13]The teacher will enjoy reading about the controversy aroused when the editors of *Webster's Third New International Dictionary* stated strongly their position about being reporters rather than arbiters of correctness. See James Sledd and Wilma R. Ebbitt, *Dictionaries and That Dictionary* (Chicago: Scott, Foresman, 1962).

kangaroo

A **kangaroo** is an animal. A **kangaroo** has strong back legs that it uses for jumping. Mother **kangaroos** carry their babies in a pocket on their stomachs. ▪

keep

Keep means to have something. Ted gave Ellen a kitten and her mother let her **keep** it. Peter **keeps** his toys in a box when he isn't playing with them. ☼*See the picture.* The teacher asked the children to **keep** quiet. The rain **kept** the children indoors.

keep

From The Magic World of Words *(New York: Macmillan, 1977).*

that whether it is pronunciation, syllabication, meaning, or etymology, there are differences depending upon which dictionary we use. Hodges (1981) gives other suggestions about ways to involve students with dictionaries.

APPROACHES TO TEACHING SPELLING

Several questions must be considered when planning how to teach spelling. The first is: How much *time* can be optimally devoted to the skill?

There seems to be agreement, the result of various research efforts, that a maximum of 75 minutes per week is most effective (Horn, 1967). While subject to the same dangers as any other educational generalization, it seems that for most average groups more time than this results in a sharp falling off of learning. The diminishing returns in terms of test scores do not seem worth the additional time and effort involved.

Another question to be considered is: *Which words* should be taught? The most common instructional procedure is for the teacher to use one of the commercially produced spelling series. How do such series decide which words to include?

Interest in which words children should learn is not new. It has been well established by several researchers that a small core of words accounts for a large percentage of those we need to know as adults (Horn, 1969). Horn speaks of the necessity of children learning what he calls the "security segment," which "may be provided by 3,000–4,000 highest frequency words which are needed in and out of school by children and adults."

What words are included in this fundamental core which all children will find of such utility when they are adults? Many researchers have concerned themselves with this problem, and a chart summarizing this research is included below.

WORD LIST STUDIES

Researcher	Year	Number of Words	Basis for Inclusion
L. P. Ayres	1915	1,000	Words used in literary writings and adult correspondence.
E. L. Thorndike	1920	10,000	Most commonly used words in textbooks, literary and other published material.
E. Horn	1926	10,000	Adult writing needs, surveyed letters, minutes of meetings, newspaper and magazine communications.
E. L. Thorndike and I. Lorge	1944	30,000	Samples drawn from magazines, the 1920 list by Thorndike, a group of 120 juvenile books, and miscellaneous adult and children's writing.
H. D. Rinsland	1945	14,571	Children's writing, both informal letters and assigned theme writing, from grades one through eight.
J. A. Fitzgerald	1951	2,650	Compiled from both children's and adults' lists, these words and their repetitions comprise 93 percent of the Rinsland list.
P. Hanna et al.	1966	17,000	Incorporated the Thorndike list of 1920 plus other, less common words.

Teaching the Basic List

Most spelling series use one or more of the above lists as a source of words.[14] Since this is so, it would seem a simple enough task to administer a spelling program. All the teacher need do is to use the commercial speller that provides the basic words children need to know. The problem is that such a circumscribed program, though unfortunately too common, meets the needs of very few children.

Capable teachers frequently make some adaptation of the basic program

---

[14]Types of lists often used are described by Markoff (1976) who also provides case studies of low-achieving spellers and suggestions for remediation.

presented in commercial spellers because they observe on an informal basis what has also been established through research, that often using only these lists is a waste of time. Frequently, many children already know part or most of the words on the list (Hughes, 1966).

For this reason, teachers interested in meeting individual needs experiment with plans, using a basic list as a departure point and providing opportunities for children to learn other words of interest to them. Three such plans follow; each is different but each provides a needed grounding in the "security segment," or basic word list, which Horn has reminded us is so crucial.

CHANGING THE PATTERN

In each of the following plans for spelling programs, details and general procedures are drawn from actual classroom situations in which experienced teachers, unsatisfied with conventional approaches, evolved new methods of spelling instruction.[15] There is no intent to provide a recipe for you to follow verbatim. Rather these descriptions are included to demonstrate that given one teacher, thirty children, and a self-contained classroom, it *is* possible to provide for differing abilities.

An Approach to Grouping

If the teacher does not feel that a totally individualized spelling approach is possible, grouping may help to meet the varying spelling abilities which exist in any classroom. The following account is illustrative of what can be accomplished.

One teacher, who had been working for about eight years in an upper-middle-class university community, wanted to challenge his children. To do this, he set up a two-group program, in which children qualified to enter the "special" group.

Each week all children took the pretest in the spelling series from the unit for that week. Research shows that such pretesting eliminates the need for children to study words they already know. This test/study/test sequence is more efficient than a study/test procedure (Loomis, 1980). If the children met the criteria, they could elect to enter the special group.[16] But even if they qualified, they did not have to enter the special spelling group. The teacher

---

[15]As a contrast, see the account included at the end of this chapter, written by a student teacher who began an individualized program.

[16]The criteria differed, depending on the difficulty of the spelling list. If it was an especially difficult list, children who had five wrong could still qualify for special spelling. On weeks when the basic list was easy, however, perhaps only one could be missed in order for a child to qualify. The criteria could change each week. It was set by the teacher and all the children knew what it was.

felt the children should be free to choose which group they would be in, depending on what they had to do that week. If a child was engrossed in an independent science project, or in making a construction for social studies, or in reading a particularly compelling book, the teacher encouraged him or her to be free to devote major attention to that.

During spelling lessons on Tuesday through Thursday (of the same duration as in ordinary programs), the teacher devoted all his time to helping individuals. Children were encouraged to work together, though this happened spontaneously, rather than by plan. Children in the regular group did the exercises in the spelling book. Those in the special group studied the words they had missed on Monday, in addition to working on the words in the special spelling list.

Where did the special group words come from? They were contributed by the children, who delighted in finding difficult words to put on the list. Words were drawn from conversations, television programs and commercials, billboards, books, subjects being studied, hobbies, and any other sources to which children wanted to turn. The teacher contributed no words to this list.

The only day this spelling approach took more time than usual was on Fridays when the final tests were given. The teacher began by reading the basic list. Children in the regular group wrote all the words. Children in the special group wrote only those they had missed on Monday. When this list was finished the children in the regular group went on to other work they needed to do, while the teacher administered the special group word list. After the tests, the children checked their own work, to receive the valuable feedback that resulted.

Though only two groups were involved in this plan, it represented one way of meeting individual needs more adequately than having all children work on the basic list. The next program provides for even more individualization.

The Multilevel Approach

The following recounts how one fifth-grade teacher in a self-contained classroom in an urban area, set up such a system.[17] The teacher, who had taught for three years, was working with a heterogeneous group of students encompassing a wide range of intelligence and ability levels.

After recognizing that a conventional spelling approach was not really challenging able children, but was frustrating slow ones, the teacher decided to establish a spelling level for each child and let the child work at that level until he or she could move to a higher level. The procedure was a simple one.

---

[17]There are research reports describing the details of this approach which attest to its success, though the method has not attained wide popularity. As long ago as 1923, a principal reported success with this method. See Ben J. Rohan, "An Experiment in Spelling," *Journal of Educational Method,* June 1923, 2, 414.

Children were first tested, using the unit tests from the commercial spelling series available in the school. The testing began with the third-grade book, the first available in that series. A few of these tests were given each day at the beginning of the school year. It was arbitrarily decided that when a child missed more than half of the words, she or he should stop at that level. Testing went on, using more advanced books, until a spelling level was established for each child. Though these were fifth-grade children, several were spelling at levels far beyond this, while others could not cope with the fifth-grade words.

When this initial placement was accomplished, each child received a copy of the book at the appropriate level.[18] Children worked at their own level, though if two children happened to be at the same level, working together was not discouraged. The same amount of time was devoted to spelling each day as in the conventional approach used in other classrooms. The teacher presented no group lessons, but was available throughout the entire spelling period to give individual help.

The testing procedure was designed to be as simple as possible. The teacher gave the test to those children working at the highest level. They in turn gave the test to those at the next level, and so the testing proceeded. After each child was tested, the children self-corrected the test, to determine what the errors were.

Another feature distinguishing this program was durational flexibility. Children worked the same amount of time each day, but if they could do two lessons in one day, it was possible to finish a unit in less time than is ordinarily the case. As soon as they mastered one unit in the book they moved on to the next.

Probably the most positive advantage of this program is the realistic challenge it provides to the participants. For the child who finds spelling easy, more difficult words (and thus more interesting ones) lie ahead. For the child who finds spelling difficult, the realistic challenge of words at a level he or she can master provides a sense of accomplishment. It is true that such a child is working below "grade level," but only until grade level is achieved. Since no one has to stay at a particular level for a specified amount of time, there is a continual challenge the children set for themselves to work their way to the next level.[19]

There are, to be sure, some disadvantages to such a program. One of the most formidable is the problem of convincing the principal, parents, and other teachers of the worth of the approach. The principal's support is neces-

---

[18]This was facilitated by the fact that the school used the soft-bound consumable type of workbook. No attempt was made to conceal from the children the level at which they were working.

[19]The whole question of the "level" of spelling words is artificial, as pointed out clearly in Ruth G. Strickland, *The Language Arts in the Elementary School* (Lexington, Mass.: D. C. Heath, 1969), pp. 401–403. Little or no agreement exists among publishers of spelling materials about how to determine word difficulty.

sary in order to sell the plan to parents, who will resist the idea of their child working below grade level. The justification for such a program can be made on the basis of amount of improvement.

In the particular instance described here, all children in the room made a year's improvement, though in some cases the child was still below grade level.[20] The problem of convincing teachers not involved in the plan remains a major one, especially if they have rather firmly established grade-level expectations.

If a teacher is successful in eliciting the cooperation of the principal, coworkers, and parents, he or she can set up this program, responsive to individual needs, using conventional materials.

Spelling Buddies

One third-grade teacher adopted an approach capitalizing on children's interest both in working with a buddy and in learning words of special interest to them. All children in her classroom, located in a small, quasi-rural school district, were assigned a partner with whom they worked during spelling periods.

On Mondays, all children took the basic test from the commercial series being used. The words missed on this pretest constituted a beginning list for each child.

The children added words from their word boxes (a three-by-five metal recipe box) to this list. They made their own choice of words from the box for any particular week.

On Tuesday through Thursday children worked with their buddies dividing words into syllables, writing the words in sentences, analyzing words to see if they followed the patterns of words already learned, and other related activities. In this as in the other approaches, teachers provided practice exercises which approximated the way adults spell. They avoided such techniques as writing words in the air, and oral spelling, which do not help children develop better visual images of the word (Johnson, 1981).

On Friday, each child gave his or her partner the test and then the process was reversed. The teacher employed self-checking for the additional learning it encourages, though each week she did spot-check several tests to make sure of accurate correction.

Two advantages resulted from this approach. First, motivation was exceedingly high. Children enjoyed working with their buddies and for the most part work proceeded in a businesslike fashion. The teacher reserved the right to change partners in the few instances where disagreements arose.

Second, many children incidentally learned the words their partners were

---

[20]That is, they managed to master the content of at least thirty-six lessons, the number prescribed for one academic year. The question of what constitutes a "year's improvement" in spelling is, of course, a rather artificial question.

learning. Each child was responsible only for the words on her or his own list. Actually, the teacher found that working together with a buddy for three days often resulted in a child's unconsciously assimilating some of the friend's words. Though no effort was made to provide for this or to measure frequency of occurrence, it happened often enough for the teacher to notice.

Spelling and Attitudes

Can the teacher interested in improving the spelling program be sure more children will learn more words in the same amount of time as do children in a conventional program? The answer is no. All the programs tried here were evolved by classroom teachers simply because they were bored with more conventional programs. None was set up in a scientific manner to assess in sophisticated fashion the amount of learning that occurred.

Then why bother? Again, the answer is a simple one: attitude. In all three cases and in that of the student teacher who wrote this chapter's supplement, improvement in children's attitude toward spelling was noted. The children who were good spellers less often slid through the list with no challenge. Those who were slow spellers less often feared the period as a time to be embarrassed by their inadequacies. Though each plan was different, each accomplished what ought to be a major purpose of any spelling program—nurturing positive attitudes.

An additional fact to be noted relates to word difficulty. When children set their own challenges, word lists tend to become more difficult. We find with individualized approaches that children often choose more difficult words than are included on commerical word lists. A group of third-grade children quite "average" in terms of I.Q. and background, voluntarily included these words on their individual lists:

chariot	distinguish
celebration	delicious
inseparable	hasten

Is it wise to advocate the use of a method that has not been scientifically researched? Specifically, is it wise to try a program the major advantage of which seems to be something as tenuous as "attitude?"

The best response to such a question comes from some authors who examined the most significant studies related to the question of method and concluded: "Evidently one still must 'make his choice and place his bets' as to what spelling strategies work best!" (Shane, 1971).

PACKAGE PROGRAMS

Teachers can find available commercial programs designed to individualize a program. An example is the *Spelling Progress Laboratory* (n.d.). A spelling teacher may not know how to individualize the program, or may wish to concentrate efforts in a different academic area, but if such is the case, the teacher can easily find several commercial packages or kits, organized to provide an individualized spelling program.

Whether this is the approach that should be used is something the individual teacher will have to decide. The approach to curriculum planning outlined in Chapter 2, which puts a premium on the teacher knowing a child well enough to plan individual objectives for him or her, questions such materials. The basic if unstated underlying assumption of this book is that the teacher chooses from an array of possibilities those more appropriate to the children. Nevertheless, it is important that teachers be aware such prepackaged materials are available, should they choose to use them.

Spelling Games

Because teacher and child alike too frequently fail to find spelling challenging, teachers often resort to spelling games to maintain interest (Sherwin, 1964). The basic motivation is laudable, but unfortunately the games must be selected with care; too many are simply not worth the child's time (Donoghue, 1971).

Many teachers have grown up with the "spelling bee," or "spelldown," which regardless of the title must be regarded as a waste of time. As Mitchell (1979) has acerbically commented: "We actually have annual nationwide contests in which scrubbed children perform like well-trained seals and outdo one another in spelling nifty and almost utterly useless words from 'abiogenetic' to 'zymurgy.'" Thousands of children have wasted valuable time in this occupation, simply because teachers who used it as motivation ignored two important requirements of any valid spelling game.

1. The game must require the children to respond in a way that approximates normal, adult spelling procedures. Adults seldom spell standing up in a line, with a coterie of peers to cheer and an opposing team to jeer. We seldom must spell a word correctly in a limited amount of time with this attendant confusion around us.

2. A valid game must engage the child in spelling, not in waiting. In a spelling bee, as in too many other "games," the child spends the majority of time waiting. If you doubt this, compute the amount of time the child actually contentrates on spelling, as compared to the amount of time spent in line, jiggling on one foot, waving arms, whispering to friends, or laughing at someone on the other team.

These two basic requirements for all valid spelling games have been explained in the context of a bad game, the spelling bee. Many of these so-called games actually do little to improve spelling ability and even less to further the self-concept of the poor speller.[21] Keeping these two important qualifications in mind, however, the perceptive teacher will be able to examine the games to determine if they will accomplish the desired purposes.

A plethora of such games is described in periodical literature (Meyer, 1978; Savage, 1970; Flasch, 1970), though if the criteria suggested above are applied, many such games will be found wanting. There are, in addition, commerically produced games which are characterized generally by their careful planning, sequential structuring, and variety.[22]

Suggestions for Further Exploration

1. Do some research on alternative forms to T. O. (traditional orthography). Several systems exist, including i/t/a and Unifon. A helpful introduction to this idea is included in *Approaches to Beginning Reading* by Robert C. Aukerman (New York: John Wiley, 1971). What advantages do these systems offer as alternatives to T. O.?
2. Locate a copy of George Bernard Shaw's *Androcles and the Lion* (Harmondsworth, Middlesex: Penguin, 1962). This edition includes a version of the text printed in an alphabet designed by Shaw as another alternative to T. O. Do you see it as more or less possible than some of the systems? Does it offer some advantages none of the other systems do?
3. The discrepancy between sounds and written symbols was discussed in this chapter. Examine several spelling series to determine how and at what levels this idea is explained to children. Which materials explain this phenomenon in a way that seems easiest to understand?
4. Design a worksheet or a series of exercises to acquaint children with the idea that many English words are borrowed from other languages. Could you explain to a group of interested parents why such an idea is important to children?
5. Make up a list of words containing silent letters. Look these up in James A. H. Murray, ed., *A New English Dictionary on Historical Principles* (Oxford: The Clarendon Press, 1933). This monumental ten-volume dictionary, a standard reference tool available in libraries, offers extensive etymological information about words. What can you learn about when the letters ceased being pronounced in the words included on your list?
6. Helping children understand the idea of homonyms (both homophones and homographs) is a difficult task which recurs throughout the spelling program. Create a homonym dictionary for children, using pictures cut from magazines. Or, if you have contact with a group of children, have them make up their own dictionary (Allen & Allen, 1976).

---

[21]Another author described this problem and dealt incisively with "Spelling Baseball." See Jules Henry, *Culture Against Man* (New York: Random House, 1963), pp. 297–302. This commentary on American society in general is stimulating. The section entitled "Golden Rule Days: American Schoolrooms" (pp. 283–322) raises important questions about conventionalized school behavior.

[22]Typical of such materials is the *Spelling Learning Games Kit* by The Riverside Press (1919 S. Highland Ave., Lombard, Ill. 60148). Provision is made for the slow and the fast learner, and for a high level of involvement of all children playing. A scope and development chart allows teachers to prescribe particular games to help children with individual problems.

7. The contention was made that spelling is best taught through an individualized approach. There are, however, articulate writers who feel that such an idea can be overdone. Read Lawrence Deacon's "The Teaching of Spelling Can Become Too Individualized," in *Issues and Problems in the Elementary Language Arts*, ed. Walter T. Petty (Boston: Allyn & Bacon, 1968). Are there advantages or disadvantaged which are ignored in the arguments? Which side seems to present the stronger case?

8. Interlingua and Esperanto are two proposed universal languages that use our standard English orthography. Write for information about each one. What factors have accounted for the acceptance or lack of acceptance of these forms? (Interlingua Institute, Box 126, Canal St. Station, New York, NY 10013. Esperanto League for North America, P.O. Box 1129, El Cerrito, Ca. 94530.)

9. The chapter referred to research which indicates that teachers' attitudes toward spelling are apparently frequently negative. Interview several elementary teachers to find out what they feel about spelling. Analyze the responses to determine if certain comments are made with regularity. What aspects of the spelling program do these teachers most frequently like and/or dislike?

Suggestions for Further Reading

Avedon, E. M., Sutton-Smith, Brian et al. *The Study of Games*. New York: John Wiley, 1971.

A comprehensive source of information about games. There is a complete section on the history of games, drawing on information from anthropology and folklore. Uses of games in many sectors of life is included, such as games in business and industry, psychology, and the armed services. The final comprehensive section treats the theory and structure of games.

Boyd, Gertrude A., and Talbert, F. Gene. *Spelling in the Elementary School*. Columbus, Ohio: Charles E. Merrill, 1971.

A succinctly written and noticeably practical paperback on planning a spelling program. There is a brief but interesting section on historical approaches to teaching spelling. The chapters on activities and spelling games, and on individualizing the spelling program are particularly helpful.

Cooney, Barbara, illustrator. *The American Speller*. New York: Thomas Y. Crowell, 1960.

The artist's charmingly evocative illustrations, done in two colors, bring to life a different world, one shaped by the pervasive influence of Webster's original blue-backed speller, of which this is an adaptation. Of value for intermediate-grade children, the book presents information about sounds and letters which most children will already know, but the words and sentences used are sure to stimulate interest in spelling. A brief biographical sketch about Webster is included.

Hanna, Paul R. et al. *Spelling: Structure and Strategies*. Boston: Houghton Mifflin, 1971.

A valuable handbook that should improve the teaching of spelling. The first part deals with theoretical foundations of spelling and provides much background material. Topics include spelling as encoding, the alphabetic principle, origins and orthography of English. The history of spelling in American schools is also detailed. The second half outlines an eight-level spelling program, sequenced to expose children to all those spelling generalizations which earlier Hanna research has revealed to be useful to children.

Hodges, Richard E. *Learning to Spell.* Urbana, Ill.: ERIC Clearinghouse on Reading and Communication Skills, 1981.

An authority long recognized in this field, the author has here turned his considerable writing skill to a brief (38 pp.) introduction that will provide teachers with much useful information. Opening with a short section on theory and research, Hodges concisely describes kinds of writing systems, provides notes on how English spelling evolved, and summarizes the new research on children's acquisition of spelling. The "Practice" section, including some 40 games organized in four different categories, will give teachers many imaginative approaches to encouraging better spelling.

Kohn, Bernice. *Secret Codes and Ciphers.* Englewood Cliffs, N.J.: Prentice-Hall, 1968.

Though not related to conventional spelling, this serves well in motivating interest in writing. Middle-grade children will be fascinated by the examination of the types of ciphers and will be challenged to learn and use these intriguing ways of disguising written communication. Though many of these codes are old, the author concludes the book with a chapter on codes of our century.

Sherwin, J. Stephen. *Four Problems in Teaching English: A Critique of Research.* Scranton, Pa.: International Textbook Company, 1969.

The author identified four areas of concern: Latin and its relation to English, spelling, grammar, and diagraming. In each area he has searched out the well-known and the obscure research reports, and analyzed them meticulously. Thoughtful reporting of conclusions, written in a delightfully readable style, results in an invaluable sourcebook for the teacher.

Steig, William. *C D B!* New York: Simon and Schuster, 1968.

A wonderfully whimsical creation, this small book with ideas and illustrations by Steig is certain to capture the imagination of young children. Working with the idea that only letters, not entire words, can communicate ideas, Steig evolves many cryptic communications that will challenge children to make up their own. By pronouncing the printed letters, the message becomes apparent. N Q = Thank you. D N S 5 X = The hen has five eggs. Can you make up another?

Taylor, Margaret C. *Wht's Yr Nm?* New York: Harcourt Brace Jovanovich, 1970.

Prolifically illustrated with black-and-white line drawings, this book for middle-grade children presents a capsule history of the evolution of writing. Ancient alphabets are examined and of particular interest is the section on how to write their names using these alphabets.

Periodical Bibliography

Ammon, Richard I., Jr. "A Practical Way to Teach Spelling." *Elementary English* 46 (December 1969): 1033–1035.

The author believes no child needs to learn to spell every word on a predetermined class list. Words a child learns to spell should be drawn from the words misspelled in writings. Ammon suggests that as the teacher finds misspellings he should write both the error and the correction on a separate slip of paper (e.g., egzakly/exactly), which prevents a child's paper from being marked up. In the beginning of the year each child is given a pack of index cards and a recipe box in which to make a personalized dictionary. After collecting from twenty to forty words, the child submits a list for study. After the list is approved and after studying the words, the child is ready for a quiz dictated and corrected by a partner.

Beers, James W., and Henderson, Edmund H. "A Study of Developing Orthographic Concepts Among First Graders." *Research in the Teaching of English* 11 (Fall 1977): 133–148.

An analysis of spelling errors made over a six-month period by first-graders. The work showed that children go through three invariant stages as they learn to spell. In stage one, students used a letter-name strategy. In stage two, they showed some refinement in ways to spell vowel sounds. In stage three, they began to use information about English writing system features. The researchers conclude that boys and girls did not lack phonetic knowledge as related to graphemes, but did lack knowledge about word structure, probably learned throughout the grades.

Blake, Howard E. "Some Spelling Facts." *Elementary English* 47 (February 1970): 271–279.

Children use many approaches when learning to spell, by reading, studying meanings of words, writing words in and out of context, oral spelling, using phonic and linguistic aids, and using a combination of some or all of these. Teachers of spelling *should* know thoroughly the intricacies of each approach and the terminology of each. Blake believes only when teachers have acquired this knowledge as well as an understanding of the potential contribution of the various approaches are they adequately qualified to teach spelling.

Bronstad, Travis, and Earp, N. Wesley. "Break Rules." *The Texas Outlook* 52 (May 1968): 32–33.

The authors deal with ways to vary spelling to meet individual capacities, interests, and needs. They point out that the conventional spelling program bores the good spellers and defeats the poor ones. They offer suggestions for providing for these individual differences. Requirements for each child should be adjusted to his or her potential. For instance, perhaps the slower student need only spell five out of twenty words correctly in order to be successful. Another necessity is that teachers help students transfer spelling skills from drills to their writing. In evaluating their spelling progress, teachers should consider children's initiative in proofreading and correcting spelling in their own writing.

Brothers, Aileen, and Hosclaw, Cora. "Fusing Behaviors into Spelling." *Elementary English* 46 (January 1969): 25–28.

The authors list five spelling behaviors to be incorporated into written work: copying a printed model, proofreading, rewriting to correct errors found in proofreading, writing a word from memory, and spelling automatically without thinking. A spelling program should provide practice in all of these. However, the traditional method of teaching spelling does not adequately satisfy these behaviors. The authors identify many weaknesses of such traditional programs.

Cramer, Ronald. "An Investigation of First-Grade Spelling Achievement." *Elementary English* 47 (March 1970): 230–237.

A study that tested the facility with which two groups of first-grade children spelled phonologically regular and irregular words and the possible influence of reading instruction on spelling achievement. Spelling achievement was examined on lists of regular and irregular words and in written composition. The reading methods used were the Language Experience Approach and the Basal Approach. The sample consisted of twenty-one first-grade classrooms. The Language Experience Approach results showed these students were better spellers, had less difficulty with the irregular orthography and their written compositions contained fewer spelling errors. The Basal Reader Approach students had more difficulty with irregular orthography and achieved lower scores on lists of regular and irregular spelling words.

Groff, Patrick. "Research on Spelling and Phonetics." *Education* 89 (November 1968): 132–135.

An attempt to test the validity of research which demonstrated that auditory discrimination plays a causal part in spelling disability and that phonetic knowledge and skill play an important part in spelling ability. Several studies have shown that children given unusual amounts of phonetic training did significantly better in spelling achievement than groups who haven't had this training. Groff's research attempted to determine if phonetics instruction for one semester would bring greater than ordinary results. His study replaced an ordinary Wednesday spelling test usually given in the textbook program. No other change from textbook procedures was used. Findings indicated that the middle-grade pupils made somewhat greater spelling gains than matched groups in the customary program.

Laurita, Raymond E. "The Road to Better Spelling." *New York State Education* 58 (February 1971): 23–24.

The author feels that poor spelling is due in part to the learner's failure to achieve a consistent method of developing an organized spelling vocabulary. The key to spelling success is mastery of a spelling process to facilitate the development of spelling categories during early exposure to language. Once an organized method has been established, the child can begin the lifelong task of adding words to already formed categories.

Lightbody, Patricia and Day, Katherine. "Order Out of Spelling Chaos." *Instructor* 79 (April 1970): 60.

The authors propose a logical, sequential approach for teaching spelling and relate several practices and characteristics of a linguistic program they have used. This program focuses on three classes of spelling words: "Predictable" words, "unpredictable but frequent" words, and "unpredictable and rare" words. Since the program is designed to stress the regular or predictable rather than the exceptions, the approach teaches children to rely on the "sound-to-spelling relationship." "Order" in spelling is achieved by means of a sequential linguistic approach. By guiding children to discover the regularities in our sound-symbol relationship, teachers can instill more confidence in young writers.

Pellowski, Anne. "AaBbCc." *Top of the News* 30 (January 1974): 144–149.

Although young children are usually fascinated by the sound of language, they are too often conditioned to speak only one and consider people who speak other languages "different." Children should be made aware of the many ways of communicating. The article describes three films about alphabets and provides a short bibliography of non-English alphabet books. After explaining how to run an alphabet program, the author appends a list of ways to arouse children's interest in other languages and alphabets.

Sharknas, Jenevie. "I Individualized Spelling." *Instructor* 79 (March 1970): 64.

Even though her class did well on tests, their compositions, letters, and other written work were full of errors. The author details each day's spelling activities: results of the program were positive. She reports a great improvement in word awareness—of pronunciation and meaning as well as spelling. There was a definite carry-over to other written work and sentence structure greatly improved, as did the appearance of the papers.

Smith, R. J. "Spelling in the Elementary School." *National Elementary Principal* 50 (September 1970): 44–51.

English contains both irregularities and regularities for which the spelling program must provide. Spelling instruction should teach the basic structural properties that underlie the spelling of many words. This can be done by incorporating spelling into many language arts activities. The teacher should find methods of motivation and reward that stimulate children to learn to spell correctly. Several such methods are described.

Unbach, Walter O. "Get Your Spelling Program Out of Its Rut." *School and Community* 57 (December 1970): 18–19.

The author views present spelling programs as routinized but he does not blame the authors of spelling texts as they have given teachers what they want—security in a stock program. Many materials can be used to teach spelling, but the important point is not the materials, but how teachers adapt these to their students. The author gives many suggestions about ways to vary the spelling program. For more honesty regarding the report card grade, Unbach suggests that is be based on the professional teacher's evaluations of the student's ability to spell in real, meaningful *writing* situations.

ANALYZING A SPELLING SERIES

This form is included because even if you do individualize your spelling program, you will probably use a commercial series as the basis for the program. If so, choosing the best text for your purposes may become a crucial issue.

This form is one way of evaluating spelling series. As you work with these series you may think of other points which need to be considered in arriving at a final decision.

	SERIES A					SERIES B				
	Poor	Fair	Good	Very Good	Excellent	Poor	Fair	Good	Very Good	Excellent
I. EXERCISES										
1. Quality, including interesting level and variety.										
2. Involves activities other than just spelling—dictionary work, hand-writing, etc.										
3. Drill: amount, type and interest level.										
4. Reviews—frequency and quality.										
5. Unit tests.										
6. Provision for individualization.										
II. TEACHER'S MATERIALS										
1. Quality of suggestions.										
2. Quantity of suggestions.										
3. Accessibility.										
III. PHYSICAL FEATURES										
1. Size and variety of type, contrast with paper for visibility; ease of use over a continued period of time.										
2. Page layout—interesting and eye-catching, but not cluttered.										
3. Indexing—of topics, reviews, adequacy of table of contents. Can you find things in it easily?										

Some Other Points to Consider

You will also want to notice the following points. While the series cannot necessarily be ranked on a continuum concerning these points, in the same way you ranked them in the first three sections, you will be able to jot some notes about these points to help you see what differences exist.

Orientation

Is the series linguistic? How effective is it in making apparent sound and symbol relationships and divergent forms?

Or does it use a story or thematic approach—with less emphasis on patterns?

Rationale

Does the series include any information about:

a. How the words were chosen? What source did the authors use to determine which words to include.[1]

b. How the authors decided on the difficulty levels of words?[2] How did they decide what grade level was right for a particular word?

ALPHABET BOOKS

One successful way of interesting young children in reading is to share with them some of the many available alphabet books. Several can be looked at and compared; discussions can ensue about which ones are liked best, and why. In addition to stimulating oral language, such an experience generates interest in learning how to make the letters.

With older children, a second use to which such books can be put is to encourage thinking about the diversity of form possible within one letter. An A, for example, can be made in many different ways. Within the basic form

JACKAL,   Oppossum,

From A Peaceable Kingdom *by Alice and Martin Provensen.*

---

[1]Several researchers have investigated the problem of which words a child "ought" to know. This has been done by investigating words children use, words adults use in writing, words most common in printed materials, and composite lists. Probably a composite list is the most sensible since there is overlap between the other lists.

[2]There is not a great deal of consistency in the grade-level placement of words. Studies concluded the same way: it is difficult if not impossible to determine with any accuracy the "grade level" of a particular word.

From A Little Alphabet *by Trina Schart Hyman.*

there are many variations possible, by changing the size, shape, proportion and weight of the parts of the letter. You can use alphabet books with older children to show the different ways artists made the letters. After you have examined the variety that is possible, the group can be encouraged to experiment with making their own letters.

Another use for these books, with older children, is as a stimulus to create their own alphabet books—which can be shared with younger children in the school. A variety of art media can be used; crayons, paint, cut paper, stencil prints, and mixed media all work well in making such books. After the books are made, their creators enjoy the experience of seeing younger children use the books with delight.

Following is an annotated list of alphabet books. By checking with more than one library you should be able to find several of these, or others, to use in the ways suggested above.

Anno, Mitsumasa. *Anno's Alphabet: An Adventure in Imagination.* New York: Thomas Y. Crowell, 1975.

A generously sized full-color book with ingenious visual illustrations. The letters (on the left page) are *trompe l'œil* foolers which seem to twist and turn. Apparently solid wood bends in ways we know it cannot. Surrounding the letter, and extending across to the illustration on the facing right page is a lacy, intricate, black ink line border. A single, colored illustration full of intricate detail on each page shows objects children will enjoy examining. No words are included.

Barry, Katharina. *A Is for Anything.* New York: Harcourt Brace Jovanovich, 1961.

The whimsical little children populating this small book encounter a variety of unusual people, including an enigmatic Indian, a jester, and a rotund king. Black ink line combines effectively with large blocks of color to create illustrations as effective as the rhymes accompanying each letter.

Boxer, Devorah. *26 Ways to Be Somebody Else.* New York: Pantheon, 1960.

This small book begins with a woodcut of an impish-looking child, and then shows him being twenty-six other things, from acrobat to zookeeper. The bold, pleasant illustrations are arranged imaginatively across the pages facing the word. Flat sweeps of one or two colors brighten the black of the woodcuts. Stark white backgrounds further intensify the colors.

Brown, Marcia. *All Butterflies*. New York: Scribner's, 1974.

The illustrator here turns her masterful woodcut technique to an array of natural objects from *a*ll *b*utterflies (on the first page) to *y*our *z*oo (on the last). Imaginative word combinations are enhanced by energetic woodcuts that crowd off the page edges. The color is more subtle than that usually associated with woodcut. The endpapers and title page provide more butterflies for fanciers of the winged creatures.

Burningham, John. *ABC*. Indianapolis: Bobbs-Merrill, 1964.

In a bright book, the illustrations for which are reminiscent of Wildsmith's, this artist takes the reader to Africa, where sultans ride elephants; to sea, where yacht sails bloom in the sun; to the top of an erupting volcano; and to an audience with a dyspeptic queen.

Carlson, Sherrill. *The Northwest Coast Indians ABC Book*. Pullman, Wash.: The State Street Press, 1972.

A black-and-white photographic survey of words special to this ethnic group, the book is appropriate for late second or third grade. Photos are clear, pleasing, and an uncluttered layout contributes to a sedate look at another culture. Order from: State Street Press, 715 State Street, Pullman, WA 99163.

Carle, Eric. *All About Arthur (an absolutely absurd ape)*. New York: Franklin Watts, 1974.

Bold, blocky woodcuts, crudely fashioned, show all the animals Arthur meets on his journey from Atlanta to Yonkers. The woodcuts are overprinted on full-color photographs of each letter, examples taken from our environment. The *a* is a neon letter, *m* is a varsity sweater applique, *n* is from a boxcar name, and *o* is chiseled in granite. An unusually imaginative combination of visual elements. The text is designed for upper-primary, unless teachers read it aloud to younger students.

Chwast, Seymour, and Moskof, Martin. *Still Another Alphabet Book*. New York: McGraw-Hill, 1969.

Designed to be a puzzle and a game in addition to an alphabet book, this bold, vibrant effort catches and holds one's attention as an attempt is made to solve the puzzle running across the bottom of all pages. Children spend hours with the captivating pictures as they learn to play the game.

Clifton, Lucille. *The Black ABC's*. New York: E. P. Dutton, 1970.

A poem for each letter of the alphabet introduces a brief discussion of the contributions of black people to American history and culture.

Coudrille, Jonathon. *A Beastly Collection*. New York: Frederick Warne, 1974.

Fanciful, though highly realistic, full-page black ink drawings face the text page for each letter. The toads are realistically depicted, though they are enjoying tea and toast in front of a television, comfortably ensconced in formal wing chairs. Some of the references are of mixed difficulty: while primary children will recognize pig, they will not recognize the peruke he is wearing. Many chuckles, if used in a group situation with the teacher present to explain.

Cranston, Margaret A. *Let's Look at the Letters.* New York: Holt, Rinehart and Winston, 1967.

Eye-catching illustrations in full color will capture children's attention, as will the open format of this unusually attractive book. The rhymes, some from Mother Goose, and others created by the illustrator, will keep children's interest.

Crews, Donald. *We Read: A to Z.* New York: Harper & Row, 1967.

Bold sans serif letters in lime green face a peacock-blue opening page, and briefly tell that all our words are made with just 26 letters. Then, each succeeding page features a concept, boldly illustrated in abstract, highly unusual fashion. *A* is for almost, to *Z* for zigzag, which stops along the way for such concepts as *grow*, *parts*, and *under.* The intense, flat color enhances the ideas (defined simply) in a way unusual in children's books.

Davar, Ashok. *Talking Words.* Indianapolis: Bobbs-Merrill, 1969.

Though this has only black-and-white illustrations, it is a striking book. Words are depicted as objects, and many are quite abstract. The presentations capture the sense of the word, and are not literal. Use with upper-primary children.

Delaunay, Sonia. *Alphabet.* New York: Thomas Y. Crowell, 1972.

Rhyming verses on one page face a highly saturated full-cover stylized letter. Imaginative letters sweep across the entire 12 x 12 inch page. Letters are distorted and elaborated for unusual visual treatment. Not appropriate for children when they are first learning their letters; this is better for older children when teachers want them to explore variety in letter shape.

Duvoisin, Roger Antoine. *A for Ark.* New York: Lothrop, Lee and Shepard, 1952.

A simple but expressive retelling of the Noah story, this full-color book exposes children to some unusual animals: vipers, nuthatches, ocelots, and jararacas. The illustrations, rhythmic with a minimum of detail, recreate the adventure with elan.

Eichenberg, Fritz. *Ape in a Cape.* New York: Harcourt, Brace, 1952.

Two-color illustrations in soft orange and blue provide fantastic settings and clothes for the animals shown. The book opens with the ape and ends at *z* for zoo. Along the way, readers see common animals like an Irish setter, and uncommon ones like an egret. The simple, descriptive phrases rhyme the animal with what it is doing.

Falls, C. B. *ABC Book.* Garden City: Doubleday, 1923. (Despite its date, this book is still in print, as is the Gag book.)

The strength of these woodcuts with their bold, blocky forms, heightened by a vigorous use of color, makes this a powerful statement. Letters and words march determinedly across the bottom of the page, while above the reader meets such unusual animals as the xiphius, yak, and unicorn.

Farber, Norma. *As I Was Crossing Boston Common.* New York: E. P. Dutton, 1973.

In rhyme with a definite rhythm, Farber tells the fanciful story of a menagerie following a leader across the common. The names are intriguing; from angwan-tibo to zibet the sounds tickle children's ears. Ink drawings, in soft gold and green, evoke a historical ambience in Arnold Lobel's predictable whimsical style. All names are actual terms for rare species of animals; a glossary is provided.

Feelings, Muriel L. *Jambo Means Hello. A Swahili Alphabet Book.* New York: Dial Press, 1974.

What a visually impressive picture book! Using the 24 letters (no *q* or *x*) of Swahili, the predominant African language, each word is phonetically spelled, including accent, followed by an informative sentence or two. Illustrations in tempera, pencil, and black ink wash in double-page spreads, visually support the text. The pictures add cultural, social, economic, and religious visual comments on African life. Use with upper-primary children.

Fife, Dale. *Adam's ABC.* New York: Coward, McCann and Goeghegan, 1971.

In simple, soft black-and-white charcoal sketches, Don Robertson depicts many aspects of the city lives of Adam and his two friends, Arthur and Albert. Most of the things boys encounter: clouds in the sky, an ebony elephant, a fire escape, a blackberry jelly sandwich, and licorice sticks, reinforce the subliminal message that black is beautiful. There is nothing particularly memorable about Fife's prose, but together with the pictures they create a useful, albeit always pleasant (and thus somewhat unrealistic) portrayal of city life.

Floyd, Lucy and Lasky, Kathryn. *Agatha's Alphabet.* Chicago: Rand McNally, 1975.

Agatha, a slightly disheveled redhead, careens through a series of fanciful environments inhabited by people, animals, and objects which illustrate capital and lower-case letters on each double page spread. Full-color pages alternate with monochrome pages. The illustrations are realistic in detail and treatment, though the juxtaposition of objects is unusual. The book concludes with a dictionary to help children identify objects they may have missed.

Freeman, Don. *Add-a-Line Alphabet.* San Carlos, Calif.: Golden Gate Junior Books, 1968.

Very simple, limited color, though bold drawings, incorporate the letter into the body of the animal. The lines of *a* form the anteater, *k* is incorporated into the kangaroo, and the *z* forms a zebra. After using the book, children will want to use paints to make their own letter-animal.

Gag, Wanda. *ABC Bunny.* New York: Coward-McCann, 1933.

Done in the artist's well-known style, this charming pastoral adventure takes the bunny through several different places until he finally returns safely home. It is done in black and white, but the bright red letters will catch children's eyes. A song about the rabbit, created by the artist, is included.

Gordon, Isabel. *The ABC Hunt.* New York: Viking, 1961.

Two children, whose adventures begin with a bowl of alphabet soup, find themselves in a variety of places looking for letters. The black-and-white photographs are very clear; a book for the literal-minded child.

Greenaway, Kate. *A Apple Pie.* London: Frederick Warne, n.d.

Another book with one theme running through from beginning to end, this may need some brief introduction to explain the illustrations. The wide-eyed children, comely in their formal clothing, are often set against a strangely empty background, adding to the air of unreality.

Grossbart, Francine. *A Big City.* New York: Harper & Row, 1966.

Flat, solid color backgrounds accompany schematic, almost silhouette drawings of objects in an urban environment.

Hoban, Tana. *A, B, See!* New York: Greenwillow, 1982.

This time the accomplished photographer uses the photogram technique to take viewers on a trip through the alphabet from *asparagus* to *zipper*. Most pages feature several items, though some pages (*umbrella*) have only one. Excellent for vocabulary development and, incidentally, spelling of the variety of words for labeling the objects presented so dramatically.

Hyman, Trina Schart. *A Little Alphabet.* Boston: Little, Brown, 1980.

In diminutive size (3¾ x 5 in.) and limited color (beige and black on cream paper), the illustrator has created a charming, object-packed world. Each miniature vignette is intertwined with the capital form of the letter, and a list is included in the front of the book, so children can check the items they have located against the complete list. Hyman's children are beguiling but not saccharine. The book will be the kind individual children return to again and again.

Jacobs, Leland. *Alphabet of Girls.* New York: Holt, Rinehart and Winston, 1969.

The author has woven an endearing garland of notable females, from Arabella to Zelda. Little girls will return again and again to delight in the rhymes, and in the game of finding the name. Now available in paperback.

Kuskin, Karla. *ABDCEFGHIJKLMNOPQRSTUVWXYZ.* New York: Harper & Row, 1963.

Another diminutive book and a visual winner. Delicate black ink line adds detail to a bold use of color. The hand-drawn letters are of interest for the variety they introduce.

Lear, Edward. *A B C.* New York: McGraw-Hill, 1965.

An exact reproduction of Lear's original manuscript, the black ink drawings and verses written in script make this book unlike any other alphabet book available. The illustrations, of another era, depict kerosene lamps, ices to eat, conical bee hives, and tops. The letters in color are large and clearly made. There is typeset copy at the end of the book in case Lear's cursive writing proves difficult to read.

Matthiesen, Thomas. *A B C*. New York: Platt and Munk, 1966.

One of the few picture books done with photographs, this is a calm and ordered look at the world in which children live. The photographs are clear, in full color and, unfortunately, lacking the kind of excitement generated by artists' conceptions. It is undoubtedly for the pragmatic child. A matter-of-fact text accompanies each illustration.

McGinn, Maureen. *I Used to Be an Artichoke*. St. Louis: Concordia Publishing House, 1973.

Fresh, full color contrasts with liberal use of white paper to create a humorous connected tale of an artichoke that was completely happy until someone criticized it. Then the metamorphoses begin, as the former artichoke becomes something for every letter of the alphabet. The imaginative use of pattern and bold color result in art that is better than the poetry which tells the story.

Mendoza, George. *The Alphabet Boat*. New York: American Heritage, 1972.

The author, a prolific writer whose output reached 100 books with this one, explores a variety of boats and the alphabetic needs they have, from anchor to zephyr winds. Fey, Sendak-esque children, a boy and a girl, inhabit detailed pastel boats and waters.

Miles, Miska. *Apricot A B C*. Boston: Little, Brown, 1969.

A circle story about the life of an apricot seed, through maturity and back to seed again, tenderly depicted in soft colors. The story is an interesting one.

Milgrom, Harry. *ABC of Ecology*. New York: Macmillan, 1972.

Milgrom depicts people and objects, primarily from the urban environment, in clear black-and-white close-up photographs and simple text that tells and asks questions about ecology. The pictures are almost full-page; brief text tells something about an aspect of ecology. Parallel questions ask children to do something (simple experiments) or think about some problem.

Milne, A. A. *Pooh's Alphabet Book*. New York: E. P. Dutton, 1975.

The characteristics and philosophy of childhood are portrayed in limericks as dolls and teddy bears animate the alphabet. Every child old enough to comprehend the subtle humor will be charmed by this new addition to the Pooh library.

Montresor, Beni. *A for Angel*. New York: Alfred A. Knopf, 1969.

Despite the angel in the title, there is nothing saccharine in this unworldly coltion of the unexpected and unusual. The artist's drawings, employing a limited palette, liberally laced with black, evoke a strange land where grandma plays a green guitar while a giraffe gulps grapes.

Moore, Margaret and Moore, John. *Certainly, Carrie, Cut the Cake*. Indianapolis: Bobbs-Merrill, 1971.

Another of those strange amalgams of children's format but adult sophistication, this unusual little book features cleverly contrived poems for each letter. The drawings are populated with intriguing and bizarre people from some indeterminable time and place.

Munari, Bruno. *A B C*. Cleveland: World Publishing, 1960.

Munari's color, splashed boldly across the pages, illustrates simply but with verve several objects beginning with each letter. Some of the alliteration is as ear-catching as the illustrations are eye-catching.

Newberry, Clare Turlay. *The Kittens' A B C*. New York: Harper & Row, 1965.

With a limited palette but using a facile wet-and-dry-brush water-color technique, the artist has created a kindle of kittens sure to delight. From alley cats to Siamese, the group is entrancing, though some of the rhymes are strained.

Parker, Fan. *The Russian Alphabet Book*. New York: Coward-McCann, 1961.

Black pencil drawings with brown watercolor wash show scenes of activities, places, and objects as each of the 33 letters are presented on separate pages. A pronunciation guide, including both upper- and lower-case letter forms (fewer differences than in our alphabet) precedes the alphabet itself. Paragraphs about four sentences in length tell about the topic for a given letter. Particularly useful in widening children's understanding of other alphabets than our Roman one.

Petersham, Maud and Petersham, Miska. *An American ABC*. New York: Macmillan, 1955.

The lithographs are done in the artists' usual, easily identifiable style. The pictures are pleasant, though the concepts of patriotism included are more emphatic than is popular today.

Rees, Ennis. *The Little Greek Alphabet Book*. Englewood Cliffs, N.J.: Prentice-Hall, 1968.

A quatrain introduces each of the letters and provides some description of the visual material. Unfortunately some of the quatrains are simply bad poetry, but the book is a good addition to a unit on the alphabet.

Rey, H. A. *Curious George Learns the Alphabet*. Boston: Houghton Mifflin, 1963.

One of an extended series of books, this one involves the inquisitive monkey learning letters from *apple* to *zebra*. The learning is interrupted periodically by George's pranks. The illustrations, in full color, are cartoonlike in quality with little visual sophistication, though the antics of George make this a popular book.

Ruben, Patricia. *Apples to Zippers*. New York: Doubleday, 1976.

Ruben pictures objects in an urban child's environment in pleasant, sometimes humorous, always unambiguous black-and-white photographs. Two to four large pictures for each letter fill the space in a pleasant page layout.

Russell, Solveig Paulson. *A is for Apply and Why*. New York: Abington Press, 1959.

Not an alphabet book per se, but rather a simplified retelling of the evolution of the alphabet, the book covers several centuries in forty-eight pages. Such an attempt necessitates omissions and generalizations, but the book is nonetheless a valuable introduction to a topic children can explore in more depth later.

Schmiderer, Dorothy. *The Alphabeast Book*. New York: Holt, Rinehart and Winston, 1971.

The dynamic graphics done in bold silhouette may not appeal to everyone but are certain to leave an indelible image in the child's mind. In a series of ingenuous steps like the panels in a cartoon, each letter is transformed into an amorphous animal painted in an assertive red and blue.

Smith, William Jay. *Puptents and Pebbles.* Boston: Atlantic Monthly Press, 1959.

Bright, simple drawings by Juliet Kepes feature large black initial letters. The text links improbable items through the poet's usual enjoyable nonsense.

Tallon, Robert. *Rotten Kidphabets* (1975), and *Zag: A Search Through the Alphabet* (1976). Both, New York: Holt, Rinehart and Winston.

In *Rotten Kidphabets* the illustrator creates a bookful of horrid children, from Awful Albert (dropping water on a passerby) to Zombiola Zachary (leashing three evil birds atop a roof). Full color makes the terrible creatures more appealing. *Zag* is a monochromatic search for the missing person. The sinister private eye goes from an airplane flown by a sour apple to a yo-yo which finally reveals where Zag is. Off-beat humor for upper-primary children.

Thayer, Jane. *Timothy and Madam Mouse.* New York: William Morrow, 1971.

Use with upper-primary children, for the large initial letters are presented in nonalphabetic order. Following the presentation of the letters, there are lines of type in which children are to pick out the letters. The line drawings, in only a few colors, are effective.

Tudor, Tasha. *A is for Annabelle.* New York: Oxford University Press, 1954.

One thread, the adventures of the doll for whom the book is named, runs through this charming pastel look at an uncomplicated world. Probably of interest only to little girls, who will be enchanted.

Wildsmith, Brian. *A B C.* New York: Franklin Watts, 1962.

The artist's usual carefree splashes, abandoned strokes of color, and infinitely subtle gradations are here turned to an enchanting picture book sure to capture children's interest from apple to zebra. Some of the animals are less well known: iguana, yak, and jaguar; all will delight the reader by their freshness.

INDIVIDUALIZED SPELLING — IT CAN BE DONE

Ellen Simsohn
Hebrew Academy of Tidewater

Often both student teachers and classroom teachers feel that mechanics, spelling, and handwriting are dull and uncreative. Nevertheless, these are subjects children are often drilled on with regularity. Perhaps this is one reason so few children really enjoy expressing themselves in writing. My feeling that the act of writing is more important than the skill areas is reflected in the placement of the previous chapters. The chapters on writing precede (being more important) the two skill chapters. I hope that motivating children to write and developing an interest in writing will precede and remain more important than mechanical considerations when you begin to teach.

Still, skills must be taught. One effective way to do this is to individualize the program, assessing which skills children need and allowing each to work independently on mastering the skills. The idea of individualized spelling is not new. Over twenty-five years ago one expert commented: "Each pupil ideally, should start at his own level and proceed at the rate at which he makes most progress. Each child should work on his own difficulties and no others" (Hildreth, 1955).

Despite such assertions, one writer has summarized the current spelling scene: ". . . far too infrequently are students placed at their own levels and permitted to move at their own paces, which is the essense of individualized spelling instruction" (Allred, 1977).

To overcome this problem, one student teacher planned an individualized spelling program. Creative and energetic, dauntless in most things, she was concerned over her responsibility to teach spelling.

This was a subject she disliked, as did her children. In the essay that follows, Mrs. Simsohn relates how she made spelling an exciting challenge for children. She launched this ambitious program at the end of her first week of student teaching. Could you plan a challenging approach to teaching one of the skill areas?

Think of this: a class of third-graders learning to spell words like lieutenant, schizophrenia, ballerina, and rhinoceros; every student's mind working to its capacity in spelling; twenty-eight children having twenty-eight different spelling lists each week. Impossible? Idealistic? Idealistic—yes. Impossible —NO! Such results as imagined above are possible through the use of an individualized spelling program. And such a program is practical, for I instituted and successfully ran one during my eight weeks of student teaching.

This was not done with a small, extraordinary group of third-graders at an experimental school. The school was in a rural area. The class was made up of fourteen boys and fourteen girls, whose talents and home environments were varied; not a unique class by any means.

I was gradually eased into my student teaching. The first week was spent in observation. The second week, I was given the responsibility of teaching one subject, the third week I was given two subjects, and so on, until I was teaching all day. My first assignment was teaching spelling—probably chosen because it seemed to be the most straightforward teaching task.

I decided that initially I would teach spelling in the manner I saw it being taught during my week of observation. The students used a workbook called *Spell Correctly*, published by Silver Burdett (1968). They all took a spelling pretest on Monday, followed by assignments in the book on Tuesday and Wednesday, a practice test on Thursday and the final test on Friday. It took less than a week for me to see that the spelling program was not all that it could be.

It was Monday's pretest that really got me thinking. The pretest was a folly, as it served no useful purpose. Although it indicated which spelling words the students already knew, they *all* did the same work during the week and they *all* took the same test on Friday. So what was the point of taking the pretest? The pretest, however, made me aware of the basic inefficiency of this way of teaching spelling. Because some of the children already knew many of the words, they were not all learning the same number of new words each week. Some students were learning only eight or six or possibly even three new words for Friday's final test, while others had to master eleven or twelve new words. Because of this inequity, you could always predict, with a reasonable degree of accuracy, who would be getting the highest grades on those tests. This just was not fair. But even more important, this inequity in learning tasks seemed to violate much that I had learned in college. I had learned that we, as teachers, should always help each student learn the most possible. Supposedly, children would grow the most when we gave them material slightly above their level, so that they would have to "reach" a little. Yet in this classroom, the brighter students were not learning as much as they could. They were not stretching their minds at all! In a very real sense, the spelling program being used allowed a gross injustice to be done to these children. So these observations—the pointlessness of the pretest, the inequity in the learning tasks, and the failure to "stretch" the minds of all the students— made it clear to me that a change was needed. But to what would I change?

It was lucky for me that the previous year I had done a research project on "The Teaching of Spelling" for my language arts method course. I had combed the literature for different methods of teaching spelling, and this was a useful resource in developing a new approach to spelling. There were many different creative spelling programs from which to choose, and I found that almost all of them were a form of individualized spelling. An individualized program seemed to be the right thing to try, for it would ameliorate the shortcomings of the spelling program previously being used. Individualization could equalize the number of new words learned and could give all students the opportunity to stretch their minds to the limit. How to go from the concept of individualization to a workable individualized program was another problem! To solve it, I again referred to my research project. I gleaned the best (or most workable) ideas from all the articles on individualized spelling, and the resulting synthesis was my very own individualized spelling program.

My program was basically quite simple. Each Monday, each student would compile a twelve-word spelling list for that week. The list would be composed of words missed on the given pretest plus some words of his or her choice. During the week, the students would do work to assure their understanding of the meaning and spelling of these words. And on Friday, each child would be tested.

With the mechanics of my program well thought out, I went to my cooperating teacher for advice and approval. She was not quite as thrilled as I was with the plan and was somewhat hesitant about its success. But she wanted me to try it. So after some minor revisions regarding the testing procedure, she sent me out into the classroom to try my new way of teaching spelling.

Preparing the students for a major change in the spelling routine was my first job. I explained the new program to them, saying that from now on they would not all be learning the same words. I told them that some of their spelling words would be words that *they* wanted to learn. We discussed the question of where to find interesting words for spelling. Possible places were books, television, and conversations. The students needed a place to compile these interesting words they found. So they each made a Spelling Wordbook from construction paper and notebook paper. Fearing that these wordbooks would not be in school when they were needed, or that they would get lost, I made the rule that Spelling Wordbooks were to stay in school. Interesting words found at home were to be jotted down on paper and transferred to the wordbook on the following day. A fellow teacher suggested that I prepare supplementary word lists, since the children might have difficulty finding words for their wordbooks at first. Using various spelling texts, I compiled lists of third-grade words, fourth-grade words, and spelling demons, which I could later give to the children if need be. Supplementary word lists also contained words from current math, science, and social studies units. The final preparation was the creation of a Word Tree, affixed to a prominent bulletin board. The Word Tree started out as a huge, leafless tree. But it would end up full of leaves, each leaf emblazoned with a spelling word that the owner was proud of having mastered.

The students were now ready to begin. On Monday, a pretest, on one of the spelling lists from *Spell Correctly,* was given. The class graded the tests together. All the girls and boys made up their own lists for the week, on a new sheet of paper which was numbered from one to twelve. They first wrote down all the words that they had missed on the pretest and then added words from their own wordbook and from my posted word lists, so that everyone's total number of spelling words was twelve. A second copy of the list was also made, to be retained by me. This second copy was a necessity. I needed it for preparing the final tests as well as for those times when students lost their own copies.

Tuesday and Wednesday were devoted to activities that would enhance the students' understanding of the meaning and spelling of their words. As a group, we worked through the exercises in the spelling book, since these exercises often emphasized phoneme-grapheme relationships, inflected forms of words, and homonyms, synonyms, and antonyms. Each student wrote sentences using his or her twelve words. This proved to be doubly beneficial, as spelling practice for the students and as an indication to me of their understanding of their spelling words. Mastering the words was done at home during the week.

Practice spelling tests were given on Thursday. Each child was given a "spelling buddy," with an approximately equal reading level. The buddies gave each other the spelling tests. I corrected the tests, although it was apparent the students had not fully realized that these lists which they had compiled on Monday were their actual spelling lists, to be learned by Friday! The remaining part of spelling time on Thursday was devoted to preparing the class for Friday's final tests. This was most crucial, for the tests were to be given in a completely new way!

In order to give twenty-eight separate tests, I utilized two portable tape recorders with earphones. Each recorder had fourteen tests on it. On the tape, I greeted each child, then gave the test as I normally would, leaving enough time for the child to write each word. The word was said three times, so that no replaying was necessary. At the end of each test, the child turned off the tape recorder, handed in the test, and called the next person to be tested.

The procedure had to run exactly on schedule, since we had a fixed amount of time in which to do the testing. It also had to proceed without me, as I would be teaching reading groups while the testing was taking place. Therefore, the class had to be thoroughly prepared for the testing experience.

So, on Thursday, the students were given a complete rundown on what to expect the next day. They were shown the testing area and told who would use which tape recorder (the tape recorders being labeled Tape Recorder #1 and Tape Recorder #2). A time schedule for the use of each tape recorder was posted. The children heard a tape of a spelling test just like the one they would hear the next day. Three rules which I instituted were discussed and their importance was stressed. Rule Number One was that no one except the two children being tested was allowed in the testing area. Rule Number Two was that there was to be *no* touching of any buttons on the tape recorder except the Play and Stop buttons. This was imperative if the testing was to go smoothly without my help. The students were told that disobeying this rule would be punishable by throwing away the test of any offender. Rule Number Three was that the completed tests were to be immediately deposited on my desk. To wind up this preparation session, all questions from students regarding the testing procedure were answered. With all this done, we were ready for Friday—final test day.

Frankly, I was afraid that the first testing session would be a disaster. But I had to go on with it. Before the actual testing started, all the children prepared their papers, noting at the top the time of their test and which tape recorder they were to use. And then we began. Seventy-five minutes later, I was ecstatic. It had worked without a hitch. I practically flew through the halls of the school to share my good news with my fellow student teachers.

In the weeks to follow, we followed the same Monday through Friday schedule, with some minor changes. Each Monday, the previous week's tests were returned, along with big, green construction paper leaves. On the leaf, the child was to write one word from the test which he or she was proud of having mastered. The diversity in words was fantastic—ballerina (from a little girl who had just started taking ballet lessons), lieutenant (this took at least three weeks to master!), Viet Nam (from a boy whose father was stationed there), to name a few. These word leaves were, of course, pinned to the Word Tree, which was bare at first but which "grew" more leaves week by week. Since Thursday was no longer needed for explaining the testing procedure, we used part of Thursday's spelling time for some good-natured competition in spelling games. Finally, every few weeks we gathered around the

Word Tree to share words. This was one of the most enjoyable activities we had. We shared words with each other, as well as discussing meanings, related words, etymologies, and unusual spellings. It was quite informal and a lot of fun both for myself and the students.

So, my individualized spelling program worked. There were some problems, however. Some were major; some were minor. Some I solved; some I didn't. One problem was the children's choice of words. Surprisingly, they did not choose words that were too easy. At first they picked words that were too hard. After the first few weeks, however, most of the children were able to pick words that were within their capacities. I would never discourage children from trying an overly hard word. Instead, I would let them try their choices for a week or two, and if their attempts proved unsuccessful, I would then suggest they drop the word. Usually the students would be more than willing to do this. There was another big problem involved with the children's choice of words. This was making sure that they understood the meanings of their words. I had the students write sentences using their spelling words in order to evaluate the degree of understanding of each word. Then I worked with those students who needed help. I found that those who drew upon their own interests and experiences in choosing words did not need help as much as those who went to the dictionary looking for "hard" spelling words.

I had a problem finding activities that would promote the learning of the spelling words. Although the students were to work on their words at home every night, there was also some time during the school day for spelling work. What kind of individual work would best help them learn those words? I tried sentence writing, story writing, sheer drill-type practice, and exercises in which the students noted the number of syllables, long and short vowels, and silent letters in each spelling word. None of these activities seemed to be very helpful.

In many spelling texts, such as *Spell Correctly*, spelling words are grouped according to some spelling pattern, e.g., words having the long /a/ sound, or words having the suffix -ly. If one used only the text, it would be easy to teach spelling generalizations, since everyone would be learning words exemplifying a particular generalization. With my spelling program, there was a problem. Since everyone was learning different words, I thought that group work on spelling generalizations would be impossible. And so, for eight weeks, we did no work of this kind. This was a terrible mistake; for if our goal is independence in spelling, it must be based on a thorough grasp of the spelling generalizations. I know of two ways to remedy this situation. The first is to somewhat circumscribe the children's choice of words, instructing them to choose words with a particular vowel sound or a particular suffix, or whatever. Everyone would then have spelling words that had something in common, and group teaching of spelling generalizations would be relatively easy. Another possibility is to let the children be completely responsible for learning their weekly spelling words at home, and then spend class time to work on this other aspect of spelling—learning generalizations. This second choice, however, does not directly tie the learning of generalizations to the weekly spelling words. Instead, it is hoped that the generalizations would carry over to the learning of those spelling words.

I found that my spelling program was not related to the other language arts. Students continually handed in stories containing misspelled words. This problem was easy to remedy, although it took some time. I kept a notebook and jotted down each child's misspelled words as I graded papers. These words could then be used in making up part of the child's weekly twelve-word list.

My cooperating teacher saw a problem in grading. Would we give letter grades, as always? The children were learning, or trying to learn, much harder words than usual. Would it be fair to give a B, when a child could receive an A in a traditional program? This was a hard problem to resolve. The cooperating teacher felt that we ought to stretch our grading scales to take into account the additional difficulty of the words. I felt, however, that you grade on *relation* to ability. Thus, children who already know the third-grade words, should not get an A for doing what is easy work for them. They should only get an A when they excell at a learning task which is challenging for them. You will have to decide this question for yourself.

There were also a few procedural problems in my spelling program. When the practice tests were given on Thursday, I had to make sure that each child knew how to pronounce his or her buddy's words correctly. And when I prepared the tape for the final tests, I had to give certain children a longer time to write their words. I felt that is was not fair to penalize any children because they worked somewhat slower than the rest. Our goal is spelling accuracy, not spelling speed.

What were the results of this individualized spelling program? The students learned to spell the "required" third-grade words plus many more advanced ones. Hopefully, the program created an interest in words. Certainly, our discussions at the Word Tree helped promote such an interest. And finally, the program was fairer and more challenging than the previous one. All the children were stretching their minds.

Certainly, this is not *the* best way to teach spelling. I don't know *the* best way. Many teachers hesitate to institute an individualized spelling program because it is too much work. Granted, there is more work involved. But the benefits are so great that it is well worth the extra effort. Do try some kind of an individualized spelling program. I am sure that you can create variations on my program, just as I created my program as a variation on the programs of others. But do try individualized spelling—it can be done.

Bibliography

Allen, Roach Van and Allen, Clarice. *Language Experience Activities.* Boston: Houghton Mifflin, 1976.

Allred, Ruel A. *Spelling—The Application of Research Findings.* Washington, D.C.: The National Education Association, 1977.

Ames, Wilbur S. "A Comparison of Spelling Textbooks." *Elementary English* 42 (February 1965): 146–150.

Beers, Carol Strickland and Beers, James Wheelock. "Three Assumptions about Learning to Spell." *Language Arts* 58(5) (May 1981): 573–580.

Beers, James and Henderson, Edmund H. "A Study of Developing Orthographic Concepts among First Graders." *Research in the Teaching of English*, 11 (Fall 1977): 133–148.

Clymer, Theodore. "The Utility of Phonic Generalizations in the Primary Grades." *The Reading Teacher* (January 1963): 252–258.

Corcoran, Gertrude B. *Language Arts in the Elementary School.* New York: Ronald Press, 1970.

Cramer, Ronald L. "An Investigation of First-Grade Spelling Achievement." *Elementary English* 47 (February 1970): 230–237.

dePaola, Tomie. *Andy (That's My Name).* Englewood Cliffs, N.J.: Prentice-Hall, 1973.

Donoghue, Mildred R. *The Child and the English Language Arts.* Dubuque, Iowa: William C. Brown, 1971.

Emery, Donald W. *Variant Spellings in Modern American Dictionaries.* Champaign: National Council of Teachers of English, 1958.

Falk, Ethel Mabie. "Interpretation of the Language Arts Program to the Parents and Community." *Teaching Language in the Elementary School.* Forty-third Yearbook, Part II. Chicago: National Society for the Study of Education, 1944.

Flasch, M. J. "Spelling Games." *The Grade Teacher* 88 (October 1970): 83–85.

Gentry, J. Richard. "Learning to Spell Developmentally." *The Reading Teacher* (January 1981): 378–381.

Gove, Phillip B., ed. *Webster's Third New International Dictionary.* Springfield, Mass.: G. and C. Merriam Co., 1961, pp. 6A–7A, preface.

Grief, Ivo P. "'When Two Vowels Go Walking,' They Should Get Lost." *The Reading Teacher* (January 1981): 460–461.

Hanna, Paul R. et al. *Phoneme-Grapheme Correspondence as Cues to Spelling Improvement.* U.S.O.E. Cooperative Research Project, #1991. Washington, D.C.: Superintendent of Documents, U.S. Government Printing Office, 1966.

Hanna, Paul R. et al. *Power to Spell.* Boston: Houghton Mifflin, 1967.

Hanna, Paul R. et al. *Spelling: Structure and Strategies.* Boston: Houghton Mifflin, 1971.

Henry, Martin. *Letters and Sounds.* London: Oxford University Press, 1942.

Hildreth, Gertrude. *Teaching Spelling: A Guide to Basic Principles and Practices.* New York: Henry Holt, 1955.

Hodges, Richard E. *Learning to Spell.* Urbana, Ill.: ERIC Clearinghouse on Reading and Communication Skills, 1981.

Horn, Ernest. *Teaching Spelling (What Research Says to the Teacher)*, No. 3. Washington, D.C.: Department of Classroom Teachers, National Education Association, 1967

Horn, Thomas D. "Spelling." In *Encyclopedia of Educational Research*, edited by Robert L. Ebel. New York: Macmillan, 1969.

Hughes, James W. "The Myth of the Spelling List." *National Elementary Principal* 46(1) (September 1966): 53–54.

Hymes, Lucia and Hymes, James. *Oodles of Noodles*. New York: Young Scott Books, 1964.

Johnson, Terry D., et al. "Characteristics of an Effective Spelling Program." *Language Arts* 58(5) (May 1981): 581–588.

Loomer, Bradley M. *The Most Commonly Asked Questions about Spelling . . . and What the Research Says*. North Billerica, Mass.: Curriculum Associates, 1980.

Markoff, Annabelle Most. *Teaching Low-Achieving Children Reading, Spelling and Handwriting*. Springfield, Ill.: Charles C. Thomas, 1976.

Meyer, Margaret. "A Spelling Olympics." *Teacher* (November 1978): 38–39.

Mitchell, Richard. *Less Than Words Can Say*. Boston: Little, Brown, 1979.

Pie, Mario. *All About Language*. Philadelphia: J. B. Lippincott, 1954.

Personke, Carl and Yee, Albert H. *Comprehensive Spelling Instruction*. Scranton: Intext Educational Publishers, 1971.

Savage, F. J. "Play Ball with Spelling." *Instructor* 79 (April 1970): 135–136.

Shane, Harold G. et al. *Interpreting Language Arts Research for the Teacher*. Washington, D.C.: Association for Supervision and Curriculum Development, 1971.

Sherwin, J. Stephen. *Four Problems in Teaching English: A Critique of Research*. Scranton, Pa.: International Textbook Co., 1969.

Spelling Progress Laboratory. Tulsa, Okla.: Educational Progress Corporation, n.d.

Stageberg, Norman C. *An Introductory English Grammar*. New York: Holt, Rinehart and Winston, 1965.

Stein, Jess, ed. *The Random House Dictionary of the English Language*. New York: Random House, 1967.

Tenney, Y. J. "Visual Factors in Spellings." In *Cognitive Processes in Spelling*, edited by U. Firth. New York: Academic Press, 1980.

Webster, Noah. *An American Dictionary of the English Language*. New York: S. Converse, 1828.

Yatvin, J. "How to Get Good Spelling from Poor Spellers." *Learning Magazine* (August/September 1979): 122–123.

LEARNING ABOUT LANGUAGE THROUGH LITERATURE

A book holds an idea still, so you can think about it as long as you want. Television moves so fast you can't think about them.

Elizabeth, fifth grader

Our purpose in this chapter is to highlight literature available to both teachers and students that will aid them in studying various aspects of our language.

Children's literature is a study in and of itself. That study is best served by other books (see, for example, Glazer & Williams, 1979). To be consistent with the purpose of this text—language as an art for effective communication—we will concentrate on how literature enhances an appreciation and understanding of language beyond a professional's concern for proper usage.

First, we will examine the functions of children's literature. Second, various aspects of our language will be defined and discussed. And last, a sampling of literature illustrating these aspects will be discussed.

THE FUNCTIONS OF LITERATURE

Literature in the classroom has three distinct functions: (1) to provide a literary experience; (2) to impart information; and (3) to provide a vehicle for developing language-related skills of memory, sequence, description, expression, comprehension, interpretation, analysis, synthesis, and evaluation. Because a misunderstanding regarding these three functions is common among teachers, it is necessary to describe each function before proceeding to a discussion of presentation and content.

The Literary Experience

The literary experience has as its sole objective the enjoyment of a book (Stewig, 1973). It treats the book as something written from the heart of the author—words and ideas put together by one who selected what was considered the right combination to make the characters come alive and to excite readers to greater insights about themselves and their worlds, past, present, and future.

Children should be allowed to take from the literary experience no more or no less than what they choose to acquire. And they should be allowed the same privileges adults exercise in their recreational reading.

Adults browse and select a book. After starting the book they might tire of it and put it away for a while, or perhaps forever. Or when reading it, they may temporarily be led to daydream if the story is reminiscent of some personally related experience, characters, or situation. If some unusually dull section occurs, they might skip over some pages to get to the more exciting segments. In the end, adults take from books exactly what they chose to take.

Children must be afforded these same freedoms. Any teacher who insists that all children look to the front while listening to a story or who treats assigned book reports as guarantees that pupils read more than the jacket, robs students of a vital experience.

The literary experience is the very heart of literature. It provides what educators and librarians have called "that spark between the reader and the story" which in unique to every individual (Bates et al., 1979).

Time should be devoted each day in every classroom to providing literary experiences for boys and girls. Literature is the most valuable content material for impressing young children with feelings concerning the past, present, and future. This experience nurtures productive minds and builds a desire to see, hear, and understand the ideas of others. Only through systematic acquaintance with books can the teacher make effective contributions to children's impressions of literature. Extensive reading is the foundation of the teacher's preparation.

It is obvious why teachers must provide literary experiences for children in initial education programs—children lack the necessary reading skills. Somehow, in too many classroom situations, children gaining skill in the decoding process parallels a gradual phasing out of the teacher's oral reading. This is most unfortunate. What about children who have not mastered the reading skills? It is equally important for teachers in all grades to provide group literary experiences so that all students can enjoy the vicarious experiences written especially with their age group's interests in mind (Sloan, 1980). This listening enjoyment also serves as a motivation to acquire reading skills once children see what literature has in store for them.

Why should this literary experience occur daily? There is ample evidence that children who have been read to regularly since birth exhibit a greater initial interest in books and school and continue to exhibit a positive reading attitude in later years.[1]

The purpose of reading is to effect a positive, lifetime, independent reading behavior, not, as some educators seem to believe, the highest measured achievement of specific reading skills. Therefore, a child must constantly see skills in light of the broader objective. A regular literary experience is the most effective guarantee that this broader objective will be met.

The Information Experience

This classroom function of literature is self-explanatory—to present factual knowledge. Information books differ from fictional works because the intent of both the author writing the book and the teacher selecting the book is different than when writing or selecting a book simply for enjoyment. The author's purpose is to give an accurate and meaningful picture of a specific topic. Therefore, thoughts and vocabulary must be limited to the subject and audience for which the author has chosen to write. Teachers have a different objective in mind. They want to measure in some way the information obtained from the book. While the literary experience is the relationship between a child and a book, the information experience is a relationship between the teacher, the child, and a book. Teachers read or assign these books for specific purposes. Information experiences are needed whenever information has to be transmitted or is sought by individual children (Sutherland, 1978).

When the child seeks information for the sheer sake of seeking, the reading experience runs a fine line between being an information or, more probably, a literary experience.

The Language Experience

The language experience uses literature in developing specific language skills. A teacher might read an accumulative story like *All in the Morning Early* (Nic Leodhas, 1963), and then ask children to recreate the exact sequence. Or assess retention by asking children to recall different parts of the story. The story could serve as a basis for extended discussion of children's related personal experiences. Or children might create different story endings. Read *Clipper* (Carter, 1981) to the point at which someone knocks on the lonely lighthouse keeper's door. Who is there? Let children finish the tale. The main function of literature in such experiences is to use content merely as a vehicle for the development of language arts skills.

---

[1]Harlan S. Hansen. "The Impact of the Home Literary Environment on Reading Attitude." *Elementary English* 46 (January 1969): 17–24. This study related parents' early literature behavior—reading to children, encouraging reading, providing materials, and modeling reading—and its effect on fourth-grade reading attitude. The bibliography refers to several other studies.

Where is the confusion? The major problem is that teachers have not seen these aspects as three separate and distinct functions of literature and have not understood the purposes of each. A teacher may intend to provide a daily literature experience for children but frequently, because of the zeal for "instruction," such an experience becomes an information experience or a language experience. Even worse, the experience sometimes becomes an indigestible melange of all three.

Perhaps the greatest abuse is to use the literary experience to accomplish one or both of the others. For example, picture the teacher who selects a story and begins, "Once upon a time, there was a baby lion named George." (Teacher, putting book temporarily out of story-reading position: "How many of you have ever seen a baby lion?" Children responding: "I saw one at the zoo." "I saw a rabbit the other day." "We have a new dog," and so on.) "George lived in the jungle." (Teacher: "How many of you know what a jungle is?" Children: "I saw an old Tarzan movie." "I played on a jungle gym yesterday." "My mom says our garden looks like a jungle." and so forth.) After a half hour of that, who can remember the story? Why should an author spend time putting down the best combination of words and ideas only to have them dissected and distorted in this manner?

Unfortunately, teachers see their role as providing children with an experience in which the gain can be immediately measured. The *literary experience* is impressional. It is measured years later by assessing the reading attitude and involvement that resulted from regular exposure to the best literature available. The *information experience* is foundational, providing information which, when added to other information, builds a firm foundation for further information. And the *language experience* is given skilled treatment so that skills of listening, expressing, thinking, and sequencing become overlearned and therefore help facilitate the intake and analysis of many communication experiences (Davis, 1979). These three levels of treatment were introduced in Chapter 3.

LITERARY PRESENTATION

There are a variety of ways to present literature to children. When involving them in the three functions, the printed page has unfortunately assumed the highest priority.

Children can benefit from a multiexposure through various media. Films, filmstrips, records, tapes, radio, television, and storytelling are available methods. These media forms can extend and enrich the three literature functions in several ways.

First, they provide a common experience for all children regardless of their reading ability. They enable children to visually experience what they may be incapable of reading. This not only makes literature available to all children but builds self-confidence as it allows them a mode of common communication with their peers. An intermediate-grade boy who loved the outdoors but who lacked reading skills was able to experience the excitement of

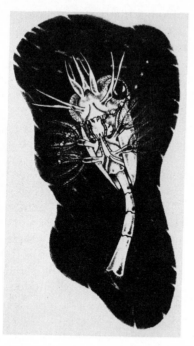

From Pagoo *by Holling Clancy Holling.*

Sperry's *Call It Courage* (1940) through the filmstrip version (Miller Brody Productions, 400 Hahn Road, Westminster, Md. 21157).

Second, exposure to literature through various media has stimulated children to go to the original source for more and continued enjoyment. Literature programs broadcast over the Wisconsin School of the Air state radio network stimulated extended reading experiences of the books used on the programs. In a sixth-grade class, taught by Harlan Hansen, the showing of the eleven-minute film, "Story of a Book,"[2] resulted in the book *Pagoo* (Holling, 1957) circulating continuously for the remainder of the school year.

Third, multimedia approaches provide for discussions of the appropriateness and value of different media. Ruth Hansen unfolded the same story of Pagoo through film, filmstrips, records, story reading, and storytelling to a kindergarten class. This laid the foundation for individual judgments of which medium best sparked individual children. It led to the discussion of disadvantages perceived in each method of presentation. The main accomplishment was an extension of literature as a study in itself—in addition to the story content as written or presented.

Finally, in our era of changing and advancing technology the use of different media expands the definition of "book" or "literature" beyond the mere printed page form. Some children have perceived themselves as failures be-

---

[2]This film and several others are annotated in the list of films following the chapter.

cause they couldn't adequately decode the alphabet system. These children need the positive feeling that they can "read" by decoding alternate visual and/or aural systems.

LANGUAGE AND LITERATURE ABOUT LANGUAGE

Language is the process by which humans communicate with each other. Lower animals communicate through signals, which relate basic areas of desire, pleasure, pain, and fear (Selsam, 1962). In humans, language adds a unique aspect to these other areas—the conveyance of an idea.

Because it is basic to all human relationships, people must understand their language at a conscious level, as well as merely use it on an intuitive level. The study and understanding of various aspects of language provide the foundation for better usage and clearer understanding.

A vast amount of literature is available for exploring, examining, and understanding our language. The initial involvement with this literature in a classroom study will fall into the *information experience* category. This organized exposure to content about language should spark a host of individual literary experiences as children seek and explore information beyond that which is expected.

When should a study of language be initiated in formal education programs? In preschool and kindergarten it is not too soon to provide some impressions about the nature of language and the various code systems. An impressional exposure at this age level not only provides early insights into a lifetime activity but puts into a broader perspective the decoding skills to come. Literature about language at this stage of study must be presented to children; they can, however, become involved in much of the content through appropriate activities.

As children learn to read they can begin more in-depth study of the history and nature of language and become much more involved in its various facets. Language is similar in characteristic to literature about language. The more often we become involved with it as we reach different ages and stages, the more new insights and adventures are opened to us.

How can children study language, and what literature is available to assist this study? Two suggested methods of study provide a look at language on two different inquiry levels. The first is the study of the means of expression of *language forms*. The second is the study of the *nature of language* in our past, present, and future.

LANGUAGE FORMS

Language forms include (1) oral communication, (2) written communication, (3) nonverbal communication, and (4) mechanical communication. A brief discussion of each form of language communication follows.

Oral Language

A focus on the *dialects* and *idiolects* of oral language unfolds related aspects of vocabulary and usage. *Dialect* refers to a regional variety of language distinguished by features of vocabulary, grammar, and pronunciation different from other regional languages and constituting together a single language (Cafone et al., 1980) *Idiolect* is the language or speech pattern peculiar to each individual.

No person can change their place of birth or the generation in which they live. The language acquired early will reflect the person's own personal phonemic style as well as the family or regional language style and will provide the basic lifetime speech pattern. The education one receives, the people one associates with, and the language uses one needs to master for particular occupations, will enable a speaker to change certain aspects of personal and cultural speech. Despite this, the opportunities to make drastic changes are not great.

Children exposed to various regional or racial dialects (Steptoe, 1980; Clifton, 1975) can understand and appreciate the roots from which specific dialect characteristics grew. In addition, such experiences sensitize children to the dialect variation they hear in their everyday environment. Literature on records provides excellent possibilities for dialect and idiolect study. Locating one story, perhaps a folktale, narrated by such famous storytellers as Carl Sandburg, Basil Rathbone, Danny Kaye, and Boris Karloff enables children to hear different dialect and idiolect patterns of the same words. Reading the Laura I. Wilder series of books on early pioneer life[3] or *Corrie and the Yankees* (Levy, 1969) about the Civil War days will add another dimension to this study. *Roosevelt Grady* (Shotwell, 1963), *Boss Cat* (Hunter, 1971), *Lonesome Boy* (Bontemps, 1955), *Uptown* and *Stevie* (both Steptoe, 1970, 1969) provide examples of black dialect from the migrant fields outside New Orleans to the streets of New York. *David He No Fear* and *Every Man Heart Lay Down* (both Graham, 1970, 1971) are told as heard from African people newly acquainted with English. *A Feast of Light* (Norris, 1967), *I Am Here. Yo Estoy Aqui* (Blue, 1971), *The Year of Small Shadow* (Lampman, 1971), and *A Little Oven* (Estes, 1955) deal with situations where children from other countries experience the problem of meeting a new culture, country, and language. *Always Room for One More* (Nic Leodhas, 1965) and *The Merry Adventures of Robin Hood* (Pyle, 1962) show speech patterns from other countries and from the past. Finally, *The Surprise Party* (Hutchins, 1969) illustrates that classic example of how a secret changes in meaning as whispered from one animal to another. Idiolect and dialect study are further

---

[3]See, for example, Laura I. Wilder, *Long Winter* (New York: Harper & Row, 1971); *Little House in the Big Woods* (New York: Hale, 1932); or *By the Shores of the Silver Lake* (New York: Harper & Row, 1953). Once children discover the delights of the author's writing, they want to read all the books in the series.

From Sparkle and Spin *by Ann and Paul Rand.*

enhanced by finding within stories several words used to mean the same thing—baby buggy, baby carriage, perambulator, pram, and others. Within regional dialects, social dialects can be frequently detected. These result from wealth, education, travel experiences, and/or the banding together of nationalistic groups.

The study of dialects and idiolects extends the usual skill program of vocabulary, grammar, and pronunciation through an in-depth exposure to its various regional and personal diversity. It also puts the term "correct speech" into proper perspective as acceptance of and tolerance for many speech patterns reinforces each child's unique pattern.

Written Language

Written language uses an intermediate written symbol in transmitting a thought to someone else. The various types of written language include: (1) graphic, (2) idea codes, (3) word-picture codes, (4) the alphabet, and (5) special code systems.

Graphic writing uses pictures as the basis for communication. Cave writing has revealed much information regarding early cave dwellers and their lives. The writing of the American Indians employed signs and picture clues which provided a meaning (Mallery, 1972). These graphic code systems function to give information as well as to provide aesthetic representation found in expressive art. Obviously, these graphic forms need to be realistic representations if they are to effectively communicate. Herein lies their limitation. Writers of the graphic form may feel they are communicating specific information through this form of written language. In actuality, the "writer" is providing possibilities for varied interpretation on the part of the "reader." This limitation is an important one for children to examine.

How Medicine Man Cured Paleface Woman (McGraw, 1956) and *The Sioux Indian* (Bleeker, 1962) are representatives of books which portray graphic forms of communication. *God's Man* (Ward, 1957) is an example of children's stories told in pictures only.

Idea writing employs symbols representing an idea. The curve sign on the road tells us not only that a bend is ahead but which direction the road is turning.[4] The symbols in our number system are idea markings that reflect a quantity which has a common meaning. This idea code system is sometimes called "memory aid writing" because it helps us keep track of items and time with a minimum of symbols. This form of writing condenses the idea into a single symbol for fast and accurate interpretation. Comic books offer examples of this form ("light bulb" signifying an idea) as do highway manuals. *Signs and Symbols Around the World* (see Bibliography, Chapter 12) provides a good foundation for both idea writing and word writing.

Word-picture writing involves children in the study of those pictures which represent a specific word. Brand name symbols are examples of this form of writing. Many grocery stores, fast food chains, department stores, and other community businesses have identifying symbols which are interchangeable with their name. Children "read" them daily in advertisements, billboards, or on store signs. This symbol-word name study capitalizes on the children's previous experiences with their environment. Newspapers and magazines provide numerous examples of word writing.

The study of the *alphabet system* takes children through an understanding of the evolution of letter code systems (Taylor, 1970). An alphabet expresses the single sounds of a language and therefore can encompass many languages in addition to our own. *What's Behind the Word* (Longman, 1968), *The Romance of Writing* (Irwin, 1956), and *A Study of Writing* (Gelb, 1963) look specifically at the alphabet code while discussing it in light of other language forms. A host of trade alphabet books, which feature content and styles ranging from Brian Wildsmith to Marcel Marceau, are readily available for children's perusal and enjoyment. An annotated list of such books is included in Chapter 10. Many young people's books are now available in foreign languages so children can compare various alphabet symbols (Hautzig, 1968, 1969).

Special code systems include such forms as shorthand and music. Music books are available in most classrooms. A shorthand book as well as a secretary serving as a resource person, will highlight the study of this special code system.

---

[4]Idea writing, also called pictograms, is explained along with ideograms and phonograms in a film suitable for fifth or sixth grade. See "The Alphabet — Mark of Man," 20m, color, available from McGraw-Hill Films.

From The Story of Ferdinand *by Munro Leaf.*

Nonverbal Language

Humans have developed a system of nonverbal communication that operates parallel to or in place of speaking or writing (Landsman, 1971). These nonverbal means are grouped into three categories: (1) haptics, (2) kinesics, and (3) paralanguage.

Haptics is the study of communication by touching. Embracing, kissing, patting on the head, shaking hands, nudging, and caressing all convey a message. These messages vary from culture to culture and are sometimes of opposing nature (Hall, 1979). To pat an American child on the top of the head is a sign of endearment. However, the top of a Thai's head is where the soul is connected with heaven and a pat there would be a grave offense. Illustrations in books and advertisements showing examples of haptics are good study possibilities. Young children as well as older ones can decode and discuss this nonverbal language form.

Kinesics is the study of body posture and movement (Birdwhistell, 1970). All movable parts of the body are involved and the message communicated may be unintentional or directed by gesture or movement. Nodding the head, winking, raising the finger to the mouth for silence all transmit an idea to the receiver. In addition, a stance might be termed masculine or feminine. It might denote happiness or unhappiness. It could show elation or anger.

Some of these movements are either spontaneous or learned, movements unique to each individual's expression pattern. However, some body movements are used for directional or interpretive purposes. The policeman, the referee, the music conductor, the deaf person, the hula dancer, and the ballet dancer all have special gestures with a common basis for communication. These are consciously learned rather than acquired intuitively and are a part of a child's out-of-school environment. The study of both forms of kinesics—the spontaneous and the learned—is vital, as body movement is an integral part of every person's language pattern, whether spontaneous or realized (McGough, 1974).

Talking without Words (Ets, 1968), *Marcel Marceau's ABC* (Mendoza, 1970), *Talking Hands* (Amon, 1968) are several of a growing number of books dealing with gestures. Referees' handbooks, music conductors' books, police handbooks, deaf sign language books (Children's Television Workshop, 1980), and books about Native American signing (Tomkins, 1969) all highlight the many facets of kinesics. Encyclopedias also include materials on gestures as communication.

Paralanguage is a signal system produced by the nonarticulated voice track. It is identified not by the oral language utilized but by its intensity, pitch, and tempo. Coughing, crying, and giggling are other examples of oral sounds which communicate an idea. Children might look for words in their stories that give clues to the paralanguage used, such as "she hollered" or "they giggled as they talked." The study possibilities of paralanguage are interesting and exciting because of these subtleties, and because many people have not seen them as separate communicators.

Mechanical Writing

This language form has recently emerged. Films, filmstrips, records, tapes, radio, and videotape all add a new dimension to language in addition to the content presented. Moods, feelings, and extended visual stimulation add new impact to the message. A film grammar is emerging which provides children ways to analyze and interpret the mechanical language form.

The use of puppets, animation, shadow figures, live animals and humans, and the iconograph means of panning the camera over book illustrations affect the film grammar. Students can compare one story in these many forms and arrive at personal value judgments. Typewriters, adding machines, braille writers, and computers are other mechanical means of communicating as well as flashing lights and teletype transmitters.

While all the above mentioned mechanical forms utilize either oral language, written language, or nonverbal language, children can profitably study the advantages and disadvantages of using a mechanical writer as well as the extent to which the message is changed in mechanical transmission.

These four language forms provide an abundance of study possibilities for many ages and many interests as our daily life is filled with examples of each. The study of language creates that necessary one-to-one correspondence between what is going on inside the classroom with what is going on outside of the classroom (see "Keystone of Language," Chapter 3). This study will not only enable children to appreciate the richness of our language heritage but to better communicate and understand others.

THE NATURE OF LANGUAGE

The study of language has another aspect—the nature and role of language in past, present, and future. This approach cuts across language forms and sees the variability of language forms within each component.

A study of the nature of language could include the following concepts: (1) history, (2) acquisition, (3) organization, (4) change, (5) roles, (6) norms, (7) acculturation, and (8) relativity. While these concepts overlap with the earlier discussion of language forms, they approach the study from another point of reference. The nature of language will be examined here to provide some ideas on which to build a more in-depth study.

History examines the origin of various language forms (Baldwin, 1970). Children can role-play the problems early people faced in their need to communicate with others. Gestures, grunts, formation of words, and pitch of voice all come into play. The importance of this historical view of language provides insights into why people needed language, the first forms available to them and how this basic system showed the need for more sophisticated means of conveying needs, desires, information, feelings, and questions (Duffy, 1970).

Acquisition deals with the manner in which young children acquire language. While many areas of this study are too complex for any but highly trained researchers, some aspects fall within elementary school-age children's understanding. Children with younger brothers and sisters can report on how they communicate and how they learned to do so. Family speech patterns, how frequently parents talk with their children, if they verbally label household items, how many new words are being learned from television, as well as exposure to brand words in the everyday environment are possible investigation areas. The start of idiolects (language or speech patterns peculiar to each individual) and how these relate to dialects can be examined. The way children acquire language in other countries or cultures may be of value in this study, especially in relationship to the availability and emphasis of public schooling. There are some excellent resources available on child growth and development to assist in this study (Kirkton, 1971).

Organization stresses the idea that language can be defined using word labels for its various parts. Paragraphs, sentences, phrases, nouns, pronouns, adjectives, and adverbs are some of the labels in use. Studying the advantages and disadvantages of this organization, including social implications, allows children to appreciate the study of organization in contrast to the usual sentence dissection method. A study of organization can motivate children to learn the specific labels, while ap reciating how these labels fit into a larger conceptual framework.

Change is inherent in language. One generation cannot always see this change taking place, especially during adolescence. Yet, our present language provides an excellent vehicle for contrasting common words children use today with those of the past. The idea that usage is an important agent of change along with people's seemingly natural desire to coin new words will facilitate understanding of this concept. The role government, technology, and the media have played in areas of usage and change is essential to examine. Resource people can greatly add to this study as can literature that utilizes language common to various times in history. Such books as *Words from the Myths* (Asimov, 1961), *People Words* (Severn, 1966), and *Culture, Class, and Language Variety* (Davis, 1972) all show how usage has changed over the years.

The concept of *roles* examines the language that accompanies various social and occupational roles. Carpenters, plumbers, policemen, engineers, teachers, athletes, and others all use language appropriate to their occupations. This language then becomes a part of the common language. For example, in a city which has a professional football team, for several months of the year such words and phrases as "split T," "tight end," "wishbone I," "free safety," and "audibles" become the language of people on the street and in the stands. Children interested in the sport will study the meanings of these words with far greater zeal than they will the word study pages prepared for them in school.

Norms deal with language which has come to be acceptable to groups of people. The child's, teenager's, and adult's needs to adapt language to the usage pattern of their peer groups is one example of developing language norms for specific groups (Kennedy, 1972). The positive or negative value placed on speech patterns at different social levels is another. It is important for children to learn how these normative patterns develop and solidify into language patterns. If this motivates children to develop extended language patterns beyond the confines of what is expected, so much the better. Literature, with its tremendous variety of vocabulary and usage, can provide a powerful tool for a child's personal language expansion.

Acculturation focuses on how our language is a part of a larger usage pattern of many people. This study also examines the way language has changed as various cultures have merged or come into proximity with each other. Such change has added new words, new sayings, new acceptance, and new usage. Books dealing with children's experiences in meeting new language situations should be utilized.

Finally, the *relativity* of language demonstrates that language means different things to different people. The person initiating the communication and the person receiving it must have the same thing in mind if the communication is to succeed. This relativity includes concepts about the nature of language. Where you were born, how and how early you acquired language, the roles and norms available and expected in certain situations, as well as the regional cultural variations all play a crucial role in a person's language pattern. Language becomes a relative factor when talking with others whose patterns were developed from a different base. If children can appreciate and understand this relativity early, they might attempt to develop their language forms to more accurately communicate what they really mean. At the same time they can remain tolerant of those who still are vague in communicating and receiving other's messages.

Indeed, language has many facets. Too often we bypass a study of these facets at the elementary school level in favor of working on decoding, encoding, and language usage skills. Whether you use the *language forms* approach or the *nature of language* approach, each intertwines around and through the other. Since we are involved with language throughout our lives, understanding the nature of our language and the various language forms will provide children with a broader foundation from which to begin extended individual language development.

Suggestions for Further Exploration

1. Take a neighborhood walk to look for graphic, idea, and word-picture writing on street signs, store name symbols, numbers, billboards, and other places.
2. Collect pictures of, or write words or phrases in as many different code systems as you can. For example, four, 4, ////, a hand with four fingers exposed; or a picture of a road with a curve, the word curve, road sign with the symbol for a curve.
3. Talk with several senior citizens in the community. Listen for and ask about word usage or speech patterns which reflect language of the past, regional dialects, and foreign language accents.
4. Select a folktale which emerged in a similar form in several countries. For example, the Gingerbread Boy is American, the Pancake is the same character in Norway, the Bannock delights children in Scotland, while the Bun is the Russian version of the story. Record the story on tape so the children can listen to the variations and compare and contrast them.
5. Tape record persons with different dialects reading or telling the same story. This provides opportunities for dialect comparison with a common word base.
6. Locate resource people who use gestures (kinesics) in their occupations: referee, music conductor, airline ground crewman, dancer, and others. Have them come to your classroom to demonstrate these gestures.
7. Begin a picture file of people using haptics and kinesics to use in discussion with children about nonverbal aspects of language. Newspaper and magazine ads and pictures are good starting sources.
8. Select some common items known to have many different words applied to them in everyday usage—baby buggy, car, stream of water, evening meal, swim suit, and others. Show the pictures of these items to at least five different people. Record the words used by each person to label the items. Are they mostly dialect or idiolect patterns?

Bibliography of Books for Children

Aiken, Joan. *The Wolves of Willoughby Chase*. New York: Doubleday, 1962.

A suspenseful Victorian melodrama about the misadventures of two young girls in the English countryside brings out the tongue-in-cheek language patterns that are a part of this literature form.

Adoff, Arnold. *MA, DA, LA*. New York: Harper & Row, 1971.

The author has composed a song in praise of humankind—the cycle of the family and of life. Resonant soundings form the basic chant, allowing readers to add words and soundings of their own.

Amon, Aline. *Talking Hands—Indian Sign Language*. New York: Doubleday, 1968.

How to speak in authentic Indian sign language. In addition, sample sentences describe the life of a typical plains boy and show how to use signs today.

Asimov, Isaac. *Words from the Myths*. Boston: Houghton Mifflin, 1961.

In addition to his *Words of Science* (Houghton Mifflin, 1959), Asimov here explores Greek myths to discover the roots of hundreds of words now in our daily language. An index includes many theological terms and modern words that come from them.

Bleeker, Sonia. *The Sioux Indians*. New York: William Morrow, 1962.

This life of the Sioux includes a description of a winter count, a historic record painted on a buffalo robe highlighting a memorable event of each year. The events are equivalent to ideographs and Indians "read" these winter counts.

Blue, Rose. *I Am Here. Yo Estoy Aqui*. New York: Franklin Watts, 1971.

The story of a five-year-old Puerto Rican girl whose family moves to the States. When she arrives at school for the first time she feels alone and strange because she does not understand the language and the things she sees are unfamiliar.

Bontemps, Arna. *Lonesome Boy*. Boston: Houghton Mifflin, 1955.

A story of a young black boy—lonesome without his trumpet—and the lesson he learns about lonesomeness. It has some flavor of the New Orleans regional dialect, especially in the speech of the boy's grandfather.

Brasch, R. *How Did It Begin?* New York: David McKay, 1965.

This fascinating book explores many customs and superstitions, mores and habits that influence us today. In so doing it looks at the reason behind many words and sayings.

Brooke, L. Leslie. *Johnny Crow's New Garden*. New York: Frederick Warne, 1964.

All the animals who come to Johnny Crow's new garden are part of the amusing rhyming words that tell their story.

Brown, Marcia. *Peter Piper's Alphabet*. New York: Scribner's 1959.

An alphabet book with a nonsense tongue twister for each letter. Excellent watercolor wash and line illustrations by the author.

Burnett, Frances Hodgson. *Little Lord Fauntleroy*. New York: E. P. Dutton, 1962.

This classic story written in the 1880s utilizes the language appropriate to England and America at that time.

Burnett, Frances Hodgson. *Rachelty-Pachelty House*. New York: Dodd, Mead, 1961.

A short book about dolls and fairies' "real lives" when people turn their backs; uses vocabulary peculiar to a time when language had a more formal flavor and different slang.

Caldecott, R. R. *Caldecott's Picture Book No. 1*. New York: Frederick Warne, 1879–1885.

Spelling unique to old England is sprinkled throughout this well-known storybook.

Carroll, Lewis. *Alice in Wonderland*. New York: Random House, 1969.

The classic story is available in a wide variety of languages and code systems, providing unlimited examples of language usage in forms for study.

Canfield, Dorothy. *Understood Betsy*. New York: Holt, Rinehart and Winston, 1916.

This well-loved story deals with Betsy's life on the Putney farm with its use of country slang common to Vermont at the turn of the century.

Charles, Robert H. *A Roundabout Turn*. New York: Frederick Warne, 1930.

An amusing tale of an adventurous toad who wants to see if the world is really round has such words as heather, gorse, braken, and feathery fronds for which children can seek out the meanings.

Cleaver, Vera and Cleaver, Bill. *Ellen Grae*. New York: J. B. Lippincott, 1967.

A story, both serious and funny, about Ellen's adventure in a Missouri town. Told in dialect.

Coggins, Jack. *Flashes and Flags, the Story of Signaling*. New York: Dodd, Mead, 1963.

An account of signals and signaling devices in everyday use—by ships, planes, trains, in sports, traffic and weather warnings—along with a glance at those of by-gone days. Helpful in looking at basic code systems.

Cox, Plamer. *The Brownies: Their Book*. New York: Dover Publishing, 1964. (First published, 1887)

This entire book in verse presents opportunities for studying the use of language in a forced verse situation as well as an opportunity for viewing language representing the late 1800s.

Davar, Ashok. *Talking Words*. New York: Bobbs Merrill, 1969.

Shows how words can be converted into many different code systems; for example, by putting eyes in the two o's in the word look. It can be used at different levels of study with all age groups.

DeAngeli, Marguerite. *Yonie Wondernose*. New York: Doubleday, 1944.

A charming, colorful picture book reflecting Amish family traditions and speech patterns.

Estes, Eleanor. *A Little Oven*. New York: Harcourt Brace Jovanovich, 1955.

Helena and Genevieve get a little oven mixed up with a little loving. This story for younger children brings out the misunderstandings in language.

Ets, Marie Hall. *Talking without Words*. New York: Viking, 1968.

Demonstrates the use of gesture in everyday life. An excellent book for the study of this too-often ignored aspect of communication.

Goodall, J. *The Adventures of Paddy Pork*. New York: Harcourt Brace Jovanovich, 1968.

A humorous story told in pictures only; children can "read" this graphic code. Paddy is lost in the woods and nearly becomes dinner for a wolf.

Graham, Lorenz. *David He No Fear*. New York: Thomas Y. Crowell, 1946, 1971.

The fearless story of David and Goliath is written as the author heard it told in Africa, using the storyteller's language. Striking woodcuts by Ann Grifalconi enhance the imaginative language.

Graham, Lorenz. *Every Man Heart Lay Down*. New York: Thomas Y. Crowell, 1946.

The story of the birth of Jesus in words and speech patterns of African people newly acquainted with English.

Graham, Lorenz. *I, Momolu*. New York: Thomas Y. Crowell, 1966.

An African boy's trip with his father from a remote Liberian village to the coast city of Cape Rogers for not only his first look at "civilization" but his first experiences with people who did not speak or understand his language.

Harris, Joel Chandler. *Uncle Remus*. New York: Schocken Books, 1965.

Humor, fun, wisdom, and humanity are combined in these superbly told stories of the nineteenth-century rural South.

Hunter, Kristin. *Boss Cat*. New York: Scribner's, 1971.

A new pet cat causes much commotion as it becomes a member of the Tanner family. The book sheds light on the dialect patterns in the characters' language.

Hutchins, Pat. *The Surprise Party*. New York: Macmillan, 1969.

"I'm having a party tomorrow," whispered Rabbit to the Owl. "It's a surprise." By the time the owl passes the message to other animals who in turn pass it along, the story changes because the message is misunderstood.

Irwin, Keith. *The Romance of Writing*. New York: Viking, 1956.

From Egyptian hieroglyphics to modern letters, numbers, and signs, Irwin examines every form of writing humans have known. From cave writing to the alphabet to numbers to musical notes, this book with over one hundred illustrations presents a deep insight into the topic.

Kerr, Judith. *When Hitler Stole Pink Rabbit*. New York: Coward, McCann & Geoghegan, 1972.

A Jewish family, separated in Germany during World War II, is finally reunited in Switzerland. They embark on an adventure that lasts years and takes them to several countries where they learn new languages, see things, and learn how to cope with wild confusions.

Kredenser, Gail. *The ABC's Bumptious Beasts*. New York: Harlin Quist, 1966.

From Aardvark to Egret to Iguana to Quail to Zenopus, this collection of journeyed creatures takes children through the alphabet. Charming illustrations by Stanley Mach.

Laker, Russell. *Anatomy of Lettering*. New York: Viking, 1966.

A lettering manual that offers children an opportunity to see letters in all styles as well as to examine the basic shapes which form the Roman alphabet.

Lampman, Evelyn. *The Year of Small Shadow*. New York: Harcourt Brace Jovanovich, 1971.

The story of a young Indian boy's stay with a white family and the problems he had with the new language and way of life.

Lenski, Lois. *Bayou Suzette*. New York: J. B. Lippincott, 1943.

A charming story told in dialect about a little French girl who lives on the bayou path in a Louisiana village and an Indian girl whom she befriends and takes to her home to live.

Lenski, Lois. *Indian Captive*. New York: J. B. Lippincott, 1941.

The story of Mary Jemison, a Caucasian girl who lived in Indian captivity for many years, gives a remarkable picture of Seneca tribal life from the inside.

Levy, Mimi. *Corrie and the Yankees*. New York: Viking, 1959.

The language of the South during the Civil War tells this story of Corrie who shelters and aids a wounded Yankee soldier.

Longman, Harold. *Would You Put Your Money in a Sand Bank? (Fun with Words)*. New York: Rand McNally, 1968.

The author examines homonyms through riddles, silly questions, nonsense conversation, and other means to involve children in words that sound alike but are spelled differently.

Longman, Harold. *What's Behind the Word?* New York: Coward, McCann & Geoghegan, 1968.

The author does much to clear up the mystery of where our words come from. He tells the story of thirty-nine words in a witty and humorous fashion and deals with how new words replace old ones.

McGough, Elizabeth. *Your Silent Language.* New York: William Morrow, 1974.

A needed book about a topic not often treated in children's information books, this covers many critical subtopics in language intermediate-grade readers will understand, despite its occasional lapses into didacticism. The author acknowledges that many nonverbal signals of the eyes, face, hands, and arms, are open to more than one interpretation. The study of *kinesics,* founded by Ray Birdwhistell, whose pioneering work is described briefly, is as yet an inexact science. McGough simplifies the adult writing of such experts as Birdwhistell, interspersing anecdotes based on her own experience. The chapters on haptics and proxemics (though not so labeled) are particularly interesting. The concluding section on cultural differences entices readers to want to know more. A list of "Selected References," all adult, is appended.

McGraw, Jessie. *How Medicine Man Cured Paleface Woman.* New York: William Scott, 1956.

This story in Indian pictographs tells how one winter a lost, sick, paleface woman was discovered by Indians, brought to their camp, and cured. This book's unique value is that it is written entirely in real Native American pictographs—the oldest known form of writing.

McGrath, Thomas. *The Beautiful Things.* New York: Vanguard, 1960.

Danny's sister Laura gave him the word "beautiful" for his birthday. To celebrate, they went out to see all the things they could find that fit the word.

Mayer, Mercer. *Frog, Where Are You?* New York: Dial, 1969.

This delightful tale is one of several books by Mayer in which the stories are told only in pictures. A boy and his dog wake one morning to find their favorite friend is gone.

Nic Leodhas, Sorche. *Always Room for One More.* New York: Holt, Rinehart and Winston, 1965.

An hilarious tale of kindness told in a Scot dialect. Lachie MacLachlan invites every weary traveler who passes by to be a guest of himself and his family of twelve in their already bulging house.

Norris, Gunilla. *A Feast of Light.* New York: Alfred A. Knopf, 1967.

This story of a nine-year-old Swedish girl's arrival in the United States has excellent examples of language in transition as she learns to speak English.

Nurnberg, Maxwell. *Fun with Words.* Englewood Cliffs, N.J.: Prentice-Hall, 1970; *Wonders in Words.* Prentice-Hall, 1968; *All About Words.* New York: New American Library, 1968.

Three books that deal in a lighthearted manner with words, their origin and meaning, and word tricks and games. Covering grammar, spelling, punctuation, and vocabulary, the books are as educational as they are entertaining.

Pizer, Vernon. *You Don't Say. How People Communicate without Speech*. New York: Putnam, 1978.

In a book for intermediate grade readers, the author describes such commonly known communication systems as finger spelling for the deaf, and other less known systems as the Adams-Ray medical diagrams. Pidgin languages, such artificial languages as Esperanto, drum communication, and the whistle language of railroaders are all described. Travel-related glyphs show the need for an internationally recognized symbol system, and a closing chapter deals with tactile and olfactory communication. An index makes finding out about a particular system possible. No pictures, but a very readable book, nonetheless.

Poe, Edgar Allan. *The Fall of the House of Usher and Some Other Tales*. New York: Franklin Watts, 1967.

Poe uses highly descriptive language to tell these stories. His lengthy sentences contain many complex word patterns and reflect the more formal language of the time.

Potter, Charles. *Tongue Tanglers. More Tongue Tanglers and a Rigmarole*. New York: World Publishing, 1964.

America's foremost authority on tongue tanglers has put together these two collections of this verse form. Included are notes about sources and variants. The tongue tanglers can provide common reference points for dialect and idiolect analysis.

Preston, Edna. *Pop Corn and Ma Goodness*. New York: Viking, 1969.

An alliterative nonsense saga about love and marriage, birth and death, summer and winter, and tears and laughter. Told in tongue-tripping words that demand to be read aloud.

Prokofiev, Sergei. *Peter and the Wolf*. New York: Alfred A. Knopf, 1940.

The print used in this edition of the children's classic is calligraphy hand-lettered by Hollis Holland.

Pyle, Howard. *Book of Pirates*. New York: Harper & Row, 1949.

The colorful language of the sea pirate fills this book of fiction, fact, and fancy concerning the buccaneers and marooners of the Spanish main.

Pyle, Howard. *The Merry Adventures of Robin Hood*. New York: Golden Press, 1962.

A children's classic is written in the language of the time.

Pyle, Howard. *The Story of King Arthur and His Knights*. New York: Scribner's, 1903.

King Arthur and his Knights use the best of language such as "thou shalt have the boon although my heart much misgiveth me that thou wilt suffer. . . ."

Rand, Paul and Rand, Ann. *Sparkle and Spin.* New York: Harcourt Brace Jovanovich, 1957.

The authors write about words in many ways, stimulating children to generate new discoveries on their own. They deal with the functions of words in everyday language as well as with how words show feelings.

Rawlings, Marjorie. *The Yearling.* New York: Scribner's, 1939.

A well-known story of a life that is far removed from modern patterns of living. It is heightened by the language of the simple, courageous people and their wild, hard, satisfying life in inland Florida.

Rees, Ennis. *The Little Greek Alphabet Book.* Englewood Cliffs, N.J.: Prentice-Hall, 1968.

An examination of the Greek alphabet and how it relates to our own. The forced rhyme often detracts from its value, yet the book offers a different dimension to alphabet study.

Rey, H. A. *Curious George Learns the Alphabet.* Boston: Houghton Mifflin, 1963.

Curious George learns the alphabet in a very unusual fashion. A good introduction to the alphabet for younger children.

Rinkoff, Barbara. *Red Light Says Stop!* New York: Lothrop, Lee and Shepard, 1974.

A light, breezy style of writing is well-matched with upbeat line drawings illustrating a variety of ways people send messages with their bodies and in writing other than alphabets. A section on everyday gestures introduces the topic, followed by a page on codes, map symbols, and a longer section on sound (i.e., foghorns) and light as communication. Means of communication among the handicapped precedes sections on other cultures (five in all) and the book closes with a series of questions to encourage child readers to experiment with the types of communication mentioned.

Scott, Joseph and Scott, Leonore. *Egyptian Hieroglyphics for Everyone.* New York: Funk and Wagnalls, 1968.

Introducing the fascinating realm of Egyptian hieroglyphics. Readers learn how to "read" hieroglyphics for use in present-day museums.

Severn, Bill. *People Words.* New York: Ives Washburn, 1966.

Here is a collection of eponyms—the persons from whom a family, race, city, or nation is supposed to have taken its name. Included are such general subjects as food and drink, clothes and fashions, science and inventions, familiar things, relations with others, mind and body.

Shotwell, Louisa. *Roosevelt Grady.* New York: World Publishing, 1963.

Roosevelt Grady was the son of migrant workers who traveled with the crop harvest. Excellent dialect as well as a classic story.

Steptoe, John. *Stevie*. New York: Harper & Row, 1969.

A story told in black speech patterns about Robert, an only child, who looks with no anticipation at having Stevie, whose parents work, as a weekday boarder in his home.

Steptoe, John. *Train Ride*. New York: Harper & Row, 1971.

An exciting story told in black speech patterns about Charles, who takes his friends on a trip to Times Square. They have a difficult time getting back home without train fare.

Steptoe, John. *Uptown*. New York: Harper & Row, 1970.

Two Harlem boys walk through Manhattan, where they see junkies, cops, karate experts, and hippies and wonder what it might be like to be any of these men. Told in black speech patterns.

Tuer, Andrew, ed. *Stories from Old-Fashioned Children's Books*. Detroit: Singing Tree Press, 1968 (first published, 1899).

A collection of stories containing many examples of various language patterns both in the narration and the dialogue.

Twain, Mark. *Adventures of Huckleberry Finn*. New York: E. P. Dutton, 1962.

In this classic story, three dialects are used: Missouri Negro, backwoods Southwestern, and Pike County.

Ungerer, Tomi. *One, Two, Where's My Shoe?* New York: Harper & Row, 1964.

Shoes are hidden in the most unlikely places in this story told only in pictures.

VanGelder, Rosalind. *Monkeys Have Tails*. New York: David McKay, 1966.

This book of homonyms is different from others in that many of the words both sound alike and are spelled alike. Told in question form with illustrated glossary.

Ward, Lynd. *God's Man, A Novel in Woodcuts*. Cleveland: World Publishing, 1957.

An ageless tragedy in the society of the 1920s and 1930s is told without words in one-hundred-and-twenty woodcuts. An outstanding example of picture writing.

West, Fred. *Breaking the Language Barrier*. New York: Coward McCann, 1961.

This book deals with language—from caveman grunts to electronic translators. The author shows how inability to speak other languages has handicapped the United States in world competition and dramatizes the way in which ability to speak languages shapes history.

Westcott, Al. *Word Bending with Aunt Sarah*. Fayetteville, GA: Oddo Publishing, 1964.

Aunt Sarah stimulates us to describe all the possible things certain words make us think of. Teachers can continue this "word bending" with children expanding the process.

Films

"Alphabet, The." (Series: Language and Linguistics) 28 minutes.

This film analyzes the English writing system and traces the origin, development, and spread of the alphabet, explaining various writing systems including Sanskrit, Chinese, and Arabic. The film discusses the significance of hieroglyphics in the development of written language. Other films in this valuable series include "Dialects," "History of the English Language," "Language and Linguistics," and "Sounds of Language." (Indiana University, Audio-Visual Center, Bloomington, Ind. 47401)

"English Language—How It Changes." 11 minutes.

This film shows changes in words; in spelling; in pronunciation and meaning; and in rules of grammar which are presented with examples. Recent examples show how change keeps our language alive, flexible, and a useful communication tool. (Coronet Instructional Films, 65 E. South Water St., Chicago, Ill. 60601)

"Language and Communication." Color. 16 minutes.

The purposes of this film are: to give an understanding of our heritage of spoken and written language and the role of this heritage in the communication of ideas; to encourage the student to develop skills in language communication; and to instill in students an appreciation of the contributions of past generations. The three historical stages of written language—pictographic, demographic, and phonetic—are described. (Moody Institute of Science, Educational Films Division, 12000 E. Washington Blvd., Whittier, Ca., 90606)

"Language of the Film." (Series: Film Appreciation) Color. 28 minutes.

We learn the importance of camera tricks and techniques in visually conveying a director's idea to an audience. Some of the tricks discussed are the dissolve, the fade, camera angle, the type of lens, screen-shape, and use of line, distance, and lighting. (Indiana University)

"Nature of Language and How It Is Learned." (Series: Modern Language Association) 30 minutes.

This film, the first in a series of five, explains the nature of language, how it is learned, and establishes the validity of the "oral approach" to teaching. The living language is shown to be speech. Examples of speech are drawn from the base reservoir of languages of the world. These examples reveal how differently languages function in their sound systems, grammatical organizations, and lexical developments. Speech is compared with writing. The series includes films on "Modern Techniques of Language Teaching," "The Organization of Language," "The Sounds of Language," and "Words and Their Meanings." (Indiana University)

"Story of a Book." Color, 11 minutes.

By opening a doorway on the intriguing behind-the-scenes creation of a book and showing the enthusiasm of its author, the film helps children to a new enjoyment and appreciation of books. This film reenacts the writing of a book. It follows a real-life author, H. C. Holling, through the exciting and satisfying process of creating *Pagoo*, the story of a hermit crab. (Pied Piper Productions, Box 320, Verdugo City, Calif., 91046.)

Bibliography

Baldwin, Gordon C. *Talking Drums to Written Word*. New York: W. W. Norton, 1970.

Bates, Sue Ann et al. *Kindergarten Curriculum Issues. Reading*. Madison: Wisconsin Department of Public Instruction, 1979.

Birdwhistell, Ray L. *Kinesics and Context*. Philadelphia: University of Pennsylvania Press, 1970.

Cafone, Harold et al. *Language Skills and Use*. Glenview, Ill.: Scott, Foresman, 1980, Book 5.

Carter, Debby. *Clipper*. New York: Harper & Row, 1981.

Children's Television Workshop. *Sesame Street Sign Language Fun*. New York: Random House, 1980.

Clifton, Lucille. *My Brother Fine with Me*. New York: Holt, Rinehart and Winston, 1975.

Davis, A. L., editor. *Culture, Class, and Language Variety*. Urbana, Ill.: National Council of Teachers of English, 1972.

Davis, James E. et al. "Responding to the Basics Movement." *Focus: Teaching English Language Arts*, 5(3) (Spring 1979): entire issue.

Duffy, G. G. "Teaching the History of Our Language." *Instructor* 80 (November 1970): 87–88.

Gelb, Ignace. *A Study of Writing*. Chicago: University of Chicago Press, 1963.

Glazer, Joan I. and Williams, Gurney. *Introduction to Children's Literature*. New York: McGraw-Hill Book Company, 1979.

Hall, Edward T. "Learning the Arabs' Silent Language." *Psychology Today* (August 1979): 45–54.

Hautzig, Esther. *At Home* (1968) and *In School* (1969). Both, New York: Macmillan.

Holling, H. C. *Pagoo*. Boston: Houghton Mifflin, 1957.

Kennedy, L. D. "Teaching Dictionary Skills in the Upper Grades; Preparing a Dictionary of Slang." *Elementary English* 49 (January 1972): 71–73.

Kirton, C. M. "Language Acquisition and Development: Some Implications for the Classroom." *Elementary English* 48 (March 1971): 406–412.

Landsman, L. A. "Man Behind the Mask." *Instructor* 80(79) (February 1971): 79.

Mallery, Garrick. *Picture-Writing of the American Indians*. New York: Dover, 1972.

Mendoza, George. *The Marcel Marceau Alphabet Book*. New York: Doubleday, 1970.

Nic Leodhas, Sorche. *All in the Morning Early*. New York: Holt, Rinehart and Winston, 1963.

Selsam, Millicent. *Language of Animals*. New York: William Morrow, 1962.

Sloan, Glenna Davis. "Developing Literacy Through Literature." *The Reading Teacher* 34(2) (November 1980): 132–136.

Sperry, Armstrong. *Call It Courage*. New York: Macmillan, 1968.

Steptoe, John. *My Daddy is a Monster . . . Sometimes*. New York: J. B. Lippincott, 1980.

Stewig, John Warren. "They Can—But Do They? (Read, that is!)" *Elementary English* 50(6) (1973) 921–924 +.

Sutherland, Zena. "Literature for Children." *The World Book Encyclopedia*. Chicago: Field Enterprises, 1978.

Taylor, Margaret C. *Wht's Yr Nm?* New York: Harcourt, Brace and World, 1970.

Tomkins, William. *Indian Sign Language*. New York: Dover, 1969.

VOCABULARY

The little red-headed boy, with the kind of indigna-
tion only four-year-olds can muster, confronted his
teacher at the lunch table. "I don't want these
peas, they're despicable," he declared vehemently.
The nursery school teacher, with apparent amaze-
ment, removed the dish of offending peas and
wondered again at the range of children's interest
in words.

The anecdote illustrates well what psychologists and students
of language have long known: that children's interest in words, and their intrepid approach to using them is indeed enviable. How a child's interest in
words is first stimulated and later encouraged and how a teacher can encourage this interest is the focus of this chapter.

AS WORDS ARE LEARNED

Children early sense the presence of sound stimuli surrounding them, and
soon begin the imitative procedures leading to early development of language. Several researchers have studied the language of very young children,
and have helped us understand the early efforts children make at emulating
sounds (Weir, 1962).

Most children utter an intelligible word sometime during the second six
months of life.[1] While such words may be difficult for other than a doting
parent to understand, the beginnning has been made; the growth that follows

---

[1] This stage in children's language acquisition is summarized in Green and Petty's *Developing
Language Skills in the Elementary Schools* (Boston: Allyn & Bacon, 1971), pp. 63–84. This meticulously researched book with many helpful references is particularly strong in the area of sequential development of language skills.

is truly amazing. From this simple beginning children progress to the point where only twenty-four months later they possess 77 percent of all sounds in adult language. Strickland (1964) reports that by the time children are three years old, they use 7,600 words per day; this increases to 10,500 words by the age of five.

LANGUAGE AT SIX

Much time and effort has been devoted to determining the size of children's vocabularies by the time they arrive in first grade. Yet it may be more confusing than illuminating to examine the results of such studies, for it is difficult to determine just what the first-grade teacher may expect. Table 12–1 summarizes a variety of studies in this area.

It is apparent from Table 12–1 that consensus in this, as in many other areas of research, is not possible. It is interesting to speculate about the factors in the research which may have accounted for these differences (see item #2, in Suggestions for Further Study).

Probably a first-grade teacher can know for sure only two things after examining this data. First, it is likely that the size of vocabulary of children entering school is larger today than in previous years. While most children may not know the 26,363 words which Shibles claims, it is safe to assume that children today do have a larger vocabulary than when Canton did his study in 1897. Some observations about society would suggest this conclusion. In the world Canton studied, neither television nor radio stimulated vocabulary development.[2] Books were expensive and scarce—it was a rare child who grew

TABLE 12–1 RESEARCH STUDIES ON SIZE OF CHILDREN'S VOCABULARIES

Year Done	Sample	Number of Words	Researcher
1897	6-year-olds	2,000	Canton
1912	6-year-olds	2,500	Terman and Childs
1926	6-year-olds	2,562	Madorah E. Smith
1936	First-grade children	2,703	F. W. Dolch
1941	First-grade children	24,000	Mary K. Smith
1957	6-year-olds	14,500	Templin
1959	First-grade children	26,363	Shibles
1960	Kindergarten children	3,728	Kolson
1964	First-grade children	12,456	Ames

[2]Since television has become an integral part of American life, several researchers have explored its effect on learning. George E. Mason, "Children Learn Words from Commercial TV," *Elementary School Journal,* March 1965, *65,* 318–320, studied the relationship between TV and vocabulary growth. He concluded that poor readers gained less vocabulary from watching TV than did good readers.

up in an environment providing this stimulus. Further, travel was severely limited, so exposure to new ideas and people (consequently to new words) was also limited. Certainly it is clear that a child's perceptual field today is considerably richer than was that of a child of seventy-five years ago.

Second, it is likely that children come to school with much of their vocabulary made up of words acquired *vicariously*—words for ideas, phenomena, and objects they have never experienced directly. For example, by watching television, children may have acquired the ability to speak such words as *module, translunar,* and *escape velocity.* Whether the children "know" such words or are simply able to repeat them in context in a superficial way is a matter to be determined by each teacher.[3] It is undoubtedly true that the presence of a large store of vicariously acquired words necessitates a different approach to teaching vocabulary than in other times when more of a child's vocabulary was learned through direct experience.

TYPES OF VOCABULARY

The typical approach to describing a child's stock of words is to discuss four major vocabularies: speaking, listening (or recognition), reading, and writing. While such finite categories are useful for discussion, obviously many areas overlap and distinctions become blurred.

A child's *speaking* vocabulary is the most useful to the majority of children so it will be considered first. As mentioned in the chapter on oral language, we communicate most frequently in speech. Because this is so, a prime concern for the teacher should be to develop, extend, or expand the child's speaking vocabulary.

As they grow, correction is constant while children are developing a speaking vocabulary. Despite correction, usually by parents in incidental and frequently noncensorious ways, many children use oral language with a fluency adults envy. Preschool children experiment with language, fearlessly try new forms, use new words, and in general feel at home with words. A teacher's role in expanding the oral vocabulary is to increase the stock of words a child can use, while maintaining this fluent approach to speaking.

Listening vocabulary is intimately related to speaking vocabulary. This vocabulary becomes increasingly important as the proportion of each day we spend in listening increases. As we gather a larger percentage of information from listening, the skill of determining word meaning from an oral context becomes more crucial. This is a more sophisticated skill than determining word meaning from print, because while listening we have little time and cannot reconsider and reflect upon words as we can in writing.

---

[3]Edgar Dale clearly defined this problem in describing procedures for measuring vocabulary size. (See "Vocabulary Measurement," *Elementary English,* December 1965, pp. 895–901.) To be able to define a word is obviously a different type of skill than being able to choose the correct definition from among several.

Once spoken, the ephemeral words are gone and subtle distinctions, especially of mood or feeling, disappear. We can examine the writer's intent and explore his or her implications at leisure. No such luxury exists with listening, so expanding this vocabulary is crucial.

A *reading* vocabulary, of concern to so many people for such a long time, is the one a child will use almost constantly while in school. Because of this, a teacher's obligation includes expanding the vocabulary a child can cope with in print.

The smallest of the vocabularies, the *writing* vocabulary, is probably also of most limited utility to the majority of students. Though some of us take delight in finding exactly the right word for the right spot to convey the precise shade of meaning we intend, for the majority of children writing will seldom be such an endeavor. This is probably appropriate, considering the small percentage of adults in our society whose careers demand an extensive written vocabulary.

THE NEED FOR VOCABULARY DEVELOPMENT

Considering the size of children's vocabularies when they come to school, why is it important that teachers concern themselves with this aspect of a child's language? If vocabulary develops to this extent before school, can't we consider it a relatively unimportant item? For two reasons, the answer to these rhetorical questions must be no.

First, vocabulary correlates most reliably with success in school. It is important to notice that in the previous sentence, the words read "success in school."

It is apparent that success in life may well be predicated on factors unrelated to size of vocabulary. There are many capable adults who function well using the 500 words on the Horn list, plus a small technical vocabulary related to their field.[4] Given compulsory school attendance laws, however, and this relation between vocabulary and success in school, the teacher's role becomes clear. Children must remain in school and the teacher must do everything possible to excite them about and arouse their interest in words, to ensure the children's success in school.

Ames (1964) stated: "Experiments have shown that vocabulary size is probably the best single index for predicting achievement in nearly all the other language skills." Ames is considering success in other language arts, but beyond this, we also have evidence that vocabulary size is related to success in other academic areas.

Petty (1968) has stated: "In the classroom the achieving students possess the most adequate vocabularies. Because of the verbal nature of most class-

---

[4]As a result of his investigations, Ernest Horn determined that the adult who knows these 500 words will know 99 percent of the words he or she needs to know, on the basis of words used most frequently. See *A Basic Writing Vocabulary* (Iowa City: State University of Iowa, 1926).

room activities, knowledge of words and ability to use language are essential to success in these activities."

A second reason for concern is the increasing rate of language change. Linguists have known for some time that a distinctive feature of any living language is change. As it is used, modified, added to, subtracted from, and in other ways altered, the language becomes unintelligible to speakers of a few hundred years earlier.[5]

Though change as an aspect of language has been noticed and commented upon before, a student of our culture rather than a linguist has summed up the startling *increase* in rate of change which now characterizes English. Alvin Toffler (1970) commented that "of the estimated 450,000 'usable' words in the English language today, only perhaps 250,000 would be comprehensible to William Shakespeare." Thus, in an interval of only about 350 years, if he were "suddenly to materialize in London or New York today, he would be able to understand on the average only five out of every nine words in our vocabulary. The Bard would be a semiliterate."

This rapid rate of language change easily leads to a particular danger in vocabulary learning, that of incomplete understanding. Graff discovered that a group of children with which she worked had indeed "learned" some words. That is, they had learned to recognize some word forms when they appeared on a list. Their learning was limited, however, to the word's commercial use. She gave children the following words, among others:

mars	lark
mound	dove
crest	raid

From children's responses to the test, she discovered that they knew the words as trade names, but were unfamiliar with the common noun aspect of the words.[6]

At least two other kinds of incomplete understandings are common among youngsters. Children will often know one meaning of a word, but not another. For example, all third graders will know the word table as an article of furniture; few will know it as a geographic term, as in water table, and fewer will know it as a verb, as in to table a motion. Similarly, most children

---

[5]Some materials that make this principle dramatically evident are the *Leaflets on Historical Linguistics* (Urbana, Il: National Council of Teachers of English, 1967). Though the text is too advanced to use with children, the illustrations of pages from such authors as Shakespeare and such works as *Beowulf* can be used with younger children to augment a study of how language changes.

[6]Virginia A. Graff, "Plenty of Words," *Elementary School Journal,* October 1967, 68, 9–12. A research report indicating quite conclusively that children frequently can respond on a verbal level, but that real understanding of both words and phrases may elude them.

know sweat as a verb common to all of us. Far fewer will know the specialized use as in the sentence, "The plumber will sweat the pipe." Clearly, one of our tasks as teachers is not simply to expand the number of words children know, but to expand also the number of *meanings* students know.

A related problem is pointed out by Saltz (1979) who says literal interpretations of the figurative language in proverbs is usually a problem for boys and girls. It is not until they reach Piaget's formal operations stage that they will be able to transcend the literal meaning of such figurative language as, "When the cat's away, the mice will play," and "Don't jump the gun." Saltz points out that students' interpretations of such expressions can show teachers their stage of linguistic development, and suggest to teachers that they use language carefully lest children misunderstand. To encourage children to think about such figures of speech, you might use *The King Who Rained* (Gwynne, 1970), a delightfully imaginative visual interpretation of the literal message of many of these phrases. Another helpful resource is Kohn's *One Day It Rained Cats and Dogs* (1965).

An alert teacher needs to be aware of such incomplete understanding of the multiple meanings of words, to expand a child's sense of words. Some suggestions about this will be made in the next section.

ENCOURAGING VOCABULARY GROWTH

The key to vocabulary growth, as with so many areas in language arts, is the teacher's own interest. If you were reading, what would your reaction be if you saw the following: *olio, shaggymane, demijohn,* or *nevus*? Would they arouse your curiosity so you'd want to find out what they mean? If so, you'll probably be able to share that curiosity with the children you teach.

Teachers whose curiosity about words sends them frequently to a dictionary to learn a new word, or a new meaning of a familiar word, can set a positive example for children. Set this example in several ways:

1. Use words without curtailing choice because of difficulty. That is, if *apprehensive* comes to mind, use it. Don't substitute *afraid*. If *courageous* comes to mind, don't substitute *brave*. This approach necessitates defining the word you have used and there are several ways this can be done. You may simply define it, saying for example: "When Dave came home from Crazy Kate's he was very *apprehensive*, or afraid, of what his dad would say" (Neville, 1963). Or you may give an example. You might say, in using *courageous:* "Remember how Swimmy felt when he was leading the rest of the fish in chasing away the Tunas? That's right, he felt very strong and powerful and brave. Another word for that is courageous" (Lionni, 1963). These are probably the two simplest ways of defining a word. Another device you can use is modification. For example, "The light blue color, *azure*, is the

most interesting one." You can also use restatement. You could say: "The woman was *frenzied*. Her overwrought state of nervous activity was obvious.[7]

2. Keep on hand a variety of dictionaries. The variety should include several different levels and several different types. The archaic practice of buying thirty copies of one publisher's dictionary does not encourage the curiosity about words that we are trying to develop. Children enjoy comparing what different dictionaries say about a particular word and learn by being exposed to the often subtle differences in etymology, pronunciation, syllabication, and definition. *Etymological* differences are apparent, for instance, in the word *tom-tom*. One dictionary reports it is of barbaric Eastern origin, while another traces it back to Hindi. *Pronunciation* differences are apparent when we compare 'nəp sh/əl/ with nŭp' shăl/, variations of the word nuptial. Syllabication differences show up when we check the words. One dictionary, for example, divides leisure as lezh 'r, while another divides it lē'shər. Similarly, one elementary dictionary divides fusion as fū'zhən, while another divides it as fyüzh'n. *Definition* differences are apparent in the following entries for the term "man Friday": (1) "a male administrative assistant with diverse duties," and (2) "a person wholly subservient to another, a servile follower." In this case, the connotations are completely different, and children's understanding of the term is enriched by exploring such differences. Even very young children can now be encouraged to turn to dictionaries, as several companies have been manufacturing dictionaries with few words and many pictures.[8] Children with access to only one type of dictionary miss the richness of meaning accessible when several dictionaries are consulted. An informal examination of dictionaries now available reveals this problem. If a third-grade teacher were using the primary level of one of the best-selling children's dictionaries, children would be limited to seven meanings of the word *cool*. By having a few copies of the intermediate level of that dictionary available, the students would encounter five additional meanings. A copy of the junior level of the same dictionary adds an additional meaning. Having

---

[7]These and other ways of defining in context are discussed at length in Lee C. Deighton's *Vocabulary Development in the Classroom* (New York: Teachers College Press, 1959). An extremely helpful small paperback book for any teacher who wants to develop vocabulary strength.

[8]A particularly fine example is *The Magic World of Words* by William D. Halsey (New York: Macmillan, 1977). The large, clear type is set off by much white space; the pictures — all four-color and helpfully detailed — are large and many. Designed for the young reader who has passed through the first stages of reading instruction, *First Dictionary* by John Trevaskis and Robin Hyman (New York: Young Readers' Press, 1973) is an inexpensive paperback so each child can have a copy. *The Rainbow Dictionary* by Wendell Write (New York: Collins & World, 1978) includes 2,300 words in a revision of an earlier work for upper-primary children with pictures by Joseph Low. *My First Dictionary* by Fernando Vianna (Boston: Houghton Mifflin, 1980) is equally attractive: 1,700 words are accompanied by one or two illustrations on each page. A contrary point of view is presented by Downing (1972), who feels that most such dictionaries are eye-appealing to adults, but in words included, and definitions provided, are not of interest to children.

subtract
divide

Subtract means to take away. *Divide* means to separate something into parts. You *divide* a cherry pie if you cut it into six pieces. If you eat a piece, you *subtract* one-sixth of the pie!

Sumi **divides** a pie when she cuts it into six pieces.

She **subtracts** one-sixth of the pie when she eats a piece!

cut

Cut can mean shorten. If you *cut* a speech or story, you shorten it by leaving a part of it out. If you *cut through* a neighbor's yard on your way to school, you are shortening the trip.

See also *shrink*.

ANTONYMS: increase (v), lengthen, add, accelerate, enlarge, extend, multiply

From In Other Words: A Junior Thesaurus *(Glenview, Il: Scott Foresman, 1982).*

copies of a different manufacturer's intermediate dictionary will add two different meanings, while yet a third manufacturer's product adds another meaning. Having three dictionaries, at three levels, lets the children be free to examine a total of sixteen different meanings of this word.

3. Use and encourage children to use other resource books. There are now thesauruses available on children's levels, though teachers of intermediate grades report good response to adult thesauruses.[9] Investing in an inexpensive paperback thesaurus results in increased vocabulary size and more effective creative writing.

4. Minimize the importance of correct spelling in written work, encouraging children to use words which may already be in their speaking vocabulary but not in their writing vocabulary. Children can experiment more freely in adding words to their oral vocabulary, simply because knowledge of the peculiarities of how a word is spelled is unimportant in speech. This is not, unfortunately, true in writing. Because of this, the teacher stresses from the first written assignment of the year the idea that in the initial stages of composition, children are free to experiment with whatever words they want to use. Attention to correct representation of the sounds in writing can come later—after the child has gained confidence by using the word in compositions.

THE READING WAY TO VOCABULARY

As already said, there are many benefits to composition in reading aloud, but it is necessary to reinforce the idea here to point out that children's vocabularies increase as they read and are read to by the teacher.

Whitehead describes the role of reading in vocabulary development in this way:

> Teachers who read to boys and girls . . . will, in the process expose them to the full beauty and flavor of the English language. The teaching need not be overt, for casual references to a particular word or phrase will often do. Indeed, children often recognize immediately a particularly melodious, rhythmic or emotional word or phrase . . . and thousands of . . . such language elements have been memorized instantly by children.[10]

As teachers share books with children, they can set the stage for each book and do some incidental vocabulary teaching. In introducing *Homer Price*, the characterization of Homer as *perplexed* when he couldn't get the donut machine to shut off will pique the children's interest. After the teacher has read this chapter, the children will have no problem in understanding the word "perplexed."[11]

---

[9]The eye-catching format of *In Other Words* by Andrew Schiller and William A. Jenkins (Glenview, Il: Scott, Foresman, 1982) makes this thesaurus for children a delight to use.

[10]Robert Whitehead, *Children's Literature: Strategies of Teaching* (Englewood Cliffs, N.J.: Prentice-Hall, 1968), p. 81. Teachers will find the leisure-time activity poll included in this book of use in assessing children's reading interests.

[11]Robert McCloskey, *Homer Price* (New York: Viking, 1949). A delightfully comic series of misadventures happens to the hero, Homer. A rather bucolic, small-town setting, unfamiliar to many children, but the humor makes it an unforgettable book.

With a little help by the teacher, children can understand what *querulous* means after an encounter with Mole in *The Wind in the Willows* (Grahame, 1960), what *imperious* means after meeting Mary Poppins (Travers, 1934): what *addled* means after hearing about the Peterkins (Hale, 1966); and what *pugnacious* means after running into Harriet the Spy (Fitzhugh, 1964).

In addition to the use a teacher makes of vocabulary in introducing or discussing a selection, the words used in the story itself will broaden the children's understanding. McCloskey uses the following words in his story:

> "Then the sherrif got *riled*."
> "That music has *pixied* these children."
> ". . . and provide the *diversion* that the trotting races have."
> "Neatest trick of *merchandising* I ever seen."
> "The aftershave lotion with the *invigorating* smell. . . ."

Some authors have suggested that vocabulary from readings, or indeed any words a teacher may wish to introduce, can be made meaningful by having children dramatize them (Duffelmeyer & Duffelmeyer, 1979). We could read *Homer Price* to our children, and then have them show in a dramatic interpretation of the scene, for instance, *how* Homer was perplexed. Though the Duffelmeyers are writing of such drama activities for older students, many of their suggestions could be adapted for use at the elementary school level. The point is that involvement with words will be more effective in actually learning the word than will the teacher's verbal definition of it.

INDEPENDENT READING

When your children want to read independently, avoid the temptation to guide them in choosing books on the basis of their reading level, although some youngsters with reading problems will need your help selecting, to avoid undue frustration.

Conversely, for the majority of readers, interest is a more crucial determinant of a child's ability to read a particular book than scores from readability formulas. Since the major purpose of independent reading should be to develop interest in, indeed compulsion for, reading, bringing a child together with a book of interest is more important than limiting that child to a book on the "right" reading level. If the child is highly motivated to read the book of his or her choice, the new words it may contain will not usually present any major problems.

Keep in mind that often we hold children to a standard we are not held to as adults. Few of us are accountable for the exact meaning of every word we read. As we read, we cull meaning from context, though precise, dictionary meanings of a word may elude us. If this interferes significantly with our comprehension, we stop to look the word up. If not, we skip over it, satisfied that we have extracted most of the author's meaning.

Seldom do we allow children such luxury. Instead, we too frequently belabor comprehension questions, insisting that children either orally define every unfamiliar word, or look each up. This is simply not the way adult readers function. The procedure thus seems questionable as we are building young readers.

DIRECT EXPERIENCES

Teachers can utilize three types of direct experience; they know a word experienced is more likely to be retained than one encountered on paper (Stewig, 1980). Direct experiences can be provided with:

1. *Objects.* Children who have cut open and eaten the succulent flesh of a persimmon or marveled over the treasure of seeds in a pomegranate seldom have difficulty remembering the names of these objects. And children who have explored the surface of piqué or percale with their fingertips while their eyes are closed will have no trouble remembering which is which. Any child who has tried to describe the difference in smell between petunias and pansies will seldom forget the names of those flowers.

2. *People.* A logical way to utilize this experience is in conjunction with the social studies program. Teachers can go beyond the usual mundane units that provide contact with the nurse, the police officer, and the mail carrier. Children are no longer challenged by this tired array of "community helpers." They would be more excited to learn about bobbins, boat shuttles, woof and warp from a weaver; about prophylaxis, amalgam carriers and wiggle-bugs from a dentist; about perlite, nodal points and friable soil from a gardener. The use of resource people in a classroom can greatly extend vocabulary learning in a painless way. An additional advantage of contact with such resource people is the logical excuse for practical writing; instruct the children to write letters to ask guests to visit the classroom and then to write thank-you letters after the visit.

3. *Environments.* In addition to having resource people visit the classroom, the teacher can frequently take children to another location for on-the-spot learning and vocabulary extension.

One kindergarten class visited the studio of an artist-in-residence at the local university. The artist told them about canvas stretchers, pigment grounds, and trompe l'œil (the kind of painting he did). When the children returned to school, they were eager to use the words in the experience story they dictated. Later on, when they read the story together, the class remembered these words, because they had experienced them.

One third-grade class enjoyed learning about the work of an architect. As they toured the office, the children encountered the words *elevation, perspective, facade, flemish bond,* and *travertine* in a way that made it easy to remember what the words meant.

Another trip, to the kitchen of a hotel, provided contact with cooking processes (sauteeing, etc.) and such equipment as quartz ovens and buffalo choppers. The children were fascinated to see how a professional kitchen operates and the experience encouraged their interest in learning new words.

It is important to emphasize that such experiences have specific purpose:

to kindle interest in vocabulary. The purpose is *not* to add, through study and testing, such arcane words to the child's vocabulary; few would have any use for such words. The value of such experiences lies in the stimulation they provide. The unusual words, some mysterious, some "funny" sounding, some euphonious, will take root in a child's imagination and keep alive an interest in and fascination with new words.

STUDYING WORD PARTS

The above suggestions have been aimed at developing a wide-ranging interest in and curiosity about words. There is, in addition, place in the language arts program for more structured approaches to teaching vocabulary.

One good way to help children broaden their vocabulary is to share with them one of the basic building processes of English, the affixes. Affixes are of three types: prefixes, suffixes, and infixes. Your understanding the word construction technique using affixes will help your students; teachers should expose children to it. There are, however, some qualifications that need to be made on how this can be done most effectively. It is not as simple as telling children that the prefix *de* means "of" or "from." Stotsky (1978) recommends teaching five of the most frequently used prefixes (un-, dis-, re-, in-, and en-). She chose these because they frequently have at least two meanings, which can be a problem to children, unless teachers focus attention on them.

Deighton (1959) treats the subject more completely in his book, and a few key ideas are included here to help teachers improve their vocabulary teaching. There are two dangers in applying the technique. The first is that one may be dealing with a word whose affix is absorbed; that is, the affix no longer means what it meant originally. The "de-" of desolate no longers means what "de-" usually means today. Similarly, the "pre-" of precept or premium, no longer means what "pre-" usually means today. Children may be misled if they apply the common or usual meaning of the affix to these words—among others. The second problem is that some words may look like they contain an affix, but they actually do not (for example: the de- of decoy). In either of these cases, students will be misled if they apply literally their too often limited information about affixes and how they work.

After extended analysis of English vocabulary, Deighton has offered some suggestions about which affixes should be taught, because of their high utility. He suggests using the following list because these twenty-six will unlock meaning in more than 200 current English words:

anthropo-	hydro-	phil- or philo-
auto-	iso-	phono-
biblio-	lith-	photo-
bio-	micro-	pneumo-
centro- centri-	mono-	poly-
cosmo-	neuro-	proto-
heter- or hetero-	omni-	pseudo-
homo-	pan-	tele-
	penta-	uni-

The following nine prefixes will help unlock the meaning of 650 words:

circum-	mal-
equi-	mis-
extra-	non-
intra-	syn-
intro-	

Noun suffixes, which always indicate an agent either living or nonliving, are also of use because of their frequent occurrence:

-eer	-ster
-ess	-stress
-grapher	-trix
-ier	

Finally, Deighton recommends teaching the following adjective forms with specific and invariant values.

-est	-less
-ferous	-able (-ible, -ble)
-fic	-most
-fold	-like
-form	-ous
-genous	-ose
-scopic	-acious
-wards	-ful
-wise	

Having recommended systematic teaching of these forms, Deighton warns of the danger in succumbing to analysis. We must remember that "The truth is that most words are more than the sum of their parts." While we give children preliminary help in investigating word meaning through study of the affixing process, we must also be careful to develop a fuller understanding of the richness and multiplicity of word meaning—which is not always accessible through simple word building (Munnelly, 1972).

Another kind of systematic study of words is possible when teachers plan a unit of study about synonyms and other such related words. Boys and girls can be introduced to such synonyms as cold and chilly, such homonyms as jet (a plane) and jet (a velvet-black mineral), such homographs as read (now) and read (past), and such antonyms as euphoric and depressed. Hanson (1972) has written a series of charming books illustrated with humorous black ink drawings and strategically placed spots of color which are useful in teaching these concepts. Each book opens with a clear definition that can be shared with your class before exploring other words they know which fit the category.

CONNOTATION AND DENOTATION

Another way to help children understand the richness of our language and develop an interest in words is to explore the idea of connotation and denotation with them. Adults use this aspect of language regularly, and yet all too infrequently learn to manipulate it consciously to make communication more effective.

When we speak of *denotative* meaning (the easier of the two to define) we mean the objective reality of a situation, the physical referent without accompanying value judgments related to it, or the simple and uncomplicated tangible aspects of something.

When we speak of *connotative* meaning (the more difficult term to define) we mean that halo of accumulated meaning, elusive because it refers less to the physical reality and more to our attitudes, perceptions, and feelings about something. Connotative meaning frequently is linked to past feelings or impressions that may remain below the level of consciousness but which, nonetheless, affect how we react to things, people, and ideas (Pei, 1969).

Some elementary series do an effective job of introducing this idea to children (Bierly, et al., 1983), but if your series does not, try to plan a unit on these two types of meaning. You can help your children see that while synonymous terms may seem to be roughly the same, their connotations make them really quite different. It has been pointed out that talkative, articulate, gossipy, garrulous, rambling, fluent, gabby, and mouthy indeed represent all points on the spectrum from favorable to unfavorable.[12]

Many words have connotations we can learn to use in order to improve language skills. We can convey innumerable shades of meaning when we choose among fat, plump, corpulent, portly, pudgy, stout, chunky, obese, and chubby. We even find that people of this physiognomy have been called Rubenesque, after the great Flemish painter whose taste ran to women of ample proportions.[13]

It is a simple procedure when children are involved in creative writing to refer them to one of the available thesauruses so they can choose the word with precisely the shade of meaning they wish to convey. After introducing the thesaurus and explaining how it works, the teacher may reasonably expect that, with practice, the children will become adept in using this tool to help them select from among a variety of words the one which exactly conveys the connotation they want.

---

[12]See Richard R. Lodwig and Eugene F. Barrett, *The Dictionary and the Language* (New York: Hayden, 1967), pp. 140–148. Though designed primarily for high school students, this well-written book contains much useful information for the teacher and can be read independently by able sixth-grade children. Most of the activities suggested can be adapted for use with elementary students.

[13]If you're not familiar with Rubens, locate one of his paintings and see which of the words above describes the women in the painting most accurately.

Down – fuzzy duck feathers   **Down** – the opposite of up

From Two-Way Words *by C. Imbior Kudrna.*

ETYMOLOGICAL EXPLORATION

One effective way to make words come alive for children and help them remember new words they encounter is to encourage etymological exploration. The term *etymology* may sound dull, but once children discover the fascinating quirks and peculiarities which lie hidden in the background of even common words, they will be intrigued with the study of word origins. Once they discover the strange original meanings of some words, it will be easier to remember what the word currently means, because the contrast is so sharp.

Two examples will serve as a beginning. When a child says something is *nice*, send him or her to the dictionary to discover that originally this now-pallid word meant foolish or ignorant. Similarly, we discover that *fond* has its origins in the Middle-English word for foolish.

For many common English words, an examination of origins reveals interesting information. It is surprising to discover that *foyer* originally meant a room with a fireplace. It is easy to remember the word if one thinks about the guests in a French chateau coming in from a cold carriage ride and stopping in the first room they entered to warm themselves at the fire in the foyer. Similarly, it is easy to remember what *recalcitrant* means if one can visualize its original meaning: the ox kicking back in rebellion—an interesting etymology hidden in the passage of years.

In talking about composition with children, I wanted to get across the idea of being *succinct*, that is, saying clearly and concisely and in a minimum of words what they had to say. The original meaning of the word is "tucking something up out of sight where it won't show." When the children visualized tucking up all the extra words and sentences that were unnecessary to their compositions, they could indeed learn to be succinct.

Alerting children to the etymologies of words and the aid these can be in remembering what a word currently means can be done casually as a new word occurs—simply by sending the children to the several different dictionaries available in the room. Or, a teacher may choose to plan a more organized unit on etymology. Few language arts textbooks for children do much with this idea, though there are many individual tradebooks, like the one by Steckler (1980), which can be helpful.

In all these examples, the intent is not that children should be asked to memorize etymologies. Rather, the purpose of this exploration and the resulting discussion is simply to pique children's interest, and in some cases to give them a "memory hook" or means for remembering the current meaning of a word.

Studying Word Geography

An easily accessible idea of exploration for children is word geography, more technically called dialect study. It is logical to study dialects with children, for we are a nation of many speech variations. Our history is even richer in dialect. At one time, California, made up of twenty-one separate Native American nations, was a land of 113 different dialects! (Ceram, 1971). There are fewer dialects today, but children are still interested in how people's speech varies. Experiences in word geography can be planned because such experiences abet the teacher's as well as the children's desire to expand vocabulary. One can easily examine with children idiolects, local and regional dialects, and the slang of particular groups.

Children enjoy collecting examples of *idiolects*, their own individual speech patterns or those particular to their families. After that, explore *local* words. For example, children in Minneapolis wait at a bus *wye*, and, if driven to school, see parents stop at the *semaphore* until the light changes to green. Natives of some parts of Indiana go to farmers' markets in the summer to buy *mangos*, not the yellowish-red succulent tropical fruit usually called by that name, but rather the common bell or green pepper.

There are, in addition, regional words which are interesting to study. Marckwardt (1964), for example, points out the regional manifestation of sweet corn as opposed to roasting ear, gutters as opposed to spouting, and sick *to* one's stomach as opposed to sick *at* one's stomach. Residents of New England have a "dropped egg" for breakfast, which midwesterners know as a poached egg. A heavy rain may be a dam-buster (Alabama), a sewer-clogger (Michigan), a mud-sender (California) or a hay-rotter (Virginia). These and literally thousands of other choices can be pinpointed with specificity by dialect experts who have devoted much time to defining regional boundaries.

In a day of rapidly increasing population mobility, a teacher may often have children from several different geographical areas in the classroom. Such linguistic checklists of regional expressions as the one included by Shuy (1967) can be used to motivate interest in dialect vocabulary.

In addition to words, students of language geography have noted some sentence constructions, or syntactical variations, peculiar to an area. A bemused new resident of Indiana commented on the following usages which she discovered were accepted as standard English in this locale:

"That's because they have so many traffic signs anymore."
"Anymore, the girls wear slacks to class."
"I would like for you to do this."
"I'll have him to call you."

As she points out, such constructions exist in colloquial standard usage in some area, but students need to be aware that they are localized, and may be scrutinized skeptically elsewhere (Robinett, 1968).

Another kind of geographic difference is evident when intermediate-grade students study British English. Many vocabulary terms vary:

BRITISH ENGLISH	AMERICAN ENGLISH
petrol	gasoline
way out	exit
flyover	overpass
loose chippings	falling rocks
bonnet (of a car)	hood

Such differences can result in sentences that seem incomprehensible, until one knows, for example, that "Don't go into the box unless the way out is clear," means "Don't enter the intersection and block it" (Lo Bello, 1980). On a simpler level, teachers can share such books as *Spot's Dogs and the Alley Cats* (Wild, 1979), for the British vocabulary they include.

The *slang* terminology of particular groups, often not shared by a community in general, is also of interest. Students at one university at which I taught go to "call-outs"—organizational meetings held at the beginning of a school year. They complain about classes in rooms far across the campus, assigned by "schedule deputies"—using the word "deputy" in a way other than it is generally used. Some of the girls become "lavaliered," the preliminary stage to becoming engaged, which involves receiving the university seal or the letters of the boy's fraternity to wear on a chain around her neck. Many groups have developed these specialized slang "languages," or at least certain specific and unusual uses of words. Children will delight in searching for examples of them.[14]

---

[14]You might find *Truck Drivers Dictionary and Glossary*, compiled by Jean M. Walker and available from the American Trucking Association, 1616 P St., NW, Washington, D.C. 20036, of interest to children. This three-part paperback is devoted to jargon, illustrations, and terminology children seldom encounter.

The Magic of Names

Beginning the school year with a discussion of your children's names, which then leads to examination of place names, is an easy way to launch into word study. Their own names hold a fascination for children, and both standard "meanings" of names and family reasons for name choices can be researched and discussed.[15]

In addition to personal names, place names can be studied. From one end of the country to the other, residents of unusually (and sometimes bizarrely) named places are fascinated by the names of their towns. Children find place names especially interesting to study. Whether one is teaching in Riddle, Oregon, or Horatio, South Carolina; Sleepy Eye, Minnesota, or Sour Lake, Texas, the lure of place name study is the same (Pizer, 1976).

Place-name study can be correlated with *social studies* when one explores the various city names in one's own state or the origin of the state name.[16] A study of cities named by Indians, the Spanish, or French explorers can also be rewarding. It can correlate with *history* as, for example, when one studies the spread of classically named cities across our continent. This classical influence spread as far as Athens, Texas; Attica, Ohio; Corinth, Mississippi; Delphi, Indiana; Rome, Illinois; and Sparta, Wisconsin. The widespread use of classical names occurred at a particular stage in our country's history and the reasons for such naming can be investigated. Or such study may be undertaken simply as a language arts activity, for instance, when children study city names to find the longest, the shortest, the most or least phonetic, those derived from people's names, or from words for geographical formations.

In studying local or area names, older residents can be interviewed who may have been present when the names were chosen (or changed, as so often happens). This activity, including planning questions before and writing reports after the interview, helps increase children's interviewing skills.

In studying more remote names, two sources exist. Children may write to the Chambers of Commerce requesting information. This helps provide practice in letter-writing skills. In doing this for several semesters with a college methods class, we have experienced between 65 percent and 90 percent response to our letters of inquiry.

You might suggest that the children write to larger cities, avoiding those

---

[15]There are so many books on the origins and meanings of names that a teacher will have no trouble locating them in any library. In addition, see Chapter 3, the letter to parents eliciting information about the child's name.

[16]Pauline Arnold and Percival White, *How We Named Our States* (New York: Criterion Books, 1965). You might begin with this volume, which moves chronologically from east to west. Given the limited space available for each state, the writing is quite effective in stimulating interest.

tiny settlements which may have picturesque names but may not have a Chamber of Commerce. Even when so warned, children frequently insist on writing to villages, and we have been delighted by responses from librarians, postmasters, operators of the only store in town, ministers, and in one case, a train stationmaster.

In addition to such primary sources, children can go to the books available on this topic.[17] There are many of these which the teacher may use to augment the primary sources children can consult.

Developing Precision

After a teacher has built interest in words and can see children using and learning new words with vigor, it is time to turn attention to developing an understanding of the precise use of words.

This must be explained further to prevent such a statement from conjuring up unfortunately repressive visions of our own former English teachers. Too many of us began our study of English with teachers who demanded one answer, who were anxious to distinguish between right and wrong. The issue of precision is quite different and a valuable one for children to encounter. That is, being able to choose the word that says precisely what the *chooser* wants to say is an enviable language skill. Too frequently, because of our own imprecise use of words, we give children the impression, albeit unintentionally, that many more words are synonyms than really are.

Think about your own use of language. Do you use the word *unique,* when unusual is what you really mean? Have you ever used *sad,* when the emotion you were trying to express was a more complex and specific one than that catchall term could express? If so, perhaps your own language precision needs a modicum of attention.

Developing precision in language is not a difficult task, if you can sense opportunities as they arise and work on them. When children use overworked and imprecise terms, it's a simple task to stop, take a few minutes to explore some alternative and more expressive terms, and wonder again at the variety English allows us.

One classroom teacher initiated such an activity with her children when she sensed an overdependence on the word *said* in her children's writing. After searching for alternatives to the word, alternatives which pinned down more precisely *how* the word was said, the class came up with 104 alternatives, ranging from answered to yelled.

In a similar fashion, the last time I taught sixth-graders, we explored the variety of ways one could describe emotion when so many of them were *mad* at

---

[17]Isaac Asimov, *Words on the Map* (Boston: Houghton Mifflin, 1962). this is another intellectually sound and fascinating book so typical of Asimov's writing. It deals with areas (New England), countries (Greece), states (Tennessee) and cities (Louisville) and in short compass (1 page) gives a well-researched account of how each came to be named.

Reprinted by permission of King Features Syndicate Division.

one another. We searched for a week, checking with dictionaries, books, families, listening carefully to radio and television, and came up with the following list:

angry	enraged
annoyed	infuriated
perturbed	furious
disgruntled	provoked
"put out"	irritated
frustrated	wrathful
indignant	"ticked-off"
peeved	

At the end of the week we shared the list and discussed the subtle shades of meaning these terms convey. We were not looking for right and wrong, and we discovered some interesting differences of opinion about the exact meanings of some of the terms. The exploration was a worthwhile experience which made the multiplicity of language more apparent to this group of children.

Tiedt and Tiedt recommend a similar activity using color words, which develops both a color sense and a vocabulary to describe colors.[18] Children, unfortunately, often do not develop the visual sensitivity and the language skill to perceive and describe colors in their environment. For children without this ability, such an activity as the Tiedts describe could be very helpful.

The foregoing has assumed, if tacitly, group participation in activities. There are times, however, when a teacher can help individual children improve their mastery of a particular word by making its meaning more specific.

---

[18] Iris M. Tiedt and Sidney W. Tiedt, *Contemporary English in the Elementary School* (Englewood Cliffs, N.J.: Prentice-Hall, 1975), p. 136. The authors' suggestion for expanding children's color sense and word competency involves looking for words and making up lists of color varieties. Related to red, children might come up with cherry, vermillion, rose, ruby, scarlet, flame, and crimson. A similar approach can be used with all colors.

A CRASH OF RHINOCEROSES

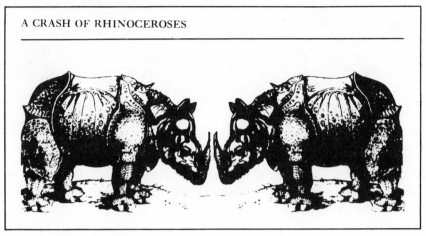

From An Exaltation of Larks *by James Lipton.*

Pinning Down Meaning

A helpful way of thinking about this problem is described by Dale (1965) in an article on different ways of "knowing" a word. Dale contends that knowledge of a word can be arranged on a continuum, as described below:

1ST STAGE →	2ND STAGE →	3RD STAGE →	4TH STAGE →	5TH STAGE
"I never saw it before."	"I know there is such a word, but I don't know what it means."	Vague contextual placing, also called the "twilight zone."	The word is pinned down.	Precise refining of differences.

Some examples illustrate this idea. For most of us, *fundular* belongs in Stage One. To understand it, we would need to look it up in a dictionary.

Stage Two might include such terms as *hugger-mugger* and *laser*. We've heard them at one time or another, but cannot fit them with appropriate referents.

Stage Three could include such terms as *hustings* (it has something to do with elections) and *bask* (it relates to the sun).

Stage Four words are those we recognize and can both use and define because their meaning is established in our minds.

Stage Five represents further refinement and development of the concept. Some people reach this stage, for example, in their use of *sympathy* and *empathy*, two words that separately vary subtly by a small but precise shade of difference.

The teacher's job is to help children continue moving words from Stage One to Stage Five. This is done by providing experiences in which the child can encounter the word in concrete manifestation.

In closing, it is important to reemphasize that the focus of this section is not on a *teacher* deciding right or wrong, but on the *child* selecting more appropriate words to convey precisely the shade of meaning he or she wishes to express. This is a sophisticated language skill, but one which can be encouraged by the teacher aware of the rewards of precision.

Vocabulary Games

As with other of the language arts, vocabulary learning can be greatly facilitated through the judicious use of games (Donoghue, 1971). Choose these carefully, to make sure they are of educational value in addition to being enjoyable.

One advantage many of these games offer is that they require little or no material or equipment. A second advantage is that, being of short duration, they can be played in the small bits of time elementary classroom teachers frequently have but seldom utilize.

Many vocabulary games capitalize on children's delight in the ways words and sounds can be manipulated, changed, altered, and experimented with, for the simple joy such experimentation gives. Lefevre (1968) points out that interest in words and sounds begins as life begins: "We all know that infants and children naturally learn language playfully. As they emerge from the cradle,

A sloth of bears

From Wild Animals *by Brian Wildsmith.*

they begin to use among themselves verbal riddles, puns, word plays, rhymes, gags of all sorts as part of their normal play."

This fascination with words continues throughout childhood, a contention documented by the extensive collection of material presented by the Opies.[19] Thus, it is easy for the teacher to capitalize on this interest by using vocabulary games. If the teacher knows some of these, they can be used in the odd moments of "waiting time," for instance, just before the art teacher arrives, or after the children come back from lunch, the time when a guest speaker is five minutes late, or when part of the group isn't back from the bathroom. Such time is seldom considered or utilized but it could be put to good use by the teacher who knows a few vocabulary games. Lake (1967) suggested several games which help develop interest in vocabulary. Our results are described here; and you may want to try your luck with a group of your children.

Lake describes "Hinky-Pinky," in which a definition must be answered by two rhyming words. Examples include: an obese rodent (fat rat); a wet hobo (damp tramp); and profound slumber (deep sleep). Trying this with a college methods class, we elicited the following:

frigid fungus	:	cold mold
elevated pig pen	:	high sty
squashed chapeau	:	flat hat
rodent abode	:	mouse house
thin bird	:	narrow sparrow

Several students in class wanted to try the idea, and from a group of fifth-grade children, they got the following results:

small evergreen	:	wee tree
recorded rock group	:	canned band
nodding bird	:	bobbin' robin
animal's false hair	:	pig wig
pale red soda	:	pink drink

A second game this author recommends is called "Tom Swifties," named after the hero of a series of boys' adventure books. The hero never simply *said* something; rather, the *way* he said it reflected what he was saying. An example is, "I'll never pet another lion," Tom said off-handedly. A teacher of sixth-

---

[19]Iona and Peter Opie, *The Lore and Language of School Children* (London: Oxford at the Clarendon Press, 1959). The results of a survey of 5,000 children in over seventy schools in different parts of Great Britain, this is a compendium of the rhymes, word tricks, riddles, parody, nicknames and epithets, jeers and torments, and secret languages used by children. It may be read for its intrinsic interest, or to notice the universality of children's language: many forms used have American English equivalents.

graders who had never tried this with students before was pleasantly surprised when her children came up with the following the first time they played the game:

"What kind of pickles are these?" she asked sourly.
"I see the ice cube," he said coldly.
"The cookies are ready," she said gingerly.
"Is that a mirror?" she asked reflectively.
"I only weight 50 pounds," she said lightly.
"My sister fainted," she said unconsciously.

In addition to those listed above, there are other, frequently more elaborate, games available from commercial manufacturers. You may want to examine those and select some to have for your children to use in their free time.

Suggestions for Further Exploration

1. To become more aware of how adult writers use vocabulary, choose two whose work you enjoy and select a sample of writing from each. Analyze the two samples in any way you like, to determine what differences exist between them. You might examine word length, use of compound words, amount and type of slang or nonstandard terms, the number of different words used, different levels of speech represented, or inflected words used. After you have done this, select two children's books, and determine how these authors' use of vocabulary differs.
2. The chart on page 397 summarizing the studies of children's vocabulary at age six is incomplete. Draw up a list of other information you would need to determine which of the studies you should accept. What would you need to know about the children, the procedures, the research conditions, and the data gathered, to determine which of the studies is most helpful? Then choose one to read and find out how much of the information you need to make a decision about the study is actually included in the report of the research.
3. The Lake article suggests doing the game "Tom Swifties" with children. College students created these: "I'll never be promoted in the Navy," Tom said admirably. "I'll always be a composer," Tom noted. "Which side of the penny did you call?" Tom asked flippantly. "I don't like wringer washers," Tom said crankily. Can you make up some Swifties as original as these?
4. Gather some data on children's vocabularies which you can analyze. You might tape record conversations with children at three different grade levels. Analyses might include incidence of various parts of speech, use of concrete and abstract terms, use of polysyllabic words, or use of compound words.
5. This chapter contends that the rate of language change is accelerating. A bit of linguistic detective work could reveal this. Talking with friends your own age, make a list of words currently used by your peers. Interview a group of high school students, to see which words are widely used by them. Then ask some people your parents' age, and your grandparents' age, to make a list of words common when they were young. Are there any words common to all lists?

6. Graff's article was written in 1967. Read it to learn about her procedures, and then replicate the study with a few children to see if her conclusions also apply to your group.
7. The chapter referred to thesauruses written for children. Could you make one, using pictures from magazines? Using it with a small group of children would give you feedback about how successful you have been.
8. The material on affixes from Deighton is useful in developing vocabulary. Could you make up a game that would be fun for children to play and would, in addition, help them learn one of the lists he suggests teaching?
9. Try to correlate dialect study with a social studies unit. Many children's books include characters speaking dialects. (See *Dingo* by Mary Patchett, Doubleday, 1963; and *Threat to the Barkers* by Joan Phipson, Harcourt, Brace, 1963.) Children's author Joan Aiken discusses this in "'Bred an Bawn in a Briar-Patch'—Dialect and Colloquial Language in Children's Books." *Children's Literature in Education*, Vol. 9, November 1972, pp. 7–23. Select a geographic area in the U.S., or a foreign country, and locate books in which the characters' language reflects the area.

Suggestions for Further Reading

Banachek, Linda. *Snake In, Snake Out.* New York: Thomas Y. Crowell, 1978.

A superb small book to develop words for concepts, this illustrates (and re-illustrates) the concept. *On*, for example, appears six times, and each time the characters—a comfy-looking old lady, her parrot, and a snake, illustrate the idea differently. Black line illustrations by Elaine Arnold show: the coverlet on the lady, the snake on the cover, the coverlet on her slippers, the glasses and the clock on the table, the bed on the rug, and so on. The next time the single word *on* appears, the scene is changed. Using only eight words (on, in, out, up, over, off, down, and under), author and illustrator collaborate to tell a humorous story about how the old lady solves her problem.

Basil, Cynthia. *How Ships Play Cards.* New York: Morrow Junior Books, 1980.

The salmon, green, and black illustrations by Janet McCaffery, done in designs stamped with soap erasers, are more interesting than the text, which tends to be "cute." The author presents fourteen riddles, which ask that children think about pairs of words (i.e., *sole* of the foot; sole—a type of fish). "When a ship reaches land, how does the ocean say good-bye? With a wave," is an example of the self-consciously clever language. Useful as a supplementary introduction to the concept of homonyms.

Belloc, Hilaire. *The Bad Child's Book of Beasts.* New York: Dover, 1961.

Another of Dover's fine reprints, this contains three of Belloc's small books bound as one. The whimsy of both the verse and the drawings, which are reminiscent of Lear, appeals to children. Vocabulary learning can be stimulated by the many unusual words the poet uses, and by contact with such unusual animals as the yak, marmoset, viper, and chamois. The last book, *A Moral Alphabet*, is for older children and could be used to motivate the creation of another alphabet.

Blumberg, Dorothy Rose. *Whose What?* New York: Holt, Rinehart and Winston, 1969.

Designed primarily for adult readers but accessible to older intermediate-grade children, this delightful accumulation of the odd bits of naming in our language will capture the imagination. Such terms as Custer's Last Stand, Gresham's Law, Hudson's Bay, Jacob's Ladder, and Mary's Little Lamb are included. An unbelievably dull format should not deter you.

Bombaugh, C. C. *Oddities and Curiosities of Words and Literature.* New York: Dover, 1961.

Of use primarily as a word game source book for teachers, this reprint of an early work contains such well-known forms as palindromes and such lesser-known forms as lipgrammata. The reading is too difficult for children, but fascinating for the teacher. The section on emblematic poetry will help in motivating creative writing.

Brown, Amy et al. *Dictionary* (Primary Dictionary Series). New York: Pyramid, 1971.

This interesting series include four paperbacks intended for children from five to twelve years of age. Each successive book contains, defined in greater depth, words included in the preceding books. The illustrations are only adequate, but the inexpensive format is convenient, since each child could have a copy.

Carlson, Ruth Kearney. "Sparkling and Spinning Words." *Elementary English*, January 1964, pp. 15–22.

Carlson provides a set of teaching suggestions based on the children's book *Sparkle and Spin*, in which authors Ann and Paul Rand examine the qualities of words. Carlson identifies ways teachers may help children write creatively by exploring vocabulary and using literature as a base for writing. She feels children's writing will sparkle when it grows from exposure to adult poetry, figurative language, and beautiful rhythms.

Charlip, Remy. *Arm in Arm.* New York: Parents Magazine Press, 1969.

Winner of the AIGA Award for distinguished illustration, this unusual book examines endless tales, reiterations, and other echolalia. After enjoying it, children may create their own words and pictures.

Dale, Edgar, and O'Rourke, Joseph. *Techniques of Teaching Vocabulary.* Chicago: Field Educational Publications, 1971.

This book contends that systematic study of organized word groups is needed in instructional programs. Its chief contribution is the variety and expressiveness of the word groups put together for the interested teacher. Teaching suggestions are provided. Chapters are devoted to suffixes, roots, synonyms and antonyms. Attention is also given to such other aspects of word study as figures of speech, semantic sources of confusion, and word games.

Davidson, Jessica. *Is That Mother in the Bottle?* New York: Franklin Watts, 1972.

An introduction to the origin and development of language, understandable to intermediate grade children. Word history is well presented, despite the unimaginative format of the book. Davidson deals with similarities and differences of language, and also with such different types as slang, idiomatic, and formal language.

Epstein, Sam and Epstein, Beryl. *The First Book of Words*. New York: Franklin Watts, 1954.

The book contains historical information, a section on the first writing, the growth of the alphabet, English in the new world and borrowed words. Children will enjoy the sections on "stuck-together" words and word tricks.

Ernst, Margaret S. *Words*. New York: Alfred A. Knopf, 1957.
Ernst's book makes fascinating reading for a child not bothered by lack of illustrations. She deals with such topics as roots, accent, slang, and suffixes. Historical information is included in chapters on The Angles, The Norman Conquest, and Modern English. The chapters on derivation of words are particularly well done.

Ferguson, Charles W. *The Abecedarian Book*. Boston: Little, Brown, 1964.

Large, elegantly designed full-page letters introduce the esoteric words for which they stand. The drawings, in fine red line, illustrate unusual words, ranging from antediluvian to zoological. A thoroughly delightful book for older children.

Fitzgerald, Cathleen. *Let's Find Out about Words*. New York: Franklin Watts, 1971.

Though it covers much the same ground as other beginner's books, the writing style and the crisp illustrations in this one recommend it. The origin of words from other countries, the creation of new English words, and a brief examination of how words sound (e.g., "crash is a noisy word") are included.

Funk, Charles Earle. *A Hog on Ice* (1948) and *Heavens to Betsy!* (1972). Both: New York: Warner Paperback Library.

Two from among several captivating books written by Funk that detail the peculiarities of English, these are valuable desk references for the teacher to use in explaining the unusual phrases which mean more than the literal meaning. Includes such common (but little understood) phrases as: to bell the cat, a Bronx cheer, a hair of the dog that bit you, and catch as catch can.

Garrison, Webb B. *Why You Say It*. New York: Abingdon Press, 1955.

This invaluable paperback provides a wealth of information about unusual words and phrases. The explanations, seldom over half a page long, detail in easily readable fashion the history and derivation of the word. Words and phrases are arranged by categories, but the index helps locate specific words for which one is searching.

Greenfield, Howard. *Summer is Icumen In*. New York: Crown, 1978.

Stimulate vocabulary study by using this book, which considers borrowed words, new meanings for old words, eponyms, euphemisms, and slang. In only sixty-five pages the author presents a wide-ranging survey of our changing

English language. The brief chapters are full of interesting details. Greenfield's clear, concise writing highlights the amusing quirks of language in an elegant format.

Hudson, Peggy, compiler. *Words to the Wise.* New York: Scholastic Book Services, 1967.

A combination information and workbook for intermediate-grade children, this illustrated paperback deals with words from many languages, the Bible, literature, and people's names and place names. The definitions and etymologies are concise and well written.

Jacobs, Leland. "Books and Children/Children and Books." *Early Years*, November 1979, 28–29 + .

The author discusses the importance of literature as an experience children can enjoy with adults which can also educate their imaginations. Through stories and poems, youngsters can come to know life in other times, places, and circumstances unlike their own. In choosing literature to share, adults must find what they themselves like, and provide a balance between traditional and modern writing. Teachers need to read to students each day, and selections need to be read and practiced before presentation. Oral storytelling by adults adds another important dimension. Writings and art created by children in response to the literature should be placed near the books where all can enjoy them. In closing, Jacobs provides ten questions useful in evaluating students' experiences with books.

Konigsburg, Elaine. "The Double Image: Language as the Perimeter of Culture." *Library Journal*, February 15, 1970, 731–734.

In these reflections upon the uses of language, the author concentrates especially on ways language shows shape and defines limits. She talks about her use of language to reflect a culture and its shape in her *About the B'nai Bagels.* In addition to defining a culture for readers, the author also sees language as a tool to poke holes in the culture's perimeter, to let readers enter deeper into the pattern of the culture.

Lambert, Eloise, and Mario Pei. *Our Names.* New York: Lothrop, Lee & Shepard, 1960.

A handy refrence for children to use in looking up what their name means, this interestingly written book can also be read in sequence as a history of naming. The chapter on names of endearment, personal name oddities, and the section on "thing" names contain material not easily available elsewhere. An additional helpful resource is *Dictionary of First Names* by Alfred J. Kolatch. New York: Perigree Press, 1981.

Lipton, James. *An Exaltation of Larks.* New York: Grossman, 1968.

An invaluable supplement to the Wildsmith books, this one for adults is illustrated with evocative old black-and-white drawings. The interesting additional feature is terms for people, including: a "diligence of messengers," a "sentence of judges," and a "skulk of thieves." The author created a "wince of dentists," and a "shush of librarians" among others. Children would enjoy making up their own.

Matthews, C.M. *English Surnames.* New York: Scribner's, 1967.

Useful primarily as a resource book, this paperback deals exhaustively with the topic. It investigates both chronological development and also such topics as nicknames, occupational and local names; a thorough tracing of each is given. The teacher may be interested in reading sections of it. For children it will serve as an interest builder as they check to see what their names mean.

O'Neill, Mary. *Words Words Words.* New York: Doubleday, 1966.

The poet, whose sensitive use of exactly the right word in the right place is enviable, has written a book containing traditional definitions of parts of speech. Despite the definitions, the charming poems interest children. The feeling poems (on such words as mean, precision, forget, hope, and happiness) are the real delight of the book, which should not be missed.

Radlauer, Ruth Shaw. *Good Times with Words.* Chicago: Melmont Press, 1963.

To help a child retain his or her own original way of saying things, the book emphasizes ways words can add colors, sounds, smells, and feelings to speaking and writing. The full-color illustrations show some funny ways words work. Several activities are suggested to involve children with words.

Reid, Alastair. *Ounce Dice Trice.* Boston: Little, Brown, 1958, o.p. Now available in an exemplary reprint from Gregg Press (Boston, 1979).

From the opening page dealing with sounds of words, to the closing page detailing the uses of firkydoodle fudge, the reader will be delighted with this book. The whole gamut of curious words from *ananals* to *ugwob* is included. The sensitive and sophisticated black-and-white drawings entrance the eye.

Shanker, Sidney. *Semantics: The Magic of Words.* Boston: Ginn, 1965.

A paperback with accompanying teacher's handbook and key, this brief examination of the topic provides valuable background for a teacher. Designed for the adult reader, the material included should enrich the teacher's understanding.

Spilka, Arnold. *A Rumbudgin of Nonsense.* New York: Scribner's, 1970.

A delightful collection of whimsical verse detailing the exploits of such diverse characters as the zinzerfoo, Milly O'Hooley (whose hair was unruly) and Little Miss Squinch. Children, who love to play with words, will enjoy Spilka's ability to do the same.

Waller, Leslie. *Our American Language.* New York: Holt, Rinehart and Winston, 1960.

Designed especially for young readers, this book presents a simple history beginning 2,000 years ago in England. The contribution of many countries is noted as is the growth of idioms and created words.

Webber, Hellen, illustrator. *What Is Sour?* New York: Holt, Rinehart and Winston, 1967.

A book with much visual impact, this deals with opposites and contains no words. It could be used very effectively for language development, especially with young children.

Weekley, Ernest. *The Romance of Words.* New York: Dover, 1961.

Another quality reprint of an early work, this fascinating, if at times eccentric, book is a good reference tool for the teacher. Use it to look up terms from *abet* to *zwilch*, or to learn about a variety of topics including semantics, word wanderings, homonyms, and metaphors. Also use it to whet the appetite of good readers in fifth and sixth grade.

White, Mary Sue. *Word Twins.* New York, Abingdon Press, 1961.

Illustrated in a pleasantly slap-dash manner, this four-color book introduces children to homophones—words which sound alike even though their spellings are unlike. It is useful in motivating children to think of other pairs and make up a book of their own.

Whitford, Harold C. and Robert J. Dixson. *Handbook of American Idioms and Idiomatic Usage.* New York: Regents Publishing, 1973.

Designed originally to familiarize students of English as a second language with the nonliteral constructions speakers of the language use. It has wider application, as a helpful supplementary paperback for the elementary teacher. The book includes over 5,000 entries of idioms, giving a definition and a sentence exemplifying its use.

Wildsmith, Brian. *Birds* and *Wild Animals.* New York: Franklin Watts, both 1967.

Two large and lovely collections of the usual lush and sensuous illustrations Wildsmith does so well. Digging through old books, he came up with unusual terms for groups of animals—unused now but common in other eras. A sloth of bears, an array of hedgehogs, and a skulk of foxes inhabit one book; a rafter of turkeys, an unkindness of ravens, and a congregation of plovers are among the birds. Either would launch children on a study of words.

Bibliography

Ames, Wilber S. "The Understanding Vocabulary of First-Grade Pupils." *Elementary English* (January 1964): 64–68.

Bierly, Kenneth et al. *Houghton Mifflin English*, Book 7, pp. 328–329; Book 8, pp. 207–358. Boston: Houghton Mifflin, 1983.

Ceram, C.W. *The First American.* New York: Harcourt Brace Jovanovich, 1971.

Dale, Edgar. "Vocabulary Measurement: Techniques and Major Findings." *Elementary English* (December 1965): 895–901.

Deighton, Lee C. *Vocabulary Development in the Classroom.* New York: Columbia University, Teachers College Press, 1959.

Donoghue, Mildred R. *The Child and the English Language Arts.* Dubuque, Iowa: William C. Brown, 1971.

Downing, John. "A Child-Centered Dictionary." *Elementary School Journal* (February 1972): 239—246.

Duffelmeyer, Frederick A. and Duffelmeyer, Barbara Blakely. "Developing Vocabulary through Dramatization," *Journal of Reading*, November 1979.

Fitzhugh, Louise. *Harriet the Spy.* New York: Harper & Row, 1964.

Grahame, Kenneth. *The Wind in the Willows.* New York: Scribner's, 1960.

Greet, W. Cabell et al. *In Other Words*. Chicago: Scott, Foresman, 1982.

Gwynne, Fred. *The King Who Rained*. New York: Young Readers Press, 1970.

Hale, Lucretia P. *The Peterkin Papers*. Ann Arbor: University Microfilms, 1966.

Hanson, Joan. *Antonyms. Homonyms. Homographs. Synonyms*. all: Minneapolis: Lerner Publishing Co., 1972.

Kohn, Bernice. *One Day it Rained Cats and Dogs*. New York: Coward-McCann, 1965.

Lake, Mary Louise. "First Aid for Vocabularies." *Elementary English* (November 1967): 783–784.

Lefevre, Carl A. "A Multidisciplinary Approach to Language and Reading: Some Projections." In *The Psycholinguistic Nature of the Reading Process*, edited by Kenneth S. Goodman. Detroit: Wayne State University Press, 1968.

Lionni, Leo. *Swimmy*. New York: Pantheon, 1963.

Lo Bello, Nino. "English Traffic Lingo," *Chicago Tribune*, July 20, 1980, Section 11, p. 9.

Marckwardt, Albert H. "Principal and Subsidiary Dialect Areas in the North Central States." In *Readings in Applied English Linguistics*, edited by Harold P. Allen. New York: Appleton-Century-Crofts, 1964.

McCloskey, Robert. *Homer Price*. New York: Viking, 1949.

Munnelly, Robert J. "Teach That Word Meanings are Open." *Instructor* 81(7) (March 1972): 57–58.

Neville, Emily. *It's Like This, Cat*. New York: Scholastic Book Services, 1963.

Pei, Mario. *Words in Sheep's Clothing*. New York: Hawthorn Books, 1969.

Pizer, Vernon. *Ink, Ark, and All That. How American Places Got Their Names*. New York: G.P. Putnam, 1976.

Robinett, Betty W. "Applications of Linguistics to the Teachings of Oral English." In *Readings in the Language Arts*, edited by V.D. and P.S. Anderson. New York: Macmillan, 1968.

Saltz, Rosalyn. "Children's Interpretations of Proverbs." *Language Arts*, 56(5) (May 1979): 508–514.

Shuy, Roger W. *Discovering American Dialects*. Champaign, Ill.: National Council of Teachers of English, 1967.

Steckler, Arthur. *101 More Words and How They Began*. New York: Doubleday, 1980.

Stewig, John Warren. "Planning Environments to Promote Language Growth," in *Discovering Language with Children* (Pinnell, ed.). Urbana, Ill.: National Council of Teachers of English, 1980.

Stotsky, Sandra L. "Teaching Prefixes in the Elementary School." *The Elementary School Journal* (March 1978): 278–283.

Toffler, Alvin. *Future Shock*. New York: Bantam Books, 1970.

Travers, P.L. *Mary Poppins*. New York: Reynal and Hitchcock, 1934.

Weir, Ruth H. *Language in the Crib*. London: Mouton, 1962.

Wild, Robin and Wild, Jocelyn. *Spot's Dogs and the Alley Cats*. Philadelphia: Lippincott, 1979.

GRAMMAR
AND USAGE

One might also overlook all the bad grammar,
although it is difficult not to wince at "could of
been," "hadn't ought to of," "not done nothing,"
"these cases is," and the like, on the part of college (people) seeking to enter a learned profession. I am told that the schools do not bother
greatly about grammar now, and I can readily
believe it. Perhaps it does not matter; if no one
uses grammar except the professors, (people) may
possibly do very well without it. (Prosser, 1939)

Those dismayed comments were not made last year by a
parent concerned that her child is not being taught the "basics," but rather
by a law professor bemoaning—some forty years ago—the lack of ability in
his college students. The concern over the place of grammar in the schools
continues today.

Few topics evoke quick responses on both ends of a continuum, ranging
from ill-concealed boredom and contemptuous indifference to zealous pro-
selytizing for dearly held views. Yet the word *grammar* arouses such
responses. Elementary school children respond with groans, a job applicant
thinks nervously about it, a mother nags when her child says a sentence in-
correctly. Are they all reacting to the same thing? To what does the term
grammar refer?

WHAT IS GRAMMAR?

One definition will not serve because the phenomenon it describes—
language—is so inordinately complex that complete descriptions elude even
professional linguists. The term itself is an old one, from the early Greek
gramma, a word for letter. This ancient word has earlier antecedents, in the

word *graphein*, meaning to write or draw. When pluralized, *grammata*, the word included a range of meanings from letters of the alphabet to the rudiments of writing (Dykema, 1963). Perhaps the following definitions will begin establishing the parameters of the term. The linguist May (1967) defines grammar as:

> A way of signaling; of showing relationships within a sentence; of organizing meaning. Grammar is also a collection of subconscious rules—rules of word order (syntax) and word form (morphology)—which guides us in the creation of new sentences.

Another linguist defines it as:

> The set of formal patterns in which words are arranged in order to convey larger meanings. It is not necessary that we be able to discuss these patterns self-consciously to be able to use them. In fact, all speakers of a language above the age of five or six know how to use its complex forms or organization with considerable skill; in this sense of the word, they are thoroughly familiar with its grammar. (Francis, 1964)

And still another says that grammar is:

> A set of statements saying how a language works. It includes, for example, a description of the principles for combining words to form grammatical sentences. (Langacker, 1973)

From the above, we can see the necessity of developing a multifaceted definition for a complex phenomenon.

THE GRAMMAR AND *A* GRAMMAR

If we distinguish between these two terms, a clearer understanding may result. When speaking of *the* grammar, we are referring to the structural system or organization that underlies the totality of the language. This structural system is made up of several components and controls in fairly rigorous ways the utterances possible in a language, and those which are not possible (or considered ungrammatical).

In contrast, *a* grammar is someone's (or some group's) written description of this language structure. The written description may range from simple to exceedingly complex, though one author has pointed out that even complex descriptions seldom deal completely with the language (Stageberg, 1965).

The distinction can be clarified through an example. In mathematics there is both *number*, the actual quantity itself, and *numeral*, the written description of, or symbol for, the quantity. The comparison can be made:

Number is to "the" grammar as
Numeral is to "a" grammar.

One widely respected linguist describes these two grammars in the following quotation:

> Grammar 1 [*the* grammar] is the system itself. This has everything to do with language performance; without that system the language could not exist . . . The study of grammar, . . . is the investigation of how the system operates. It is not, and never has intended to be, a miscellany of shibboleths of usage.
>
> Grammar 2 [*a* grammar] is some kind of a description and explanation of that system. This has nothing to do with language performance . . . we are able to use it without being able to explain how the system works. (Schiller, 1969)

COMPONENTS

There are many ways of writing *a* grammar of English; the most influential of these grammars will be described later. No matter what one's persuasion, it is incumbent upon any grammar-maker to describe the three basic components of language: phonology, morphology, and syntax. These are components in any language, though the nature and importance of each varies according to the language being considered.

Phonology is a first consideration because sound is basic to language. The word *phonology* means the study or science of speech sounds. It comes from the ancient Greek word *phone*, meaning voice. Any grammar will include some description of phonology, the sound system of the language. The basic sound unit is the phoneme, defined as:

> [a class] of sounds that contrast with other classes of sounds, and a single phoneme can be defined as a class of sounds whose phonetic differences are incapable of distinguishing one meaning from another. (Dineen, 1967)

Phonemes are the smallest distinctive speech sounds. In the words *dip* and *din*, the /p/ and the /n/ are identified as separate and distinct phonemes.[1]

These small speech sounds, phonemes, are also called *segmentals*, or segments of sound. There is another way we add meaning to this basic set of speech segments, through the use of *suprasegmentals*. This term refers to three ways we vary the basic segments to give more definitive meaning to speech. The three suprasegmentals in English are pitch, stress, and juncture.

Pitch refers to the different levels of sound between the highest and the lowest sounds any given speaker can make. Two speakers will have different vocal ranges, with some overlap. For example, women's voices usually have

---

[1] It is an agreed-upon linguistic convention that when writing about sounds, / / are put around the letter used to represent the sound. This indicates sounds are being talked about, *not* letters.

a higher vocal range than do men's (Figure 13-1). How the speaker changes pitches within the range is an example of pitch variation. In English we most commonly use pitch to distinguish between questions and statements, a rising pitch contour usually signaling a question.

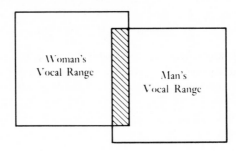

FIGURE 13-1

Stress refers to the intensity or loudness with which a word is said. There are four degrees of stress in English:

1. primary (´)
2. secondary (\ )
3. tertiary (∧)
4. weak (⌣)

Say the following sentences to yourself:

1. The invälid was difficult to care for.

2. The invalid argument presented by the speaker did not convince us.

Did you notice the difference in the way the word was stressed in each sentence? In addition to stressing speech segments (phonemes) differently, we sometimes stress entire words differently to convey meaning and indicate parts of speech. Say the following two sentences to yourself:

1. The loud speaker was defective and we couldn't hear.

2. He was a loud speaker because of an unfortunate hearing loss.

Other examples of this are given by Elkins (1974).

Juncture is the term we use for the suprasegmental which signals a transition from one phoneme to another, from one syllable to another, from one word to another, and from one sentence to another. It is the vocal element that makes it possible to distinguish between the identical segmental sounds in the following pairs of sentences:

430

1. The *night rate* for sending telegrams is very reasonable.
2. The presence of *nitrate* in the compound was disturbing to the scientist.

1. The *ice cream* melted before the diners had finished the main course.
2. "*I scream* loudly," Sara said, "but no one ever listens!"

Juncture is one of several components of grammar which Schroth (1978) feels can be taught to children by using the writings of Dr. Seuss. Despite the usefulness of Schroth's suggestions, the complete understanding of phonology is very complex; indeed, many universities offer a sequence of courses dealing only with this one aspect of grammar. While it is impossible in this chapter to offer anything approximating a complete description, additional reading will help further your understanding of this facet of language.

Morphology is another component of the grammar of a language. The term has roots in the early Greek word *morphē*, which means form. English words have a distinctive morphological, or form, system that can be taught to children.

Morphemes, the basic unit in morphology, are the smallest meaning-bearing units of language. In the word "goats," there are two morphemes, goat and -s. The example illustrates that there are two types of morphemes:

1. *free*, e.g., the word goat appears independently and carries meaning.
2. *bound*, e.g., the -s does not appear independently, though it does carry meaning: the idea of plural.

Other bound morphemes include the -'s and -s' attached to nouns, the -s, -ed, and -ing attached to verbs, the -est attached to adjectives, and the -er attached to adverbs. In each case, these bound morphemes signify meaning, though they never appear independently (Ross & Ross, 1973).

You can see that while free morphemes are virtually limitless, bound morphemes are limited in number. Though we can and do make up new words, the number of bound morphemes and their meanings remain relatively constant. Some authors of elementary series have devised imaginative ways to present this concept to children (Easton & Klein, 1981).

Syntax, the third large component of language, is the word order in sentences. The origin of the word comes through the French *syntaxe* from the Greek word *tassein* which means to arrange or put in order.

English, a word-order or distributive language, offers flexibility of this word order, but not as much flexibility as other languages called inflectional languages. Latin provides a clear contrast. In Latin, it makes no difference whether one says: "*Puer puellam amat*," or "*Puellam puer amat*." The meaning is identical, i.e., The boy loves the girl. This is because the endings or inflected forms at the ends of the words tell us who is doing what and to whom. The order, or syntax, is unimportant.

The same is not true of English. Because English is a positional language, there is a considerable difference between: "The girl ate the hamburger," and "The hamburger ate the girl."

Though all languages are made up of these components, in some, one component is more important than the rest. For example, in Vietnamese (as in other Eastern languages) the direction of the pitch signals meaning. One small two-letter word can mean six different things, depending on how the pitch is manipulated.

$\overrightarrow{ma}$	$\overset{\nearrow}{má}$	$\overset{\searrow}{ma}$
(ghost)	(cheek)	(but)
$\overset{\nearrow}{ma}$	ma	ma
(tomb)	(horse)	(rice-seedling)

For English speakers, unused to such subtle meaning-bearing pitch indicators, learning such a language is difficult. We are used to different meaning signals.

Usage

Often people mistakenly use the term grammar when they are in fact referring to the choices individuals make between two possible alternatives for a particular position in a sentence. We can say either "I brung the teacher an apple," or "I brought the teacher an apple." About such choices, one author said:

> The dialect of some groups of people includes "brung" as the past tense of bring. Since these two words have equal signaling power, i.e., they both signal the past tense of bring, they are both grammatically "correct." Yet, to most of us only one of them seems proper and elegant. (May, 1967)

Such a choice is one of usage and does not represent a grammatical error. One may affirm that it is an error; in fact, most standard English speakers would think so. Nonetheless, it is crucial to remember it is a usage, not a grammatical, issue.

Other usage choices include:

"I ain't going," or
"I am not going."
"May I use the car?" or
"Can I use the car?"

The whole issue of usage choices is a very emotional one because people, especially those who have made a conscious effort to improve their language, tend to look down upon those who have not.

Like it or not, language is one way American society makes class distinctions, and less-acceptable usage choices are heavily penalized by those in power. Attitudes about usage are slow to change, though students of language point out that change is occurring. The rate may change, depending on social conditions. During the decade of the 1960s, nonstandard forms were more widely accepted than they are today, when arbiters of the language are calling for more attention to "correct" language (Newman, 1976; Safire, 1980).

Perhaps one of the most helpful changes is the increasing use of the term *non*standard English, to substitute for *sub*standard. Though the difference may not be readily apparent, considerable philosophical difference exists between them.

The older term, *substandard*, suggested a hierarchy in which standard English was at the top, and all variants were below, and thus inferior to it.

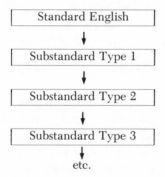

Linguists, and particularly those interested in studying language variations (dialectologists) believe that the term *nonstandard* indicates a different concept of ordering.

Rather than implying or stating the value position that there is one standard to be attained, this position says that several variants of equal worth in different settings are possible.[2]

---

[2]One author has stated that while attitudes in this area are changing among language students, little change has occurred among speakers of English, as most still view variants as inferior to standard English. See Phillip S. Dale, *Language Development* (New York: Holt, Rinehart and Winston, 1976), pp. 271–273. This section on sociolinguistics includes much of interest to teachers.

The question of what schools should do about helping children improve their usage has been debated hotly, and cannot be settled here, though Chapter 14, on language for the culturally divergent, delineates the issue clearly.

The problem faced by the elementary teacher is: What usage problems are important enough to deserve attention? Within a limited amount of time available, which should be the subject of individual or small-group work?

Any teacher who has tried it will tell you it is difficult to make even minor changes in a child's usage. This is easy to understand if you keep in mind:

1. Kindergarten children have spent between four and six years of total immersion in their home culture and language; language habits are well established and difficult to change.
2. Even the school-age child continues to spend the major portion of waking hours in the home-language environment. He or she may spend a maximum of six hours at school, compared to at least ten waking hours at home.
3. Often there are psychological reasons why children are uninterested in changing usage patterns. Family and peer groups may exert a tremendous inhibiting force against usage change.
4. Much of the practice experienced in school will have been ineffective. Usage drill consists, for the most part, of the written exercises prescribed by language textbooks.

The problem is not simplified by the approach taken in too many elementary language arts materials. These tend to take a "scattergun" approach and give minimal attention to a wide variety of problems. One thing we know for certain about children's usage problems is that they will not yield to a one-page written drill. Despite this, language arts books are filled with such drills.

Another reason the teacher must use such materials discriminatingly is that even today they frequently prescribe fine points of usage unrelated to the real world of communication.

One recent elementary series includes the following:

May and *Can*
Do You Remember?
   May is used to mean "be permitted to."
   May is also used to mean "have a chance to."
   Can is generally used to mean "to be able to."

While it may be of use for some adults to make this distinction, to recommend that the elementary teacher take up children's time with such is indeed a mistake.

Another series recommends some even finer distinctions in its sixth-grade book.

"Who-o-om, who-o-om?"

D. Hand in the Christian Science Monitor © *TCSPS*

Are you aware of the following *Do's* and *Don'ts?* Careful speakers—

DON'T	DO
1. Say: What *kind of a* car he drive?	1. Say: *What kind* of car does he drive?
2. Say: I *sort of* thought you would go.	2. Say: I *rather* thought you would go.
3. Say: I was *kind* of tired.	3. Say: I was *somewhat* tired.

How the authors decided that the usages included in the recommended column are representative of standard English is difficult to determine. Further, suggesting that item 2 or item 3 in the "Do" column are desirable for young children, exposes the authors' lack of contact with the way normal children speak.

A further distinction the book recommends is the following:

this and *these* refer to nearby things.
that and *those* refer to things farther away.

As a result, saying "Bill likes *those* kinds of shoes," is incorrect if one is pointing to some on a rack near you. Is such a distinction any longer a functioning part of English? It is difficult to believe that such is the case.

Even methods books for teachers are not immune to such dreamlike speculation about the way language ought to be.[3] The following example is taken from a book published by a widely known language expert.

Of and *from*
The prepositions of and *from* are never used with the adverb *off* such as:
   "The men jumped *off* the boat." (correct)
   "The men jumped *off of* the boat." (incorrect)

   "The men jumped *off* the log." (correct)
   "The men jumped *from off* the log." (incorrect)

Such distinctions as these are difficult if not impossible to defend, simply on the basis of common oral usage. The first example is obviously irrelevant in other than literary written English at this time. The form labeled incorrect is, in fact, in widespread use. The second example labeled incorrect could certainly occur in response to a question. For example, "Where did the men jump from?" While the second example may be less acceptable to language purists, it is certainly arbitrary to label it as incorrect. In the final analysis, neither is worth the time of elementary school children.

A problem related to overly prescriptive elementary texts is the teacher's own perceptions of error. What is acceptable to teachers does not always coincide with which is acceptable to professional authors and editors. Green and Petty (1975) refer to a group of studies dating to 1949, which bear out this point. Usages rated unacceptable by teachers are often in fact judged acceptable by those who make their living using the language.

Realistic Approaches to Usage

Many of the above recommendations, found in materials currently widely used, seem unrealistic to classroom teachers. The materials attempt to teach children some very fine distinctions of language usage that may be of value to a small segment of the adult population but are of questionable usefulness to most children.

Thus, the first thing teachers must do is to examine critically what resources are provided in the school to which they can turn *if* they are appropriate. Once you develop this attitude toward the materials, begin at the best place to begin—the children's oral speech.

Diagnosis of children's usage errors is important and must be done in a variety of speech situations. Listen carefully, at first in a general way, and pick out the most common usage errors made by the group as a whole. Jot

---

[3]This appellation is applied to much grammar teaching by James C. Bostain, in "The Dream World of English Grammar," *NEA Journal* 55 (September 1966): 20–22. He makes careful distinctions between valid grammatical knowledge and equally useful, but different, social knowledge gained by understanding usage differences.

these down. At the end of a week or so review your list and note which errors are the most serious. Once you have established some priorities, make a more specific diagnosis to determine which children make the usage errors you have focused upon. Note down these errors on a simple checklist, such as Figure 13-2.

Usage Error Incidence

Type	Alice	Tim	Margy	Sara	Tom	Roger	Alan	Joyce	Bob
he done									
this here									
she don't									
he was									
brung									
ain't got none									
has took									
they knowed									

FIGURE 13-2

The next step is to organize the children into small skill groups, to provide intensive practice in drill on a particular usage error. Because problems of this nature are most pronounced in speech, the drill is oral with less attention given to written practice. The skill group meets together, drilling in a variety of ways, until the teacher feels the children have mastered the particular problem usage. Then the group is disbanded.

Many children may need work of some nature, and this intensive oral practice in small groups results in more improvement in usage than do several years of occasional written practice.

All of the foregoing is based on a tacit assumption that you, the teacher, identify problems, form groups, direct practice, and make corrections with *tact*. An implicit understanding, which governs any attempt to modify usage, is that it is done by teachers who respect the integrity of the child. Though some teachers feel any attempts to modify usage are in fact criticisms of the child, one authority reacts this way: "Constructive suggestions about a youngster's talk—when offered with considerateness and sensitivity—won't undermine self-esteem" (Work, 1981).

Usage is the child's language at work. But what of his or her *under-*

standing of the language and how it works? There are wide differences of opinion about how much, if any, understanding a child needs to have about the inner workings and structure of the language. Eloquent statements have been made by those who claim with accuracy that a child can be enviably fluent with no understanding of how language works. Equally eloquent statements have been made by those who feel a conscious understanding of the grammar of language is important. In the following section we shall examine three ways to describe *the* grammar, or the structural system of English, and some suggestions about how to teach grammatical ideas to children.

TRADITIONAL GRAMMAR[4]

Many who read this will have grown up with what is commonly called traditional, or *prescriptive*, grammar, while a few readers will have had the unusual experience of studying one of the other two types described later.

Traditional grammar, with deep roots going back many hundreds of years, is nomothetic. That is, it attempts to tell people, or prescribe, how they should speak. Originally based on Latin models, this type of grammar is concerned with categorizing sentences according to their purposes and words according to their classes, among other more technical considerations. Some of the earliest grammars of English, including those of Jesperson, Curme, Poutsma, and Kruisinga, were lengthy analyses. These were not taught to children, but ideas from them were adapted by textbook writers.

Of course, no school attempted to teach these extensive and highly sophisticated treatments in toto. Instead, a variety of interpreters produced what are called *school grammars*, which diluted and often distorted scholarly efforts. Chisholm (1969) commented trenchantly:

> Adaptation is really not the right word; bastardization would be fairer, if severer. For the most part they were faulty representations of careful traditional-historical technique . . . presented frequently with gross oversimplifications and . . . the good in them was usually obscured by irrelevant and trivial sections on good manners on the telephone and decorum in the library. . . .

One aspect of traditional grammar, diagraming sentences to uncover underlying structural/syntactical relationships, has been a part of many children's English experiences in school. This is true, despite the fact that quite conclusive evidence exists that such exercises have no demonstrable relationship to effective speaking or writing (Sherwin, 1969). For a while,

---

[4]A more complete detailing of the nature of traditional grammar and the problems it presents is included in John R. Searles, *Structural and Traditional Grammar* (Oshkosh: Wisconsin Council of Teachers of English, 1965), 1–20.

school grammars were free of such exercises, but unfortunately recent revisions of some commercial materials have mistakenly reincluded this activity, in an effort to convince parent pressure groups that they are indeed teaching the "basics."

STRUCTURAL GRAMMAR

The year 1933 marked a significant change in direction in grammatical descriptions by professional linguists. That year a leading linguist published a book destined to have profound effects on the work of many scholars for several decades. Leonard Bloomfield, and other structural linguists who followed him, emphasized the importance of studying spoken language. This is a major difference between structural linguists and traditional linguists who are more concerned with written language.

A second major difference between the two approaches is that structural linguistics is *descriptive* rather than prescriptive. Instead of beginning with a written description of how people *should* speak and searching for examples, the structuralists often begin with a corpus of material (recorded speech) and derive from this a description of how people *do* speak. Unlike traditional grammarians, structural linguists are uninterested in making value judgments about how people should speak. Rather, with the dispassionate attitude of a scientist, they study a natural phenomenon so they can record their observations.

Structural linguists have concerned themselves with *sentence patterns*, though there is not universal agreement among them as to the number of patterns that exist.[5] A sample pattern is N V Adj (The tree seems scrawny). The most common sentence patterns include:

Pattern One: NV (Noun and verb)
   This is the simplest, most basic pattern in English, e.g., Girls sew. Children are playing. Common variations include: NVA (Noun, verb, adjective), e.g., The door slammed shut; and NVAd (Noun, verb, adverb), e.g., She sang sadly.
Pattern Two: NVN (Noun, verb, noun complement)
   This also is a very common pattern, e.g., The girls drank lemonade. Mary eats candy.
Pattern Three: NVNN (Noun, verb, noun, noun)
   The girls call the dog Oscar, or Alice gave the chickens corn. A variation of this pattern is NVNA, e.g., They stained the house brown.
Pattern Four: NLvN, NLvA, and NLvAD (Noun, linking verb and noun, adjective or adverb). Mary is a singer. The girls are intelligent. Tom is away.

---

[5]For a concise explanation of how this idea can be taught, see Verna L. Newsome, *Structural Grammar in the Classroom* (Oshkosh: Wisconsin Council of Teachers of English, 1961), 12–16. Though Newsome's approach is for children in sixth grade and above, her explanation is of help in increasing the teacher's competency in this area.

The above patterns have been presented as though they are the only recognized ones. Such is not the case, for in this, as in many aspects of linguistics, there is some difference of opinion. In examining the work of several structuralists, we find the number of sentence patterns given varies from four (Lefevre & Lefevre, 1965) to ten (Roberts, 1962).

In addition to sentence patterns, structuralists are also interested in word classes, or parts of speech. Rather than relying on traditional means of determining parts of speech, they have evolved an approach using *slot* and *filler* technique. Sentence, or test frames are created with a word missing. All the words which can fit into the slot, or blank space, belong to that word class, or part of speech.

A noun is a word like *vase* in a sentence: The green (*vase*) is broken.
An adjective is a word like *tall* in the sentence: The (*tall*) tree is blighted.
A verb is a word like *ran* in the sentence: The dog (*ran*).
An adverb is a word like *sadly* in the sentence: The girl returned home very (*sadly*).

Structuralists are quick to remind us that this one test is not definitive in determining word class. Some words that do belong in a particular class will not fit in the examples given above. More than one test to determine word class is often necessary.

Nouns as a class are defined quite differently than the conventional definition of "a person, place, or thing." It is readily apparent that this definition is so loose as to be almost useless for teaching purposes, especially for young children. The "or thing" part of the definition contributes to much misunderstanding when children try to work with the definition. Structuralists, in contrast, would define a noun in the following ways:

1. It inflects following certain predictable patterns, e.g., nouns are words which accept -s, -'s, and -s'.
2. It is preceded by particular function words, like determiners, e.g., a, an, one. (Hamp, 1979)
3. It occupies certain positions in a sentence, e.g., between a determiner and a verb, in the slot and filler construction, a _____ ran.
4. It is formed by the addition of certain derivational suffixes to adjective forms, e.g., add -ness to roots like kind and bold.
5. It sometimes is indicated by a contrast in accent pattern with a similar word in another class, e.g., "I suspect we go," as contrasted with "The suspect was in jail."

Many structuralist concepts are currently included in elementary text series material for children. For example, word forms and position can be taught to intermediate-grade children. This can be done using real words or nonsense words (Johnson, 1979).

TRANSFORMATIONAL GRAMMAR

A more recent development in grammar description was evolved by two linguists, Zellig Harris and Noam Chomsky.[6] Their work provided the impetus for development of a new direction and fostered much writing and some research.

Transformational linguists believe there are two kinds of sentences:

Kernel sentences, which are a relatively small number of basic sentence types which form the core of grammar. These cannot be derived from any other sentences or sentence types underlying them.

Transformed sentences, which are formed, using kernel sentences as a base, by applying a series of transform rules that give direction for changing, adding, deleting, substituting, and combining basic, or kernel sentences.

These transform rules, commonly written in a conventionalized notation system, range from very simple, e.g.:[7]

$$S \rightarrow N P + V P,$$

to very complex, e.g.:[8]

$$\text{Aux} \rightarrow \text{tense} + (M) + (\text{have}) + (\text{Part.}) + (\text{be} + \text{ing}).$$

A complete understanding of transformational grammar is beyond the capabilities of young children, but some less complex aspects of the approach are being taught. The underlying assumptions of the system include:

1. There is a finite number of basic kernel sentence types and transform rules, but an infinite number of variations or actual sentences which can be made, or generated, as a result of using the transform rules.[9]

---

[6]A statement of the principles of this approach to grammar is Chomsky's *Syntactic Structures* (The Hague, Netherlands: Mouton, 1957). An admittedly difficult to read, technical discussion of the original theory underlying transformational grammar, this book is historically important.

[7]The notation reads: "Sentence is rewritten as noun phrase plus verb phrase." The arrow is standard linguistic notation for: is made from, consists of, or is rewritten as.

[8]Example is taken from Paul Roberts, *The Roberts English Series* (New York: Harcourt Brace Jovanovich, 1970), Teacher's Edition for the Sixth Book, p. 34, which was an innovative attempt to introduce linguistic concepts in a systematic fashion to children.

[9]This use of the term generate, or generation, to make or create using a basic kernel sentence, illustrates why this approach to grammar is sometimes called transformational-generative grammar.

For example, if we take the transform rule, which is *finite*,

NP → DAN (determiner, adjective, noun),

we can generate an *infinite* number of actual sentences from this rule.

2. Everyone possesses an understanding of this process because even young children each day generate many sentences they have never heard before. They know the rules intuitively and use them in creating new sentences.

Despite the enthusiasm with which linguists have espoused this grammatical description, there are some linguists who raise questions about its validity (Derwing, 1973).

In the last decade, teachers serving on textbook selection committees had to choose which of the three approaches they wished to teach. Today, however, teachers examining current elementary language arts textbooks will soon realize that most do not present either the traditional, structural, or transformational points of view alone. Rather, the approach recently has been to adopt an eclectic stance, incorporating some elements of each of these grammatical descriptions into the texts. Unfortunately, with loud and too often uninformed public outcries for return to the "basics," however poorly defined, publishers are tending to allow traditional grammar to crowd out structural and transformational ideas.

EVEN NEWER APPROACHES

One aspect of linguistics, which makes it exciting to professionals and intimidating to the uninformed, is the rate at which new knowledge is being discovered and new ideas generated. Linguists are theorizing, writing, and experimenting constantly. Such new ideas as tagmemics (Lefevre, 1970), stratificational grammar,[10] and case grammar (Slobin, 1979) are being developed. Will these new formulations eventually be adapted to the elementary school, as structural and transformational ideas have been? It is too early to tell, but this exciting area of English is apt to continue to be one in which much is happening.

IS GRAMMAR TEACHING USEFUL?

To answer this question, another must be considered first: What is the *purpose* of teaching grammar to children? As pointed out in Chapter 2, until one identifies both purposes and underlying assumptions, it is difficult to

---

[10]Most grammatical descriptions have to this point been limited to the sentence, or smaller units. A truly adequate description must give attention to units larger than the sentences; stratificational grammar attempts to do this. The description in Lefevre, *Linguistics, English and the Language Arts*, pp. 330–331 is intelligible to novices.

determine effectiveness of any educational idea. Two reasons are often given for teaching grammar to children.

1. Because grammar exists, it can be and should be studied. Like geography or physics, a body of knowledge exists in linguistics, of intrinsic interest if it is clearly and systematically presented to the learner, at whatever age. Despite the stance of elementary language arts textbook writers and publishers, professional linguists will continue to seek more effective ways to describe our language.

2. Improvement in speaking and writing is, logically enough, often given as a reason for teaching grammar. Conscious knowledge of the structure of language is a means of improving oral and written compositions. Despite the logic, such improvement does not seem to result.[11] Research studies done, beginning with one by Hoyt in 1906, suggest that this reason for grammar teaching must be discounted.[12]

The studies mentioned above examine the relationship between knowledge of formal, or traditional, grammar and the expressive arts of writing and speaking. There is certainly the possibility that research examining the relationship between these arts and the newer structural and transformational grammars may well discover some cause and effect relationship. The influence of structural and transformational grammar in schools is as yet too new to have resulted in a significant body of research (Marquart, 1968).

CLASSROOM APPLICATIONS

Until researchers' findings suggest instructional strategies more clearly, many teachers will remain uncertain about what to do regarding grammar. While it is difficult to justify a full-scale attempt to teach a grammatical system to children, there are many ideas which can be borrowed from linguists for use in classrooms. These ideas are of interest to children, and exposure to them often results in beneficial understandings about language.

Children can experiment with the *slot and filler technique* borrowed from structural grammar to show the idea of word class. The teacher prepares flash cards with words of different classes (Murray, 1975). Several children take these word cards which can be arranged to make a sentence. The

---

[11]Though students do get better at grammar exercises, such exercises do not lead to significantly better speaking or writing. A summary of research studies is included in Harry A. Greene and Walter T. Petty, *Developing Language Skills in the Elementary Schools* (Boston: Allyn & Bacon, 1975), pp. 37–38.

[12]Franklin S. Hoyt, "Studies in English Grammar," *Teachers College Record*, November 1906, 7, 467–500. Hoyt compared the written compositions of two groups of children (one of which had two years' drill on formal grammar, the other had none). The groups were equal in compositional ability. Later studies by Rapeer (1913), Boraas (1917), and Asker (1923) confirmed Hoyt's findings.

children stand in the front of the room with their cards forming a sentence. After the sentence is made, one child steps out of line. The teacher asks who has a card that will fit into the slot. This child becomes the filler. Then the teacher sees if anyone else has another word that will fit. This can be repeated several times. The activity can lead into a discussion of what the words which fit into a particular slot have in common. Another approach to this idea is described by Scott (1968), who reports his experiment teaching first-grade children the word classes by manipulating blocks.

Other morphological aspects of English can also be studied in quasi-game formats, even by young children. Ashby-Davis suggests an imaginative approach to helping students study comparative and superlative forms of the adjective.[13]

The idea of transformation of basic, or kernel, sentences can be taught to children. Given a kernel sentence, e.g., "The dog chewed on his bone," children can transform it in a variety of ways.

1. It can be made passive:
   The bone was chewed on by the dog.
2. It can be made an active question:
   Did the dog chew on his bone?
3. It can be made a passive question:
   Was the bone chewed on by the dog?
4. It can be made negative:
   The dog did not chew on his bone.
5. It can be made a negative question:
   Didn't the dog chew on his bone?
6. It can be made an emphatic statement:
   The dog did chew on his bone.

Note that the transforms do not change the tense, but only the form of the sentence. There are other, more complex, transforms which do change tense and other aspects of kernel sentences. May (1980, p. 120) gives a very complete list of these.

Another technique children enjoy and from which they learn is that of *expansion*. Any kernel sentence can be expanded in a variety of ways. One approach to expansion is suggested by Wolfe (1972), who says the technique can either be done orally, or the children may write their responses. He suggests children take a simple (or kernel) sentence and ask themselves several questions, in the following manner:

---

[13]Ashby-Davis, Claire. "Popular Media and Reading: Television Commercials." In *Drama News*, Spring 1980, 3(1), 2–3. The newsletter, published by the drama special interest group of the International Reading Association, presents practical ideas for integrating the arts through language.

SENTENCE: I bought something.

1. *When* did you buy it?
   I bought it yesterday.
2. *What* did you buy?
   I bought a pencil yesterday.
3. Can you add a *color* word?
   I bought a yellow pencil yesterday.
4. Can you tell *where*?
   I bought a yellow pencil yesterday at the grocery store.
5. Can you *reverse* the word order?
   Yesterday, at the grocery store, I bought a yellow pencil.

With older children who have had some experience with sentence parts and their functions, a slightly different approach can be used:

SENTENCE: The girl sang a song.

1. Expanding the noun phrase:
   The large girl sang a song.
2. Expanding the verb phrase:
   The girl sang a song very loudly.
3. Expanding both the subject and the predicate:
   The dark haired girl sang a song in a very raspy voice.
4. Expanding through coordinating:
   The girl *and* the boy sang a song and did a dance.
5. Expanding through subordinating:
   Because the girl sang the song, several people left the hall in a hurry.

In this exercise, as in many others, the sentences given are samples and not the *one* right answer for which a teacher should strive. There are many possible alternatives to most of these processes.

The purpose of the above techniques is to show children the flexibility and richness of language. It is widely agreed that the major difference between skilled and unskilled communicators is their ability to say what they want to say in more than one way (Loban, 1963). Rather than being locked into the first way they say something, those children who are fluent speakers and writers seem to be able to recast their thoughts in several ways. Conscious instruction in transformation and expansion should help develop this fluency. Other ideas for expanding sentences are given by Heilman and Holmes (1972) in a book notable for the many practical classroom ideas it includes.

The idea of sentence *movables*, an aspect of syntax, can be explored. It is true, as mentioned earlier, that because English is a word-order language, fewer syntactic arrangements are possible than with other languages. Despite this, many sentences in English can be arranged more than one way.

Adverbs, for example, can frequently be located in several different slots. Such multiple positions allow for stylistic variations.

> Fortunately, the girls were able to maintain happy relations with the villagers.
> The girls, fortunately, were able to maintain happy relations with the villagers.
> The girls were, fortunately, able to maintain happy relations with the villagers.
> The girls were able, fortunately, to maintain happy relations with the villagers.
> The girls were able to maintain, fortunately, happy relations with the villagers.
> The girls were able to maintain happy relations with the villagers, fortunately.

Each of the above creates a slightly different effect because of the sentence order. This example of an adult sentence has counterparts on a child's level as seen in the Nebraska Curriculum (1966).

Another idea borrowed from linguistics is *sentence combining*, which can be done by grade school children at all levels. Most elementary language arts series have begun including such exercises. See, for example, Wiggins and Peterson (1979). These activities are particularly helpful for children who write short, choppy sentences strung together with "and's." We might take some sentences from *The Story of Ferdinand* (Leaf, 1936).

> His name was Ferdinand.
> He sat down in the bull ring.
> He liked to smell flowers.

Children can combine these sentences in many ways. Some possibilities include:

1. In the bull ring Ferdinand, who liked to smell flowers, sat down.
2. Ferdinand, who liked to smell flowers, sat down in the bull ring.
3. Ferdinand liked to smell flowers. He sat down in the bull ring.
4. A bull who liked to smell flowers sat down in the bull ring. His name was Ferdinand.
5. His name was Ferdinand and he liked to smell flowers. He sat down in the bull ring.

There is some evidence that, with seventh-graders, such experiences in sentence combining result in significant gains in syntactic maturity and reading comprehension (Smart & Ollila, 1978). Ney (1980) has summarized several other studies about sentence combining.

SUMMARY

Grammatical descriptions of English can be taught and learned by elementary school children. Traditional grammar has been taught, with indifferent results, to decades of children. Now, newer approaches, drawn from the work of structural and transformational grammarians, are being introduced into the elementary curriculum. This takes place primarily through the commercial language arts series, most of which incorporate ideas from all three grammatical descriptions, in an attempt to provide an eclectic approach. Most recently, traditional grammar descriptions have tended to crowd out newer approaches.

There is no doubt that children *can* study and learn traditional grammar as well as the newer structural and transformational grammars. Should they? This is a larger philosophical question, requiring that groups of teachers think deeply about purposes. Why should children study the nature of their languages? Are there better things for them to be doing during the limited amount of time they spend in schools? It would be folly for a writer to prescribe what an individual school system ought to do, without knowing intimately the nature of that system.

Such philosophical questions are absolutely essential if groups of teachers are to make informed curriculum decisions. Perhaps the questions raised above suggest another which can help lead teachers out of a yes/no decision concerning grammar teaching. A more critical question probably is: How much, and what kind of grammar, for which children and when? An assertion contained in an important British publication provides a context for considering this issue:

> Formal study of grammar will have little place in the primary school, since active and imaginative experience and use of the language should precede attempts to analyze grammatically how language behaves. (Central Advisory Council, 1967)

Perhaps the information presented in this chapter will help you when you are asked to be on a curriculum committee confronted with such questions.

Suggestions for Further Exploration

1. Read some of the new linguistic prescriptivists (see Newman and Safire in the Bibliography). In what specific ways are their recommendations different than your own use of oral or written language?
2. Several definitions of the word *grammar*, varying in different respects, were included in the chapter. Examine a number of elementary series for children to see if and how these explain this term.

3. Visit a classroom and listen to the children's speech, keeping a tally of the types of usage errors you hear. Tabulate the frequency of these: which are the most common?
4. Try teaching the idea of expansion or transformation to a group of children. Have another student who can serve as observer work with you. How did the children respond to the idea? What, if anything, was difficult about the concept?
5. Find several children's books that provide sentences to use in the combining process explained in the chapter. Try them out with a group of children to see how many variations can be created using this process.
6. One author has identified eight basic sentence patterns. See Catheryn Eisenhardt, *Applying Linguistics in the Teaching of Reading and the Language Arts* (Columbus, Ohio: Charles E. Merrill, 1972). How do these eight compare or contrast with the patterns described in the chapter?

Suggestions for Further Reading

Algeo, John. "Grammar: A Contemporary View of What Should be Taught." *NAASP Bulletin*, April 1981, 12–17.

The "back to basics" movement has produced new interest in the teaching of grammar. Algeo comments that grammars which distinguish between language options can provide the "traffic rules" of English. Reasons for teaching grammar include: (a) to change usage; (b) to expand the range of grammatical structures students use; (c) to provide a language for talking about writing; and (d) to help students understand how language works. He then describes the three major types of grammar taught and concludes with a brief section on teaching strategies.

Clapp, Ouida H. "Why Color It White?" *Instructor*, October 1970, *80*, 74–75.

The author comments on the controversy surrounding the question of black children's speech and lists some differences between that speech and standard English. She draws attention to the built-in racism underlying bidialectical language programs and makes suggestions for teachers whose black children speak nonstandard English.

Keipe, Ashtoreth and Wood, Roger. "A Comparative Study of Achievement between a Linguistics Program of Generative Transform Grammar and a Traditional Program of Grammar." *Elementary English*, April 1970, *47*, 535–539.

An attempt was made to determine which grammatical description leads to more growth in English and reading achievement. The study was limited by a small sample size (59 students) and a short (four months) treatment time. There were no significant differences in the gains made by groups.

Keyser, Samuel J. "The Role of Linguistics in the Elementary School Curriculum." *Elementary English*, January 1970, *47*, 39–45.

Keyser contends that grammar study could lead children to make, critically examine, and reformulate hypotheses about language, surely a far cry from typical activity in language classes today. Sample lesson plans are included. The author asserts that linguistic information is available to all, thus teachers should be able to plan lessons of this nature despite the lack of commercial materials.

Kreidler, Charles W. "The Influence of Linguistics in School Grammar." *The Linguistic Reporter* (Newsletter of the Center for Applied Linguistics), December 1966, 8(6).

A short article dealing with discrepancies between the Latinate description of our language and newer linguistic approaches. The author describes the work of the NCTE in encouraging language scholarships and the problems of writers in working with publishers. Over 20 linguistic materials for children are analyzed.

Lamb, Pose M. *Linguistics in Proper Perspective.* Columbus, Ohio: Charles E. Merrill, 1977.

A conscientious attempt to interpret for classroom teachers linguistic terminology and thought. The book is especially good for the reader with little or no background. The chapters on the relation of linguistics to reading, spelling, and grammar should be of help to many teachers.

Lefevre, Carl A. "A Multidisciplinary Approach to Language and Reading: Some Projections." In *The Psychological Nature of the Reading Process*, edited by Kenneth S. Goodman. Detroit: Wayne State University Press, 1968, 289–312.

The author raises the question about whether the newer linguistic diagrams and notation may not simply be a new form of pedantic busywork. While these may be of interest to scholars, their usefulness for children is questioned. Lefevre considers the question in a dispassionate manner.

Mehta, Ved. "Onward and Upward with the Arts: John Is Easy to Please." *The New Yorker*, May 8, 1971, 47, 44–48.

A combination of chatty anecdote and scholarly analysis presenting a many-sided view of the life and thought of Noam Chomsky, a leading transformationalist. Supportive but not adulatory, the article describes the arguments Chomsky's ideas have provoked.

Mountain, Lee Harrison. "Telling Parents about Transformational Grammar." *Elementary English*, May 1972, 49, 684–687.

A markedly creative analogy comparing this grammar system with packing clothes in a suitcase. In short compass the author explains, in a fashion designed to intrigue middle-grade children and their parents, a rather complex grammatical description.

Pike, Kenneth. "A Linguistic Contribution to Composition: A Hypothesis." *College Composition and Communication*, May 1964, 15, 82–88.

Another statement appears in October 1964, pp. 129–135. The two articles summarize tagmemic theory with suggestions for teaching composition and literature, including sample exercises for students.

Rycenga, John A. "Understanding Linguistics." *Catholic School Journal*, June 1967, *67*, 27–31.

A comprehensible summary of several complex ideas. The ground covered is considerable: from the work of Rask (1818) through the current transformational grammarians. The linguistics reading program appended should be invaluable to teachers.

Shugrue, Michael F. *How the "New English" Will Help Your Child.* New York: Association Press, 1966.

A helpful book to use with groups of parents who may be unclear about why the English their children learn is so unlike what they themselves learned. It describes with clarity and brevity not only several different linguistic descriptions but also usage and the relations between these components.

Sklar, Robert. "Chomsky's Revolution in Lingustics." *The Nation*, September 9, 1968, *207*, 213–217.

A very thorough review of Chomsky's ideas and the book in which they are presented. Written in nontechnical language, this thoughtful analysis provides an accessible introduction to the works of a leading linguistic scholar.

Thomas, Owen. *Transformational Grammar and the Teacher of English.* New York: Holt, Rinehart and Winston, 1965.

The author's emphasis is on teaching, rather than theoretical concerns. His purpose is to present those aspects of transformational grammar which have the greatest usefulness to teachers and future teachers. The explanations are clear and numerous illustrations are given.

Wilson, Sloan. "Why Jessie Hates English." *Saturday Review*, September 18, 1976, 11–13.

Father of a voracious reader who writes often and well, Wilson here describes the reasons his child dislikes the English program in her school. Disparaging remarks about the Madison Avenue, superslick visual techniques used to sugarcoat an intensive dose of grammar, begin the article. Wilson goes on to denounce the lack of fine literature as only brief "snippets" of recognized writers are included. Page after page of dismal grammar exercises and tests are offered, and the author claims he could not pass most of them, despite earning his living as a writer. He contends that terminology (derivational suffix, subjective completion, terminal clusters, and chain linking) is irrelevant to producing effective child communicators. He concludes: "The fact that it is necessary to learn to speak and write grammatically does not mean that one must devote much time to the abstract study of grammar."

Bibliography

Bloomfield, Leonard. *Language.* New York: Henry Holt, 1933.

Central Advisory Council for Education. *Children and Their Primary Schools* (The Plowden Report), Vols. 1 & 2. London: Her Majesty's Stationery Office, 1967, p. 612.

Chisholm, William S. *The New English.* New York: Funk & Wagnalls, 1969.

Derwing, Bruce L. *Transformational Grammar as a Theory of Language Acquisition*. Cambridge: The University Press, 1973.

Dinnen, Francis P., S.J. *An Introduction to General Linguistics*. New York: Holt, Rinehart and Winston, 1967.

Dykema, Karl. "Where Our Language Came From." In *Perspectives on Language*, edited by Rycenga & Schwartz. New York: The Ronald Press, 1963, 98–111.

Easton, Lois Brown and Klein, Marvin. *Expressways*. Oklahoma City: The Economy Co., Book 6, 1981.

Elkins, William R. *A New English Primer. An Introduction to Linguistic Concepts and Systems*. New York: St. Martin's Press, 1974, 9–10.

Francis, W. Nelson. "Revolution in Grammar." In *Readings in Applied Linguistics*, edited by Harold Allen. New York: Appleton-Century-Crofts, 1964, 69.

Greene, Harry A. and Petty, Walter T. *Developing Language Skills in the Elementary Schools*. Boston: Allyn & Bacon, 1975.

Hamp, Eric P. *Language Basics Plus*. New York: Harper & Row, 1979, Book 5.

Heilman, Arthur W. and Holmes, Elizabeth Ann. *Smuggling Language into the Teaching of Reading*. Columbus, Ohio: Charles E. Merrill, 1972.

Johnson, Ken et al. *Language*. Lexington, Mass.: Ginn, 1979, Book 5.

Langacker, Ronald W. *Language and Its Structure*. New York: Harcourt Brace Jovanovich, 1973.

Leaf, Munroe. *The Story of Ferdinand*. New York: Viking, 1936.

Lefevre, Carl A. *Linguistics, English and the Language Arts*. Boston: Allyn & Bacon, 1970.

Loban, Walter. *The Language of Elementary School Children*. Champaign, Ill.: National Council of Teachers of English, 1963.

Marckwardt, Albert H., editor. *Language and Language Learning*. Champaign, Ill.: National Council of Teachers of English, 1968.

May, Frank B. *Teaching Language as Communication to Children*. Columbus, Ohio: Charles E. Merrill, 1967.

May, Frank B. *To Help Children Communicate*. Columbus, Ohio: Charles E. Merrill, 1980.

Murray, Elizabeth A. "Sentence Building with Manipulative Board Cards." *Instructor*, March 1975, 66–67.

The Nebraska Curriculum Development Center. *A Curriculum for English*. Lincoln: University of Nebraska Press, 1966.

Newman, Edwin. *A Civil Tongue*. New York: Bobbs-Merrill, 1976.

Ney, James W. "A Short History of Sentence Combining: Its Limitations and Use." *English Education*, February 1980, 169–177.

Prosser, William L. "English as She Is Wrote." *English Journal*, January 1939, 41–42.

Roberts, Paul. *English Sentences*. New York: Harcourt Brace Jovanovich, 1962.

Ross, Charles S. and Ross, Mary M. "Linguistics in the Elementary School Classroom." In *Linguistics for Teachers* (edited by J.S. Savage). Chicago: SRA, 1973, 175–186.

Safire, William. *On Language*. New York: Times Books, 1980.

Schiller, Andrew. "A Few Words about Grammar in General and This Book in Particular." In *Language and How to Use It*. Chicago: Scott, Foresman, 1969, Book 5, p. x.

Schroth, Evelyn. "Dr. Seuss and Language Use." *The Reading Teacher*, April 1978, 748–750.

451

Scott, Robert Ian. "Teaching Elementary Grammar with Color-Coded Word Blocks." *Elementary English*, November 1968, *45*, 972–981.

Sherwin, J. Stephen. *Four Problems in Teaching English*. Scranton, Pa.: International Textbooks Co., 1969.

Slobin, Dan Isaac. *Psycholinguistics*. Glenview, Ill.: Scott, Foresman, 1979.

Smart, W. Douglas and Ollila, Lloyd O. "The Effect of Sentence Combining Practice on Written Compositions and Reading Comprehension." *The Alberta Journal of Educational Research*, June 1978, *24*(2), 113–120.

Stageberg, Norman C. *An Introductory English Grammar*. New York: Holt, Rinehart and Winston, 1965.

Wiggins, Antoinette and Peterson, Sue W. *Effective English*. Morristown, N.J.: Silver Burdett, 1979, Book 2.

Wolfe, Don M. "The Sentence Building Game in Action." In *Language Arts and Life Patterns*. New York: Odyssey, 1972, 307–320.

Work, William. "Viewpoints: Listening and Talking." *Language Arts*, February 1981, 153.

LANGUAGE AND THE LINGUISTICALLY DIFFERENT CHILD

Who are these children? They are rich and poor, settled and nomadic. The children speak one or more of about 3,000 different languages. Of every 100 children, about 19 speak Chinese; about 7 speak English; 6 speak Hindi; and slightly fewer speak Spanish. (McHale et al., 1979)

The authors of the above quote were speaking of children worldwide, though our focus here is somewhat narrower. Teachers in the United States are—to a degree rare when this century began—encountering linguistic diversity in their classrooms. For example, the percent of non-English speakers in classrooms varies from a low of 6 percent in Alabama to a high of 42 percent in Hawaii (Kloss, 1977). More and more elementary teachers must learn to deal with language differences.

Who are the linguistically different? What characteristics do they have in common? What makes them unlike children who come to school speaking standard English proficiently? In what ways are children who don't speak standard English disadvantaged in the school milieu?

To some extent, everyone is disadvantaged, or lacking in advantages (Goodman, 1971). The army brat who lives in seven states by the age of five lacks the "advantage" of growing up in one neighborhood. The child who does not move until he or she goes away to college may miss the "advantages" that come with living in a variety of environments and meeting different people. The only child in a family may be deprived of the spirit of cooperation and camaraderie found in large families. These examples illustrate relatively minor disadvantages when the child comes to school. A more critical problem is when the child does not speak "school talk" or standard English.

Generalizations are hazardous; exceptions abound, but *generally* children who speak a language other than standard English as a first or home language, also suffer economic and social discrimination. Such children are often members of minority groups, some of whom lack the means of attaining the privileges of the majority. Because a child is a member of a minority group, however, does not necessarily mean that he or she is disadvantaged; the full gamut of "advantagedness" can be found in every identifiable sector of American society.[1] However, many children who encounter some educational problems because of their language are members of minority groups including blacks; rural and inner-city whites[2]; Mexican Americans; American Indians; Puerto Ricans; and migrant workers of all types.

In contrast to the relatively minor disadvantages of the middle class, the problems of linguistically divergent children seem overwhelming. When these problems are compounded by social and economic limitations, defeatism and despair are logical outcomes. In *The Other America* Harrington (1962) depicts the nearly overwhelming difficulties of large segments of the American population. If there is to be a large-scale improvement in the quality of life for these millions of people, education must be integrally and vitally involved.

PROBLEMS OF THE LINGUISTICALLY DIFFERENT

Life for inner-city poor children differs markedly in some respects from that of the small-town or rural disadvantaged; generalizations thus tend to be foolhardy.[3] Several educationally significant problems seem to be common, however:

1. Standard English is frequently not spoken and a nonstandard dialect is used in the home.
2. Experiences upon which school is based are lacking.
3. Community and school conditions are bad and slow to improve.

---

[1] A concurring statement is by Leonard Kaplan, "Ain't No Such Thing as Culturally Disadvantaged," *Instructor* 81 (February 1972): 18–20. The author points out in incisive fashion the importance of the school valuing and building on the experience the child has had.

[2] In a brief chapter like this, some diverse groups, which indeed have quite distinct characteristics, must be combined. For example, poor whites form three unlike groups, depending on geographic location. See: "Whites," by Alvin L. Bertrand, in *Reading for the Disadvantaged*, ed. by Horn (New York: Harcourt, Brace and World, 1970), pp. 21–28. Particularly helpful are the sections on specific language characteristics of minority groups.

[3] Suggestions for teachers of rural poor are included in R. A. Saudargas et al., "Prescriptive Teaching in Language Arts Remediation for Black Rural Children," *Journal of Learning Disabilities* 3 (July 1970): 364–370.

Language Problems

Often a child from a disadvantaged home has limited opportunities to hear or speak standard English. Frequently, large families and crowded conditions prevail. Any infant babbles and makes a wide variety of sounds, only some of which will be needed in the language later spoken as an adult. If someone speaks to a child regularly, the appropriate sounds for the dialect are reinforced and random babbling develops into words. Poor children are not often enough talked to by an adult concentrating on the task. Large blocks of time may be spent in the presence of an indifferent caretaker or older siblings. Thus, for linguistically different children, the problem of developing standard verbal English may be hindered by the lack of reinforcement and inconsistency of models.

A further language problem accrues from the nonstandard dialect spoken in many minority homes. Loban (1968) explains:

> As long as class societies remain stable, the variations in language cause few problems. In fact the language deficiencies support and stabilize class societies. In any kind of society language represents tremendous social power, and the Establishment speaks one kind of dialect, the established standard dialect. . . . Closed societies have always used language and education as one means of maintaining the *status quo* and of perpetuating a large class of peons or peasants. . . . Even in an open society such as ours, however, where individual worth and aspiration are intended to count for more than fortunate or unfortunate birth, language still operates to preserve social class distinctions and remains one of the major barriers to crossing social lines.

Experiential Background

Consider the following: John and Willie are born on the same day in the same hour. When John leaves the hospital he goes home to an eight-room house where a four-year-old sister eagerly awaits him. His father is an electrical engineer; his mother, a travel consultant, has a leave of absence to care for the new baby. Later, though she is gone from the home, John is left with an experienced sitter, who understands the importance of talking to young children. Though John's mother works, she makes a conscious effort to talk to him, read to him, and take him shopping with her. By the time he enters kindergarten, he will have been to the zoo, art galleries, symphony concerts, puppet plays, and big-league baseball games. Many times John has ridden in the car with his family to visit his grandmother in another state; once he has flown there.

Willie leaves the hospital and goes home to five rooms in which his mother and father, grandmother, uncle, five brothers, and four sisters live. Willie's father is a kitchen worker in a large restaurant; shortly after Willie was born a fire destroyed the restaurant and Willie's father was unable to find work for many months. His mother is a domestic worker who cleans houses six days a week. To get to the houses, which are located in the suburbs, she leaves her house at 7:00 A.M. and seldom returns home before six o'clock. Willie's mother loves her children, but her long hours of work enable her to spend very limited time with them.[4] Willie sleeps in the same room with his brothers and his uncle; it is stifling hot in summer and cold in winter. He is kept clean, but Willie's clothes are the ones outgrown by older siblings. Willie's family doesn't own a car. Although he is adept at getting around on the bus, Willie has never been beyond a four-mile radius of his house.

Both of these children have come to school with a background of many experiences. In all probability, only one set of experiences will be built upon by the school. Thus the urban poor, many of whom are also members of minority groups, do not lack experiences. They do, however, lack the kind of experiences too many schools typically expect students to have (Carter, 1971).

Haas (1980), in describing a trio of children of varying social, economic, ethnic, and language backgrounds, suggests teachers ask themselves such questions as:

1. How are . . . these young people alike?
2. How are they different?
3. What social forces have played a significant part in their lives?
4. How can the school curriculum . . . meet . . . the needs of these students, considering the social settings from which they come?
5. How would you, as the teacher of these . . . students, deal with the similarities and differences they bring. . .?

Community and School Conditions

The environment of the linguistically different child is often limited. Crowded living conditions are common, a problem compounded in the inner city by the density of population in the neighborhood. High noise levels contribute to a state of uproar, sanitary facilities are often inadequate, and visual and olfactory pollution are common.

Schools, which should be of the highest quality, are often of the poorest quality. The following conditions are common in inner-city schools:

1. Facilities for both education and recreation are inadequate.
2. The buildings are generally older than those in other areas.
3. The schools are less likely to provide remedial facilities and programs than those in higher-income areas.
4. Substitute teachers provide much of the instruction.

The problem of parents' limited time, especially in relation to influencing school programs is discussed more fully in William R. Harmer, "To What Extent Should Parents be Involved in Language Programs for Linguistically Different Learners," *Elementary English* (November 1970): 940–943.

5. The high rate of turnover among teachers and the reluctance of experienced teachers to teach the poor result in a high proportion of inexperienced teachers in these schools.
6. Teachers spend almost as much time disciplining as they do on instruction. (Ragan et al., 1972)

Another condition in the school occurs because of double-edged ignorance. Students are ignorant of how to survive within the system; antagonism and, as children grow older, often violence, is the result. Teachers are unaware of the cultural mores of the students and ignore the distinct cultural contribution the home could make.

Community and school conditions do not improve rapidly for such children and their families. Although there are a number of contributing causes, one stands out above the others: the urban and rural poor have no political leverage. Sadly, funds allocated to improve conditions have in some cases been misused and abused with few reprisals to the guilty. Feelings of distrust for outsiders, alienation, and helplessness often result. Such problems are compounded by recent shifts in dominant political ideology resulting in diminished federal funding of education programs.

Positive Education Aspects

Descriptions of minorities usually revolve around negative aspects of the situation—the word "disadvantaged" itself is a negative word. There are significant features, however, that have been identified.

Based on an examination of creativity among the poor, Torrance (1971) found that in many ways:

> . . . the life experiences of disadvantaged children prepare them for creative achievement. Their lack of expensive toys and play materials contribute to their skill in improvising with common materials. The large families and lifestyles of disadvantaged families develop skills in group activities and problem-solving. Positive values placed by their families on music, rhythm, dance, body expressiveness, and humor keep alive abilities that tend to perish in more advantaged families.

In elaborating these ideas, Torrance and Torrance (1972) identify some "creative positives" they have found among learners too frequently considered disadvantaged by teachers:

1. Ability to express feelings and emotions.
2. Articulateness in role-playing and storytelling.
3. Enjoyment of and ability in creative movement, dramatics, and dance.
4. Expressiveness in speech.
5. Expressiveness of gestures and "body language."
6. Richness of imagery in informal language and creative writing.

These features suggest exciting possibilities to those who teach such youngsters. As specific activities are planned for learners, these data can be considered in establishing an atmosphere to foster creativity.

ATTITUDE OF THE TEACHER

The attitudes and feelings of people are crucial in situations dependent upon the quality of interaction among people. To focus attention on attitudes, ponder the eight unfinished statements below. How would you complete them? How do you think others might complete them?

1. Most Jews _____ .
2. Italians never _____ .
3. _____ usually cause trouble.
4. Puerto Ricans are _____ .
5. _____ are aggressive, pushy.
6. Mexicans always _____ .
7. _____ are lazy.

If you are willing to attribute qualities and characteristics to groups of people in these statements, it *may* indicate an attitude of prejudice. Prejudice is a prejudgment made without adequate basis. If you are prejudiced toward a person, you tend to lump that person into a group and attribute characteristics without really knowing the person. You *assume* certain things to be true about the person because you see him or her as a member of a particular group even though you *know* very little about the individual.

The tendency toward overgeneralization leading to prejudice has its origin in the complexities of life. In his classic work, *The Nature of Prejudice*, Allport (1954) says:

Overgeneralization is perhaps the commonest trick of the human mind. Given a thimbleful of facts we rush to make a generalization as large as a tub. . . . There is a natural basis for this tendency. Life is short, and the demands upon us for practical adjustments so great, that we cannot let our ignorance detain us in our daily transactions. We have to decide whether objects are good or bad by classes. We cannot weigh each object in the world by itself. Rough and ready rubrics, however coarse and broad, have to suffice.

Thus, categorizations and judgments based on scanty evidence abound and feelings of prejudice often result. Allport explains:

Man has a propensity to prejudice. This propensity lies in his normal and natural tendency to form generalizations, concepts, categories, whose content represents an oversimplification of his world of experience.

Prejudice is often accompanied by fear. In fact, fear and prejudice often are reciprocal; we are frequently prejudiced against what we fear and fear what we are prejudiced against. The teacher who plans to work with culturally diverse learners needs to ask: Are there factors in this situation that frighten me? Are they justified? How can these fears be overcome?

Fear based on ignorance is not uncommon among prospective teachers of minority children. Very few teachers were discriminated against in school when they were children. Most teachers were good students, received the rewards of the system and found satisfaction enough to continue through secondary school and college. It is difficult under such conditions to empathize with students who despise school and teachers alike, and who are unable or unwilling to fulfill the expectations of school.

> The discontinuity between the culture of the home and the school makes it
> difficult to develop in these children the desire for competence in the school
> environment which is necessary for a continuing positive interaction there.
> The children have entered school without the skills on which the curriculum
> is founded, and furthermore, they find it difficult to see the point in making
> an effort. Thus, for them, the school becomes a place which makes baffling
> demands, where failure is a rule, and a feeling of competence is rare. (Taba
> and Elkins, 1966)

Ignorance of the conditions causing such student attitudes can contribute to a subtle fear in teachers of students who hold these attitudes.

If teachers honestly examine their inner thoughts, they may find feelings of prejudice and fear for the culturally different. When teachers want to overcome these feelings, they need to engage in activities that enable them to remedy this ignorance of conditions influencing the children. Involvement with minority children is imperative, so observation and interaction can occur. Tutoring students, working in local volunteer groups, observing at community centers or day-care facilities can be most helpful.

Inferences, unfortunately, are often made about a person's intelligence because of language. Certain dialects are considered "uneducated" while others are considered to be "educated." If this attitude prevails among teachers, a child may be evaluated as having limited abilities merely because of dialect. According to Russell (1956) although there is a close relationship between language and thinking, they are not identical. Shuy (1967) says:

> That people speak different dialects in no way stems from their intelligence
> or judgment. They speak the dialect which enables them to get along with
> the other members of their social and geographical group.

It is sad, but true, that teachers too often make such judgments about children's intelligence based upon their language patterns. For upwardly mobile teachers from lower-middle or lower classes, standard English is seen as a means of mobility. Too often such teachers look down upon the nonstandard varieties of English spoken by the disadvantaged children they teach (Shafer, 1976).

In addition to inferences about verbal language, teachers may also be tempted to make inferences about nonverbal communication. In Caucasian, middle-class school culture, looking at the teacher is taken to signify interest and attention. In contrast, however, Blackfeet Indian children won't look directly at their teacher when addressing him or her, as the Blackfeet consider this a mark of disrespect (Katz, 1981). Obviously, a Caucasian teacher working for the first time with a Blackfoot child would need to know this to avoid misinterpreting the child's nonverbal communication.

As this section has attempted to illustrate, an honest examination of teacher attitudes is essential in dealing with linguistically diverse minority speakers. One fact stands out above the others: the attitude of the teacher toward linguistically and culturally different children is the key element in the teaching-learning environment. The best materials and conditions available cannot overcome the negative attitude of a teacher toward students. On the other hand, lack of facilities will have minimal effect on an educational environment where the attitudes are positive.[5]

From the foregoing, it is possible to assume that children would be better served by a teacher from their own culture. While this seems logical, the reality is that some minority children are widely dispersed; there may not be enough students in a community to make it possible to provide a teacher from their own culture. This is related to the fact that there is a dearth of minority teachers.

Saville-Troike (1978) feels that this logical truth may in fact not be true. She states:

> It is not at all certain that teachers from a similar cultural background to the students' will teach them more effectively, although research in this area is still far too sketchy to draw definite conclusions. (pp. 8–9)

At the conclusion of her book, a succinct yet engrossing consideration of the cultural diversity teachers face, the author presents a checklist of cultural competencies necessary for the effective teacher of linguistically diverse children.

NONSTANDARD DIALECTS

In examining one's attitude toward minorities, it is essential to consider one's attitude toward language. The first impression of another person often

---

[5]Other statements of the importance of the teacher's attitude are included in John Holt, *The Underachieving School* (New York: Dell, 1970); James Herndon, *The Way It Spozed to Be* (New York: Simon & Schuster, 1968); Herbert Kohl, *Thirty-Six Children* (New York: New American Library, 1968); and Esther Rothman, *The Angel Inside Went Sour* (New York: Bantam, 1972).

stems, if unconsciously, to a great extent upon the person's use of language. Based in part on the dialect spoken, a person's language may pique our curiosity and hold our attention or we may conclude that there is little about him or her to interest us. This impact of language was illustrated delightfully in the musical *My Fair Lady*, based on George Bernard Shaw's play *Pygmalion*. Professor Higgins's modifications of Eliza's dialect could even, with older children, become subject matter for a study of dialect differences.

In all likelihood the most perplexing language-related problems facing the teacher of culturally diverse students revolves around dialects. Typically, disadvantaged students speak a nonstandard dialect, viewed by many as inferior (Pertz, 1971). Loban (1966) says:

> Whereas regional differences in language are usually acceptable and delightful, social class dialects offer a difficult problem to American schools in which equality of opportunity for all pupils is accepted as an aim. Economic and social lines have always been difficult to cross, and language is one of the strongest barriers to a fluid society . . . all speech communities tend to feel hostility or disdain for those who do not use their language. . . . American teachers acknowledge that most children need to perfect or acquire the prestige dialect—not because standard English is correct or superior in itself but because society exacts severe penalties of those who do not speak it.

CHANGING ATTITUDES TOWARD DIALECTS

Within the past ten years, there has been significant change in professional attitudes toward dialects (Granger, 1976). Prior to this time, dialects had been described in terms of *deficiencies*, for which the child had to compensate. Schickedanz, et al. (1977) are among those who speak strongly about the importance of the teacher valuing the child's language: "Any attempt to modify directly the child's native language upon that child's entrance to school is not only inappropriate but may also prevent further growth."

An example of the changing attitude toward dialect is the issue of *precision* in language. A decade ago, some writers were commenting on the inability of minority speakers to produce complex and precise statements, contending that children use language globally, speaking undifferentiated "giant words" with less exactness than speakers of standard English. Today, in contrast, Davies (1977) contends there is:

> . . . no data showing that children from linguistically disadvantaged homes . . . cannot elaborate the basic linguistic forms . . . They are able at times to elaborate complex linguistic constructions, they can at times be as explicit and precise as children from more advantaged homes. The point is that they do not so frequently make complex constructions, and they are not as explicit as frequently, perhaps because their early upbringing does not demand it.

A further statement of this problem is provided by the respected language educator Joan Tough, who speaks of "provoking the child into explicitness." Her section of the book, "How Shall We Educate the Young Child?" is particularly useful. The chapters contributed by different writers and responded to by various discussants, are complex reading, but important.

A recent helpful development has brought attention to the concept of "registers." This is the notion that all of us speak in different ways at different times in different situations, depending on the relation and status of the people to whom we are speaking. A decade ago many minority children were labeled "nonverbal," because experts ignored the context in which this judgment was made. Minority children, placed in an intimidating context of an alien culture classroom with an unfamiliar teacher, did in fact often say nothing. With the development of the concept of registers, and more attention to the kinds of language minority children use among themselves in situations in which they are comfortable, such judgments decreased. Houston (1970) is one of the experts who points out that research methods used with lower-class children are often unfair to them. The researcher asserts that such children really have two registers at their disposal, a School Register and a Nonschool Register. Of the two, the School Register is the only one that is limited, giving few insights into the rich capacities possessed by the home language.

Given Loban's analysis of the limitations of American society, it would appear that a goal of democratic education is that students should be able to use standard English if social and economic mobility are to become realities. Given the changing professional attitudes about dialect, this ability to use standard English should be developed without disparaging the student's home dialect, or extinguishing his or her ability to use it in appropriate situations. Teachers of nonstandard speakers can best achieve this goal if they apprise themselves of the major ways in which nonstandard dialects differ from standard English. Figures of school enrollment indicate that speakers of black English are the most prevalent group of minority students, though the percentage of Hispanic students is increasing dramatically. It is likely that you will, during your teaching career, encounter speakers of both black and Hispanic dialects. To help acquaint you with some of the language features of these groups, we will discuss features of several nonstandard black dialects. This will be followed by a section on bilingual programs for Spanish speakers, and other less common minority speakers.

BLACK DIALECTS

Not uncommonly, it is assumed that there is a single black dialect. It is equally as absurd to believe there is one black dialect as it is to assume there is one Caucasian dialect. The tendency of some of us to overgeneralize about dialects may be symptomatic of prejudice as described earlier in this chapter; we may overgeneralize when stereotypes about language are formed. For example, someone using a nonstandard form 20 percent to 30 percent of the time is often perceived to be using this form 100 percent of the time.

According to Labov (1967), three major *phonological* variables commonly found in black dialects can be identified:

1. *r-lessness.* When an *r* appears in the medial or final position of a word, it becomes a schwa or it disappears. For example:
Carol = Cal
Paris = Pass
guard = god
terrace = test

2. *l-lessness.* In a manner similar to the loss of the *r* in pronunciation, the final *l* is often not pronounced.
toll = toe
rule = rue
help = hep
all = awe

3. *Simplification of consonant clusters at the ends of words.*
Although many consonant sounds are dropped at the ends of words, those represented by *t* and *d* are very commonly omitted.

past = pass	mend = men
hold = hole	field = feel
laughed = laugh	mash = mass
meant = men	gasp = gas

This type of simplification is also a characteristic of disadvantaged Caucasian Southern speakers (Horn, 1970, p. 163).

Several major *grammatical* counterparts of these phonological variations can be identified. For example, l-lessness can result in the absence of indication of the future tense in speech.

you'll = you
they'll = they
he'll = he
she'll = she

Likewise, the elimination of the final consonant sounds represented by *t* and *d* can result in the absence of indication of the past tense in oral language.

missed = miss
picked = pick
raised = raise

Another systematic examination of a black dialect was conducted by Loban in a longitudinal study. In his conclusions, Loban identifies ten significant variations betwen the nonstandard black dialect and standard English. The five most prevalent include:

1. Lack of verb agreement, third person singular (excluding *to be*)
   He *say* he's going home.
   They boy *don't* look happy.
   The mother *look* at television a lot.
2. Lack of auxiliary verbs
   He (is) running away.
   How (do) you know he isn't there?
   He (has) been here.
3. Inconsistency in use of tense.
   One time when I was sick my mother *comes* to see me.
   She knew if she *does* something bad he would find out.
4. Nonstandard use of verb forms
   He has *ate*.
   I *seen* him yesterday.
   He *don't* be there much.
5. Lack of agreement using *to be*.
   I *is* going inside.
   There *was* two girls.
   Here *is* two dogs. (Loban, 1966, pp. 8, 10, 14, 16, 20)

Through such thorough analyses of dialects, specific variations from standard English can be identified. Once identified, alternatives can be proposed.

Many teachers of the disadvantaged will not come in contact with the specific deviations from standard English described here. They may teach students with an entirely different set of dialect features. It is highly important that these be identified and described if the problems of nonstandard dialects are to be addressed seriously. Other descriptions are provided by DeStefano (1972) and Stoller (1975).

It is critical to remember that not all black speakers will manifest the characteristics described above. Barnitz (1980) points out that nonstandard features are found more frequently in lower socioeconomic communities. Teachers with middle class black students will find that often these children will have acquired standard English.

BILINGUAL EDUCATION PROGRAMS

In addition to speakers of black English, teachers often encounter students for whom Spanish is the first, or home, language. In fact, Kloss (1977) asserts that Spanish speakers are now the most numerous minority. He estimates there are some seven million children in schools for whom a variety of Spanish is the home language.

At one time, given the popularity of the "melting-pot" concept of American society, it was assumed that such children could of course be expected to speak English in the schools. However,

> . . . many of the problems facing adolescents . . . had their roots in early school experiences since many of these children were unable to meet the middle-class expectations of the English-speaking public school system. They were often retained in the lower grades and classified as slow learners or retarded. (Nedler, 1975)

Because of a growing awareness that conventional, standard English-only classrooms cannot adequately meet the needs of such boys and girls, bilingual programs have been mandated by law.

The Bilingual Education Act (Title VII, 1967) was the first federal legislation in our nation's history designed to promote the preservation of non-English languages spoken in the United States by encouraging their use as mediums of regular instruction in public schools. Like many pieces of federal legislation, it is "masterfully ambiguous" (Gaardner, 1977).

The U.S. Office of Education, formerly so named, currently entitled the Department of Education, interpreted bilingual education officially to mean:

> the use of two languages, one of which is English, as mediums of instruction for the same pupil population in a well-organized program which encompasses part or all of the curriculum and includes the study of the history and culture associated with the mother tongue.

Because of the lack of specificity in both the Act and its official interpretation, a variety of positions (and resulting instructional approaches) are possible, along a continuum representing quite different outlooks about the importance of the home language.

These range from: ⟶ to ⟶

Those who want to produce full literacy in children maintaining/ developing the mother tongue on a par with English.	A variety of other medial	positions which also	affect instruction.	Those who want to focus hard on English, permitting the mother tongue only as a quick, expedient bridge to English.

There is not, thus, universal agreement about the purposes, or forms of bilingual education. Mackey (1977) has commented that indeed, "Bilingual education in early childhood has taken a number of different, and often *contradictory* forms" (italics added). Programs try to (1) assure efficient foreign language learning; (2) assure that minorities get at least part of their education in their mother tongue; (3) transfer the medium of instruction from the home language to the national language, or (4) implement a national policy of bilingualism. It is apparent that these purposes are in some ways contradictory, and would in fact need to be accomplished through distinctly different instructional strategies. As Mackey points out, too frequently programs have been established at considerable cost in schools which make the assumption that there is one best approach applicable everywhere and under all circumstances.

Affective Considerations

Bilingual programs are often advocated on the basis that the child's mother tongue, the dominant language when they come to school, is the logical medium for learning. The contention is that more cognitive development occurs more quickly if the child is developing thought in the home language.

There is another rationale for instruction in the mother tongue, however. That is the effect such instruction has on the affective domain. An expert in bilingual education, Von Maltitz (1975) observed that:

> Encouragement of the use of mother tongues . . . demonstrat(ing) respect for a child's cultural and familial roots has an effect not only on how children think, but also on how they feel. And feeling right, feeling good and confident about oneself, is usually of great importance in the capacity of any . . . child . . . to carry out a task successfully, in school or out.

We have been considering the nature of bilingual *programs*. This is because it is more often the case that a school will offer special bilingual classes, than that individual classroom teachers will be asked to deal with a single bilingual child. Such programs, planned at the school district level, often involving input from parents, most effectively hire teachers who are themselves bilingual. That is because Hispanic parents have been politically active, and effective, in convincing school boards of the need for such special programs and staff.

Bilingual teachers can make use of research evidence about parental teaching styles: "As teachers, Chicano mothers made greater use of nonverbal instructions and included a higher percentage of original adult wording than Anglo and Chinese mothers." (Stewart, 1981)

By adapting teaching styles to reflect the home, and by using the home language, bilingual teachers can be more effective with Spanish-speaking children. In fact, as Stewart points out, being able to communicate either orally or in letters with the Spanish-speaking parents greatly increases the credibility of bilingual teachers.

Let us now consider the second label often appended to such programs, frequently designated *bilingual-bicultural*. This is an effort to reinforce the pride in the home culture which comes from a realization that simply learning a second language is not enough. To develop fully functioning adults, we must help boys and girls retain a pride in the originating culture.

Such cultural and linguistic elements are densely interwoven. As Gonzalez-Mena (1976) pointed out, if a child has a problem learning a language, the problem may not only be linguistic. That is, learning the words may in fact be conceptual, if a particular concept does not exist in the home language. The student may not perceive the difference between two things, and then cannot readily learn a word for a difference, words being labels for perceptions.

Early efforts at developing bilingual programs of necessity focused on such purely linguistic concerns as identifying the elements in the two languages which were contrastive. More recent efforts have wisely gone beyond such initially important concerns to also incorporate a wide-ranging concern for the interaction of culture and language. An engrossing account of the development of one such program over a period of years is provided by Nedler (1975).

As programs of many varieties have grown, nourished by federal legislation and funding, the need for evaluation has become apparent. The teacher working with bilingual children has today many tools to use in evaluating their language. These evaluation instruments include project-developed, commercially published, and noncommercial sources. Teachers can assess bilingual speakers' ability in phonics and spelling (Fullerton Spanish Language Test); vocabulary comprehension (Santillana Pre/Post Language Development Test); complete sentences (Informal Language Assessment); listening (Pimsleur Spanish Proficiency Test); and reading (Prueba de Lectura), among others. These and other tests are described in a booklet that provides data about availability, grade level, means of administering, date of publication, cost, and length. The guide is descriptive, not evaluative (DACBE, 1977).

In addition to assessing how individual children are learning English in a particular program, there is need for another kind of evaluation. Differing approaches to bilingual education need to be compared, to determine if some are more effective than others. It is at this level that government law and regulations have been lacking. Our government ". . . has spent over half a billion dollars on bilingual programs, and less than one-tenth of one percent of this amount on basic research needed to improve the quality of programs" (Center for Applied Linguistics).

Until we make serious efforts to evaluate both pupil progress in programs, and also the effectiveness of varying approaches to bilingual education, school districts will continue to experiment in ways which could be more effective. There is another, equally critical task, however. We must reexamine our own attitudes as adults toward those who speak a language different from our own. Such reexamination asks that we look at attitudes embedded deep within the dominant Anglo culture.

It is clear that, regardless of the particular approach to bilingualism espoused, the success of such programs will be inextricably linked to the relative social and cultural status of the groups. If students are "subjected to various forms of discrimination and disvaluation of their language and culture during a critical developmental period," they will not make rapid progress, while "students who have escaped this experience quickly overcome the language barrier and function successfully. . . ." The difference is whether bilingualism is *subtractive* or *additive* (Troike, 1978).

Increasingly, better-prepared bilingual (if not also bicultural) teachers are entering the school system equipped to meet the needs of these minority children. While Wolfgang in 1977 lamented: "Unfortunately, there are few teacher training institutions that offer intensive training programs to prepare teachers for the multicultural or multiracial classrooms," the situation is much better today. There still are not enough bilingual teachers, but more and more Hispanic children are learning with teachers who are knowledgeable about and sensitive to their language.

NATIVE AMERICAN SPEAKERS

Less geographically widespread than bilingual programs for Hispanic speakers are the programs for Native Americans. Though some have dispersed to cities, the majority of Native Americans are clustered, often in areas served by schools administered by the federal government.

Described by a single term, the group of peoples so labeled present unique problems for bilingual education. Unlike other minority groups, this term refers not to a relatively homogeneous group, but to over 400 officially recognized tribes, and over 200 still extant languages (Parker, 1978). Some of these groups use their first language in everyday life; as a consequence, children come to school speaking little or no English. In other groups, religious prohibitions and related reasons lead to a tribal position that native languages are not to be used in the classroom. Obviously, these different beliefs result in substantially different approaches to curriculum.

Although culturally distinct, Simpson-Tyson (1978) contends one thing links these disparate learners: they "may be the most disadvantaged of all cultural groups." She points out that Native American children function up to three years below white students in vocabulary, syntactic complexity, and conceptual understanding.

Clearly part of the problem, once again, is that Anglos designing curricula do not understand the minority culture to be served. For example, Philion and Galloway (1971) point out that Indian homes seem to promote highly developed nonverbal communication skills. The child learns to pay attention to nonverbal clues from the parents in doing concrete tasks. The modeling by adults does not include verbal instructions. The cultural disparity that occurs when such children move into the predominantly verbal Caucasian classroom is evident.

A second example of cultural difference is given by Allen and Remley (1978), who point out that Navajo attitudes toward direct eye contact, and toward verbal language are very different than whites exhibit. Concerning nonverbal aspects, Navajo children look down as a mark of respect, avoiding the kind of direct, open-face look which middle-class whites see as "honest." One can imagine the problems a teacher unfamiliar with such tribal conventions faces. In commenting on oral language, the authors point out that to the Navajo: "Language is a holy thing . . . not, essentially, as it is with most white men, a means of communicating personal wishes, of defining and solving technical problems." If the Navajo values silence itself as an important means of communication, Anglo teachers working with such children will have to be aware of such values in order to be effective.

One author has been specific in identifying ways classrooms for such learners must change. In a study involving the Indian children on the Warm Springs Indian Reservation, Phillips (1970) came to the conclusion that the structure of the classroom needs to be changed to take into account the fact that the sociolinguistic rules of Indian children differ from those of non-Indian children. For example, situations in which the child was required to speak when the entire class was listening, such as having to answer questions in front of everyone and participate in "sharing time" need to be minimized and opportunities to ask and answer questions with the teacher at her desk without an audience, and working in small groups rather than with the entire class, need to be maximized.

Finally, two tasks confront teachers concerning Native American speakers. The teachers whose work puts them in contact with these learners must devise sensitive ways to alter curricula to accommodate divergent learners. There is an equally important task, however, for those teachers who may never encounter a Native American child in the classroom. That is to provide vicarious experiences through literature; to enrich all children's understanding of the linguistic and cultural diversity in the United States. Such books as the one by Lass-Woodfin (1978) annotate other books that describe various aspects of the lives of Native Americans. In this particular reference, books are listed alphabetically by the author and there is also a subject index. Annotations summarize content, but also comment on possible uses and list strengths and weaknesses in several areas. Such reference tools can help teachers bridge the "culture gap" for children in a single culture classroom.

MAINSTREAMING

Differences we have been considering to this point have been those that arise primarily because the child is from a culture other than the Caucasian school culture. In addition, teachers now find themselves dealing with another kind of difference not directly linked to the students' culture. As a result of so-called "mainstreaming" laws, more and more children with learning disabilities are being placed in classrooms. Teachers find it difficult to meet the needs of such children, who may be physically handicapped, cognitively handicapped, or emotionally handicapped.

Mainstreaming has been defined as the placing of physically and/or mentally handicapped students in the "least restrictive environment."

The process is one of the latest and most controversial developments in education. In 1975 Congress passed Public Law 94-142 and subsequently the Department of Health, Education and Welfare issued rules and regulations which mean that many teachers without any specific training in handling such children are finding them in their classrooms. Most elementary teachers are inadequately prepared to work with mainstreamed pupils (Morsink, 1979).

One author suggests that in fact the terminology used to describe such children may affect our perception of them. Askew et al. (1981) suggest that using the term "special needs child" may help us focus on what we, as teachers, need to provide, rather than focusing on the limitation itself.

Another author has recommended some techniques she feels can help a classroom teacher accommodate the individual capabilities of special needs children in a regular classroom:

1. *Pretest* at the beginning of the year, determining students' abilities in each of the language arts.
2. Use small *groups*, establishing a task for each member of the group at varying levels of ability.
3. Make use of peers for *tutoring.*
4. Vary assignment *due dates* to provide for the necessary additional time slower students will need.
5. Adapt *reading assignments* for some children, i.e., Learning Disabled (LD) students who may be very competent verbally but have severe reading problems.
6. Teach and test in *alternative ways*, to go beyond the verbal presentation and written response so common in schools. (Dodd, 1980)

Taken together, Dodd's suggestions form an approach to individualizing instruction, adapting modes of presentation, requirements, and means of meeting them, to individual students who may enter the classroom with physical, mental, or psychological limitations.

Dodd's brief article deals with mainstreaming in general, but teachers with special needs children can turn to a variety of more specialized and more extensive books dealing with particular conditions.

For example, teachers encountering a deaf, blind, or mildly mentally handicapped student for the first time might read the suggestions of Gearheart and Weishahn (1976). In each chapter the authors consider the equipment necessary, ways to adapt the classroom environment, and alternative teaching strategies. The writing is easy to read, and the suggestions seem eminently practical.

Dealing with listening, speaking, and writing in succession, Turnbull and Schulz (1979) point out the types of difficulties special needs children may have with these, and offer alternative classroom strategies. The three types of oral language assessment they suggest include annotations of tests. The authors point out that some children have communication difficulties because of physical disabilities (cerebral palsy), sensory deficits (hearing-impairments), and intellectual deficits (mental retardation). Alternative activities are suggested, though many are variations of ideas presented elsewhere in this book. For example, they suggest: "Fill boxes with various objects; listen to the objects as they are shaken," an activity also included in the listening chapter of this book. They also give suggestions for teaching handwriting, noting that some mentally handicapped children who do not excell in more cognitive areas can do well in this motor skill. For children who have perceptual or neurological problems, specific ways of adapting handwriting exercises are given. The chapter concludes with a strong recommendation of the language-experience approach.

Even more extensive consideration of two aspects of encoding written language—handwriting and spelling—are given by Hammill and Bartel (1978). In providing an entire chapter on each skill, the authors give a description of usual development in children without problems, consider diagnostic techniques, and then describe at length remedial activities to overcome problems.

In a quote well summarizing this overly brief section, Sapon-Shevin (1978) challenges educators: "Many aspects of regular education—that is, of the 'mainstream' itself—will need to be reassessed and modified if successful mainstreaming is to occur." Fortunately, many universities are developing courses designed to help future classroom teachers understand special needs children. Nationwide, school districts are planning in-service programs to help teachers develop the capabilities of meeting the needs of such children.

PURPOSES AND STRATEGIES FOR LANGUAGE INSTRUCTION

The classification of humans into groups labeled "disadvantaged," "advantaged," "genius," or "EMR," stirs the conscience because it is basically *de*humanizing. A number of descriptors can be applied to any one group of people resulting in the multiple classification of individuals. Thus, among other possibilities, a youngster may be classified as male, ten years old, identical twin, average IQ, minority. The last classification *may* be the least relevant. Therefore, to consider teaching strategies for culturally diverse boys and girls as though this was the most pertinent bit of information about them is unwise.

Linguistically different students profit from good teaching just as more advantaged students do. This book suggests many effective strategies for teaching language to students. All of the suggestions can be incorporated into teaching linguistically different sutdents because the basic principles of good teaching are applicable to any level of learning at any socioeconomic level (Edelsky & Rosegrant, 1981).

In the sections that follow, a sampling of the many goals for language instruction based on the cognitive, affective, and psychomotor taxonomies is presented. These are the three taxonomies described in Chapter 2. You may wish to review the more complete descriptions included there before reading this section. In addition, strategies to attain language goals are described for the skills of listening, speaking, reading, and writing. Most of the strategies are appropriate for individual or small-group instruction as well as large-group instruction.

Listening

Emphasis on teaching children the skills of language must not overshadow time for receiving language. Teachers should read to children daily. All humans have greater receptive control than productive control (Goodman et al., 1979). Children will be able to understand more through reading and listening than they will through speaking and writing. They should therefore be read to in both languages they are learning. "This provides them with fine

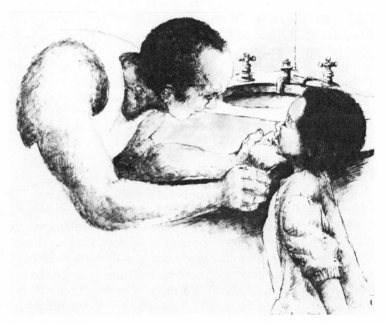

From Daddy *by Jeanette Caines.*

literature they cannot yet read for themselves, and it tunes their ears to structures of language and knowledge they cannot get through reading on their own" (p. 37). In selecting books, teachers should choose widely to expand children's experiences. It is critical to read to the children books about the culture from which they come. Such books are more widely available now than previously (Chall et al., 1979). It is not necessary, however, to exclude books simply because they represent something the children may not have experienced firsthand; it is important not to assume too narrow a definition of relevance. Cazden (1972) tells about the impact of *The Story about Ping* (by Marjorie Flack, Viking, 1933) on a Navajo reader, despite the fact the tale is about a duck on the Yangtze River in China. Geographic and cultural differences did not interfere with the impact of the author's message; superficial differences were unimportant.

Children will also be interested in listening to books by other students. Such books as *I Heard a Scream in the Street* (Larrick, 1970), featuring poems written by black students, and *Ah, Man, You Found Me Again* (Gross, 1972), featuring poems and stories by black and Hispanic students, are both useful.

Among important goals for listening are the following:

COGNITIVE : The student should be able to:
listen for differences
listen for likenesses
listen accurately
listen critically
PSYCHOMOTOR : The student should be able to:
listen attentively
discern relevant sounds (e.g., hear the
teacher's voice amid many voices)
AFFECTIVE : The student should be able to:
listen appreciatively

As the suggestions below indicate, students should have an opportunity to hear many sounds, not just the teacher's voice. Students can talk or read into a tape recorder and listen to their own voices; they can listen to musical records and raise their hands every time they hear a specified instrument (the use of popular records will heighten motivation). They can be given a sheet of paper divided into rows of cells, and can take turns giving such directions as:

1. "Start at the upper lefthand corner. Count 3 squares over, two squares down, and draw a cat."
2. "Find the bottom righthand square. Count four squares up and write your name."

473

Stop everything that is going on. Ask the children what small sounds they hear (clock ticking, noises in the hall, etc.) that are usually inaudible. Read a list of words, all of which begin with the same sound except for one. Instruct your students to identify which word begins differently than the others. This can be done with final sounds, rhyming words, words with a specified number of syllables, etc. Play musical records of various moods. Have your students express the way the music makes them feel, through dancing, creative movement, role playing, drawing, or painting.

There is a common saying that once you have learned to ride a bicycle you never forget. The same isn't true for listening. Once "taught," it does not remain "learned." To acquire good listening skills, activities that explicitly allow for their acquisition are required throughout the school years. Upper-grade teachers cannot logically expect that all necessary instruction in listening will have been accomplished in the primary grades.

Speaking

Oral language is a major avenue by which people express their ideas, feelings, and values. Speaking skills play an important role as we seek to reach our full potential. The majority of intentional communication is transmitted through speech. One of the major responsibilities of education, then, is the development of students' speaking abilities.

From Stories Julian Tells *by Ann Cameron.*

Students need many opportunities to talk in school if they are to develop and refine speaking skills. All adults speak in a variety of "styles," depending upon the situation. We talk differently with husband or wife, with employer, with public official. Culturally diverse students should be able to talk with other students in their classes, with older students, younger students, and people in authority because each situation requires a different speaking style, or register.

The use of nonstandard dialects and the need for standard English to achieve economic and social mobility pose instructional problems for teachers of the linguistically different. Several questions persist: When should students be taught standard English? How should it be taught?

For early elementary students, the major goal should be free oral expression. If there is mutual understanding of what is said among students and between the teacher and students, there is little need to be concerned about dialect. The child should feel comfortable with the home dialect, and his or her ability to express ideas in it.

As children advance in school, the ability to express ideas in standard English becomes more important. In the later elementary years, in the middle school and secondary school, instruction in standard English is necessary to provide students with another dialect in addition to their first language.[6]

The concept of alternatives is important. Language and emotions are intertwined. If a person's language is criticized, the inner self may be threatened. The aim of instruction in standard English should not be to *replace* the dialect of the student but to provide an *alternative* dialect if the child chooses to use it. Although there may be occasions in the secondary school when standard English is required, the choice is ultimately up to the individual as to whether he or she will speak standard English. Students only have a choice, however, if they know standard English.

In commenting about such conscious choosing, Gaardner (1975) has pointed out a distinction between freely choosing, and having to learn a new language. He feels that for most college students who choose to learn a new language, the process is ". . . an elitist gesture of cultural enrichment," while for most children whose home language is not English, it is a "form of assimilation which they would find almost impossible to avoid." He goes on to note that the reason most bilingual programs are "self-destructing," is that only the minority child is learning a new language, and as soon as possible the child is integrated into all-English learning. A useful opportunity is lost when standard English speakers in the classroom do not learn at least some of the language of the minority speaker.

Methods of instruction in standard English vary. The identification of how dialects vary specifically from standard English is prerequisite to

---

[6]The question of *when* instruction in standard English should be introduced is one of many unresolved questions discussed by Dorothy S. Strickland in "Black is Beautiful vs. White is Right," *Elementary English*, 49 (February 1972): 220–223.

thorough instruction. The most common variations can then be altered through drill. Older students can be taught generalizations and then apply them. For example, Loban (1966) identified lack of verb agreement, third-person singular (excluding *to be*) as a major deviation from the standard English dialect he examined. The standard verb forms for the third-person singular can be presented with the students actually memorizing the standard forms. They can then be asked in an analytical approach to substitute the standard forms for nonstandard forms as in the following examples:

She *go* to the store.
He *say* he will be there tomorrow.

This suggestion is similar in approach to one called "English Now," described at length in Hammill and Bartel (1975, pp. 194–198). Following this, based on synthesis, students can make up their own sentences using the standard form. Clearly, the true indication of students' *willingness* to use standard forms will not likely occur within the classroom, but their *ability* to do so can be ascertained.

Other goals for speaking may include:

COGNITIVE : The student should:
know a variety of words for expressing
   thoughts
be able to express thoughts orally
PSYCHOMOTOR : The student should be able to:
enunciate clearly
articulate clearly
make the sounds of standard English
speak audibly
AFFECTIVE : The student should be:
willing to speak in small and large groups
willing to speak standard English (at an
   appropriate age)
willing to participate in discussions about
   dialects and attitudes toward it

Halliday (1978) suggests having students explore their own attitudes, to see that dialect can be a subject of rational discussion, instead of a means of categorizing humans.

The following suggestions may be useful in developing standard English facility among culturally diverse youngsters:

Provide a set of common experiences to talk about. Walks around the school neighborhood and longer field trips can be taken. Films, filmstrips, records, and TV programs can also provide a stimulus for conversation.

The teacher can have the students look at interesting and thought-provoking pictures. Students can make up stories about pictures (individually or in a group) or they can make up questions to ask about the pictures.

A student can be asked to say a word that pops into his or her head. Another student can repeat this word and say another that has the same beginning sound. This can be repeated until the group has suggested as many possibilities as it can.

The students can sit informally in a circle. One student can start out by saying something like, "I see a green book. Mary, do you see it?" Mary has to find what the first student saw before she can have a turn.

A student can be blindfolded and asked to describe an object which she or he can feel.

If students are hesitant to speak before others, they can talk "through" puppets.

The students can be asked to experiment with saying a sentence in many different ways. For example, the sentence "I will be there in five minutes" can be whispered, shouted, stated emphatically, or stammered.

Another way the same spoken sentence can have different meanings is through the emphasis put on words. The students can be asked to emphasize different words in a sentence such as: "*I* am going home now," "I *am* going home now," or "I am *going* home now" (Teigenbaum, 1970). The last two abilities can be incorporated into informal classroom drama, when children enact a story they have read, or one of their own making. Noble et al. (1977) demonstrated the benefits dramatizing offers to minority children. The researchers discovered that black seven- and eight-year-olds, after only six hours of drama lessons, were significantly more aware of their own individual behavior and potential (future) behavior.

We nurture oral language abilities because we know that success in one of the language arts is related to success in the others. As Wilson (1981) points out, students who are effective speakers will also be successful in listening and reading skills.

Reading

Reading requires breaking the code of a symbol (written word) for something else (object, idea, feeling). Decoding a written word and understanding its intent is a complex process that requires a background of experiences and a knowledge of words.

The problem is that, even for speakers of standard English, there is a significant discrepancy between the oral language spoken and the written language encountered in books. The problem is larger when the home dialect is different than the standard English presented in reading books. One author says:

There are some remarkable differences between the sorts of things children say, the kinds of conversations they engage in, and the texts they are expected to learn to read from. In the children's speech samples, there is a rich system of organization whereby utterances are tied to meanings—present events, previous events, persons, objects, causes and effects. In the reading texts there is a near total disregard of such organization. The point of such texts, apparently, is to present forms of language that use a small inventory of elements. . . . The object is certainly not to say anything a child would be likely to think of saying. (Oller, 1979, p. 414)

Another complication is that some minority youngsters come from homes where there are no books. They may rarely see a person reading. For these youngsters, reading-readiness activities may appropriately extend throughout the first years of school. The early years of schooling for such children should stress vocabulary and oral language development; encoding, and decoding someone else's written language may not be relevant until the intermediate grades.

It would seem obvious . . . that particularly in the primary years children should be given every opportunity to learn to use standard American English with ease and agility. It is not enough for them to acquire an enriched vocabulary in a socially unmarked dialect alone. They must learn to manipulate language in meaningful and efficient ways. . . . Language skills should be established before the reading program commences. (York & Ebert, 1970)

After language skills have been developed, several approaches for teaching reading to the disadvantaged seem worthy of consideration. The language-experience approach can be effective because it builds on the unique experiences of each child as he or she learns to read by decoding what has been dictated (Lee & Allen, 1963). The initial teaching alphabet (ITA) can also be effective with minority youngsters. The alphabet consists of 44 symbols each of which represents only one sound. Children who know the twenty-six letters of the alphabet may be slightly confused by ITA, but many minority children may not know the alphabet when they enter school. The regularities of sound-symbol relationship can be stressed with ITA, reducing the confusion resulting from the inconsistencies of the English language.

It is important to note that regardless of the approach used in teaching reading, the teacher's attitude is paramount. The method that seems best to the teacher will likely be the one that is most effective for her or him.[7]

The specific strategies utilized in reading instruction will vary according

---

[7]See *The Reading Teacher* (May 1966). The entire volume is devoted to summaries of the twenty-seven studies of first-grade reading, supported by U.S.O.E. Different problems are handled in different ways; no definitive answer was reached regarding the "best" way to teach reading. All studies concur on the importance of the teacher favoring the method being used.

to the basic approach adopted in the school; therefore, no strategies will be presented here. The following goals are among those which could be, however, incorporated into the reading program.

COGNITIVE : The student should:
    know generalizations about the symbol-sound
      relationships of English
    be able to apply knowledge of generalizations
      in attacking new words
PSYCHOMOTOR : The student should:
    have the necessary eye coordination for
      reading
    be able to read aloud smoothly
AFFECTIVE : The student should:
    be interested in reading

Direct Instruction

In contrast to some of the preceding ideas, which assume that the children's own language forms a logical base for the learning of another language variant, a different approach does not rely on the language of the students. Becker (1977) has written convincingly about the benefits of what is called "direct instruction," a highly structured, organized approach that emphasizes small-group, face-to-face instruction by a teacher using carefully sequenced lessons. The method is characterized by rapid-paced, teacher-directed instruction, and monitors student progress through biweekly tests and reports. Becker describes educationally important gains in spelling, reading decoding skills, and vocabulary that resulted in low-income students in the program performing at or near national norms on all measures. The author closes his article with the contention that schools, designed to teach middle-class children, must be redesigned to teach all students.

Writing

Writing is an important process for recording language. It makes permanent thoughts and ideas which in oral form have only momentary existence. A thought or a spoken word always precedes the written word. Thus, instruction in writing should be minimal until the student's oral language is fluent.

When instruction in writing does become appropriate, two basic types should be considered: the functional and the creative. Functional writing is the presentation of expository material. It should be clear and concise. Generally, formal English is used in functional writing. Knowledge of punctuation and other mechanics is required if the written word is to communicate accurately. Knowledge of sentence and paragraph structure also becomes important as students advance in their writing ability.

Creative or imaginative writing can take many forms. Free verse, haiku poetry, short stories, fairy tales, and puppet plays are only a few ways in which children can write creatively. Minority children may excel in creativity. Among the creative positives two authors have identified for such children are "richness of imagery in informal language and creative writing," and "originality of ideas in problem-solving and brainstorming" (Torrance & Torrance, 1972). It is critical that parents understand the importance of praising students' creative efforts at writing, at home and in school ("Como Ayudar," n.d.).

An important facet of writing is spelling. If written words are to communicate they need to be spelled correctly. The use of nonstandard dialects in oral language can cause spelling problems in written language. For example, *l-lessness* in oral language may result in the absence of the final *l* when a word is written. Knowledge of dialects spoken by students is requisite in analyzing such spelling errors. If students spell words as they pronounce them, they are making the transition from the spoken to the written word with consistency. Their spelling errors are not likely to be corrected until they recognize the patterns of variation from standard English in their speech. If the spelling errors do not follow the pattern of their dialect, the problem could be caused by any of the factors commonly associated with spelling errors (Graham & Rudorf, 1970).

Another aspect of writing is penmanship. Other than the possible lack of practice with pencils or crayons prior to entry in school, minority students should encounter no special problems in this area.

Goals for writing can include:

COGNITIVE : Students should:
know basic punctuation
be able to use punctuation appropriately
be able to write a sentence
be able to spell appropriate words correctly
be able to express ideas creatively

PSYCHOMOTOR : Students should:
be able to write legibly

AFFECTIVE : Students should be willing to share their ideas
and feelings in writing

The following suggestions can be used in teaching writing:
Students can write down stories dictated by younger children.
Pen pals in another school or another city but from the same culture can be identified and letters can be exchanged.
Students can make puppets and write stories for the puppets to tell.
Students can write titles for, and stories about, thought-provoking pictures.

SUMMARY

Characteristics of linguistically diverse students can be described and conditions in which they live can quite accurately be postulated. In doing this, however, it must not be overlooked that minorities have far more in common with advantaged groups than there are differences between them. The differences between advantaged and disadvantaged youngsters can be meaningful, but they should not become overpowering. In designing curricula for teaching language skills to a diversity of speakers, characteristics of the group should be considered as one of many bits of relevant information. Regardless of how well researched these characteristics may be, however, the assessment of *individual* characteristics of *individual* learners remains the essential task. A major goal of teachers working with linguistically diverse children is to plan learning strategies that do not demean the language of the child, or the home culture (Shield, 1979).

Suggestions for Further Exploration

1. Choose one of the "creative positives" identified by Torrance. Plan a language lesson built upon that strength. If possible, teach the lesson to a group of disadvantaged children to test its effectiveness.
2. Make a tape of yourself having a conversation with a friend. Analyze your language to determine what nonstandard forms you used. Is there any difference of opinion regarding this? If several different people analyzed the tape, would the tally of nonstandard forms agree?
3. Make a collection of pictures that you feel would be thought-provoking for linguistically diverse children. Can you justify your choice of pictures as appropriate for the target group of children? Identify the language motivation uses to which the pictures could be put.
4. Visit an inner-city school and a rural school that have impoverished students. Compare and contrast the student bodies, the facilities, the learning problems presented, and the environments.
5. Search census reports, newspaper files, and school records to determine how many and what types of poor people live in your community. Is there some way you could determine what these different groups have in common, and how they differ?
6. Read the Granger article (see Bibliography) and also "Some Approaches to Teaching Standard English as a Second Language," by Charlotte Brooks, *Elementary English*, November 1964, pp. 728–733. Observe in an inner-city school. Make lists of evidences of language differences, of language deficiencies. Which do you find more prevalent?

Suggestions for Further Reading

Alexander, Clara Franklin. "Black English Dialect and the Classroom Teacher." *The Reading Teacher*, 33(5) (February 1980): 571–576.

The first priority of the teacher is developing an understanding of the language and how it reflects a culture. Demonstrating to students that you believe they are capable of handling two or more dialects will give them an incentive to learn. When speaking to students, use a normal conversational tone. When reading orally, have them read aloud silently. This provides a standard English model, and lets students notice differences in dialects. Dictating passages that contain standard English constructions provides practice in punctuation, capitalization, and spelling.

Ashton-Warner, Sylvia. *Teacher*. New York: Bantam Books, 1963.

This warm, sensitive account of teaching Maori and white children in New Zealand details the language-experience approach to teaching reading. Although loaded with information, it is not presented in typical textbook fashion.

Bordie, John G. "Language Tests and Linguistically Different Learners: The Sad State of the Art," *Elementary English* 47 (October 1970): 814–828.

Teachers in disadvantaged schools are plagued as are all teachers with annual administration of standardized tests. For many such children, these tests are unfair at best. The author analyzes such tests, pointing out weaknesses. The conclusion reached is that few accurately assess such children's language ability.

Cheyney, Arnold B. *Teaching Culturally Disadvantaged in the Elementary School*. Columbus, Ohio: Charles E. Merrill, 1967.

Many practical suggestions for teaching language skills to disadvantaged students and pertinent information on characteristics of these students and the role of teacher attitude.

Clark, Kenneth B. *Dark Ghetto: Dilemmas of Social Power*. New York: Harper & Row, 1965.

Clark speaks freely of the problems facing both blacks and whites in American society. It is a well-written, informative, gutsy book.

Cole, Robert W., Jr. "Ribbin', Jivin', and Playin' the Dozens." *Phi Delta Kappan*, November 1974, pp. 171–176.

Cole interviews Herbert Foster, author of a book about the games of verbal abuse which originate in black male street-corner behavior and are brought into the classroom to challenge and test teachers and administrators who do not understand the games. Foster, who taught in Harlem High School for 17 years, describes ribbing games, in which a youngster taunts, for example, by asking "Are those SAs?" SAs refer to Salvation Army clothing, and this is a sample of the kind of specific vocabulary with which teachers are often unfamiliar. *Floods* are pants worn too high above the shoes. Another game is the "dozens," in which antagonists say insulting, often sexual, things about the mother (wife, etc.) of the victim. Foster describes this as a subtle form of verbal game playing which many whites outside the inner city don't understand. He feels that teachers needn't participate in such games when students initiate them, but that showing they understand them can win respect. Included are examples of how successful inner-city teachers have used their knowledge of the games to regain control of classes disrupted by such verbal games.

Coleman, James S. *Equality of Educational Opportunity.* Washington, D.C.: U.S. Government Printing Office, 1966.

The Coleman Report focuses on educational opportunities for the disadvantaged. Data regarding school environments, school enrollment, pupil achievement and motivation, and school integration are presented.

Gonzales, Philip C. "What's Wrong with the Basal Reader Approach to Language Development." *The Reading Teacher*, March 1980, 668–673.

An examination of the conditions that promote and inhibit language development, noting that inadequate language development can lead to inefficient reading. Children learn language when they are involved in using it to participate in situations of interest to them. Conditions inhibiting language learning closely resemble basal reader talk, which features little opportunity for spontaneous talk. Isolated drill, emphasis on correct pronunciation and grammar are characteristic of such readers. Instead, spontaneous talk, in which an experience provides the context for child/adult language, is more effective in developing language skills.

Imhoff, M. I. "Preparation of Language Arts Teachers for Ghetto Schools." *Viewpoints* 47 (March 1971): 125–135.

The author prescribes what he feels is the most successful way to prepare teachers of the culturally disadvantaged. Read this for some contrasts it offers to the suggestions made in this chapter.

Kozol, Jonathan. *Death at an Early Age.* New York: Bantam Books, 1967.

The subtitle of the book describes it as dealing with "The destruction of the hearts and minds of Negro children in the Boston public schools." This destruction is detailed in a heart-rending account that should be read by teachers of advantaged as well as minority learners.

Masland, S. "Black Dialect and Learning to Read: What is the Problem?" *Journal of Teacher Education* (March/April 1979): 41–44.

Does black dialect interfere with reading? Apparently neither dialect nor vocabulary contributes to poor reading. Rather, it is the mismatch between syntax that results in a reading problem for black children. Children comprehend material significantly better when it is written in language structures that appear frequently in their own language. The teacher's response to dialect is a powerful determinant of whether a particular child will learn. Often teachers correct what they perceive as random errors. These efforts to teach "correct" English have at least two negative results. *First*, evidence suggests that teachers find more errors than are actually there, prompting children to view themselves as more of a problem reader than is actually the case. *Second*, children may feel they are in a hostile environment, and speak less. Teachers may view the silence as another example of incompetence or obstinacy. Teacher-training institutions

483

and elementary schools must provide opportunities for teachers to examine their language biases and make positive changes. First, teachers could listen and respond to taped black dialect and standard English speakers, rating these on a number of variables and compare ratings. Or, educators might view videotapes of black and Caucasian children, again rating speakers and comparing ratings. Before attitudes toward language can be changed, they must be discovered and acknowledged. The second step is to show teachers the structure and consistency of black dialect, so they can recognize differences and similarities to standard English.

Report of the National Advisory Commission on Civil Disorders. New York: Bantam Books, 1968.

This report by the Kerner Commission, established by the federal government, provides data on conditions of the disadvantaged that Americans in general and educators in particular cannot afford to ignore.

Skeel, Dorothy J. *Children of the Street: Teaching in the Inner City.* Pacific Palisades, Calif.: Goodyear Publishing, 1971.

Conditions of the classroom and qualifications for teachers are discussed prior to suggestions for teaching language arts and other areas.

Snyder, Alice B. "Let's Do Drama!" *The Pointer, 21*(3) (Spring 1977): 36–40.

The author, a learning disorder specialist, points out that books on creative drama for the regular classroom do not offer much help to teachers of LD children. The activities suggested offer: (a) too many choices for children; (b) too few controls; and (c) goals which are not sufficiently concrete. She tells how teachers must structure space so LD children can do drama, and suggests using easily heard signals for beginning and ending an activity. At the beginning, such children must have a limited number of possibilities from which to choose. They should choose only after watching the teacher demonstrate what they are to do. Following these general guidelines, there are suggestions for specific sound stories, pantomime activities, and role-playing activities appropriate for LD children. Speech is added last of all in this sequence which should make it possible for classroom teachers to involve LD children in drama.

Teague, Bob. *Letters to a Black Boy.* New York: Lancer Books, 1968.

Teague, a black newscaster, had fewer obstacles to overcome in rising to the top of his profession than many others, yet he is fearful of the hurt ahead for his young son. In a series of sensitive letters, sometimes moving, sometimes comical, he tries to prepare his son for what lies ahead. Fast but worthwhile reading.

Uhl, Norman P. et al. "Receptive and Expressive Vocabularies of Upper-Middle and Low SEL Children." *Elementary English* 49 (May 1972): 725–729.

The authors identify some important vocabulary differences and similarities between the two groups being studied. Suggestions for vocabulary teaching techniques are included.

Webster, Staten W. *Knowing and Understanding the Socially Disadvantaged: Ethnic Minority Groups.* Scranton, Pa.: Intext Educational Publishers, 1972.

A book of readings particularly useful because it includes articles not only on black Americans but Mexican Americans, Puerto Ricans, American Indians, Chinese, and Japanese.

Bibliography

Allen, Paula, and Remley, David. "Literature and Writing for Native American Students." In *Problems in Applied Educational Sociolinguistics* (G. G. Gilbert and J. Ornstein, eds.). The Hague: Mouton, 1978, p. 103.

Allport, Gordon W. *The Nature of Prejudice.* New York: Doubleday, 1954.

Askew, Judy et al. "The Dis-enfranchised Return to the Mainstream." *Childhood Education,* May/June 1981, p. 281.

Baratz, Joan, and Shuy, Roger W. (eds.). *Teaching Black Children to Read.* Washington, D.C.: Center for Applied Research, 1973.

Barnitz, John G. "Black English and Other Dialects." *The Reading Teacher,* April 1980, pp. 779–786.

Becker, Wesley. "Teaching Reading and Language to the Disadvantaged." *Harvard Educational Review,* 47(4) (November 1977): 518–543.

Carter, T. P. "Cultural Content for Linguistically Different Learners." *Elementary English,* 48 (February 1971): 162–175.

Cazden, Courtney B. *Child Language and Education.* New York: Holt, Rinehart and Winston, 1972.

Center for Applied Linguistics. *Bilingual Education: Current Perspectives. Law.* Arlington, Va.: Center for Applied Linguistics, 1977.

Chall, Jeanne S. et al. "Blacks in the World of Children's Books." *The Reading Teacher,* February 1979, pp. 527–533.

"Como Ayudar a su Nino a Escribir Mejor." Urbana, Ill.: National Council of Teachers of English, n.d.

Cullinan, Bernice. *Black Dialects and Reading.* Urbana, Ill.: ERIC Clearinghouse on Reading, 1974.

Davies, Alan (ed.). *Language and Learning in Early Childhood.* London: Heinemann, 1977.

DeStefano, Johanna. *Language, Society, and Education.* Worthington, Ohio: Charles Jones, 1973.

DeStefano, Johanna. "Productive Language Differences in Fifth-Grade Black Students' Syntactic Forms." *Elementary English* 49 (April 1972): 552–558.

Dissemination and Assessment Center for Bilingual Education. "Evaluation Instruments for Bilingual Education: An Annotated Bibliography." Austin, Texas: Dissemination and Assessment Center for Bilingual Education, 1977.

Dodd, Julie. "Mainstreaming." *English Journal,* April 1980, pp. 51–55.

Edelsky, Carole, and Rosegrant, T. J. "Language Development for Mainstreamed Severely Handicapped Non-Verbal Children." *Language Arts,* January 1981, pp. 68–76.

Gaardner, A. Bruce. "Bilingual Education: Central Questions and Concerns." *New York University Education Quarterly,* 6(4) (Summer 1975): 2–6.

Gaardner, A. Bruce. *Bilingual Schooling and the Survival of Spanish in the United States*. Rowley, Mass.: Newbury House, 1977.

Gearheart, Bill R., and Weishahn, Mel W. *The Handicapped Child in the Regular Classroom*. St. Louis, Mo.: C. V. Mosby, 1976.

Gonzalez-Mena, Janet. "English as a Second Language for Preschool Children." *Young Children*, November 1976, pp. 14–18.

Goodman, Kenneth et al. *Reading in the Bilingual Classroom*. Rosslyn, Va.: National Clearinghouse for Bilingual Education, 1979.

Goodman, Y. M. "Culture of the Culturally Deprived." *Elementary School Journal*, 71 (April 1971): 376–383.

Graham, Richard T. and Rudorf, E. Hugh. "Dialect and Spelling." *Elementary English*, 47 (March 1970): 363–373.

Granger, Robert C. "The Nonstandard Speaking Child: Myths Past and Present." *Young Children*, September 1976, pp. 479–485.

Gross, Mary Anne. *Ah, Man, You Found Me Again*. New York: Beacon Press, 1972.

Haas, Glen. *Curriculum Planning: A New Approach*. Boston: Allyn & Bacon, 1980.

Halliday, M. A. K. *Language as Social Semiotic*. London: Edward Arnold, 1978.

Hammill, Donald D., and Bartel, Nettie R. *Teaching Children with Learning and Behavior Problems*. Boston: Allyn & Bacon, 1978.

Harrington, Michael. *The Other America: Poverty in the United States*. Baltimore, Md.: Penguin Books, 1962.

Horn, Thomas D. (ed.). *Reading for the Disadvantaged*. New York: Harcourt Brace and World, 1970.

Houston, S. "A Reexamination of Some Assumptions about the Language of the Disadvantaged Child." *Child Development*, 1970, pp. 947–963.

Karlsen, Bjorn. "Black Children and Final Consonant Sounds." *The Reading Teacher*, February 1974, pp. 462–463.

Katz, Joseph. "Bridging Values." *Childhood Education*, January/February 1981, pp. 131–139.

Kloss, Heinz. *The American Bilingual Tradition*. Rowley, Mass.: Newbury House, 1977.

Labov, William. "Some Sources of Reading Problems for Negro Speakers of Nonstandard English." In *New Directions in Elementary English* (edited by Alexander Frazier). Champaign, Ill.: National Council of Teachers of English, 1967, pp. 143, 148–152, 155–157.

Labov, William. *The Study of Non-Standard English*. Boston: Little, Brown, 1974.

Larrick, Nancy. *I Heard a Scream in the Street*. New York: M. Evans, 1970.

Lass, Bonnie. "Speaking Black and Reading Standard." ERIC Document Reproduction Service No. ED 140 221, May 1977, pp. 2–10.

Lass-Woodfin, Mary Jo (ed.). *Books on American Indians and Eskimos: A Selection Guide for Children and Young Adults*. Chicago: American Library Association, 1978.

Lee, Doris M., and Allen, R. V. *Learning to Read through Experience*. New York: Appleton-Century-Crofts, 1963.

Loban, Walter. *Problems in Oral English*. NCTE Research Report No. 5. Champaign, Ill.: National Council of Teachers of English, 1966.

Loban, Walter. "Teaching Children Who Speak Social Class Dialects.' *Elementary English*, 45 (May 1968): 593.

McHale, Magda Cordell et al. *Children in the World*. Washington, D.C.: Population Reference Bureau, 1979.

Mackey, William F. "Free Language Alternation in School." In *Bilingualism in Early Childhood* (edited by Mackey and Andersson). Rowley, Mass.: Newbury House, 1977, pp. 333–348.

Mays, Luberta. "Black Second Graders' Perception of Their Dialect Speech." ERIC Document Reproduction Service No. ED 123 600, 1976.

Morsink, Catherine. "Implementing PL 94-142: The Challenge of the 1980's." *Education Unlimited*, 1(4) (October 1979): 20–22.

Nedler, Shari E. "Explorations in Teaching English as a Second Language." *Young Children*, September 1975, pp. 480–488.

Noble, G. et al. "Changing the Self-Concepts of Seven-Year-Old Deprived Urban Children by Creative Drama or Videofeedback." *Social Behavior and Personality*, 5(1) (1977): 55–64.

Oller, John W. *Language Tests at School*. New York: Longman, 1979.

Parker, L. Leann. "Current Perspectives." In *Bilingual Education: Synthesis*. Arlington, Va.: Center for Applied Linguistics, 1978, pp. 1–62.

Pertz, Doris L. "Urban Youth, Nonstandard English and Economic Mobility." *Elementary English*, 48 (December 1971): 1012–1017.

Philion, William E., and Galloway, Charles G. "Indian Children and the Reading Program." In *Teaching the Language Arts to Culturally Different Children* (edited by W. W. Joyce and J. A. Banks). Reading, Mass.: Addison-Wesley, 1971, pp. 168–177.

Philips, Susan U. "Acquisition of Rules for Appropriate Speech Usage." In *Report of the 21st Annual Round Table Meeting on Linguistics and Language Studies* (edited by James E. Alatis). Washington, D.C.: Georgetown University Press, 1970, pp. 77–101.

Ragan, William B., Wilson, John H., and Ragan, Tillman J. *Teaching in the New Elementary School*. New York: Holt, Rinehart and Winston, 1972.

Reiter, Arlene. "The Possible Interference of Black Dialect on the Comprehension of Standard Reading Materials." ERIC Document Reproduction Service No. ED 098 552, October, 1974.

Rupley, William, and Robeck, Carol. "Black Dialect and Reading Achievement." *Reading Teacher*, February 1978. ERIC Document Reproduction Service No. EJ 173 373.

Russell, David H. *Children's Thinking*. New York: Blaisdell, 1956.

Sapon-Shevin, Mara. "Another Look at Mainstreaming: Exceptionality, Normality, and the Nature of Difference." *Phi Delta Kappan*, 60(2) (October 1978): 119–121.

Saville-Troike, Muriel. *A Guide to Culture in the Classroom*. Rosslyn, Va.: National Clearinghouse for Bilingual Education, 1978.

Schickedanz, Judith A.; York, Mary E.; Stewart, Ida Santos; and White, Doris. *Strategies for Teaching Young Children*. Englewood Cliffs, N.J.: Prentice-Hall, 1977.

Shafer, Susan. "Messin' wif Language." *Elementary School Journal*, May 1976, pp. 500–506.

Shield, Portia. "The Language of Poor Black Children and Reading Performance." *The Journal of Negro Education*, Spring 1979, p. 207.

Shuy, Roger W. *Discovering American Dialects.* Champaign, Ill.: National Council of Teachers of English, 1967, p. 5.

Simpson-Tyson, Audrey K. "Are Native American First Graders Ready to Read?" *The Reading Teacher*, April 1978, pp. 798–801.

Stewart, Ida Santos. "Bilingual Education, Family and Society." *Childhood Education*, January/February 1981, pp. 138–143.

Stoller, Paul (ed.). *Black American English: A Book of Readings on Its Background and Its Usage in the Schools and in Literature.* New York: Delta Division of Dell, 1975.

Taba, Hilda, and Elkins, Deborah. *Teaching Strategies for the Culturally Disadvantaged.* Chicago: Rand McNally, 1966.

Teigenbaum, Irwin. "Developing Fluency in Standard Oral English." *Elementary English*, 47 (December 1970): 1053–1059.

Torrance, E. Paul. "Are the Torrance Tests of Creative Thinking Biased Against Or In Favor of 'Disadvantaged' Groups?" *The Gifted Child Quarterly* (Summer 1971): 27.

Torrance, E. Paul, and Torrance, Pansy. "Combining Creative Problem-Solving with Creative Expressive Activities in the Education of Disadvantaged Young People." *The Journal of Creative Behavior*, 6 (First Quarter, 1972): 2–3.

Troike, Rudolph C. *Research Evidence for the Effectiveness of Bilingual Education.* Rosslyn, Va.: National Clearinghouse for Bilingual Education, 1978.

Turnbull, Ann P., and Schulz, Jane B. *Mainstreaming Handicapped Students: A Guide for the Classroom Teacher.* Boston: Allyn & Bacon, 1979.

Von Maltitz, Frances Willard. *Living and Learning in Two Languages.* New York: McGraw-Hill, 1975.

Wilson, Velez. "Nurturing Language Diversity in the School." *NASSP Bulletin*, April 1981, pp. 6–11.

Wolfgang, Aaron. "The Silent Language in the Multicultural Classroom." *Theory into Practice*, 16(3) (June 1977): 145–152.

York, Jean and Ebert, Dorothy. "Primary Level: Grades 1-3." In *Reading for the Disadvantaged: Problems of Linguistically Different Learners* (edited by Thomas D. Horn). New York: Harcourt Brace Jovanovich, 1970, pp. 186–187.

INDEX